"SOMEONE IS GETTING AWAY WITH MURDER.
WHY ISN'T SAM SHEPPARD IN JAIL?
GET THAT KILLER."
—Headline in the *Cleveland Press,* in 1954

"AFTER LIFE OF NOTORIETY AND PAIN, SON
TRIES TO SOLVE HIS MOTHER'S MURDER."
—Headline in the *New York Times,* in 1996

Sam Reese Sheppard was only seven when his life was shattered. His mother was killed, his father was sent to prison for murder, newspapers slandered both of them, and the young boy had to fight to keep from believing what the world said was true.

Sam Reese Sheppard won that fight.

And now, together with a tenacious investigative reporter, he has written a book to tell the world the truth about the woman who was his mother, the man who was his father, and the case that represented our legal system at its most hysterically prejudiced and flagrantly unjust. Following the trail of evidence year after year, the authors have at last identified the man who killed Sam Reese Sheppard's mother and destroyed his father. Specially updated with newly revealed evidence and new witnesses, this eyeopening book reveals the complete inside story of the murder case that would not die.

"THE EVIDENCE THAT THE AUTHORS HAVE
UNCOVERED IS COMPELLING."
—*Cleveland Plain Dealer,* in 1996

MOCKERY OF JUSTICE

THE TRUE STORY OF
THE SHEPPARD MURDER CASE

by CYNTHIA L. COOPER
& SAM REESE SHEPPARD

AN ONYX BOOK

ONYX
Published by the Penguin Group
Penguin Books USA Inc., 375 Hudson Street,
New York, New York 10014, U.S.A.
Penguin Books Ltd, 27 Wrights Lane,
London W8 5TZ, England
Penguin Books Australia Ltd, Ringwood,
Victoria, Australia
Penguin Books Canada Ltd, 10 Alcorn Avenue,
Toronto, Ontario, Canada M4V 3B2
Penguin Books (N.Z.) Ltd, 182–190 Wairau Road,
Auckland 10, New Zealand

Penguin Books Ltd, Registered Offices:
Harmondsworth, Middlesex, England

Published by Onyx, an imprint of Dutton Signet, a division of Penguin Books
USA Inc. This is an authorized reprint of a hardcover edition published by Northeastern University Press. For information contact Northeastern University Press,
272 Huntington Plaza, 360 Huntington Avenue, Boston, MA 02115.

First Onyx Printing, May, 1997
10 9 8 7 6 5 4 3 2 1

 REGISTERED TRADEMARK—MARCA REGISTRADA

Printed in the United States of America

ACKNOWLEDGMENTS

This collaboration is unusual because it encompassed much more than the writing of a book. Also involved was an intense investigation that lasted several years and necessitated searching out new sources, plunging through years of yellowing materials, and digging through the wells of myth and misinformation that surrounded the Sheppard case. The responsibility for research and investigation was largely that of Cynthia L. Cooper, who also wrote the bulk of the text. Writings by Sam Reese Sheppard have been integrated at various points in the book, and throughout his perspective has served as a guide to the material, offering insight, family documents, contacts, and a human context for understanding both the seriousness of this effort and the magnitude of the tragedy of injustice.

AMSEC, an investigative service of great integrity, provided invaluable assistance, particularly in the last two years of the investigation. Terry Gilbert, a Cleveland attorney, offered critical perspectives during the five-to-six-year period in which the material for this book was gathered.

Countless individuals who have been touched by the Sheppard case also helped. Some people cannot be named—one in particular—because their information was provided confidentially or anonymously. Our deepest respect and appreciation is held for these sources. Many of the hundreds of people who eased our path cannot be acknowledged here because of sheer space limitations. Nonetheless, their comments, thoughts, tips, and encouragement sustained us through long and difficult challenges and provided threads of information that were vital to weaving the full story. We thank them for coming forward.

In addition to those named in the text and notes, we want to acknowledge the following individuals: Mildred Adams, Randall Dale Adams, Jim Amman, Ruth Andrews, Pat Bane, Hugo Adam Bedau, Ron Bernstein, Michael Blau, Barbara Bloomquist, Nola Bonecutter, William Bowers, Dave Channon, Dr. James Chapman, Kathy Chavez, Lillie

Clark, Pat Clark, Jennifer R. Clarke, Stephen W. Cooper, Richard Dalrymple, Lyn Date, Rev. Alan and Beatrice Davis, Dr. Peter R. De Forest, Marie Deans, Micki Dickoff, Joe Dirck, Patricia Dugan, Janet Sheppard Duvall, Kathy Engel, Erika Fine, Lory Frankel, Jean Gardner, William Gaul, Erica Goldman, Luther Grisso, Bob Gross, Merritt Harrison, Jack Healey, Larry and Joyce Heaton, Martha Hellander, Henry Heller, Miriam Holmes, Sonia "Sunny" Jacobs, Marietta Jaeger, Ernest James, Jr., Mary Kirk Janke, Michael angel Johnson, Jim Kershaw, Anita Kirk, James Lader, Jacqui LeBeau, the Leimbach family, Cindy Leise, David Lerner, Don Lowers, Bill Lucero, Deborah Ludwig, Kevin Lund, William G. Manning, Teresa Mathis, Keith McKnight, Marge Mellon, Philip Mellon, Sherri Miller, Larry Monaldo, Evelyn Moore, Howard Neal, Alison Stair Neet, Anne Nunamaker, Meave O'Marah, Harold Lamonte Otey, Sally Peck, Bill and Judy Pelke, Dr. John Plunkett, Debbie Pollack, Susan Pollack, Michael L. Radelet, Sunshine Richards, Ralph Ristenbatt, Alma and Sy Rosen, Michael Ross, Andrea Rudner, David Russell, Vince Russo, Jeanette Schoenfeldt, Julie Schofield, Larry Scripp, Dr. Robert Shaler, Mary Ann Sharkey, Ariane Tebbejohanns Sheppard, Dorothy Sheppard and family members Jean, Margaret, and Richard, Steve and Betty Sheppard, Russell Sherman, Martin Short, Barbara Sonnenblick, Matt Stella, Lynda Sturner, Charlie and Pauline Sullivan, Christina Tafero, Ashima Thompson-Scripp, Deborah Thompson-Scripp, John Thornton, Linda Thurston, Judyth Ulis, Margaret Vandiver, the Weigle family, Ted and Wylene West, Andrea Westervelt, George White, Tom White, Judy Williams, Gunner Wood, and Renette Zimmerly; and the following organizations: Amnesty International, American Friends Service Committee, Capital Jury Project of Northeastern University College of Criminal Justice, Cleveland State University, CURE (Citizens United for the Rehabilitation of Errants), Cuyahoga County Archives, Family Awareness Program at MCI Norfolk, The Lifers and Long Termers Group at Bay State Correctional Center, Massachusetts Citizens Against the Death Penalty, Murder Victim Families for Reconciliation, National Archives, National Coalition to Abolish the Death Penalty (especially state affiliates in Arkansas, California, Georgia, Indiana, Iowa, Maine, Nebraska), Ohio Supreme Court Library, Parents of Murdered Children and Other Homicide Survivors, Riptide, Rocky River Police Department, and Western Reserve Historical Society.

Special thanks to the editorial staff at Northeastern University Press who extended themselves in personal and professional ways to complete this project, including William Frohlich, Jill Bahcall, Scott Brassart, and Ann Twombly; and at Dutton Signet, Michaela Hamilton and Laura Turley. In addition, a special nod of gratitude goes to our agent, Carol Mann.

CONTENTS

DRAMATIS PERSONAE

Victims and Survivors

Sam Reese Sheppard, or Sam R.	*Son of Dr. Sam and Marilyn*
Marilyn Sheppard	*Murder victim*
Dr. Sam Sheppard	*Husband of victim*
Kokie	*Dog, part Irish Setter*

Family

Dr. R. A. Sheppard	*Dr. Sam's father*
Ethel Niles Sheppard	*Dr. Sam's mother*
Dr. Stephen Sheppard	*Dr. Sam's brother*
Betty Sheppard	*Married to Stephen Sheppard*
Dr. Richard Niles Sheppard	*Dr. Sam's brother*
Dorothy Sheppard	*Married to Richard Niles Sheppard*

Neighbors and Friends

Esther Houk	*First to scene*
Mayor Spencer Houk	*First to scene*
Larry Houk	*Son of Esther and Spen Houk*
Dr. Lester Hoversten	*Doctor staying at Sheppard home*
Nancy Ahern	*Guest prior to murder*
Don Ahern	*Guest prior to murder*

Coroner's Office

Dr. Samuel Gerber	*Coroner, 1936–1986*
Mary Cowan	*Lab technician*
Dr. Lester Adelson	*Chief Pathologist*
Dr. Elizabeth Balraj	*Coroner from 1986*

Bay Village Police

John Eaton	*Bay Village police chief*

Fred Drenkhan   *Bay Villiage officer*
Jay Hubach   *Bay Village officer*

Cleveland Police
Frank Story   *Cleveland police chief*
Henry Dombrowski   *Cleveland scientific investiga-
                     tion unit*
David Kerr   *Cleveland captain of
                     homicide*
James McArthur   *Cleveland inspector*
Robert Schottke   *Cleveland officer*
Pat Gareau   *Cleveland officer*
Michael Grabowski   *Cleveland scientific investiga-
                     tion unit*

Sheriff's Office
Carl Rossbach   *Deputy sheriff*
Dave Yettra   *Deputy sheriff*

Judges
Judge Edward Blythin   *Trial judge, 1954*
Judge Francis Talty   *Trial judge, 1966*
Judge Carl Weinman   *Federal district court judge*
Justice Tom Clark   *U.S. Supreme Court*

Attorneys
John Mahon   *Main prosecuting attorney, 1954*
John T. Corrigan   *Prosecuting attorney, 1966*
William Corrigan   *Defense attorney, 1954–61*
Arthur Petersilge   *Sheppard family attorney*
F. Lee Bailey   *Defense attorney, 1961–66*
Russell Sherman   *Defense attorney, co-counsel,
                     1963–66*

Expert
Dr. Paul Leland Kirk   *Criminalist*

Writers
Erle Stanley Gardner   *Court of Last Resort*
Paul Holmes   *Author of two Sheppard
                        books*
Jack Harrison Pollack   *Author of Sheppard book*

Jan Sheppard Duvall   *Dr. Sam's niece, researcher in 1980s*

Richard Dalrymple   *Journalist, researcher in 1980s*

Other Cases

Ethel May Durkin   *Murder victim*

Richard Eberling   *Widow washer, Durkin murderer*

Pat Bogar   *Witness to false Durkin will*

Bev Scheidler   *Witness to false Durkin will*

Dale Scheidler   *Witness to false Durkin will*

Vincent Kremperger   *Police officer, Durkin case*

Donald Joseph Wedler   *Convict, Florida*

Reinvestigation

AMSEC   *Private investigative firm*

Monsignor   *Ad hoc investigator*

Terry Gilbert   *Attorney, Cleveland*

CHRONOLOGY

July 4, 1954
Early A.M.   Marilyn Reese Sheppard murdered by
                            severe beating in her bed. She was four
                            months pregnant.

5:50 A.M.   Bay Village mayor Spencer Houk and his
                            wife, Ethel, arrive at the Sheppard home
                            after getting a call from Dr. Sam Sheppard.

6:02 A.M.   First officer, Fred Drenkhan, arrives at
                            the Sheppard home and murder scene.

6–7:30 A.M.   Police officers, relatives, press, and
                            neighbors troop through the house.
                                Samuel Reese Sheppard, seven years
                            old, then called Chip, is carried away from
                            the house by his uncle Richard.
                                Dr. Sam Sheppard, in pain, is re-
                            moved to Bay View Hospital.

8:00 A.M.   Coroner, Dr. Sam Gerber, arrives.

9:30 A.M.–3 P.M.   Dr. Sheppard, under sedation and
                            being treated for shock and neck injur-
                            ies, which he said resulted from his
                            struggle with an intruder, is visited sev-
                            eral times and interrogated by the coro-
                            ner, coroner's investigator, local police
                            chief, two Cleveland police officers, and
                            Bay Village police. By midafternoon,
                            Cleveland officer Schottke tells Shep-
                            pard, "I think you killed your wife."
                                Sheppard home sealed and closed off
                            to Dr. Sheppard until after Sheppard is
                            convicted.

July 7, 1954   Funeral of Marilyn Sheppard. Son, Sam R., does not attend because of extensive press coverage.

    Prosecutor criticizes Dr. Sheppard for refusing to permit immediate questioning, although he has already been questioned on several occasions.

July 8, 1954   Headline: "Testify Now in Death, Bay Doctor Is Ordered"—one of hundreds of articles, many with untruths or inadmissible information, printed in the next few months.

July 9, 1954   Front-page story: "Doctor Balks at Lie Test."

    Sheppard leads a contingent of officers through the house, showing them what occurred.

    Window washing company employee Vern Lund leaves town.

July 10, 1954   Sheppard voluntarily gives a formal statement, taken at the Cuyahoga County Sheriff's Office, with several officers in attendance.

July 20, 1954   Front-page editorial: "Someone Is Getting Away with Murder"—part of the unabated editorial attack calling for Dr. Sheppard's arrest and conviction.

July 21, 1954
A.M.   Front-page editorial: "Why No Inquest? Do It Now, Dr. Gerber."

P.M.   Dr. Gerber calls inquest.

July 22, 1954   Beginning of three-day inquest staged in local school gymnasium to accommodate large crowds, reporters, live television and radio crews; Dr. Sheppard searched in full view of crowd; Dr. Sheppard's lawyer is not permitted to participate and is ejected altogether when he tries to introduce evidence.

July 23, 1954   Cleveland police formally takes over the investigation of the murder from Bay Village police and, for the first time, sends out its scientific investigation unit.

July 26, 1954   Headline: Police Captain "Urges Sheppard's Arrest."

July 28, 1954   Editorial: "Why Don't Police Quiz Top Suspect?"

July 29, 1954   Vern Lund joins service, reports to basic training in Florida.

July 30, 1954
A.M.   Front-page editorial: "Why Isn't Sam Sheppard in Jail?"

10 P.M.   Dr. Sheppard arrested and taken to suburban city hall, where hundreds of newscasters, photographers, and reporters await his arrival.

August 1954   Massive press coverage, including cartoons, editorials, rumor, innuendo.

August 16, 1954   Judge finds no evidence and releases Dr. Sheppard on bail.

August 17, 1954   Dr. Sheppard indicted for murder. Grand jury foreman Bert Winston complains that members of the grand jury were under enormous pressure. Dr. Sheppard is rearrested—his last day of freedom for nearly ten years.

October 9, 1954   Editorial criticizes defense counsel's poll of the public to show local bias for a change of venue motion, saying it "smacks of mass jury tampering."

October 18, 1954

Selection of jury for Dr. Sheppard's trial begins. Courtroom is outfitted with a long table in front of the bar, three feet from jurors, for seating of twenty press representatives. Three of four rows of benches are assigned to press. All New York news media, Chicago media, press syndicates have representatives, including "star" reporters such as Dorothy Kilgallen. Representatives of news media use all rooms on courtroom floor, with private telephones and telegraphic equipment installed. Radio station sets up broadcasting facilities on another floor, next to the jury room.

October 19, 1954

Radio debate broadcast live in which reporters accuse Dr. Sheppard of trying to block prosecution and assert that he conceded his guilt by hiring a prominent criminal lawyer. Continuance of the trial is denied.

October 23, 1954

Front-page, two-inch headline: "But Who Will Speak for Marilyn?" calling for "Justice to Sam Sheppard."

October 28, 1954

Jury sworn in.
   First day of trial, massive coverage of jurors' visit to Sheppard home; a reporter travels with the jury.

October– December 1954

Jurors are not sequestered during trial; have their names and photos in the papers over forty times; and are not queried about media accounts they have heard.
   Police, prosecutors, witnesses, judge, juror families give interviews and appear on camera. Trial transcript made available and reported daily.

November 21, 1954	Radio broadcast calls Dr. Sheppard a perjurer, comparing him to Alger Hiss. Judge refuses to question jury about whether members heard it.
November 24, 1954	Eight-column headline: "Sam Called a 'Jekyll-Hyde' by Marilyn, Cousin to Testify"; no such testimony is presented.
November 1954	National broadcaster Walter Winchell reports that woman under arrest in New York was Dr. Sheppard's mistress and had had an illegitimate child by him. Two jurors admit having heard the broadcast; judge takes no action. The report is false.
December 9, 1954	Police issue a press statement calling Dr. Sheppard a "Bare-faced Liar."
December 16, 1954	Testimony ends. Prosecution seeks guilt on first-degree murder with the penalty of death in the electric chair.
December 17– 21, 1954	Jury deliberates. Jury is sequestered for the first time, but there are no female bailiffs to caretake the five women. Jurors are permitted to make unmonitored telephone calls home at night. Chaos outside and around the jury room prevails.
December 21, 1954	Jury returns verdict of guilty in the second degree, ending what was then one of the longest criminal trials in American history.
	Sheppard, incarcerated since his arrest, is sentenced to life imprisonment.
	Five volumes of newspaper clippings from Cleveland are collected from trial and pretrial period.
	Sheppard home returned to family.

January 7, 1955	Ethel Niles Sheppard, Dr. Sheppard's mother, commits suicide by shooting herself.
January 18, 1955	Dr. Richard Allen Sheppard, Dr. Sam Sheppard's father, dies of a hemorrhaging gastric ulcer and suddenly worsened stomach cancer.
January 22, 1955	Dr. Paul Leland Kirk, California criminalist, visits Cleveland and Sheppard home.
March 1955	Dr. Kirk returns a report that discusses evidence of a third person, blood spatter, and other items.
April 1955	Hearing on motion for new trial, in which affidavit of Dr. Kirk is presented; motion taken under advisement and then denied.
Summer 1955	Dr. Sheppard moved from jail in Cleveland to maximum security prison near Columbus, Ohio, one of two in which he will stay until 1964.
July 13, 1955	Dr. Sheppard's appeal to the state court of appeals is rejected, and the denial is upheld in subsequent appeals, including one to the U.S. Supreme Court, despite commentary by every reviewing court criticizing the conduct of the trial and the media.
November 1959	Richard Eberling arrested for larceny, including theft of Marilyn Sheppard's ring from her brother-in-law's house.
July 1961	William Corrigan, original defense attorney for Dr. Sheppard, dies; F. Lee Bailey of Boston takes over defense within the next year.

August 1961	Publication of *The Sheppard Murder Case* by Paul Holmes, questioning the conviction of Dr. Sheppard.
February 13, 1963	Thomas Reese, father of deceased Marilyn Reese Sheppard, commits suicide with a shotgun.
April 13, 1963	F. Lee Bailey files a new habeas corpus petition in U.S. district court; prosecution represented by John Corrigan (no relation to William Corrigan, prior defense attorney).
September, 1963	"The Fugitive," a highly popular television series inspired by the Sheppard case, according to most observers, begins on ABC.
July 16, 1964	Dr. Sheppard released from prison, after federal district court judge Carl Weinman rules that Sheppard was denied a fair trial.
June 6, 1966	U.S. Supreme Court agrees with federal district court judge Weinman, ruling in *Sheppard v Maxwell* that the trial of Dr. Sam Sheppard was a "carnival" and that Dr. Sheppard was denied a fair trial because the judge failed to take steps to control the courtroom atmosphere and prevent jury bias from excessive press coverage.
October 24, 1966	Dr. Sheppard's second, and fair, trial begins.
November 16, 1966	Jury finds Dr. Sheppard not guilty.
August 27, 1967	"The Fugitive" runs its final episode. Ratings have declined since Dr. Sheppard was found not guilty. Daily reruns of the 120 episodes begin shortly after.

April 6, 1970   Dr. Sam Sheppard dies at age forty-six; Dr. Paul Kirk dies within a few months.

1981–82   Spen Houk and Esther Houk, divorced in 1962, die.

January 3, 1984   Elderly widow Ethel May Durkin dies, six weeks after being hospitalized for a fall at her home.

July 1989   Richard Eberling, an interior decorator and the former window washer at the Sheppard home, is convicted of aggravated murder in the death of Ethel May Durkin.

October 1989   Sam Reese Sheppard, only child of Dr. and Mrs. Sheppard, first speaks out publicly about the injustice he has suffered and begins an effort to solve his mother's murder.

March 1990   Sam Reese Sheppard meets with Richard Eberling at the Lebanon Correctional Institution in Ohio.

August 1993   The movie *The Fugitive,* starring Harrison Ford and based on the old television series about Dr. Richard Kimble, an innocent man wrongly convicted of the murder of his wife, is released.

November 1993   AMSEC joins in helping Sam Reese Sheppard reinvestigate the murder.

October 13, 1995   Cuyahoga County Prosecutor Stephanie Tubbs Jones announces an investigation into the murder of Marilyn Sheppard.

February 22, 1996   The first court hearing in over 30 years on the Sheppard case takes place before Judge Ronald Suster in Ohio.

GREATER CLEVELAND

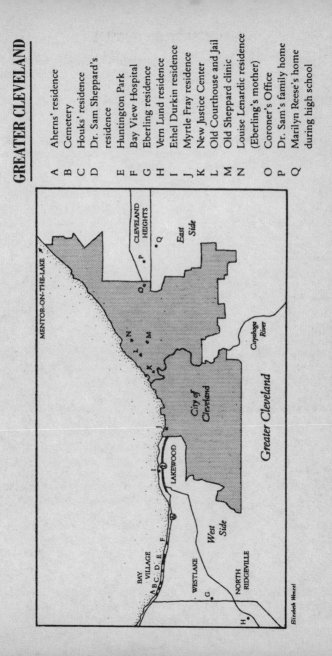

A Aherns' residence
B Cemetery
C Houks' residence
D Dr. Sam Sheppard's
   residence
E Huntington Park
F Bay View Hospital
G Eberling residence
H Vern Lund residence
I Ethel Durkin residence
J Myrtle Fray residence
K New Justice Center
L Old Courthouse and Jail
M Old Sheppard clinic
N Louise Lenardic residence
   (Eberling's mother)
O Coroner's Office
P Dr. Sam's family home
Q Marilyn Reese's home
   during high school

PART ONE

COVER-UP

Prologue

A chill came from the lake with intermittent sleet and rain—more like Halloween than Valentine's Day, 1955.

They all went for a "real" Chinese dinner somewhere near downtown Cleveland—he and his cousins and his aunt and uncle—for fun. And he had fun: tea, steaming pots of food in the middle of the table, the five of them sitting in a circle. He had tried to use chopsticks and, for a seven-year-old, had managed fairly well.

On the way back to the West Side, Uncle Steve mentioned that his dad was nearby, in the county jail. That's where his dad was waiting, following his conviction. They all were waiting. The appeal would make things all right, set his dad free, and make up for this huge, horrible mistake that kept them apart.

So close by. Uncle Steve said he would just go in for a minute, for a hello.

They drove to the large, ominous building that served as courthouse, with the jail on top. Uncle Steve parked in the empty lot and said he would return soon.

His dad! But he couldn't go see him. For over six months now, since his dad was placed in the county jail, he had not been allowed to visit.

The rest of them stayed in the car, played a spelling game, "Three-Thirds of a Ghost." He lost; he couldn't concentrate. He kept looking outside the car to the parking lot, a black space but for one spotlight that lit a utility pole in silhouette. He looked for their ghosts—his mother and dad.

He hated the game. He just wanted his mother back and he wanted to see his father, and instead he had to play their stupid game.

At last, Uncle Steve returned. Out of the cold, he brought an envelope and passed it back.

Inside was a tall card, a Slim Jim. There were hearts on it—from his dad, with love. He sent it just to him, for him to show to everybody or pin up or hold, alone, in his room.

Later, he called it his Valentine's card from the Fourth of July, because the Fourth is when it all happened, in 1954.

"Valentine" was the name that she left on his new answering machine, on a night in 1989. "I hope I have the right Sheppard. You'll want to talk to me. I know some people and I have something."

Her hello is husky, scratchy, deep with age when he calls back. He announces himself: Sam Reese Sheppard. The Reese—his mother's maiden name—distinguishes him from his father, Dr. Samuel Holmes Sheppard, a point that leads to much confusion and occasional contention. He objects vehemently to being called Sam Junior, and even more so to "Chip," his childhood nickname.*

Sam Reese Sheppard stands in his single room, the rooming house in Cambridge, Massachusetts, that has become home. Next week he will be taking one of the biggest risks of his life by speaking publicly in Cleveland, Ohio—a city that holds his nightmares.

Valentine seems to arrange her words before she speaks. "I . . . have something . . . that will solve the case."

The case. People always call it "The Case," as if it were an abstract notion that has nothing to do with him, that has not landed in his life like a violent storm spinning off Lake Erie and refusing to leave. Three and a half decades later, the damage can't be calculated; pain still sears.

July 4, 1954, the date the case began, is the date on the

*Sorting out the confusion of names in this story is no easy matter. For the purposes of this book, Sam Reese Sheppard is called Sam R. or young Sam; his father, Dr. Samuel H. Sheppard, is called Dr. Sam or Sheppard. (Sam Shepard, the popular playwright and actor whose given name was Samuel S. Rogers, is not related to Dr. Sam Sheppard.)

obituary for his mother, Marilyn Reese Sheppard. She was thirty-one years old. He was seven, asleep in the room next door while she was murdered during the night.

The allegations against his father began immediately. Cameras, press, media people accusing Dr. Sam, as everyone called him, in editorials with blunt headlines: "Get That Killer!" "Somebody Is Getting Away with Murder." "Why Isn't Sam Sheppard in Jail?" A rush, a blur. His father's arrest, trial, and incarceration, all of it wrong. Twelve years later, a successful appeal, a fair trial, and an acquittal finally came, but some people ignored it, refused to accept the verdict. The wrongful trial was massively publicized; the acquittal is less known. His father died less than four years later, disheartened and confused. Dr. Sam was forty-six at his death, sixteen years of his life stolen by the case and its aftermath. Now his son is forty-two, and the aftermath still lingers.

"I don't know you," he says to Valentine. His voice has a slight quaver, the same quaver that people say his father's voice had, emotions too close to the surface.

"I knew him in Columbus after he got out." Valentine speaks in a stage whisper. "I knew the family he lived with. The couple, the son, the daughter. Used to chat with the girls at the beauty parlor. You know the beauty parlor?"

Sam understands the implications of Columbus. In the 3,575 days of prison, in the 85,800 hours that Dr. Sam spent locked away from his son, his profession, his family, he had gotten to know many men. Prison was filled with hardened men. In ten years, his dad got to know some of the toughest, even some in organized crime.

It is hitting him that, no matter what, he is the son, and his poor dad won't be left alone even twenty years after his death. This Valentine reverberates with ghosts of the past.

Her few sentences are enough to let him know that she could be dangerous, a threat. Anything at all could be expected next.

"I have a statement from your father. Signed by your father," she says. She pauses, wielding her punch line. "It's a confession."

"Oh, really? I didn't know there was such a thing."

"I'm writing a book. We're going to put the confession on the cover of our book. We want you to write a chapter."

He inhales a deep one. He does not believe her for an

instant, but over the years he has learned to hold on, to listen, to find out what more he can.

"Well, that is interesting. I'm pretty busy at the moment. But I'd like to take a look at it."

After he hangs up, the flush rises. He closes his eyes for a minute and sees the image of his father, always described as handsome, well built—a cross between Henry Fonda and Marlon Brando, said one reporter. What Sam R. sees when he closes his eyes, though, is the mixture of relief and fright and kindness and disbelief that coalesced in his father's face when he greeted his son at visiting hours in those days of his imprisonment. People often remark that Sam R. bears a resemblance to his dad. Although Sam R. is tall, with a cleft chin and wisps of blond hair, he slips more comfortably into anonymity, using the eyeglasses he wears as a protective shield.

For a moment now, Sam R.'s eyes burn, the way his father's had in the courtroom in 1954 when forced to look—"on advice of counsel"—at the giant projected color images of the death scene.

Valentine isn't the first, of course. Over the years there have been hundreds upon hundreds of letters, calls from supporters, fans, cranks, nuts, buffoons. Shakedowns. Opportunists. Publicity seekers. People with their opinions, no matter how ill informed. The ones that offer hope are the hardest to take.

Dear Sir. I killed your wife. I can't sleep. I don't want to fry. I am living now in New York. I can't give you my name and address. Flushing, New York. A fraud.

Dear Friend Sam, Just a few lines to let you know that I am very sorry for what I did to Marilyn, but it was nothing but constant fighting between you and her, your own brother knows that I did it. . . . It's a damn shame you have to pay for something you didn't do. But they will never take me back to Cleveland. A.L.C., Pittsburgh. A false statement.

As if the notoriety at the time of the trial were not enough, a popular 1960s drama had kept the story before the public eye. "The Fugitive," a television series about a doctor convicted of murdering his wife, was modeled on the case, some say; some say it was not. Every week, the voice of William Conrad penetrated living rooms: "Dr. Richard Kimble, an innocent victim of blind justice. Falsely convicted for the murder of his wife. Reprieved by fate when a train wreck freed him en route to the death house. . . . Freed him to run before the relentless pursuit of the police lieutenant obsessed with his capture.''

Wrongfully convicted like his father, yes, but not locked behind iron grates and steep walls. Running, but not dealing with the shock of it, the hurt, and the crippling of the heart that never leaves, never goes away.

Stashed in an overnight bag in his clothes closet, along with some towels, Sam R. keeps the quilt on which his mother died, a regular-size, red-and-white diamond-and-triangle pattern of snowflakes with two large stains, darker than burgundy, each about twelve inches long and about six inches wide. He pulls it out.

Shortly after he received the quilt last year, from boxes that could no longer be stored in Cleveland, he tried to wash the blood out of it, the stains then over thirty-five years old. The water darkened as he plunged his hands into the remnants, into the memory of his mother's blood, his mother whose death caused so much anguish in so many lives. She was the victim; it was not her fault. But still there persisted people who blamed her. Maybe, they said, she brought it on herself, maybe she had been too pretty, or too free, or maybe a little too haughty or vain.

Now, for a moment, he fingers the quilt.

How to stop the lies and the Valentines? How to solve the case after years of neglect? Only recently has he even met another human being outside of relatives who knew the agony of dealing with a murder in the family. And he has just begun to realize and cope with the effects of childhood exposure to the prison system, the general unease with certain quarters of society that he could not explain. In groups such as Murder Victim Families for Reconciliation, the National Coalition to Abolish the Death Penalty, CURE prison reform, Amnesty International, he has at last found others with like experience.

The stains remain on the quilt, even after he has tried hard to soak it, like the stigma of the Sheppard case. He knows that the quilt could be put away again, but he will continue to be identified with the case. The rumor and innuendo about his past will relentlessly pursue him; he can never expect to lead a quiet, private life.

But to take on the whole of it is too daunting—not just to establish that his father was not guilty, as the jury had

said in a fair trial, but to explain *why* his father was innocent and how the system had failed. To answer the unanswered questions. Who killed his mother? Who, on July 4,
1954, entered his home and violently beat his mother? Who
staged a burglary and stood by mutely to let his father go
to prison, his family explode? What stands before him is
the task of resolving the case. That will prove more than
difficult to accomplish—near to overwhelming. Not just because of the years gone by, but because it means challenging American myths, the ones that take easy comfort in
homilies that the innocent are freed, the guilty get what
they deserve, the truth will out.

"One of the most common American myths is the belief
that innocent people are not convicted for crimes they have
not committed," wrote Edward D. Radin in *The Innocents*.
"Most newspapers help foster this illusion by reporting only
a handful of such cases a year, and many of these are obscure items deep on an inside page where they are easily
overlooked. It is only occasionally that a case with a particularly strong emotional appeal wins national publicity and
the public becomes aware that a miscarriage of justice
occurs."

Especially now. People are more frightened by crime
than ever, and they want quick-fix answers—ones as easy
as a fast burger or an instant food mix. Clean resolutions.
Sure, if they thought about it, they realize the myths are
only myths. They know from their own experiences of getting turned down for a job or being accused of cheating on
a test in junior high or getting a parking ticket even though
the meter was broken. Mistakes are made. The system errs.
The bureaucracy can be harrowing. Getting officials to listen, to change, can be impossible. But it is as if people see
only themselves as wronged, as if they can't imagine those
small-scale injustices happening on a bigger scale. On television the bad guys are always caught or trapped by some
miserable fate. The good guys, even if bungling or sarcastic,
are ultimately vindicated. The resolution comes to an end,
the music rises, they ride away on a horse or speed away
on a motorcycle, and are victorious. Right wins again. The
American myths demand it.

The real world is different. People see their lives eroded.
"Countless men and women get arrested for murders they

did not commit," write the authors of *In Spite of Innocence.*
Innocent people are even sentenced to death.

The attorney in Dr. Sam's fair trial in 1966, F. Lee Bailey, had wanted to pull a coup from fiction and nab a Perry Mason–style confession on the stand. The jury acquitted Dr. Sheppard, but there was no third-act drama, no curtain pulled away as the true murderer stood up and took the rap. When the trial was over, Bailey told Sam R. that it would be up to him to put the matter finally to rest. Others, like the writer Dorothy Kilgallen, had a different perspective: "Don't try to solve the mystery of Marilyn Sheppard's murder!" she wrote. "My guess is that it will never be solved." Even if there were a way to resolve the case, this wasn't like a game show, with the right answer solidly positioned behind some door, certain to appear if only you could guess the clues correctly.

The case had been "exceptional." That was the term used by Erle Stanley Gardner, the author of the Perry Mason mysteries, in 1957. But there are thousands more cases and faces, murders that live briefly in headlines, the victims' families trying to live on. Hundreds of murders on television each year. Casual treatment of the victims' families. When Sam R. finally began to understand the social context, to meet people like himself who had dealt with the hurt and loss to violence, he saw his own pain reflected by too many more.

Why had the case, of all cases, taken on such prominence? That was part of the mystery. But the Sheppard case was also a microcosm of the American judicial system: murder, media, courtroom drama, legal appeal. "I have been asked by the press if I felt that Dr. Sheppard had a fair trial," said Gardner. "I think [the jury] made a most commendable attempt to keep from being affected by the terrific publicity which could well have generated a species of public hysteria. Our system of justice, however, isn't infallible. . . . the case of Dr. Sam Sheppard is a controversial case and it is a highly exceptional case. . . . In every prison, there are *exceptional* cases."

A combination of events powerful enough to break the case, to pry open the belief in the American myth, was remote. There were always the long-lasting hopes of Sam R.'s uncles and his father: a confession by the guilty, a dogged investigator who would not be shaken, a previously hidden clue suddenly unearthed, a collaboration of people and events that would plumb the deep pit of mysterious lethargy to yield a name, a face, an explanation. Luck.

And so much of the case was a fog to young Sam. Names, accusations, emotions. Newspaper articles that were not fact at all, but merely fiction parading in newspaper fonts and black ink. And his own reality—he could remember none of the actual event.

What happened to the doctor who had been staying at their house until the day before the murder? Where was the newspaper editor who so voraciously had gone after his father? Or the coroner who had fabricated the nature of the weapon to make his father seem guilty? What was the relationship between his parents that had caused so much attention to be drawn to them, that had led some to say his father had committed adultery but was tried for murder? Or the neighbors who had been the subject of a later grand jury inquiry but never charged? What about the confession from the petty criminal and drug user in Florida that seemed so real at the time? And what had he heard from his aunt, the only Sheppard relative left in Cleveland, about some other man in Ohio who had worked in their home and was recently arrested for another murder?

Sam R. folds the quilt back into the place where he keeps it.

That night he begins putting the finishing touches on his speech for Cleveland. The electronic word processor is the only luxury in the room. He types some of the words of Justice Tom Clark of the U.S. Supreme Court, the man who in 1966 finally denounced the trial that had resulted in his father's wrongful conviction: "massive, pervasive, prejudicial publicity"; "a carnival atmosphere"; "bedlam."

Even if he found rock-solid proof, some people would never be convinced. Their minds were made up so long ago that their opinions have calcified. Once a defendant is convicted, people have stakes in the conviction. Jurors, prosecutors, witnesses, and judges become entrenched: "Few are willing to admit the possibility that they were in error," says one study of erroneous convictions. And in the Sheppard case, added to the mix were the reporters who didn't want to admit error and were clinging to opinions argued long ago in articles and editorials. Vested interests with deep emotions and deep pockets. At least with the courts, there were higher courts that would hear an appeal. How to convince the press to clear its preconceptions, to rewind the tainted history, stand back, look at something fresh; how to change the minds of those who know nothing, those who think they know everything?

To reopen the wounds, to look again at the case, to enter his parents' history with a magnifying glass and a microscope—nothing easy about it. Only in the past year has he come forward at all, speaking tentatively for murder victim families who oppose the death penalty. He agrees with their ideas, but exposing himself publicly, after all these years, brings bouts of fear and panic. This next step will require him to reach in and to reach out in ways he can barely imagine.

Reality does not come as neatly wrapped and tied as fiction. Sam R. knows that firsthand. His life has been built around the rough edges. He has tried to carry on, but wherever he turns, the case is there, staring at him. Reality, old and new, on one canvas—him. The old: his mother's murder is unsolved, and his father, wrongfully convicted at first, is innocent. The new: he, their only child, Sam Reese Sheppard, named after both his father and his mother, will have to do something to silence the Valentines.

ONE

Deeds Will Rise

Cleveland had shrunk considerably from 1954 to 1989. The city dropped from the seventh largest metropolitan area in the United States to somewhere below the twentieth. To Sam R. it mattered little. The city was overwhelming, not because of the size but because of the power it packed in his life.

Staying on the East Side, far from where his parents had lived, seemed like it would make things easier when Sam R. returned to face Cleveland on his own in 1989. But markers of his family, he soon realized, were everywhere.

Cleveland is a city that divides from east to west, almost like two cities joined at the head by a downtown. When people say they are from Cleveland, the first question bounced back to them is: "East Side or West Side?"

Bay Village, the place most closely identified with Sam R.'s family, is on the West Side. The Sheppards had opened Bay View Hospital there, the first osteopathic facility on the West Side and part of the dream of Sam R.'s grandfather for an expanded osteopathic center comparable to the Mayo Clinic. Sam R.'s grandfather, Dr. R. A. Sheppard, his two uncles, Dr. Richard and Dr. Steve, and his father had all worked there. Sixteen miles from downtown, Bay Village saw itself as a pleasant township of a certain affluence, more than a suburb of a decidedly urban city. His mother's murder had totally bewildered the community and its tiny suburban police force of five full-time officers.

Sam R.'s family had roots on the East Side, where both

12

of his parents had grown up in the suburbs. In the early 1940s, the popular duo had graduated from Cleveland Heights High School, a large, well-known school. His grandfather's original clinic had been in the inner city on the East Side, at East Thirty-first and Euclid.

Coming to face Cleveland on his own in 1989, Sam R. was staying less than a mile from his grandfather's old clinic. Gone from the East Side was the old arena where major-league hockey and basketball teams had played. The Sears store was torn down, and even some of the majestic churches along the avenue had disappeared. True, the Cleveland Playhouse had opened a new space on the East Side. And there was a huge medical facility, the Cleveland Clinic, but much of it was walled off from the community.

For the most part, the inner city of the East Side had lost its vibrancy. Affluent African Americans had moved to suburbs, as had the potpourri of European immigrants before them. Vast expanses of empty lots lined the major streets where abandoned buildings had been torn down. This was a sign of civic improvement to Clevelanders anxious to be rid of fire hazards, eyesores, homes for rats and drug dealers. To Sam R., the vacant lots made it look barren, pockmarks on the face of an urban desert.

As city edged to suburbs on the East Side, Sam R. recognized the church with the distinctive copper spire. The "oil can" church, his mother used to call it, when they rode together to visit relatives. Nearby were the art museum, orchestra hall, and Case Western Reserve University. There too was the morgue, and, above it, the offices of the coroner. Sam R. had been taken there to give "testimony" as a child. From there, the ugliest aspects of the case still hung in the air. The coroner, Dr. Samuel Gerber, had had as great a hand as any in wrongfully accusing Sam R.'s father. Now Gerber's name was inscribed on the building.

Downtown, where Sam R. was to speak at the City Club, east and west joined. The recession years had been rough, although a new civic pride was trying to put life back into the city. Six or so office towers poked into the sky, ringing the old Terminal Tower, a fifty-two-story clone of New York's Empire State Building. The Terminal itself had had a major reconstruction, adding Tower City, fountains, and a mall. Once-industrial warehouses in the Flats at the edge of downtown had been refashioned into art shops and upscale restaurants. The multiagency Justice Center, a brick structure filling a city block, replaced the old courthouse and police station and jail that the Sheppards had unwillingly come to know so well.

To get to the West Side from downtown, the road crosses over the Cuyahoga River (pronounced Kigh'-ya-ho'-ga). *Cuyahoga,* also the name of the county, is said to be a Native American term for "crooked," supposedly referring to the snaking path of the river. Given Cleveland's history, "crooked" could have more than one meaning, as well.

The river flows to the one feature that spans east and west—Lake Erie. Sam R. remembered it well. Filling the northern vista, the lake has a spectacular sweeping breadth and high rolling waves that crash. Fifty-seven miles across to Canada, 241 miles in length, the lake's crescent-shaped shoreline spreads as far as the eye can see.

For all of its overpowering natural grandeur, Lake Erie had been largely ignored by the city. The lake was simply there, clinging to the city's backside like the trunk on a car. Even at the Lakefront Stadium, where the Browns once played football to eighty thousand of the world's most dedicated fans, people might not see the lake unless they happened to be sitting on a riser high in the sky or flying over in a blimp. Until the 1980s, when city leaders finally made plans to build a festival park along the downtown harbor, featuring the Rock 'n' Roll Hall of Fame, the lake had been seen only as a utilitarian aid for commercial traffic.

To enjoy the lake as a body of water, people had to make an effort. Sam R.'s parents, Dr. Sam and Marilyn, did. When they were sweethearts in high school, Marilyn spent her summers at her grandparents' cottage at Mentor-on-the-Lake, a distant suburban town that had one of the few accessible swimming beaches on the East Side. For a good swimmer like Marilyn, the waves were ocean without the salt, and swimmers bounced up and down as if they had found the Atlantic. On summer nights Sheppard would borrow his brother's car and drive out to be near her, sometimes spending the night at a beach house rented by his high school fraternity.

Equidistant on the West Side, Bay Village rose on the cliff over the lake, providing stunning panoramas from above and beaches for swimming and boating below. For those who could not own property along the lake, Huntington Park offered public access. The park was a mere 250 feet—one house, two lots—from the home that Dr. Sam and Marilyn bought.

Samuel Holmes Sheppard and Marilyn Reese—her real name was Florence Marilyn Reese, but she had dropped the "Florence" as a bit flat—left Cleveland as East Siders in the mid-1940s and came back as West Siders in the early 1950s. Married, parents of four-year-old Sam R., more confident, they moved to 28924 Lake Road in Bay Village, near the hospital begun by Dr. R. A. Sheppard.

For several years they had lived in Los Angeles, where Dr. Sam had attended the Los Angeles College of Osteopathic Physicians and Surgeons. He asked Marilyn to come and join him, and they married in California in February 1945. There they discovered a sporty, freewheeling lifestyle that fit their personalities. As a couple, sometimes with son in tow, they would head for beautiful ocean sites like Malibu, where they swam until the fog rolled in. Often, after the tragedy, as Sam R. came to call his mother's murder, it was easy to look at their paths and say, "If only this," and, "Because of that": if only they hadn't moved back to Cleveland; if only they had not been exposed to the fresh openness of the West Coast.

The compensation in moving back to Cleveland, perhaps, was the lake. They found an expansive Dutch Colonial home that was modest on the inside but luxurious in its embrace of Lake Erie. The house had a porch on the bluff above the water, its own beach, and was the only house among the neighboring homes to have a changing house by the lake. Dr. Sam swam practically every morning in good weather. And in the evenings and on weekends, he and Marilyn practiced the new sport of water skiing, flying down the lake despite its bumpiness, waving broadly to strangers and neighbors. They celebrated by buying each other the joint Christmas gift of a powerful outboard motor.

The house they bought even had a front door that faced the lake, a factor that caused continual confusion in the trial that came later, particularly since the street was called Lake Road, or sometimes West Lake Road. "We are calling the lake door the front door," an attorney tried to explain to one witness. The other door, the one that faced the street, was considered the back door.

If they were reluctant to return to Cleveland, Dr. Sam and Marilyn at least had a perfectly splendid lake view.

Sam R. had quietly returned with no fanfare earlier in 1989. He had been on a focused mission to retrieve boxes of family papers. That was when his aunt first showed him the articles about the interior decorator and former window washer who was under arrest for the murder of an elderly woman in a West Side suburb. On that trip, Sam R. had stopped by Huntington Park, where he studied the lake from more or less the same view that he had had from his second-floor bedroom window as a child.

This fall visit to Cleveland was about more—about opening boxes and windows, expanding personally, and letting fresh air breathe on the case. It just wasn't so easy. Cleveland held too much of his history. Too many powerful images gripped him, filtering into every sight.

Most outsiders find Cleveland not nearly so dreary or dumpy as the jokes that dog it. The snide remarks (Q: "How does Cleveland differ from the Titanic?" A: "Cleveland has a better orchestra") melt away.

A niceness pervades Cleveland. But a person couldn't forget that it was the place where robber barons and Mafia and Teamster arm twisters also made their way, hidden and sometimes protected. Beneath the niceness, a brutal argument could erupt on the street, at City Hall, in the courthouse.

A murder could happen in the middle of the night and never be solved. A trial might take place and certain evidence might be ignored and suppressed. And a person couldn't ignore the images of all those abandoned lots along the East Side.

The irony was that for Sam R. the negative reputation of Cleveland held true, not because of dumb jokes or bad public relations, but because of specific bad experiences. Here was the place where the newspapers had actually mounted a campaign to send one man, his father, to prison or to the electric chair; and when his father was finally released and acquitted through the efforts of outsiders, the same papers had abandoned any attempt to solve the murder of his mother, which had so devastated the community, his family, and him.

No agency had repaid them for the loss, his dad's years

in prison. No official had ever offered regrets, said the simplest of words: "We're sorry." None had held out a hand, given an understanding pat, offered to help patch the wounds, speed the healing.

Sam R. Sheppard was hoping that at least some of Cleveland would listen.

Standing at the podium of the City Club on October 27, 1989, Sam R. readied himself to deliver his speech: "Mistrial, Prison Reform, and the Death Penalty." These three ideas were the magnets that drew him to speak up. Later, he would talk at a program arranged by CURE, the prison reform group that had originally suggested the trip. There the audience would be more predictable. Here he wasn't sure what to expect. He had researched carefully, crafted his speech as he wanted. The message: based on his father's own brush with it, Sam R. opposed the death penalty. The feelings he could supply on his own. The facts he sometimes had to look up, since his own recollections were based on impressions gathered at an early age and then held inside for many years.

The City Club was a tradition in downtown Cleveland dating to 1912. The guest appearance of Sam R. was facilitated personally by the then-executive director, Reverend Alan J. Davis. Davis had grown up in Cleveland Heights with Dr. Sam, where they had been neighbors and school buddies, the kind of friends that go way back and never go away.

Davis could remember when Sheppard and Marilyn Reese met at Roosevelt Junior High School. Even though Marilyn was a year and a half ahead of Sheppard, they seemed destined to marry each other. Reverend Davis could remember Dr. Sam as the gracious successful athlete, the popularity contest winner, the darling of the Sheppard family.

Dr. Sam had been a do-right fellow at the vortex of a large circle of friends. He was elected president of virtually every club he joined and was voted class president every year. A high school newspaper once teased that Sheppard had "made it his ambition to aid the school by being connected with as many beneficial activities as possible," listing thirteen. In the sports teams photos, he was dreamily attractive, with hazel eyes and Hollywood poster-boy looks, and he was usually in the center, surrounded by teammates. He had lettered in varsity football, basketball, and track, with his relay team making it to the state competition. At graduation he secured the title he coveted: Most Valuable Athlete.

In his last year of high school, Sheppard was jokingly called "Skidmore" by some of his friends because he was so close to Marilyn, then attending Skidmore College in New York. If anyone was more popular than Samuel Holmes Sheppard, it might have been Marilyn Reese. In the summertime, boys from other high schools gathered around her out at the Mentor beach, and in the winter she had her pick from the varsity boys. She was good in sports, too, and was readily pledged into fashionable sororities. Later Dr. Sam recalled how she dated only the "best fellows," older boys whom he admired. "The fact that she was now my constant companion in a way placed me in their class, which was sort of an honor," he wrote. They exchanged school pins with deep reverence. Occasionally they had tiffs, usually over another fellow seeing Marilyn or another girl dating Sheppard. But after a sorority dance and scavenger hunt and a long walk on a moonlit road lined with poplar trees in 1940—Dr. Sam could recall the date, October 11, more clearly than his wedding date— Marilyn told him she loved him. No girl had ever said that to him before.

Although Marilyn was already a college woman, she came back to Cleveland Heights to see the graduation ceremony for the class of 1942. Sheppard, as class president, was the designated student speaker. He echoed the high-minded values of his civics lessons. He exhorted his classmates to "strive for greater learning, greater tolerance and better understanding, for in these lie the hope of the future."

Reverend Davis knew what kind of person Dr. Sam Sheppard was; his belief in Dr. Sam's innocence never wavered.

Members crammed the City Club, and as executive director Davis worked the crowd with a professional hand. Friday lunch forums at the City Club were broadcast on 156 radio stations across the country. Newspaper reporters attended every week, and when the speakers touched a local nerve, such as today, television cameras appeared as well.

Sam R. was leery of the press. He had personal reasons, and good ones, to feel cautious. The U.S. Supreme Court had even validated his reasons. Thirty-five years earlier, the *Cleveland Press* had printed 399 Sheppard articles in a six-month period: front page, accusatory, sensational. The other two daily papers had kept pace. Television reporters had found a new use for the medium. Dozens of reporters from around the country had taken over the courtroom with the consent of the judge. Loudspeakers had been installed in the courtroom to amplify the proceedings, and the constant coming and going of reporters had still created a disruption. The judge had permitted jurors to be photographed over forty times and had brazenly violated courtroom decorum by setting up a special table for the press in front of the bar, next to the jury box and the witness stand. These same reporters had for months mobbed Sam R.'s family, crowded onto their lawns, stationed themselves outside their homes. Sam R. could still remember cameras clicking when, as a sleepy seven-year-old, he had been led away from the early-morning murder scene.

Sam R. intended not just to face the press but to face down the press. The press had always had an important place in Cleveland. The city was so-named because of a newspaper's arbitrary decision. Unable to fit the correct spelling of namesake Moses Cleaveland on its masthead, a letter was dropped. "Cleveland" without the first *a* was the version that stuck. In Sam R.'s view, that was a minor matter compared with how the press had vilified his father.

Cindy Leise, a reporter for the *Chronicle-Telegram*, wasn't one of the old-guard reporters. The newspaper she wrote for was published in the small city of Elyria but had a large West Side readership. Leise's managing editor, Arnold Miller, had worked for the *Cleveland Press*, although after the days of the Sheppard murder case. But the Sheppard mystery was inculcated in Miller while he was at the *Press*, and it lingered after he left. Leise, with ten years at the *Chronicle-Telegram*, had stepped up from beat reporter to investigative pieces. At the urging of Miller, she read the old clips. She was tantalized by the way that, over the years, with the slightest prompting, the Sheppard case would be revived. But Leise came at the story fresh.

"For too long the public has depended on faulty information about this case from a prejudiced, unthinking, and

careless press. At least now a new generation of news-
people seek the true story in the interests of fairness," Sam
R. planned to say in his speech.

The sparks that were reigniting the Sheppard case right
then came from a different murder case. The homicide of
Ethel May Durkin had taken place in another West Side
Cleveland suburb, Lakewood. Richard G. Eberling (pronounced EBB-er-ling) had been tried and convicted of murder in the Durkin case less than three months before Sam
R.'s visit. Eberling had been a prosperous, active, even
prominent, West Sider before moving to Tennessee with
his close friend and companion, Obie Henderson, not long
after Durkin died.

A couple of times the *Chronicle-Telegram* had run articles about Eberling and the way that he had transformed
a former farmhouse on the West Side into a "homes and
gardens" tour showpiece. What specifically interested
Leise's editor was that Eberling had been a window washer
in 1954 at the home of Dr. Sam Sheppard. The nature of
his business gave him access to homes and people all along
Lake Road. He knew the interior and exterior of properties
well. He told a tale about having cut his hand in the Sheppard home a few days before the murder, and claimed to
have inside knowledge about who committed the murder.

The Durkin homicide itself was a peculiar case that might
have been borrowed from an Agatha Christie story, since
it seemed both too odd and too pat to happen in real life.
Ethel May Durkin was an elderly widow who died in 1984
and from whom Eberling had inherited three-quarters of a
million dollars. Initially, Durkin's death came under no special scrutiny. While alone with a caretaker, she fell in her
home in 1983. The caretaker called the paramedics, but
Durkin died after six weeks in the hospital. Only years later
did the death come to be charged as a murder, with the
caretaker, Richard Eberling, as defendant. After a trial and
conviction that summer, Richard Eberling was sentenced
on September 13, 1989. By coincidence, Sam R. arrived in
Cleveland five weeks later.

Not many reporters had followed the Durkin case
closely, and Cindy Leise had no great love for trial coverage. She had skipped most of the month-long trial. The
only surviving daily paper in Cleveland, the *Plain Dealer*,

had run a few stories each week of the trial, usually carrying them without great hype in the Metro section.

The Sheppard case was of far more interest. The *Plain Dealer* devoted considerable space in the month of July to thirty-fifth-anniversary coverage of the Sheppard case, turning to the same tired reporters who had editorialized for Dr. Sam's conviction in the first place. They ran a picture folio, a review of the murder and trial in 1954, and a slight mention that Dr. Sheppard had been found not guilty after all in 1966.

Added to the retrospective this summer had been a revived call by Sam R.'s uncle, Dr. Steve Sheppard, for Cleveland officials to find the murderer. Dr. Steve had long ago moved to California. He was weary of the case, and young Sam's interest came as a welcome relief.

Local authorities were not likely to heed Dr. Steve. Even in 1989 the local prosecutor was the very man who had prosecuted Dr. Sam in 1966, John T. Corrigan, called "John T." or "J.T." by those who worked with him. After the fair trial in 1966 that had freed Dr. Sheppard, John T. proclaimed that Dr. Sam was guilty anyhow. His son, Michael Corrigan, a judge in Cleveland, later reiterated the point when John T. became incapacitated. "My father believes that the man that killed Marilyn was Sam Sheppard without a doubt. They had the right guy." Young Sam was hard pressed to see a glimmer of possibility that any official in Cleveland would do anything at all.

Outside Cleveland, even modest distances away, the treatment of the Sheppard case had often been different. One of the biggest critics of the media coverage in 1954 had been a newspaper in Toledo, Ohio. Cleveland reporters had become so prosecutorial, the Toledo paper had said, that they had a vested interest in the conviction. The sensationalism of the press was overstepping the bounds of freedom and interfering with the conduct of fair trials.

From the perspective of many who stood a distance from this city, by either geography or time, there was a maze of wonder layered on top of the puzzle of murder. The question was not only "who done it" or why, but something much deeper, more fundamental, touching on matters of justice and the judicial system. These were the issues that troubled Dr. Sam Sheppard, too, as he sat in jail awaiting his trial. "Is this the free country, U.S.A., that we studied about in school, where a man is innocent 'til proven guilty? It hasn't seemed like it in the past six weeks." As if inherited, the same question confounded Sam R. as he stood to speak before the City Club.

The Durkin case was receiving a much more cautious treatment from the *Chronicle-Telegram* than Sheppard had received from the Cleveland newspapers. The paper waited until the guilty verdict was returned against Eberling before publishing the copyrighted stories Cindy Leise had put together about Eberling's background and his connection to the Sheppard case. The articles were accompanied by a graphic with the caption "Shadowed by Death." The *New York Times* came out with a folksy country journal report later in August 1989, noting how interest in the Sheppard case, the "crime of the century," picked up as if the Sheppard trial had ended the day before and not decades before.

A judge had once tried to describe the Sheppard phenomenon: "Murder and mystery, society, sex and suspense were combined in this case in such a manner as to intrigue and captivate the public fancy. . . . Circulation-conscious editors catered to the insatiable interest of the American public in the bizarre. . . . In this atmosphere of a 'Roman holiday' for the news media, Sam Sheppard stood trial for his life." The paragraph was repeated often, but to Sam R. even it was not enough to explain away the events that engulfed his life.

In an entirely different context, an explanation was offered by a witness in the case, Dr. Lester Adelson. The chief pathologist at the coroner's office, he had conducted the autopsy on Marilyn Sheppard. In 1960 Adelson published an article reflecting on Shakespeare's *Hamlet.* "It has been said that 'Everyone can find in this play something to stimulate his speculative nature and stir his imagination.' " And so it was with the Sheppard case.

Sam R. was also a fan of *Hamlet,* but he was moved by another part of the play, a speech that called to him through the years: "Foul deeds will rise, Though all the earth o'erwhelm them, to men's eyes."

Unlike Dr. Adelson and many of the principals of the Sheppard case who went on regular speaking engagements, Sam Reese Sheppard had not spoken publicly about the Sheppard case since 1966, when his father was acquitted. The acquittal spoke for itself, he thought. There was no need to go around and explain that his father was not guilty. Slowly, Sam R. was beginning to discover that "not guilty" was not enough for some people.

Leise joined the crowd at the City Club, curious to hear whether Sam R. would indulge in Hamlet-like speculation and imagination. Leise thought she might try to get an interview. And there was the distinct possibility that Sam R. would be interested in the letters she had received from Richard Eberling.

After the introductory formalities, Sam R. started with 1954, the beginning of a saga that was still being unraveled. Changes had come about as a result: how defendants could be treated, how the press could cover trials, how the law would be interpreted. The saga had changed his life, and it was still going on.

"The Fourth of July, at dawn, my mother lay dead, just down the hall from me as I lay asleep. On the shore of the lake below our house, my father lay half in and half out of the water, viciously knocked unconscious . . ."

TWO

Emergency

Bay Village police had never investigated a murder before 1954. People lived in Bay because it was a friendly, safe community, filled with young families on the rising side of middle class.

Accidents were not uncommon. Police were used to rushing to car crashes. All the main arteries traveling west from metropolitan Cleveland went through Bay Village, and although Lake Road was a residential street, it was also a state highway.

Boating and swimming accidents on Lake Erie were frequent occurrences, too. In June 1954 a concerned Marilyn Sheppard called neighbors Esther and Spen Houk (pronounced HOW'k) at one o'clock in the morning. "I hear cries out on the lake," Marilyn said. "I can't go back to sleep and I can't wake up Sam." The Houks went to their window. They heard the cries, and even though they knew Dr. Sam was a notoriously deep sleeper, they told Marilyn to roust him. When she did, Spen and Sheppard pushed their boat into the water and rode into the darkness, rescuing a frantic fisherman who was stranded with a broken motor on his boat.

In 1954, when a car accident occurred, the police would immediately call the police physician for the city. That was Dr. Sam Sheppard. Sheppard would hop in a jeep that the village had purchased at his urging for emergency situations, and head out. Dr. Sam helped set up an emergency plan for Bay Village, was a member of the civilian defense corps, and in his wallet carried a card from the coroner's office that identified him as a qualified assistant coroner in the event of emergency.

If the accident victims needed assistance, they were rushed to Bay View Hospital, which had the nearest emergency room. Dr. Sam would scoot over and zip into medical gear. Bay View was only about two miles east of his home on Lake Road.

Sometimes when accident calls came in, Dr. Sam rang the town's safety director, who was also the mayor of Bay Village and his neighbor, Spen Houk. They'd ride out to the scene together. Under the village system, the police were supervised by the safety director, and the safety director was appointed by the mayor. Mayor Houk had appointed himself.

Older than Dr. Sam and Marilyn, with two teenage children, Spen and Esther became mentors and friends of the Sheppards. Dr. Sam was a frequent fixture at the Houks' home, sometimes just dropping by for coffee, other times patiently ministering in-house calls to Spen's mother, who lived there. The Houks' son, Larry, had made Dr. Sam into a role model, and their daughter, Lynette, had come to see Marilyn as a big sister.

Together, Spen and Dr. Sam invested in a boat for lake outings, each supplying his own motor. The two couples had vacationed together in 1952. Houk, a butcher with a nearby shop, often stopped by to have a cup of coffee with Marilyn. In February 1953, when a fire broke out in the Sheppard basement, Dr. Sam ran to the Houks to sound the alarm.

On the morning of July 4, Dr. Sam called Spen Houk with a different kind of emergency. "Come quick! I think they've killed Marilyn," he blurted out.

Saturday, July 3, 1954, had been an ordinary, if extraordinarily busy, day for the Sheppards. Dr. Sam had left in the morning for surgery at the hospital. His friend Dr. Lester Hoversten was staying at their house and was to join him.

A medical-school chum of Dr. Sam's, Hoversten had arrived at the Sheppards' on July 1, having been released from his duties at a hospital in Dayton as of June 30, 1954. Hoversten had been a resident at Bay View for a period, too. Marilyn wasn't fond of the bachelor, who could be a sloppy and inconsiderate houseguest. Still, when Hoversten asked to stay, Dr. Sam, intensely loyal, said yes.

Hoversten was assigned the master bedroom, which, like all the bedrooms, was on the second floor. Stairs to the second floor could be reached from the kitchen or the living room, each of which had three stairs that joined at a landing and rose in a northerly direction. Hoversten's room was to the east and south, reached by walking through a small dressing room filled with Dr. Sam's weights.

During warm weather, Dr. Sam and Marilyn slept in a room with a breeze off the lake, slightly to the west and north from the top of the stairs. If the door to the room were open, a person climbing the stairs could see into it. Like much of the Sheppards' house, the room was sparsely furnished, with twin beds, a rocking chair, a night table.

Slightly to the east of the stairs on the north side was the room where young Sam slept. Although it adjoined the "twin" bedroom, the rooms were buffered by a three-foot-thick closet on each side.

Dr. Sam's scheduled operation on Saturday was for the removal of a blood clot from the hand of an older patient. As he had the day before, on July 2, Hoversten drove separately to the hospital.

On Saturday, July 3, while at the hospital, Hoversten was seized with the notion of spending the night with friends in Kent, Ohio, about forty miles away. Dr. Sam and Marilyn were throwing a hot dog roast for the hospital interns on the next day, and Hoversten wanted to avoid the uncomfortable comments that might arise about his lack of job prospects. He left.

Before Dr. Sam could wrest himself away from the hospital, a man ran into the emergency room holding a limp boy in his arms. The boy had been hit by a utility truck. Dr. Sam rushed the small child into the operating room, cut open his chest, massaged his heart, and ventured a variety of emergency resuscitation efforts. None were successful. With sadness, he had to inform the father that the boy was dead. Physically and emotionally drained, Dr. Sam stopped by to visit his parents and then headed home.

For Saturday evening, Marilyn had arranged a pleasant summer dinner looking out at the lake with a neighbor family, Don and Nancy Ahern and their two children.

The Sheppards often entertained. People were in and out: family, neighbors, hospital employees, cops on the beat. Sometimes they dropped by to pick up medical supplies; other times, to say hello. Dr. Sam converted a room over the garage into a "clubhouse" for teen boys. Mostly football players, they often slept in the clubhouse overnight or played basketball in the driveway or used Dr. Sam's boat. Even workers on the property, such as Richard Eberling, said they were warmly greeted.

Since Dr. Sam and Marilyn were fixing dinner, the Aherns, five lots away, hosted cocktails in advance. But almost as soon as the Sheppards arrived, one more emergency called Dr. Sam back to the hospital. Another boy had been injured in a home construction accident, this time suffering a broken thigh bone.

Both families finally reconvened at the Sheppard home. Dr. Sam and Don took the children down to the basement and showed them a punching bag. They ate a sociable late dinner, adults on the porch, children in the kitchen, and it seemed that everything was finally on track for the Fourth of July holiday.

After dinner, Don Ahern took his children home, tucked them in bed, and then returned. Young Sam put on his pajamas and hung around downstairs while Dr. Sam fixed a broken toy airplane for him. At nearly ten o'clock young Sam was scooted up to bed. Later, Sam R. confessed that he didn't go to sleep right away.

Cool winds brushed up from the lake, whipping up the waves. The giant pre–Fourth of July fireworks were shot off over the lake. Spen and Esther Houk later said that they had gone down to the water and climbed onto a breakwall on their property to watch the fireworks.

The Sheppards and the Aherns relaxed in the living room, an odd L-shaped area, with the long end running east to west on the lake side. Don perched against a portable radio to pick up the action in the Cleveland-Chicago baseball game at the Stadium. The others clicked on the early-model black-and-white TV to watch the movie *Strange Holiday*. A 1945 film by the minor auteur-director Arch Oboler, it starred Claude Rains in a post–World War II nightmare about a man who goes on vacation only to come back and find the country taken over by the Nazis.

The title of the movie was one of those little things that

haunted over the years. *Strange Holiday* traced the confusion of a character who finds his identity perverted and lost overnight by forces greater than he and which he cannot understand. Dr. Sam tried to maintain a mild interest. To him, such stuff was pure fantasy. Still, Saturday night movies on television were the latest thing, and Dr. Sam and Marilyn cuddled. She sat in his lap on an oversized chair in the living room for a while.

Since announcing her second pregnancy, they had been more inclined to public displays of affection. Whatever slight rifts existed in their marriage had been mended. She was dressed casually in a pair of shorts that were almost her trademark, a sporty California style that suited her still-girlish figure. Dr. Sam wore lightweight summer pants, a white T-shirt, a casual corduroy sports jacket, moccasin-type shoes. How and where and when the sports jacket ended up folded on the couch and what happened to his T-shirt later became major points of contention.

During the movie, Dr. Sam decided to stretch out on a daybed that was next to the staircase wall, on the short side of the room. His energy depleted from trips to the hospital, and aware that on a holiday weekend there might be many more, he fell back on a technique that the Aherns were used to: taking a snooze wherever he was, no matter who was there. The Aherns left sometime after midnight, exiting by the Lake Road door and giving their good-byes to Marilyn. Dr. Sam didn't stir. He was still on the daybed, asleep.

That was the last peaceful moment in Dr. Sam Sheppard's life. Or in Marilyn Sheppard's life.

Marilyn prepared to turn in for the night. Dr. Sam thought she may have touched him and said that she was going on up. This wasn't unusual for either of them, and it was a lot easier than trying to awaken him. Before settling down, she removed her nail polish, leaving little cotton balls in an ashtray. Upstairs, she turned on a light in the dressing room. Customarily, the light was left on when Dr. Sam was out on call; now he was just "out" on the daybed. In the twin bedroom where she was sleeping, the shade and window on the north side were raised four inches so the lake air could keep the room refreshed. Sometimes it was said that young voyeurs would steal views of her undressing. Crawling into a pair of diamond-patterned two-piece pajamas, she tossed her shorts, shirt, panties, and bra on a small pile of clothes already accumulated on a rocking chair in the corner of the room. She folded back the sheets on the west bed by the wall so that Dr. Sam could easily crawl in when he came up, and, as was her custom, she slipped under the quilt on the bed closer to the door.

Sometime later, Dr. Sam didn't know how long, his sleep was pierced. The audible whoosh of the waves and the heavy-breathing winds of the lake commonly filled the house at night. But this was different. Marilyn's voice called: "Sam! Sam!" The sound penetrated the deep haze of the night. Like a cold slap of water on the face, his mind clicked: Marilyn was having convulsions, as she had in the early days of her previous pregnancy.

"Sam!" cut through the murkiness of slumber. Dr. Sam pulled himself up from the daybed, trying to collect his mental faculties, alert himself to medical procedures he might need to take, while heading up the familiar stairs.

He had no idea that he would come upon the scene that then appeared.

As he reached the top of the stairs, he confronted a confusing image. Marilyn was in her bed next to the door, but another person, a form he couldn't quite see, brushed across his field of vision. In their room. What? Who? A form with a light top of some type. The only illumination was the dim fifty-watt light in the dressing room on the second floor, many feet behind Sam as he ran to help his wife, and he was trying to grasp hold of what it was that he was seeing while concentrating on why she was calling.

He stretched forward with his body. Moans, groans—from Marilyn? Boom. Suddenly, he was hit on the back of the neck. Not even sucker-punched in front, where he might have a shot at hitting back, but hard on the neck. He fell, not gently, but violently. Boom. Thrown to the floor, knocked out, trying to fit this scene into the world he knew, hearing painful noises from somewhere—no, not from somewhere but from Marilyn. Boom. Everything was going black, but he resisted it, resisted it, trying to figure out what was happening. And why.

Consciousness returned slowly. How long he lay there, he did not know. He opened his eyes and in the dull light saw the glint of the badge he carried as police surgeon lying on the floor. The badge was usually pinned inside his wallet. His wallet, of brownish leather, was on the floor. Stiffly, he sat up, then stood. And then he saw a sight so unreal that he thought he must be having a nightmare, must still be unconscious on the ground or asleep on the daybed, anywhere but here in their bedroom. Blood was everywhere. A pool of blood on the bed. Her face. Her hair. Instinctively, medically, he reached for her neck to take her pulse. None.

He swung away quickly and ran to Sam R.'s room to assure himself that young Sam was okay. A sound. Downstairs. He didn't hesitate. He ran down the steps and, rounding into the living room, caught a glimpse of, yes, a form, a person who was now making haste toward the door that headed out toward the lake, to the north. Numbed by the smash to his neck and the sight of his wife, he pulled together all his energy and bolted after the figure. He ran through the porch, headed out the same door as the intruder, ran the twenty or so feet to the steps that led down to the bathhouse and beach, steps newly reconstructed last year after the fire. At the top of the steps he lost sight of the person he had seen. He clipped down the fifty-two steps as quickly as he could go, past the beach house, and on to the beach. And there it was again—the figure.

Dr. Sam lunged toward him, getting the best look he would have of this figure, and not a very good one. The clothing from behind seemed dark. A white man. A large head. Longish hair standing up on top of his head. Not like a 1960s hippie with long hair that went in every direction, or like the 1970s Afro bush that became so popular among blacks and hip whites. No, this was a 1950s kind of bushiness—a longish crew cut, hair that, unlike Dr. Sam's neatly groomed, standard part, went up in the air. A bushy appearance. The bushy-haired intruder.

When Roy Huggins created "The Fugitive" several years after, he had first called for a "red-haired" intruder. Too much like the Sheppard case, TV lawyers told him. The one-armed man was born. But on the beach, Dr. Sam saw a man with two arms, who used them both against Dr. Sam.

Later, when Dr. Sheppard tried to describe what he had seen, he displayed the extraordinary weakness of the medical profession. It didn't matter that he was a D. O., a doctor of osteopathy, and in constant struggle with M.D.'s, medical doctors. Both branches had a similar problem: an inability to communicate in ordinary words, even in life-and-death

situations. Too often he would revert to stilted language
and authoritative-sounding words that seemed clinical and
distant, too much the scientist in action. Trying to be precise, but armed only with groggy impressions, he would say
things like "I visualized" or "I perceived" or "I was stimu-
lated to respond" or "I ascended" or "I pursued."

And as he perceived it, the form was taller than Dr. Sam,
who was six feet tall. A big man, six feet one or two or
three. The impression of a very large head. A relatively
large form. And at that moment, a stronger man, too.

In the darkness, they struggled on the beach. The lake
waves crashed. Dr. Sam grabbed and tackled the form,
thought he had the best of him. Sheppard was athletic, fit.
He had a reputation for excellence in sports—trophies,
medals. Maybe he was not as fit as in his younger days, as
a younger man, as someone who did manual labor, worked
out. His energy was low, he was still dazed from being
struck in the bedroom, but like a football player hit with a
rough tackle and then sent back into the game, he put his
body into it. The figure overpowered him. There was a
choking sensation. He hit the beach like a punching bag
cut off its tether.

Light was beginning to filter through the sky when Dr.
Sam felt the water rushing over him. The lake. He was
lying belly down, legs and feet were in the water, head
toward the beach at the water's edge, a twisting sensation
in his throat. Low waves were wallowing back and forth.
He pulled himself up on the sand, out of the water. His
neck hurt. He braced his head with his hands. How did he
get here? Confusion. He was bare from the waist up; his
pants and shoes were wet. Light was breaking; he could see
the public park's Huntington Pier, about fifty yards away.
Dazed, he staggered to his feet and then back to the house,
remembering being aroused abruptly from his sleep, recalling something awful he had seen, unless, perhaps, yes,
maybe it was a nightmare, a movie, a piece of fiction. A
horrible dream.

As he entered the house, there was some disarray, but
he had no time for that now. There was one thing he had
to see. He climbed the steps to the bedroom, dripping with
water. He saw his wife, thirty-one years old, motionless,
in bed.

Her head was halfway down the bed, lying in a pool of

blood, her face battered and bruised. Her legs dangled over the bottom edge of the bed. The walls, the bed, the sheet, the bedspread—all were bloody. She was practically naked, pajama bottoms pulled down, top pushed above her breasts. He checked her again. He put his knee on the bed, leaned over, took a pulse. It was true. She was gone. As if by medical rote, he pulled the bedspread over her lower body. Marilyn was so modest about things like that. Again, a reality check. He went into young Sam's room. Sleeping. That was what he remembered from before. He wandered downstairs.

Clasping both hands behind his neck, trying to understand what was going on, choking back tears, he now noticed his medical bag upturned, a general mess in the den. Shaken beyond explanation, he thought maybe he would wake up. In a haze, he didn't especially notice the drawers pulled out, lying on the floor, his wife's watch also there, the bowling and track trophies knocked down. Nor did he take any special notice of the papers that were scattered about, or the lid of the desk that was lying on one of the upholstered living room chairs. He didn't think about his keys, the chain he kept in his pocket. He was trying to grapple with what was going on. How had this happened? How had he failed to stop it? He tried to think. What to do. Think. Think. There was nothing like this in his experience. Think. A telephone number came into his mind. The safety director, the mayor, his friend. He called Spen Houk.

THREE

Sounding Out

Three days of events in Cleveland whirred by quickly for Sam R. in 1989. The speech at the City Club had gone well, packed in with interviews, events, television appearances, before and after.

How intense the days must have been for his father in the three days after the murder. Sam R. had been isolated. He knew little of what was going on. Relatives thought that was best. Because the media were already spinning out of control, Sam R. didn't go to his mother's funeral. Television cameras would be there, photographers, radio and print reporters.

On the very first day, his father, in the hospital and injured, had been interrogated several times. Accused. And again the next day. And the day after. One set of officers had tried to question him the day after that, but Dr. Sam was at his wife's funeral. At any rate, officers from another jurisdiction were standing guard beside him as he mourned.

In these three days in 1989, Sam R. had traveled the state. With each event, he was finding insights about the case, himself, the world that inhabited him. In Columbus he had visited the old Ohio Penitentiary. Closed for good, it had been home to his father. Nearly every day his father had written to him. Sam R. meant to write every day as well, but he had not managed to be quite as diligent. Standing in the shadows of the old prison in 1989, he could remember the days when he climbed out of the car with his uncle Steve after the four-hour drive for the monthly visit with his father. He was eight when he was first allowed to

33

come. The visitors were brought into a closed, windowless room, which was lined up and down with picnic tables. His father, like all the prisoners, had to sit on the inside corridor. Sam R. and his uncle were placed on the other side. He had not even been able to sit next to his dad.

Inside, his father was simply known as "Doc." Sam R. imagined momentarily the cheer that roared throughout the prison when Doc was finally released. But the toll it had taken on him hadn't been known, even then. Sam R. visited his father's grave, a simple headstone in a cemetery near Columbus. It said "Endure and conquer," but he had died too young, too disillusioned.

Other moments on the trip had made deep impressions. He met Randall Dale Adams and Adams's mother. The connection was visceral. Adams's own ordeal of being wrongfully convicted and sentenced to death in Texas, exposed in the movie *The Thin Blue Line,* reverberated.

At a college, Sam R. spoke to a history club. His topic was prison reform and the death penalty, and he tied in strands of historical references about politics, power, the ascent of prosecutors to judgeships, and his personal observations of the criminal justice system. The professor came up afterward, disappointed that Sam R. had not discussed whether his father was guilty or innocent. Sam R. nodded politely and shrugged, but he wanted to scream. The U.S. Supreme Court had decided the case, written an opinion! A jury in 1966 had come to a verdict of not guilty! Sam R. said he was sorry that the professor hadn't known the topic in advance.

And there was the moment in Cleveland when relatives on his mother's side had caught up with them at a speaking engagement to say hello. They were cousins, his own age and younger, bringing words of goodwill. But he had a hard time with the memory of two aunts on his mother's side who had turned against his dad. Sam R. remembered that when he had been briefly called as a witness in his dad's trial in 1966, he could see the aunts through a crowd of reporters and noticed how they had aged. Now he was grateful, pleased once again to see the cousins.

Sam Reese Sheppard was beginning to understand more clearly his own unique perspective. His life was a bridge of victims and prisoners. They were not two opposing sides, separate and distinct, but two halves of a whole. His words and experiences could touch others with wounds to heal.

Quite honestly, he was drained by the constant pull on his emotions, and he was not anxious to take the phone call that came on his last night. He had accepted the offer to stay with Reverend Davis and his family in their East Side apartment. Tired, glad for the quiet, Sam R. was ready to bed down on the pullout couch in the den when Davis tapped on the door.

"There's a call, Sam. I think you should take it."

On the phone, he heard the voice of an elderly man.

"This is Monsignor," the man said.

Another crank?

"Look, I'm really sorry . . ."

"Is this Sam Sheppard? 'Chip,' as they used to call you?"

"Not 'Chip.' I don't use 'Chip.' "

"Let me run something up and down your psyche."

"Who are you?"

"Do you want to be in touch with Richard Eberling?"

"Well . . ." That self-conscious caution. Could he do it? What was involved? Should he do it?

"Do you know what I'm talking about? I said, Do you—"

"Yes. Yes, I think so." Don't say no, he reminded himself. Keep the doors open. Get the information.

"Good. That's the right answer. That's good. I'm in touch with him. He will contact you."

"Who are you?"

"I'm the world's greatest investigator. Just to show you I'm genuine, let me read you a letter."

Monsignor proceeded to read a letter from Dr. Steve Sheppard, his uncle. The letter was written on Sam R.'s behalf. Yes, yes, it was genuine. It was about the sailing trip that Sam R. had wanted to take after he graduated from high school in 1965, when media attention was again focused on his family as his father awaited a hearing by the U.S. Supreme Court. Private information, Sam R. thought. He didn't realize until later that the letter was part of the public file in the probate court. His uncle had cleared the trip and expenditure of money by writing to the judge, since Sam R. was still underage and Steve was his guardian.

Hearing the words read over the phone, Sam R. was impressed that this elderly-sounding man knew so much.

"Your grandfather hired the agency I worked for years ago. I worked on the case then. This is the greatest case in the world. I want to solve it. Do you get my drift?"

Monsignor said that Dr. R. A. Sheppard, Sam R.'s grandfather, had retained his agency to find new clues on the case. Monsignor intimated that the hire came after Dr. Sam's conviction in December 1954, but Sam R.'s grandfather had lived for only a few weeks after that. Later, Monsignor would describe going to the police department and talking to Captain James McArthur, the chief inspector, something that would have happened *before* the wrongful conviction. The agency that Sam R.'s grandfather had hired, he said or implied, was a major national detective agency, which he named. Sam R. had no way of knowing whether the information was true or not. In 1955 he had been dealing with second grade in a new school, a new living situation at his uncle's, the loss of his mother, grandmother, grandfather, and great-grandfather, and the removal of his father, his home, and his dog. He listened to the information, decided to try and ferret it out later.

Who this Monsignor really was and what he really wanted became something of another mystery. He refused to be seen in person; the phone was his instrument. The biggest clue eventually came from his license plates, which included the word WEB.

Soon it became clear that Monsignor's real name was James R. Monroe, and although he would only say he was "older than God," that meant God was about seventy at the time. Because he was in "deep cover," he didn't use his real name. At all times, Sam R. was supposed to call him "Monsignor." The name helped, he once confided, since contacts sometimes confused him with an official of the church, which he definitely was not. Sometimes Sam R. or others would talk to people about the case and they would mention that they had been contacted by some priest.

Monsignor lived in Lakewood, a suburb on Cleveland's West Side, and operated out of his home. Previously, he had a life as a private detective that he described, over time, as adventures in politics and labor management in

New York, London, Cuba, maybe even Siberia. He seemed to have spanned the world.

But later, when AMSEC came onto the scene, the dash and mystique surrounding Monsignor began to melt away, a diversion from the real task at hand. AMSEC, an investigative firm that was owned by a company traded on the New York stock exchange, handled largely corporate security. Everything it did was professional, upright. Reports were typed. Information was documented. Sometimes privacy was needed, but not code names. Conferences were in person.

Monsignor sent notes written in a large cursive hand, accompanied by articles underlined with red, and engaged in endless circular telephone conversations. He was not registered as a private detective in New York, as his stationery said, or in Ohio. He once said that he had attended the University of Dayton, although the school had no record of his having graduated.

Sam's uncle, Dr. Steve, had no recollection of him. "I doubt if we hired him," he said. A detective had been hired after the 1954 trial, but he was a private investigator in New York City, Harold Bretnall, who had died in 1963 before he had completed his final report. William Corrigan, the original defense attorney, had engaged private investigators from time to time to check out sporadic points, according to his files. But none was James R. Monroe or the firm that he named. Mrs. Nellie Kralick had been a secretary to Arthur Petersilge, the longtime Sheppard lawyer who handled all the family's business affairs. There were few things that Dr. R. A. Sheppard did without contacting or checking with Petersilge. And Mrs. Kralick had never heard of Monsignor; she was sure that she would have.

Later, Sam R. learned more about Monsignor. Court records indicated that years of litigation had surrounded his house, which was under foreclosure with over a dozen liens from judgments entered on credit cards, loans, taxes, and charge accounts. And it became increasingly clear that the one person who had paid him was Richard Eberling. While in prison, Eberling kept in constant and frequent contact with Monsignor.

The web that he was weaving spun in a half dozen directions. The question was, Who or what was he trying to catch?

Despite the nebulous history, Monsignor did have a grip on certain investigative techniques, even if his skills were slightly pre–computer age. Every phone call, it seemed, was taped; every document was scrutinized. He spoke in long, windy sentences that reflected the meanderings of the elderly and inserted yesteryear slang and a brittle "heh-heh-heh" chuckle after every sentence or two to let you know that he was enjoying himself, even if his listener was not. He worked with "operatives," and they also had code names, like Granny Goose and Stardust and Mason. He referred to them as "my people."

Though Sam R. never saw Monsignor in person, he was able to gather little bits of information here and there. He lived with his wife, Jayne, who almost always had the television on in the background. He had a dog named Old Chap, a pug. He knew Eberling from a mutual acquaintance, a woman who owned a carpet store and supposedly had once been a secretary to Monsignor. He was not tall—five feet, nine inches, with gray hair, blue eyes. He drove an old Cadillac El Dorado.

Eberling claimed to have seen him once, and that he was a little man who wore a green beret. When asked about it, Monsignor only gave his heh-heh-heh response and said, yes, in fact, he had berets of many colors, red, green, blue.

His letters came on bright red stationery that said "Kings Cross, Consultants" and listed offices in London, New York, and Miami, none operative, and had a phone number in Cleveland that was so out of date that it used the old alphabet prefix instead of numbers. For unknown reasons, the names of the presidents of "Licensed Detectives" associations of New York and in London were on the letterhead. On the top line, it said, "Enquiries—Verifications—Audio Research."

"I don't have any money," Sam R. said to the elderly man, a bit tentatively. So many people thought of his family as wealthy, expected him to have money flowing on tap. In the best of times they had been financially secure, although not nearly so rich as people seemed to think. And whatever they had had was now long gone. Sam R. was only keeping his head above water, working part-time as a dental hygienist, spending his free time now on anti–death penalty work. He had no savings, little disposable income, nothing to pawn or sell. He lived a spartan life that suited him. He had no car but managed quite well by bicycle, riding almost everywhere in Boston except in the most horrendous winter weather conditions. He lived in a rooming house, where he had a room to himself and shared a bathroom with others. At times it occurred to him that he had replicated the nearly ascetic conditions of the prison that had been home to his dad.

"I'm doing this to prove I'm the world's greatest investigator. To my cronies. Of course, most of them are dead." Monsignor chuckled. "But around the world, they'll know that I solved the most famous case. This is international. Can you think of a greater case? So, do you have any new information? Anything to check out?"

"Maybe." Sam R. remembered the Valentine call just before he left. "There is one thing I could use help on."

"Good. I'll be in touch when you get back to Boston. You'll get a package from me. And after you digest it, I want your observations. I think you know what I mean. Are you with me?"

"Okay." Sam R. had no idea what he meant.

"And," he told Sam R., "you let me know when you hear from Richard Eberling. I want to know what he says."

"Okay."

"But don't think you can get away."

Saying little, Sam R. slipped back to the den at Reverend Davis's, where the pullout couch awaited him. He felt as though he had stepped out of a long sleep with this trip, speaking out, stretching; now with this call, he had been personally pulled out to a different level. What level it was, where it would lead, he wasn't sure.

Going solo on an investigation of his mother's murder seemed impossible, especially after three days in Ohio. His feelings were too tender. And there was no place, really, to turn; no center for reinvestigation, no cop or prosecutor to call up and say, "Hey, have you heard about thus-and-so?" Victims and survivors had nowhere to turn, except to themselves, their strengths, their resources.

What could happen if he had some people to help him? He didn't know. He had been alone for so long. He lived alone, was currently without a steady relationship. Even in the days when he had tried his hand at music, he had been a solo performer.

Maybe what he needed was a band. A musician friend had once explained a formula for getting the right people together in a band. A lead, a bass, a drummer: people who could play together and play off one another. Maybe the same concept applied to the case. The notion of building a team, of reaching out to different players, seeing how they sounded together, adding or replacing as needed, was an attractive one.

Later, he began to fill out the idea. A writer from Canada never materialized; a writer from California came and went. And then the elements of a band, a team. Terry Gilbert stayed. He was an attorney Sam R. had met in Cleveland. An activist criminal defense lawyer, he had come to the Equality and Justice conference at Cleveland State University where Sam R. had delivered his address against the death penalty. Gilbert came up, shook Sam R.'s hand, and later Sam R. called him to see if he would provide legal representation in Ohio. Cynthia Cooper, a writer living in New York City, stayed too. She was originally from Cleveland, and her background as a lawyer attuned to social justice issues had drawn her to the story. She had contacted Sam R.; the two eventually met for coffee in Cambridge, and they slowly built a working alliance. And Monsignor: he stayed for a long time, until he seemed stalled in riddles and circles. Sam R. finally became frustrated. Through luck, AMSEC appeared on the horizon and stepped in on the investigative end, providing necessary expert guidance.

For now, Sam R. was leaving Cleveland, well, with an idea. If he could get a team of people to help, he might actually make progress on the case. At least, he had nothing to lose by trying.

He had hardly been back in Cambridge for a day when he found the letter in his post office box.

Prison letters were easy to spot. The plain envelopes, the bulkiness, the way they never seemed to be glued flat, the slightly dangerous feel about them, like stolen property or counterfeit money. Secrets. Heavy, no matter how much they weighed. When he saw Richard Eberling's envelope in his box, Sam R. was so nervous about the letter's possible contents that he spun away, forgetting his keys still dangling in the lock.

The writing on the letter was small and in such faded

gray pencil markings that it gave the appearance of words trying to disappear, shrinking to hide from themselves. Sentences were choppy. They were not even sentences. Misspellings fell like droplets throughout the text. Reading it was slow.

Oct. 29, 89, Sat.

Dear Sam,
 . . . The good Lord certainly writes with a crooked line. How very strange when I met you and your father. Eating breakfast thirty six years ago. About this time in Oct.
 Never in my wildest of thoughts would have dreamed. I would be writing to you. Let alone be found guilty of a murder. Then my life taken from me. Such as it has been.
 Your family has been with me a long time. . . . Sam, yes I do know the entire story. . . .

The letter continued for a few short paragraphs. Elusively, Richard Eberling said that he knew who the real murderer was. No, he said, it was not Dr. Sam. But he, Eberling, had been party to private conversations with both of Sam R.'s parents, and each had shared personal information that gave him alone the details and solution to the murder. "Something you should know about me People for some unknown reason Confide with me." He had not come forward before because he had promised not to tell. Now he could. He would like to meet Sam R. He signed off: "I Remain, Richard Eberling."
 Sam R. read it and put it down. Read it again. Again. What did it mean? What was he talking about? What was written between the lines? Could this man, now in prison for murder, unlock the gates to this murder, after all these years, all the miles traveled, all this turmoil?

FOUR

Red Dye

Nerves were on edge again in 1966. Sam R., then eighteen, sensed it before he got the letter. The letter, received on coming into port in mid-February in Madras, India, months along in his around-the-world trip, confirmed it. Eager for the news, he slit the envelope at once.

The letter was from his dad: his case was being heard by the U.S. Supreme Court on February 28, 1966, less than two weeks away. Sent separately was a letter from Ariane, the German-born woman who had become his father's second wife after a prison romance. Confidentially, she wanted to tell Sam R. that his father needed support and was hurt that Sam R. was not close by. Sam R. gave away most of his belongings and flew back.

Light snow flurries fell when they mounted the steps to the Supreme Court building in Washington, D.C., on February 28, 1966. Together they posed for the media people gathered outside: young Sam, his father, Ariane, and his father's attorney, F. Lee Bailey. From the steps they walked into the marble portico and anteroom with a breath of awe.

Inside, a quiet, an implied stillness. People spoke in whispers, if they spoke at all.

The route here had been neither quick nor easy, and now the Court held the final decision in its hands. Dr. Sam had been released from prison on July 16, 1964, based on the order of a federal district court judge in southern Ohio, Judge Carl A. Weinman. Weinman, perhaps because he was two hundred miles or so from Cleveland, was not intimidated by the history of the case and its trail of bad press. He ruled that Dr. Sam's constitutional right to a fair trial had been violated in 1954.

The opinion by Judge Weinman included pages of the frenzied articles that Cleveland experienced in 1954, untrue stories filled with rumor, innuendo, fabrication.

QUIT STALLING—BRING HIM IN

GET THAT KILLER

ISN'T THIS MURDER WORTH AN INQUEST?

TIME TO BRING BAY SLAYING INTO OPEN

WHY DON'T POLICE QUIZ TOP SUSPECT?

BUT WHO WILL SPEAK FOR MARILYN?

Screaming headlines and slanted articles insisted that Dr. Sam was guilty, the judge noted. Regardless of an individual juror's perspective, the community was so prejudiced that a fair trial could not be had. Jurors, allowed to go home each night, were bound to hear the negative information, and their very ability to serve was compromised.

"If ever there was a trial by newspaper, this is a perfect example," wrote Judge Weinman. The newspaper acted as judge, jury, and prosecutor. The biased reportage was, said the judge, an injustice not only to Sheppard but to the community as well.

The trial of Dr. Sam Sheppard, Judge Weinman concluded, was worse than unfair; it was "a mockery of justice."

Almost ten years after his arrest and incarceration, Dr. Sam finally walked freely outside the walls and gates. Judge Weinman's ruling was the only thing that stood between Dr. Sam and E. L. Maxwell, the warden of the Ohio Penitentiary. Judge Weinman had given Dr. Sam sky and water, breathing room, and time with a son he barely knew.

The State of Ohio was not happy and immediately decided to appeal. In May 1965 the appeals court voted two to one to reverse Judge Weinman. Dr. Sam was ordered back to the Ohio pen.

A hearing was set on the issue. Dr. Sam came prepared with the little bag that he kept packed beside the bed during his nine months of freedom. Unlike his first incarceration in 1954, he now knew the ropes. He knew what items he would need. Miraculously, Dr. Sam was allowed to remain free on bond as the case notched up to the next level in the system. That was the U.S. Supreme Court.

While an impressive structure, the Supreme Court looked small compared with the White House or the Capitol or the Pentagon. A compact building, it had a mere 188 seats for observers. At the front would sit the nine justices empowered to interpret the Constitution. This was the last stop. Even if only five Justices agreed and four disagreed, their word became precedent to be followed by every other court in the country.

And the Justices held the power to make a decision that could change forever Dr. Sam's life.

People always say, "I'm going to take this case all the way to the Supreme Court"—as if it's a simple matter of making up one's mind and going ahead and doing it. Not at all. The Supreme Court doesn't take many cases. Each year, 4,000 to 5,000 requests for a hearing are presented to the Court; only 150, less than 4 percent, are selected. Of those, only a handful will be criminal cases.

To be among the chosen, a person files a petition for a "writ of certiorari." Special reasons are urged to explain why the highest court in the land should spend its time hearing an appeal on the case. Justices look for cases that will settle an important constitutional issue.

F. Lee Bailey, who had taken up Dr. Sam's case in 1961 after trial attorney William Corrigan died, wrote an impressive petition for "cert." Bailey explained why the trial judge, Judge Edward Blythin, had failed to provide Dr. Sam with a fair trial in 1954, free from the invasion of the press.

The American Civil Liberties Union joined on Dr. Sheppard's side, even though it usually took the point of view of the press. The ACLU explained that as communications technology and the public thirst for details of notorious criminal trials both grew, courts needed guidelines. If the Court didn't do something, every case could be like the Sheppard case, tried in the press instead of the courts.

The Court agreed to accept the case.

Although he had been involved in the legal system for nearly eleven years by the time the Supreme Court announced it would hear the Sheppard case, Dr. Sam was still learning what it meant. On January 14, 1965, he scribbled:

"Much reaction over Supreme Court ruling to hear case. I was not aware of the importance of this step."

The scene was set. The case highlighted the conflict: the First Amendment and freedom of the press versus the Sixth Amendment and the right to a fair trial.

Dr. Sam's trial attorney, William J. Corrigan, had pressed the issue initially, in 1954. Corrigan objected time and again during the trial to the outrageousness of the press's conduct. A criminal defendant generally cannot later appeal an issue if objections have not been made at the trial, where the problem can be corrected in the first place.

Corrigan spoke up vociferously. He objected to the press's takeover of the courtroom. He objected to the loudspeakers, to TV cameras, to photographers. The judge always responded in the same way: "Overruled."

Judge: And let the record show that counsel for the defendant and the defendant, himself, have been voluntarily photographed in the court room from time to time during the progress of this trial.

Corrigan: I haven't been voluntarily photographed. Neither has the defendant. We have been compelled to be photographed. We can't escape it.

Judge: Oh, no, I don't think that is so, Mr. Corrigan, and the court will say to you that the defendant is not to be photographed in the courtroom at all without your consent.

Corrigan: Well, if there has been any consent by anybody in this matter, the consent is withdrawn.

Whatever criticisms there were of William Corrigan's defense of Dr. Sam, and there were many, his staunch stand against courtroom abuse by the press was impressive. In other publicized cases of the time, such as the trial of Julius and Ethel Rosenberg as alleged spies in 1953, similar objections were not made. As a result, Marshall Perlin, the attorney who handled the Rosenberg appeals, could not use that issue for appeal. In Sheppard's case, the groundwork was laid, even if the objections were summarily denied during the trial.

Dr. Sam registered what was going on only in the middle of the trial. "The realism of what has happened has just hit me in the past week or two. I see that these people now are going to try to railroad this thing through to protect the papers and officials who have gone out on a limb," he wrote in a journal.

The judge himself became a subject of controversy at the Supreme Court. Judge Edward Blythin had been up for reelection and needed good publicity. F. Lee Bailey gathered statements that showed the judge had been biased against Dr. Sam. The judge had a son who was on the Cleveland Police Department's homicide unit, which was trying to convict Dr. Sam. A clerk, Edward T. Murray, and the reporter Dorothy Kilgallen revealed prejudicial comments that the judge had made before the trial.

Kilgallen, known for her celebrity role on the television game show "What's My Line?," covered the trial and was shocked by the guilty verdict. But it wasn't until years later that Kilgallen also described how the judge called her in on the first day of the trial: "He shook hands with me and said, 'I am very glad to see you. I watch you on television very frequently. . . . But what brings you to Cleveland?' And I said, 'Well, your Honor, this trial.'" Kilgallen explained that she was intrigued by the mystery as to who had committed the crime. The judge responded, "Mystery? It's an open and shut case. . . . He is guilty as hell. There is no question about it."

By 1966 Dr. Sam's prospects had improved considerably. Although every court on appeal had been critical of the press and its effect on the trial process, no court prior to Judge Weinman would overturn the verdict on that basis. Bill Corrigan had even tried to take the Sheppard case to the U.S. Supreme Court in 1956, ten years earlier, but the Court wouldn't hear it.

Times changed in the early 1960s. In 1961 Paul Holmes, a Chicago writer, published a book that said the trial "rubbed luster from American jurisprudence." Earl Warren became the Chief Justice of the Supreme Court, and began to take action against overreaching by police and prosecutors. In one decision after another, the Court ruled that defendants had a right to an attorney and to confer with their attorney prior to being questioned; to be protected from evidence gathered in illegal searches being used against them in court; and to be advised of their right to remain silent.

Expectations about what the Warren Court would do in the Sheppard case were high that morning. Fears also were high, especially Dr. Sam's.

Dr. Sam, Ariane, and Sam R. seated themselves, in that order, on the cushioned benches set aside for observers. To their dismay, Ohio Attorney General William Saxbe showed up personally to argue the case. Dr. Sam turned nervously to Bailey, but Bailey tossed it off. The Attorney General hadn't done the real work of preparing the brief. His appearance was an act of political grandstanding that would backfire, Bailey predicted.

The chamber itself was stern, austere. The light was dim. Other people began to step in.

Bailey stood in front of the bar, nodding to and quieting the other attorneys on the Sheppard side. Russell Sherman, his Ohio co-counsel, came in. Together they stepped to the front and, with white quill pens, signed in as counsel for the defendant. Later, Bailey presented his pen to Dr. Sam.

Then, it happened. Like a whisper, a gust of wind, the Justices whooshed to their places, the clerk calling all to rise as the Justices took their seats on high benches above them. Here were some of the most prominent, most powerful names in the nation. Earl Warren. Hugo L. Black. William O. Douglas. Tom C. Clark. John M. Harlan. William J. Brennan, Jr. Potter Stewart. Byron R. White. Abe Fortas.

The hearing began. "For the Petitioner, Your Honor, Dr. Samuel H. Sheppard."

Bailey was first. He had perfected the arguments, speaking eloquently with a measured voice. Facts rushed by: Bay Village, busy and successful doctor, guests, asleep on couch, said goodnight to Marilyn, "and she was never seen alive again."

Attorneys had only thirty minutes to argue their case, getting in their points and answering any questions that the Justices might raise. Only a short span of time to make an impact on the nine.

Bailey was interrupted. In the middle of describing how Dr. Sam rushed upstairs to see a white shape or form, a question came. The tone sounded too much like the prosecutor.

The Court: Is there any question about whether this form was a human being or not?

Bailey: I think the inference is that it was a human being. Dr. Sheppard said he could not be sure, except that it had a white top as it stood next to the bed.

Briskly, Bailey carried on. He told how Sheppard was interrogated extensively and the newspapers began to run the story with ferocity. One editor "unleashed his editorial artillery."

The kind of powerful courtroom speaker who gets portrayed in movies, Bailey hit his stride. Then the questions from the Justices came pummeling. Which articles was he complaining about? Are they in the record? What page? Was this brought up at trial? Why wasn't the jury sequestered, in a large city like Cleveland?

His time was up in a flash. How had the arguments fared? Sam R. and Dr. Sam couldn't tell. The Justices gave away nothing.

Next, the Ohio ACLU lawyer, Bernard A. Berkman, spoke for Sheppard. More questions. What could the judge have done? Can't you tell us specifically? Berkman answered dryly, without the flair of Bailey, but scoring legal points as if throwing darts at balloons.

Saxbe, the attorney general, representing the other side, followed. Bailey had prophesied correctly. He got off on the wrong foot, sidetracked on whether the state had agreed to the authenticity of the Dorothy Kilgallen statement about the judge's bias. He was confused. Saxbe began to look foolish.

After an hour and a half, recess was announced. Dr. Sam, Bailey, Ariane, and Sam R. headed for the coffee shop in the basement. As usual, Bailey was buoyant. Dr. Sam and Ariane sat grim-faced. Bailey wanted a moment with them.

Sam R. was sent to get coffee. When he returned, his hands were shaking so badly that the coffee cups rattled on their saucers. He nearly dropped the entire tray.

The afternoon session began with county prosecutor John T. Corrigan—no relation to defense attorney William Corrigan—taking over for Saxbe. The prosecutor had a gruff style, a dislike for Dr. Sam, and a greater antipathy for Bailey, the out-of-town attorney. He tried to show how the Sheppard case was different from and not as serious as other cases of prejudicial publicity. The Justices were testy.

With only fifteen minutes to go, Bailey had the last shot.

But he was left clearing up the silly points about why a notary was not present when Dorothy Kilgallen had given her statement. With the clock winding down, Bailey tried to summarize, expressing his consternation. Then his time was up.

The spectators were summoned to rise. No hint was given of the Justices' reactions. Their decision would not be issued for months to come. The Justices disappeared behind a wall. The chamber was empty.

Sam R. and the others walked back out on the steps, meeting the very entity under attack, the press. They gave interviews, but Sam R. was constantly aware of the cameras pointing at Saxbe across the way.

"We have concluded that Sheppard did not receive a fair trial . . ."

The Supreme Court opinion was released June 6, 1966—eleven years, eleven months, and three days after the murder of Marilyn Sheppard. The opinion could hardly have been more favorable to Dr. Sam Sheppard if it had been written by Bailey himself. As it was, it was written by Justice Tom Clark. Eight Justices signed the opinion; the only holdout, Justice Black, wrote no dissenting opinion.

The Justices clearly and plainly meant this decision to set a firm precedent across the nation. And it did. By the 1990s the opinion had been cited nearly two thousand times by other courts and written about or cited in nearly one thousand scholarly legal articles. This is not usual, even for Supreme Court cases. It set the precedent for other high-profile cases, such as the Rodney King incident and O. J. Simpson trial.

In a rare flourish, the language of the decision was emphatic. Sheppard's case, the Court said, was infected by "massive, pervasive and prejudicial publicity." Solemnity should attend a trial, but it had not for Dr. Sam. "The fact is that bedlam reigned at the courthouse." These disruptive influences, the Court said, sparing no disdain in its choice of words, created a "carnival atmosphere."

Much as Judge Weinman had done, the Court listed all the things that were wrong in the Sheppard trial: The publicity was enormous. A judge and prosecutor were running for office. The names and addresses of the prospective jurors were published, resulting in anonymous letters and calls. A table for reporters was set up in front of the bar, the area reserved for official court proceedings—"unprecedented." Media personnel overtook the courtroom and the courthouse. A radio station had broadcasting facilities next to the jury room. Reporters roamed in and out of the court proceedings, causing confusion. Sheppard and his attorneys could not have private conversations. Every juror except one had read about the case. Not sequestered, jurors were subjected to countless stories in the media. Jurors were asked to pose by the bailiff, and their photographs were in the papers more than forty times. During deliberations, bailiffs allowed jurors to make unmonitored phone calls. Untrue stories and incriminating articles were the norm. Sheppard had been examined for five hours at an inquest without the benefit of counsel, and it had been televised live, a unique event in an era of unsophisticated television.

After its litany of things that went wrong, the Supreme Court announced fair trial–free press guidelines for courts to use to deal with the "virulence" of the press. These guidelines explained what judges should do if another case like Sheppard's should arise:

- Continue the case
- Transfer a highly publicized case to another county
- Sequester a jury
- Adopt strict rules for courtroom conduct
- Insulate witnesses from outside influences
- Control the release of leads, information, and gossip to the press that might come from people who work for or have a duty to the court
- Order a new trial if publicity threatens the fairness of the proceedings.

Dr. Sam's name was inscribed in legal history. By now, it was a small consolation. Upon being released from prison on the order of Judge Carl Weinman, a reporter asked Dr. Sam how much it had "cost" him. "Ten years," Dr. Sam responded, his voice shivering. The reporter persisted. No, he said, how much did it cost you in *money.* "Money could not possibly repay me for my mother's life. How much would it cost to bring her back?"

Ethel Niles Sheppard, Dr. Sam's mother, might have appreciated the Supreme Court opinion. Quoted in it was

Justice Oliver Wendell Holmes, after whom she had given
her youngest son, Samuel Holmes Sheppard, his middle
name. But she was no longer alive.

Five days after he was convicted, Dr. Sam wrote his
mother a gentle letter, full of inspiration:

> Dearest Mother,
>   We have been the victims of a great injustice, but due
> to the wide publicity this injustice has been realized by
> many people all over the country if not the world. Bill
> Corrigan feels that I have been chosen to go through
> this experience in order that measures might be taken to
> prevent future injustices. He is confident of a favorable
> outcome and *so am I*. . . . Things are dark now but . . .
> Keep up the great and wonderful spirit you have. . . .
>
> > Love always,
> > Sam.

The effort to be upbeat did not succeed. Less than two weeks
later, Mrs. Sheppard shot and killed herself. In another two
weeks, Dr. Sam's father died at age sixty-five of a bleeding ulcer
brought on by suddenly worsened stomach cancer. Some people
claimed the deaths were signs that they felt their son was guilty;
Dr. Sam knew that was not true. They had died of shock at the
public persecution he had suffered and they had witnessed.

Finally, the Supreme Court, in a roundabout way, had paid
a tribute to the woman who believed so deeply in justice. The
Court repeated Justice Holmes's admonition that every conclusion in a case must be reached only by evidence in court and
not by outside influences, whether private talk or public print.

Still, public opinion had been influenced beyond correction in 1954. In 1994 Neil Postman, the noted writer and
cultural observer, described a parallel process. Red dye in
clear water, he pointed out, is not a mere additive. Red
dye is ecological: it changes everything. Even when Dr. Sam
was acquitted in a fair trial, some people persisted in quoting the old prejudicial tripe.

And even the Supreme Court, with all its clarity of vision, could not have had X-ray vision to see through the
layers of ineptitude and deception, the pieces of information conveniently buried, forgotten, lost, misconstrued.

That was going to be up to Sam R. to try to correct. And
he knew already that he was up against formidable forces.

FIVE

Circumstances

Monsignor called Sam R. after he returned to Boston in 1989, as promised. Sam R. gratefully gave him the number left by Valentine. Monsignor called back. She was not to be trusted, he said, and Sam R. could trust Monsignor on that.

Now he had some questions for Sam R.

"What did you see that night?"

Sam R. sighed. These old, old questions. Did he have to deal with them again?

"Nothing," he replied.

"Nothing?"

"Right."

"You slept through it?"

"Yes."

"You must have heard something."

"No."

"You were in the room next door."

"I know I was in the room next door."

"Then you couldn't have heard nothing."

"I didn't hear anything, damn it!"

"Nothing? *Nothing?*"

"Just lay off, okay?"

He had slept through everything. Of the two closets that separated his room from the twin bedroom, his was stuffed to the top with his comic book collection. Like his father, Sam R. was known as a sound sleeper. Even their neighbor Esther Houk recalled how young Sam had slept through fire engines and great commotion without so much as a little groan.

Not long after the tragedy, on July 24, while Sam R. was away at a Pennsylvania summer camp, Coroner Samuel Gerber had him called back to Cuyahoga County. Barely in second grade, young Sam was finger-printed, and, with only Aunt Betty at his side, he was interrogated at the office above the county morgue on the East Side. When Sam R. read excerpts from the transcript as an adult, he couldn't remember the interrogation and at first doubted whether it had occurred.

> *Gerber:* Will you tell me what you know?
> *Sam R.:* I don't know anything except in the morning I just found out about it.
> *Gerber:* And what did you find out?
> *Sam R.:* That my dad had a bad bump on his head; my mother's face was cut up and my dad had a bad bump on his head.
> *Gerber:* Go ahead and tell me what else you found out.
> *Sam R.:* I don't think I found out anything else.

Esther and Spen Houk drove up to the Sheppard home, three doors from theirs. That the couple had taken their tan Ford station wagon instead of walking was one of those matters of curious speculation later. Driving would be faster, they said, pointing out that Spen had a game leg from youth. Lake Road had no sidewalk on its north side.

But it was only one of many questions that later arose about their conduct. Why had they taken so much time to get dressed? They hadn't, they insisted. Why had they both come? She heard him answer the phone and sensed that she could help, she said. Why didn't they call the police immediately, from their own home? Didn't it occur to them that if someone was murdered the murderer could still be in the house? How well did they know the house? And how well did they know the Sheppards—more specifically, how well did Spen Houk, who seemed to stop by to visit Marilyn often, know Mrs. Sheppard?

The Houks entered by the Lake Road door, by which the Aherns had left at 12:30 A.M. Now it was about 5:50 A.M. The door was closed but not locked.

* * *

A fingerprint officer for the Cleveland police, Michael Grabowski, later testified that there were no fingerprints in the house, and he added that he saw a grainy line on some of the furniture, as if someone had "wiped it down." This became the popular myth. Few considered the obvious discrepancy: there had to be at least the fingerprints of whichever Houk opened the door, unless the Houks had wiped them off afterward.

A 1990s examination of the police records revealed a story different from that which the public heard in 1954. It wasn't that there were *no* fingerprints, Grabowski reluctantly admitted under cross-examination; what he said was that there were no *identifiable* fingerprints. Actually, there were a lot of prints. In some areas, there were too many prints—on the door, on the doorknob, on the medical bag that was overturned in the hallway; too many prints on the desktop in the den with the drawers pulled out.

But by the time the information was wriggled out of the police at the trial, the press had had a field day with the subject. The entire community was convinced: the house had been wiped down. It became a matter of lore, often repeated like the untrue tale that Dr. Sam refused to be questioned, like so many other tales that tilted the scales unfairly.

When Sam R. and his team began to reinvestigate, Dr. Peter De Forest, one of the top forensic criminalists in the country, looked through the old Sheppard file. "I'd question whether the house was wiped down," he cautioned. "It's common. The police sometimes say the house was wiped down when they want to point to a person living in the house."

On cross-examination, William Corrigan finally eked an admission out of a reluctant Grabowski. Yes, Grabowski finally admitted after trying to avoid answering, he had found fingerprints. No, he said, he didn't identify them.

And, it turns out, Grabowski saw many fingerprints on the glass top of the desk but didn't bother to lift them. He saw fingerprints on the windowsill in the murder room but decided they were smudges and not useful. He had the powder to lift prints off paper, but he decided not to use it on any of the letters scattered about. A palm print on the desk was too limited. The medical bag had a "pebbly" surface, he claimed—not good. He didn't want to disturb the blood spatter in the murder room, thinking that the police might send in someone to do a scientific examination of that. He could have done it, but he didn't. And it was never done by the police. Nor did he think of examining the bed in the murder room, the door or walls, the inside of the closet. And the bloody fingerprint that Bay Village officer Jay Hubach saw on the bannister that morning simply disappeared.

Only the first version, that the house had been completely wiped down, was printed in the papers. Grabowski, who also carried a camera with him, seemed not to have photographed the supposed minute lines that he claimed to have seen on the furniture and said looked as if they had been made by sandpaper or a cloth. When no one photographs it, pointed out Dr. De Forest, you don't know what is there. Wiping off a drinking glass is fairly simple. A house is virtually impossible to wipe down.

But the conclusion took on the pall of proven fact. Even some people close to the events came to accept it.

If the police had reason to want to solve this case, and fast, at least part of it had to be to deflect attention away from the frighteningly poor handling of the crime scene that morning.

The Houks immediately confronted signs of disarray. Spen saw Dr. Sam sitting slumped in a red leather chair in the den that was to the east of the door. Dr. Sam was barechested, holding his neck. He was moaning.

Spen asked him what happened. Dr. Sam was dazed. He said that he didn't know. But someone should do something for Marilyn, he said.

Spen stood, seemingly frozen. He could not turn, did not move, said nothing. Esther spun around and headed back through the kitchen, to the west of the entryway from the Lake Road door, and up the stairs. How she knew where to find Marilyn remained mysterious. She noticed water on the steps.

At the top of the steps she saw what Dr. Sam had seen—a numbing sight. Blood was all around Marilyn's head and had soaked into the sheets and mattress in a large splotch. The marks on her were counted later: thirty-five wounds, including fifteen blows to the head; a broken nose; nine abrasions on the hands, arms, and fingers. Esther, in a state of near shock, picked up Marilyn's arm, intending to check the pulse. She realized there was no point.

Esther fled downstairs. She told Spen to call the police, an ambulance. "Call everybody." Spen didn't ask questions and didn't go upstairs. The expression on Esther's face was enough. He went to Dr. Sam's phone and called Bay Village emergency services.

Dr. Sam sat, still holding his head, occasionally stood, ventured into the kitchen. He thought he had a broken neck, he'd say. Mumbling. He was muddled and in undertones would talk erratically about running upstairs and being hit on the head and chasing someone, things that didn't make sense to the Houks. And he kept repeating, "I've got to think." His disorientation was palpable.

Esther reached into a cupboard in the kitchen where she knew a bottle of whiskey was kept. She poured a glass and offered it to Dr. Sam. He declined. "That won't help. I have to think clearly," he said. Esther gawked. She believed, and the prosecution ultimately argued, that it was unusual for a man in pain, as Dr. Sam appeared to be, to refuse a glass of whiskey at 5:55 A.M. Esther stood, thinking she would like to either wake up from the nightmare or, if she was awake, just pass out. She drank the whiskey herself.

Dr. Sam muttered something about his son, and Esther again headed upstairs, finding Sam R. snuggled asleep in his bed, his back to the door.

Spen's calls brought Bay Village police officer Fred F. Drenkhan to the scene. He'd been on patrol since midnight, along with Roger Cavanaugh, and was at the combined fire-police center when Houk called at 5:57 A.M. Next to arrive were Bay Village firemen Richard Sommer and Richard L. Callihan. The firemen unloaded a stretcher, then realized that it wasn't really necessary. Stretchers were used to take someone to the hospital by ambulance; Mrs. Sheppard was beyond assistance.

Spen continued to make calls. Someone at the house suggested that a doctor be called, and Spen reported that Dr. Richard N. Sheppard, Sam's oldest brother, was on his way. When he entered, Richard bounded up the steps with police officers in tow. Then he stumbled back down and went to his brother. "Sam," Richard said, "she's gone."

"Oh, God, no," said Dr. Sam, collapsing on the floor of the den.

Later, when under pressure himself, Spen Houk said he heard Richard say to Dr. Sam, "Did you do this?" or maybe, "Did you have anything to do with this?" "No!" Dr. Sam supposedly answered. Dr. Richard flatly denied the exchange or that he ever considered the possibility that his younger brother might have committed this crime.

Houk walked back home and made more calls. He phoned the Aherns. He woke up his sixteen-year-old son, Larry, who was close to the Sheppards.

Neighbors and strangers gathered on the lawn, attracted by the calls from their mayor and the accumulating police cars, ambulance, and other vehicles on the Sheppard property. People were numb, slightly dazed. The middle brother, Dr. Steve Sheppard, arrived with a gun, his wife, and a doctor he had picked up from Bay View Hospital in case medical support was required. Soon-to-retire Bay Village police chief John Eaton showed up, as did patrolman Jay Hubach.

Houk went back to the Sheppards'. Soon his son, Larry, appeared on the scene and walked through the house. He might have touched some things in the kitchen; he couldn't quite remember, he said later. If so, he needn't have worried, since Grabowski was not in a fingerprinting mood. Larry went upstairs. He saw Mrs. Sheppard, still lying in her bed. Then he went and sat in his father's car, nauseated.

More curious onlookers came into the yard. Patrolman Drenkhan had an idea that this might be beyond the department's ability. He suggested to Houk, who as mayor and safety director was his boss, that the Cleveland force, which had more experience in handling homicide, should be asked to come out to Bay Village, even though it had no jurisdiction there.

There was a void in Cuyahoga County. Greater Cleveland had—and still has—an incredibly inefficient division of police services. No metropolitan police force existed. Cleveland and each of its fifty-nine suburbs were separate entities, each with its own police force. The county government, which included the city and suburbs, had no fully trained police. The sheriff's office served the entire county, but it was poorly funded, and deputy sheriffs had jobs like handling prisoners, guarding the courthouse, serving subpoenas.

The large police department of Cleveland had its own

scientific investigation unit. Small police departments like
Bay Village's had no such facilities. All departments relied
on the county coroner to conduct laboratory tests and forensic examinations. The coroner had about one trained
investigator.

Cleveland police officers arrived. So did reporters and
photographers, who would later argue over who was the
first reporter on the scene.

Someone from the coroner's office needed to be called,
and Drenkhan, who had recently gone through a course of
formal training, did so. After a couple of hours, the coroner, Dr. Samuel Gerber, arrived with his investigator, Ray
Keefe. More reporters came. No one seemed in charge.
There were just people, lots of people.

Before the crowds arrived, Drenkhan questioned Dr.
Sam. Drenkhan was a friend; Dr. Sheppard had run out
to many police emergencies with him. They socialized on
occasion, with Dr. Sam inviting the police crew over.

Dr. Sam was in obvious pain, confused. Drenkhan noted
that he appeared to have been hit around the face on the
right side. The officer observed small cuts on the inside of
Dr. Sam's lip and inside his mouth.

In a broken fashion, Dr. Sam told him the events of that
strange holiday morning. This was his first statement to a
police officer. Essentially, it never changed. Again and
again he was asked to tell it. Each time, he described how
he heard Marilyn scream, ran upstairs in the near dark, saw
a figure, was knocked out, regained consciousness, checked
his wife, heard a noise downstairs, ran down, chased a form
out the door, caught up with the form on the beach by the
lake, grappled with the figure, was knocked out again.

He was questioned at least four times that day, and yet
the newspapers began running banner headlines stating that
Dr. Sam Sheppard was refusing to be questioned. None of
it was true.

The house was beginning to get congested when someone
remembered young Sam R., still asleep. He didn't stir until
he was awakened. Even then, his uncle Richard already
had him on the stairs, clad in his pajamas, before he became conscious of the goings-on in any fashion: other people in the house, a lot of people, cars in the driveway and

the yard, people very grim, no one smiling or saying hello, just hollow faces. A foggy memory.

They piled Sam R. into the car, with few explanations, a vague, frightening conglomeration of people, upset, hustling.

> *Gerber:* Who woke you up?
> *Sam R.:* My uncle Richard.
> *Gerber:* Was that just before they took you to your uncle Richard's house?
> *Sam R.:* Yes.
> *Gerber:* Did you see anyone else that morning?
> *Sam R.:* I saw the doctors.
> *Gerber:* You saw the doctors?
> *Sam R.:* Yes.
> *Gerber:* Did you see anyone at the house, at your home, at your house? Who else did you see?
> *Sam R.:* I didn't see Kokie, my dog.

Kokie became another feature of the case, a case so circumstantial that the police scrounged for any evidence, a case pieced together with inferences piled on inferences, which were in themselves made from the slightest of information. Forensic scientists only later came to recognize the importance of understanding the probability or "order" of deductions, a term used by Charles R. Kingston, a professor and specialist in the field. In this case the "science" part was elusive and, for now, it was all about Kokie. Kokie was a dog that merged with the background, always there, rarely noticed. People even got her name wrong.

"Koko was a sort of lie-in-the-corner kind of dog," Nancy Ahern said. She couldn't recall where Kokie was the night before, or if the dog sneaked out the door when they had left.

Sam R. noticed that morning, though. Kokie was part Irish setter, not unlike the dog Dr. Sam had had as a child. After she was hit on Lake Road the year before, Dr. Sam had set her badly fractured leg until they could get her to the vet. Kokie still walked with a limp sometimes.

Why hadn't Kokie barked? Dr. Sam was asked. He didn't know. He thought about it. Actually, he had no idea if Kokie had barked or hadn't barked. He didn't even know if Kokie was inside or outside; sometimes Marilyn let the

dog out for the night and Dr. Sam was to let her back in
if he went up to bed late.

An animal writer even psychoanalyzed the dog, suggesting that dogs of Kokie's temperament were not excit-
able. Richard Eberling, who washed the windows at the
Sheppard home in 1953–54, recalled, "I would talk to the
dog. The dog only wagged its tail. It would lay on the chair
in the living room. It was the friendliest dog."

In one statement, Esther Houk testified that Kokie was
inside the house when they arrived. This was one of the
small factors that began to implicate Dr. Sam. But later, in
an unpublished interview with a journalist, Richard Dalrymple, Esther gave a different version. "The dog must
have been out of the house at the time we got there. Because I didn't see the dog anyplace," she said.

While Dr. Richard was bundling up young Sam R., Dr.
Steve looked over Dr. Sam. He didn't look good. He
thought he had broken his neck. Dr. Steve told Officer
Drenkhan that he was going to take Dr. Sam to the hospital. Drenkhan nodded.

When Dr. Steve said "the hospital," there was no question which hospital was being considered. He meant Bay
View, the hospital that the Sheppards ran and that provided
Bay Village with emergency services. With the help of the
young doctor he had brought along from the hospital, Dr.
Steve led Dr. Sam to his car. Later the papers alleged this
move was part of an elaborate cover-up on the part of the
Sheppards to isolate Dr. Sam, to hide him in a circle of
protection, cared for by his family and friends. A Cleveland
police officer volunteered that Cleveland police always took
people from crime scenes to their *own* hospital; in this case,
Bay View was the hospital that the police used.

What neither young Sam nor his father could know when
they were led out to cars that morning was that they were
closing the door for good. The house was seized by the
police; the Sheppards and the defense were barred.

A camera was brought in. Fred Drenkhan began shooting
the crime scene. Already things were happening out of
Drenkhan's control. Chief Eaton or someone else clumsily
knocked over drawers that were stacked up on the floor.

A woman's watch was spotted on the floor of the den.
Officers picked it up and handled it before realizing that it

was evidence. Then it was decided that there was no point in looking for fingerprints.

Other people were standing around. Newspaper photographers were permitted to roam the house, even go into the murder room while Mrs. Sheppard's body still lay there.

Dr. Steve returned to the house and asked if anyone had been in the basement. No one had. He led Chief Eaton downstairs. Lights were on—very unusual. No one knew what to do.

Officer Patrick Gareau, from Cleveland, took Grabowski down to the beach. There were footprints there. Grabowski had the equipment to make plaster casts. He didn't think these impressions were strong enough. He measured a couple, took some photos. Others he decided probably were not relevant and didn't bother taking photos of them; accidentally some showed up in his photos anyhow. Officers looked at a footprint in the bushes near the house, but nothing was done with it.

People seemed to be looking everywhere and doing almost nothing, nothing useful.

Dr. Steve found some canvas gloves with dark stains under a ledge outside the house. A Bay Village officer made a note that the deep underbrush on the hillside between the house and the lake had a fresh swath through it. This statement was contained in a report written later that summer by Captain Harold Lockwood of the Cleveland police. It was never released to the defense. Its true significance was to be pieced together by Sam R. and his team many years later. The brush was completely cut down later in the day.

Hubach and others saw the butt of an unfiltered cigarette in the toilet upstairs; it disappeared.

The body of Mrs. Sheppard was lifted off the bed by employees of the Pease Funeral Home to be taken to the morgue. Underneath her body, the coroner found two white objects: teeth. They were portions of an upper right medial incisor and a part of the occlusal surface of the upper left medial incisor. Dr. Gerber, who later set the time of death as 3 to 4 A.M., claimed that he tried to fit the teeth to Mrs. Sheppard's mouth, but rigor mortis had already set in and he couldn't open the jaw. The coroner concluded that the teeth were not from her mouth. This was one of several mistakes that had to be corrected.

These were not mere chips but teeth, broken at the root. They were from Mrs. Sheppard's mouth, but the police never wanted to focus too much attention on them. Clearly, Mrs. Sheppard had fought someone and had probably bitten the person. But Fred Drenkhan and all the officers had said there was no sign of struggle in the room. The teeth didn't fit into the prosecution theory. They were conveniently ignored in accounts of the case.

The coroner picked up a pillow case at the top of the bed. The pillow case lay above the spot where Mrs. Sheppard's head had been. The pillow was bloody on both sides. The coroner thought he saw something, an imprint of a weapon. Later he said the weapon was a medical instrument, although what medical instrument he could not say. The defense said he was seeing illusory images in the pattern of blood. Twelve years later, in a fair trial, Gerber admitted that he couldn't identify it as a medical instrument at all.

The crime scene was near chaos. Everyone was walking through the house, recalled Jim Redinger, a teen in the neighborhood. The police were very loose about security. Piles of materials were dumped on the floor. A boy under ten wandered through the first floor, looking for a turtle that Dr. Sam had found for him.

Officers didn't look closely at the murder room. Not until the end of July were other critical pieces of evidence found right under the bed in which Mrs. Sheppard lay. There was a piece of leather that was freshly broken off; a tooth chip that matched neither Mrs. Sheppard nor Dr. Sam; pieces of red chips that were first identified as fingernail polish, but analyzed after the 1954 trial to be lacquer. There were items that never made any public reports, like matches and tinfoil.

What happened in the next two hours may have determined the course of events for the next twelve years.

At nine o'clock Dr. Gerber completed a summary inspection of the scene. He went to Bay View Hospital, about a mile away, along with at least three police officers. Dr. R. A. Sheppard, the senior Sheppard, was at the hospital when Gerber arrived.

Dr. Gerber confronted Dr. Sam, and again Sheppard repeated the predawn events. Gerber inspected Dr. Sam's face, hair, eyes, mouth, eyebrows, hands, fingernails. Dr. Sam's clothing was handed over to the coroner—the trousers, wallet within, still wet; belt; undershorts; shoes; socks.

Clothing now became a major issue in the case: clothing without blood; clothing placed or misplaced; clothing lost; clothing found. Everywhere in the murder room, blood was splattered, and whoever killed Mrs. Sheppard would have had to have been covered with blood. None of Dr. Sam's clothes were splattered with blood: not his pants; not his leather belt. It's hard to wash blood out of cloth (and even then it can be seen microscopically), but it is virtually impossible to remove blood from leather.

The only blood on his clothing was a splotch, which matched perfectly a mark on the sheets where Dr. Sheppard said he had leaned over his wife to check her condition. On the sheets was a water-and-blood mixture that verified what he said: the pants were wet from his having been knocked out in the lake. And, matching Dr. Sam's description of events, sand was found in his cuffs and pockets, accumulated, no doubt, when he was left unconscious on the beach.

The Aherns said that when they left, Dr. Sam was asleep on the couch, wearing a white T-shirt. When the Houks arrived, he wore no shirt, and ask as people did, and try as he might, Sheppard had no recollection of what had happened to his T-shirt or when he had last had it on.

Days later, a T-shirt washed up on the pier of the Schueles, next door. It was ripped completely down one side seam. But when lab analysis showed that it had no blood on it, officials discounted it and said that it was not Dr. Sam's.

The corduroy jacket that Dr. Sam had been wearing became the greatest source of contention. The jacket was found in the living room, but whether it was lying on the floor or folded at the end of the couch or in the middle of the couch was in dispute. Officer Drenkhan said that it was folded on the end of the couch. Dr. Steve said he remembered stepping over it on the floor. Esther Houk saw it in the middle of the couch, but she didn't say anything about it until an unpublished interview in the 1980s. She said that she didn't think it was important.

Dr. Sam said he didn't remember when he took it off.

The jacket became important because the prosecution

tried to use it as circumstantial evidence to link Dr. Sam to the murder. At one point, for example, the prosecution claimed that Dr. Sam had heard his wife screaming and had casually arisen and removed his jacket and neatly folded it on the edge of the couch before responding to his wife's screams. Yet at the same time, the prosecution argued that Dr. Sam had committed the murder, and if so, he would not have been responding to his wife's screams. The dot-to-dot pseudologic never seemed to be a bother.

The Aherns would testify that Dr. Sam was wearing his corduroy jacket when he fell asleep on the couch. Only the police and prosecution could have known what was in Don Ahern's original statement on July 5, 1954, and they did not tell. After pressing to get unreleased police files, Sam R. learned about the statement thirty-nine years later.

On July 4, after visiting Dr. Sam, Gerber went back to the Sheppard house. One officer claimed Gerber said, "I think Sam Sheppard did this, let's go get him, boys." Gerber denied it.

By eleven o'clock, Cleveland detectives Robert Schottke and Pat Gareau and Bay Village police officers Eaton and Drenkhan were back at the hospital, interrogating Dr. Sam. Despite his injuries, Dr. Sam was trying to recall any detail that might aid the police in a thorough search for the killer.

But that was not what these detectives had in mind. Schottke and Gareau left the hospital, only to return in less than two hours. They wanted to know about rumors of marital affairs. Detective Schottke leaned over to Sheppard, pointing his finger. "I think you killed your wife," he said.

Dr. Sam didn't know it, but from then on, anything he said or did would be added to the swirl of innuendo and rumor that would be used to make him seem guilty.

A lot of the pieces of evidence didn't fit Dr. Sam. But with the decision made, any serious analysis ended. Calls to the police with contrary information were ignored. Forensic clues were rejected. Assumptions piled up. Mistakes mounted. Evidence was covered up. The thoughtful sifting of evidence—the type of impressive detective work you see on television shows—was skipped.

"This should have been a routine investigation. It was a small community. If properly conducted from the first hour, it could have been solved easily," said John Burkholder, one of the investigators working for AMSEC in 1994 to help Sam R.

Ray Keefe, the investigator for the coroner, immediately wrote a report that was not revealed until Sam R. saw a copy in 1993. "My only suggestion is to establish a central office where all leads, tips, and evidence should go through due process." It was never done.

Five jurisdictions eventually poked their fingers into the investigation, each doing disconnected bits and pieces: Bay Village police, Cleveland police, the county sheriff's office, the coroner's office, and the county prosecutor's office. No one was in charge; it was a mess.

Police forces committed classic mistakes. Cleveland Police Captain David Kerr gave lectures on procedure. "The investigation for and the preservation of physical evidence at the scene of a homicide requires a great amount of time-consuming care and attention to detail," he would say. In the Sheppard case, there was nothing of the sort. The biggest mistake detectives could make, he would explain, was to jump to conclusions. "Jumping" was an understatement.

Suspense and detective story buffs probably could recite proper procedure without hesitation. Their Cleveland counterparts were lacking. John H. B. Troon was a top detective at Scotland Yard in Great Britain, familiar with procedures at that time. He offered his observations in 1993. "The first forty-eight hours are crucial," he said.

In a sticky case, you would form a murder squad—forty to fifty persons. The scene is sealed off. You do house-to-house inquiries on every house or dwelling within a square mile, nonstop. You open a murder room with four to six officers and a civilian staff. You have a detective sergeant/officer-in-charge. You have teams outside. Every snippet of information, irrelevant or not, comes into the room. Everything is put on a specially adapted card reference system. It's cross-referenced. You disseminate all information and narrow it down. It's supervised. Among the phone calls, all have to be looked at and eliminated. You look at the type of crime—if there is anything on record. The information has to be assessed and incorporated. The senior investigating officer reads through all the evidence.

The senior officer works very closely with the pathologist. A forensic pathologist comes to the scene. After all the forensics are done, the body is removed. The forensic pathologist would ask a police officer to take notes, then do a report.

As a matter of course, you would look to see if there is a sexual motive. In ninety-nine out of one hundred cases, that is the motive, especially if there is a female victim. If a woman is found in bed, the top motive must be sexual assault. If in bed, and bedclothes are in disarray, this is especially so. It would be common for a murderer to make it look like a burglary. Then if he is suspected, there wouldn't be a sexual motive. You'd have swabs taken all over. A dental odontologist should be consulted.

As an investigator, you look at all possible suspects, not only to convict people, but to eliminate people as well.

Troon allowed that there is one exception, or perhaps, more accurately, one consistent failure, in conducting such a complete murder investigation. That's when the case is designated first as a "domestic"—a case in which the only suspect is going to be the husband.

Fundamental flaws that would jeopardize Sheppard's freedom continued through the day.

At the morgue, Dr. Lester Adelson, the chief pathologist at the coroner's office, did something careless. Dr. Adelson had a good reputation for his autopsy work. As usual, before conducting the autopsy, he arranged to have forensic photographs taken. But to see the wounds better, he washed them off. He did not test for foreign particles that might give clues to the as-yet-undetermined weapon.

From that point on, many questions about the wounds would remain a mystery, permitting open speculation. Which wound came first? Was Mrs. Sheppard killed in a series of rapid blows, one to thirty-five? Were the hands hit first or the face? Were there two sets of blows—one first, interrupted by Dr. Sam's running up the stairs, then continued?

More importantly, critical information about the weapon could never be determined exactly. Was it wood, or metal, or plastic? Were any bits of the red chips found on the floor also in the wounds, creating a link to the weapon? Were there any of the fibers discovered under the fingernails also in the wounds? Any hairs like those found on the bed sheet? Or any material similar to the leather scrap found under the bed? No one would know.

"Murderers have been run to earth by means of fewer clues than were discovered in this case," Bill Corrigan charged later.

Sheppard made mistakes, too—but not the ones that were publicly attributed to him. In retrospect, it is almost impossible to understand how one action, so seemingly normal, was suddenly considered obvious evidence of guilt. At the time, it was cause for scandal. After the detectives at the hospital accused Dr. Sam of murder, Dr. Sam's father called the family attorney, Arthur Petersilge, who did not hesitate for a moment. He called a criminal defense lawyer, one with experience—Bill Corrigan.

The media sounded an alarm. Only a guilty person would hire an attorney, the papers exclaimed. One reporter said, "I suppose many people, most of them police reporters at heart, thought that when Corrigan was hired, the guy was guilty." Community opinion was stoked.

One of the key players at the coroner's office echoed the sentiment. And in one front-page article, the police complained bitterly that no suspect would talk to them anymore since they had seen that Dr. Sheppard had hired an attorney.

The more the investigation went out of control, the more frustrated Dr. Sheppard and his family became. In a medical hierarchy, the doctors were accustomed to being in charge. Trying to assert control, they alienated people. "You guys are out on a limb," brother Steve supposedly told a reporter. "We'll see that's sawed off. . . . You don't care who committed the murder."

Dr. Sam failed terribly in perceiving the circumstances. He believed in the cops. He was a police surgeon. He believed the words of the idealistic speech he gave at his high school graduation. He believed that right was right and that the truth would come out.

Captain David Kerr later described the number-one fallacy of homicide investigation: the belief that Murder Will Out. It's surprising, he said, how many people subscribe to this belief. "Actually, we have thousands and thousands of unsolved murders."

Dr. Sam didn't know these things. As the victim of a crime and the husband of the murder victim, he was initially confident that the police would take his information and do a crackerjack job. The system had served him well, and he trusted it.

He was confused when the police came, one after another, into his hospital room with an accusatory tone, asking personal questions about lovers or potential scandals that seemed less directed at finding the killer than at embarrassing him. And there was something that he preferred not to have publicized, although it was hardly a secret.

Dr. Sam had had affairs. Marilyn and he had talked about his extramarital relations. She described the situation to friends, not in anger, but with a calm distance. If she was not enthusiastic about his straying, she at least knew and had turned the other cheek. After giving birth, Marilyn was uninterested in, even afraid of, sex. She was trying to revive her sexual desire and, at least for the time, excused Dr. Sam's dalliances. There was no threat to their marriage, no talk of divorce, no harsh recriminations, no plans to seek another life. Marilyn adopted the message of a popular tune: wherever you roam, just remember you belong to me.

Dr. Sam had no motive to kill. He, more than anyone, knew that he had none. He and his wife were deeply bonded, as friends as much as lovers.

At first he denied the affairs. That was a lie. For Dr. Sam, it was a lie that, like the pounding of waves on the lake beach, became a constant eroding factor. No amount of explanation later—about trying to protect the reputation of the woman he was seeing or, the unstated but more likely concern, about trying to protect his doting and sensitive mother—mattered. During his escapades with a lab technician, Susan Hayes, or with others, he had never anticipated a situation like this.

Dr. Sam tried to get the police to understand his point of view. He was a doctor; he tried to save people's lives, he said. He would not bludgeon someone to death. Surely the authorities, police with experience, could see the distinction between having an affair and this heinous, hideous crime. He didn't use the concise words that a judge used later, but his plea was the same: "A philanderer may have propensities for peacefulness."

Dr. Sam didn't understand that the way things seemed to others could hurt him as much as, or more than, the way things really were. A man who had been naturally successful, who had moved through his world with the grace bestowed on those with good looks and charm, failed to comprehend what happened when hardship arose, when those qualities were not enough. Had he been more streetwise, had he grown up in poverty or adversity, he might have known about police abuse, overreaching, about how simple pieces of information could be made into a different shape, strung, twisted, used against him. His state of shock over the murder evolved into shock at the system.

To some newspaper editors, the Sheppard case was a ripe example of values in disarray. An editor of the evening daily, the *Cleveland News,* carried on privately about "the rather peculiar morality practiced by persons in Dr. Sheppard's set." The editor said that "the general inference by investigators" was that Dr. Sam traveled with people who were not content "to play musical chairs" at their parties. This aura of sexual familiarity was read as evidence of spiritual and moral bankruptcy.

Affairs, denial—rocket fuel. At once, the investigation went askew. Officers became more interested in proving whom Dr. Sam might have slept with than in his wife's death. Investigators flew to California, seeking to take lie-detector tests of everyone who knew Dr. Sheppard, including acquaintances that predated Dr. Sam and Marilyn's nine-year marriage.

Rumors were passed off as fact. There were the stories of a "key club" in Bay Village, wife swappers, a cult of sexual deviants. There were rumors that Dr. Sam was sterile, that Marilyn was having affairs, that her pregnancy was the result of sex with another man, that young Sam, in fact, had been fathered by someone else. In the middle of the 1954 trial, the national broadcaster Walter Winchell aired a story about a woman under felony arrest in New York who said she had had a child by Dr. Sam. None of it was true.

The fantasy of television and movie images also had a subtle role. Subliminally, Marilyn Sheppard was equated with Marilyn Monroe. Mrs. Sheppard was called Marilyn, not Mrs. Sheppard. Mrs. Sheppard was described as beautiful, as if this were her only attribute, and often referred to as a blonde. She was attractive, no doubt, but at least as much for her personality as for her looks. She was clearly, undeniably, a dark-haired brunette.

Had Dr. Sam Sheppard's wife used the first name Florence, which preceded her middle name, Marilyn, the overwhelming press hype may have never occurred. When the *Cleveland Press* ran an eight-column headline, "But Who Will Speak for Marilyn?," it was hard to imagine the same impact from "But Who Will Speak for Florence?"

On the afternoon of July 4, teenage boys from the neighborhood were rounded up. Although the Sheppard home was packed with police officers, a crew of teenagers was assigned to search for evidence. The boys put on their bathing suits and dragged the bottom of the lake. Then officers told them to cut the brush in the backyard in hopes of finding a murder weapon. The path that a Bay Village police officer reported seeing earlier in the day was destroyed, with no attention to its possible significance at the crime scene.

In the brush, at a point about fifteen feet higher than the bathhouse and seven or eight feet to the east of the steps, Larry Houk spied a dark green cloth bag, six inches wide by thirteen and a half inches long. Standing with him was Jim Redinger. They didn't immediately call over the police. Instead, Houk and Redinger nabbed the bag, opened it, and poured out its contents. Redinger later recalled having fingered the items, and expressed puzzlement over the police statement that they couldn't find any fingerprints. He knew his were there.

Inside the bag were items of jewelry and personal property that belonged to Dr. Sam Sheppard. A man's watch with a broken band was there. Also found was a yellow metal chain with several items attached to it, including a knife in a yellow metal case, a gold football charm, a yellow metal tag, a charm from Los Angeles County General Hospital, a yellow metal charm with the Greek letters Sigma Alpha, five keys, and a fraternity ring with a metal crest superimposed on a black stone; the stone had a diagonal crack and several chips. Combined with the discovery of a woman's watch inside the house, on the den floor near pulled-out drawers, jewelry now became an issue.

From Dr. Sam's perspective, the appearance of the green bag verified exactly what he was describing. After being knocked out upstairs, he came to and heard someone rummaging downstairs. The bag itself had been lifted from a desk drawer downstairs. Motorboat tools that had been in it were laid out on the floor. Mrs. Sheppard's watch was right there, as if overlooked. Dr. Sam had seen the person trying to escape down the hill to the beach. Obviously, the person dropped the bag by accident, or threw it, or deliberately placed it under the bushes.

This was not obvious to the police. They pounced on another conclusion. Dr. Sam had committed the murder, they said, and then tried to make the assault on his wife look like a burglary; Dr. Sam had placed the items in the bag, then put the bag in the brush so he could claim a burglary had occurred, or else so he could retrieve his property later. Dr. Sam, in other words, had plotted out the entire murder of his wife, but the detectives had foiled him by having teenage boys go through the brush and search for evidence.

Had the jewelry been planted there, Dr. Sheppard would surely have drawn attention to it right away. A plant is ineffective otherwise. But the truth was that until it was mentioned, Dr. Sam had not even noticed that the items were missing.

How did the items get in the bag? they asked Dr. Sam. He answered. He didn't know.

The watch in the bag and the watch in the den became central items in the circumstantial case argued first before jury and judge, then again in hearings for a new trial and appeals, and yet again in the fair trial in 1966. Was there blood on the watches? Whose? Dr. Sam's? Mrs. Sheppard's? The blood of a third person? How was the blood type determined? What happened to the notes on the original blood analysis conducted in the coroner's lab? Why did the cards say that the blood analysis was inconclusive?

Other questions weren't even raised until Dr. Sam was convicted. How did Dr. Sam's watchband get broken? How was the ring cracked? How was the key chain ripped out of Dr. Sam's pants pocket in a downward fashion, something that would have been physically impossible for a person wearing the pants to do?

A serious search for the truth had not begun and had already ended by the time the green bag was found at 1:30 P.M. Whatever was found, it was found to weigh against Dr. Sam.

By three P.M. Dr. Sam's eyes were swollen with black-and-blue marks. His lip and lower face were distended. X rays showed his neck was damaged. Now officer Schottke was accusing him of murder.

In less than a twelve-hour time span since the murder, Dr. Sam's world was falling apart.

The officers left. Dr. Sam broke down in tears.

SIX

Inquisition

In 1989 the newspaper photograph of two sons standing outside a Texas prison was still crisp in Sam R.'s mind. When he had seen it seven years earlier, the photo unexpectedly sent a shudder through him. His response to stories about the death penalty was visceral, and seeing the photo brought up a feeling even more intense than the incomprehensible reactions he had experienced when reading, in 1979, about the execution of Gary Gilmore. Now, helping to reinvestigate the case, reinvolving it in his life, he was experiencing in 1989 even more of those moments in which feelings and memories from the past ripped into the present, often without warning. He heard someone refer to it as PTSS, post-traumatic stress syndrome, the type of flashbacks that Vietnam soldiers encountered upon returning home.

Sam R. was living in Maine in 1979 at the time that he first read *The Executioner's Song,* Norman Mailer's book about Gilmore and the first legal execution after a period during which they had been prevented by rulings of the U.S. Supreme Court. Three years later, in Boston, Sam R. saw the photograph of the two young men, another marker on a continuum of events, catalysts to slow-gathering change and momentum.

The Sheppard case stayed with him every day, but for so long there seemed to be no place to go with it. In Maine he worked, wrote, played music, lived a simple life with a woman friend. When a television movie about the Sheppard story was broadcast in 1976, he watched it once. The woman he lived with found it difficult and asked that he not watch it again. That was fine; he had no real desire to. By the time the Gilmore book came out in 1979, the relationship was starting to unravel. The feelings he had held in for so long were rocked in an uncomfortable way. Deeply held emotions began to show through. By 1981 the relationship was at a breaking point, and he moved back to Boston, shaken.

When Sam R. looked at the newspaper image of the two college students, African American, standing vigil, he saw himself and his dad. He recognized the expression of bewilderment. The students were waiting, powerless, while their father, Charlie Brooks, Jr., was being readied for execution, the first by lethal injection in the United States. Brooks had been one of two defendants charged with the murder of a man during a Texas robbery. It was not clear which man had wielded the weapon. Brooks was convicted, and was sentenced to die. The other man ultimately made a plea agreement and was given a prison term instead of the death penalty. Although the circumstances were vastly different, Sam R. knew that it could have been his dad who was sentenced to die. The headline "State Asks Death Penalty for Dr. Sam" floated in and out of the edges of his memory. The terror of Brooks's sons swept through Sam R. From a place inside, he understood that sons and daughters needed a voice.

When first speaking up about his opposition to the death penalty in 1989 and then talking about his decision to help reinvestigate the case, more inexplicable feelings would come rushing. Sometimes they were little things, such as the sudden panic he experienced when a newspaper photographer wanted to take a photo outdoors. Sam R. had not anticipated that. He had new glasses with special lenses that filtered the light and darkened in the outdoors. He realized they would look like sunglasses. All he could think of were the pictures that the newspapers published over and over in 1954 of his dad in dark glasses, selected, it seemed, to make Dr. Sam look shady, somehow guilty. After the photo session, he placed a priority order for another pair of glasses, ones with clear lenses. Next time, he would be prepared.

He was not prepared at all for the contents of the manila envelope from Monsignor. Monsignor was calling and writing regularly now, discussing the case in conversations that sometimes wrapped around themselves. On the "Kings Cross" letterhead were handwritten notes: "Enclosed are the facts of the autopsy on your mother, and needless to say, there is considerable cause for speculation on the facts submitted by the coroner," it said. Sam R.'s eyes jumped to the bottom. The letter was signed: "Kindest regards, Msgr." Regards, perhaps. As for sending the autopsy—"kind" was not the adjective Sam R. would have used.

Sam R. let the documents sit in their envelope for some time after receiving them. Finally, he took them out. They were large pieces of paper, legal-size photocopies reduced from even larger sheets. Some of the papers were printed forms, with things like "The State of Ohio, Cuyahoga County," "Case No.," and "Coroner's Verdict." He had never heard of a coroner's verdict.

With cursive strokes, Monsignor had underlined and circled various points. Already Sam R. understood that Monsignor would interrogate him about these points: What did they mean? What did he know? Had he ever seen the document before? What did he think?

Looking more closely, Sam R. saw how the preprinted lines would drop off from point to point, and a word or two would be typed to fill a gap or complete a phrase, giving the document the feeling of being generic and specific all at once. "Be It Remembered That on the *4th* day of *July*, A.D. *1954*, information was given to me, S. R. Gerber, M.D., Coroner of said county, that the dead body of a ["man" was x'd out] woman supposed to have come to her death as the result of criminal or other violent means, or by casualty . . ."

His mother was described, but only by the most superficial of characteristics: thirty-one years of age, a native of America, hazel eyes, brown hair, five feet seven inches in height, 124 pounds.

There the form stopped and thick lines of typing took over, reeling out blasts of detail:

> The said Marilyn Sheppard was found lying on the bed in the 2nd floor bedroom, located in the northwest side of the house. Her head was about one third down from the head of the bed. The legs of the deceased extended over the end of the bed and hung downward to the floor.

The chest was partially covered with a pajama jacket and the right leg of the pajama pants was on the right leg and the left leg of the pajama pants was not on the left leg, but was lying alongside the right leg. The top of the pajamas were below the rim of the pelvis. The bed clothes were partially over the lower part of the body and on the floor. The anterior chest and abdomen were uncovered. The head and face was covered with blood and there were multiple wounds in the area of the forehead, the head and the face. There were multiple wounds on the hands and the finger-nail on the left fourth finger was torn loose. The bed sheet was covered with blood beginning at the head and extending downward to the foot of the bed. The blood had soaked through on the mattress. The walls and doors of the room were splashed with blood. The pillow was at the head of the bed and had blood spots on both sides of the pillow slip.

A blank space on the front had been filled in: "see other side for marks." Listed on the back were thirty-five "marks and wounds," each one numbered, with each sentence beginning with the words "There is" like a religious mantra:

1. There is a contused abraded laceration measuring 1 x 1/2" in the left frontal region, centered 2 1/2" from the midline.
2. There is a contused crescentic laceration measuring 1 x 1/4" in the left frontal region, centered 2" from the midline. . . .

Merely skimming the "There is's" on the list stirred a kind of gut agony. Sam had been in his thirties before he even saw the pictures of his mother's battered body. Thousands of others had viewed them closely, and the chief medical examiner, Dr. Lester Adelson, had made high theater in the courtroom when the lights were turned off and slide projections of his mother's wounds were magnified on a screen. Supposedly, Dr. Adelson still presented a slide show with the pictures of his mother at various events in Cleveland all these years later.

Sam R. knew the description of the wounds well enough by now: four long gashes, curved, on the left forehead; two serrated gashes on the upper right forehead; abraded lacerations on the back and top of the head; skull fractures (but without bones being driven into the brain); bruised eyelids; broken nose; two broken teeth but no wounds on the exterior of the mouth; bruises on the shoulder, arm, hands, and wrist. They sickened him to think about.

Whenever Sam R. made a television appearance or spoke to a newspaper reporter, he would ask that brutal images be omitted and that his mother be treated respectfully. He would ask that they call her Mrs. Sheppard and not the overfamiliar Marilyn. Once, in Cleveland, he had agreed to a live television interview, one of his first. But he was caught off guard. A studio interview was introduced with a "package" of historical footage that left him spinning. When the camera turned to him, he was barely able to speak. Now the coroner's description had the same effect.

But this document was more than a medical analysis. The coroner's *verdict* meant something else, and as Sam R. read on, he began to see how it shifted and changed beyond the boundaries of a mere autopsy. The document went on to describe "information received from Dr. Samuel H. Sheppard" about his encounters that night and adopted a slightly sarcastic tone, such as that he was "rendered unconscious" and "was not able to 'visualize' who had struck him."

Sam R. recognized the sleight-of-hand right away. It had the tinge of selective characterization, always selecting the circumstances that would make his father look worst.

. . . it was found that the apparent appearances and signs of burglary and robbery were not probable or possible, and that these conditions were arranged by the person who had beaten the said Marilyn Sheppard to death. Doctor Samuel H. Sheppard was given opportunities to state "what he knew about the death of Marilyn Sheppard." . . . He also called in two attorneys sometime on July 4th and 5th, 1954.

And then a determination of death.

I find that the said Marilyn Sheppard came to her death as the result of "multiple impacts to head and face with comminuted fractures of skull and separation of frontal suture, bilateral subdural hemorrhages, diffuse bi-

lateral subarachnoid hemorrhages, and contusions of
the brain."

But there was more. The next line was the clincher: the
coroner's opinion. The coroner's *verdict*.

> I find it impossible to believe the explanation . . . as
> told by her husband Dr. Samuel H. Sheppard. . . . I
> further find that the injuries that caused this death were
> inflicted by her husband Dr. Samuel H. Sheppard and
> that death in this case was homicidal in nature.
> S. R. Gerber, M.D., Coroner
> Case No. 76629

Monsignor called, as predicted. "The coroner fingered
him," he said. "Have you ever seen such a thing? Have
you ever?"

He had not. But then he did not make a habit of reviewing autopsy reports.

"This is illegal," Monsignor said. He wanted Sam R. to
call the Plain Dealer in Cleveland and have it print the
coroner's verdict. This seemed like a crazy idea; Monsignor
was beginning to suggest a lot of crazy ideas. Sam R.
balked. Later he learned that Monsignor was incorrect. The
coroner's verdict was not illegal, just 100 percent wrong.

What was peculiar about the coroner's verdict was that
such a thing even existed. The coroner's verdict, declaring
that Dr. Sam Sheppard had committed homicide, was issued well before the trial, even before the investigation,
such as it was, was complete; before the arrest, before the
grand jury indictment. There was no "innocent until proven
guilty" with the coroner's verdict, no presentation of a defense. This was not merely a report of the time and place
of death or the medical examination, but a judgment, a
pronouncement. It was the criminal justice process,
hotwired.

In 1954 Dr. Sam did not fully comprehend the power of
the coroner in Cleveland. Few people did. For all the pages
of newsprint on murder, not one story was written exposing
the ugly, excessive power of the coroner in Cuyahoga
County, power greater than that of any coroner or medical

examiner in the entire country. In the 1990s, Sam R. learned, the situation was still the same.

The power of the coroner's office made it subject to abuse, and abusive it became in the Sheppard case. The public was barely aware of the existence of the office of the coroner, let alone its potential for abuse. Sam R. knew.

The coroner's office held the power of life and death. It could turn someone into a crime suspect. It could pass judgment on evidence and individuals. And it had no accountability to anyone on a daily basis. The only way to exercise control over the coroner in Cuyahoga County was to refuse to reelect him or her. As long as the coroner kept the support of the newspaper editors, prosecutors, and other powerful people, that wasn't likely.

The person who exercised this dictator-like authority in 1954 was Dr. Samuel Robert Gerber, the elected coroner of Cuyahoga County since 1936. He died in 1987, having served fifty years on the job. When first elected, he was a small, feisty man who had a slightly Groucho Marx air about him, with a mustache, dark wavy hair, and glasses. By 1954, at age fifty-six, his face had already condensed into puggishness and, the mustache removed, displayed a narrow slice of an upper lip and a permanent smirk.

Gerber's early medical career began with fits and starts. He attended a medical college in Cincinnati, Ohio, with the unlikely name of Cincinnati Eclectic Medical College, becoming one of the last practitioners to train in the branch of "eclectic medicine." Gerber moved to internships in Brooklyn, a residency in Manhattan, and work with a New York ambulance service. He became a ship's surgeon, traveling to South America, and then headed for Scott, Ohio, where the previous physician was leaving. But Scott had only four hundred people, hardly enough for an aggressive young doctor with political aspirations. He secured a job in the public health service in Ohio's biggest city, Cleveland. In 1925 he began a series of government jobs in Cleveland, working at a correctional farm, a tuberculosis facility, and at the Department of Child Hygiene.

Gerber's arrival in Cleveland came only two years after Dr. Richard Allen Sheppard, the patriarch of the Sheppard family, moved there from Upper Sandusky, Ohio. R.A., as he was called, was a pioneer in the field of osteopathy. Known as D. O.'s rather than M.D.'s, osteopaths would take the same or similar medical exams and had specialties, such as surgery or gynecology or pediatrics. Like M.D.'s, osteopaths served internships and residencies, prescribed drugs, and ordered X rays. But osteopaths also believed in the integration of treatment, approaching the body as a whole and incorporating body manipulation with other treatment options.

More than one person thought that Dr. Gerber harbored a grudge against the Sheppards because of their success as osteopaths. Horace Don, D.O., said that Gerber told him before the murder of Marilyn Sheppard that he was going to "get" the Sheppards one day. Edward Murray, D.O., an intern at Bay View Hospital in 1954, could remember the fierce animosity of medical doctors toward osteopaths.

Gerber was an ambitious man with a tremendous drive, according to medical insiders. His first effort to run for coroner on the countywide Democratic ticket flopped, but, undaunted, he tried again two years later, in 1936, and prevailed.

Coroners rarely get noticed, but Gerber did by thrusting himself into the investigation of the "torso murderer" in the Cleveland area. This wicked serial killer dismembered the bodies of at least twelve victims, leaving heads, arms, legs, bodies in a dry creek bed. Victims were often drifters. The new coroner described the killer as someone who knew how to use medical implements because of the clean cuts on the limbs. The coroner even implied that it might be a medical person looking for bodies for experimentation.

The killing stopped before a murderer was identified. Crime writers believed that a derelict with surgical knowledge who hanged himself in the county jail may have been the killer, or a medical doctor who committed himself to an insane asylum. But the case was a stepping-stone for Gerber, who was pictured in the papers and used the torso killer for the centerpiece of a book he wrote.

Dr. Gerber wanted more: publicity, respect, possibly a higher office. After the Sheppard case and all its publicity, he even tried to push his name forward as a mayoral candidate. Just before the Sheppard case, he opened a new million-dollar facility with taxpayer bonds in 1953. The new "center"—he hated the word morgue—was not downtown by the police department, but near the medical school, where the coroner could affiliate with important medical people.

But just as he was building up the coroner's office, other jurisdictions were getting rid of their coroners in favor of a medical-examiner system. Even in England, where the coroner system began in 1170, changes were under way. Coroners were outmoded. Originally coroners were fee collectors for the crown—a corona—who declared whether or not a death resulted from criminal activity. If it did, the king was entitled to seize the property of the person accused. But in eight hundred years much had changed.

In 1937, just after his first election to office, Dr. Gerber formed a high-profile blue-ribbon committee to make recommendations for the coroner's office. The recommendation: that the coroner's office be abolished and a medical examiner's office like the highly regarded one in New York be established. The recommendation was ignored.

Gerber had good reasons to turn the recommendation away. A coroner had vastly more power than a mere medical examiner. A medical examiner had one simple function: to inquire into the causes and circumstances of any unnatural or otherwise suspicious death. The medical examiner made findings and turned them over to a prosecutor for an independent evaluation of the case. Coroners had the same power as medical examiners to inquire into the causes and circumstances of death, and much more.

One example of this greater power was the coroner's verdict, the very document that puzzled Sam R. in 1989. Without having to confer with any other authority or subject evidence to any type of legal review of even a minimal nature, the coroner had the power to accuse a person of homicide. Another power of the coroner was the use of the inquest—the power to "investigate" deaths by calling witnesses and presenting evidence. And in Cuyahoga County, Gerber's inquest power was also the greatest of any coroner in the country—and in the world.

On Wednesday, July 21, 1954, the *Cleveland Press* ran one of its characteristically inflammatory front-page editorials: "Why No Inquest? Do It Now, Dr. Gerber."

Gerber was friends with *Press* editor Louis Seltzer, according to a former Gerber secretary who made lunch appointments for the two. Seltzer held so much sway among the city's power elite that he was sometimes called "Mr. Cleveland." He had personally made the decision to pursue the Sheppard case to the hilt. The newspaper made it clear that pursuing the Sheppard case meant pursuing Dr. Sam Sheppard. On Tuesday, July 20, the day before, it had printed a front-page editorial with an even bigger headline: "Getting Away with Murder."

Exactly whom the *Press* was going to hold responsible was made clear on Wednesday. Visions of a disintegrating political career must have hit Gerber between the eyes when he picked up his afternoon paper:

> "Why hasn't County Coroner Sam Gerber called an inquest into the Sheppard murder case?
> What restrains him?"

Gerber scheduled an inquest later that same day.

Inquests are not well understood in today's world. Even in Cleveland, coroner office employees cannot recall an inquest being held since 1981. They are not often conducted unless there is great public pressure, said one official.

An inquest is defined as a fact-finding hearing to determine the cause of death. In almost every inquest system, a jury of ordinary citizens, usually six people, is impaneled to hear evidence and to issue a verdict. In that respect, the process is meant to imitate a trial; indeed, the original Perry Mason stories were set at inquest hearings.

But there is a dark side to inquests. The word *inquest* is related to *inquisition,* and inquests came to their greatest prominence in witchcraft trials. Coroner's inquests, in particular, came into disrepute precisely because they failed to protect the rights of individuals.

If the inquest system could lead to abuse, the implementation of them in Ohio had greater potential for abuse because, in Ohio alone, the coroner was given unusually strong powers. And there were no checks upon those powers. The safeguards of the American judicial system were completely absent, and the system was colossally out of step with modern standards.

Ohio, unlike virtually every other jurisdiction, did not use inquest juries: the coroner alone was empowered to issue a verdict. The coroner was the sole questioner at an inquest hearing. The coroner was permitted to compel people to testify and to exclude witnesses. The coroner also could prohibit cross-examination and could even deny the right of an attorney to be present—no Perry Mason in Ohio. The coroner could make public charges, and the coroner's verdict was not subject to appeal.

In an Ohio inquest, the coroner presented the "case" and called the witnesses, like the prosecutor in a criminal trial; ruled on the proceedings and whether testimony was admissible, like the judge; and decided and wrote out the verdict, like the jury. An autocrat could have no greater power than that of prosecutor, judge, and jury.

As if this were not enough, Ohio's coroners were entangled in electoral politics. Even those dwindling few experts who supported the concept of a coroner system decried *elected* coroners. Elected officials were placed under public pressure to act, to do things. What pressure should there be on someone to do a proper autopsy? A scientific inquiry need not be voted on.

The overactive press corps in 1954 was so busy scrutinizing the possible affairs of Dr. Sam that no reporter ever looked deeper to see the truly shocking system that was in front of them.

When the *Cleveland Press* released its editorial artillery, Gerber snapped to attention. He set an inquest to begin at nine o'clock the next morning. Dr. Gerber scurried out with subpoenas, served late that night by Bay Village patrolman Gerhard H. Deutschlander. Dr. Sam was subpoenaed, as were his parents, his brothers, his brothers' wives, and the neighbors. Only young Sam R. could not be served the subpoena that had his name on it: he was away at summer camp in Pennsylvania.

Inquests were usually quiet affairs, held in inconspicuous circumstances. Gerber responded to the *Press* editorials with flair. He set this inquest in the gymnasium of Normandy school in Bay Village, where public spectators could fill the bleachers of the gymnasium, and television cameras could film it.

The inquest was pressed even though, as papers released in 1993 showed, Gerber knew that the prosecutors had rejected an indictment earlier on the same day as the *Press* editorial. A report by Cuyahoga County Sheriff Carl Rossbach described a meeting with the prosecutor on July 21, 1954: "We were informed that at this time, both their office and this office had not received sufficient evidence with which to seek an indictment."

People lined up outside Normandy school to get seats for the spectacle. Photographers had their bulky cameras with headlight-size flashes draped around their necks.

Gerber played to the crowd. He set himself up at a table, front and center. Members of the coroner's office who had conducted the autopsy were not even questioned. He humiliated family members, probed love affairs, asked for rumor and hearsay.

Reverend Alfred Kreke of the Bay Village Methodist Church, a mild-mannered man, had baptized Marilyn Sheppard a few years before the murder in a special ceremony. He was on vacation when the inquest began. "We returned to find our community the center of an open inquest with a miniature McCarthy at the head of what seemed from all appearances to be a carefully planned persecution of not only one individual but the defamation of an honored family name."

As the sole questioner, Gerber got into the ridiculous. He probed Bay Village firefighter Richard Sommer about his observations of Kokie, the family dog. Gerber, clumsy in his questioning, cut off people if their testimony pointed to someone other than Dr. Sam. He refused to call as witnesses those whose testimony would have been favorable to Dr. Sam, like Dr. Charles Elkins, a man who had given Gerber a personal report of his examination of Dr. Sam on the morning of the fourth. Elkins concluded that Dr. Sam had suffered fairly serious damage to the back of his neck.

Gerber, who had attended night law school, asked questions that would make a law professor cringe. He pursued hearsay relentlessly, with no regard to evidentiary rules. In court, hearsay rules are designed to keep rumor out of the proceedings. For the most part, people are limited to testifying to what they observed, and not what they heard from someone else. But there were no rules of evidence or procedure for the inquest, except what Dr. Gerber made up himself.

Larry Houk, sixteen, understood the inappropriateness of hearsay better than the coroner. When Gerber asked Larry if he ever noticed Dr. Sam get angry, Larry responded that he had always observed Dr. Sam to be mild tempered and not likely to get angry when others would have. He had, he said, heard a story once. Gerber pressed him to tell. "This is strictly rumor now, Larry protested. "Go ahead," Gerber responded. Reluctantly, Larry told a sketchy story about the brother of a friend who said he saw Dr. Sam sitting in his car one day, revving the motor, and that Dr. Sam told the boy that he'd had an argument with his wife. The story was not confirmed.

One of the cruelest moments in the entire episode of the Sheppard case came at the inquest. Dr. Gerber not only demanded that R. A. Sheppard testify, although he had little to add, but also insisted on parading Dr. Sam's mother, Ethel Niles Sheppard, in front of the crowds. Less than six months later, she would commit suicide.

Dr. Sam's mother was timid. Gerber had to ask her repeatedly to speak up. She was shy of the press and had never spoken a word publicly about the case. A woman to whom faith and religion meant a great deal, she was frail and distraught. Marilyn was as close as a daughter; Dr. Sam, her youngest, was her darling.

Gerber made her describe the morning of July 4 and the calls that awakened her husband. She could tell by his voice that he was alarmed. "I asked him what it was, and he said something has happened at Sam's. 'I don't know what, but you go on and rest a while, and I will be back and tell you.'" Gerber asked if Marilyn ever talked to her mother-in-law about difficulties in her marriage, and the senior Mrs. Sheppard politely described how Marilyn talked freely about many little difficulties, but never anything that was terribly upsetting or distressing.

After two days of testimony, Dr. Sam was called. Newspapers geared up for days' worth of sizzling headlines, charging up the story just when the subject had the possibility of quieting down. "Doctor in Tears on Stand As His Story Is Challenged." "Doctor Relates Murder Day Actions." "'I Heard Her . . . Screaming My Name' Dr. Sheppard's Own Story at Inquest."

For five hours, Sheppard testified. Highlights were printed in the *Cleveland Press*. He answered questions about how he met Marilyn Reese in junior high school and about their courtship and marriage. He told about the birth of young Sam, Marilyn's difficult pregnancy, the determination that she was Rh negative, a possible danger signal for pregnancy. And he told about the night of July 3 and the

morning of July 4—the same story he had told again and
again to investigators and police and deputy sheriffs. He
told about his medical history, about being in a car accident
in 1951, about water skiing and swimming and bowling; he
told about the diseases he had had as a child, about not
shopping at the May company where a clerk claimed he
had purchased a hunting knife; he told about the lights in
the house; he told about the dog. And he repeated the one
untruth that would follow him—he said that he had not
slept with Susan Hayes.

Dr. Sam's attorney, William J. Corrigan, was not by Dr.
Sam's side. Earlier, faced with the inquest's mounting im-
proprieties and scorn for due process, he had spoken out
loudly, questioning the whole proceeding. He had demanded that he be permitted to represent his client, to
cross-examine those who were testifying. After all, even
in medieval England cross-examination had been allowed
at inquests.

Gerber responded in a typical fashion: "Remove him,"
he ordered. Sheriff's deputies Rossbach and Yettra grabbed
the arms of the senior attorney and dragged him out of the
school gymnasium, while cameras whirred and whizzed.

To the court reporter, Gerber read into the record: "Mr.
William J. Corrigan repeatedly interrupted the process of
this trial, and has been informed on numerous occasions
not to interfere. . . . He refused to sit down and I therefore
ordered him removed or ejected from the hearing room."

The response of the audience was that of a basketball
crowd when a slam dunk is scored. They cheered as Corrigan was expelled, and afterward people hugged and kissed
Dr. Gerber on the cheek. They cared little for fairness or
decorum. They were in a hanging kind of mood.

Reverend Kreke could not understand what was going
on: "I was mortified at the subtle innuendoes and implications suggested in the questioning, which was not conducted
as an inquest, but as a trial with a prosecutor suggesting
most of the questions. There were all the earmarks not of
an inquest, but of a medieval inquisition. The morbid, sadis-
tic attitude of the audience reminded one of the blood letting arenas of Nero days. . . . When one says that it's pretty
difficult to believe in people any more, I think I
understand."

The inquest set a tone that could never be eliminated.

Thirty-nine years later, a caller to a phone line set up by Sam R. left a message: "I went to the inquest. I think you should give up. I think they did the right thing."

If Clevelanders lost perspective about what constituted fairness, perhaps they were influenced by the McCarthy anticommunist hearings that were going on in Washington, described by one author as a "carnival-like four-year spree of accusations." The words are reminiscent of the "carnival" atmosphere that the U.S. Supreme Court attributed to the Sheppard trial. In Cleveland, the McCarthy hearings were second rate; Clevelanders had Sheppard.

On the third day of the inquest, even Dr. Gerber seemed to be having second thoughts about the hysteria it was generating. He called the final witnesses to his office above the morgue, with only himself, the prosecutor, and a court reporter present. Those called in private included young Sam, brought back from summer camp in Pennsylvania and accompanied by his aunt, and Thomas S. Reese, father of Marilyn Sheppard.

Gerber's manner of questioning did not improve in private. Thomas Reese, a scientist and inventor accustomed to precision, gave his only testimony there. He was baffled by the coroner. Asked repeatedly if Marilyn had told him that she was having difficulties with her husband, Reese answered no, and no again, several times. "She appeared to be very happy." The coroner asked him to describe a visit he made to Dr. Sam in the hospital on the morning of the murder.

> *Reese:* Well, I was, of course, upset at the time and I don't know as I can repeat the conversation verbatim, but I went into the room, and my brother-in-law went in with me. I went over to the bed and took his hand, and said, "My God, Sam, what has happened?" And he was, his face was swollen up and his eye closed, and he had this collar-like affair on, and he was rolling back and forth in the bed. . . . he was obviously under a severe emotional strain, and apparently in some pain. . . .
>
> *Gerber:* Did he say that he recognized anything on the beach?
>
> *Reese:* No, we did not discuss it in that detail, Dr. Gerber. . . . my conversation with him that morning was very brief and under severe stress on both of our parts.

> *Gerber:* Did Dr. Sam ever tell you that he cried or yelled for help at any time?
> *Reese:* No, he did not.
> *Gerber:* Called for help?
> *Reese:* No, he did not tell me that.

Dr. Gerber, in his 1950 book *The Coroner and the Law in Ohio,* had waxed reverently about the importance of coroner's verdicts. "It is to be remembered that the coroners' verdicts are factors in the administration of justice." Now he seemed to have forgotten his own words. From that time forward, the momentum that would push Dr. Sam to prison could not be stopped.

Three decades later, Richard Eberling would learn some hard lessons about the power of the coroner in the Durkin case, as well. One link between the murder of Marilyn Sheppard and the murder of Ethel May Durkin, for which Eberling was convicted, was the extraordinary power of the coroner in Cuyahoga County.

The circumstances were different for Eberling. Durkin's death was adjudged "accidental in nature" by Dr. Gerber on January 4, 1984, the day after she died. Eventually, a new coroner, who had been designated personally by Gerber to become his successor, had ordered the body exhumed and conducted an autopsy. The coroner's verdict was changed. This time, "accidental fall" was crossed out, and "homicide" was inserted.

Throughout the Sheppard case, Dr. Gerber kept his records sealed. Bill Corrigan repeatedly demanded copies, and repeatedly he was refused.

After the trial, with Sheppard in prison, Dr. Gerber kept the clamps on. When world crime experts gathered in Cleveland for a conference of the Science of Law Enforcement Institute at Western Reserve University, Gerber imposed a blackout on any discussion of the Sheppard case.

Even in 1993, thirty-nine years after the murder and with a reinvestigation under way, the new coroner, Dr. Elizabeth Balraj, would not open up files on Marilyn Sheppard's murder, despite the Ohio laws allowing for freedom of information. When the law was pointed out to her, she brushed it off: "So sue me," she said.

SEVEN

Mistrial

Now that Sam R. was reinvestigating the case, Dr. Steve was retiring, so to speak. Young Sam could represent the family in the future. By the 1990s Steve had had his fill of the case. He sent a packet to Sam R. with articles, letters, old *Argosy* magazines with their Sheppard stories and the advertisements of the 1950s man who wins the dance contest, gets the girl, and smokes the best, Sir Walter Raleigh's pipe tobacco: "smells, packs, smokes," the ad bragged. Sam R. could remember his father's love of pipe smoking. In their house in Bay Village, Dr. Sam kept a rack with several pipes in the den, and the aroma of the tobacco would fill the house sometimes.

Meanwhile, Monsignor was smoking out a theory. There had been a conspiracy by members of a Masonic organization to convict Dr. Sam, Monsignor said. He had collected the burial sites of various now-deceased police officials, along with that of Louis B. Seltzer, the editor of the *Cleveland Press*. Sam R. wasn't sure that he bought it. In fact, his grandfather Dr. R. A. Sheppard had been a Mason.

One evening, the call was urgent.

"Friend Sam?"

"Yes?"

"I think you know who this is. We have something to discuss."

Monsignor's voice had the air of "this is a matter of the most serious consideration." A woman reporter who claimed to be a great authority on the case was trying to get a national television segment aired, Monsignor said.

Sam R. remembered hearing the woman's name.
Through the years she had written many articles, often hob-
bling together selected pieces of skewed material to make
her point, which was that no matter what anyone said, Dr.
Sam was really guilty, after all. She seemed to be on some
kind of long-running vendetta.

Would Sam R. talk to her? Monsignor asked. Sure, Sam
R. said. He was still of the opinion that he should talk to
everyone. Any piece of information might help. Monsignor
gave him the number.

Reaching her answering machine, Sam R. left a message
with his name and number, saying that he understood from
a certain party that she wanted to talk to him, and he would
be glad to do so. He never heard back.

A few days later, Monsignor called again. The reporter
called the FBI to complain that he was harassing her, Monsignor said. Sam R. was shaken. One call, one message.
Later, Sam R. wondered if even that was true, or if Monsignor was trying to block the possibility that he and the
reporter would ever compare notes.

Pressure Cooker

The intensity of the inquest was only a prelude, the Sheppards were to learn in 1954. By the minute, the murder
was becoming inextricably entangled in political wrangling.
As the media successfully pushed the buttons of politicians
and police, the editors decided to flex their muscles even
more.

"The family was under siege," said Nellie Kralick, secretary to the Sheppard family attorney, Arthur Petersilge.

Any trick was used to keep the story on the front page,
she recalled. The *Cleveland Press* promised Dr. Sam that it
would stop the lurid front-page headlines if he would answer a list of questions. Petersilge, unused to media sav-
agery, convinced Dr. Sam to go along. The questions were
answered; the attorney personally delivered the response.
The next night, the paper ran another of its accusatory,
front-page editorials.

Now the newspaper wanted the City of Cleveland to take
full charge of the investigation. The newspaper insisted that
Bay Village was offering "protection" to Dr. Sam. Cleveland police were in Bay Village on the day of the murder
and, in fact, had bungled much of the eighteen-day-old in-

vestigation by ignoring forensic evidence and jumping to premature conclusions. The scientific unit officer it sent to the scene was inept. But the newspaper wanted Dr. Sam arrested and subjected to the third degree: the Cleveland police could get tough.

The media created an impression that Dr. Sam was refusing to be questioned. This was not true. Sheppard had been questioned extensively. In the first week after the murder alone, he was interrogated by police on July 4 (four times), July 5, July 6, July 8, July 9, and July 10. On the ninth, he reenacted the events of the murder morning for a gaggle of officers from multiple jurisdictions; he spent all of July 10 at the sheriff's office being freely questioned and signing a several-page formal statement. Officers swarmed his house, going through gutters and scouring the lake repeatedly. One report that Sam R.'s team read in 1993 from Ray Keefe, an investigator for the coroner's office, showed Keefe went out to Bay Village on July 4, 5, 6, 7, 14, and 15; Mary Cowan, a lab analyst, was there on several days; Gerber had set up an outpost at the Houk home, three doors away. Sheriff's deputies and prosecutors were actively involved.

A few resisted the pushiness of the mainstream press. A member of the Bay Village City Council, George Serb, refused to vote for turning the case over to the City of Cleveland. He thought the media were intent on creating a circus and that Sheppard couldn't possibly get a fair trial. The *Cleveland Press* ridiculed him. Serb's voice was drowned out.

Cleveland police were under the gun, too. Bad press dogged the department. Confidence had been undermined by a vice squad scandal that the department had handled poorly. An ugly image of corruption and police insolence was still making headlines. Cleveland police knew they had to put a cap on the murder case fast, and that meant one thing—arresting Dr. Sam, as the papers wanted.

Chief Frank Story and the Cleveland police were formally given authority over the Sheppard case as of July 21. But Justice of the Peace Stewart S. Sanderson refused to sign an arrest warrant for Dr. Sam for "investigation" when Cleveland police demanded it.

Finally, Acting Bay Village Mayor Gershom M. M. Barber signed the arrest warrant on July 30. Mayor Spen Houk had withdrawn. Houk was under pressure: not only did he know the Sheppards, but he had come under suspicion himself. Barber's order was eventually thrown out because of bias, but in the interim, police raced reporters over to the senior Sheppard's home and grabbed Dr. Sam. He was handcuffed and led out while his parents stood by. Dr. Sam later wrote a chilling account: "A crowd collected around the house, on the porches and peering in the windows. My poor mother was petrified as flash bulbs flashed at the windows and voices broke above the crowd 'murderer' and 'go get him.' "

Dr. Sam was taken to the county jail. Intensive all-hours grilling began. Four rotating teams of police interrogators questioned Dr. Sam for twelve hours at a time. They used every trick in the book, said Dr. Sam.

Interrogators thrust pictures of his wife's beaten body in front of him. They hounded him to take a lie detector test, which his attorney had advised against because he did not think police officers would be fair. Officers berated his father, screamed at Dr. Sam, talked about trying to "get something" on his brothers.

> Others jabbed me in the ribs with their fingers and called me every name in the book. . . . One of the last questioners was Becker. He suggested a plea of manslaughter again. I asked if he would accept a confession from an innocent man. Officer Becker broke down and displayed tears saying that "Sam if you're innocent you stick to your guns and God will help you."

Judge William Thomas was finally assigned the case for a preliminary hearing on August 16. Presented with no evidence by the prosecutor, he ordered Dr. Sam to be released on bail. The police began making threats. They told reporters they were shocked and had never heard of a murder suspect being released on bail. An anonymous postcard sent to the judge read, "Get off the bench, you don't belong there. Get a job sweeping streets."

The release was short-lived. The prosecutor rushed to seek an indictment on August 17, so that Dr. Sam could be rearrested. The newspaper printed grand jury testimony, which is supposed to be sealed. Cleveland police inspector James McArthur rejected any theory of a third person being in the house. "There is no physical proof of anyone else being in the house at the moment of the murder besides the victim, her husband and her sleeping son."

The names of grand jurors were printed in the paper, and they were called and stopped on the street. Returning the indictment, grand jury foreman Bert R. Winston said: "The pressure on us has been enormous."

"It's obvious," Bay Village patrolman Howard Nickel said in late August, "that everything is being stacked up against [Dr. Sam]."

Character Assassination

All those who decided Dr. Sam was guilty had one item, some tiny piece of circumstantial evidence or some quirk in Dr. Sheppard's character, to which they clung as their "proof." Underlying validity was rarely questioned.

The truth was that Cleveland police and prosecutors were engaged in a mad scramble to find any evidence at all. Although the bedroom in which Mrs. Sheppard was murdered was never analyzed for forensic evidence until after Dr. Sam was convicted, police officers were dispatched to peer into Dr. Sam's love life like Hollywood gossip reporters.

Police had to come up with some answer to "why?" Why would Dr. Sam Sheppard, in the middle of the night, suddenly murder his wife with such viciousness and violence? An answer was not available. Dr. Sam was mild-tempered, rarely agitated, happy. According to Esther Houk, he was easily the most popular person in Bay Village.

The "other woman" scenario was not working as well as police had hoped. Initially police were ecstatic to have found "Miss X," Susan Hayes. A lab technician at Bay View Hospital who left in 1953 and moved to California, Hayes at first denied having had an affair with Dr. Sam. Officers told her, untruthfully, that Dr. Sam had told all, and suggested that since she had committed adultery, a crime in Ohio, she would be charged criminally if she didn't cooperate. Hayes described the affair. Her many encounters with Dr. Sam, occurring in his car, in the apartment above the Sheppard clinic, in California, were clearly "sexsational" copy for the tabloid writers.

Police elation was followed by a certain disappointment. Hayes did not supply a strong motive. The "other woman" was supposed to be lusted after, causing obsessiveness, spousal arguments. Dr. Sam wasn't about to enter into a permanent relationship with Hayes, and she didn't expect it. He said he loved his wife. Hayes didn't think that she ever loved him. They never exchanged passionate words. He didn't promise her marriage. Hayes wasn't demanding, wasn't rich. Theirs was a sexual liaison.

And Sheppard was not a desperate man who had something to gain by murdering his wife. He had nothing to inherit. The prosecution tried to claim that his family objected to divorce, but he had no heavy chains to cast off. The reality was that Dr. Sam had it pretty good.

In an effort to paint a portrait of Sheppard that was as dark as possible, the police began an all-out search for more "extracurricular" activities, as they called them. Officers flew to California, looking for other liaisons. Newspapers, eager for incriminating stories, printed it all.

A slight arm twist was all that was needed to get Dr. Lester Hoversten, the friend who was staying at the Sheppard home during early July, to provide the names of possible lovers. Hoversten was justifiably afraid of being implicated. Divorced himself, he turned around the details, saying that it was Dr. Sam who had been having marital troubles. He was easy to pressure. Upon hearing that he wanted to go to Europe, police confiscated Hoversten's passport.

Other characterizations spread. Maybe Mrs. Sheppard was having affairs, some officers hypothesized. Cleveland police officer Harold Lockwood wrote a several-page report, which Sam R. was able to see in 1993, that threw out wild scenarios. The officer suggested that the baby Mrs. Sheppard was carrying was not her husband's but that of a local man, although the coroner had already pinpointed the time of conception as occurring when Dr. Sam and Marilyn were in California together. Dr. Sam was really sterile, the officer said. Or they chased after the stories of a woman named Dill. She claimed that she had had a conversation with a stranger who might have been Mrs. Sheppard and who told her that she was having an affair with another man and how unhappy she was in her marriage. Newspapers and police indulged the tale for weeks. It turned out to have no foundation.

Sex angles did have one long-term effect that lasted

throughout the history of the Sheppard case and its many reincarnations. Sex could effectively shift the focus away from the murder and from what the scientific clues demonstrated to sleazy speculation dressed up as "circumstantial" evidence.

And while bedroom inquiries gave reporters plenty to write about, the real link between sex and the murder was ignored. There was an ugly sexual aspect to the murder. The scene was brutal: a woman murdered in her bed, pajamas pulled off, exposing her genitals. Blood smears were on her abdomen. Was a sexual assault in progress, a rape, an attempted rape? A complete sexual analysis by the coroner's office had not been done. Swabs were not taken to examine for semen; a chemical analysis was not conducted; sheets were inspected only "visually." Psychiatric observers speculated that sexual assault was at the root of the murder; Cleveland police and prosecutors preferred to obscure the issue.

The violence obvious at the scene also did not fit Dr. Sam. The police went for characterization again. Finally, the prosecution got Tom R. Weigle, a second cousin of Marilyn's, to testify. Initially, when contacted by police, he had nothing to offer, according to reports recovered by Sam R. in 1994. Then Tom's brother, a radiologist who years later was known to suffer from a severe addiction to the drug Demerol, was mentioned as a suspect. As a result, Tom was pressured into testifying and became the only witness to contradict the parade of people who, again and again, described Dr. Sam's moderate nature, calm demeanor.

Later, Weigle said he regretted it. Weigle's sole trial testimony was that he had once witnessed Dr. Sam discipline his son very harshly. Sam R. recalled nothing of the kind.

The Tom Weigle testimony was painted in bright colors before he took the stand: "Sam Called a 'Jekyll-Hyde' by Marilyn Cousin to Testify," the newspaper headlined. No such testimony was presented. In an unpublished interview in 1981, Weigle said he was "set up," coached in advance, and didn't realize how the testimony was being used. "It was trumped up," he said.

Trials and Mistrials

Immediately upon taking over, the Cleveland police realized that the scientific end of the investigation had been dangerously ignored.

On the morning of July 23, Detective Henry Dombrowski of the scientific investigation unit was grabbed by his superior Harold Lockwood and told to get out to the Sheppard home right away with all his equipment. By 9:15 A.M., when Dombrowski arrived with two other officers from his unit, a dozen other Cleveland police officers were already there.

Dombrowski was one of the few officers with a college degree. He made two critical findings and filed a report the next day, which he gave to his superiors. Half the information in the report was not released. If it had been, it would have blown the entire prosecution case out of the water. Until 1994 this half of his report mysteriously disappeared.

The part of Dombrowski's report that *was* publicized had to do with so-called blood trails. The blood trails became some of the most misused and misunderstood evidence to appear in the entire case. The blood trails could have solved the case definitively, except that they were never fully analyzed.

Dombrowski used benzidine tests, luminol, and a new black-light probe to analyze whether spots on the stairs and carpet were blood. Cleveland police had never used a black-light probe before, and the newspapers were excited by this scientific panache.

The spots were indeed blood, Dombrowski concluded. He found as many as forty-five tiny spots of blood on the treads or risers of the steps from the murder room to the kitchen and from the kitchen to the basement: the blood trails. In other areas of the house, blood spots were discovered near the drawers that had been pulled out of the desk and the upturned medical case, according to an account by Captain David Kerr.

More blood droplets, Dombrowski thought, circled around a low-hanging light fixture or chandelier on the first floor. Its location suggested that former owners had placed a dining room table under it, though the Sheppards had arranged the room differently. A tall person, even someone of ordinary height, could not walk under the free hanging light without bumping his head. These droplets might mean that a person had walked around the unusually placed light. Someone unfamiliar with the property would not be likely to do so.

Later, in 1994, Detective Dombrowski admitted that the

blood stains on the living room carpet were never very clear. He was not so sure that they were blood.

The conclusion that the murderer was someone familiar with the property was something on which nearly all police and forensic investigators agreed. Error was made in leaping to the conclusion that that someone could only be Dr. Sam Sheppard.

Other things pointed to someone who knew the Sheppard property. Someone knew, for example, the path to the second-floor bedroom from the kitchen. Someone knew that running out the porch door and down to the lake was a good escape route because the yard was covered by bushes, and below, on the shore, passage in either direction could be navigated without observation.

If familiarity with the property was the prime consideration, there were numerous people who fit the bill: family members, overnight guests, neighbors, visitors, interns from the hospital who would awaken Dr. Sam for emergency surgery. Boys used the room above the garage. Home deliveries were common—bread, milk, newspaper. Workers were on the property, rebuilding after a fire, doing cleaning, baby-sitting, landscaping, tree trimming, and window washing.

Richard Eberling, a window washer, could make a more architecturally accurate drawing of the property even thirty-eight years later than could any of the investigators or Dr. Sam in 1954. Workers should be able to do that, he insisted, in interviews in the 1990s. When names of other workers who might have been on the property were mentioned to him in 1991, he boldly suggested a test for them: "Since they were in the house, have them give a layout."

Never contacted by the police in 1954, according to police reports, Eberling maintained that he was in the basement, for example, more often than Dr. Sam. "I don't think he ever was in the basement," said Eberling.

Although Dr. Sam had been in the basement, even the night before, he was not likely to do household maintenance. Officers who went through the house with him on July 9 noted that Dr. Sam demonstrated a general lack of knowledge about much of anything other than the location of his medical bags. Keeping order in the house was the province of his wife, he explained.

Eberling, on the other hand, knew the basement well,

since he used the cellarway entrance from the outdoors to the basement for removing screens from windows. In the basement were a washer, dryer, utility tubs, and furnace, he said. "It was a summer cottage basement. . . . There were no windows in the basement. It was a dark dingy room." A person in the basement could not be observed from the street. From the basement, a person could walk upstairs into the kitchen. The kitchen had three steps that went up to a landing, from which rose the stairs to the second floor (the living room had a parallel set of three steps). Someone could enter from the basement and go to the second floor without passing through the living room or by the daybed on which Dr. Sam rested that night, said Eberling. The cellarway entry was overlooked on every police drawing.

The identification of the blood trails could have been significant. But it was only the beginning. No one ever did a full analysis. Using luminol on the scene, Dombrowski answered question one: Was this blood? Yes. Question two: Was this human blood or animal blood? Dombrowski had to go back to the lab to analyze that. He cut out pieces of wood from a basement stair. Yes. At least some of the blood spots were human blood, especially on the basement steps.

But then comes question three: *Whose blood was it?* No one knew and no one ever tried to find out. The blood was never typed to see if it matched the blood type of the victim or of any possible suspect.

Blood typing was beyond Dombrowski's expertise. Blood typing for everyone in the county was done by the Cuyahoga County Coroner's Office. The scientific investigation unit could not complete lab analysis. Mary Cowan, the lab analyst at the coroner's office, was not trained as an investigator, even though she, too, cut out wood chips from the stairs to test stains on them. For example, on August 9, 1954, she took a sample from the basement stairs, third step from the top, which later became state's exhibit 84. She identified human blood on the sample. Cowan also went to the trouble to test a slight amount of blood on the two watches to determine blood type, yet she claimed that there was not enough blood on any stair samples to conduct a blood typing test.

The prosecutors circumvented what should have been the

real question by pressing a theory that held little scientific sway. The blood trails, they claimed, were created when someone walked through the house with a dripping weapon, or else with clothes dripping with blood. If those scenarios were true, the blood would have proved to be that from the assaulted Mrs. Sheppard. Blood on the weapon would have been from the weapon coming into contact with her body; blood on the clothes of the assailant would also have her blood, splattered as she was bludgeoned. Blood typing would have supported the prosecution thesis—locked it in.

Or blood typing could have shown clearly that a third person was in the house.

Scientific analysis by criminalist Dr. Paul Leland Kirk was not conducted until after Dr. Sam was convicted. Kirk showed, through scientific experiments, that neither blood from a weapon nor clothes with blood on them would have dripped and left the blood trails. Blood so carried would have congealed in a short period of time, could not have dripped the distance that it took to walk several dozen stairs, and would not have created similar-size spots in all locations, even in the basement, by drawers, and near the medical bag.

Only the blood from a bleeding person would have dripped for the length of time it took someone to walk all the way down to the basement and left droplets that did not diminish in size.

Who had bled? Mrs. Sheppard, who was definitely bleeding, could have walked throughout the house. This was a somewhat absurd theory proposed by Sergeant Harold Lockwood, who thought that the assault began downstairs and was continued upstairs. The theory had little credibility, given the physical condition of Mrs. Sheppard, the state of her clothing, and the blood in the murder room.

If Dr. Sam had been the one to bleed throughout the house, the blood could have been typed to see if it fit his blood category. But Dr. Sam was not bleeding on July 4. He was injured, but he had no open wounds. Dr. Gerber had seen that for himself when he examined Dr. Sam in the hospital on the morning of July 4.

In fact, the blood trails provided conclusive proof that Dr. Sam Sheppard was innocent. Blood trails had to come from a bleeding person; Dr. Sam was not bleeding. The evidence was totally overlooked and misconstrued in 1954.

And if the blood trails were that of a third person, this fact coincided exactly with Dr. Sam's description of events. A third person with an open wound had walked throughout the house; a third person familiar with the property walked around an unusually low-hanging chandelier in the dark or semidark. That would have ended the prosecution's case against Dr. Sam.

From his jail cell, Dr. Sam, who was never credited for his scientific acumen, had a much clearer head about the blood trails than did his attorney. William Corrigan argued that the blood was dog blood belonging to the poor beleaguered Kokie, who had never been spayed. In early September 1954 Dr. Sam wrote to Corrigan with urgency: "I think it would be wise to perform an experiment with the presence of some objective person in regard to how far a hand or weapon will drip when immersed in whole non-oxalated blood. If there is evidence of human blood beyond 20 feet from the bedroom, I may have caused a bloody nose or such on the assailant. Whole blood coagulates too fast to drip very far."

During the trial, Dr. Sam tried again. On November 29 he wrote a pressing note: "If this is human blood on the basement steps—he [the intruder] must have gone down there to clean himself up a little and he knew he could have the light on down there without anyone seeing in, etc. He may have been bleeding himself from nose or bite?"

Although the analysis by lab people was utterly insufficient, the newspaper readers would never know this. Exciting, hot-breath stories told about ingenious investigators using revolutionary techniques to turn up blood trails and foil Dr. Sam. "Find Killer's Bloody Trail," the paper headlined, describing how the "magic of modern science has permitted Cleveland police to smash through the clever cover-up." There were articles about a secret fluid, a special solution, about finding a trail of blood to the Sheppard cellar.

The exaggerated press did have an unanticipated impact several years later. Skating over the superficiality of the scientific analysis, the press, if nothing else, brought out some strange admissions. Richard Eberling, for example, was arrested in a West Side suburb in 1959 for burglary.

He suddenly told a story about having cut his hand while washing windows in the Sheppard house a few days before the murder of Mrs. Sheppard. He had, he said, dripped blood on the stairs. But Dr. Sam was already in prison, and documents released in 1994 show that after cursory questioning, Eberling was sent home and the matter was dropped.

Nor did the public learn of Henry Dombrowski's other major find. He did not testify about it. He never mentioned a word about it to the grand jury that indicted Dr. Sam, or to the jury that convicted Dr. Sam in 1954. In fact, what he found in the basement on July 23, 1954, was a closely held secret. Sam R. and his team had to dig it up much later, and by then it was far too late to help Dr. Sam Sheppard.

Lock-Out and Propaganda

The defense was effectively precluded from helping Dr. Sam. Even the scrappiest of defense attorneys faced significant obstacles. For one thing, in 1954 prosecutors and police could hide evidence. No legal rule at the time required prosecutors or police to open their files to the defense. The other side could be shut out. Even evidence of innocence—and Sam R. would learn in 1994 that it existed in police files—didn't have to be shown the light of day. Not until 1963, in a case known as *Brady v. Maryland,* would the U.S. Supreme Court rule that police and prosecutors were required to share with the defense any material evidence that tended to prove innocence. But in 1954, Corrigan was blocked out.

At the trial and beforehand, Corrigan demanded files and records. The requests were ignored or denied. Only by accident did Corrigan learn of Leo Stawicki and Mr. and Mrs. Richard Knitter, people unknown to each other, in separate cars, who drove by the Sheppard home on the night of the murder and reported seeing a bushy-haired man by the side of the road. The Knitters' description was specific enough for a drawing to be made.

At the same time, the Sheppards and their lawyers were barred from the murder scene. "It was one of the most unfair things I have ever seen," said Nellie Kralick, Petersilge's secretary.

At first, Dr. Sam willingly let the police have control of

the property without the officers having to seek a warrant. But Sheppard did not foresee that police could then lock him out, even when he was defending his life in a murder trial.

Officers, and the reporters they let in, wandered through the house at will. When a second fingerprint expert was brought out to the house in late July, the most prominent print he found was that of a police officer on the door frame of the murder room. The coroner's office removed practically every piece of furniture in the home, including beds and the closet doors from the murder room.

Thousands of people were reported to be driving by the home, on a street that was already a busy artery. Neighbors complained about accidents. Bay Village officers were spending more time directing traffic than working on the murder.

Dr. Sam wrote a letter from the county jail in August, asking for the house to be returned. "I did not interfere with your possession in any way, or attempt to gain possession of my home, or protest about the action, because I desired to give the authorities every opportunity to make a complete examination of my home, its contents, and the premises surrounding it, in the hope they could discover some clue that would lead to the murderer of my wife. . . . You have now been in possession for 50 days, which is ample time to make any necessary inspection." The request was denied.

When the trial was ready to begin, Arthur Petersilge again asked for entry. At first the prosecutor agreed to turn over the keys to the property, and then reneged. Sheppard's attorneys renewed the demand again in the middle of the trial, after the prosecution had rested. Surely there could be no claim that the prosecution could suffer interference at that point. The judge agreed with the Sheppards at first, but when the prosecutor balked, the judge changed his mind, too. The request was denied.

The house was turned back to the Sheppards, but only after Dr. Sam was convicted. That was the first time that the Sheppards were able to bring in the kind of forensic expertise the case needed.

While they had it under their control, police had no problem using the house to conduct a propaganda campaign with reporters. Officials conducted a pretrial "demonstration" in the house. The demonstration had no basis in science, but it was effective in convincing any skeptical members of the press corps that Dr. Sam was guilty. Reporters never questioned the premise of the demonstrations. They seemingly never doubted the demonstrations' scientific validity or the propriety of their being conducted without the presence of the defense.

The demonstration would begin when Dr. Gerber or Cleveland police chief Frank Story lay on the daybed where Dr. Sam was sleeping on the night of the murder. Then Captain Kerr or another officer would stand upstairs where Mrs. Sheppard was beaten to death. Kerr, pretending to be swinging at the bed, would call out the number of swings: one, two, three. Dr. Gerber or Chief Story would jump up, run up the steps, and try to get upstairs before thirty-five was reached. The idea was to show that Dr. Sam was not really responding to his wife's screams because he would have reached the top of the stairs before she was murdered and could have done something about it.

From this, it was supposed that the crime could not have happened as Dr. Sam described. Ray DeCrane, the assistant city editor of the *Cleveland Press,* told a reporter in 1989 that the pretrial demonstration had a significant influence on his opinion that Dr. Sam was guilty.

Bill Corrigan pointed out at the time that the simulation would be more realistic if the police officer running up the steps were bashed in the back of the head as he reached the top, in order to observe what a dazed man would do under those circumstances.

The demonstration was overtly unscientific. Criminalist and professor Dr. Charles Kingston notes that to have value, an experiment must have a basis. Good forensic science is built on "objective probability," or measurable analysis—not "subjective probability," or conjecture about what someone might do under the circumstances. For example, to determine how far blood flies from a particular type of weapon, tests are done in a laboratory with weapons, blood, and measurements. To determine skid distance on the road, cars are repeatedly driven, stopped, timed, skid marks measured. The results of these tests then set models for objective analysis of similar crime situations.

Subjective analysis is done when an officer looks at a

scene and comes up with a theory. Guessing that a car might go only five feet after the brakes are hit is not a scientific experiment. Nor was this. Science cannot measure on what blow a woman being hit with an unidentified weapon would call out. It would be patently absurd for a police officer to hit many people over the head in order to measure when they first scream or for how long.

The police experiment was based on a huge number of unacknowledged presumptions: that the victim screamed on the first blow; that the victim's mouth was not covered; that a scream would last so long and be so loud; that x number of screams would likely occur between blows; that x amount of time would pass between blows; that the sound would travel in a certain manner; that a person would be roused on the instant of hearing the sound under those circumstances; and a multitude of things that were not and cannot be tested. The demonstration was conjectural, based on an officer's subjective feeling about what he would do under similar circumstances—in short, less scientific than a game of Clue.

But the demonstration effectively showed another thing: the basic underlying motive of the police. The trial strategy of police and prosecutors was to pollute the atmosphere with propaganda, to pick Dr. Sam's story apart, to avoid presenting direct evidence, and to convict Dr. Sam at any cost, whether based on logic or fact, or not.

A Camouflaged Prosecution

The selection of the jury began on October 18, 1954. Judge Edward Blythin, up for election in two weeks, was eager to get under way and would consider no delay.

For the fledgling television medium in 1954, the case offered opportunity. Through TV magic, the Sheppard story put "true crime" onto the small screen for the first time, its events broadcast daily across the nation. Reporters had a debate, not over guilt or innocence (guilt was assumed), but over which press organization should get the most credit for "getting" Dr. Sam.

One writer, Sidney Andorn, finally began to question the fever of his press colleagues. "What is there . . . that frenzies us into an orgy of salacious sensationalism. . . . Does Cleveland need mass psychiatry?"

The jury was selected in twelve days. All but one of the

jurors admitted having read articles about the murder and Dr. Sam in the newspaper. One prospective juror said he made a special point of reading everything that was printed so that he could be "prepared." The judge did not find that sufficient to excuse him. Another juror begged to be excused after he was selected because he was personally caught in the muck of tabloid press. "Morals" charges that were brought against the juror years earlier were printed in the paper. The juror said he thought the publicity would lead him to have a nervous breakdown. "In fact, I am just about ready for one right now." The judge dismissed him and seated an alternate.

The trial had elements of the drama that makes up television movies. At the same time, the trial was deadly dull, since most of the testimony had already been printed in the newspaper and usually in a more exciting, if unrealistic, fashion.

The case was a challenge for a defense attorney. The prosecution was going to try to show guilt by relying on the inferences created from dozens upon dozens of tiny points. To succeed in battling this type of circumstantial network, the defense was going to have to refute each point, a tedious task.

To make matters worse, Corrigan, sixty-seven now, was an arguer who quibbled about irrelevancies. By the time the trial started, he was already aggravated, justifiably, with how his client was being treated. A defendant is supposed to enter the criminal arena with the benefit of the presumption of innocence on his side. Not only was Dr. Sam not getting a "benefit," but he wasn't even permitted a level playing field. He was presumed guilty; the trial was a mere formality.

Corrigan was joined at the defense table by Fred Garmone, a lawyer with a backroom reputation; Corrigan's son, Bill Jr., a recent law school graduate; and Arthur Petersilge.

The prosecution had a table even more full. The lead attorney was John J. Mahon, an assistant prosecutor who fared so well with the pretrial publicity that he was elected to a judgeship in the middle of the trial, despite previous ballot failures. He also found a new partner and ended up marrying an assistant prosecutor, Gertrude Bauer, who did much of the trial preparation and later appeals. Two more assistant prosecutors, Saul S. Danaceau and Thomas J. Parrino, both to become judges later, represented the State as well, along with Inspector James McArthur, who sat with the prosecutors as a constant reminder to jurors and witnesses of where the police stood on this case.

After twenty-eight days of testimony, the case was said to be the longest criminal trial on record in America, although undoubtedly it has since been surpassed untold times.

The prosecution began with gruesome pictures of Mrs. Sheppard, projected on a screen, while Dr. Adelson from the coroner's office testified about the injuries Mrs. Sheppard had suffered. Dr. Sam cried. Later, the coroner's office carried into court a wax model of Mrs. Sheppard's head to demonstrate the murder blows. Dramatically carved into the model were deep gouges to indicate the wounds.

After showing that a murder did indeed occur, the major effort of the prosecution went into trying to prove that Dr. Sam's version of events was vague and full of holes.

Neighbors Don and Nancy Ahern each testified that Dr. Sam had fallen asleep with his jacket on, although, unknown to the defense and uncovered by Sam R. years later, Don had stated otherwise to police shortly after the event. Double hearsay was elicited from Nancy Ahern and allowed by the judge. She said that Marilyn had told her (hearsay) that a California friend had told Marilyn (hearsay) that Dr. Sam had told the friend (hearsay, possibly allowable as an exception) that he had considered a divorce but had decided against it. Permitting the testimony was chastised on appeal, but not considered a basis for reversal.

Three Houks testified. Esther and Spencer Houk described the events of the morning. To imply that Dr. Sam was being untruthful about being knocked out near the water, Esther Houk was asked if his shoulder was dry when she touched it. "Yes," she said. Years later, Esther said she had noticed that Dr. Sam's hair, shoes, and trousers were wet, but that no one had asked her about it when she was on the stand. Spen explained that he had been hospitalized with a nervous breakdown about a month before the trial began. Their son, Larry Houk, described finding in the Sheppard yard the green bag that had Dr. Sam's watch and jewelry inside.

Bay Village police officers Drenkhan, Hubach, and Eaton and firemen Callihan and Sommer testified. Cleveland officers Dombrowski, Poelking, Grabowski, Gareau, and

Schottke, along with county deputy sheriffs Rossbach and Yettra, also testified.

Gerber and Cowan took their turns as well. Gerber had one surprise to hand to the defense: he had decided from the stains on a pillow case on Marilyn's bed that a bloody weapon had been placed on it, leaving an imprint of a weapon. The imprint on the pillow, he claimed, showed two blades, each about three inches long, joined in the middle like a wishbone, and separated at its widest part by two and three-quarters inches, each blade having a toothlike indentation at the end.

The imprint, Gerber said, showed the weapon to be a surgical instrument. This description spun the case directly toward the surgeon on trial in a most damaging way. Since Gerber did not have the weapon and could not be specific about what surgical instrument it was, even the judge was startled and, in a rare moment, interjected to ask questions. The coroner didn't really mean to imply that the weapon was a surgical instrument, did he? Gerber held fast: either a surgical instrument or "something similar."

Key to the prosecution's case was the claim that there were no signs of forcible entry into the Sheppard home— no break-in. A significant amount of testimony was spent discussing whether the Sheppards commonly left one or more doors to the home unlocked, and whether they had that night.

And the highlight for the rumor mill, of course, was the testimony of Susan Hayes, who spoke about her sexual affair with Sheppard.

The defense featured medical people and character witnesses. Doctors who had examined Dr. Sam's injuries testified. The prosecution, having given up on trying to show that Sheppard was not injured, did not even bother to call the three doctors who had done evaluations for the police after Dr. Sam was arrested. To explain away the injuries, the prosecution now decided to claim that Sheppard had injured himself in a desperate suicide attempt.

Dr. Charles Elkins, who saw Dr. Sam on the first days that he was in Bay View Hospital, described a spinal cord injury in the region of the second cervical vertebra, either a chip fracture or a contusion. In addition, he saw facial, jaw, and body bruises and a possible concussion of the brain.

Records released in 1994 show that Elkins told Gerber in mid-July 1954 what he had found. Five other doctors, a dentist, and several nurses described a chip fracture, swelling at the base of the skull, a swollen eye, a possible thumb mark on the Adam's apple, shock, puckered feet, numbness in the arms and fingers, and lacerations inside the mouth.

One doctor was located for the prosecution, Dr. Richard Hexter, to support the claim that Dr. Sam's injuries were superficial. Hexter had completed only a partial examination, and he admitted on cross-examination that he didn't look at the spine or neck area because he had no experience in neurology.

Sheppard family members testified. Betty Sheppard, married to Dr. Steve, described how she had discovered Marilyn's open wallet sitting on a shelf next to the bread box. A long string of character witnesses testified to Dr. Sam's good nature and the general normality of the relationship between Dr. Sam and Marilyn. Marilyn's aunt and surrogate mother, Mary Brown, described the joy that Marilyn expressed about being pregnant, only four days before the murder.

People who had been in the area the night of the fourth testified on both sides. Mrs. Arthur Paine testified that she saw lights go out at twelve-thirty A.M.; Doris Bender was called by the prosecution to say that she had seen lights on in the house at two-thirty A.M., but police reports recovered later show that she wasn't at all sure about the date or which lights she saw on. Two fishermen talked about seeing three teenage boys on the park pier early in the morning. Teenagers who had been on the pier that night, but not in the morning, testified. Yet the prosecution skimmed over the information in Bay Village files recovered by Sam R. that these teenagers saw five cars parked at Huntington Park, even though prosecutors tried to depict the neighborhood as isolated and uninhabited. The drivers who had seen an odd man walking along Lake Road early that morning were called to the stand by the defense.

Unexplained items found at the scene of the crime were conspicuously *not* mentioned in court, or were minimized and overlooked. And whatever didn't fit, the prosecution leapt over. Both sides brushed over the T-shirt that washed up on the next-door neighbors' pier immediately after the fourth and that was dismissed by the police because it had no blood on it. Ignored were tooth chips, the red chips on the carpet, and physical evidence that could have solved the crime but didn't fit Dr. Sam.

A red frayed fiber found on July 11 by Mary Cowan on the bottom edge of the desk could be matched with no clothing in the household, so it was ignored as evidence. A piece of leather found under the bed supposedly could not be matched with any item in the home, so it was pushed aside. Yet, by simple visual inspection in 1994, investigators saw a match to the inner pocket of Dr. Sam's wallet. No "fresh stains" of blood could be found on the green bag, so it was considered worth nothing. Hairs, fibers, and sand in Dr. Sam's pockets were not worthy of testing.

Fibers found under the fingernails of Mrs. Sheppard were ignored or summarily dismissed. The victim's hands were severely bruised. One finger was nearly torn off. The injuries indicated a vicious struggle. Mrs. Sheppard's hands may have held the answer to the murder, for they surely came into contact with the person who murdered her.

Cowan did analysis on the fingernail scrapings, but when copies were read by Sam R. and those working on his behalf in 1993, it was apparent that in each successive report the importance of the items was diluted. At the time of the trial in 1954, the coroner's office provided only cryptic information to the defense. Its "Microscopic Examinations" report merely read, "Scrapings removed at autopsy from underneath fingernails of Marilyn Sheppard: No significant fibers or hairs noted."

But an earlier twenty-eight-page trace-evidence report described red material, blood, hair, a plant fiber, a dark blue wool fiber, a red wool fiber, a fine blue fiber, thin pieces of wood. Cowan did not test any of the items because she decided that they were not significant. They were not considered significant simply because they did not match anything belonging to Dr. Sam Sheppard.

Dr. Sam was exasperated. He wrote plaintive notes to his attorney, begging for attention to various details: "My track trophy which was broken and Marilyn's bowling trophy also broken were not in sight—these should be brought *to court.*"

Or, "Why not a picture depicting the relative position of prints on beach in relation to the rest of beach. Why not a picture displaying condition of beach?"

Or, "The blood stain [on the pillowcase that Gerber said was the impression of a surgical instrument] that Gerber refers to is obviously due to blood caught between the creases of the pillow. To substantiate this the streak in the middle should be noted."

Or, "Why were these fibers not photographed through a microscope? This is often done and would allow the jury to see evidence which they otherwise cannot see with the naked eye.

Dr. Sam testified on his own behalf, taking the stand for three days. Although he could not shake his stilted style, he told the events of the morning again. His frustration at the spectacle filtered through on occasion, especially when the prosecution tried to provoke him.

Prosecutor Mahon: Is cold water more effective to remove blood from clothing than hot water?

Dr. Sam: I am certainly no authority on that. And I never tried to remove blood from clothing, sir.

Prosecutor: Now, Doctor, the injuries that you received, Doctor, didn't you receive those injuries from jumping off that platform down at the beach?

Dr. Sam: No, sir. I think that would be impossible, sir.

Prosecutor: Why impossible, Doctor?

Dr. Sam: Because a spinal cord contusion, sir, is something that is the result of a rather forcible force and would necessitate very—almost definitely—a force from the back of the neck unless there was injury to the top of the head in conjunction with the production of the spinal cord contusion.

Prosecutor: And couldn't such a blow be administered to the back of the neck if you fell on it, Doctor?

Dr. Sam: No, sir.

Prosecutor: No, Doctor, isn't this the fact: that you beat your wife that morning?

Dr. Sam: No, sir.

Prosecutor: And that after you had killed her you rushed down to that lake and either fell on those stairs or jumped off of the platform down there, out to the beach and there obtained your injury?

Dr. Sam: That is absolutely untrue, sir.
Prosecutor: That is all sir.
Dr. Sam: And unfair.

The trial ended with a whimper. In concluding arguments, the attorneys had little vision; cohesiveness was lacking. Nit-picking was prominent.

The defense picked at the prosecution's case, hoping to poke holes here and there, but a strong weaving and explaining of evidence was utterly missing. Corrigan floated off into discourses about democracy and the press, but he did not pay enough attention to the facts in evidence that showed Dr. Sam to be innocent.

The prosecutor also picked away, but at Dr. Sam's version of events, hammering at the questions that Dr. Sam could not answer. Why hadn't he turned on the lights as he ran upstairs? Why was his jacket folded on the couch? Why hadn't his son awakened? Why hadn't Dr. Sam shouted "murder"? If there was an intruder, why had the intruder taken only small items and put them in a bag instead of pockets? Why had the intruder taken Mrs. Sheppard's watch off her wrist but not her rings off her fingers?

Sarcastically, prosecutor Mahon concluded: "Why, this house was full of phantoms that night, I think, ladies and gentlemen, the phantom burglar, the phantom killer, and then they charge this defendant with the murder. The phantoms did all that, ladies and gentlemen."

In the end, one decision mattered and that was the jury's. The prosecution is supposed to prove that the defendant committed the crime. In this case, the prosecution successfully proved that Dr. Sam was there, which, of course, he did not deny.

The amazing fact was not that Dr. Sam was convicted, but that the jurors refused to back a first-degree murder conviction. The state asked for the electric chair, based on a verdict of first-degree or premeditated murder. The jurors came back with a verdict of second-degree murder, intentional but without premeditation.

Without a blink, the burden of proof had been shifted. A member of the jury later told a reporter that jurors thought Dr. Sam's version of events was "fantastic": "Dr.

Sam was the lone adult in the murder house. His child couldn't have done it. It had to be Sam." Another juror proclaimed even in 1993 that Dr. Sheppard had never "proven" his "innocence."

The jury had expected or wanted Dr. Sam to prove that he had not committed the crime. As the writers of the Bill of Rights knew, it is virtually impossible to prove that you did not do something, especially if you do not deny being present and physically able to have done it. For this reason, American prosecutors, powerful representatives of the government with resources at hand, are required to actively prove that a defendant did something, not the other way around.

What was the motion picture version of what happened that night? How could the evidence be reconciled so that all of it fit, and none of it was eliminated? Roll the tape in the mind's eye and there was always a major glitch that set off the eject button.

The prosecution never tried to fully explain what happened. Every version had a hitch. The coroner claimed that Dr. Sam used a surgical instrument to kill his wife. No such instrument was kept in the bedroom. If the weapon was not nearby, Dr. Sam could not have acted in a sudden rage, as implied by the second-degree murder verdict returned by the jury. Nor did the jury ever accept that Dr. Sam got into an argument with his wife, went downstairs and got a surgical instrument, went back upstairs and found her still in bed waiting for him, and then bludgeoned her to death—which would have shown premeditation. Nor did the prosecutor argue or jury accept that Dr. Sam, coolly and calmly, waited for the neighbors to leave, decided that this was the night to end his wife's life, marched upstairs with a surgical instrument in hand, and killed her.

No, all the prosecution could say was that he was there. That maybe he didn't run up the stairs fast enough when he heard his wife scream. That there was supposedly no evidence of forcible entry into the home. That he had taken his coat jacket off, an act of great deliberation.

The prosecution's presentation of evidence was full of inconsistencies. The police claimed that Dr. Sam went down to the lake to wash blood off his trousers, but blood doesn't wash off, and anyhow there was a sink in the basement. And if he was going to wash off his pants, why not wash off a T-shirt? Or, since he was at home, why not put on a new T-shirt?

The weapon was never found. The police dredged the lake, using teen boys, divers, metal detectors. All sorts of things were found, including a toy gun and an iron pipe. But no weapon. A dozen police officers poked through the yard and the house and the garage and the park nearby and lugged in item after item for scientific testing. Golf clubs and wood and barbells and medical implements from doctor's bags were all carried away. None matched. The weapon was not on the premises. The likely reason was that someone carried the weapon into the Sheppard home and took the weapon out the door in fleeing. In order to support the idea that Dr. Sam had committed the crime, the prosecution had to construct an elaborate scenario that involved a cover-up by Dr. Sam's brothers or others. Nothing in the evidence supported that, either.

Dr. Sam was injured. First the prosecution denied it. Then it claimed that he had tried to kill himself by jumping off the rocky hillside behind his house, although there was no flattened ground where he might have landed or any scrapes on his body that would indicate a jump, nor was such a scenario consistent with his injuries. Years later, the prosecution changed this version of its case and implied that Dr. Sam had been injured in a fight with his wife; yet that hardly explained a damaged cervical vertebra.

Run the screen version, tell the story—the prosecutors never could. The reason: Dr. Sam was innocent. And if they had bothered to carefully review the evidence and read all the reports from the Bay Village and Cleveland police, the Cuyahoga County Sheriff's Office, and the coroner's office, if they had used rigorous honesty, they could have discovered the same.

On December 21, 1954, the foreman of the jury, James Bird, read the verdict: guilty of second-degree murder. It carried a sentence of life in prison.

For the jurors, who spent the week of deliberations sequestered for the first time, the ordeal was over in time to celebrate Christmas. Prosecutors Gertrude Bauer and John Mahon, the latter now a judge-elect, were able to get married before the holiday. And the *Cleveland Press*, its editor bragged in a trade journal, sold thirty thousand extra copies on the day of the verdict.

EIGHT

Scientific Track-Down

Horrible. The only word young Sam had to describe Christmas was horrible.

Thanksgiving of 1954 had been bad enough. But people were hopeful. People smiled. There was no denying that there was trouble, but still the adults said that the family would win and be triumphant in the end.

And then it was Christmas. The trial was over. Instead of being right, the jury made a mistake. The adults said that it was wrong. His dad sat in jail sentenced to life imprisonment. They said they would appeal it, that it wouldn't take long to set things right. But they didn't laugh much or smile. They were stony faced and moved through the day by habits so established they need not think. This couldn't happen here, not in the United States. They all said that. How could the jury make such a horrible mistake?

Sam R. tried to fit into his new role. He was living with his uncle Steve and aunt Betty. He was no longer the only child. There were his cousins, too, Janet and Carol. Everything was different.

Christmas was organized in an orderly fashion. He or Janet or Carol would play Santa and pick out one gift per person from the pile. The Santa would hand it to the person whose name was on it. Then the person who received it would open the gift, one at a time, one person at a time, so all could see. As it went on, each child made a list of each gift received and who had given it. That way, they could write their thank-you notes appropriately.

This was not like the Christmases that Sam R. had experienced. Somehow it was painful; he felt he was among strangers. Somehow he wished he could be far away from it all, somewhere where he belonged. He belonged at home, with his parents and with his dog, Kokie. Kokie had been given away to some nurses, they said. And people said his mother was dead, but really, secretly, he didn't believe them.

As they went around the circle it became increasingly clear that he had many more presents than anyone else. This was awful, too. Janet and Carol just stared as his list got longer and longer. From someone, he got a beautiful fire engine that was four or five feet long, with removable parts. He didn't really want it. He had presents from complete strangers saying things about "faith" and "God" and "the truth will come out." And then there was a gift card from Mrs. Ahern that had twenty dimes in a dot-to-dot picture on the card and cheerily wished him to buy something "happy." The adults stared in disbelief. This woman had testified against his dad. Now she had sent him a card with dimes in it, telling him to be happy.

From jail his dad sent him a little drawing and a sailor hat. That was the best present. He put the hat on and refused to take it off. He wore it every day and slept in it. Eventually they made him take it off for meals. He wanted to be at home, or, if not, he thought he would rather be in jail with his dad.

For his son's sake, Dr. Sam was determined to turn the case around even after he was convicted. The month after the jury returned the guilty verdict was another hard one. On January 7, 1955, and then on January 18, 1955, while living in a cell in the Cleveland jail, he learned that first his mother and then his father had died. His mother committed suicide; his father died of a suddenly worsened cancer of the stomach. "Don't ever give up," R. A. Sheppard had said to Dr. Sam in a final conversation.

Later, Dr. Sam remembered those desolate days and how he had carried on. "I realized I *must* live on and prove my *complete innocence* for my son's sake, if not my own. . . . Many people claim to have considered suicide. . . . Death would have been sweet, so very easy in 1954, '55 & '56."

There was plenty of time for reflection about what went

wrong. Too much time for Dr. Sam. Too much time alone for young Sam. Sam R. was surrounded by family, but no one knew how to fill the void inside. Even Sam R. didn't understand how deep it went, wounds so hurtful that he could not be consoled.

The axis of his world shifted on a monthly basis. His mother, his father, his home, his pet. H. P. Blake, his mother's grandfather, had died during the trial. And then his grandmother Sheppard; then grandfather.

He identified with Dondi, the orphan child in the Sunday cartoon strips. He would find solace in an imaginary conversation with his mother. Adults would chastise him for daydreaming, and he would try to look like he was paying attention. Relatives, women in particular, tried to mother him, and he hated it. He disliked their kissing him, pretending to smooth over the gullies of grief. Mere touch was painful.

He wrote his dad letters and got letters back. But it wasn't the same as a dad who cheered at home plate during Little League.

There were no victim groups, no survivor support systems, no programs for children whose mothers had been murdered or fathers wrongfully convicted and locked up in prison.

No one talked about it. It was best to just get on with life, the adults thought. No one knew any better.

At one point, during his ten years in prison, Dr. Sam confessed. His guilt was palpable, painful. Still, this was a private confession, in a journal. Sweet and soft, it was the confession of a guilt so inconsequential that it rises unbidden only from those who have suffered irredeemable losses. "When this tragedy first occurred and for several months thereafter I gave not a thought to love, except Marilyn, and I could never love again like I did M. I'd never consider serious love again. I had feelings of remorse that I had not been more tender to M. at times and that I had not taken time to enjoy home a little more."

The evidence that Dr. Sam was innocent began to rise slowly from the depths. But some evidence was so deeply buried that it took years and years of sifting through files and reports, public information requests and interviews, to dredge it up. The "phantoms" in Dr. Sam's house that night began to look more and more real.

By the time Paul Holmes's book *The Sheppard Murder Case* was published in 1961, a full seven years after the murder, members of the public were beginning to have second thoughts. What if Dr. Sam didn't do it? Magazines from *Life* to *Parade* to *Man's World* were zeroing in on an American atrocity; publications in Europe and even Russia decried the way that Dr. Sam had been treated.

Dr. Sam went over the case again and again in his mind, searching for clues not just to what happened that night but to how and why he was found guilty of a crime he did not commit. Shortly after his conviction, he wrote out seventeen points in his favor, which he was certain would have shown him innocent if only the jury had understood them.

His list focused mainly on failures in the scientific understanding of the case: failure to examine the wounds for foreign material or the sheets on the bed for semen, hair, or foreign material; failure to analyze fibers of cotton and wool under Marilyn's fingernails, and the red chips from the floor, none of which were associated with anything belonging to the Sheppards—"Where from?" he wrote; failure to analyze a broken tooth found under the bed that could not be matched to Dr. Sam or his wife; failure to explain how the lack of blood on his pants, belt, socks, and shoes showed innocence; failure to explain his own injuries, of being waterlogged and having a spinal cord injury.

Dr. Sam wrote: "My deep seated emotion, if permitted expression, will be toward the step-by-step *scientific track down* of Marilyn's *murderer,* to be followed by proper conviction and punishment. This should pave the way for a recount of just exactly what happened to me, and questions 'why?' "

The evidence in his favor was actually much more voluminous than even Dr. Sam could imagine. But the undoing of a criminal trial was also much more difficult than he imagined.

In the desire for a fully scientific analysis, Dr. Sam finally had a counterpart in Dr. Paul Leland Kirk. Dr. Kirk entered the Sheppard case in January 1955, after Dr. Sam was convicted.

With bachelor's and master's degrees in chemistry and a doctorate in biochemistry, Kirk had an impressive résumé. He had been part of the Manhattan Project, was a consultant to the army and the Atomic Energy Commission, and was a professor at the University of California at Berkeley, where he founded a department of criminalistics, opened a criminalistics lab, and wrote the premiere text on criminal investigations.

Kirk first became interested in applying science to law enforcement when perplexed police in California sought his help in solving a particularly ugly rape of a young girl. Officers were about to arrest a man after a cigarette lighter found on the scene was traced to him, but the police chief was uneasy. Kirk microscopically identified a pubic hair found on a handkerchief at the scene. It did not belong to the man; the man it did belong to confessed within a week. A thousand cases later, defense attorney Bill Corrigan contacted Kirk about Dr. Sam Sheppard.

When studying a case, Kirk had one concern: What items, what proof, what scientifically verifiable materials, could be collected to show who had committed the murder? His textbook, *Crime Investigation: Physical Evidence and the Police Laboratory,* was a "must-have" in virtually every police department in the country. It taught police officers how to recognize and collect evidence that could be examined in a lab. The biggest problem in crime investigation, Kirk found, was that police officers did not understand what could be done in a lab, and so failed to preserve or collect vital pieces of evidence.

"Wherever [the criminal] steps, whatever he touches, whatever he leaves, even unconsciously, will serve as silent evidence against him," wrote Kirk. Fingerprints, footprints, hair, clothing fibers, tool marks, paint, blood, semen—all are witnesses to the crime. A fiber can be traced to a manufacturer and to an item of clothing and then to a person. The tear in an item of clothing can be replicated to learn how it was ripped. "This is evidence that does not forget. . . . Physical evidence cannot be wrong; it cannot perjure itself, it cannot be wholly absent. Only its interpretation can err. Only human failure to find it, study and understand it, can diminish its value."

Police err most often because they fail to think small. Lab evidence is microscopic. Gross physical evidence will often be absent from a crime scene. But microscopic evidence is present in almost all cases. For example, examining a wound can tell much about the type of weapon, but microscopic evidence will connect the weapon with the perpetrator.

The beauty of microscopic evidence, according to Kirk, is in its obscurity: criminals, like investigators, overlook it. Even a criminal who attempts to plan every move leaves a silent trail of hair, fibers, tool marks, scratches. Controlling every aspect of an environment is virtually impossible, and the evidence can remain on a scene for months and years.

When he was first asked to study the Sheppard murder, Dr. Kirk assumed that Dr. Sam was guilty, he wrote in private notes in the late 1950s. Kirk was in northern California during the trial; like others across the country, he had seen the headlines. From what the newspapers told him, he thought Dr. Sam told an implausible story, had inflicted injuries upon himself, and had wrongly refused to take a lie detector test. As a result, Kirk, who normally worked for the police and prosecution, agreed to look at the evidence in the Sheppard case only if it were understood that he would come to his own conclusions, and that they might not favor Dr. Sam. Corrigan agreed to this condition.

Kirk worked methodically. Method was not just a part of Kirk's approach; it was his entire approach. Microscopic detection was serious work to him, but, just as precisely, he carefully distinguished himself from a detective.

Detectives, he explained, operate by finding witnesses and conducting interviews, piecing together the movements and motives of various individuals. Detectives come up with hypotheses and try to prove them. Criminalists such as himself come up with facts that lead to theories. Criminalists are interested in a scientific solution based on provable facts. Kirk even created the word *criminalist* to carefully differentiate the role of the forensic scientist from that of the detective. Criminologists are an altogether different breed, despite the similarity in name. Criminologists are concerned with broad behavioral and sociological theories about deviance, crime, and punishment.

Kirk lived by the premise that one fact was worth a thousand theories. In any investigation there are opposing alternatives. The correct conclusion in the end has to explain or be consistent with every known fact. If a theory is contradicted by a proven fact, then the theory is wrong.

The contrast in approaches between detectives and criminalists can be stark. Although Kirk did not have access to it, the police report by Sergeant Harold C. Lockwood that Sam R. obtained in 1993 demonstrated the difference. Lockwood listed fourteen "facts" of the Sheppard case (although many of these "facts" were unproven rumors), each followed by a "contention." The contentions were really imaginative guesses, and even Lockwood conceded in the end that they were "purely theoretical" possibilities. Fact three, for example, described how Mrs. Sheppard's watch and two broken trophies were found on the floor of the den. From this, Lockwood's "contention" was that a fight had begun downstairs. Lockwood did not acknowledge that this theory was contradicted by the universally accepted forensic evidence that the assault occurred in the bedroom. Lockwood's "possibilities" were a far cry from proof, especially proof beyond a reasonable doubt.

Mary Cowan also had a different view of her role as lab technician at the coroner's office. She gave a lecture under the title "Debunking the Laboratory." Cases could not be solved in the lab, she insisted. She rejected the "Quincy"-style approach of the creative thinker in the lab. The role of the person in the laboratory was simply to test whether something was or was not what it appeared to be, she argued, not to come up with theories. Kirk, on the other hand, pioneered scientific crime scene reconstruction, using all the tools of the scientific technique. His work paved the path for a new generation of crime busters.

In late January 1955 Dr. Kirk traveled to Ohio. Before anything else, he wanted to know what scientific evidence had been presented at Dr. Sam's trial. He began by reading the trial transcript of the prosecution's witnesses. Defense testimony, he decided, would be useless, since the defense had not done any independent examination of the evidence, but had relied solely on trying to rebut the prosecution's case.

Entering at this stage, Kirk allowed three possibilities. He would have to: (1) find facts that had eluded the police; (2) find errors in the interpretation of evidence; or (3) conclude with the prosecution that Dr. Sam was guilty.

As he immersed himself in the case, Kirk understood

how police suspicions initially arose around Dr. Sam. Here was the victim's husband, in the house, in a world in which husbands accounted for far more deaths of women than strangers. Statistics worked against Sheppard.

At first glance, the circumstances must have seemed peculiar: the missing T-shirt, the folded jacket, the awkward burglary. Dr. Sam's injuries, without further inquiry, might have been viewed as the result of a struggle between Dr. Sam and his wife. Add to this the adultery, soon discovered. On at least a surface level, without further scientific study or examination, surrounding factors pointed in Sheppard's direction.

Dr. Sam's supposed lack of cooperation at first seemed troubling, but Kirk soon saw that Sheppard had expressed willingness to cooperate with the authorities and had done so. The continual parade of comments about Dr. Sam's refusal to talk was really an expression of frustration that he did not confess.

Kirk analyzed further. He recognized that no single item was conclusive of guilt. "Combined, they constituted only a set of extremely suspicious circumstances."

To have had any chance at the trial, the defense had needed to offer a satisfactory explanation for every element of circumstantial evidence. Instead the trial had become mired in a huge amount of irrelevant material. The jury easily could have been confused.

Dr. Sam's description of events was vague and sometimes illogical, and this also bothered Kirk "until," he said, "it occurred to me that the reason must be that it was true." He saw that Sheppard's narrative of events was consistent; in multiple statements, he said the same thing. The only point on which Dr. Sam had reversed himself was his affair with Susan Hayes.

Proceeding meticulously, Dr. Kirk set as his first task a determination of what, if anything, in Dr. Sam's explanation could be independently verified or negated. He made a list.

- Aherns as guests the night before, and Dr. Sam falling asleep on the couch: verified.
- Dr. Sam's description of his wife's screams: unprovable.
- Vagueness about what occurred: consistent with sudden awakening.

- Dr. Sam's statement that he saw a form with a light garment as he ran up the steps: confirmed when Kirk did tests simulating the light on the morning of July 4 and saw a whitish "form," exactly as Dr. Sam described it; verified.
- Knocked unconscious from unseen blow behind him: injuries were compatible with this point; verified.
- Awakened and saw his wallet on floor: unprovable at that time.
- Second encounter with an intruder on the beach: the injuries to Dr. Sam on both front and back of the head (eyes, mouth, face, and neck) lend credibility to two attacks, but this could not be definitely determined.
- Knocked into the water: water seen on the steps from the beach and porch; sand in his pants, which would not have been the case had he merely waded in the water (i.e., to "wash off"); clothes and wallet waterlogged; sand pressed into the toes of shoes more than heels and consistent with lying face down—definitely verifiable.
- Second visit to bedroom to check on wife: blood on left knee of trousers, which exactly matched the description of how he checked his wife's condition; further confirmed when Kirk found diluted blood at that location on the bed sheet which he believed came from the lake water on Dr. Sam's pants; verified.
- Key chain and jewelry (found in the green bag) that Dr. Sam had looped around his belt and sunk in his pocket; the rip on Dr. Sam's pants pocket demonstrated that the items were yanked from his pants, and experiments with the direction and tears of ripping cloth showed that Dr. Sam could not have yanked the chain off himself while wearing the pants; definitely verified by testing.

The remaining elements of Dr. Sam's story were things that he did not know or could not remember—that is, negative statements. Dr. Sam's version of events was largely confirmed; what could not be confirmed were the voids. By a positive statement, Kirk meant an action. If, hypothetically, Sheppard had said that he had taken off his T-shirt and left it on the kitchen counter, that would be a positive statement. Then, either the T-shirt was found on the kitchen counter and the positive statement was verified, or it was found elsewhere or not found as described and was not verified. But what Sheppard said was that he hadn't any idea what happened to his T-shirt—a negative statement. It was not something in which an action was involved. This type of negative statement could be neither verified nor disproved. In general, Kirk concluded that Dr. Sam's positive statements were either confirmed or consistent with the known facts.

Kirk knew that Sheppard's failure to take a lie detector test had hurt the public perception of him. Even though polygraph testimony was so unreliable that it could not be used in court, people had grand illusions about its ability to "solve" a crime. In this case, Dr. Sam was right to refuse, Kirk realized. The situation was too traumatic. Whether guilty or innocent, Dr. Sam was emotionally close to the crime. "If he did not commit the murder, he could not escape an intense feeling of guilt from his failure to protect his wife. To the latter would be added many more emotions—grief, anger, despair, desperation, fear, and a hopeless feeling of loss."

If a competent operator—and Kirk maintained there were few in the nation at the time and none in northern Ohio—were to give a reliable test that indicated guilt, how then could the operator discern whether the guilt was from participation in the murder or from having failed as a husband or protector? Participating in a polygraph exam under those circumstances would have been a bad decision.

With his mind clear, Dr. Kirk began the search for evidence that the police might have missed or misinterpreted. He began with the room in which the murder was committed, a room the police had largely neglected. They had searched up and down the hillside and the stairs, dredging the lake, and ignored the very room in which the crime took place. Detective Henry Dombrowski, who had tested blood on the stairs, admitted at the trial that blood spots on the carpet and walls in the murder room had not been analyzed because there was too much blood, and he hadn't seen why it would be significant. This was exactly the type of common mistake that police made in failing to understand the significance of scientific evidence, thought Kirk.

The analysis of the flight and impact of blood in a murder room can literally be the writing on the walls to solve a case. With every blow, blood is thrown, and that blood has to land somewhere, whether on a wall, a carpet, or a person. The blood had left a record, and much of this evidence remained untouched. "The real story of the Sheppard murder had yet to be interpreted, and . . . this room held the story," he said.

As if conducting a thorough medical exam on every part of the house, Dr. Kirk undertook to analyze the murder room. He observed everything. No microscopic blood spot or fiber was beyond his scope. He conducted on-the-scene experiments and collected materials to take to his lab in California. Using a special vacuum cleaner with a filter, he swept the rug, finding fragments that had been completely ignored. He made a drawing of the room that included every blood spot he found.

Blood was dispersed throughout the room. Small droplets of blood were on the covers of the second bed, which was still neatly made with the covers folded back, as it was on the night of the murder. The wall beyond that bed, on the west, had the fewest drops. The north wall, at the foot of the bed where Mrs. Sheppard lay, had twenty blood spots. On the east, closet doors only a few feet from the first bed were heavily coated with blood, which formed a low triangle on the closet doors. The door to the room, also on the east, had obviously been fully open and pushed against the wall at the time of the murder, since the normally outward side was splattered. The south wall at the head of the bed was splattered.

Kirk's analysis began with an understanding of the qualities of blood and what story it could tell. Blood flies through the air like a bullet. Upon landing, blood spreads or splatters on the surface. Blood spots can be elongated or rounded, thicker or thinner. Three factors affect how blood spreads out and are reflected in the shape of the spot: the angle of the impact, size, and speed.

Skilled scientific investigators, by analyzing the shape of the spot, can determine the arc of the blood, the direction of blows, and the force with which the blows were delivered. Scientists such as Paul Kirk come to their conclusions through laboratory analysis, recreating situations and examining the results.

Blood striking at a right angle to the surface will create a round spot. Blood landing at a different angle will create a spot that extends, like a bowling pin, in the direction that it is flying. If beads are visible around the spot, they are an indication of a rapidly moving drop, which has thrown smaller droplets on impact.

Radial blood splatter is a pattern of distribution that Dr. Kirk also understood, with larger drops in the center and smaller droplets around the periphery. Radial blood splatter originates from a solid object striking a bloody surface, such as a weapon hitting a bleeding wound, causing compression and forcing blood to be ejected violently. Kirk saw this pattern in the murder room. From it, he could conclude that the victim had not been moving at the time the blows were delivered; she was already unconscious. The viciousness of the murder was even worse than had been thought.

Kirk could also distinguish blood thrown off from a weapon. Blood drops from a weapon are larger, since the weapon is coated with blood every time it reconnects with the bloody surface. The backswing throws off the largest portion because it is then that the direction of movement is switched. Unlike the radial pattern, the pattern of these spots is elongated and reflects the arc of the moving weapon. In the murder room, the blood on the closet doors was largely weapon throw-off.

Immediately, Dr. Kirk could tell where the murderer was standing. Since flying blood will land on whatever object is there to intercept it, a person standing will also intercept the blood. The murderer acts as a freestanding wall. This was not startling: all investigators agreed that the murderer of Mrs. Sheppard would have been coated with blood.

Those who saw Dr. Sam as guilty pointed to his missing T-shirt, which they said he had discarded because it was bloody, then washed himself off. Those who knew Dr. Sam was innocent pointed out that he had no blood on his belt, his shoes, or his socks, and no blood splatter on his pants. As prosecution witnesses admitted, blood is virtually impossible to wash off fabrics and leather, and even when washed can be seen under a microscope or with a chemical agent.

Attorney Arthur Petersilge commented that he always thought the absence of numerous small spots of blood on Dr. Sam's pants was "one of the strongest indications of Sam's innocence." The prosecution also began to retreat. On appeal, the prosecution seemed to abandon its claim that Dr. Sam had washed off his clothes. One judge at the oral argument asked prosecutors how they accounted for the fact that there were no blood spots on Dr. Sam's pants. They answered: "We don't know if he had his trousers on." Petersilge saw their answer as the rankest kind of speculation. "This sudden shift shows clearly that they were wrong in the beginning, that they realize the absence of small blood spots on the trousers is fatal to their case, and that they are clutching at straws."

The murderer's pants would have been splattered from above the knees, Kirk determined. Even an untucked T-shirt could not have covered all of the affected area of the pants. On the other hand, Kirk said, if the prosecution experts had found blood splatter on Dr. Sam's trousers, that would have been clear evidence of his guilt.

When the murderer acts as a receptacle for flying blood, the objects behind the murderer will show an absence of blood splatter. A cut-out pattern, like a shadow, is left behind. Kirk found the area quickly on the east wall, north of the closet door. The killer stood with his back to the east, at the lower part of the bed, and delivered the blows while facing Mrs. Sheppard's head.

Now Kirk was able to go further in recreating the scene. Knowing where the murderer stood, and with the throw-off blood from the weapon behind and to the left of the killer, Kirk knew that the blows were delivered from the left side. The swing of the weapon started low in a left-sided swing, rose through an arc, and struck the victim with a sideways blow, rather than blows that rained down vertically from above.

Blows delivered from the left side meant that the murderer either held the weapon in his left hand and delivered forearm blows, or held the weapon in his right hand and delivered backarm blows. Dr. Kirk was convinced that a backhand swing was not possible because weapon throw-off spots were low. With a backhand stroke, he believed that the swing would necessarily come from the left shoulder and the weapon throw-off would be high in the arc. Kirk believed that the killer was left-handed.

When Dr. Kirk's findings were made public, officials did not disagree with his conclusions. Dr. Gerber had said something similar early in the investigation. Sheppard was right-handed. Rather than dispute Dr. Kirk's findings, the prosecutor released a picture of Sheppard eating with his left hand at a picnic. Then he released another of him water-skiing with Marilyn and holding the ski bar with his left hand. According to the prosecutor, these showed that Dr. Sam was ambidextrous.

Dr. Charles Kingston, a specialist in probability in crime analysis, considered Dr. Kirk's reconstruction of the direction of the swing. A reconstruction, said Kingston, is an attempt to find "the most probable sequence" of actions from the evidence observed. Kirk's conclusion that the killer was left-handed employed differing "orders" of deduction.

In probability terms, Kingston said, a first-order deduction follows directly from the evidence and is usually correct. The direction of travel of the murder weapon was a first-order deduction, since it was directly related to the blood pattern on the wall. The deduction that the murderer held the weapon in his left hand was a second-order deduction that didn't follow directly from the blood pattern; it was a probable explanation of why the weapon was swung in that direction. A backhand swing with the right hand was an equally likely explanation. To then deduce that the person was left-handed was a third-order deduction, based on the correctness of the first two deductions. But, explained Kingston, "it is not improbable that a right-handed person might wield a weapon in his left hand."

Dr. Kirk's left-handed analysis was adopted and used successfully when Dr. Sam was tried and acquitted in 1966. F. Lee Bailey and many other supporters of Sheppard were convinced that the killer was left-handed. They asked first, whenever a prospective suspect emerged, whether or not the person was left-handed.

Kingston's analysis shows that Dr. Kirk was exactly correct in determining that the weapon was swung from the left-hand side, but whether it was a left-handed person, a right-handed person using the weapon in the left hand, or a person using a backhand swing of the right hand is uncertain.

One other factor Kirk may not have weighed in his analysis was the possibility that a right-handed killer had injured his left hand before delivering the death blows. Such a person, finding himself on the east side of the room, enraged, having silenced Mrs. Sheppard and then having had to fight off her husband, might have delivered forceful backhand blows with his right hand, using a swing that was horizontal, instead of raising the weapon up to his shoulder.

Tracking down clues, one by one, Kirk turned his attention to the weapon. Although Dr. Gerber claimed in the trial that the weapon was a "surgical instrument," he had previously suggested a pipe, a piece of wood, or one of "hundreds" of other objects. Gerber really knew only that the weapon was a blunt instrument.

Unlike other investigators who had gathered dozens of objects for testing, Kirk sought to narrow the search first. The length of the weapon could be determined. He knew where the attacker stood, where the victim lay, the proportionate length of arms. With these variables, he learned that the weapon could not have been more than one foot long.

The shape of the weapon could be analyzed. The autopsy showed a weapon with a blunt edge that caused lacerations but did not cut cleanly. Many of the wounds had a half-moon shape, described as "crescentic." This pointed toward a cylindrical object.

Power and weight could be put into a range. The autopsy showed that while the skull was fractured, none of the fractures had been driven into the brain, and the covering over the brain, the dura, had not been penetrated. The weapon, Kirk concluded, was not heavy.

Now he worked logically with the known facts. He supposed that the killer went to the bedroom and, for whatever reason, flew into a rage. Marilyn's killer had few options: he used something from the room as a weapon; he left the room to find something; he used something he brought with him. Whether an intruder or Dr. Sam, the same thinking applied.

There was no evidence to show that something from the room was used as a weapon, and it was improbable, Kirk thought. Documents viewed in 1993 showed that the coroner's office did test the arm of a rocking chair, but no results were ever released. The idea that the killer left the room to find a weapon was unrealistic because Mrs. Sheppard would have risen. The most reasonable conclusion was that the killer brought the weapon into the room.

An intruder very likely would have carried a flashlight. A flashlight is less than a foot long, not heavy, and cylindrical in shape. Kirk raised his own objection to this possibility, noting that there was no broken glass, such as might have come from a smashed bulb cover. But, he thought, if the murderer used the back end of the flashlight as the weapon, no glass would have broken. One wound, like a gouge made by a sharp-pointed object, might have been formed from the bending of the thin metal cap at the bottom of the flashlight. It was also likely that an intruder would carry a flashlight, but that Dr. Sam would not.

The exact weapon could not be determined with available information, Kirk said, but he was certain that it was in no significant respect similar to the surgical instrument that Gerber claimed was the weapon from impressions he supposedly saw on a pillow case.

Other pieces of forgotten and ignored evidence fascinated Kirk. Teeth were among them. At least one tooth chip was discovered under the bed and never identified as having belonged to anyone. The laboratory and microscopic examination report that was presented to the defense by the coroner's office did not even mention the tooth chip. Unfortunately, given the state of the prior investigation, Kirk found that there was little he could do with this tooth chip. Today, capable forensic scientists can get mitochondrial DNA from a tooth chip and can match it individually to a possible suspect, according to Dr. Owen Lovejoy, a biological anthropologist and forensic analyst at Kent State University.

Gerber also found two pieces of teeth on the bed, and it was these on which Dr. Kirk concentrated. These teeth were found to be two of Mrs. Sheppard's upper front teeth. While in Ohio, Kirk visually examined the teeth, held by the prosecution, and was surprised at how large the pieces were, since in testimony they had been described as "chips." They were almost whole teeth, broken cleanly at the gum line. But how? That was what Kirk wanted to know.

Mrs. Sheppard's mouth, like her entire lower face, had no exterior bruises or injuries. Only a small scrape was found on the inside of the lower lip. The autopsy seemed to indicate that there had been no blow to Mrs. Sheppard's mouth that could have knocked the teeth in. If the teeth had been smashed by a blow to her mouth, marks would have shown on the mouth and the teeth would have been knocked back into her throat and not ejected from her mouth, Kirk believed.

Back in California, Kirk designed an experiment to test how the teeth could have been broken. He collected extracted incisors from dentists and mounted them in a metal frame to simulate a jawbone. The teeth were then struck, tapped, pulled, pushed. Through testing, Kirk determined that the teeth that were found on the bed had been pulled from the inside out, and not struck, as was assumed. Mrs. Sheppard had sunk her teeth into some object, such as a finger, hand, or arm, and the teeth had given way as the object was yanked away.

"That Marilyn bit something must be accepted as fact," said Kirk.

The determination that she bit something led to a scenario. The killer, Kirk believed, tried to stifle Mrs. Sheppard's cries by putting his hand over her mouth. She bit. The killer snatched away his injured hand. The motion pulled out her gripped teeth.

This information also made sense when connected to the blood trails throughout the house. Through actual experiments, Kirk determined that the blood on the "blood trails" was not shed from clothing or tracked by shoes. Clothing would have absorbed the blood; shoes would have left a distinct imprint. Neither was the blood from a dripping weapon, as the prosecution asserted. Blood on a weapon would have drained off, dropping larger spots followed by smaller ones. But the blood trails on the steps found by detective Henry Dombrowski were of a uniform size from the second floor all the way to the basement.

"Whenever an experienced investigator sees a distinct trail of blood, he knows that the person who left it was himself bleeding," commented Kirk. "If the murderer left trails of blood in remote parts of the house, it is a certainty that the deposits were his own blood."

Analysis of the way that the teeth were pulled out further explained how the blood trails came to be. The killer's hand had been bitten and was bleeding; the killer walked through the house.

Other examinations conducted by Kirk found details that had completely evaded the thirty or more police officers who had worked the case. These included:

Tear on pants. A three-and-a-half-inch tear on the right pocket of the pants extended directly downward from the pocket. It was here that Dr. Sam normally carried the key chain (with five keys and items of jewelry) that was found in the green bag outside. Normally, Dr. Sam looped his keys around a belt and sunk them in the bottom of his right pocket. The tears in the reinforced seam were made from downward or outward jerking that pulled out the keys, Kirk determined. Unless an individual is a contortionist, the human anatomy makes only an upward and outward motion possible. Dr. Sam could not have ripped the keys out himself and caused the tear. The tear was fully consistent with another person tearing off the key chain from a prone body.

Victim's pajamas. During the trial, little attention was paid to the disarray in Mrs. Sheppard's bedclothes. Kirk found it significant. Blood had accumulated at the bottom of the pajama pants, showing definitively that they had been pulled below her genitals before the murder. The crime started as a sex attack, rather than as a murder. The way that Mrs. Sheppard was left in a near-nude condition was so "highly characteristic" of a sex crime that the conclusion was inescapable, he said.

Pillow. The pillow with the "imprint" showed both more and less than Gerber tried to claim, Kirk said. A proper look at the pillow revealed that blood was on both sides of it. He knew that the side opposite to the "imprint" faced up during the murder, because it had blood splatter on it. The killer would have had to turn the pillow over after the murder and lay the weapon there. Kirk was definite that the pillow was in contact with blood before the murder, and was used either by the assailant to muffle outcry, or by the victim as a shield from blows. The side with the so-called weapon imprint came from a fold in the pillow that created a "mirror image" blood impression, said Kirk.

"Nail polish." The coroner's office had tested numerous small red particles collected from under Mrs. Sheppard's bed. Dr. Kirk referred to this as one of the pieces of "embarrassing evidence." Mary Cowan had performed virtually no investigative analysis of these items. Cowan looked at them under a microscope and decided that the particles were nail polish and concluded they were insignificant. She compared them with fragments found under Mrs. Shep-

pard's fingernails. Mrs. Sheppard was not wearing fingernail or toenail polish. Cowan made no comparison with polish in the house.

The particles were embarrassing, according to Kirk, because they demanded an explanation, and yet they had been totally disregarded. They had no connection to Dr. Sam.

In his vacuum sweep of the room, Kirk found more particles that fit the same description, and he took them to his lab. Like Cowan, he looked under a microscope. He compared the items to nail polish in the house, but none matched. Now he stopped himself and decided to check assumptions.

He realized that he had assumed that the material was nail polish because it had been so confidently labeled as such in the courtroom. But when he checked further, he realized the chips were not nail polish at all but commercial lacquer. Nail polish has an organic dye and allows light to pass through it. Lacquer has mineral and organic pigments and is opaque, deflecting light.

Commercial lacquer is used for painting hardware and metal. Some flashlights have a red coating on the cylinder, which may have been the source of the red lacquer. Before the trial, Detective Dombrowski referred to the material as a "paint chip." Gerber claimed on July 7 that material "resembling a chip of paint" was found near the bed and that it may have come from the murder weapon.

Leather fragment, tinfoil, match. The tiny triangular fragment, Kirk noted, was definitely leather and appeared to have been torn off recently. Here was another bit of "embarrassing evidence." Kirk was not allowed to test it further. A visual inspection by investigators in 1994 revealed that the scrap may have been ripped from the inner lining of Sheppard's wallet, which would have supported his description of awakening and seeing his wallet flopped open on the floor. Nor could Kirk do anything with a match and a piece of tinfoil that had been picked up in the murder room by Detective Dombrowski. They had been completely discounted as evidence.

Fingernail scrapings. Among the microscopic evidence sadly ignored were the fingernail scrapings. The fibers found under Mrs. Sheppard's nails were a direct link to the murder, and the two blue fibers in particular might have provided valuable information. Kirk noted that Dr. Sam was wearing a white T-shirt, tan trousers, and white socks. There was nothing blue. A sharp laboratory technician today might be able to take a single fiber and from it trace the source to a manufacturer of the product. The fibers were held by the coroner's office, and Kirk could not test them.

Green bag. A person setting up a scene probably would not abandon the green bag in the weeds. "Rather, its abandonment was the act of a person in an unnatural hurry, as would be true of an intruder being pursued."

Kirk pointed out that the prosecution never commented about the lack of blood found on Dr. Sam's ring in the bag. Yet if Dr. Sam had committed the murder, there most certainly would have been blood on it. He was not persuaded by the statement of Mary Cowan, who tested a small cutout of the green bag for blood, that it contained no "fresh" stains. The bag must have had at least dried blood chips because blood would have flaked off the watch inside, which had blood on its face.

Watch. Claims about the man's watch, which the prosecution considered to be its most convincing evidence, were utterly inconsistent, noted Kirk. Identifying blood on the face and water under the crystal, the prosecution claimed that Dr. Sam had gotten blood on the watch during the murder and water under the crystal by washing himself off in the lake. But tests by Kirk proved that blood on the face would have been washed off if it had been submerged in water. From photographs, he thought the water under the crystal was condensation. A report secured under freedom of information laws in 1994 demonstrated that the prosecution already knew that, but kept it quiet.

One ignored fact about the man's watch was how the band was broken. Since it had not been broken earlier in the evening, when the Aherns were dinner guests, it was definitely connected to the events of that morning. Did Dr. Sam Sheppard strip the watch from his own wrist with such force that the band was broken? Or did someone else jerk it off while Dr. Sam was unconscious? "The breaking of the watch band combined with ripping of the pants in removing the key chain gives a distinct impression that this was the work of a person who was not wearing these items."

Trophies. Trophies belonging to Dr. Sam and Marilyn were snapped from their bases and tossed to the floor. It was not believable for Dr. Sam to deliberately break his own and Marilyn's trophies, Dr. Kirk thought. "It is completely consistent only for someone who hated the Sheppards, or who was jealous of their athletic tendencies and abilities."

Dr. Sam's own nostalgic remembrances unintentionally showed the deep reverence he had for his trophies. The track trophy was from his 1941 high school team, which won the Ohio state title, a first for his school. He celebrated with Marilyn. "She was so happy about the track trophy. I gave her the medal which was awarded to me. Marilyn wanted to make a bracelet out of the awards from various athletic events but I asked her not to. . . . I felt the medals should not be treated as trinkets, and she agreed."

The destruction of the trophies was a "retaliatory" action, said Dr. Kirk. Likewise, the medical bag would not have been maltreated by Dr. Sam, as medical bags are a doctor's prized possession.

Burglary. The burglary issue was wrongly debated, Kirk believed. The prosecution always emphasized what was *not* taken—but much was. Marilyn's watch was removed, if dropped; there was an effort to remove her rings, which were pulled to her knuckle; Dr. Sam's watch and ring and accessories were removed; his wallet was removed and money was stolen from it, and Marilyn's wallet was found with money removed from it; trophies were broken; the medicine ease was overturned. A panicky husband might do some of these things, Kirk reasoned, but not others. The actions were more likely those of a person who needed to conceal the true intent of the crime and his identity from both authorities and Dr. Sam.

Kirk believed the person who committed the crime probably was someone known to the Sheppards, aware of Mrs. Sheppard's physical attractiveness, and familiar with the layout of the home and habits of the family.

One final point made by Kirk became the subject of great contention. In looking at the closet doors in the murder room, he found one blood spot that looked different from all the others. It was larger in diameter and, unlike the elongated shape of other blood spots, it was round. There was no secondary splatter beading, which meant that it did not hit hard enough or fast enough to break up into smaller drops. The spot landed with such minimal velocity, it almost looked as if the blood had been poured there.

Back in his laboratory, Kirk began testing to see how blood might make such a formation. He dipped weapons in blood and tried throwing it off, but never produced the same type of spot. Only when he lightly tossed blood in his hand onto the surface did he get the same shape. He was convinced that the blood came not from a weapon but from a wound on the attacker's hand or arm. This was further confirmation that the killer had a cut that was bleeding; Dr. Sam had not.

The California criminalist had scrapings from this particular blood spot sent to him in sealed vials from Cleveland, as well as samples from other blood spots in close proximity to it. With these, he wanted to attempt to type the blood by category. Typing dried blood was difficult, especially in 1954.

Using the available science, Kirk wanted to know if this one spot had different characteristics from the blood of Mrs. Sheppard. If so, it might indicate the blood type of the third person that he believed was in the room. Marilyn's blood was group O; Dr. Sam's was group A.

Kirk used agglutinogen tests, which were different from the agglutinin tests used by the coroner's office in Ohio. Agglutinogens are the substances found on the outer surface of the blood corpuscles. Agglutinins are the substances found in the plasma or serum, and Kirk avoided this test because agglutinins are lost very rapidly in many bloods.

In conducting the tests, Kirk noticed differences in the characteristics of the blood from the large unique spot and those of the smaller ones. The blood from the smaller spots started to dissolve at once, while the blood from the large spot dissolved slowly. The solubility was very different. After dissolving, both samples were grouped by Kirk as group O, but they reacted differently. More important, this suggested to Kirk that the two spots were definitely not blood from the same person.

Later, Dr. Kirk used a method of paper electrophoresis, new at the time, to determine the protein composition of the blood samples. The blood in the round spot, he again concluded, was from a third person.

Prosecutors challenged this conclusion. Dr. Roger Marsters gave a statement that asserted that Kirk's tests could not be reliable because eight months had passed since the blood was shed. The blood could have become contaminated. Dr. Marsters, however, had very little, if any, experience typing dried blood, since he worked with fresh blood for transfusions.

Blood grouping can determine only a broad category to which the person belongs. Under the ABO system used in 1954, there were four blood categories—A, B, O, AB. Kirk was working with a more discriminating analysis to find individual blood characteristics beyond those broad typing categories.

Dr. Peter De Forest noted in 1994 that the solubility test that Kirk was using was valid for the time period, but crude compared to what is available today. Blood can lose enzymes over time, said De Forest. Dr. Kirk attempted to account for this by using a comparison spot, which would have been exposed to the same conditions. Dr. De Forest said that Kirk could have further supported his thesis by doing independent testing with different blood samples to measure enzyme loss, but this technology was not available until six or seven years later.

There was one factor, in addition, of which neither Kirk nor Marsters seemed to be aware. While the blood in the murder room was undisturbed and ideal for testing, the closet doors with the blood spot had been disturbed. The doors had been wholly dismantled, removed, and taken to the coroner's office. What was done with them there was never explained. They were then moved back to the Sheppard home. Unlike the walls, the doors could have been contaminated. Still, surfaces would have been affected equally, and would have done little to change Dr. Kirk's conclusion that the blood of a third person was unaccountably in the murder room.

Dr. Kirk wrote up his findings in a fifty-six-page report that included nine appendix entries of tests that he had done. He submitted it to Bill Corrigan on March 18, 1955. His conclusion was riveting: "Taken together, the only explanation that actually is consistent with all the facts is the one given by Dr. Sam, vague and uncertain though it may be."

Dr. Sam was elated. The report documented points that he had tried to raise, and it did it scientifically, without rumor, innuendo, and inference. Kirk had many findings that changed the entire face of the case, that challenged every bit of the prosecution. On April 24, 1955, Dr. Sam wrote, "Reread Kirk's report—it is the real stuff. It should *really* do the trick."

On April 25, 1955, Kirk returned to Cleveland and his report was converted into a twenty-seven-page affidavit to be presented to the court as part of a supplemental motion for a new trial based on newly discovered evidence. The trial judge, Edward Blythin, was to hear the motion. Kirk was prepared to testify. The judge said it was not necessary, and that he could make a ruling based on the written materials.

Police and prosecutors mounted a news blitz to decry Kirk. His work amounted to a "good college thesis," said Inspector James McArthur with obvious derision. Only four days after his spirits had soared, Dr. Sam began to deflate. "Reaction by the Prosecuting Attorneys to Dr. Kirk's work is absolutely a disgrace," wrote Dr. Sam. "I'll say there's no justice left around here at all."

Blythin denied the motion for a new trial on May 9, 1955. It was appealed. No appellate court would consider the evidence, either. The appellate court said that the same information could have been presented at trial, and just because Dr. Sam and his lawyers had not done so was no reason to put the state to the strain of a new trial. That the Sheppards had not been allowed to take possession of the property was not considered a sufficient excuse. One appellate court was especially harsh in its attack on Kirk.

Like Dr. Sam, Kirk was astonished by the reaction and stung by the criticism. Regarded as one of the most prominent people in his field, he could not understand how the courts could be so unyielding. In a letter to Bill Corrigan, he expressed his disappointment: "That the court [said] that it had no intention of re-trying on the facts, but only of passing on the legality was the saddest thing of all, because it is the facts that should be re-tried, and the facts are all on our side."

The scientific understanding of bloodstain patterns at crime scenes was advanced by Kirk's work on the Sheppard case, according to experts in the field. But Gerber, furious over Kirk's scientific swipe at the coroner's office, went on an anti-Kirk rampage, deriding his work to professional associations for years afterward. Kirk wrote that he had taken a "very bad beating" over the case, losing a research grant and the editorship of a journal. Dr. De Forest, a former student of Kirk's, recalled how Gerber, a board member of the American Academy of Forensic Sciences, kept Kirk out, even though he was obviously qualified as a member.

Kirk finally got his day in court, but, like Dr. Sam, he didn't see it until 1966, nearly twelve years after the conclusion of his work.

And even though he died in 1970, still blocked by Gerber from the forensics academy, there was a posthumous victory. The academy decided to establish a yearly award for excellence in criminalistics. It was named "The Paul L. Kirk Award."

NINE

Enduring

The letters that young Sam first wrote his dad were necessarily simple, crafted in the blocky, deliberate printing of a second-grader, sometimes accompanied by a pencil sketch. They spoke of everyday things but said nothing about the confusion that he was experiencing nearly every day. Even between the lines, he could not describe the strange world into which he had suddenly been thrust. It was better to keep a chin up, not to make his Dad worry too much; this is what the adults told him.

May 17, 1955
Dear Daddy,
I might ride my bike today to school.
How are you!
I am fine.
We went sailing Sunday [drawing of boat].
I'm going on a camping trip.
Love Sam

June 28, 1955
Dear Daddy,
I'm having a nice time. I caught a lizard.
Love Sam

Oct. 21, 1955
Dear Daddy,
How are you!
Fine I hope.

Thank you for the present.
I played football.
Janet and I just got through looking at funny books.
I want to play football today.
Lots of love,
Sam

Dr. Sam's responses were equally upbeat, with tips or advice given from afar. At the time, prisoners were not allowed phone calls. He would describe his activities in prison or the people he had met or things he had read.

There were few of the lines that Dr. Sam put in a personal journal about his gnawing abhorrence of the justice system and his feelings of betrayal and loss. "Father's day card from Sam made me cry. I recall last year when Marilyn and Sam gave me a fine new pipe," he wrote in 1955. Or, "The grief of the past eight months has been so great that the small effect of poor food and attempted personal degradation [by jail officials] rarely penetrates the great emotion tied up with wrongful conviction and the death of three of the individuals I loved most in this world."

In his letters, Dr. Sam added drawings to amuse young Sam. But just as often they might include very adult requests for young Sam to please call someone or do something that the regulations prohibited a man in prison from doing for himself, such as pass on a message to a relative who was not on his formal correspondence list. After an aunt sent a gift, Dr. Sam wrote his son, then nine: "Will you please call her on the phone and thank her for me?"

Whatever they contained, the letters were precious to Sam R. Each letter that he received, he carefully folded away. More than words on paper, they were *his,* his connection, his link.

1954
Sam Dear,
I got your pictures today and have three of them stuck up on my wall. They are all very good.
There is a man here who was a crew member of a submarine during the war and has a lot of experiences to tell. He said it looks like this: [drawing of sub] The name was the seahorse.

My thoughts are with you most of the time. Keep up the good job of being a little man.

Love, Daddy.

1956

Dear Sam:

. . . Uncle Rich told me all about the way you got up when you slept on the boat and caught the fish for breakfast. They told me how you had to wake everyone up. Sure wish I could have been there so we could have water skied in the bay in front of the camp. Well, there'll come a day.

Love, Dad.

1957

Dear Sam:

Your most recent, fine letter came the other day and I was very happy to receive it, as I always am to hear from you. In this way I know that you are thinking of me and that is a big help.

I was glad to hear about your nature scrap book and I also got word of your objection to the increase of game birds which are to be shot. That is fine and I sure agree with you all the way. A friend of mine always goes hunting with a camera-gun, rather than one with bullets. We'll give it some thought when we want to go hunting together.

Wish we could get into baseball shape together this Spring, but guess we'll have to wait for another.

Love, Dad.

Sam R.'s letters gradually changed from printing to the slow handwriting of a grade-schooler and then to the more sophisticated style of a teenager. The subjects changed to training for a track meet and dating. Even the return address changed in eighth grade when Sam R. began attending a military prep school in Indiana that his uncle thought offered a better environment.

Dr. Sam's letters had a certain constancy: his jobs in prison, his interactions, some words of wisdom. They were all on regulation stationery and carried 98860, his prison number.

Both father and son began to sign off with the same code, one that spoke of hope tempered with patience: V.Q.P. The Latin initials for "Vincit Qui Patitur" were adopted from a gift sent to Dr. Sam by a supporter, and meant "He who endures, conquers." They were trying to endure.

The appellate process was not going well. Dr. Sam was suddenly aware of the connections among the politically powerful, the way the judges were appointed or sat on the board of a panel that gave a citizenship award to the editor of a newspaper. "I have been so bounced and battered by this type of injustice that at this point I'm really numb," he wrote in June 1955.

He had been a neophyte in understanding the limitations in the appellate process. As the convicted person, he had to prove that major legal errors had occurred. The jury and judge were presumed to have decided properly. New evidence was not to be considered, unless he could show that the evidence could not possibly have been presented at the trial. And at every level, the appeals were opposed vigorously, not only by the prosecutors who had convicted him but also by the newspapers and the police and the coroner. Once convicted, he began to see, Joshua at Jericho was needed to tumble the conviction down. "I don't dare hope and count in any way on honesty and justice for fear that the hammer will fall again and knock me apart. . . . This wait until the decision is the worst yet, mainly because it represents the continuous wonder as to whether our higher courts are what they claim to be or not."

Weeks and months and years passed. Two separate appeals, one on constitutional and legal errors in the trial and another on newly discovered evidence, worked their way through the multiple layers of the system. They were consistently denied.

Confident at first that a wrong would be rectified, Sheppard opted to stay in the county jail in Cleveland. He was placed in solitary confinement, away from even the other prisoners. He heard that in the penitentiary, he could hold a job and get exercise. Worn down with the process and isolated in the jail, in June 1955 Dr. Sam requested a transfer to the pen.

Special transportation was arranged so that the press could get good photos. Sheppard was marched out in handcuffs and driven away.

The biggest practical change in Sheppard's circumstances was a shift of public opinion. Dr. Sam, his supporters, and his family would not go away. They made appeals. They spoke out. They continued to investigate, digging up pieces of information big and small. Their legions grew, while at the same time the hysteria of 1954 began to wear off.

From 1956 to 1962 articles championed Dr. Sam. They were written almost universally by writers who were not from Cleveland: *True Detective, Man's World, American Weekly, Parade, The Lowdown,* magazines in Germany, Britain. Dr. Sam, for his part, held his ground: he was innocent, he said again and again. Dr. Sam was becoming known as the man who was wrongfully convicted.

Harold B. Bretnall, a New York private investigator, was hired in October 1955 by Dr. Sam's brothers to solve the case. A former investigator for Senator Estes Kefauver's crime committee, Bretnall wrote coded "trenchcoat" letters to the Sheppard brothers, often signed merely "Bret." In 1957 he said he had solved the case. He was convinced of Sheppard's innocence and had a suspect. He had new clues that involved Marilyn Sheppard's red bedroom slippers and a "small blue bordered towel." He never explained their significance.

Bretnall was putting his information into an exposé called "The Big Frame" at the time of his death in 1963. His thesis was never fully made public, and the big frame was largely a big secret. In 1993, Sam R. got an inkling of the content of Bretnall's work but by then most of Bretnall's materials had vanished.

As Sam R. came to learn, Bretnall was convinced that the police themselves wiped off the fingerprints in the house. He also challenged a claim by Cleveland police investigator Jerry Poelking that a partial palm print found on a desk in the Sheppard living room belonged to young Sam. Leading independent experts who compared young Sam's palm print and a photograph of the desk print, he said, found that they could not be matched with any certainty. The palm print had weighed little in the trial, but a truer interpretation of it may have pointed to an intruder, Bretnall felt.

In 1956 Bretnall also alerted defense attorney Bill Corrigan to overlooked blood identification testimony that favored Dr. Sam. Corrigan began a state habeas corpus action, seeking to have Dr. Sam released from prison because of these irregularities. It was soon thrown off track. The essence of the issue had to do with blood grouping tests done by Mary Cowan on blood smears found on Dr. Sam's and Marilyn's watches. Cowan first testified that the efforts to group the blood on both of the watches found on the Sheppard property was "inconclusive."

The blood on the watches was presumed to be that of Mrs. Sheppard, but standard ABO testing had not proved that to be true. Had the blood been that of a third person, for example, an intruder with a bleeding hand, it would have undermined the prosecution case.

When cross-examined about the blood type on the man's watch, Cowan implied that it scientifically matched that of Mrs. Sheppard. But this was based on an inferior and statistically irrelevant test, and the statement was highly misleading. Unfortunately, Corrigan completely missed the point during the trial. The perception had been left and was widely published that the blood on Dr. Sam's watch matched Mrs. Sheppard's blood, with the implication that the blood landed there during an assault.

Blood grouping is a limited investigative tool, especially in 1954. Blood grouping cannot match a sample of blood found on the scene to a person's actual blood. If successful, it can only say that a blood sample fit a category of blood, each category containing millions of people. A person might be excluded from the crime scene by blood grouping if the blood found on the scene does not match the individual's blood. By contrast, DNA testing used today is individualized and can match a blood sample found on the scene with an individual's actual blood to a high degree of probability.

Several types of blood grouping, or "typing," systems were in effect in 1954. The predominant method of typing blood was the Universal ABO system. About 43 percent of the population is group O; about 40 percent is group A; about 14 percent is group B; and about 3 percent is group AB. In blood typing, red corpuscles are mixed with anti-A and anti-B sera to see whether they clump with one, both, or neither. A or B blood will clump when mixed with the other; O will clump only when mixed with both; AB will not clump at all.

Another, less useful way of grouping blood at the time was through the MNS system. In addition to the ABO types, blood corpuscles also contain agglutinogens known as M and N factors. Three groupings are possible: M, N, and MN. The MNS system's usefulness in crime detection is exceedingly limited, however, since the M factor is found in both M and MN blood, or 80 percent of the Caucasian population. MNS typing is also far more difficult to do successfully.

The evidence on the blood typing of Dr. Sam's and Marilyn's watches was so obscured that not until 1993, when the trace-evidence report was finally made available for viewing to Sam R. and those working with him, was it moderately clear what Cowan had or had not done. Cowan had tested the blood on the watches under the ABO system on July 7–8, 1954. There was slight clumping of the A cells and the B cells, but none with the O cells. The results were so unsatisfactory that Cowan declared the tests inconclusive. No blood type was determined. On "Laboratory findings" given to the defense, Cowan did not mention the ABO tests at all.

Despite the clear deficiencies of those tests, and the fact that MNS elements are harder to determine, Cowan worked with Roger Marsters, Ph.D., to do MNS typing on July 16, 1954. Marsters had not typed dried blood before. The conclusion they reached was that an M factor was present. This determination is statistically irrelevant, because four of five people have the M factor. The only possible value of doing the test would have been to exclude a link, had the blood proved *not* to have the M factor. That not being the case, any conclusions based on the test were absurd.

In testimony, Cowan was led by the prosecutor in a way that breezed past the M typing's statistical insignificance. In criminal trials today, the defense attorney would probably have an opportunity not only to challenge testing information in a pretrial hearing without the jury present, but also to have access to blood samples for independent testing. Corrigan did not have those opportunities, and the prosecution effectively pulled the wool over his eyes.

When Bretnall pointed out in 1956 that a work card used by Mary Cowan indicated that the initial blood typing was inconclusive, Corrigan was adamant that the card had not been presented at trial. Had he seen the card, he said, he would have certainly cross-examined Cowan extensively. This maneuver, he felt, was part of a "brazen effort" to suppress material evidence. He filed the state habeas corpus petition, but in this effort Corrigan again misunderstood the scientific implications, believing that the test showed that the blood was of a B grouping, which was not so.

This new legal effort sank into a quagmire. The coroner's office refused to turn over Cowan's twenty-eight work cards. The card relating to the blood tests on the watch disappeared altogether, then mysteriously appeared in an appellate court file, where it should never have been. Finally, in 1960 the Ohio Supreme Court brusquely rejected the issue altogether. Bretnall, waiting to write his big exposé, was frustrated on the sidelines.

And Dr. Sam also waited, by then spending his sixth year in prison, his son turning into a teenager in the same year.

Even in 1956, Dr. Sam began to fret about the toll the case was taking on his family. His brothers and close family were suffering more than he was, he thought. "They feel my incarceration as if part of them were, or are, locked behind these walls. They and their personalities are, in truth, partially cut away as long as this great wrong continues."

For himself, Dr. Sam was beginning to see the long haul ahead. He found a grim reality in prison. There were not innocent people or guilty people in prison. There were only prisoners and guards.

Early on arrival, Dr. Sam stood out. Already he was known to people who were strangers because of the publicity. Yet his life experience was different from that of many others. Prisoners wanted to know where he would stand. Would he be a stool pigeon and sell out the other inmates? Or would he stand by the convicts who befriended him? Dr. Sam realized that he would have to prove himself.

Athletics helped. From his sports background, he knew how to be a team player while still playing fair and square with the other side. And he knew that, whatever the game, he had to maintain his own personal integrity.

Bit by bit, Dr. Sam won respect "on the inside." His first assignment was to teach car mechanics. His knowledge of the subject was limited, gained mostly from tinkering with his own cars, but he applied himself with great energy, studying and planning lessons. The classes went well. Prison authorities were impressed. They gave him an office job.

But even more important, the prisoners liked him. He wasn't a rat, and he stayed true to his word. That was what counted. He was selected as the master of ceremonies for the annual prison pageant. Soon everyone was calling him Doc. He was well liked, popular, and prisoners would brag to their families back home that they had gotten to know Dr. Sam.

After he was less than a year inside the pen, the need for more hospital help in the prison became apparent. An assistant to the warden inquired: Would Dr. Sam do hospital detail if he were asked? If asked, he said, he would. Prison officials moved him to the hospital dorm. Although he was assigned a job as duty nurse, he was scrubbing in as first assistant to the overworked physicians. They appreciated his medical knowledge, and for Dr. Sam, it felt good to do what he was trained to do and to be back in the operating room. When emergencies arose, he was on-site to help. He saved lives. He set up a blood bank and organized donors. Unpublicized, he volunteered to do an experiment in solitary to help NASA scientists. When Sloan-Kettering Cancer Institute proposed a medical experiment that involved injecting live cancer cells into their bodies, no prisoners would consent. Dr. Sam took the bold step of being the first to volunteer; trusting him, nearly two dozen other prisoners followed his example.

Through it all, he tried to keep his presence of mind. He remembered the words of his father, Dr. R. A. Sheppard, who had advised him never to give up. "All I can say, I'll keep punching and do all the good for the men that I can while I'm in here," Dr. Sam wrote in his journal. "But this has become such a political football that I'll expect something good only *when it happens!*"

People began writing to the Court of Last Resort almost as soon as Dr. Sam was found guilty. The Court of Last Resort was not a real court, but a creation of Erle Stanley Gardner, a lawyer and the author of the Perry Mason books. Gardner set up the "court" to probe real-life cases in which innocent people may have been wrongfully convicted. Activities and results were published in *Argosy*, a popular men's magazine in the 1950s.

Public persistence finally pushed Gardner to get involved in 1957. He had one stipulation. Before making any sincere investigation into the facts of the case, he wanted Sheppard's brothers to submit to lie detector tests to determine if they had been involved in any cover-up. Gardner didn't want to take up the case if he thought perjury or manipulation was involved.

Dr. Steve and Dr. Richard and their wives, Betty and Dorothy, all agreed. They traveled to Chicago, where Gardner arranged for tests by the four most prominent polygraph experts in the country: John E. Reid, H. B. Hanscom, Alex Gregory, and Dr. Lemoyne Snyder. All of the Sheppards passed. The unanimous opinion of the examiners was that members of the family had in no way hidden any evidence, and that they sincerely believed that Dr. Sam Sheppard was innocent. When these developments were reported publicly, Dr. Samuel Gerber was furious.

Gardner carried on. His plan was to take a lie detector test of Dr. Sam, then incarcerated in Columbus, Ohio. Ohio Governor C. William O'Neill agreed to allow it.

Almost at once, another development occurred. Donald Joseph Wedler, a criminal in Florida, confessed to the murder of Marilyn Sheppard. His was not the first confession, but the Florida authorities were convinced that it was to be taken seriously. Gardner dropped everything and arranged for his team to fly to Florida. Now Gerber was even angrier, decrying any possibility that anyone other than Sheppard had committed the murder.

After polygraph testing, Gardner was not certain whether Wedler had been involved. Gardner returned to his original game plan. He sent his polygraph examiners to Columbus to test Dr. Sam, as agreed. But by the time they arrived at the prison, Governor O'Neill had changed his mind. Permission was withdrawn. Although the governor gave no reason for his turnabout, Gardner recognized a political whammy when he saw one. Frustrated with Ohio politics, Gardner announced that he was pulling the Court of Last Resort out of the state. He publicized the state's orneriness, but it seemed to have no effect.

The intervention of the Court of Last Resort was another episode of hopes raised and dashed. What was left for Dr. Sam turned up in a file, years later: "*The Case*, a three-act play by #98860" (the number was Dr. Sam's prison identification number). In the theatrical version, Dr. Sam takes the in-prison polygraph tests while the warden, police captain, and others watch, and Dr. Sam is cleared. Real life was, however, infinitely more complicated than the play version.

Not surprisingly, no one in power in Ohio paid any attention when Gerard Croiset made statements that tended to support Dr. Sam's version of events. From Holland, Croiset was an international phenomenon because of his uncanny ability to solve difficult crimes through extrasensory perception. Police forces across Europe took impossible cases to him. His exceptional success rate was tracked and documented by a university in Utrecht. Many factually oriented investigators who rejected other "telepathic" intervention had respect for Croiset.

As described by the writer Jack Harrison Pollack, Croiset would take an object from a victim and recount a series of scenes in rapid pictures, sometimes verbalizing them, sometimes sketching them quickly. In 1958 Harold Bretnall arranged for an intermediary, a New York police detective, to present Croiset with a pair of red slippers that had belonged to Mrs. Sheppard. The origin of the slippers was unknown to Croiset. As he held them, Croiset immediately described his images: a home, a body of water, a big city in America. And, he said, the slippers belonged to a woman "murdered by a bushy-haired man." The man, he said, was "not her husband." He said nothing more.

The story raised Dr. Sam's spirits. But he knew by then that no official was going to listen.

When Bill Corrigan died on July 30, 1961, legal action on the Sheppard case was at a standstill. All avenues of appeal, state and federal, had been approached, and all had failed. Dr. Sam's best hope was his eligibility for parole, which would come in 1964, after ten years in prison.

Within days of Corrigan's death, the first edition of *The Sheppard Murder Case,* by a Chicago newspaper writer and lawyer named Paul Holmes, came out. Erle Stanley Gardner wrote the introduction. Holmes, who had covered the 1954 trial, gave an absorbing account of the case, concluding with his own personal observation that it was, "in its most literal and reverent sense, a God-damned shame." The book reawakened public attention to Dr. Sam.

F. Lee Bailey was only one year out of law school when he encountered Paul Holmes, who was impressed with his abilities and energy. After Corrigan's death in 1961, Sheppard had no representation. Bailey picked up the ball.

Bailey turned his attention to new strategies. He was convinced that Dr. Sam had gotten a raw deal. He appealed to the new governor, Michael V. DiSalle, seeking permission for Dr. Sam to be hypnotized in prison. Permission was denied.

Dr. Sam's new counsel then focused on legal rather than investigative efforts. He proceeded with the petition for habeas corpus in federal court. Pressure mounted. This time politicians were nervous. Dr. Sam Gerber, Sheppard's longtime nemesis, sent a letter recommending that Sheppard be paroled when he became eligible after ten years of incarceration. Observers thought it was an indication that Gerber was feeling shaky about the possibility of Bailey succeeding with his aggressive legal strategies. As Sam R. learned in 1993, Gerber had also had some encounters with possible suspects that may have rattled him.

Bailey gathered statements about the bias of Judge Blythin at the 1954 trial. He tightened and freshened the voluminous legal briefs prepared by Bill Corrigan. The case trekked its way to the U.S. Supreme Court.

After the Supreme Court overturned the conviction, the prosecutors had the option of trying Dr. Sam again. Prosecutor John T. Corrigan would not let it go. Twelve years after the murder of Marilyn Sheppard, Dr. Sam would have to stand trial again. The trial was scheduled to begin in October 1966.

A master trial strategist and communicator, Bailey had a focus that defense attorney Bill Corrigan had lacked. Working with local co-counsel Russell Sherman, he was going to make the prosecution prove that Dr. Sam was guilty. He was not going to let them get away with half-baked statements like the inference that a medical instrument was the weapon, or the damaging innuendo that arose from sexual affairs, or the completely unsupported statements that Dr. Sam was not injured or injured himself trying to jump off the cliff. He would present testimony about how shoddy the investigation had been. He would lean heavily on the scientific evidence and the analysis of Dr. Kirk. And Bailey had a secondary plan: to try to provide an alternative theory as to who might be the real murderer.

To these ends, Bailey dispatched a prized investigator, Andy Tuney, to Ohio in the summer of 1966 to see what new information he could dig up. Tuney had been a detective with the state police in Massachusetts. He had been the chief investigator in the "Boston Strangler" case, which had resulted in the arrest of Albert deSalvo.

One person Tuney searched out was Richard Eberling. Tuney was tracking information that Eberling had been found with a ring belonging to Marilyn Sheppard when arrested for larceny in 1959. Tuney's initial information was that the ring had been stolen from Dr. Sam's house, and he was less interested in what Eberling had to say when he learned that the ring had been stolen from the home of Dr. Richard sometime after the murder of Marilyn. Tuney and Bailey discussed the possibility of having Eberling testify about how easy it was to get access to the inside of the Sheppard home. Ultimately, Eberling didn't testify before the jury.

Tuney also located Jack Krakan, a bread deliveryman who said that he had seen a man who was not Dr. Sam in the Sheppard home, hugging and kissing Mrs. Sheppard. On one occasion, he said, he had observed Mrs. Sheppard give this man a key to the house. This fit in well with Bailey's theory about who committed the murder, and Krakan would be Bailey's first witness, even if the testimony was cut short before the man was named. The judge in this trial, Judge Francis J. Talty, was determined not to let the trial stray into peripheral issues. Tuney said later that he was less confident about Krakan's testimony than was Bailey. Dr. Sam opposed the idea of having Krakan testify because he saw it as sullying Marilyn's reputation.

John T. Corrigan, as prosecutor, was joined by assistant district attorney Leo Spellacy. Some of the same witnesses would testify, including coroner Samuel Gerber, lab technician Mary Cowan, pathologist Lester Adelson, and investigator Henry Dombrowski. But some of the evidence that had been undermined over the years was dropped, and the interpretation of other evidence was changed. Sheppard's version of events remained the same; the prosecution created a new "story." And prosecutor Corrigan had one new piece of forensic evidence that he considered devastating. Once again, it involved Mary Cowan and the blood on the man's wristwatch that had been found in the green bag.

This time, though, Cowan came forward with a different theory. Projecting a slide of the watch enlarged to giant size, Cowan described small droplets of blood splatter on the watch, which, she claimed, could only have landed there from flying blood. Although the coroner's office previously had completely dismissed the blood analysis work done by Dr. Kirk, Cowan was now trying to use his methods. She said that she had noticed elongated dots of blood on the man's watch. The information was designed to prove that the splatter got on the watch when Mrs. Sheppard was being murdered.

Under cross-examination, Cowan fumbled. She was forced to admit that she had little experience in examining blood splatter, had never conducted experiments herself, and had not examined the murder room for its blood splatter.

If the prosecution thought that Cowan would be its dynamite, it had not fully factored in the atomic power of Dr. Paul Kirk. By then, Kirk had worked on two thousand cases around the world, published 240 articles, and written four books. He had waited a long time to testify in this case. After Kirk crisply described the forensic evidence that he had uncovered, Bailey asked about the blood on the man's watch. Kirk, the leading expert in the world on blood splatter, stated that he believed that the blood had probably gotten there by contact with a bleeding person, not by blood flying in the air. He pointed to two factors: flying blood leaves a symmetrical tail. The blood spots pointed to by Cowan were not symmetrical. This type of "dysymmetry" was an effect that was just as likely to come from partially coagulated blood. The second factor was that blood had slipped into crevices and depressions along the rim and band of the watch, which would indicate a contact transfer from flowing blood. The collection of blood in small dots was caused by partially coagulated blood, which, because it was sticky, did not flow or deposit regularly.

Kirk's testimony was bolstered by the cross-examination of a prosecution witness, Dr. Roger Marsters, when Bailey was able to draw him into admitting that spots on the watchband were inside the links of the band. The spots were located in such a position that, if the watch were on someone's wrist, flying blood could not have landed there.

Bailey established that the blood on the watch could not have gotten there from impact splatter that flew when the murder was being committed because of where the blood was located (on interior links that would have been clasped shut) and how the blood droplets were shaped (without symmetry when symmetry is the sign of flying blood). Instead, the watch had come into contact with dripping blood, such as blood from a wound that flowed onto the watch after it was pulled off Dr. Sam's wrist and that, in a sticky state, had dropped down between the links and around the rim in microscopic dots. Combined with Dr. Kirk's testimony that the person who murdered Marilyn Sheppard probably had a bleeding hand, the watch testimony was turned against the prosecution. Someone who was bleeding had handled the watch; Dr. Sam was not bleeding.

Bailey kept the trial short and to the point. He got Gerber to admit that, after twelve years of searching medical supply outlets, catalogs, and drawers, he could find no surgical instrument like the one he claimed in 1954 was the murder weapon. Bailey held the line on diversionary testimony about sex, and Dr. Sam's various affairs were not made part of the testimony. He had young Sam make a cameo appearance that showed he was in full support of his dad.

For several reasons, Bailey decided that Sheppard should not take the stand. At the time he told Dr. Sam that his story had already been told enough times, that it would open him up to unfair cross-examination, and that it would allow the prosecution to try and drag out some prisoner who would claim that he heard a cell confession. That was, in fact, the prosecution's plan. Dr. Sam did not testify, nor did the prisoner with the supposed story, a man known as Frenchie Flout. While Bailey may not have said so, Dr. Sam was not in condition to testify, either.

In the end, Bailey told the jury a classic story that crystallized the long-standing problems with the case. Investigator Andy Tuney could recall its power years later: "Lee summed it. . . . He said there was a woman standing under the street light and she's looking all around. And another woman comes walking down the street, and she said to the woman looking around, 'What are you looking for, what's the matter?' And she answered, 'Well, I lost a dollar bill, I dropped a dollar.' 'Where did you drop it?' 'Oh, fifty yards down the street.' 'Well, what are you looking here for?' 'Well, the light's better here.' And that's what the police did. The light was better there, they never looked down the street."

The jury didn't have to deliberate for long. After getting instructions from the judge on the morning of November 16, 1966, the jury returned at 9:10 P.M. that night. The foreman, James Vichill, read the verdict. It was pointed and poignant and unambiguous: "Not guilty." A reporter, Mike Roberts, remembered the uncommon roar of jubilant voices that fell from the sky, down from the cells in the jail block on the top floors of the courthouse, as the word was heard: Doc was acquitted.

Soon after the acquittal, Bailey made one more effort to get authorities to reopen an investigation into the murder of Marilyn Sheppard. He wrote a fifteen-page letter to Bay

Village authorities, giving his opinion about who had committed the murder. William R. Pringle, foreman of the grand jury at the time, convened a hearing, and a handful of people were called in to testify.

In his letter, Bailey described information that he had not been allowed to present at the trial. Jack Krakan, the bakery man, had not just seen a man hugging Mrs. Sheppard, but he said he had seen Spen Houk kissing her. Bailey reported on the results of a hypnotic examination of Dr. Sam that he had arranged prior to the trial by Dr. William J. Bryan, Jr., a California medical doctor, and how Dr. Sam relived the scene of July 4, 1954, under hypnosis. In that state, Dr. Sam recreated being thrown violently to the floor and feeling his neck crushed under someone's foot. He heard someone talking about whether or not to kill him. Dr. Sam was said to have remembered that the person who went through the door to the lake was limping slightly. The Houks—Esther and Spen together—had committed the murder, Bailey suggested.

The grand jury heard a few witnesses, including Spen Houk, and decided that there was no case. Houk had a limp that was so bad, said Pringle, that he could not have run down the incline to the beach as Dr. Sam indicated someone had. The grand jury took no action.

But after all the years of working on the Sheppard case, presenting it so effectively to the highest court in the land and to a local jury, Bailey still did not know the extent of evidence that had been hidden away and suppressed. Uncovering that evidence was finally left to Sam R. many years later.

The weekly television series "The Fugitive," starring David Janssen as Dr. Richard Kimble, was canceled at the end of the 1966–67 season. Dr. Kimble, the fictional doctor wrongly convicted of killing his wife, had spent years on the run, having escaped from prison after a train wreck. The *New York Times* reported that, despite the enormous popularity in prior years that ranked it as one of the most-watched television programs, the show suffered from declining interest. The newspaper speculated that after the acquittal of the real-life Dr. Sam, the plight of the fictional Dr. Kimble lost some of its spark and tension. Still, the two-part finale in 1967 racked up enormous audience shares.

In the final episode, Dr. Kimble and the small-town Lieutenant Gerard find the true killer, a one-armed drifter who falls to his death from the top of a carnival ride as they chase him. As the show closes, Dr. Kimble walks away from the courthouse, a free man. He hesitates slightly at the sight of a police car. Shaking off his years of being a fugitive, he realizes it is an inoffensive patrol, nods to say hello, and walks on. The message: everything will be fine.

For Dr. Sam, life was not so easy as fiction. Ten years in prison, nearly a quarter of his life, had changed him. Undoing those years was not simple. Even though he was acquitted, media people and prosecutors and backyard talkers still insisted that he had committed the murder. They were unrelenting.

He tried to pull a life together, but his usual success was elusive. As soon as the prison doors opened, he had married the former Ariane Tebbenjohanns, a German woman who had corresponded with him and helped him through the years of the Bailey appeals. For the first years, he was on tenterhooks: waiting, waiting for the Sixth Circuit Court of Appeals decision that almost sent him back to prison; then for the U.S. Supreme Court decision; then for the new trial. His bag, packed for prison just in case, was always by his bed. Until the legal ordeal was over, he was unable to resume his work life, since his medical license had been suspended upon conviction. His health was not the same; he was in constant pain with a slipped disk that he had let go until he was on the outside and able to see a medical friend whom he could trust to operate. Sloan-Kettering said there were no aftereffects from the cancer studies, but others were not so sure.

Dr. Sam testified in Congress about the disregard for human life that he had witnessed in the prisons. After the acquittal, his own story came out in a book, *Endure and Conquer,* written by a ghostwriter with Dr. Sam's notes. Lawyers were needed to petition for his medical license to be reinstated, and more waiting was necessary. When his right to practice was finally restored in Ohio and he secured a position in a small-city hospital, publicity followed him. Two malpractice suits were pressed, and he felt he was being targeted. The insurers said they couldn't afford to cover him for surgery, and almost at once his ability to practice was limited to tongue depressors and aspirins. Old friends from prison, some with organized crime connec-

tions, had other ideas for him, but Dr. Sam was not interested. He tried to assuage his pain with liquor, too much.
Mood swings began, then grew out of control.

Acquitted but not vindicated, he was hounded wherever
he went. Twelve years of bad press, from 1954 to 1966,
years of "massive pervasive prejudicial publicity," did not
simply fade away. Like the red dye in clear water, like
the negative years in prison, the negative stories were now
embedded in people's minds, and he was trapped on the
outside just like he was inside the prison.

And there was one more thing that made him different
from Dr. Richard Kimble. Yes, he had finally been acquitted. But in some ways, he was back to square one, back
exactly where he was at 5:50 A.M. on July 4, 1954, not knowing what had happened and who had murdered his wife.
Who would or could, after all these years, after the depleted funds, the drain, the ups and downs, find the intruder
who had taken his wife's life?

Unable to put back the pieces that had been smashed so
thoroughly, Dr. Sam's marriage to Ariane broke apart. Afterward, he began living near Columbus, Ohio, with a couple he
had befriended, George and Betty Strickland. In the summer
of 1969 Dr. Sam took up team wrestling as if still fighting the
intruder on the beach, and toured the Saturday afternoon
venues with George as his manager. Near the end of 1969
George's daughter Colleen went with Dr. Sam on a motorcycle trip to Mexico; they came back and reported that they
had married, although legal validity was doubtful.

On April 6, 1970, Dr. Sam died. He was forty-six years
old. On his death certificate the cause of death is listed as
Wernicke's acute hemorrhagic encephalopathy, medically
described as a disease brought on by acute nutritional defi-
ciency and once linked to alcohol. Medical terms don't fully
capture what killed Dr. Sam. He really died of a broken
heart and a spirit that found no solace.

After his death, Dr. Sam's case still lived. Mythology took
over. He was pictorialized, editorialized, anthologized.
Courts cited the Supreme Court decision in the Sheppard
case by the hundreds. It became precedent for such famous
cases as those of O. J. Simpson, William Kennedy Smith,
and the officers accused of beating Rodney King, and it
came up whenever prejudicial publicity threatened to taint

the right to a fair trial. F. Lee Bailey's book *The Defense Never Rests* told the lawyer's version of the story; Dorothy Kilgallen's *Murder One* gave the celebrity journalist's view. Jack Harrison Pollack's recap of the story in a book, *Dr. Sam: An American Tragedy,* was used as the basis for a three-hour television drama starring George Peppard, *Guilty or Innocent: The Sam Sheppard Murder Case.* Encyclopedia Britannica told the story to students in a film version; the cable TV series "American Justice" gave a modern video review. A scholarly book, *Crime and Science,* told the Sheppard case from the point of view of its pioneering forensic work by Dr. Kirk.

Several of those involved used the case as a platform, giving lectures and speeches: Dr. Adelson, police officers of all ranks, even a juror. Some had slides and photographs that seemed to be pulled directly from official files.

The investigative efforts did not end. But even more so than before, there seemed to be nowhere to go with the information that was dislodged.

Cowan, Gerber, and Adelson were still the principals at the coroner's office in 1982 when fireplace tongs were brought to them for testing. On November 17, 1982, Paul Vargo and his son found the tongs while digging a trench on their property on Lake Road in Bay Village, property owned until 1961 by Spen and Esther Houk, who divorced in 1962. When the tongs were found, both Houks were dead—Spen for two years, and Esther for four and a half months.

The Vargos said they found the tongs four to five inches below ground. The implement was twenty-three and a half inches long, weighed one and three-quarters pounds, and was made of brass, with its two arms held together by a steel pin. At the end of each arm were six inch-long clawlike fingers. The tongs were discovered only one day after a rerun of the television movie about Dr. Sam was broadcast locally.

Questions abounded. How old were the tongs? How had they gotten in the ground? Who had put them there? Was this a hoax, a plant, a weapon, a find?

Unlike other weapons discovered over the years, the tongs were taken by the Bay Village police to the FBI, as well as to the coroner's office. At the coroner's office, Mary Cowan used the wax replica of Mrs. Sheppard's head to compare the claws to the wounds on the right side, which were described as "rosettes." Some similarity was noted.

The weapon did not match the four long, curved gashes. Peter Gray, then chief of the Bay Village police, thought the tongs could be the weapon or one of two weapons; Gerber did not. The tongs were compared to a tracing of the pillow case "imprint." The tongs were smaller than the tracing, reported Gray.

The FBI reported back to Chief Gray. Microscopic analysis uncovered one brown Caucasian head hair on the tongs and one white Caucasian head hair on the brown wrapping paper which the Vargos had used. Although the hairs were not weathered in any way, they were mounted for possible future hair comparison. No latent prints were found, nor could any manufacturing information or logo be located. The FBI was unable to date the tongs because, it said, brass was resistant to corrosion.

In a further effort to determine the age of the tongs, Bay Village contacted a local metallurgist, Robert Haddad. Focusing on the steel pinbolt, Haddad concluded that the tongs could not have been buried for twenty-eight years, given the corrosive soil in the area. In that length of time, the pin would have decomposed. Apparently, no effort was made to contact either of the Houk children to learn if they recalled the implement.

Jan Sheppard Duvall jumped into the Sheppard case with zest in the early 1980s, joining with California journalist Richard Dalrymple and New York criminalist Jim Chapman. Dalrymple planned to write a book. His efforts were shelved after the death of a supportive financier, and Jan pursued the idea on her own for a while longer before the effort wilted.

Jan, the older daughter of Dr. Steve Sheppard, had been a fourth-grader in 1954, when she saw her family embroiled in turmoil and experienced the taunts of friends. She was the first to wonder why her grandmother did not answer the door on the day that Ethel Sheppard committed suicide. Although she had moved away from Cleveland, a growing need to resolve the case caught up with her.

Jan, Dalrymple, and Chapman conducted two dozen interviews of people involved in the original case. Chapman used voice stress analysis on some of the interviewees to measure inaudible vocal responses that might indicate unusual anxiety in certain responses. They collected the original files of Dr. Kirk. They heard from former Bay Village police officer Jay Hubach about photos he took that disappeared: of abrasions on Mrs. Sheppard's wrist where the watch was ripped off, of what seemed to be a hand-print on the bed sheets. But as often as not, they heard theories and suppositions that Dalrymple described as loaded with prejudice and empty of fact.

The process was hard. Dr. Lester Adelson urged Jan to drop it all. "You can't put toothpaste back in the tube," he said, advising her to go on with other things in life. "I told him that hadn't worked for 27 years," Jan wrote in her notes. She pressed on for as long as she could.

Jim Chapman was intrigued by the pillow case "imprint." Was it blood that was folded like an ink blot, as Kirk suggested? Or the imprint of a weapon, as Gerber insisted? New techniques of computer photo enhancement gave him an idea. Computer enhancement worked by projecting different shadings of colors on the image, making visible things that could not be seen with the naked eye. A new enhancement and matching system had been developed in New Mexico to identify which assailants had committed specific acts of violence in a prison riot. Computer enhancements were used to identify the shape and formation of the wounds of those assaulted—guards and prisoners. The crude instruments collected from prisoners, and other weapons, were photographed and then projected side by side with the enhancements of the wounds for electronic matching.

Chapman thought the technique might work with the pillow case imprint, and New Mexico technicians agreed to give it a try. Their report found two possibilities. One was that the "imprint" was a fold. The other was that it was a weapon similar to an industrial flashlight with a flanged end, a heavy-duty commercial model commonly owned in the 1950s.

The Bay Village Police Department still got the occasional call. Some were written down into notes; others were written off as nuts. Police still had their opinions and their hunches. Whether Dr. Sam was dead or alive, few were without an opinion. But if the murderer were still out there, he could feel relatively safe that no Lieutenant Gerard from "The Fugitive" was breathing down his neck.

TEN

Suppressed

By the time an average American child in the 1990s reaches the age of eighteen, the youth will have witnessed 20,000 murders on television, media analysts estimate. None of the stories are like those that Sam R. heard in the support groups for murder victim families.

Solace was the name of the first group of victim families that Sam R. visited. He was over forty years old at the time, but the pain of murder did not simply dissolve as easily as people would like. In these and other groups, he finally heard the stories of others like himself who had suffered losses by murder.

There were parents whose children had been murdered. There were sisters who lost brothers and husbands who lost wives. There was the crane operator whose grandmother had been murdered by several young girls. There was the peace activist whose small daughter had been kidnapped and murdered by a man who later phoned to taunt the mother. She had kept calm and conversational, even compassionate. The man was so moved that he continued to call; as a result police were able to locate and arrest him. There was the successful entrepreneur who, along with his wife, was assaulted. She was killed; he became the focus of police suspicion. There was an African-American man, a student and opponent of the death penalty, who was grieving the death of his sister, killed by violent means. The murder was not solved.

Victims were not always fun people to be around. They relived their fear and relieved their hurt in the groups. Telling their stories, family members and survivors tried, bit by bit, to reestablish some personal equilibrium.

But even in those groups, understanding was not a guarantee. Sam R. told one woman, whose child had been murdered, why he had come to the group. She turned to him and said, "Oh, but that was so long ago."

It wasn't. It was right there with him. It did not just "go away" because the pages flipped off the calendar like in the old movies. He could not just "get on with it" until "it" was resolved: the pain, the hurt, the confusion, the shock, the trauma, the quandaries and question marks.

There was no use comparing tragedies. Members of the victim and survivor groups all had them. And there were plenty outside these groups too: many had suffered for many reasons. But he knew how devastated children could be when faced with a tragedy, while still forming a world-view, still trying to comprehend much simpler things, such as how to swim or what happened when the dog was hit by a car or why kids at school were snickering in the corner. Children were too young to understand, he would sometimes hear. Or people claimed that they were resilient. No, the children picked it all up, by osmosis, by the unspoken. Children hurt. Who but the children would suffer the longest? If they survived, children could be sentenced for life.

He had been the kid in the next room. He realized he was always off to the side. He was there, but he had no voice. Every generation, a few murder stories slip out of control in the media; his was one. The grown-ups in his family hadn't had time to grieve. They had not been able to get a handle on the situation, grip the rapid pace and enormity of what was happening. How were they to deal with him? And everywhere Sam R. went, to visits from one relative to another, his presence reminded them of their loss, of his mother.

Now, through victim and survivor groups, Sam R. was letting the hurt rise and flow through him, sharing, and then trying to reach out to others, especially the children.

Despite the seeming ease with which television detectives solve their mysteries, knowing how to investigate a case does not come naturally. Reinvestigating an old case is even more difficult. Evidence is stale, perplexing to locate. Contraditions arise. The truth can be shrouded, and some of it can be painful.

Whom do you contact? Whom do you believe? How do you separate those with agendas that are counterproductive, contrary? From the inception of his decision to help reinvestigate the murder in 1989, Sam R. stepped gingerly into the role of family spokesperson and lead contact, aware that emotional land mines could rock him at any moment, but not always able to spot them far enough in advance to avoid them.

Where was the evidence that had been presented at trial? What still existed? What was on record? And where were the records? Getting the original, unfiltered material on the case was important, Sam R. realized from the outset. But how?

Papers were scattered everywhere in 1989.

Almost by accident, Sam R. had secured vital documents early in the summer, before he knew he was going to put them to use. He had simply responded to a call to get them or forget them. He went to get them.

As it turned out, Ariane Sheppard, his father's second wife, had had Dr. Sam's memorabilia stored in Cleveland all through the 1970s and 1980s, even though she had returned to Germany. Now she was making a special trip to liquidate. She contacted Sam R. Did he want anything? In making the hasty trip to Cleveland, his intention initially was straightforward: he hoped to reclaim the prison letters that his father had written to him and which Sam R. had maintained meticulously for many years. At some point he had put the letters in the care of his father, and they had been passed, person to person.

In one hurried weekend in the summer of 1989, Sam R. pored through huge boxes of papers. Much more than letters was there: family diaries, baby books, wedding albums, photos. His mother's college diary was there. He pulled out the mortgage loan payment record for their house. Folded away was a letter from grandfather Reese, his mother's father, excited to hear about a grandchild on the way. On yellowed paper was a letter to his father as a child from great-grandmother Sheppard, telling the five-year-old he must do "good and wonderful things for the men and women of the world who need you."

He also tripped upon evidence envelopes, some preserved, others ripped open, empty. Tags from the coroner's office lay like dry leaves between pieces of paper. Dusty pieces of his parents' past looked out at him. He saw, held in his hand, the supposed "evidence." There was a glass vial with a small item inside, a piece of wood or something, he wasn't sure. His father's wallet was there, the brown leather one that Dr. Sam had seen on the floor on the morning of July 4 upon regaining consciousness. In it were all the membership and business cards that item by item formed a picture of Dr. Sam's life before the tragedy.

As quickly as possible, Sam R. sorted through the boxes, grabbing what he could for preservation, trying not to be overwhelmed by the stories that each article told. Back in Cambridge, he encountered a different obstacle. His single room had scant storage space. He hardly relished rolling over in the morning to see the remnants of his father's life and his mother's murder piled on the floor.

Finally, he arranged to store them at the criminal justice department at Northeastern University, which was interested in documenting criminal cases. A five-drawer file cabinet was set aside. When the reinvestigation was under way, he knew the files would need serious review.

Whenever something was found, it became a resource for the team working on the case. Materials pried from old archives not only gave a reconstruction of what had happened, but were put under a 1990s lens to be analyzed anew. Volumes of legal documents were collected: U.S. Supreme Court files in Washington, D.C.; Sixth Circuit Court of Appeals and federal district court documents at archives in Chicago; Ohio Supreme Court papers in Columbus. Sometimes a little dollop of information could be extracted.

Newspaper files were huge, but newspapers would no longer open their morgues, which catalogue articles by subject. Although the old morgue collection of the *Cleveland Press* was archived as a whole at Cleveland State University, the Sheppard files had been "removed." Tedious scanning of microfilm was necessary.

Anita Kirk, the daughter of Dr. Paul Kirk, searched her parents' basement. As it happened, most of Kirk's files had been delivered to Sam R.'s cousin Jan. When Jan and her collaborators, Dalrymple and Chapman, shipped their materials, Kirk's findings were waiting there, too. The most recent author to have published a book on the Sheppard case, Jack Harrison Pollack, was no longer alive, but his daughters, Susan and Debbie, dragged out boxes packed in a barn on Long Island. Upon opening one, Sam R. pulled out his mother's red satin slippers. Momentarily, he reeled.

Attorneys who worked on the case had died, moved, moved on, but colleagues checked their storage bins. F. Lee Bailey said he had passed his files on to author Paul Holmes, who had since died. His widow, Miriam, living in Texas, was eager to help, but she had winnowed her husband's research to a meager selection. Andy Tuney explained that he never put things in writing when investigating for Bailey. Bailey wanted only oral reports. Russell Sherman made his trial notebook available.

The files of William J. Corrigan had been sent to the Western Reserve Historical Society by Corrigan's children. Attorney files, even when in the physical custody of the lawyer, are supposed to "belong" to the client. Neither the society nor the Corrigans had thought to contact anyone in the Sheppard family before opening the files to the public.

At first, the opportunity to review Corrigan's files seemed like a gold mine. On closer look, they were dreadfully empty. Except for an odd piece of detail here or there, there were no fresh answers from the defense side.

What was missing were police reports. The official version of what officials had and had not done in the case— the records of police, prosecutors, sheriffs, the coroner—was a void. No one was willingly making those available.

Monsignor was putting together some new theories. One was about a conspiracy by the "Irish mob." The who-what-where-when-how was getting more difficult to comprehend. Monsignor always promised details of his various claimed insights into the case, but they never came, or if they did, they would be snips of photocopied photographs, with nothing to explain what they meant. "Advise me of your evaluations," a note inside would say.

Terry Gilbert, the attorney Sam R. met after giving a speech in Cleveland, thought about the problem of getting records. Why not try formal requests under the Ohio public records laws, he suggested.

Freedom of information laws, passed mostly in the early

1970s, require public officials to open up their records to the press or the public. It seemed that no one had ever formally pursued the police files on the Sheppard case under public records laws, even though the files were practically antiques.

Ohio's law was broad—at least on paper. The law permitted access to records and copies of them. Records requests could be denied only if there were specific exceptions in the law. Cynthia Cooper, who was by now doing much of the day-to-day footwork, made requests to Ohio law enforcement agencies to see their Sheppard files. The requests were promptly rejected.

The Cleveland police were unable to assist because, the police said, they did not retain any documents. The county prosecutor's office claimed that none of its files were open to the public, even decades later. Bay Village was especially inventive. The murder, it said, was still an open case—"an on-going criminal investigation"—and claimed that for this reason, the documents were not subject to release under public records laws. Of course, Ohio laws did not say that records requests could be rejected because of an "open" case. And Bay Village could describe no investigative work that it had done on the Sheppard case in years.

The refusals to disclose the records flew in the face of law and common sense. Gilbert went ahead with the only other option, filing a lawsuit with Cooper as the plaintiff. The action came thirty-eight years to the day after Dr. Sam Sheppard was found guilty in an unfair trial.

"Do you actually believe that you will find anything new in police files?" reporters pressed Gilbert and Cooper at a news conference announcing the lawsuit.

Because of legal maneuvers by the Cuyahoga County Prosecutor's Office, the lawsuit languished in the courts for more than a year. The matter was on deep stall.

The Cuyahoga County coroner, Elizabeth Balraj, was not named in the lawsuit that Gilbert filed. She initially offered to make her files available. But when the time came to honor the offer, she presented only portions of the files. Still, some documents were new, never having been opened to the Sheppards or their attorneys. When it came to making copies, as the law allowed, Balraj flatly said no.

In addition, the word began to filter back that the coroner's office had many more files than it was letting on. A woman at the county archives stated that all its files had been removed by the coroner, and were kept by the coroner's office in a vault under lock and key. Balraj admitted they might be there but claimed that she couldn't release them because they belonged to other government agencies—the police, prosecutor's, sheriff's office. The other agencies were doing little to assist.

The specter of coroner Gerber was rising again. Old-time employees at the coroner's office had a joke about the vault. Whenever Gerber had had his office door closed, employees used to whisper, "Oh, he's probably playing with the Sheppard files again."

The license plates on Monsignor's car with "WEB" on them were becoming more troubling. Sam R. faced a growing quandary. He had given Monsignor his unswerving word: Monsignor was the investigator, and in consideration, he would get credit.

But now it was 1993, and the case simply wasn't getting solved. Monsignor called frequently. In scattered analyses, he would bring up a subject or a name and then would launch into several stories, pushing psychological buttons, peppering his monologues with "aren't I doing a great job?" A constant rush of conversations took place, yet answers were scarce.

Seeing the attitude of public officials, Sam R. knew that there were people waiting in the wings to attack at the slightest false move. Substantiating every point was going to be critical.

Sam R. began to try to get verification from Monsignor. Monsignor claimed to have discovered the weapon. Demanding confidentiality, Monsignor announced his find: the telephone in the bedroom. An old, standard-issue black dial phone, it had stood on a bedstand between the beds of Marilyn and Dr. Sam. According to Monsignor's scenario, the base of the phone was wielded in the killer's hand, with the four metal holders of the cradle on top turned downward as a weapon.

Monsignor pointed to the four curved wounds. The fairly regular distance between them had led some people to speculate over the years about a multipronged instrument; Kirk never bought the idea. Monsignor claimed that Mrs. Sheppard was dialing the telephone, and that the killer had ripped the phone from her hands, causing the severe finger injuries. The killer then used the phone to kill.

How had it been overlooked? Monsignor's explanations would digress into a cover-up, with someone switching the phone in the murder room with another phone. Monsignor would not say how he came to this conclusion. He offered no supporting documentation, other than an informal comparison of the distance between the prongs of the phone to the distance between the curved wounds. Monsignor could sound convincing; Terry Gilbert, who had a large criminal practice, remained skeptical.

Many questions were left hanging. Whatever information could be gathered about this theory was presented to Dr. Peter De Forest. He was familiar with the telephones of those days—made of Bakelite, he reported. But the possibility that one was the weapon that killed Mrs. Sheppard was remote, De Forest said. The phone had many surfaces which were made of many materials, including two cords, dial, receiver. There would be a clear indication if a telephone had been used as a weapon, De Forest said, and even the most inept of investigators on the scene would notice it. A telephone was large, he pointed out, compared to microscopic evidence, like fibers or paint chips. The proximity of the phone to the bed also meant that it would be in the blood splatter radius: either blood splatter would be on the phone or, if it had been the weapon, blood splatter would be on the items that had sat below it—table, phone books. Blood and hair would be on the phone, and cleaning it completely would not be possible. A large amount of forensic information would be generated if the telephone had been the weapon. "My gut feeling," said Dr. De Forest, "is that it is all speculative, and there is nothing to support that at all."

At the same time, Sam R. was hearing other statements about Monsignor that were creating an uneasiness. These statements were coming from Richard Eberling, of all people. Eberling, before being sent to prison, had amassed a handsome sum of money. He said that he had paid Monsignor to investigate aspects of the Durkin case, for which Eberling had been convicted of murder. Monsignor did not deny that Eberling had paid him, but presented himself as a double agent. Now Eberling started saying that he had paid Monsignor to solve the Sheppard case, too. Why he had done this, he could not say. In total, it was not a comforting picture.

Sam R. had come to enjoy Monsignor's blustery war stories, his sometimes preposterous, sometimes exasperating calls. They had become a regular feature of his life. Monsignor had kept him informed of the goings-on in Cleveland and was a connection to case events. But something was awry. Sam R. had faced so many disappointments; this was looking like one more. He didn't know how he would proceed, but it was time to move on.

Slowly, things were turning around. The public records lawsuit was beginning to pay off, as was the publicity that it generated. Bay Village dropped its "open case" claim and was now interested in settling. Lawyers for the suburb finally sent Terry Gilbert a list of documents that Bay Village held, divided into those that they would release without a fight and those that they would not release, based on a claim of confidentiality.

Two months later, Bay Village's "nonconfidential" files began to creak open. Pieces of information that previously had been hidden now surfaced in the hundreds of pages of information. The question that reporters had asked—could there be anything new?—was now answerable.

Small points in the Bay Village documents belied the prosecution case against Sheppard. The use of Dr. Sam's sports jacket as incriminating "circumstantial" evidence was one. The first statement of Don Ahern immediately after the murder showed that Dr. Sam had not awakened and removed his corduroy jacket and folded it calmly before the murder, as the prosecutors insisted, while they brandished the jacket in front of the jury.

Police: Did you observe whether Dr. Sam Sheppard had changed any of his wearing apparel that night from the first time you saw him until you left and saw him lying on the couch?

Ahern: Yes, he had removed his Khaki jacket during the course of the meal and up to the time that he decided to sleep on the couch he was wearing a brown Corduroy Sport Coat. *At the time we left Dr. Sam did not have his*

Corduroy jacket on but it was visible near the couch. [Emphasis added.]

The defense never saw Ahern's July 5 statement.

Much ado was made at Dr. Sam's trial that not "enough" was stolen to qualify as a burglary. The prosecution cleverly checked off everything that had *not* been stolen.

Bay Village documents show that it took a bevy of investigators days to find the things that were not stolen. Even then, as Chief John Eaton of Bay Village reported, Dr. Sam had to tell them where to look: "The rest of [July 4] I spent searching the house with others. $32.00 was found in a copper mug on a shelf in the den. . . . On Monday [July 5] the house and grounds were searched again several times. . . . Dr. Sam Sheppard claimed there was money in a secret part of his purse. I found $60.00 there. He also claimed a pocket secretary in his desk had some money in it. A second search of this revealed $100.00."

The prosecution had asserted that the wallet was evidence of a *lack* of theft, saying that it contained $1,063.00. The sum came from three single dollar bills that had been crumpled in Dr. Sam's pocket; a $1,000.00 check from the Sheppard Clinic made out to Dr. Samuel Sheppard that few thieves would be stupid enough to steal; and $60.00 cash, hidden so well that even the chief of police couldn't find it.

Bay Village police documents showed that police, prosecutors, and the coroner knew full well that Dr. Sam had suffered serious medical injuries, even though they persisted in saying otherwise. On July 7, 1954, officers, prosecutors Mahon and Parrino, and Gerber all met confidentially with Dr. Charles Elkins at the Sheppard home. A respected medical doctor who was not affiliated with Bay View Hospital, Dr. Elkins had treated Dr. Sam on July 4, 1954.

"Dr. Elkins stated that there was injury to the spinal column of Dr. Sam, or indications to indicate it, as he could not use left hand or arm freely and there was definite lack of reflexes on that side of the body," wrote Bay Village police officer Fred Drenkhan. A mere two weeks later, Gerber refused to call Dr. Elkins at the inquest.

*   *   *

There were other details that the prosecution did not make known. For example, on July 19, 1954, Bay Village patrolman G. H. Deutschlander filed a report about accompanying Mary Cowan, lab technician at the coroner's office, to visit a watch expert. Of the woman's watch, expert Carl H. Bee said that the case over the face had been damaged—"sprung, possibly by strong tension on the band." Of the man's watch, Bee stated that "the water on the face seemed to be normal condensation. . . . There was no water in the watch." This did not stop the prosecution in 1954 from claiming that Sheppard had washed himself off in the lake after a failed suicide attempt and then placed his watch in the green bag. They knew at the time that the water under the face was not from the lake but was condensation. The prosecution preferred innuendo to the truer picture: the watch was never in the water, but was stripped from Sheppard's wrist earlier by a third party.

The coroner's office also held documents and materials that painted a picture different from the one that Dr. Gerber and allies presented publicly. Some were made available for viewing in 1993.

The full "Trace Evidence Report" had never been released to the defense. This report was a complete analysis of forensic testing done by the coroner's office on items that could be traced to the murder. Until 1993 only those inside the coroner's closest circle saw the report, single-spaced, twenty-eight pages long. By contrast, the summary given to Bill Corrigan in 1954 was a scant two pages.

The coroner's office wrote up reports on the same trace evidence in three different ways: (1) the twenty-eight-page trace-evidence report; (2) a two-page "Microscopic and Laboratory Examinations" report, with no detail, the only document released in 1954; and (3) Mary Cowan's lab cards with the raw information collected as testing was under way. Under close examination, an inconsistency of information was apparent.

A document kept inside the office gave one perspective, those presented to the defense gave another. The analysis of the fingernail scrapings showed how the information could change and transform. For example, the scant report released to the defense said, "Scrapings removed at autopsy from underneath fingernails of Marilyn Sheppard: No sig-

nificant fibers or hairs noted." Card TE 95 prepared by
Cowan, however, listed blood, four wood fragments, a
"pink material—nail polish?," and fibers—brown, red, blue,
and dark blue.

"Wood" was a particular surprise. Never was the presence of wood mentioned to the defense. Cowan scribbled
that the wood was apparently from a toothpick used to
remove the fingernail scrapings. Criminalists say that is unlikely. If crumbling toothpicks were used in such a way,
they would defeat the purpose of the microscopic examination. At any rate, it would have been easy enough to identify whether the wood matched a toothpick used by the
pathologist on the staff.

Wood may have had a connection to the nature of the
murder, though, possibly pointing to a wooden item used
as a weapon or to a tool partially made of wood that was
used as a weapon—a screwdriver with a wooden handle,
for example. Other wooden items were brought in for testing by the coroner's office, including an old wringer washer
roll and "a piece of curved wood that appeared to be broken free from a rocking chair." Unlike the surgical instrument about which there was so much fake information
none would have tied the murder to Dr. Sam.

The information about the fingernail scrapings was further sanitized in its progression through the coroner's office. On a second card, also marked TE 95, the fingernail
scrapings for the left hand omitted wood fragments altogether. Listed were dried blood, fragments of red nail
polish, and a new addition—a brown plant fiber. The trace-
evidence report even gave an abbreviated version of the
second card, listing only blood and the plant fiber. By the
time the defense received the lab report, the language had
metamorphosed into "no significant fibers."

Although she did not disclose her results, Cowan, who
worked at the coroner's office until 1995, had in 1954 tested
many other items, including the clothes of a tree trimmer,
Horace H., and of another man, Dr. C. Other testing was
done on a variety of possible weapons: golf clubs, an iron
pipe, a riding whip, a tire iron, a file found wrapped in a
July 8 newspaper in a Bay Village yard. More: a T-shirt
found in the city dump; a pair of ladies' hose found by a
reporter "in or about the Sheppard home"; towels; a strip
of carpeting; the white porcelain soap dish from the bath-

room; two hairs that were on Mrs. Sheppard's left hand; two other hairs picked up from the mattress on which she was murdered. About all this mass of material collected and tested and detailed on the trace-evidence report the defense knew nothing. Dr. Gerber was asked on the stand by Bill Corrigan if he had any report on all the items the office has processed. "Yes," Gerber replied, "in here," and pointed to his head.

The information from Bay Village and the coroner's office began to demonstrate the ways that the prosecution had unfairly boxed the case around Dr. Sam. Still, they were smaller points, none of them explosive.

Then, documentary dynamite came in the mail to Cynthia Cooper in 1993; a plain manila envelope, with no return address, no letter, and no name. Inside were copies of a series of police and sheriff reports that had not been released before, clearly collected from an official source.

Among the documents was hidden information—suppressed evidence that would have disproved the entire basis for the prosecution case, that would have shown its foundation to be a sham. The reports could have changed every assumption about the events of July 4, 1954, at the home of Dr. Sam and Marilyn Sheppard.

One document in the manila envelope, among those of lesser consequence, was a report of several pages by Sergeant Harold C. Lockwood of the Cleveland police. It had one overlooked piece of evidence that took on new import in the reinvestigation. In 1954, no one mentioned to Sheppard that a path might have been seen through the underbrush behind his house, although rumors had arisen from time to time. Cleveland police officer Pat Gareau mentioned later that footprints had been found at the location of the green bag.

Lockwood's report went further. He described a path from the top of the cliff "at a point about 20 feet east of the stairway" to the boathouse. "This path continued all the way down the cliff, stopping just short of the place where the stairs end and the boardwalk starts. This path in the underbrush was apparently *newly made* on the night of the murder." [Emphasis added.]

The green bag that contained Dr. Sam's jewelry, Lockwood states, "was found near the point where the path in the underbrush down the side of the cliff ended."

The fresh path was fully consistent with Sheppard's statement that he chased someone out the porch door and then lost sight of the person until he reached the beach. It added credibility to the description of an intruder, who had filled the bag with stolen jewelry and then, in a panicked flight, dropped or discarded it. Dr. Kirk had insisted that the disposal of the bag pointed to a person who, escaping, dumped things of no value to him. "Burglars, similarly pursued by the police, frequently discard their entire loot in an attempt to protect themselves," he noted.

The startling statement in the plain manila envelope was in yet another document. The item, a single page, looked innocuous, a standard-issue report filed by officer Henry E. Dombrowski of the Cleveland Police Department's Scientific Investigation Unit. Dombrowski's clean looks, college education, and calm demeanor had made him an excellent witness for the prosecution at both Sheppard trials.

Dombrowski was not brought into the investigation until the Cleveland police took it over from Bay Village in the third week of July 1954, over two and a half weeks after the crime. The only other member of the Scientific Investigation Unit who had previously been on the scene was Michael Grabowski, the officer sent there on July 4, whose work was thoroughly incomplete. Mary Cowan had been sent on one occasion by Dr. Gerber, but no serious scientific study of the property had been undertaken by trained personnel. Throughout July, the house was under the full and exclusive control of the police.

By the time Dombrowski was sent to the Sheppard house with all his equipment, much had happened on the case. Dr. Sam had been accused by Cleveland detectives, the *Cleveland Press* was running continually accusatory front-page editorials, and other papers were trying to keep pace. Gerber had convened the sensationalized inquest on July 22 and was about to release his coroner's verdict. Cleveland Police Department captain McArthur had made statements to the press, declaring that he knew who the murderer was. No one thought he meant anyone but Dr. Sam. Everyone wanted Dr. Sam under wraps, fast, and the pressure was on the Scientific Investigation Unit to come up with some usable evidence. Captain McArthur perhaps had not counted on Dombrowski to be so thorough.

At the house, Dombrowski performed magnificently. Despite the volumes of documents on the Sheppard case, this one was not released before. The full report said:

POLICE DEPARTMENT
Cleveland, Ohio
DEPARTMENTAL INFORMATION

Dist. Zone DB SIU   July 23, 1954
Examined by (signature) Robert Blaha Rank Sgt. 7-24-54
From: Henry E. Dombrowski, Det. #120
To: David L. Cowles, Supt.
Subject: Examination of Scene of Homicide of Marilyn Sheppard

---

Sir:

At 8:15 A.M. this date together with Detectives Elmer Reubal #210 and Poelking #28 went to 28924 Lake Road, Bay Village City, Ohio to examine the scene of the homicide of Marilyn Sheppard.

Examination of the home disclosed the following. Spots of what appeared to be dried drops of blood and upon testing with a benzidine reagent gave a positive reaction, were found at the following locations: on the third tread and the sixth tread from the bottom of the basement landing of the stairs leading from the basement to the kitchen, on both metal bands on the face of the treads and both risers of the steps leading from the kitchen to the first landing of the stairs leading to the second floor; on the face of the first tread and both risers going from the living room to the first landing of the same stairs leading to the second floor; and there were spots on several of the risers leading from the landing to the second floor hallway.

Similar spots were also found on the tread of the Living room door leading into the screened in porch on the north side of the building. Spots were also found on the porch floor in the area adjacent to this door.

Examination of the red leather chair in the Doctor's Study disclosed several thin film-like spots on the face of the cushion and the area below it. These gave a positive test with Benzidine reagent.

Scrappings of blood were brought to the Laboratory from the basement and kitchen stairs.

A plasticine impression was made of what appears to be a freshly made tool mark in a door at the foot of the basement stairs. This door leads to a crawl space at the front of the house. Mark appears to have been made by a chisel or wedge like tool of more than ⅞" in width which is the length of the impression, however this does not show both edges of the tool. [Emphasis added.]

Respectfully,
Henry E. Dombrowski, Det. #120

Time and again the prosecution emphasized that there was no evidence of forcible entry into the Sheppard home. That point was the most powerful piece of circumstantial evidence used to convict Dr. Sam.

Dr. Sam and his defense team did not know about Dombrowski's report, nor did they have access to the property for their own independent investigation. Given these circumstances, the primary emphasis of the defense had been to show that the doors were often unlocked and that "force" was not necessary to enter the Sheppard home. Dr. Hoversten testified that the Lake Road door was open the night before. Dr. Sam testified that it was their habit to leave it unlocked unless he was away, in which case a key was placed in a small basket beside the door. The Sheppards did not even bother with carrying keys to the door. The front door out to the porch and lakeside was often unlocked, as well. The prosecution countered with testimony by the Aherns that the doors may have been locked before they left, although the Lake Road door was open when the Houks arrived in the morning. After the 1966 trial, Bailey noted that a key might have been handed out, for example, to Spen Houk.

But, indisputably, the *lack* of evidence of any forced entry could not be eradicated from people's minds. It permeated the atmosphere, hung there, until it dropped down as the one catch-all to lock up Dr. Sam. No evidence of forced entry; one person—Dr. Sam—was definitely there.

This central chord was struck early. The *Cleveland Press* brayed on the front page on July 30, 1954, the day before Dr. Sam's arrest, but seven days after Dombrowski delivered his report to his superior officers: "Nobody yet has found a solitary trace of the presence of anybody else in his Lake Rd. house the night or morning his wife was brutally beaten to death in her bedroom."

Gertrude Bauer Mahon, the prosecutor in the 1954 trial who carried forward with most post-conviction matters, argued on appeal to the highest courts of Ohio that the most damaging evidence against Sheppard was that there was *no evidence of forcible entry into the house.*

John T. Corrigan, prosecutor in the 1966 trial and acquittal, had urged Dr. Sam's conviction because, he said, there was no sign of forcible entry or breaking in of the Sheppard home.

And Mary Cowan, when asked what, from a laboratory standpoint, pointed toward Dr. Sam, answered: "There was no evidence demonstrated of any outsider."

The door to which Dombrowski's report referred was indeed a basement door. From the inside, it went out to the lake side of the house, always considered the front. On the outside of the house was a small, hatchlike door known as the cellarway. Rising about a foot above the ground, it angled up toward the wall and opened to the side. It was on the north side, accessed on the exterior in a cutout area to the east of the porch. Someone entering the cellarway could comfortably do so without being seen by anyone on the street, by neighbors, or even by persons inside the Sheppard home.

The cellarway entrance was designed to allow workers to gain access to the furnace, washtubs, and storage space in the basement without having to walk through the kitchen or the first floor. In order to enter from the exterior, a person opened the outer door, walked down six steps, and then faced another door. This door opened into the basement.

It was the inner door to which Dombrowski referred. There were no windows in the basement, no other doors, and no other entrances or exits to the outside, according to Ann Leusch, who with her husband was the most recent owner of the house in 1993. She remembered the basement entrance vividly.

So did the former window washer on the property, Richard Eberling, who always used the outside cellarway door to enter the basement and to carry screens or windows in and out. The outside door to the basement, he said, "was never locked." He made a drawing of the property in 1992 to show exactly where the basement door was. His version was more accurate than all the drawings of the investigators who inspected the property. A man who worked for Eberling in the 1950s, Ed Wilbert, confirmed that they often used the basement door and that the exterior door was never locked.

After entering the basement from the outside through the cellarway door, someone could easily walk from the basement up to the kitchen, and from the kitchen up the steps to the second floor, completely bypassing the daybed where Dr. Sam slept on the night of the murder.

Officer Dombrowski had also identified the blood trail on the stairs, which revealed that someone walked between the second-floor murder room and the basement, dripping blood on two flights, and seemingly knowing exactly where he was going. Mary Cowan had shown the same thing. Both Dombrowski and Cowan had cut out portions of the wood on the basement steps and tested them to prove that the drops were human blood, although they neglected or were unable to determine a blood type.

On July 4, after the murder, Dr. Steve Sheppard accompanied Police Chief Eaton to the basement, where they noticed the lights were on. No one else had been in the basement before them that morning. Having no explanation for the lights, they assumed that Dr. Sam and Don Ahern had left them on the night before. Lights in the basement would not have been visible on the street, unless the basement door to the kitchen was left open so that the light could have filtered into the kitchen.

Dombrowski considered the marks on the basement doors significant enough that he went to the trouble of making a Plasticine cast. Plasticine is a synthetic molding clay used to make an impression at the scene; the impression is then used in the lab to make a plaster cast. Dombrowski never mentioned making a cast in any of his testimony, to the grand jury, in the 1954 trial, in the 1966 trial.

The discovery of this door on July 23, 1954, not only showed entry from outside but also gave evidence of a tool—a possible weapon, one that was carried in by an intruder who most likely carried it out. All the dragging of the lake and use of metal detectors and digging through the gutters were not going to find a weapon removed from the property.

The tool described, said criminalist Jim Chapman, sounded very much like a pry bar, which he said was commonly used by burglars in the 1950s. Not unlike a crowbar, a pry bar, explained Chapman, was about 15 to 18 inches long. One end was flat, like a screwdriver or tire iron. The other end had two claws that could be used by a carpenter, for example, to pull out nails. The width of the tool mark described in Dombrowski's report was seven-eighths of an inch, an apt description of a pry bar or crowbar, said Chapman.

Henry Dombrowski left the Cleveland police in 1969 to work for the state. By 1994 he was retired and still living in a suburb of Cleveland. It was there that Cynthia Cooper knocked on his door, carrying with her a copy of his police report of July 23, 1954.

An active senior, Dombrowski was widowed and lived alone in a modest home on a large lot that rose up a hill above a well-trafficked street. In his living room, he had rigged up chairs and items so that he could exercise—therapy after a hip replacement. A nice-looking man, he frequently lunched with friends and several times every year participated in elder hostels, where he took courses at college campuses in different parts of the country. Twice he had studied the Polish language to explore his heritage.

In thirty-three years he had worked on thousands of cases, he said. "Thousands." Reluctant to discuss the Sheppard case and the past, he said he "always called it as he saw it."

Dombrowski denied at first that he had ever taken a Plasticine impression of tool marks in the basement. But looking at the report, he could not deny it. Yes, the report was his, he said.

As for the tool mark: "Evidently," he said slowly, "it was there." Officer Dombrowski was not the type of police officer to fake a report.

Once a Plasticine cast such as this was made, Dombrowski said, the investigator on the scene ordinarily would go back to the lab and make a plaster cast. Dombrowski had no recollection of doing that. He had no recollection of

doing anything further at all with the Plasticine cast of the
tool mark on the basement door. He had no idea what had
happened to the Plasticine cast. "It would have been
handed over to the property room. . . . But evidently
there wasn't any more work done on that." He went on:
"We had nothing to compare it with. If we don't have the
tool submitted, there is no comparison. Nothing more was
done with that."

Why not? "I don't want to go back and be a Monday
morning quarterback," he said. "There were so many reports. We were out there a number of times. When you
come into a scene like that, you take anything. If nothing
develops, you disregard it." He continued: "That cast, evidently it made no impression on me. It was there, we took
it, nothing ever developed."

As for who else saw the report, Dombrowski wouldn't
say. He worked at the old police station at East Twenty-
first and Payne, on the third floor. His superiors, he said,
were good. Chief Frank Story was a good chief. "If you
think I'm going to criticize anybody, you can stop asking
questions now," he said.

This much was clear: Dombrowski, a scientific investigator, one of the first with true skills sent to the scene, saw
something that no one else had. He did his job. He made
a Plasticine cast. He wrote it up in his report and submitted
it to his superiors. The report had been located with files
containing official police documents. Some superiors read
the report. The report was never made public, never released to the defense, to the jury, to Dr. Sam Sheppard.
The report contradicted the very basis of the prosecution
of Dr. Sam Sheppard; it cut out the foundation of the case
against him altogether.

"If you have a homicide and you have fresh tool marks
on a door, you just can't *dismiss* that," said Chapman, who
teaches investigative analysis for law enforcement. A pry
bar, a flashlight to see the way, a way to enter. "Now they
have pry marks, and any competent investigator will look
into it."

"There's your smoking gun," he said. "This is your smoking gun."

PART TWO

PHANTOMS

PHANTOMS

ELEVEN

Who

The Journey of Hope in the summer of 1993 was a turning point for Sam R.

Events, some planned, some unexpected, brought a new focus on him and the case. Planned was the march in Indiana with the organization Murder Victim Families for Reconciliation. The organizers named it the Journey of Hope. Unexpected was that the house in which his mother was murdered would be smashed to rubble at the same time

Sam R. was keenly aware that the next year, 1994, was the fortieth anniversary of his mother's death. For four years now he had extended himself. He had facilitated. He had made phone calls, done interviews, listened, sometimes read more than he could handle. The investigation was only inching forward and at times was tied up in tangles and knots. In the meantime, he had sometimes wanted to crawl into himself, even as the case became more public.

A memory from childhood summoned up the feeling of parallel lives. As a child, Sam R. had faced the same concerns as other kids about school and homework and friends, while simultaneously swirling all around him were matters of huge proportion. There were lawyers and investigators and appeals and prison visits and courts and heady discussions. After his father's acquittal, he had tried to move along one path, living a regular life, fulfilling his own goals.

Now he was thrust back into the sensations of those other years. His days were filled with totally average things, going to work, paying the rent, and at the same time he was swept up in the twists and turns, the ups and downs, of the reinvestigation.

The first Journey of Hope in Indiana that summer was both more and less than a metaphor. Members of Murder Victim Families for Reconciliation marched and conducted teach-ins. They hoped to educate people about the horrors of death, and with death, the death penalty. Not all victims' families wanted the death penalty for killers, they explained, even if that was the impression given by the mainstream media.

Events collided in the most unforeseen way. Just as the Journey of Hope participants were settling in for a serious discussion about philosophy, the press was calling from Ohio. Members were discussing forgiveness, and Sam R. was mentally engaged in defining how reconciliation differed from forgiveness. Forgiveness seemed rooted in pardoning someone for past acts, giving up any claim of harm that had been done. Reconciliation seemed poised on restoring harmony, adjusting differences, and moving forward. The nuances were of little concern to the media. Reporters only wanted to know how Sam R. felt about the house being torn down. The property owners were demolishing it. What did he have to say?

In truth, specific clues in the house, its layout, its entrances and exits had arisen; they needed to be checked out. And he had hoped to walk through the property, once, as an adult, to get a sense of the place of his mother's death.

The house had been up for sale for quite some time. The sales agent, an old Bay Villager, promised to let Sam R. know before it was transferred to new owners. Instead, the owners pulled the property from the market and decided to build a new house on their bluff above the lake. Quietly, they sought a demolition permit, and were thrown when it brought out media people and cameras and souvenir seekers in droves. The promise to contact Sam R. got lost in the shuffle.

Sam R. did the Ohio interviews. Yes, he was saddened. Yes, there were things about the house that might have aided. Yes, he was disappointed that they had not contacted him. Yes, he could understand that the owners wanted to build. And yes, he would continue with a reinvestigation of the case.

Like the Journey of Hope, he had come this far. He had made strides. And sometimes there were obstacles to overcome. He was learning that the road was long, and that the longer the road, the deeper he had to dig.

For Sam R., being able to touch the documents that had been hidden away in private files for thirty-nine years was incredible.

A handful of documents recovered by public records laws and the concern of an anonymous person proved what he had always known. His father, Dr. Sam Sheppard, was an innocent man. Not just innocent, but provably innocent. Not just provably innocent, but provably the victim of government misconduct.

Not all the police records were secured. The coroner's office not only had more documents, it may have had evidentiary samples, too. Forensic pathologist Dr. Robert Challener, whose tenure began well after the 1966 Sheppard trial, said that blood slides were intact; later, the coroner's office stonewalled and denied it.

Who knew what else lay in their offices and drawers, what other secrets of the government and its prosecution of Dr. Sam had been sealed away? Didn't they understand? In 1959 Dr. Kirk had implored:

Can American citizens, supposedly protected by a long list of Constitutional rights designed to protect innocent persons, afford to permit the miscarriage of justice without a feeling of guilt?

If the circumstance of a person's unintended presence at the scene of a crime can be interpreted as being indicative of guilt to the extent that police surveillance is directed toward no other person, then we—you and I—have just cause to be fearful that our laws might once again not protect the innocent from self-serving public officials.

Five documents, twenty documents. In one way, to Sam R., it didn't matter. Just one was enough.

Who was guilty? Who deprived a man of his life, his liberty, his family, his hope, his dignity, his constitutional rights? Certainly people who should have known better.

And there was left a huge, enormous, haunting question to be answered still. Who had killed his mother?

As Sam R.'s connection with Monsignor dwindled, almost as if by magic, an investigative firm with an opposite approach appeared on the horizon. AMSEC, based in Middleburg, Virginia, near Washington, D.C., became part of the team. Unlike Monsignor, AMSEC sent agents out into the field; unlike Monsignor, its work was to be specific. They were going to focus on the suspects who had been overlooked.

The real business of AMSEC was in corporate security and investigation: armored car robberies, theft, computer fraud, embezzlement, kidnapping, executive security. In that respect, the work of the firm was not unlike that of Harold Bretnall, the specialist in corporate security who had undertaken an investigation of the Sheppard case from 1955 to 1961. Through a chance meeting, AMSEC's marketing director, Jim Kershaw, heard about Sam R.'s efforts and mentioned them at the home office. The interest was tangible; something about it touched the soul of AMSEC.

The president of AMSEC, Mark Lowers, had founded the firm in 1980 with his two brothers. Using former agents for the FBI, ATF, CIA, and local jurisdictions, AMSEC carefully planned each investigative project. By intermingling sophisticated techniques with plain common sense, AMSEC got results. Closing cases was its purpose and intent.

Sam R.'s predicament caught the attention of Andy Carraway, who held the joint titles of general counsel and director of investigations. Andy's understated presence personified the style of AMSEC. A lawyer, he listened quietly, speaking up only when necessary, and then followed through with meticulous attention to detail. Andy was the same age as Sam R. and, like Sam R., was an only child. He had grown up in a Maryland suburb of Washington, D.C., that was as seemingly pastoral and middle class as Bay Village in the 1950s. Close to his parents, even following his father's footsteps into the law, Andy was struck by how different his life would have been if murder had intervened. He thought AMSEC could provide the investigative muscle needed to finalize the case.

After making an initial plan, an AMSEC investigator shared the firm's thoughts by phone with Sam R., asking him not to say anything publicly until the firm could get rolling. As soon as he hung up, Sam R. had a call from Monsignor, with whom interaction had become markedly less frequent. "Is there something you want to tell me?" Monsignor prodded. Sam R. tried not to sound on edge; he said nothing.

Soon afterward, in November 1993, Sam R. met with four AMSEC investigators in New York City. He was impressed. They were professional and businesslike, not prone to speculation or influenced by rumor. They had the perspective of geographical distance from Ohio. They just might be able to break through the logjam that blocked the further resolution of the case.

AMSEC needed a full briefing on the case, and that meant gathering and collating the pieces of information that had been collected. Sam R. had paid meager attention to the loose pieces of "evidence" he had picked up from Ariane in Cleveland. There seemed to be little point in it.

Now he and Cynthia Cooper delved into the files stored at Northeastern. They pulled out one item that by its very existence breathed new possibilities into the case. Inside a tiny, one-inch-by-three-inch manila envelope was a small glass vial, half the size of a cigarette. Still sealed, the vial had its original evidence markings. A close look inside revealed a gray sliver of wood, and a comparison with the transcript of the 1954 trial showed that the vial matched state's exhibit number 84, which was a wood chip with blood on it that Mary Cowan had extracted from the third basement step on August 9, 1954. This chip seemed to contain a spot of blood—the very blood that was never typed by investigators, and that Kirk hypothesized probably came from the bleeding hand of the killer. But time had become a friend now, and new technology had vastly increased the reach of forensic science.

Dr. Peter De Forest, a former Kirk student and criminalistics professor in New York City, put the vial under a microscope. The wood chip was still intact. He could see a spot of what appeared to be blood on it. Advanced DNA testing might be possible, he explained. DNA is in every cell (excepting red blood cells) of every person, and is unique to each individual. In criminal cases, "DNA fingerprinting" is used to match a sample with a subject. DNA can be tested from a sample of blood, semen, saliva, tooth, or even a hair: anything with a human cell.

Its specificity is worlds beyond the type of blood grouping done in 1954. DNA testing can be done successfully even after the passage of time. DNA might link the blood from the crime scene to a suspect.

But De Forest cautioned that it was possible that only one test could be conducted with the wood chip. Merely testing the sample for DNA blindly would be useless, he pointed out, unless the sample on the wood chip could be matched to possible suspects or sources of the blood drop. For this reason, it was wiser to hold off on testing the drop of blood on the wood chip until other relevant samples could be collected. And in order to do this, it would be necessary to make a clear and thorough analysis of all the possible suspects in the case.

Just like this wood chip, finding the possible suspects meant looking over the original documentation, as well as that gathered over the years, with new eyes. What was known about murderers in general? And what was known about the murderer in this case? Every clue needed to be considered: physical, environmental, forensic, psychological.

In multiple statements, Dr. Sam, who was six feet tall and weighed 170 pounds, had described the intruder as a man larger than he was, probably white, with a large head and hair with a bushy appearance. Later, Dr. Sam said that maybe he had only thought the person was large because the individual had so readily overpowered him on the beach.

Other witnesses who had driven by the Sheppard home described seeing a tall man with brushlike hair that was cut close at the neck, walking along the roadway. One description by Mr. and Mrs. Richard Knitter was specific enough for a composite drawing of the killer to be made.

Forensic evidence could have been used to focus the search for the intruder. The murderer surely would have been covered with blood on the upper part of his body. Dr. Kirk believed that the disregarded fibers under Mrs. Sheppard's fingernails may have pointed to a person wearing a light blue mercerized cotton shirt and dark blue wool slacks.

The wounds probably had not been delivered by extremely strong blows, since the dura of the brain was not broken. Yet the killer had to have had the physical ability to swing a weapon thirty-five times (or less if a multi-pronged instrument was used) in close proximity to one another. The killer was either somewhat weak or, more likely, in a weakened condition, perhaps injured and not using the full strength of the arm or his normal dexterity. Dr. Kirk believed that the killer was left-handed; others were certain that the blows were delivered from the left side, but not necessarily by the left hand or by a left-handed person. Mrs. Sheppard's broken teeth indicated that she had bitten someone and had fought back. The killer would have had to be muscular enough to overpower her, since she was athletic and in good physical condition.

The person also had to be powerful enough to fight off Dr. Sam, or be in league with a second assailant who did so. Dr. Sam was undoubtedly strong. Although in the first encounter he was hit blindly on the back of the neck and in the second encounter he was already injured, the person with whom he struggled on the beach needed a certain brawniness to overcome him. The killer had run down the hillside to the beach, indicating a robust runner.

Kirk was certain that the murderer had a cut on his hand, finger, or arm, and that there might be a resulting scar. The perpetrator might have smoked, since a nonfilter brand cigarette was seen in but never recovered from an upstairs toilet.

Evidence of actions at the scene of the crime might have created a profile of the killer—or killers, since there was the chance that more than one killer was involved.

The killer was probably familiar with the Sheppards and the property, knowing entrances and exits and the surrounding neighborhood. The intruder might have known, for example, about the porch exit that led to the path to the beach, and that the beach was a good exit route. If the droplets on the floor of the living room were human blood, the killer may have known to walk around the low-hanging chandelier. The killer might also have known that the basement had its own entrance, unlocked and hidden, and also a washtub for cleaning up. The dog, if she were present, did not bark at familiar people.

The disfigurement of Mrs. Sheppard's face might be an indication of the type of killer who depersonalizes the victim, thus separating himself psychologically from the violence and pain he inflicts. And the breaking of the athletic trophies, Kirk believed, showed clear evidence of someone with feelings of jealousy toward Dr. Sam and Marilyn and their athletic accomplishments.

The sexual aspects of the murder were insufficiently analyzed by investigators at the scene, Kirk thought. The denuding of Mrs. Sheppard's body was clear, direct, and forceful evidence of an attempted sexual attack. Mrs. Sheppard's pajamas had been completely removed from the left leg and partially from the right leg. The pajama top was rolled up over the victim's breasts. Most sex murders, according to the FBI, are committed by people of the same race as their victims.

William J. Walker, a New York attorney who lectured about crime issues in the 1950s, also believed that sexual motives were indicated. He thought the murderer of Mrs. Sheppard was a mentally deranged person who was periodically seized with a "compulsion psychosis" to kill a woman.

Howard Winter, the manager of the William J. Burns International Detective Agency, did an independent analysis of the case for a men's magazine. He wrote that the killer of Mrs. Sheppard was a "sex-obsessed criminal" who tried to assault her sexually and then killed in a maniacal frenzy when she resisted. Winter described the murderer as a man of unstable emotions who, unknown to Mrs. Sheppard, had observed her and developed a growing lust for her. In modern parlance Winter was talking about a stalker who had had casual interactions with Mrs. Sheppard.

The understanding of violent crime has proceeded slowly. In the 1950s it was a subject far less well known. The public, along with police officers and judges, had a preconceived notion of what a killer looked like and acted like and sounded like. Ideas changed substantially over the years through research by criminologists and psychologists, and through the pervasive influence of crime movies and books.

In the early 1990s the FBI completed a ten-year study to aid investigators in solving violent crimes. Homicide was divided into four categories based on defining characteristics of the victim, crime scene, and forensic and investigative data. The four categories are criminal enterprise, personal cause homicides, sexual homicide, and group cause (i.e., cult) murder.

Each has subcategories, as well. For example, a situational felony murder is unplanned, committed out of panic or impulse in the course of committing another crime. In an "erotomania-motivated killing," the killer has fantasized about a relationship with the victim, who is possibly well known, or of a higher status, or a superior at work.

The FBI also identified the crossover in crime categories, for example, between burglary and murder. Sexual homicide, FBI experts noted, often involves "secondary criminal activity (e.g., robbery)."

Jim Chapman explains that crimes don't always fit into neat patterns. Burglars sometimes get sexually aroused in the act of surreptitiously entering someone else's home at night, not knowing exactly what will be encountered. "Does a person commit burglary for monetary gain or for sexual gratification?" he asked. There is no ready answer.

In 1954 these classifications of murder were not well understood. The prosecution in the Sheppard trial of 1954, for example, argued that a burglar would not be likely to commit murder, and that a murderer would not commit burglary. This view was even adopted by no less of an authority than the judges of the Ohio Court of Appeals, who wrote on an appeal in the Sheppard case: "It is difficult to believe that a sex maniac, after discovery, would take the time to set up the appearance of a burglary, or that a burglar would throw away the only property found to have been taken from the house." This misunderstanding of the very nature of crime, and especially murder, was a damaging force in taking the Sheppard investigation so far astray.

A good psychological profile of the killer could have provided significant clues. This was a technique that Gerber used in the "torso" murders when he first took office. Early in the Sheppard murder investigation, Gerber described the murderer as a schizophrenic. The person, he said, may have built up Mrs. Sheppard in his mind as someone to be destroyed. Gerber later dropped that description.

Since 1954 research in forensic psychiatry, along with that in other social sciences, has grown enormously. Researchers have begun to develop working models of violent personalities and to identify the characteristics that are common to many killers. Research goes in many directions, from studying causes rooted in family violence, child abuse, sexual abuse, abandonment, or adoption, to an analysis of medical symptoms, such as neurological impairment or injury.

Some see differences between violence in men and women. In the United States, men commit more than nine murders for every murder committed by a woman. Similarly, of women victims, only one in ten is killed by a woman. Although women kill less often, their victims are more often family members. British author and policy researcher Anne Campbell believes that men use aggression spontaneously to assert control and assume authority over frightening forces, while women become aggressive only after a long struggle for self-control that slowly builds to a breaking point.

Canadian forensic psychologist and psychophysiologist Dr. Robert Hare studies psychopaths. He began his work inside prisons. Psychopathy, Dr. Hare stresses, is a syndrome, that is, a combination of related symptoms. In some but not all cases psychopathy results in criminal behavior. Dr. Hare defines the key traits of psychopathy as lack of empathy, lack of remorse or guilt, grandiosity, superficiality and glibness, deceitfulness, manipulation, and emotional shallowness, combined with impulsiveness, behavior problems, a need for excitement, and a lack of responsibility. Despite this long list of symptoms, psychopaths can be socially engaging, notes Dr. Hare, but at their core show a deep inability to experience empathy or a full panoply of emotional response.

Dr. Joel Norris, a psychologist and author, has directed much of his work to understanding serial killers, or those who engage in episodic aggression, killing first one person, then later killing another or several others. Through his interviews and existing research, Dr. Norris developed a list of behavior patterns of episodic killers. Dr. Norris said that he found "patterns of parental abuse, violence, neglect, childhood cognitive disabilities, and alcohol and drug abuse." Among those at risk for episodic violence, said Dr. Norris, are neglected children.

Some researchers, Dr. Vernon Mark among them, have made correlations between psychomotor epilepsy and repeated aggression. The possible relationship of epileptoid behavior and violence was advanced even in 1954, causing

Bill Corrigan to seek a list of all epileptics that Dr. Sam had treated as a doctor, thinking the killer might be among them.

Among the more sophisticated researchers of violence is Dr. Dorothy Otnow Lewis, a medical doctor and psychiatrist who has conducted comprehensive studies of adults and juveniles on death row. She has identified characteristics, including medical, psychological, biological, and sociological, that are more likely to occur among murderers and violently aggressive people. No single characteristic could be said to "make" a killer, but a group of characteristics together seemed to point to violent aggressiveness: "a constellation of vulnerabilities," she called it.

In the juveniles that she studied in the late 1980s, Dr. Lewis found that homicide was not the result of a single outburst of violence in an otherwise contented childhood, but was caused by people with significant existing problems. Among the characteristics that she said were evident were neurological or head injuries, such as seizures, encephalitis, severe accidents, and traumatic deliveries; neurological impairment, such as dizzy spells, severe headaches, and lapses of awareness; episodic psychotic symptoms or psychiatric indicators, such as severe depression, hallucinations, extreme mood swings, paranoia, and racing thoughts; a history of having been sexually or physically abused; and a history of family violence.

Another study, which Lewis co-authored on adult murderers, also found similar characteristics. In a high percentage of cases, the murderers suffered from physical and sexual abuse as children, and murderous acts by parents toward them in half the cases. The killers had been subjected to ongoing hostility, neglect, and abandonment throughout childhood and adulthood.

By 1994, the development of psychiatric expertise offered directions for solving the Sheppard murder that were not understood by investigators in 1954. Identifiable personality traits were clues that might lead to possibilities, give ideas, point in a direction, but they were only part of the job. Attaching a name—finding one killer or, as the case might be, two killers—was the more difficult task. Still, the profiles expanded the understanding of "who" in the murder of Sam R.'s mother.

But while more information was being amassed, some was disappearing. Sam R. was all too familiar with evidence that evaporated. Newspaper files, official photographs, sheriff's records, and more had vanished, and the entire murder scene had been wiped out by the shovel of a wrecker's crane. People connected to the case died, ranging from police officers, investigators, and court personnel to actual and potential witnesses. What if other information was slipping through the cracks? How would Sam R. ever know if there was a person who had clues and wanted to come forward and provide information?

If no official was going to pursue the case, and no police officers or prosecutors were doing any work on it except to fight the effort to get records, the least Sam R. could do was make a direct public appeal. He decided to start a "Sheppard Case Line" in Cleveland. Using an answering service, a number was made available for people to call and leave messages with tips or information that might solve his mother's murder.

Calls began almost instantaneously.

TWELVE

Confessors

The Fourth of July made Sam R. shudder every year. The red-white-and-blue banners going up on the light poles, stars and stripes, people calling with their party invitations, all bubbling about their plans for barbecues and beaches. Holiday sales. Deals. That upbeat tone of a day off work crackled through the city, always punctuated with the promise of fireworks, lest anyone should forget.

The anniversary of his mother's death was bound to feel somber. Every year, growing up, the newspapers filled with anniversary stories, pictures of his dad and his mom, wrapups and summaries and "where are they now." Sometimes there would be a picture of young Sam, too, as if his personal tragedy were a subject for their public consumption. The anniversary would have been bad, whatever the date. Independence Day made it worse.

As an adult, he tried to carve out a patch of privacy for himself on the Fourth of July, away from the crowd, sometimes with a friend who understood. He knew himself well enough to stay away from the social obligations of friends and families: he is not good company on Independence Day. And on more than one occasion he has spent the day alone, staring at the sky, not for the summer blue or nighttime bursts, but simply to be silent with his grief.

Calls to the phone line flowed constantly at first. Most were well meaning; some had information; others were downright nasty. At least it was a way of keeping the door open for possibilities. No stone should remain unturned, Sam R.

believed, although he had not always contemplated just
how many stones there were on any given path.

> *Anonymous, woman:* It was in that night I was threat-
> ened by a man over my six-year-old son. At a transient
> circus. Threatened me with an ax. It's been on my mind
> all these years and I'm a little more at ease.
> *A man. Name and return phone number:* My uncle did
> time with Sam Sheppard at the Ohio pen. My uncle died
> recently but he told me some things. Some things that
> Dr. Sam told him.
> *A woman. Nickname and return phone number:* I do
> have information. I lived around the corner. My parents
> would not allow me to give it.
> *Woman. Name and return phone number (synopsis):* I
> lived near another woman who was murdered. I believe
> the same man murdered my neighbor as murdered Mari-
> lyn Sheppard. I found my neighbor beaten. It's something
> that's been haunting me.

Over the years, names had floated in and out. Some confessed to killing Mrs. Sheppard. If the police took the person seriously, a report might be written, finally filed as an
"uncharged suspect." It seemed to Sam R. that there were
probably three or four.

The inventory of police documents released by Bay Village had a surprise. *Twenty-five* uncharged suspects. Names
were blocked out; much of the information was excluded
as confidential. But even the list itself was instructive: it
was clear that the Bay Village police had not been so certain that Dr. Sam Sheppard was the murderer.

Nineteen uncharged suspects were listed in 1954. Reports
were taken even the week before the murder trial. And
then there was uncharged suspect no. 24, who was not listed
until 1959. There was no activity on uncharged suspect no.
24 for another thirty years, when a sudden spate of interest
was expressed by another jurisdiction on Cleveland's West
Side. Uncharged suspect no. 24 had not been questioned
in 1954.

Coroner Sam Gerber told a reporter for the *Cleveland
Press* on July 19, 1954, "I'm convinced that the killer is still
in Greater Cleveland reading every newspaper account of

the investigation and chuckling over his shrewdness—if he remembers that he committed the crime." His conclusion about the killer's identity may have been wrong, but the words would reverberate through the years.

There were many possibilities among the uncharged, some convincing, some merely strange. Helen K., thirty-five, called the Bay Village Police Department promptly on July 11, 1954, to confess. Deputy Sheriffs Rossbach and Yettra went to her home in an East Side suburb. She was quickly dismissed as a "mental case," having been in practically every institution in Ohio, they said.

George Ennis confessed, too—sort of. He called a Cleveland reporter from Baltimore in July 1954 to say that he had been offered one thousand dollars to kill Mrs. Sheppard, but that he had refused it. Then he was offered five hundred dollars to get a professional killer, he claimed. Ennis said that he had worked at Bay View Hospital as an electrician. None of it was true. Ennis was a petty thief on probation, had never worked at the hospital, and admitted that he had "cooked up" the story to "impress" a woman friend.

Louis Winner came to the Bay Village police station to confess on August 1, 1954. The fifty-nine-year-old Winner explained that on the morning of July 4 he got up about 2 A.M. and started drinking. He was "burned up" about the medical bills from Dr. Sam, who had fixed Winner's broken arm, and he decided to get even. Taking a two-by-two piece of wood, he drove to the Sheppards' and walked in an unlocked door. He saw Dr. Sam asleep in a chair and hit him on the neck with the crude club. Dr. Sam slumped down. Winner heard a noise upstairs. He went up and saw a woman lying there who he feared could identify him. "I hit her with the club about twenty times," he said. Then he left and went back home. Winner couldn't describe the layout of the house, couldn't remember what he did with the two-by-two, and couldn't remember if his clothes were bloody.

Winner was locked in the local jail while officers checked out his story. Winner's wife said that he was home that night and was sober. A friend verified it. Winner's son said he had accompanied his father to the hospital with a broken arm and confirmed that Dr. Sam treated Winner. But

it was not at all a bad experience. Winner rather liked
the doctor.

When confronted, Winner admitted that he was lying.
He felt sorry for Dr. Sam, he said, and he was an old man
and didn't have anything to lose. Winner signed a waiver
and was sent home.

A tip from Trenton sent Dr. Steve Sheppard on a flight
to New Jersey in September 1954, where he heard the confession of a jailed con named Williams. An African American, twenty-seven years old, Williams said that he had
definitely killed Marilyn Sheppard. He had been in Cleveland around that time, and on July 5 he inexplicably woke
up with cuts and abrasions on his body. Previous to that,
he said he had stolen a doctor's car in Florida to escape a
sticky situation that developed when he had gone into a
strange home and climbed into bed with a man and woman.
Now the Marilyn Sheppard thing was bothering him. He
couldn't describe the house or its contents, but he would
come back and reenact the crime, he said. He added that
he was a schizophrenic and had periods of not knowing
what he had done.

The list of names and of leads mounted, but so many
seemed to lead to dead ends. Hopes rose, hopes crashed.

Tree trimmers were featured for a short while. Mrs. Seh-
uele, who lived next door to the Sheppards, said that the
day before the murder she had seen a man hanging around
trying to peddle tree-trimming services. Two out-of-state
tree trimmers who had been arrested for intoxication on
July 29 in the nearby town of Lorain were sought by Bay
Village officers in August. But the tree trimmers had bailed
out the morning after their arrest, and hadn't been seen
since. No further inquiries followed.

A man by the name of Henry F. went into the Elmwood
Place, Ohio, police station on November 21, 1954, and identified himself as a former convict. On July 3, 1954, he said,
he had met up in a bar with another former convict, known
to him only as "Pal." Pal was a rough character. They got
drunk and Pal suggested they "knock off a joint." Pal said
he would "get some money if he had to beat someone's
brains out." They drove out to Bay Village.

Pal got out of the car with a large screwdriver, a pinch
bar, and a small flashlight. He was wearing a dark jacket

and dark trousers, had a big head and black bushy hair, was six feet two, and weighed 190 to 200 pounds. Henry didn't go with him because he planned to steal Pal's car, but Pal didn't leave the keys. Soon Henry heard loud yelling. A burglary gone bad, Henry thought, and he ran, ending up in Detroit two days later.

Officers were dubious. "Has anyone prompted you with promises of some type of remuneration for making this statement?" they asked. Henry said no.

As an ex-con who admitted being in Bay Village on July 3, he was charged with the questionable crime of being a "suspicious person" in the community in violation of a local ordinance. The complaint was signed by the mayor, Spen Houk. Cleveland police took over and got Henry to admit that the story was a hoax in an effort to gain sympathy and get work. On July 4, 1954, Henry had actually been in Knoxville, Tennessee, where he had been serving time in the workhouse for loitering. Interestingly, he had a description of weapons that was quite feasible, according to later scientific analysis.

A woman who would give her name only as "Jane Doe" wrote to Reverend Al Kreke, the family minister connected to the Sheppards, on Valentine's Day 1955 to report what she knew. She began: "[Dr. Sam Sheppard] did not kill his wife. I did not kill her, but I was an unwilling witness to the act. It was my husband who did it." In a three-page typewritten letter, the woman described how her husband, suffering from severe headaches, left the house that night. Following him by car, she watched him enter the Sheppard home with a large flashlight and crept after him.

She was "shocked beyond all senses when I saw my husband strike her with the flashlight. He seemed to have instantly turned into a maniac. The woman rose from the bed and he put his hand over her mouth and started beating her. She bit him and he took his hand from her mouth, and she called, 'Sam, Sam.' I tried to stop him but he struck me also. Soon a man came running up the stairs and he turned and attacked him."

The woman left and later found her husband walking on the road, all bloody. He could remember nothing. After that, he was discovered to have a brain tumor, and he died at the end of 1954. She felt now she had to speak out, but could not give any more details because it would break the hearts of her husband's aged parents. "I pray that God and the Sheppard family will forgive my husband, who was not responsible for what he did."

Jane Doe, it so happens, accurately described scientific findings that Dr. Kirk would arrive at only later, including the killer placing his hand over Mrs. Sheppard's mouth and her biting the hand. Reverend Kreke turned the letter over to the police. Whoever Jane Doe was, this was the end of the matter.

There were more: A man who had lived nearby supposedly resented Dr. Sam because Sheppard prevented him from committing suicide. He died in a car accident.

Another man did commit suicide on July 19, after two weeks of despondency. Some thought he should be looked into.

A woman in Oklahoma, while on the operating table, said she heard her doctor admit killing Mrs. Sheppard. This story was intertwined with another one about her teen son being declared dead after a car accident when he was still alive and hidden away. She had one compelling point: she included a copy of a gasoline charge slip with Marilyn Sheppard's name and signature from May 1954.

Suspects. Informers. Women and men. All kinds of theories—one suspect; two; maybe three. Suspects were disqualified, considered liars or not clever enough. Informers were crazy. Some suspects kept reappearing and denied any involvement. Names were forwarded of people who had done bizarre things on July 4, 1954. One person called Sam R.'s phone line to "inform" on a "one-armed man," cross-pollinating Dr. Sam's description of a bushy-haired man with the fictional tale of a one-armed man told in "The Fugitive."

People heard sounds and saw things, or thought they did. People claimed to have found weapons. Even in 1993 calls about weapons came to the phone line.

A woman: The day after the killing, a man came out of the woods with a club.

A woman. Anonymous. Very confident. Very definite. Possibly African-American: There was a light blue station wagon never brought up that was involved. A light blue station wagon. In the rear of the station wagon, the rear

seat, right hand side, that's where the murder weapon
was stuffed, down in the seat.

Nearly everyone connected to the case had a "favorite"
suspect. Not all of them could have committed the crime—
even if the slaying had been like Agatha Christie's *Murder
on the Orient Express,* in which many people converge to
commit a single crime.

Marilyn's cousin, a doctor later found to have a drug
habit, was considered a suspect at one point. There were
boys in the neighborhood who hung around. Young Sam,
with his child's eye, felt particularly strongly about one.
This boy, a left-hander, was one of the teens who used the
clubhouse above the Sheppard garage and seemed to have
a crush on Mrs. Sheppard. At the same time, he would
bully young Sam, one time ramming Sam R.'s head into a
tree to "test" a football helmet.

One-time Bay Village police chief Peter Gray, who
served in the 1980s, thought the most likely suspect was
the so-called "Spyglass Killer" in Chicago, a man named
Barry C., who was suspected of bludgeoning various women
victims around the head and face.

Russell Sherman was inclined to believe a story told to
him in a clandestine meeting in the Terminal Tower with
a former East Side suburban cop. The cop, once institutionalized, whispered information about two men on death row
for a Cincinnati murder. They had been casing Bay Village
the day before the murder, the cop said, and were charged
with soliciting without a license. Sherman tried to locate
them.

Other people suggested that Dr. Sam was covering up
for someone else. In 1993 Jim F., a man who said he was
once a chauffeur for the coroner's office, called the phone
line to report that investigator Ray Keefe had said that the
coroner knew Dr. Sam was innocent, but that Dr. Sam
knew who had committed the crime.

And then there was James F. There were few things
about the tales of his mother's murder that could make
Sam R. laugh. James F. was one. James F. contacted the
Bay Village police department in 1967. He had done a good
deal of thinking about the Sheppard case and wanted to
share his analysis. The likely murderer, he suggested, was
someone who had great animosity toward Sheppard, was

in a position of power, and had a substantial knowledge of drugs. He admitted the evidence was somewhat circumstantial and could not be "considered as definite." The murderer, he announced, was coroner Sam Gerber.

Some of the stories were familiar to Sam R. Most were new. But he tried to learn, to ferret them out. Maybe one word, one thought, one detail would provide a glimpse into the murder, even if it would not deliver up the murderer.

Turning stones.

Stones like the man who made contact in 1990. He was seriously ill with stomach cancer and wanted to make a statement directly to Sam R. before he died. Already he had spoken to the police and they had brushed him off. There was a tone that was very earnest. How to know? Was it real? Were the police right?

Sam R. struggled, a strand pulled each way in the emotional back-and-forth between the easy negativity that wrote off every tip and the much harder pursuit of possibilities that might evaporate.

He could still remember the momentary lift that came back in 1957. A pinlight had flickered, a crack had let in hope, even unbidden. In one transitory shift of events, it seemed that the troubles might end.

THIRTEEN

Strangers

Sam R. had just turned ten years old and was headed for fifth grade when the mood in his uncle's house shifted. He first grasped what was going on from listening to the transistor radio in his bedroom at Uncle Steve's. A radio announcer talked about the guy in Florida who had come up in the Sheppard case.

This seemed real. It was even on the radio. A kind of buoyancy filled Sam R. Everything was clear. Get the guy who did it, put him in prison, and get his dad out.

Sam R. heard more about it at the prison. Sitting in the dark subbasement visiting room with his uncle Steve next to him and his dad across the wide table, he heard the conversation turn from subject to subject. In the prison, circumstances required that Sam R. be fully elevated to adult status. His dad and uncle quickly shared the month's news. An urgency, an optimism, flew between the men. Sam R. grabbed onto it.

It seemed so great. So simple. A guy named Donald Wedler had confessed. He was the right size, he sometimes did drugs, he was a criminal, and he said he had done it. He confessed. And, his uncle said, the best part was that the Court of Last Resort was looking into it. So it was really serious. Erle Stanley Gardner himself was flying to Florida to meet the guy and personally take his confession. This was exciting; this was real.

Donald Joseph Wedler gave his statement in July 1957 in De Land, Florida, three years and eleven days after the murder of Mrs. Marilyn Sheppard. De Land was a small community, about twenty-five miles inland from Daytona Beach, on the eastern coast of Florida.

The sheriff of Volusia County, Rodney Thursby, first contacted the Cleveland homicide squad when Wedler wanted to talk. The Cleveland police told Thursby to forget it. A bit surprised, Thursby pursued the matter anyhow. He wasn't going to just forget a murder confession. Thursby got in touch with a local osteopath, Dr. John Hull, and explained his dilemma. Hull knew the Sheppards and contacted Dr. Steve. The ball was in motion.

Wedler was a classic small-time hoodlum. Born in Washington, D.C., in 1933, he was only twenty-three years old in 1957 and already had a string of prison time, jail time, and reformatory time going back to age fifteen. At first his charges were small, for stolen cars, or "unauthorized use of a motor vehicle." These were followed by vagrancy, robbery, and escape charges. He joined and was kicked out of the army. He joined the air force, and that ended quickly with an arrest, too. In fall 1954 he was sentenced to ten years for a robbery in Tampa. He ended up in De Land after having twice slipped out of custody.

Between prison stretches, he roamed. He snagged rides from town to town, hitchhiked. He did odd jobs: working in a café, as a mover's helper loading and unloading furniture, sometimes using the alias Donald Joseph Helms.

Physically, he was tall, slender—about an inch taller than Dr. Sam at six feet one, but, in 1957, only 150 pounds. He was white, good looking, with well-proportioned features and a cleft chin. He was left-handed. His blood type, it was learned later, was A, Rh negative. His blond hair was slicked back in a greasy "Kookie" style, and he sported long, rakish side burns. Gardner described him as having "a massive mane of lion-colored hair." He turned up the collar on his shirts, and his eyelids often drooped as if he was bored with everything around him. Considered intelligent, he had something of a sly snicker when photographed, even in mug shots.

In March 1954 Wedler was released from prison. He went to his grandmother's in Virginia for two months. Then he took off, going to Colorado Springs, Cheyenne, Los Angeles before heading east again, to Omaha. At the end of June he hitchhiked to Cleveland.

According to statements he made in 1957 to Sheriff Thursby and others, things started getting a little out of hand in Cleveland. He arrived on July 1, 1954, and just slept wherever he could find a place to lay his head. He had about fifty dollars from helping a truck driver and went out on the town. On July 1 he met a girl in a café near downtown (Wedler didn't want to identify her because he didn't want to cause her any embarrassment). He walked her to her apartment and stayed all night. The next two days he wandered around downtown. He saw the popular hit *Three Coins in a Fountain* at a movie theater. On July 3 he met a man named Charley Freemont, a former marine who had been injured in Korea and was getting a disability pension.

On the evening of July 3 he went over to Charley's apartment, a second-floor walkup. A couple of other fellows were there, too. From the windows at Charley's he could see the lights of the Stadium in downtown Cleveland, where the Indians were playing. He shot up with heroin, then he and Charley left and went to a saloon. Wedler had his two suitcases—"grips"—with him. After only fifteen minutes at the bar, Wedler decided to get out of town.

He walked around, looking for a car to steal. Finding one with the keys in the lock, he hopped in. He said it was a 1949, '50, or '51 model four-door Ford, dark blue, that he found on the street in Cleveland. He started driving around, going over a viaduct or bridge in the center of the town. He was starting to feel very high. "I never had the same feeling before or since," he said in one statement. "Something seemed to be urging me on. I was excited."

Broke, he decided to burglarize a house. He was near the lake, and entering a residential district, saw houses with large front yards. The houses were white. It was a "very good part of town." He parked the car and walked along. Wedler wanted a place he could get into without making too much noise.

He found a two-story wood-frame house, he said, that seemed to be built right down to the ground. It was on the lake. He noticed a large tree on the street side that was about two and a half feet in diameter, and there was a driveway that led to a garage at the side of the house. "I went to the house and tried the door." It opened.

Wedler was wearing a dark blue shirt, khaki pants with shorts underneath, tennis shoes, and yellow-and-gray argyle socks. He was carrying a piece of pipe with a flange on both ends. The pipe was square, one inch by one inch, with sharp corners. It was bent at a forty-five-degree angle and was about nine inches long. He had picked up this pipe in California and carried it with him. Wedler made a drawing of the pipe for investigators.

As he entered, he went into a hall and through a living room. He saw a man asleep on the couch. "I went upstairs—went into a bedroom. I was in there such a short time that it is hard to remember detail. I noticed a woman asleep on a bed. I noticed slippers beside the bed and a chair with a dress on it. Light was reflected through the doorway of the bedroom from an electric light which was burning somewhere outside the room."

Looking for money, Wedler opened a dresser drawer. "I was just in the act of closing it when the woman in the bed made some kind of noise. I figured she was going to do something. I hit her with the pipe. I hit her three or four times. I have been shown pictures which indicate she was hit a number of times. If I hit her more than three or four times I don't remember it." He thought she was about thirty years old, and not a fat woman. All the blows, he said, were struck from the left side.

Wedler heard someone coming up the stairs. He was still in the bedroom. At the top of the stairs, he encountered the person and hit him with the pipe on the side of the head. It was, he said, the man who had been sleeping on the couch. "He started to fall and I pushed him out of the way."

Now Wedler ran down the stairs to the first floor. He saw a doctor's black bag and dumped it out, but didn't take anything. He was downstairs only a minute when he heard a noise on the stairway. He rushed out the door to the bluff over the beach and ran down wooden steps. He ran along the beach in the opposite direction from where the car was parked. "I ran about 50 steps and then threw the pipe into Lake Erie about 25 to 30 feet." He then swung back around on the beach, reversing his direction. He came past the steps he had come down and went to the "2nd or 3rd house, went up through the yard. It was a white house." He walked around to where the car was parked.

Question: Did you see any blood on the woman after you hit her?

Wedler: Yes, I saw some blood.

Question: Did the woman scream?

Wedler: No, she didn't do anything after I hit her with the pipe.

No, he didn't think he could find the house again. Yes, if someone showed him the house, he could pinpoint where he threw the pipe.

He was covered with blood, Wedler said. His left sleeve was covered to the elbow, and there were spots of blood on his shirt and pants. He drove away, changing his clothes while riding in the car and selecting other items from his suitcase. Deciding it would be better to leave the car behind, he parked it and started hitching.

Heading south, he got two rides, one after the other, each about thirty-five miles long. About then, he thought he should get rid of the bloody clothes in his suitcase. He rolled them up and stuffed them in a drain pipe that ran parallel to the highway.

Next picked up by a sailor in uniform, Wedler went to eat with him at a café. The sailor played some tunes on the jukebox, including a favorite of Wedler's, "Sh-Boom." Wedler rode with the sailor to Norfolk, Virginia. "It was there I read about the Sheppard murder. I had been thinking of what I had done. I didn't know she was dead and had no intention of killing her."

He stayed with relatives here and there, for a day in one place, a week in another. Finally, he arrived in Tampa. His second suitcase he pawned at a bar in Tampa. In early August he was arrested in Tampa for vagrancy and spent two weeks locked up. Police records showed he had been jailed. Barely out again, he went into a café and wrote a note to the cashier saying that it was a holdup and he had a gun. For that he was sentenced to ten years and sent to a road camp. In 1957, after an escape, he was picked up in June in De Land.

The young con said he read about Dr. Sam's conviction but took the attitude that the police must have known what they were doing. "I tried to put it out of my mind. It kept coming back. I had to get it off my mind." Wedler said that in prison, from September 20, 1954, to February 1957, he had had no access to newspapers or magazines. He had not read much about the case, he said.

While in jail in De Land, Wedler had spoken to the jailer to say that he thought it was quite possible that the woman he had hit over the head was Marilyn Sheppard.

Meanwhile, Erle Stanley Gardner had just completed lie detector tests of Dr. Sam's brothers. He had both feet into the case when Wedler surfaced. At once he arranged for his top polygrapher, Alex Gregory, to go and run a test on Wedler. Gregory telegrammed his conclusion: Wedler showed no evidence of falsehood. The excitement level at the Sheppard home rose. But what Gregory actually meant was that Wedler either was telling the truth or sincerely believed that he was telling the truth.

More things started to fall into place. A woman by the name of Ellie Fryfogle contacted Gardner. She lived in the greater Cleveland area. She said that her husband, a truck driver, had seen a dark blue car parked by the Sheppard home on July 4, 1954. The car had no lights on and was parked so badly that he had to swerve to avoid hitting the car. Her husband confirmed. He was driving west to his home in Avon Lake between 3:30 and 4:00 A.M. The car he saw was a 1948 to '50 dark sedan, either a Pontiac, Chevrolet, Ford, or Plymouth, not a large car. Fryfogle said he was going about sixty miles per hour, so fast that he didn't really get a good look at the car. He had said nothing right away, but in August 1954 he went to the Bay Village police, he said. They told him it was irrelevant, to forget it, and that Dr. Sam had done it. Now he came forward again.

A California truck driver chimed in. He identified Wedler as a hitchhiker he had picked up. The bar owner in Tampa weighed in. He remembered the suitcase that Wedler had pawned. There were parts of Wedler's story that hung together very well.

The crack in Dr. Sam's prison wall was opening a little farther. The Sheppards were quietly elated. Sheppard wrote to his attorney from prison. "Naturally I have been following things as close as possible and hoping. It is hard to think that anyone could possibly know some of the things this man states in his confession unless he was there. You always said that it would have to come out."

There was one trick, though. Gregory, the polygrapher, knew as well as anyone that lie detector tests did not always work and could only go so far. Wedler admitted using drugs, although he denied that he was a drug addict. Still, drugs could distort a person's perception, and that might be reflected on the polygraph test.

Gardner was anxious to talk to Wedler face to face, as was Bill Corrigan. They headed down to Florida separately. Cleveland officials wanted to meet Wedler, too, but for an entirely different reason. Gardner wanted to know if Wedler could be the murderer. Cleveland officials debunked the idea even before speaking to him. Dr. Gerber decided to go to De Land with retired police captain James McArthur and another Cleveland officer.

Before meeting Wedler, Gerber said that Wedler was a psychotic and that this condition would invalidate the lie detector test. Gerber didn't change his opinion after meeting Wedler He announced that Wedler was a faker.

When Wedler spoke to Corrigan, he offered to waive extradition and to submit to lie detector tests. His formal signed statement specified that the tests be administered "by anyone . . . except the Cleveland Police Department or the Coroner. From my contacts with them it would be a waste of time." Wedler said that when Cleveland authorities talked to him they were only interested in getting him to admit that he was not telling the truth. He said that they were not at all interested in the things that he could remember. Captain McArthur, he said, became abusive. "They seemed to have some kind of a hatred for Sheppard."

Nonetheless, there were discrepancies in Wedler's tale. Portions of Wedler's story did not mesh entirely with the known facts of the case. He said nothing about removing Mrs. Sheppard's pajamas. The number of blows delivered to Mrs. Sheppard was far more than the "three or four" that Wedler described. He did not mention stealing jewelry, trashing trophies, putting items in the green bag, or throwing the bag down in the bushes. There was only the house of Charles Bryson to the east of the Sheppards' before the park, while Wedler described passing two or three and running back to the road through another yard.

Still, Wedler described the type of house and grounds accurately. He was right about the blunt instrument: a pipe could have been the weapon. Even Dr. Gerber at one point early in the case had used a metal pipe to demonstrate the murder instrument. Wedler described the bloody clothes, which were a certainty; admitted being in a drug-induced state; and did not have a "model citizen" background. He was of the height of the person Dr. Sam first described, and without the grease, his hair would have been very bushy. In 1954 he would have been an agile twenty years old, a potentially tough match for the thirty-year-old Dr. Sam. And he was left-handed, which fit in well with Dr. Kirk's theory at the time.

Wedler was questioned, but not heavily. No hair or other samples were taken. One of the members of the Court of Last Resort came up with an interesting hypothesis. Suppose, he said, Wedler committed the crime as he described, knocking out Dr. Sam. Dr. Sam awakened, recognized that his infidelity would put him in a vulnerable position as a possible suspect, and took steps to enhance the "burglary" aspect of the scene.

Whatever the scenario, Wedler had enough to offer that Gardner thought the case deserved a fresh analysis, including a lie detector test of Dr. Sam in prison. Politically connected but a non-Clevelander, Ohio appellate attorney Paul Herbert felt that the governor would agree.

Dr. Gerber objected vociferously to a lie detector test of Sheppard. Wedler did not commit the crime, he and McArthur said; Dr. Sam did. No test of Dr. Sam should be allowed. He was a convict, and that was it. No special privileges should be granted. Eventually, the local politicians prevailed over Gardner, an outsider. The Ohio governor refused to allow testing of Dr. Sam. Gardner was disgusted and frustrated with the reaction of Ohio authorities.

As quickly as it opened, the crack in the case that Wedler represented was cemented over. Ohio authorities turned their backs.

The Court of Last Resort ended its efforts. The last resort for Dr. Sam had not lasted long.

As an adult Sam R. could vividly remember Wedler, whenever the name of a suspect arose. Who knew what Wedler had done? And why did he confess with such sincerity if he had not done it? Why did people confess? Did they seek attention? Were they hoping to be found out—about something else, if not this?

So many of the confessors told a similar story: they were bent on doing something bad, such as burglary, drugs. They saw a place that looked like an easy mark, the home of people who were more successful. The house was secluded from the road, but on a main street, so there was plenty of traffic to keep one car from standing out too much, as it would on a tiny side street. There were many doors to the house, and security measures were lax. They entered, maybe high on drugs or alcohol or insanity. Things got rough. Surprised, they acted out, spontaneously. Other details were vague.

The stories of these confessors were of the garden variety, filled with clichés and standard plots. They had a franchise feel to them, a mad-lib plot. By comparison, Dr. Sam's description of events was quirky. Although he was vague on points, the specifics were unusual, such as being knocked out twice, seeing his police surgeon badge on the floor with his wallet, nearly drowning on the beach. Little details. These were not the things that a person intent on making up a story would conjure. Even in "The Fugitive," the crime had been generic. The true murderer was one of the "confessor" types, a sneak thief caught in the act, who grabbed a lamp base for a weapon. So bland was the television crime that the 1993 movie version took extra pains to complicate it with a not-entirely-understandable mystery about medical experimentation, a drug company, and fake data.

The confessors were a subsection of society who wanted to stand up and say they were guilty for all to see. The angst and guilt of the Wedlers thrived inside them, and they hitched their internal hysteria onto the most public case of the time. They recognized a "dark side," an evil within them that was capable of committing a horrendous act, an ugliness that frightened even themselves. Maybe they had killed, done something else too terrible to remember or to tell.

And maybe confessing helped them release some hidden demon. Wedler, after confessing, had become a model prisoner. Once he was released from prison, nearly six years after confessing to Mrs. Sheppard's murder, he never returned to the Florida prison system again.

On April 9, 1963, Wedler was released from Raiford prison in Florida, where he had been incarcerated. Thirty years old at the time of release, Wedler listed his next address as Washington, D.C. He faded and was not heard from again; efforts to locate him in the 1990s met no success. Up and down the east coast, throughout the south, even the country—no Donald Joseph Wedler, born October 25, 1933, could be found, dead or alive. Without a death certificate, the Federal Bureau of Information will not release to third parties what information it may have on a private individual, and it declined to give information about him.

Was Wedler using another name? Was he now a completely different person? Prison authorities and parole officers long ago closed out his case. Sheriff Thursby, who had tried to keep some track of him, died in 1992.

Had Donald Joseph Wedler murdered Marilyn Sheppard? Or merely imagined that he had?

In 1957 Wedler represented the worst to Sam R. He was a possibility, a prospect, a crushing defeat. Sam R. would not allow himself the latitude of daring to hope for so much again.

FOURTEEN

Friends

Prison was no mere abstraction in the victim reconciliation and anti-death penalty organizations that Sam R. joined in the 1990s. They were dealing with prisoners, and the prison world framed many discussions. Wardens appeared as speakers. Some members, like Sam R., got involved in prison reform; others visited prisoners, especially those on death row.

Murder victim survivors who visited prisoners wanted to understand the what and the how and the why of their loved ones' deaths, as peculiar as it seemed to those who had not gone through the experience. So many things were unexplainable, and survivors wanted to know as much as possible. One woman in Murder Victim Families for Reconciliation had lost her parents to murder and started writing to the incarcerated killer. She arranged a visit and, upon meeting him, was struck with how lost and pathetic the man seemed, with no family and no connection to the world. She continued to keep in touch with him.

Even as the reinvestigation into his mother's murder moved on, Sam R. decided that he wanted to do those visits. A note, a bar of soap, a tube of toothpaste, a pack of gum were precious gifts to a prisoner, Sam R. knew. A visit offered an irreplaceable link, a small thread of human contact. But now that he was searching for clues to the murder of his mother, Sam R. could also learn. His uncle Steve, in the late 1960s, had trained in psychiatry, and in 1971 he went to work at a maximum security psychiatric facility in California for several years. Perhaps it was the same kind of search. People who had committed murder might grasp a single aspect of the Sheppard case that had eluded others. Murderers were resources.

Each visit to a prison for Sam R. meant walking through a chamber of powerful memories, of waiting rooms with floors polished by prisoners to a TV-ad shine, of being searched, of metal doors with ominous signs and the buzzing sounds of the electronic safety devices. Once he was the only visitor a death-row prisoner had had in years.

For Sam R., prison had an unusual sense of comfort. In a way, it was like home. If he had been denied the relationship with his dad that other boys could claim, he had something that others never had. He and his dad couldn't hug or touch, but in the prison visits and in the letters from his dad, Sam R. learned adult truths and deep convictions at an early age.

Allegiance was a common theme. "Many people live a long and so-called 'full' life, but never know or find one real brother, sister, or friend, in the truest sense of the word. . . . In their faith and knowledge of my innocence in the face of lies, twisted facts and cruelty, I am really and truly a very rich man," his father had written to eleven-year-old Sam R. Dr. Sam constantly exhorted him to be kind to Marilyn's aunt Mary Brown, who with her husband, Bud, had been so supportive of Dr. Sam and his family after the murder. And, he would advise, "Never let anyone sway you from what you know is right."

Rarely, but occasionally, Dr. Sam would take a different tack. Once, upon receiving a picture of young Sam at camp, holding a big snake, he wrote, "That picture of you and your friend the snake is sure the best. Just remember that snake is more of a friend than many people who claim to be your friend." But Dr. Sam did not make a point of speaking about those who had betrayed him, hurt him, or of those who had refashioned their friendship into a tool to be used by people willing to corrupt the truth.

Although unanticipated, the pain that his father must have felt swept through Sam R. in 1993 when he encountered, on paper, Dr. Lester Hoversten.

Sam R. vaguely remembered the man who had occupied the room down the hall on the days before his mother was murdered. His parents' friend didn't seem to like kids much. His presence was that of a cranky, bothersome uncle, someone who was around a lot and somehow always in the way. Maybe that was the sense that Sam R. picked up from his mother. She didn't camouflage her disdain for Hoversten, and that was unusual. She, like Dr. Sam, was very much a people person, an upbeat, good-golly personality. Normally their home was an open house, people always around. She liked having guests, whether the neighborhood teens or the cops who would drop by. Hoversten was the exception.

Hoversten represented another forgotten character in the Sheppard case. He was so forgotten that no one closely connected with the case could remember hearing of him or from him since 1955 or thereabouts. The word was that he had left for Europe immediately after his debut role as a prosecution witness at the trial of Dr. Sam.

The letter that Sam R. found in the files he brought back from Cleveland stirred an uneasy memory.

Saturday, August 7, 1954

Chief of Police
Cleveland, Ohio
Dear Sir:
    . . . It is my opinion that a person who was questioned by the Bay Village authorities at one time, so I understand, should be re-questioned in the case. His name is Dr. Lester Hoversten. . . .

Sincerely,
Thomas S., D.O.

Lester Tillman Hoversten had come into the life of Dr. Sam Sheppard when they were in medical school in 1944. He was born on March 3, 1911, in Iowa, and his name, pronounced "Hoe-ver-sten," was constantly misspelled. Hoversten had taken a premedical program at the University of Iowa, then finished his undergraduate studies at the University of Southern California. His family had moved to Glendale, California, and Hoversten decided to enter the College of Osteopathic Physicians and Surgeons in Los Angeles in the fall of 1944.

Then thirty-three years old, Hoversten was significantly older than the young college graduates who made up most of the class. Samuel Holmes Sheppard was only twenty, having accelerated his college education during the war years. Already, Sheppard was on a fast track when he began medical training.

Even though he was thirteen years younger than Hoversten, Samuel Holmes Sheppard had a lot more going for him. From his family, Sheppard already had a good solid indoctrination into osteopathic medicine. He had worked at his father's East Side Cleveland clinic since he was a teenager and had observed operations for years. Although sometimes he had struggled for good grades through high school and college, he sailed through medical school. His brother Steve was just finishing up at the school, his brother Richard was a graduate, and his father was a guest lecturer. His grades were at the top of the class, his professors adored him, and his classmates were drawn to his warm personality.

Hoversten and Sheppard became bachelor friends in a class of a mere thirty or so. But soon after he began medical school, Sheppard added a new dimension to his life that Les lacked. Sheppard asked Marilyn to come to California, and in early 1945 the couple married, affirming the pledges they had taken in high school. Marilyn worked as the medical secretary to a woman osteopath and typed up Sheppard's notes and papers. She was as fluent in medical terminology as any of the students who clustered around their Sichel Street apartment. "You could talk about anything, even medical subjects, and she would chime right in," said Dr. Bob Bailey, another student at the osteopathic college.

Hoversten was not nearly so well positioned. He was always awkward, a bit of a loner. Although not bad looking, an air of gloom accompanied him, like a permanent five o'clock shadow. His medical school photographs betrayed depression and despondency. He had a way of grating on the nerves of those around him. "He was what you call an eccentric. Like an old maid, an old fuddy duddy," said Dr. Bailey.

"He stayed by himself," said Dr. Edward Murray, another osteopath who came to know Hoversten in Ohio in the 1950s. Murray described Hoversten as tall, with a blond, bushy crew cut, a prototypical "German-type guy."

Long-term relationships were difficult for Hoversten. He approached women aggressively, and if they pushed him away, he continued to pursue them. He wrote down the names of stewardesses if he flew anywhere and was constantly switching one woman for another. Or was it something different he was really seeking? "The reaction to women was in my opinion a result of lack of women companionship or a cover for a homosexual tendency which had been noted by me and Dr. Miller," said Dr. Sam.

A confidential local informant to the police department in August 1954 had a similar tip. "Dr. Hoversten who was staying with the Sam Sheppard family for a period of about one week is known or supposed to have homosexual tendencies."

But just as he had befriended some of the lonely characters in his high school class, Dr. Sam was compelled to reach out to the odd man. "I always felt sorry for Hoversten for some reason, realizing he was a misfit and had had difficulty in his life," said Dr. Sam. Sheppard had opened his life, his home, his generosity to Hoversten. It may have been a mistake.

Marilyn's distaste for Lester Hoversten dated back to 1949, in California. Dr. Sam was just beginning his internship and the hours were long. Days blended into nights as the hospital became his home, an endless whirl of emergencies, patients, surgery, diagnoses, reports to professors. At this time of great intensity for Dr. Sam, Marilyn suffered acute appendicitis. Friends helped through the convalescence. Dr. Sam urged Marilyn to make a trip to Ohio with baby Sam R. so she could rest up.

While she was gone Dr. Sam was staying at the hospital, so he gave Hoversten the keys to their apartment. Hoversten took a date over and they made themselves comfortable. But Hoversten was something of a slob and definitely lacking in tact. Although he made full use of Dr. Sam and Marilyn's bed, he didn't give the slightest thought to cleaning up or changing the sheets. Marilyn came back to find soiled and dirty linen. She was not pleased. "That is when Marilyn first began to dislike Hoversten," Dr. Sam recalled.

Hoversten remained close to Dr. Sam. Dr. Sam had confided in Hoversten, as he had in others, that sex had changed for Marilyn after the birth of Sam R. She was more timid, distant, less interested in sexual activity. At the same time, Dr. Sam was stepping into his physician role, growing in confidence.

Hoversten encouraged Dr. Sam to fulfill his sexual appetite away from home. He squired Dr. Sam away. If Marilyn was out of town, Hoversten would suggest that Dr. Sam take another date to a class party. Dr. Sam began to do so. His straying days had started. The two of them, Les and Sam, wore dapper suits, carved stylish profiles. While Hoversten was dull, Dr. Sam had charisma and brought life to their friendship. When Marilyn went to Cleveland for another vacation in the summer of 1950, "Hoversten loomed up again with suggestions to date some girls he knew. I didn't want to and said no. Hoversten had a date to a school dance. As it turned out, he had to work that night. He asked me if I would go and take his girl. He said she was very nice. He encouraged me, saying everyone would understand since Marilyn was away. Hoversten was very insistent, so I took Margaret to the dance."

Marilyn could not help linking her husband's infidelity to Hoversten. Dr. Sam added to that impression when he wrote to Marilyn in Cleveland to describe his encounters with Margaret. There was nothing more than a friendship, Sam said, but he wanted Marilyn to hear it from him so that she wouldn't get the wrong impression. When Dr. Sam mentioned the letter, Hoversten became agitated. He told Sam not to write it. Marilyn might think Hoversten had led Sam astray, Les said, and she might think about a divorce. "I told him not to be silly, that Marilyn was not as unreasonable as he thought," Dr. Sam recalled. It was in this letter, Hoversten would later testify, that Dr. Sam said he wanted a divorce.

At the time the letter was written, Hoversten was justifiably concerned. Dr. Sam's family had not only connections but also jobs for osteopaths. Hoversten wanted to stay in the family's good graces. Hoversten was supposed to drive to Cleveland with Dr. Sam, and the trip would be a chance to see about getting a job there. The worst that Hoversten could anticipate, in fact, happened: Marilyn showed the letter to her father-in-law, Dr. R. A. Sheppard, who immediately called Dr. Sam and told him not to bring Hoversten to Cleveland. R.A. did not want Hoversten staying in his home. "Hoversten was very upset about this and broke down a time or two. I assured him that I would square him with my parents," said Dr. Sam.

Dr. Sam finally did "square it" with his parents, but it took years. After his internship and residency at the Los Angeles County Hospital, Dr. Sam moved back to Cleveland in 1951, took his place at Bay View, and worked on his family about giving Hoversten an opportunity.

In the meantime, Hoversten's postgraduate career was stumbling at the Los Angeles County Hospital. Hospital officials abruptly told him that his services were no longer needed. Hoversten placed the blame on the desire of the hospital administrator to hire a relative.

Personal relationships were troubling, too. In late February 1951 Hoversten married Barbara R. in San Marino. The best man at the wedding was his friend Dr. Sam Sheppard, but most friends and associates never learned he was married. The marriage was short-lived. By the middle of May, with a baby on the way, the couple decided to separate.

In late fall of 1951, when Hoversten was the father of an infant son, Dr. Sam was able to write about a potential offer from the clinical group at Bay View Hospital. "The groundwork has been laid," Dr. Sam wrote to him. By July 1952 Les and Barbara Hoversten had entered into a formal separation agreement, and Hoversten moved to Cleveland alone.

The job that Hoversten was finally given at Bay View was something less than what he or Dr. Sam had hoped for initially. Dr. Sam thought maybe he could get Hoversten a job as an assistant to a retiring doctor, an eye, ear, nose, and throat specialist. Instead, Hoversten was offered a position as surgical resident-in-training, although already a fully trained doctor. "We called him an educational bum. He was taking a residency there and he had already completed two or three residencies," recalled Dr. Murray.

Upon arrival, Hoversten moved in with his friend, Dr. Sam, against Marilyn's better judgment. Again, Dr. Sam felt sorry for him. "His marriage had not worked out, he lost his residency at the County Hospital and he was very depressed," he wrote. While he lived at Dr. Sam's, Hoversten had his meals at the hospital. On rare occasions Marilyn would ask him to eat with them.

According to neighbor Esther Houk, Marilyn couldn't stand Hoversten. "She made no bones about the fact to anybody," said Houk. "Marilyn may have had excellent reasons for disliking Les. She said she couldn't stand him sitting around the house staring at her all day. She couldn't turn around and he would be sitting there quietly just staring at her."

Hoversten was familiar with Dr. Sam's dallying, and what he didn't know he made up. He rubbed it in to Marilyn constantly. In her earshot he would ask a coy question about "Sue," or wonder whether Dr. Sam had heard lately from "Margaret." He would corner Marilyn in the daytime and chatter on with stories of Dr. Sam's conquests. Esther Houk thought that Hoversten would have enjoyed it if Sam had dropped Marilyn and just taken off with him.

Marilyn's dislike for Hoversten grew. Dr. Sam said he tried to explain that this was "a sort of pathology with him and he didn't mean to be malicious about it." Marilyn didn't really care. She just didn't like him. According to Dr. Sam, Marilyn later told him that Hoversten made advances to her during his stay.

When a vacancy in the apartment above the Sheppard-operated Fairview Clinic finally opened up after three months, Hoversten moved out. Hoversten shared the apartment above the clinic with Dr. Robert Stevenson. Stevenson was then engaged to Susan Hayes, the lab technician who was having a sexual liaison with Dr. Sam.

Although Dr. Sam had advocated for his friend, things were still not working out for Hoversten. The confidence of the Sheppards in his abilities was very low. He was not of the caliber they expected. Dr. Sam was nervous. His father had high standards, but Hoversten exhibited "a lot of stupidity," said Dr. Sam. He wasn't dependable. He would pull the phone jack out so no one could reach him at the clinic, completely undermining the goal of having a surgical resident. He didn't know what he was doing. And he griped about the "fellowship" program that they had set up especially to accommodate him. The Sheppards breathed a collective sigh of relief when he applied for a residency in Dayton and was accepted. "It overcame the distasteful job of terminating the work," said Dr. Sam.

Hoversten left Bay View for Grandview Hospital in Dayton on October 15, 1953. Little went well for him there, either. Quickly, Hoversten earned a reputation as a strange man. One doctor said that he would show pictures of Marilyn Sheppard and young Sam R. and claim that they were his wife and son.

In the meantime, his own divorce became finalized in February 1954. When the hearing came about in Cleveland that winter, Hoversten asked Dr. Sam to appear as a character witness. Dr. Sam did. Later, Hoversten would testify against Dr. Sam, saying that Dr. Sam had talked to him about divorce. Yes, said Dr. Sam, they had talked about divorce, but it was Hoversten's divorce they had discussed.

In Dayton, Hoversten suffered from ailments—most particularly sinusitis. He longed to be in New Mexico or California. He had X-ray therapy on his face and began taking Demerol to ease the pain. Headaches persisted. He had codeine prescribed. On other occasions, he was unable to sleep all night. A plantar wart on his foot called for injections of procaine and codeine.

Dayton was lonely. Hoversten would make frequent trips back to Cleveland, staying either with the Baileys in the old Fairview Clinic apartment or with Dr. Sam. Visiting Dr. Sam's was one of his panaceas. He interrupted Dr. Sam's life without regard to anything else that was going on. On one occasion, feeling in need, he drove to Dr. Sam's to be consoled, not recognizing that it was the night of Dr. Sam and Marilyn's wedding anniversary.

Other problems were coming up at the hospital in Dayton. In February Hoversten was chastised by another doctor who implied that he was negligent. The charge was that a tampon was not removed from a woman's vagina prior to difficult surgery. In another surgical incident, a doctor became irate that Hoversten did not know the patient's history. Another doctor became "irked" with him for not providing fluids for a patient as the doctor ordered; Hoversten insisted that he had heard no such order. He began to feel paranoid. People were out to get him. One doctor, he thought, was "nasty" to him without reason. Hoversten was accused of deceiving the hospital on autopsy reviews and of not looking at reports that he was supposed to read. He denied it.

Hoversten never admitted an error. His version of what happened was constantly at variance with others', and some questioned his veracity. He had a constant stream of excuses that pointed to the doctors that complained about him, and he protested vigorously to Dr. Sam, spreading rumors that Dr. Sam knew were untrue. Dr. Sam began to wonder if Hoversten might not be doing the same thing about the Sheppards.

Already, by the end of March, one of the top doctors was asking to have Hoversten's contract at Grandview terminated early. He was "tagged by the Surgeon in chief as incompetent," said Dr. Sam. The majority of the surgeons at the hospital signed a petition. One doctor spoke to Hoversten: hadn't he said he would resign if that happened? Not true, Hoversten replied.

As these events were going on, Hoversten's other troubles multiplied. Hoversten was headed for Dr. Sam's at Easter when the rear wheels on his car started to slide off the pavement in the rain near Springfield, Ohio. He collided head-on with a truck. He never made it for Easter. Afterward, his physical ailments increased. His hand, forehead, and knees were swollen.

In May Dr. Hoversten was sinking. He wrote in his diary for Monday, May 17, 1954: "very depressed—wish my life were over." He wrote a letter to his good friend Dr. Sam Sheppard. He was depressed. He had money troubles, and might need financial assistance. Maybe Dr. Sam and he could visit South Africa together, he said wistfully. After the murder, the last statement was snatched up by police and reporters to show that Dr. Sam was unhappy, rather than the obviously unhappy writer. In the same letter, Hoversten threw in, sarcastically, that he hoped to visit Dr. Sam after leaving Dayton, but "your beloved wife's attitude to me in the past still fills me with an aversion to staying at your house." The implication was not subtle. If only Les could spend more time with Dr. Sam, if only Sam were a free man . . .

"Hoversten had tried to talk about divorce to me many times. My reply was that I could find no one better than Marilyn for me," wrote Dr. Sam while in jail awaiting trial. "I allowed Hoversten in my home because I felt his reaction was and is part of a psychosis or psychoneurosis which drove him to talk about other people and tell untruths in order to build himself up."

On Thursday, May 27, Hoversten's residency in Dayton was terminated by the vote of the hospital's board of trustees. The next day, hospital officials informed Hoversten that his contract would be terminated as of July 1, 1954, well before one year was up in October.

Hoversten's immediate response was to drive to the home of his friend Dr. Sam. When he arrived, Dr. Sam and Marilyn were on their way out. They didn't really have time to spend with him. Hoversten wrote somewhat glumly in his calendar-diary: "Vis. S.H.S. but Marilyn & Sam were going out to their dinner dance." After he wrote it, he crossed out the "their," realizing perhaps how possessive and envious it seemed, so that it read, "*a* dinner dance."

Hoversten stayed with a friend that night, but couldn't sleep. In the morning, he asked to watch Dr. R. A. Sheppard perform surgery, as if by proximity he could earn his way back into the Bay View family. Bay View had no intention of taking him back. The pressure on Les Hoversten was building.

In June Hoversten's distress was not abated. He tried to talk to people about the Grandview decision, how unfair the termination was. Little sympathy was passed his way. He wrote a few letters seeking employment, but if anything, they may have indicated how poor his judgment was. In a letter to Dr. Dominic Aveni on June 15, 1954, on Grandview stationery, he only said: "I am leaving Grandview Hospt. July 1. What opportunities do you have at this time?" Dr. Aveni, it so happened, had no opportunities for Lester Hoversten. In fact, he had little respect for Hoversten. He told Bay Village police that Hoversten was "a frustrated man who could not settle down to anything."

On July 1 Hoversten left Grandview Hospital for good. "His mental outlook was not good, due to his discharge from his residency," wrote Dr. Thomas S. of Dayton. He thought Hoversten had some kind of mental disorder.

Hardly any more disturbed person could have landed in the Sheppard household two days before the murder of Mrs. Marilyn Sheppard.

Hoversten was not exactly the person Marilyn most wanted to see. Marilyn said that if he stayed there, she refused to be burdened by making his bed or cooking for him, Dr. Sam and others recalled later. Dr. Sam wrote, "I said OK but we'd let him sleep there if he wanted." Indeed, after the murder, police investigators noted that the bed in Dr. Hoversten's room was unmade, even though Hoversten had supposedly slept elsewhere. Hoversten indicated it had not been made earlier in the day either. It apparently never occurred to him that he might do it himself.

Dr. Hoversten's movements in Cleveland in the few days before the murder were not as clear-cut as he liked to make them seem. He arrived on Thursday, July 1, at seven-thirty in the evening, maybe eight o'clock. Sometimes he said four P.M. Dr. Sam, Marilyn, and young Sam were doing homey things together, like weeding the lawn and planting flowers, he said. Right away Hoversten was reminded of everything that he did not have: the tight little family unit at which he had failed so miserably, a partner who loved him, a child who was part of his life, a salary to live on, even a place to call home. There was no way he was going to persuade Dr. Sam to leave and go to South Africa. Sam and Marilyn seemed happier than ever. It was salt in the wound.

Instead of staying at the house for dinner on July 1, he went out and returned after Marilyn had gone to bed. Hoversten came in the unlocked Lake Road door. Dr. Sam was watching television and then quickly joined Marilyn, who was sleeping.

Dr. Sam had invited Hoversten to come and watch him perform surgery in the morning, both on Friday and Saturday, July 2 and July 3. Hoversten said that he got up on Friday morning, had breakfast with Dr. Sam and Marilyn, and then "accompanied" Dr. Sam to the hospital. Dr. Sam said that he left at eight-thirty; Hoversten was to follow but did not arrive until ten, after Dr. Sam had already completed the operations. His time was unaccounted for. The same thing occurred on Saturday morning.

Visits to Bay View Hospital on Friday and Saturday with Dr. Sam were bitter reminders of Hoversten's failings. Dr. Sam was successful. Hoversten was without a job and had no prospects for one. Interns and residents clustered around Dr. Sam, learning from his medical grace. Dr. Hoversten was pushed aside.

Bay View Hospital was not going to take Hoversten back, as became vividly clear on July 2 and 3. Everywhere he went in the hospital, he was treated coolly. His reception may very well have been due to the negative attitude of Dr. Sam's "beloved wife." Marilyn's visibility had grown. She was now the head of the Women's Auxiliary of Bay View Hospital. Hoversten could easily imagine that Marilyn had made disparaging comments about him, that she was trying to "get him," just like the doctors in Dayton had done.

On Friday and Saturday, Hoversten talked with a couple of other doctors in Cleveland about job prospects. Hoversten was forty-three years old now. Starting over was getting tiresome. Dr. Aveni was one of the doctors he met with. Things did not look good.

On Friday evening, Hoversten was not included when Dr. Sam and Marilyn went to a little dinner party at his brother Steve's, even though Hoversten also knew Steve from medical school and Bay View Hospital. Instead, Hoversten went out to dinner with a doctor and his wife on the East Side.

When Les returned to the Sheppards', Kokie did not bark. Hoversten entered through the Lake Road door. The door was not locked, said Hoversten. Marilyn called to him from the bedroom and told him to leave the door unlocked because Elnora Helms, the occasional housekeeper, was expected in the morning. Helms, as it happens, had been scheduled at the last minute and had to cancel.

While at Bay View Hospital on Saturday morning, July 3, Hoversten had a sudden change of plans. He got on the phone with Dr. Robert Stevenson. Stevenson had moved to Kent, Ohio, about thirty miles south and east of Bay Village, where he was in practice with his aging father. Hoversten decided to go to Kent for the night.

Perhaps it was an escape from the turmoil that was overtaking him at the Sheppard home and the hospital. Dr. Sam and Marilyn continued to make plans that excluded him. He didn't care about Marilyn, but Dr. Sam was one of the few people he could cling to. Now Sheppard was closer than ever to Marilyn. Even their sexual problems seemed to have been resolved. Hoversten may well have known that the previous night, Dr. Sam and Marilyn had made love in their twin room, after Les had gone into his room down the hall.

In addition, on Sunday, July 4, there was to be a hot dog roast at the Sheppard home with all the hospital interns. Dr. Sam and Marilyn could have planned no more humiliating activity. The interns, many of whom knew Hoversten from Bay View, would ridicule his short tenure at Dayton and belittle his lack of plans for the future.

In the middle of Saturday afternoon, Hoversten went back to the Sheppards'. Marilyn was there baking a blueberry pie, a small surprise for Dr. Sam, she said. Hoversten was hasty, disorganized. He grabbed a few things. He left so quickly, in fact, that he forgot his shaving kit and toothbrush. Fastidious about his hygiene, he was unlikely to overlook anything so essential.

On his way to Kent, Hoversten said, he stopped at a driving range and hit some balls. At any rate, two or three hours were idly passed with little accounting. He arrived at Stevenson's house. Dr. Stevenson and Susan Hayes had broken off their engagement before she headed for California at the beginning of 1954. Stevenson wanted her to "settle down," he said, but she was not willing to give up her party life.

The two bachelor doctors passed Saturday night uneventfully. They had dinner at home with Dr. Stevenson's parents. They listened to the Cleveland baseball game on the radio. After the late-running game ended, they went to bed. Or did they?

Hoversten admitted that he got up in the middle of the night. He said that Stevenson's Dalmation dog was in his room and that the dog was making yawning sounds that disturbed him. Hoversten, a sometime insomniac and a light sleeper who awoke with the slightest provocation, said that he took the dog down to the kitchen, locked it in, and returned to bed. Dr. Sam later noted, more caustically, that "Dr. Hoversten is a light sleeper and also a known pathological liar."

Whether Hoversten might have or could have slipped out in the night was subject to debate. The younger Dr. Stevenson was like Dr. Sam, a man who fell into deep sleeps and was difficult to wake. He might not have heard Hoversten slip away. Dr. Stephen Sheppard told a reporter in late July that the older Dr. Stevenson was deaf. Still, Mrs. Stevenson, the younger doctor's mother, claimed that she heard Hoversten both get up with the dog and go back to bed.

One thing is clear: had Hoversten stayed in Bay Village that night, events may very well have been different on the morning of July 4.

On that morning, Hoversten arose at approximately eight o'clock and, with the male Stevensons, drove to the Twin

Lakes Golf and Country Club for eighteen holes of golf. After returning to the Stevenson home at two-fifteen, he had a call from authorities in Bay Village, who wanted to talk to him at once. Hoversten decided to sit down and have a sandwich first.

Dr. Thomas S., who believed Hoversten should have been a suspect, told the Cleveland police that he thought Hoversten had a mental problem. "This situation could have created a mental condition in which Dr. Hoversten could have returned to Cleveland during the night, and possibly could have committed the crime," he suggested. He had a new car, a 1954 V-8 mainline Ford, purchased with the insurance proceeds from his Easter accident. In an easy drive of thirty to forty-five minutes each way, Hoversten could have made a round trip to Bay Village between 12:30 A.M., when the Aherns left, and 5:50 A.M., when the Houks arrived.

Dr. Hoversten knew the Sheppard house well—after all, he had lived there and had every opportunity to check out its latest condition. Kokie did not bark at him. He would have been aware of the signal that Marilyn sometimes used when Dr. Sam was not home: she would leave the dressing room light on, as she had that night, even though he was downstairs. The house was no problem to enter; he knew the Lake Road door would be unlocked. If it were locked, he knew to find the key in a basket beside the door. During his many weeks at the Sheppard home, he may have become familiar with the basement and its cellarway entry as well. Even if he had seen Dr. Sam sleeping on the couch, Hoversten knew that Dr. Sam slept through almost everything. And he had set up an excellent alibi: he was supposed to be in Kent.

Perhaps Hoversten had spontaneously and obsessively driven back to the Sheppard home, ostensibly to retrieve his toiletries. Unaware that Dr. Sam was home or knowing that he was unwakable once asleep, he went upstairs to get his kit. As he went by the "twin" bedroom, he saw Marilyn lying there, inside the open door. He entered. She had rejected him and all his approaches over the years. But now, vulnerable on the bed, he decided to disrobe her. She screamed. Dr. Hoversten panicked.

Or perhaps, with his anger and rejection fueled by Marilyn's icy attitude toward him, he planned this event. He needed to do something to change things and to get Dr. Sam back in his corner, like their days in California. On Saturday morning he had an idea. He arranged a situation in Kent that would not be considered suspicious, an alibi to deflect attention. He knew that he could sneak out from there during the night without detection. He had whatever weapons or implements he needed in his car, and, with other items, he tossed them out the car window on the way back to Kent, making them nearly impossible to find. When told of Mrs. Sheppard's death on July 4, he feigned surprise, but could not bring himself to show emotion. He sat down and had lunch before even returning to Bay Village at the request of officers.

A large man, Hoversten matched in size the person Dr. Sam described. But he was not as athletic as Dr. Sam, and somewhat older, not as strong. Whether he could have knocked Dr. Sam out twice, inflicting bruises on the face and neck, was questionable. Also, his hair was receding, not overflowing, although the long crew cut may have had the "bushy" appearance Dr. Sam described. He had no known history of violence or crime. And there is a solid probability that Dr. Sam would have recognized him, even in the dim light at the bedroom door or in the predawn darkness of the beach.

Dr. Kirk had described how the likely murderer was someone who was afraid of being identified. Hoversten definitely fit into that category. Marilyn would have readily recognized him; the ramifications would have been severe. He would have had every reason to want to get rid of Marilyn, but not Dr. Sam. He had to hope that Dr. Sam had gotten no look either, although he could not bring himself to do him harm. The klutzy burglary, the broken trophies were things that fit in with his love-hate relationship with Dr. Sam and Marilyn.

Yet none of these things occurred to police when they talked to Les Hoversten on July 4. They did not check his car or his clothes. When surgical instruments became the coroner's preoccupation as the possible weapon, Hoversten's were not checked. When golf clubs were tested by the dozens, Hoversten's were not. Police did not make a visual inspection or interrogate him closely about his activities. No one noticed whether he had cuts on his hands, abrasions, any teeth needing repair. That he was an emotional powder keg was not of the slightest interest to them, even though it was one of the first things to come up with neighbors.

A report by Cleveland detective Pat Gareau on July 4, 1954, that Sam R. obtained in 1993 showed that the police learned immediately "from a confidential source" that Hoversten "was supposed to be infatuated by Marilyn Sheppard and that his advances were spurned by her."

When Dr. Hoversten arrived in Bay Village that afternoon, he showed not the slightest bit of emotion at Marilyn's death. He was taken to the house and was shown her blood-soaked mattress. He didn't flinch; he didn't cry or even sigh deeply. Mayor Houk was practically in shock; his wife, Esther, had downed a shot of whiskey without thinking. Hoversten merely did as he was told, made a perfunctory survey of his clothes and belongings at the Sheppard home, decided that nothing had really been disturbed. Most of the money he had was in checks; fifty dollars tucked away in a suit pocket was still there.

On July 5 Hoversten visited Dr. Sam in the hospital. Sam burst into tears, blurting out: "My God, I wish they'd have killed me instead of Marilyn. [Young Sam] needs Marilyn more as a mother than he does me." Hoversten told this to the detectives who first interviewed him. Hoversten had replied to Dr. Sam that he should try to control his emotions. "Excessive grief could tear you apart," he said. Hoversten himself was very calm.

At the very least, Les Hoversten knew one damaging thing about himself. He knew that Marilyn Sheppard despised him, and this he wanted to conceal. If he was worried that his friend Sam was being blamed for the murder, he was more concerned about not being implicated himself.

And if psychological state had been a consideration, Dr. Hoversten would have been at the top of the list of suspects. Put Hoversten in an emotional lineup and he was uranium, glowing with motive. If police knew this, they used it only to lean on Hoversten to build a case against Dr. Sam.

On July 6 Hoversten gave a formal statement to sheriff's deputies Carl Rossbach and Dave Yettra. Although their questions were aimed at getting damaging information about Dr. Sam, they did ask one direct question. Had Hov-

ersten ever had any misunderstanding with Dr. Sam or
Marilyn? Hoversten answered with a clipped "No."

Of course, he did have misunderstandings, and they were
deep, hurtful ones. Hoversten would soon have to find stories to cover that up. He adjusted his answers, saying that
there were misunderstandings—not between Hoversten and
Marilyn, but between Dr. Sam and Marilyn. He would say
that Dr. Sam talked about divorce, when the divorce under
discussion had been Hoversten's.

On the evening of July 6 Hoversten went to the Saxton
Funeral Home to view Marilyn's body. His observations
were clinical. "She did not look natural," he noted in his
diary. "Head on l. & face swollen." The rest of the week
he passed his time attending the funeral, playing golf, and
doing one very curious thing. On Friday, July 9, he saw a
dentist. "There were an awful lot of people having dental
work around then," noted an investigator with AMSEC,
working with Sam R. in 1994.

Toothwork was interesting only because of the evidence
found later in July under the murder bed. Tooth chips discovered under the bed never were identified. Hoversten
wrote that his dental appointment consisted of fillings and
teeth cleaning. But immediately after his dental appointment on July 9, he was taken to the prosecutor's office for
an interview with two Cuyahoga County prosecutors, who
had in a most unusual way joined the investigative side of
the case, and the two Cleveland detectives who had supposedly been pulled off the case.

On Saturday, July 10, Hoversten was called to the sheriff's office. He was made to wait for many hours, until six
o'clock, while officers completed an all-day interview with
Dr. Sam. Hoversten was questioned for only an hour, and
then he was on his way. He agreeably complied with everything that the police requested, while quietly and unemo-
tionally making plans to leave the country.

On Monday, July 12, Hoversten packed up his car. He
visited Dr. Sam. "Sam thanked me for standing by and for
my advice re. control of emotions," he wrote. Hoversten
left the next morning for Iowa City, headed for California.
On the way, he became oppressively ill and had to take to
bed for days. His temperature rose to 103 degrees.

As soon as he arrived in California, Hoversten was writing anxious, strange letters. One was postmarked July 24,

written on stationery from Grandview Hospital, the Dayton facility that had dismissed him. He sent it to Mabel Moyers, a friend who worked at the Bay View Hospital. She thought it was peculiar enough to turn it over to the police, who put it on file but did little more with it.

> Please write & send me the news. . . . How's Sam?—do not mention to him that I inquired as I'll write him myself next week and the Sheppards fear I may be a source of too much information to their Calif. friends anyway. Did the questioning of employees reveal anything unusual? . . .
>
> My best to you all,
> Sincerely, Les H.

On the first possible day after his arrival back in California, Hoversten went to Glendale Public Health Office to get typhoid, smallpox, cholera, and tetanus shots. Hoversten was intent on getting out of the country. By August 4 he had booked passage on a ship for Berlin.

On August 10 the Los Angeles police came to his home and told him he was wanted for interrogation in Cleveland. The prosecutor was trying to get evidence together to present to a grand jury.

Hoversten was flown back to Cleveland on August 11, arriving at 10:30 P.M. after an exceptionally long flight with a three-hour delay. At the Cleveland airport he was met by prosecutor Mahon and Cleveland police sergeant Lockwood. They went downtown and were joined by the chief of police, chief prosecutor, head of the homicide unit, and deputy inspector, all questioning Hoversten until 2:15 A. M., according to a diary Hoversten kept at the time and obtained by Sam R.

When he could go on no longer, Hoversten was taken to the Carter Hotel in downtown Cleveland, where Sergeant Lockwood stayed with him all night. The next morning he was awakened and sent back for more interrogation. He was questioned all day for the next three days.

Hoversten was not an especially strong man. The detectives began to see an opportunity and pushed him to tell them something. The middle-aged former resident doctor found it easy to comply with their wishes. If they wanted the names of other women that Dr. Sam Sheppard may have seen, he was ready to give them. Intimacies, reveal them. Confidences, tell them. Stories, he could improvise and embellish, change the characters to switch his own and Dr. Sam's roles. He would do whatever was necessary to get out of this situation.

If Hoversten feared that the top brass were out to get him, he need not have worried. By the time Hoversten was brought back to Cleveland, the coroner had declared that Dr. Sam was the murderer and Dr. Sam was under arrest and in jail, being questioned on a nearly round-the-clock basis. Cleveland authorities were fully committed to convicting Dr. Sam.

Still, they squeezed Hoversten for more and more information, whether true or fabricated. He gave a revised story of his July 5 visit to Dr. Sam with more sinister overtones, claiming that Dr. Steve had come in and tried to stop Hoversten from talking to Sam. When Dr. Sam interposed, Steve stormed out, then came back. Now, Hoversten said, Steve told Sam to "go over his story" in his mind several times a day to get it straight. This statement by Hoversten, to which he testified on the stand, added to the impression of Dr. Sam as a man who was concocting events, or at least of a man whose brother was encouraging him to do so. With each day of interrogation of Hoversten, the newspapers crowed: "Hoversten Tells More"; "Hoversten Talks."

On Friday, August 13, Hoversten was given a lie detector test by Officer Conneley. In his diary Les noted that he got certain "card numbers" wrong both times. The defense was never informed about this. The newspapers reported that he took two lie detector tests; his diaries show only one. Chief Story declared them a success and gave to the press his synopsis of the positive results of questioning Hoversten.

Hoversten was under twenty-four-hour police guard. The authorities wanted to make certain that he was available to testify before the grand jury. In one absurd public moment, one officer had to replace another in the third inning of a doubleheader at the Stadium that Hoversten was attending. People stared, and Hoversten panicked and abruptly left before the game ended, the replacement officer following.

Hoversten was suffocating. Daily he called various people at the prosecutor's office and police department. When could he leave? he wanted to know. When could he go back to California?

Finally, on August 16, he spoke for about an hour before the grand jury. The grand jury finished its work to the prosecution's satisfaction, returning an indictment for first-degree murder. On August 19 Hoversten was at last allowed to leave Cleveland.

He was boarded on a red-eye flight, but not until after the visit by Mr. Lamkin of the State Department and Mr. Kirchner of the Immigration Department. They wanted his passport. The police made it clear: his plans to travel abroad were canceled. He cooperated, or he would not be traveling at all.

As soon as he landed back in Los Angeles, Hoversten called his lawyer. Nine days he had been under watch by the police. It was more than enough to let him know what he had to do.

The rest of the summer and fall creeped by. With no work, Hoversten played golf, traveled up and down the coast, went to a rifle-shooting range, played tennis, went swimming. His former friend Dr. Sam sat in a cell, his life in the balance, but Les lived a free and easy life. On October 4 he started work for a California doctor, but it ended almost as quickly as it began, on October 16.

Waiting in the West Coast wings to testify in the Sheppard trial, Hoversten had become the subject of some leafleting in Ohio. The fliers, everyone said, were passed out by cranks. A letter with one was sent to Dr. Sam's father and signed by Amad No-Ra Heavedoy of Cleveland. Another one that had apparently been handed out to members of the jury had the name All-A Yodheavauhe of Cleveland on the top.

The flier contained a collage of newspaper articles, typewriting, and two newspaper photos. On the left side of the page was a pained picture of Dr. Sam in the hospital on July 4 or 5, his face obviously beaten and swollen. A typewritten comment below said: "Lovely Marilyn would never strike anyone, much less do this to her Lover." To the right was a photograph of Hoversten and Police Chief Frank Story talking amicably. It had been printed in the August 14 *Cleveland Plain Dealer*. Below these photos were reproductions of two articles—one from the *Cleveland Press* titled "Catholic Man of the Year Award Goes to Worthy

Individual" from September 23, 1954, about an award from the Greater Cleveland Knights of Columbus to Sheriff Joseph Sweeney. The other was two columns of a September 20 article about the bail hearing on Dr. Sam and how Hoversten had been immediately dismissed as a possible suspect. Here the typewritten comment remarked on how successfully "Brother" Mahon, the lead prosecutor, had changed the subject of interrogation from a focus on Hoversten.

The top of the flier made its point in typewritten sentences: "The Marilyn Murder is not a minor, local, individual Case. It is an International, Historical, New Era starting point—The Death Struggle of The Popes' Phallic 'universe,' and the Birth Pang of an Honest and True 'INFINIVERSE.' WITHOUT THE POPES' CONTROL, OUR OFFICERS WOULD SOON ACQUIRE NORMAL INTELLIGENCE."

This sentiment was punctuated elsewhere with a comment about not believing "THE LYING KNIGHTS ABOUT HOVERSTEN'S ALIBI."

This 1954 conspiracy seemed to claim that the Catholic brotherhood of the Knights of Columbus was being used as a blanket to hide Dr. Lester T. Hoversten as a suspect.

The fliers shook up Hoversten. His will was weakening. He was still in California when a *Cleveland Press* article came out on November 2: "Hoversten Bares Divorce Talk." In big fountain pen strokes he wrote, "Newspaper reports re. my knowledge of Marilyn & Sam Sheppards relationship markedly distorted & false."

On Saturday, November 6, he got the call from prosecutor Parrino. The time for his appearance was at hand. On Sunday he went to church, as was often his habit. Then, on Wednesday, November 10, he was back in Cleveland. Reporters stood waiting at the airport. He was placed at the Carter Hotel, again with a police guard, but was moved two days later through a back exit to the University Center Motel. He met with prosecutors, but still more waiting was required. Days droned by; the trial dragged. On November 19 Hoversten had to cancel his December 1 sailing for Europe, opting instead for a ship leaving on January 13.

Finally, on November 22, he took the stand, soon after star witnesses Dr. Adelson, Dr. Gerber, and Detective Schottke.

Once he took the oath, Hoversten began to hedge. But

it was too late. The newspapers had already printed every damaging statement he had made to the police. His testimony, no matter what, was going to be used to smear the character of a man he practically idolized. Motive, sex stories, a diversion from the lack of forensic evidence were what the police wanted, and in Les Hoversten they got all three.

The judge even allowed Hoversten to testify about what he said were the contents of the letter that Dr. Sam had written to Marilyn in Cleveland in 1950. The letter was not on hand. Hoversten said that Dr. Sam wrote to Marilyn that "he was concerned regarding his marriage and wanted to tell her how he felt, and he felt, according to his views with me, that he wanted to consider the possibility of a divorce."

Bam!

There was more. Hoversten was permitted to repeat what Dr. R. A. Sheppard had supposedly said to his son in a telephone conversation—more hearsay.

> *Question:* Did he tell you what his father had said to him over the phone?
> *Hoversten:* No. I do not recall exactly, except it was to this effect: That he felt that Sam should realize his responsibility as a husband and a father in this marriage situation.

On cross-examination, Hoversten tried to soften the innuendo about Dr. Sam's infidelity. He did not know of any specific instance in which Dr. Sam was intimate with any woman other than his wife; he did see him in the company of various women, including Margaret, but always as a guest of his, Hoversten's. In addition, he had never seen Dr. Sam angry, he said on cross-examination; Dr. Sam was even-tempered.

All the questions about Hoversten, his neurotic background, his failure as a doctor, husband, father, his meanderings, his depression, the reasons for his job dismissals, including dishonesty and incompetence, his rejection by Marilyn, his discomfort at their house combined with the longing to be there, his wish to flee the country—none of that was raised.

Dr. Hoversten was given his ticket back home. On December 24 he got a Christmas present: now that Dr. Sam Sheppard was behind bars, Les could have his passport back, said Captain James McArthur.

On January 5, 1955, Dr. Sam had no more kindness for Lester Hoversten. "All I have to say about him is limited at this time due to the restraint currently applied to all things & people, but Marilyn was entirely correct about him," he wrote from jail to his brother.

Hoversten did leave for Europe. "He disappeared like a ghost," said Dr. Edward Murray. "Everybody wondered what happened to Les. . . . he just never entered into the picture at all." Nobody ever heard of him after that time, said Esther Houk, who kept scrupulous track of Sheppard events. Dr. Steve Sheppard had no recollection of hearing from Hoversten again, either.

By the time Dr. Kirk was allowed to conduct tests on the Sheppard property in early 1955, Hoversten was gone. But in 1956 a message came from him, postmarked Newcastle-on-Tyne, England, a shipbuilding town of working-class people that also boasted an osteopathic community. By 1993 no old-timer in osteopathy could remember any American taking training there in the 1950s. Something of a semireligious apology, the letter that Hoversten wrote could not have been comforting to Dr. Sam, then in prison: "Words, written or spoken, are often so inadequate to express what one feels and thinks; therefore, I should like nothing better than to see you and to shake your hand and to wish you well as I last did when I bid you Goodbye the evening before I left for California in July 1954."

Hoversten seemed to have forgotten about how he testified against Dr. Sam in November 1954, and that was the last time he saw Dr. Sam. Dr. Sam was sitting with his lawyers, struggling to combat a case glued together with rumor, innuendo, and the revisionist history of Les Hoversten. "There are of course many questions in my mind; I hope that somehow you will be able to surmount all the problems, that you will succeed in your appeal," wrote Hoversten.

Finally, Hoversten asked if he could send some records or literature from Europe. "No doubt," he said, in the same old catty Hoversten style, "you have all that money and a loving family can provide, but if I can send you anything from here please do not hesitate to ask." He ended with religious quotations.

Words could do nothing to make up for the damage that Hoversten had inflicted. Whether he was a bona fide suspect himself who tried to point blame in another direction, or was simply a man too cowardly to stand up to the police, too self-involved and worried about his own image, Hoversten had shattered a tremendous friendship and stoked the fuel of the railroad train that ran down Dr. Sam.

Les Hoversten did not, in fact, entirely disappear. In 1958 he wrote to a medical colleague from Sweden. Then, apparently, after several trips back and forth to Europe, he went back to California. Dr. Bob Bailey had some vague recollection of his opening a clinic in southern California and just as suddenly closing it up and, without warning, sending his patients to Dr. Bailey. In 1963 he showed up as a practitioner at the Presbyterian Medical Center in San Francisco.

In 1975, eight days after his sixty-fourth birthday, Hoversten became licensed as a medical doctor in California. Like two thousand other osteopaths, he took advantage of legislation passed in California that allowed D.O.'s to transfer their licenses to those of M.D.'s simply by paying a transfer fee. Moving to San Jose, Hoversten practiced as an anesthesiologist. In 1987, at the age of seventy-six, he died there after being hospitalized for a heart ailment. Thirteen years older than Dr. Sam, he had outlasted him by seventeen years.

There was one final, seemingly unanswered communication from Hoversten to Dr. Sam after he was finally acquitted in 1966. Buried deep in Dr. Sam's files that had been collected by his son was a telegram from San Francisco:

CONGRATULATIONS I HOPE RETURN TO SURGERY—AND TENNIS—WILL INCREASE YOUR JOY

LESTER HOVERSTEN

As for his own role, the police had never seriously looked at Hoversten. People who knew him were contacting the police, reporting that he had the emotional stability of whipped-up storm waves on the lake. Like so many other persons who might have real information about what happened in the murder room, Les Hoversten's silence was secure.

In 1994 Hoversten's son wrote this short note: "My dad . . . only spoke a few times to me about Sam Sheppard, concerning his court case. He indicated to me that because he was associated with Sam Sheppard that his medical career had suffered some."

FIFTEEN

Neighbors

If the phone line that Sam R. had opened in 1993 was any indication, the former mayor of Bay Village and his wife had made an indelible impression upon the case. Almost as many people had opinions about the mayor and his wife as about Dr. Sam and the murder itself

> *A man:* I think the mayor did it. The mayor did not call the police till three hours later. The proof came out in court.
> *A man:* I was a friend with a man who was a part-time policeman. The feeling of the police was that the mayor was a prime suspect.
> *A woman:* I just strongly feel the mayor did it. He lost his business, his wife divorced him.
> *A woman:* The mayor at Bay Village, he killed her, I have no doubt. They used that poker. The bushy-haired intruder was the mayor.

Esther Houk and J. Spencer Houk, usually known as Spen, cast long and powerful shadows in the Sheppard case. Their memories held fast in Bay Village. Like nearly everyone else, Sam R. heard much about them during the years after the murder when he was growing up on the West Side of Cleveland. Richard Eberling, too, knew the Houks. He said that he had worked for them at one time, and when he was convicted of murder in 1989, he decided that he wanted to talk about them. And one of the callers to the phone line was the grandson of Spen and Esther, who de-

scribed how a continual swirl of Sheppard stories had infil-
trated his life, as if part of his inheritance. The grandson
wasn't even born until 1968, fourteen years after the murder and two years after the trial in which Dr. Sam was
acquitted.

The names of the Houks were brought to the fore in the
summer of 1954, and again through the later 1950s and
early 1960s, and again in a grand jury inquiry in 1966, after
which no action was taken, and again in 1982 when fireplace tongs were found buried on their former property,
and yet again in the years after 1989 when the former West
Side window washer began to talk about the Sheppard case.

Two main factors had put the Houks in the suspect category. One was their strange behavior after the murder. The
other was the close attachment that Spen had to Marilyn
Sheppard prior to the murder, the kind of attentions that
might provoke gossip and jealousy that flared up like oil
on hot cinders when she was found dead.

One moment in the fall of 1954 captured the intensity of
the cross fire between the Sheppard case and the Houks.
In September a bail hearing was set to determine whether
Dr. Sam Sheppard would be required to stay in jail during
the entire period of his trial. Already there had been the
inquest, the arrest, the grand jury hearing. Now more witnesses were called to testify. The trial was nearing and the
media were raring to go. Esther Houk took the stand to
repeat the events of July 4, but J. Spencer Houk was nowhere to be found. He had testified at the inquest at the
end of July; now he was unavailable. The reason was that
he was having a nervous breakdown and had checked himself into a local hospital, one on the East Side, far from his
Bay Village neighbors.

On the morning of July 4, 1954, Spen and Esther Houk
opened the Lake Road door to the Sheppard home, only
three doors from theirs.

"I cannot recall what Mr. Houk or Mrs. Houk said when
they first came in," said Dr. Sam when questioned at the
inquest about three weeks later in July. "I don't recall talking to Mayor Houk or Mrs. Houk. They may have asked
me what happened; I don't recall."

When Dr. Sam urged that someone do something for
Marilyn, Spen stood paralyzed. Esther ran upstairs, al-

Four years after graduating from Cleveland Heights High School in 1941, Marilyn Reese married her high school sweetheart, Sam Sheppard.

Dr. Sam Sheppard graduated fourth in his class from the College of Osteopathic Physicans and Surgeons in 1949.

Two-year-old Sam Reese Sheppard poses with his parents, Marilyn, twenty-six, and Sam, twenty-five, in 1949.

The Sheppard home in Bay Village was unusual in that the back of the house, above, faced the road. The home's front overlooked Lake Erie.

Coroner Sam Gerber examines the desk in the Sheppard living room. (*Courtesy of the* Plain Dealer, *Cleveland, Ohio*)

The Sheppards were not wealthy, as they were portrayed in the media. The television was one of the few items of furniture that was not on loan.

Late in the evening prior to the murder, Dr. Sam, exhausted from hospital emergencies, fell asleep on a daybed in the living room. He did not wake until he heard his wife screaming.

A police artist drew this sketch after three people reported seeing a man walking along Lake Road in the early morning hours of July 4, 1954.

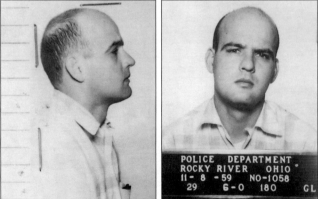

These mug shots were taken after Richard Eberling's 1959 arrest for theft. At the time of his arrest, Eberling was in possession of a ring that had belonged to Marilyn Sheppard.

Eberling was found guilty of the murder of Ethel May Durkin in 1989.
(*Courtesy of the* Plain Dealer.)

Ethel May Durkin died on January 3, 1984, after what was at first described as a fall. Caretaker Richard Eberling was the only one present when Ms. Durkin sustained her injuries. (*Drawing by Erica Bobone*)

Vern Lund, left, worked for Eberling's company in the summer of 1954. On July 2, he washed windows at the Sheppard home.

Dr. Richard Sheppard, Sam's father, puts his arm around his son, while Sam rests his hand on top of his father's as they talk during a quiet moment of the ill-fated 1954 "circus trial."

During the trial, jury members were taken to see the Sheppard home. A newspaper reporter accompanied them, photographers lined the property, and a helicopter flew overhead. (*Courtesy of the Plain Dealer.*)

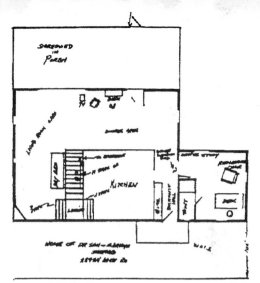

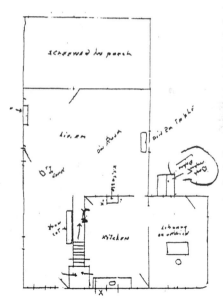

A 1954 police drawing, above, depicts the first floor of the Sheppard home. From a prison cell thirty-eight years later, Richard Eberling made this eerily accurate drawing, below, of the same area from memory. (*Reproduction Courtesy of AMSEC International, Middleburg, VA*)

Attorney F. Lee Bailey, foreground, exits the Cuyahoga County Courthouse with Dr. Sam Sheppard, left, and co-counsel Russell Sherman during the 1966 trial in which Dr. Sam was found not guilty. (*Courtesy of the* Plain Dealer.)

Dr. Paul Leland Kirk, the nation's leading forensic scientist, was brought into the Sheppard case after Dr. Sam's 1954 conviction. Dr. Kirk's testimony at the 1966 trial was critical in showing Dr. Sam's innocence.

though she could not explain how she knew where to go, and found the body of Mrs. Sheppard. She returned to the first floor. Spen, at her instruction, called the police. Spen was the Safety Director and, as such, supervisor of the police and fire forces. Why Spen and Esther had not called the police at the instant that Dr. Sam called them, or the moment that they walked inside the door, they could not say.

Later, Esther described the moment of suddenly encountering the aftermath of such violence upstairs. "I impulsively grabbed her wrist. . . . And I looked again and, well, I must have gone into shock. . . . It was, well, you know, it still didn't seem real. 'Cause I saw Madame Toussaud's in London. And all I kept thinking of was that this is something out of a museum or something. . . . And it's funny, that was all I could think of. Something like you see in a wax museum. It isn't real. It just wasn't real."

Esther stayed in the house or on the grounds all morning while the house filled with police, family, neighbors, even her son, Larry, who went upstairs and all through the house. Spen made calls, returned home, made more calls, returned to the Sheppard home—a nervous parade of events.

Dr. Sam saw Spen and Esther going back and forth. "It was all a mass of confusion," he said.

Esther was so upset that, before Bay Village police officer Fred Drenkhan arrived, she poured a glass of whiskey for Dr. Sam, but he declined it. Esther swallowed the double shot herself, washed the glass, and completely forgot about it for years. "I was hoping I'd either pass out or wake up. It was just not real. I wanted to do one or the other," she said in an interview in 1981. She remarked to neighbors all through the morning how peculiar it was that Dr. Sam turned down the whiskey, a point that the prosecution emphasized in its closing argument in 1954.

If Dr. Sam remembered confusion, it was even more confounding to young Sam. But when questioned by the coroner in late July, he could remember seeing Spen and Esther and Larry Houk in his house that morning. Unlike some of the others roaming the house and the lawn, he knew them. They were friends. They were neighbors.

Although neighbors since late summer 1951, the Sheppards and Houks didn't become friends until the winter of that year. Dr. Sam wrote a letter to the mayor of Bay Village, offering his services as police surgeon. Spen arranged to meet Dr. Sam. The connection to Bay Village politics that Spen offered was important to Dr. Sam. Bay View Hospital was building community relations and business by providing emergency services to the local suburban communities. Dr. Sam was keen on associating with Bay Village, and Spen was key to that goal. Dr. Sam invited the Houks over for cocktails, and Esther and Marilyn were added into the mix.

Houk, mayor of Bay Village since 1950, owned a butcher shop at the Bay Village shopping center, about a mile from the Houk and Sheppard homes. The Houks were three doors to the west of the Sheppards. Dr. Sam and Marilyn were a good decade younger than the Houks, but newly relocated from California and not knowing many people on the West Side other than family members and hospital personnel, they welcomed the neighborliness.

Quickly, the Sheppards' effusive personalities enchanted the Houks. The Houks' teenage children, Larry and Lynette, found the Sheppards exciting and attractive. "She was a fun person . . . she could talk to kids," Larry recalled in 1980. Larry, sixteen years old in 1954, was a sturdy football player, and one of the boys who used to congregate at Dr. Sam's to play basketball or spend the night in the "clubroom" above the Sheppard garage. Later, when he became a doctor, Larry acknowledged that his choice of career was at least partially influenced by Dr. Sam. Lynette, highly impressionable, thought of Marilyn as a big sister. Like other teens in the neighborhood, she often came by to talk with Marilyn about typical problems of school and dating.

Esther Gearhardt Houk had the longest history in the tiny suburb. She grew up in the community, went to high school there. Her father had owned a hardware store, and when it suffered difficult financial times, he worked as an electrician. Esther and Spen met in high school and developed a friendship as much as a love interest.

Spen, sometimes simply called J. S. or Jess by his wife, had suffered from childhood osteomyelitis, a bone infection that resulted in a fused right knee. He had a big scar on his leg and walked with a limp, but it was not always noticeable unless a person watched closely. Because of this medical condition, he had not been eligible for military service.

Neither Spencer nor Esther was especially good looking. They were a bit like Jack Sprat and his wife in reverse. She was small, birdlike. When upset, her face became pinched and tight; if she was feeling happy, her mouth spread wide, her high forehead became prominent. Esther was a nonstop talker and, it seemed, sometimes more ambitious than her laconic husband.

He was overweight and had a droopy face with bags under his eyes, a protruding lower lip, and a billowy double chin. Although he had bulk and was five feet and nine or ten inches tall, he was not at all athletic. But he was congenial, a natural conversationalist who was especially skilled at working out compromises when people clashed. "He was a good politician. He was a good double-talker," said Esther.

Spen and Esther married on October 14, 1933, when she was twenty and he had just turned twenty-three. Five years later, John Lawrence, called Larry or Lare by his mother, was born; Lynette Marie, called Lyn, was born two years after that.

Spen's father had had a stall in the West End Meat Market until a fire caused calamity. In 1949 the butcher shop reopened in Bay Village, and son Spen eventually took over. Spen and Esther had moved to the Lake Road house in about 1950.

Regardless of the moralistic picture of the 1950s painted later, Houk presented an image entirely different. He had a reputation as a ladies' man. His affairs were so widely known among the men of the town that they called him "Lover Boy." Even during his first year of marriage, he would disappear from a party with an attractive woman, infuriating his wife. When he was first considered as a mayoral possibility, some of the town leaders fretted about whether his marital indiscretions would invalidate him as a proper candidate.

The Houk and Sheppard friendship grew. Marilyn, who had an aversion to being alone that extended back to her childhood, would drop by Spen's meat market and go into the back for a cup of coffee. If he paid special attention to her, she did not mind, at least at first. She would call him "Dad" if he seemed to be moving too close.

The Bay Village city council members were initially not enthusiastic about Dr. Sam becoming police surgeon, according to Esther. Some council members had fought against Bay View Hospital opening up altogether back in 1948 and were not about to encourage its growth and development now. Gershom Barber, who was later to sign the warrant for Dr. Sam's arrest, was one of those who opposed naming Dr. Sam. Never mind, said Spen. He named Dr. Sam as a police surgeon through a mayor's appointment.

The Houks invited the Sheppards to a Decoration Day picnic, and Sam and Marilyn began to socialize regularly with friends of the Houks. Otto Graham, a Cleveland Browns football hero, and his wife, and Cliff Lewis, another football player, and his wife rounded out the circle of friends. The four couples bowled together on Sunday nights and then went back to the homes of one couple or another and talked sports.

Unlike some of his neighbors, Spen Houk was not terribly successful financially. His house was old. Like many along Lake Road, it was a former summer cottage for East Siders. The Houks bought it cheap, planning to remodel, but somehow the remodeling never got very far.

"The Houks were carefree. Their house was ready to fall down," said Richard Eberling, who said that at various times he provided window service and indoor wall cleaning to the Houks. "The living room floor was on an angle. If my memory serves me correctly, they paid twenty-five thousand dollars for the house and the lot was worth fifteen thousand dollars. It was one of those old summer cottages. No door on the bedroom, just a curtain that drew across. Tacky."

Still, like the Sheppards, they had the lake, and Spen loved the water. Before they became friendly with the Sheppards, the Houks had enjoyed taking a boat out onto the choppy lake waters, launching from the cement retaining wall below their property. The sound of the lake, especially on windy nights, was like an ocean roar, with waves crashing against the breakwater and wind whipping up the bluff. On the best of days, the sandy part of the beach was narrow along this curve of the lake, but it was practically nonexistent at the Houk property. Summer squalls frequently arose without warning, and one such storm had snatched the Houks' boat from its moorings and washed it away. Spen didn't quite have the cash to buy a new boat, so it was a perfect solution when Sam and Spen had the idea to buy a boat together. They got a fourteen-foot aluminum boat which, they hoped, was light enough to pull up on the bank when weather got bad. Each family had its own motor.

Dr. Sam and Marilyn bought a zippy twenty-five-horse-power motor for Christmas in 1952, one that would speed their way to expertise as some of the first practitioners in the sport of water skiing. The motor came with a green bag of tools that Dr. Sam kept in a desk drawer in the house—the bag later found in the bushes. As ski enthusiasts, Dr. Sam and Marilyn made water skiing practically mandatory for every summer guest, eagerly giving lessons. With no qualms, Dr. Sam let Larry Houk and friends borrow the motor so they too could stand on the water and ride victoriously behind the boat. That was curtailed, though, in the summer of 1953 after an unfortunate incident of roughhousing when one youth nearly drowned. Marilyn, unhappy, told Dr. Sam, who withdrew permission for the boys to use the motor. Larry was not pleased.

The boys had one other clash with Dr. Sam, which Larry mentioned briefly in his inquest testimony. Dr. Sam learned that the boys were committing some small-scale thefts and then coming back to the clubhouse above the Sheppard garage. Dr. Sam didn't get angry, Larry reported, but he did lecture them about values. When it came up in the inquest testimony, coroner Samuel Gerber inquired no further. On another occasion, Larry said that Dr. Sam and Marilyn were irked that boys would bring dates over to the clubhouse for long night stays.

The easy visiting from home to home and the relationship of the two families continued to develop. Dr. Sam made house calls to Spen's mother, who lived with the Houks. Her complaints were calls for attention as much as for physical relief, and he always delighted her with his treatments. Sometimes Dr. Sam would drop by the Houks' and take off his shoes, lie back, and watch sports on TV. And Spen often stopped by the Sheppards' on his way to work and had coffee with Marilyn. He sometimes did little chores that seemed to elude Dr. Sam, as a favor to Marilyn. He came to know the house better than Dr. Sam did. He brought deliveries from the meat market and cashed checks for Marilyn so that she wouldn't have to make a trip to the bank. One check was not cashed until after Marilyn died.

Late in the summer of 1952, the four of them decided to go on a fishing trip together on Pointe au Baril, an island on the Canadian part of Lake Erie, where the Houks had a cabin. The children were not along; this was a couples' holiday. Each day, Spen and Marilyn would get up early and go out fishing together; Dr. Sam and Esther were left behind to sleep late. Two weeks were planned. Dr. Sam, slightly bored and finding Esther a bit disagreeable, felt compelled to leave more than a week early for a medical emergency at the hospital. After he left, a nasty argument broke out between Spen and Esther. The remaining trio, having lost its spirit, decided to pack up early and go home.

A couple of weeks later, Marilyn somberly repeated to Dr. Sam a conversation she'd had with Spen earlier in the day. Spen said he was in love with her, had fallen in love on vacation; that was why he and Esther had argued. She could not reciprocate, Marilyn told Spen. After this recounting, Dr. Sam sat down. Perhaps it would be better to put a little more distance into their friendship. Dr. Sam and Marilyn decided to branch out into other social circles and to pull away from the Houks.

More subdued, the friendship continued. When the Sheppard home caught on fire, Dr. Sam ran to the Houks'. He called the fire department; Esther called Spen, who gathered up the civic-minded men at city hall to fight the fire. Even Gershom Barber, who voted against the Sheppards' hospital, assisted. When it was time to move back in, the Houks were there to help.

Marilyn reported that Spen pouted when the Sheppards began to spend more time with other couples, such as the Aherns and a slightly younger Bay Village group. Yet shortly before the murder, Dr. Sam and Marilyn had invited Esther and Spen out to dinner at a restaurant, a rare event. As they had to the closest family members, the Sheppards announced that Marilyn was pregnant.

Spen's fondness for Marilyn was not a secret. Everybody in Bay Village seemed to know that the mayor had a keen interest in Marilyn. Jim Redinger, a member of the crew of boys that hung out at the Sheppards', said that even as kids they were aware of the dark rumors about Larry's dad,

Mayor Houk. "It wasn't unusual to see his station wagon in the driveway in the afternoon," he said.

"She was a swell person. Just a hell of a nice person," said Spen Houk of Marilyn Sheppard in an interview in March 1981, just months before he died. He was living in Florida with his third wife, Selma. "Well, she was just a hundred percent straight. And she knew Sam was playing, but I would be willing to stake anything that she didn't do any playing. She was straight all the way."

Esther didn't think that Spen and Marilyn were sleeping together, she said later; she just thought he was acting like a public buffoon with his visits to Marilyn Sheppard. He thought that if his car was parked right there, no one could accuse him of having a clandestine affair. But it only meant that everyone knew he was there. "I told Spen he was making a darn fool of himself," she said.

But Marilyn's attitude toward Spen was less clear. From her perspective, Spen was a father figure. She was as close in age to his son as she was to him. Some people thought that his advances made her uncomfortable. Dr. Bob Bailey, a confidant, said that she didn't like Houk. Others were convinced that Marilyn and Spen were having a sexual liaison.

Was she or wasn't she? Most saw something that fell somewhere in between: Spen was attracted to Marilyn; Marilyn accepted his affections and attentions, but sex was not a part of it. Marilyn was having problems with sex in general, and Spen was not a likely mate to break the barrier. "She wasn't interested in sex at all," said Esther Houk.

The most controversial visit of Spen's, because it was recounted by the occasional housekeeper, Elnora Helms, occurred one day when Marilyn was sick. The time was April 1954, only three months before the murder. Spen came by, made Marilyn something to eat, and proceeded to take it to her in bed. This stretched the limits of propriety and friendship. Spen said he did this at the insistence of Dr. Sam, who had called him at work and asked him to check on Marilyn. Helms thought it unusual enough that she mentioned it to another member of the Sheppard family, who also employed her.

Jack Krakan, a bakery delivery man, was positive that he had seen the mayor kissing Mrs. Sheppard inside her home. On another occasion, he said, he had overheard Mrs. Sheppard give Houk a key to the house and say that he must not let Dr. Sam know about it. Krakan told his tale before the 1954 trial to Katherine Post, a reporter on a small local paper, and also to Bill Corrigan. When Dr. Sam was put on trial for a second time in 1966, F. Lee Bailey called Krakan as a witness.

A babysitter who lived across the street, and who had grown deeply attached to Marilyn, visited her every morning. The babysitter noticed that Marilyn was less friendly to Houk shortly before the murder. Previously when Houk came to visit, the babysitter was supposed to take a cue to disappear. Of late, Marilyn had told her to stay.

This suburban romantic intrigue stirred up razor-sharp rumors. The biggest: Spen Houk was the real father of the baby that Marilyn was carrying at the time of her death. But even Dr. Gerber had pinpointed the time of conception in March, when Dr. Sam and Marilyn were in California. This coincided with statements made by Marilyn before her death and with the information given by Dr. Sam, who said that they had finally overcome some of their sexual difficulties in the latter part of that trip.

Yet another conundrum confused matters even more: Dr. Sam's sense of honor. Whether or not Marilyn was having an affair with Spen, Dr. Sam was going to protect her reputation. He would cover up for Marilyn, in the same way that, after discovering her body nearly nude and beaten, he pulled a sheet over her legs and exposed genitals to protect her modesty. Out of a sense of personal honor, Dr. Sam wanted Marilyn to remain pure and her memory, especially in her son's eyes, to be spotless. When first asked on July 4, 1954, if Marilyn had any male admirers, Dr. Sam had simply answered yes, several, but that he was certain that she was faithful to him. He was irritated that the officers were trying to somehow "blame" his wife. During the 1966 trial, Dr. Sam recoiled when his attorney wanted to introduce evidence that might lead people to think that Marilyn was unfaithful. He let them go forward, but in his own writings, Dr. Sam never allowed that Marilyn was having a sexual encounter. And, in reality, it did not seem likely. While Marilyn's openness and freshness was attractive to men, she was never sexually adventurous.

Once Marilyn Sheppard was murdered, however, stories

of Spen Houk's sexual energy, the undercurrent of lust that he represented, spread uncontrolled through Bay Village gossip. But the real question, like the infidelities of Dr. Sam Sheppard, was whether the gossip told anything at all about the identity of the killer.

Other strange coincidences and unusual activities of the Houks at the time of the murder raised eyebrows. "You don't know how many times I wished we weren't even in Bay Village that night . . . [I wished I were] in Timbuktu or something," said Spen in 1981. Dr. Sam's call to him that morning required a series of decisions, actions, movements. And a lot of people thought he and his wife responded poorly, even oddly.

Why hadn't Spen simply hustled out the door in such a dire emergency instead of hesitating to wait for Esther? Why did they not lock their own doors on the way out? Did they know what they would find? Did they know that the killer was not there because they had inside information—very inside, very personal—about who the killer really was? Why had they not taken a weapon along? At the Sheppard home, why had Spen stayed downstairs, and Esther, without being told, run upstairs to the bedroom, even though she claimed that she had never been upstairs in the Sheppard home before? Why had she said that Marilyn's right arm was dangling, when by everyone else's account it was folded over her stomach? In taking items from the cupboard of a crime scene—liquor and a glass—was Esther trying to establish that her fingerprints might be found at the scene? Could it have been one of them who wiped away the bloody fingerprint that Officer Jay Hubach saw on the bannister when he arrived? Why did Spen encourage his son, Larry, to come down to the scene of such a hideously gruesome crime? Why did Larry view the body of Mrs. Sheppard, touch other items in the kitchen, and then go outside, nauseated?

"Jeez, I used to get crank calls in the middle of the night. Somebody'd call me up . . . 'Hey, Houk, I want to kill my wife, would you help me?' " said Spen in 1981. "It damn near drove me up a tree. And I'd go to the office and try to work and everybody, 'What have you heard?'—about this, about that. I'd stay at home and get crank calls. I'd go over to the market and try to work there, and people would say, I heard this and I heard that. Blah, blah, blah, blah, blah. It was unreal. Just unreal."

Later in the summer, Houk threatened to commit suicide. He said goodbye, as Esther screamed that no way was he going to leave her and the two children holding the bag. Ominously, he walked down to the beach. When he returned, nothing more was said.

Another day, Houk came home, went to his room, and lay down in his bed and sobbed. Spen was haunted. He could not stop sobbing. Esther finally called a doctor, who came out and gave him a shot of tranquilizer to calm him down.

When the pressure was on by the Cleveland police and the Cleveland newspapers for an arrest warrant to be signed, Spen Houk bowed out. He stepped down, claiming conflict of interest, and Gershom Barber, later ruled to have been biased, did the deed.

The Houks gave various statements about who was at home and who was not on the night before. In their final rendition, Spen and Esther walked down to the beach at about ten o'clock and watched fireworks from the breakwater attached to their property, even though the weather was cool and the lake was wild. Esther later watched a television movie, then read until 2:30 A.M., when she headed for bed. Spen did not watch the movie and went to bed earlier. The one thing they agreed upon was that Spen and Esther were sleeping in separate bedrooms.

Sometimes Esther said they were all home together. Sometimes, Larry said he had been on a date and then came home and listened to the ballgame, but he could not remember if Lynette was there, and he couldn't remember what movie he and his date had seen. Esther said that she and Lynette had watched the movie *Strange Holiday,* but Larry and Spen had not. Rumors rolled through the community: that Lyn had a guest that night who had been sent home at two-thirty in the morning; that Spen was fishing; that Spen was setting up a Fourth of July fair; that Larry was out with a girl who was supposed to spend the weekend with him, but the Houks had refused to allow her to stay.

Other details of the murder morning shifted, like the sandy prints that Esther saw on the porch but no policeman ever photographed. Esther said in 1954 that Kokie was in the house when they arrived; in an interview in 1980, she said the dog was not there. Esther said that she saw Dr. Sam's coat neatly folded at the end of the couch; later, she made no comment even though she noticed that it had been moved and was photographed in the middle of the couch. What difference did it make, she thought.

And there was controversy about the fire. Why did the Houks have a fire in the fireplace that morning? Were they trying to burn evidence? Esther claimed that it was cool, and that she loved to have fires. She said that she was burning cannel coal, but reporter Katherine Post, in the Houk home that day, said she saw the ends of large logs.

How is it that Larry Houk coincidentally found the green bag in the brush? Had someone from the Houk side planted it? Questions, human quirks, actions that under the glare of press and publicity didn't seem right.

One decision, one day, is stunningly difficult to understand: July 7, the day of the funeral of Mrs. Marilyn Sheppard. Marilyn Sheppard had visited practically every day with Spen Houk, she had been a friend and neighbor to Esther Houk, she had been a companion and role model for their two children, she had been if nothing else a constituent and associate of the mayor of Bay Village. Yet on the day of her funeral, the Houks stayed at home.

> *Question:* Did you and Spen go to Marilyn's funeral?
> *Esther:* No.
> *Question:* Why is that?
> *Esther:* I don't know. I was trying too hard to . . . trying too hard to be objective. And keep all of that into perspective. And I was afraid [that] if I actually went to her funeral I'd get hysterical. And I said, there is no point in me going to her funeral, this has just been so ghastly, I'm trying to be objective and not get emotional about this whole thing. And, really, we were so tired and worn out with, like I say, detectives and reporters, and we weren't getting any sleep . . .

Afterward, the Houks made their home into command central. The coroner was invited to set up shop in their living room, and he did. Every day for nearly two weeks, Gerber was there. Esther fed him meals. This was, at a minimum, an error in judgment on the coroner's part.

Police officers were encouraged to make their reports

directly to Safety Director Houk at home. Esther often sat in on the conferences. On other occasions, the mayor made a point of going to the police department and reviewing the work on the Sheppard case. Was it then that photographs disappeared? wondered Bay Village police officer Jay Hubach.

Could the Houks have committed this murder? How? Two possible scenarios developed over the years:

Scene 1. Spen Houk decides to drop by the Sheppard home sometime after 12:30 A.M. when the Aherns, his neighbors to the west, have returned home. He believes from seeing the light in the dressing room—the "signal" that Dr. Sam was not home—that the coast is clear for a little good-night encounter. His sense that he will be safe in this endeavor is confirmed when he sees that one of the cars is missing. Although it is Dr. Hoversten's car, he assumes that Dr. Sam and Hoversten are together. He enters by the Lake Road door—either because it is unlocked or because he has a key. Kokie, if present, barely opens an eyelid to see the mayor there, yet another time. Spen doesn't see Dr. Sam asleep on the couch and, from this entrance, doesn't have to pass him. He goes upstairs, believing that he can enjoy a few moments with Marilyn. Perhaps he is so bold as to pull down her pajama bottoms. She begins to scream. Some people envision Spen and Marilyn voluntarily entering into a passionate embrace. This argument is usually prefaced by the statement that Spen did not know that Dr. Sam was downstairs. But if Spen didn't know, Marilyn certainly did. Even if she desired to engage in extramarital affairs, she most certainly would have selected a better time and place than this.

Spen panics, either at her screams or the sound of Dr. Sam awakening, and begins to strike her with some sort of implement that he carries with him—a flashlight or screwdriver or pair of pliers. Dr. Sam runs upstairs. In his fright, Spen strikes Sam. Although he is not as tall as Dr. Sam, and is older, he is a butcher and has a strong arm. After Dr. Sam is knocked out, Spen, suddenly remorseful, begins to clean himself up and set the stage for a burglary.

Spen, of course, knows the house and the property thoroughly, as a practically daily guest. Now he uses that knowledge.

When Dr. Sam returns to consciousness, Spen rushes out the porch door. He only has to get down to the lake, and then he can cross over to his own property along the beach. Whether it is light is of no concern; Spen is frequently on the beach in much greater darkness. It is familiar territory. Dr. Sam chases him, and again, on the beach, Spen struggles with him. His head is big; his hair can bush out. Is this the bushy-haired man that Dr. Sam cannot quite recognize? Spen gets the better of Dr. Sam, who, because he is injured, doesn't put up a good fight. Houk leaves Dr. Sam unconscious in the water, goes home, burns his bloody clothes in the fireplace, and hides the weapon. Since no one ever searches his property, these efforts are unnecessary.

When Dr. Sam phones in the morning, Houk is amazed to know that his neighbor, left for dead on the beach, is alive, and surprised to be the first contacted. But now he must pretend that he has no idea what has happened, and he tries to be the mayor again. But little moments, like his inability to go upstairs, betray his activities earlier in the morning. Given his role as safety director, he believes he will be able to control the situation. Houk carefully arrives at the scene with his wife, and makes certain that he cannot be recognized or identified before calling police in. When Bay Village police officer Drenkhan immediately acts to call in county authorities and the Cleveland police, Spen becomes nervous. His emotions get the better of him. Before the summer is over, he has a mental collapse.

Scene 2. Spen enters the Sheppard house. Esther, furious with his dalliances, trails after him. Because of the darkness, she has grabbed a good-size flashlight. Or, just mad enough to be paranoid or fearful, she carries an implement, a weapon, such as a fireplace poker or a heavy kitchen utensil.

Spen is upstairs. Esther goes in and finds him there. She is enraged. At her presence, Spen backs away and Esther begins to vent pent-up frustrations by beating up her friend in bed. Marilyn cries out. As Dr. Sam rushes up the steps, Spen leaps out and knocks him down. Spen and Esther, faced with one dead body and another unconscious one, and fearful for their own lives and the futures of their children, try to make a plan.

Esther, a smoker, lights up and then drops her cigarette in the toilet bowl. Later, when the two clean up and arrange to cover up, it is a clue they forget. While Esther has inflicted the damage, the chase down to the beach involves Spen. Esther and Spen, according to this scenario, are locked forever in a deadly silence of guilt and violence.

Dr. Sam, in some subconscious recess, recalls seeing them when he awakens, and he places his first call to them. They return to the Sheppards', and when the cigarette is discovered, Esther flushes it.

Allegations began flying in all directions that summer. Houk told Dr. Sam that he should plead guilty, perhaps to a lesser charge. Dr. Sam and his brother Dr. Steve suggested that Houk might fit the psychological profile of the murderer. Houk lost his control, started screaming, "Lies, lies," at Dr. Steve, and even tried to take a swing at him. Dazed by the encounter, Houk then entered a barbershop, sat down, got up, and left, all in seeming shock.

Spencer Houk took two lie detector tests. The newspapers reported that he had not "passed" on questions about whether he was telling the whole truth and about a T-shirt. The tests weren't given until August, when Dr. Sam was already under arrest. Years later, a man claiming to be Officer Jerry Poelking of the Cleveland Police Scientific Investigation Unit told Dr. Steve Sheppard that Spen had completely failed the lie detector test.

Esther, on the other hand, neither failed nor passed a polygraph test. She was asked at one point to take one but never did. She didn't see what purpose it would serve.

Both Houks contradicted themselves on whether they had been upstairs in the Sheppard home before July 4, 1954, and whether they had been in the bedroom in which Mrs. Sheppard was murdered. Spen, in particular, had to backtrack once Elnora Helms described his upstairs visit to take Marilyn lunch. Spen first said he had not seen Mrs. Sheppard's body that morning; later he had to admit that after going home and coming back, he had gone upstairs and viewed the body.

Esther later gave yet another account of how she knew to go upstairs. She said it was just logical, since she could see the living room, den, and kitchen and didn't see Marilyn. Other times, she suggested that Dr. Sam mentioned the stairs, and that was her cue.

As for the fast exit, Spen couldn't have fled down the

steep steps, said Esther. In fact, she said, the reason they had driven to the house, three doors away, was because of Spen's leg. Spen drove virtually everywhere for that reason. Indeed, Spen's car was so often at the Sheppards' that it provoked regular tongue-wagging. But Larry Houk disagreed about just how bad Spen's leg was when interviewed in 1980. His father, he said, was not an invalid and without a doubt could have run down the stairs.

After some of Dr. Kirk's analysis of the crime scene became public, Esther became worried. Kirk's theory that the weapon was a flashlight seemed to grate on her. In June 1955 she wrote a letter to Sam Gerber suggesting that he look for a certain medical instrument that supposedly belonged to Dr. Sam. It might be the weapon that the coroner was looking for. She called it "Sam's 'Skull Cracker' " and said she had only recently heard about it from a friend. Made of chrome-plated metal, it would be easy to clean off, she noted. Dr. Sam supposedly used this item to crack plaster casts. She described it in detail, as if she had measured it: eight to ten inches long, straight at the top, curved at the bottom to a depth of two to three inches in the middle, and so on. Dr. Sam carried it at the bottom of his medical case, Esther asserted, and took it on night emergencies. Since Dr. Sam was already convicted, there was little to gain from passing on this information, unless she was suddenly nervous that Kirk's affidavit would be taken seriously. Esther later said that Gerber informed her that no such instrument, or prototype of one, was located.

The male Houks were predominantly left-handed, although Spen had ambidextrous abilities. Later, there seemed to be a good deal of confusion about which Houks were right-handed and which were left-handed. After Sheppard's acquittal in 1966, F. Lee Bailey asked for an inquiry into Esther Houk, suggesting among many points that she was left handed *in 1954,* and that a left-handed killer was consistent with Paul Kirk's forensic analysis. Bailey's emphasis on 1954 seemed to concede that she was right-handed in 1966. Other criminalists feel that it is not definite that the killer was left-handed. And in interviews with Esther and Larry Houk in the 1980s, Esther denied flatly that she was ever left-handed. In 1994 her grandson remembered distinctly that she was right-handed because she had helped teach him how to write.

Still, other details of the murder led some observers to
consider whether a woman had committed it. The blows to
Mrs. Sheppard were not enormously powerful—while they
had fractured the skull, the bone fractures were not driven
into the brain and the blows had not penetrated the covering of the brain, or the dura. Esther Houk, however,
forty-one at the time, was petite, hardly athletic, and barely
fit physically. The person Sheppard described was about
double her size. Not only was she smaller than Marilyn
Sheppard, but forensic evidence also showed that Mrs.
Sheppard put up a strong fight. Fit, trim, strong, she would
have easily overwhelmed Esther Houk. And had the crime
involved Esther alone, there was no credible explanation
for the evidence pointing to an attempted sexual assault.

Another piece of evidence that raised a woman's involvement were imprints of a woman's bare feet in the sand,
found by Patrick Gareau, a Cleveland detective, on the
beach on July 4. A photograph was taken, but nothing else
was done with it.

In addition, the tiny red chips found on the floor of the
murder room were initially identified as nail polish, suggesting the presence of a woman other than Mrs. Sheppard.
But after extensive analysis, Paul Kirk discovered that the
chips were paint. "There was some speculation as to
whether or not the 'nail polish' implied the presence of a
woman other than Marilyn in the room the night of the
murder. In light of the actual nature of the material, this
supposition also became meaningless. However," he wrote,
"the absence of nail polish would not prove that another
woman could not have been in the murder room."

Dr. Kirk had also described the clear likelihood that the
killer was bleeding. Neither Esther Houk nor her husband
was known to have cuts or wounds on arms or hands. Esther said in 1981 that her blood type was A positive; Spen's
remained unknown.

During the 1966 trial, Bailey prodded the Houks about
their actions on the morning of the murder. Spen and Esther Houk had divorced in 1962. Spen had been drinking to
excess and suffered another nervous breakdown. No longer
mayor, he had given up the meat-selling business, remarried, and was selling cars.

Bailey's goal was to raise for the jury the specter that
there were ways to solve the murder that did not point to

Dr. Sam. As the defense attorney, Bailey's only job was to defend his client, not to solve the murder. That task usually takes all the resources of the state—to interrogate people, get search warrants for evidence, conduct testing. But Bailey also knew from the trial in 1954 that juries can sometimes shift the burden of proof and expect the defendant to prove his innocence unless the defense provides the jury with some possible explanation for the crime. The actions of the Houks showed the jury that there was more than one way to read ambiguous evidence. Through Bailey's skillful cross-examination of the Houks, doubts crept into the courtroom in unnerving ways.

Bailey: How frequently was it your custom to visit the Sheppards in their own home, let's say, in the six months preceding Marilyn's death?

Spen: Well, on numerous occasions.

Bailey: Did you always visit the two Sheppards together, or were there times that you saw one or the other there?

Spen: There were times when I saw one or the other.

Bailey: Which one?

Spen: Marilyn.

Bailey: Were you apprehensive about going over there [after having received the call from Dr. Sam early on the morning of July 4]?

Esther: No.

Bailey: Did you and Mr. Houk have any conversation relative to taking a weapon with you?

Esther: No.

Bailey: Did you have any conversation relative to calling the police?

Esther: No.

Bailey: Was there any reason why you did not choose to call the police at that time?

Esther: Sam called for help. He could call the police.

Bailey: But was there a reason you decided not to call the police?

Prosecutor: Objection.

Judge: Sustained.

Bailey: When you approached the house and pulled into the driveway, did you see anyone from the outside?

Spen: No, sir.

Bailey: Did you look around the outside of the house at all before you went into the Lake Road door?

Spen: No, sir.

Bailey: Did you observe anything unusual about the exterior of the house or its entrance?

Spen: No, sir.

Bailey: Did you have any reason to believe that there was nothing lurking as to danger as to the safety of you and Mrs. Houk behind that door?

Spen: I didn't even think about it.

Bailey: So that you had no concern about one or more killers walking on the premises as you entered the Sheppard home, is that right?

Spen: As I say, I just didn't think about it.

Bailey had other reasons for believing that two people had committed the murder. After Dr. Sam was released from prison, Bailey had engaged Dr. William Bryan, Jr., a California medical doctor who specialized in hypnotism, to regress Dr. Sam to the night of the murder, according to a letter Bailey wrote to Bay Village police chief Fred Drenkhan after the 1966 trial. On that occasion, Dr. Sam was taken to the moment of being attacked in the bedroom, and repeated a conversation between two people in which he supposedly heard: "Should we kill him too?"

Bailey also believed that motive pointed to Esther. He asserted that Spen was having a liaison with Marilyn Sheppard and that Esther had reacted in what Bailey said was a typical "feminine jealous hatred," which, he tried to claim, provoked women to kill. Esther would have this reaction, in Bailey's view, because she was uncommonly unattractive. He also suggested that Esther Houk had dental work done soon after Dr. Kirk's information about tooth chips was made public in 1955.

Esther admitted that she had her upper teeth replaced in July 1955, but it was because her fillings had started dropping out. The Sheppard case was the cause, she said—not because she was involved in the crime, but because of poor diet and worry. And she told a story about having a chipped tooth, but said that it was chipped when she and Spen first married, in some horseplay when he held out his fist and she "walked" into it.

But none of this was connected to the murder of Marilyn,

Esther said firmly. "To have anybody think I would kill and that sort of thing, really . . . I wouldn't swat a fly," Esther said in an interview. "If I was going to clobber anyone I would have clobbered Spen, not Marilyn."

A grand jury convened in 1966 and, according to William Pringle, the foreman, heard evidence about Spen Houk. Houk even testified. "We had the fellow in front of us and had him run in the jury room. He couldn't run—he was a lame man." Of course, it was now twelve years after the murder and Spen was in his late fifties. Nonetheless, Pringle said the grand jury members were convinced that the former mayor had not committed the murder. No indictment was issued, and the case remained unsolved and inactive.

After another sixteen years, in 1982, a fireplace tool was found buried on the former Houk property. Was this the weapon, secreted under the ground? For some, it completed the circle that led to the Houks. But for most, it was merely another mystifying aspect to the Sheppard case.

Picking up the unsolved case in the early 1980s led journalist Richard Dalrymple back to the Houks. Joined at times by Jan Sheppard Duvall, he set up interviews. Spen was in Florida, Esther and the Houk son in Cincinnati, their daughter in the Greater Cleveland area.

Although he consented to an interview with Dalrymple, Spen showed indifference and an unwillingness to discuss the case. He was sick of it. Larry reluctantly gave one of very few interviews. Lynette described the impact of the murder on her own personal life, but had no new insights. And Esther talked repeatedly, repetitiously, about the Sheppards, the trial, the events of 1954, opening up a trunk of things she had collected, including books, magazines, newspapers, letters telling her or Spen to confess, and the letter that she had written to the coroner's office in 1955.

In hours and hours of interviews, Esther claimed variously that Dr. Sam was guilty; that Sam had gotten violently mad at his wife because he wanted oral sex and she bit his penis; that the whole murder was a mystery that would never be solved (that is, that Dr. Sam was not guilty); that everyone would have been much better off if only patrolman Fred Drenkhan had not suggested calling in another jurisdiction. The case should have died a quiet and simple death there in Bay Village, she said.

Jim Chapman participated in several interviews, with the goal of conducting tests on the PSE, or Psychological Stress Evaluator, an alternative to the polygraph invented in 1971. A polygraph detects physical nervousness and body movement, such as unseen twitches that might result from anxiety or agitation. Questions on a polygraph require a yes or a no answer. If the subject shows a reaction while responding, the polygrapher knows that the question is creating stress. Stress does not mean the person is lying, which is why polygraph tests are rarely admissible in court. The indication of stress tells the polygrapher to investigate further.

The PSE detects verbal twitches, that is, stress-related components of the voice. "There are A.M. frequencies that we hear, superimposed on F.M. frequencies that we can't hear. Involuntary responses or muscle microtremors show a pattern when there is stress," explained Chapman. In a PSE test, a person speaks into a microphone, which measures frequency modulations, shown graphically in a printout. Wild reactions, or spiking, indicate stress. As with polygraphy, stress does not necessarily mean a falsehood, but it raises a red flag about something that needs to be followed up with further investigative work. Chapman believes the PSE is a much better tool for investigators than the polygraph.

Esther's PSE tests registered something slightly peculiar. "The charts showed a great deal of stress on related questions," said Chapman, who did not believe that she had committed the crime but perceived her to be holding back, possibly covering up. He couldn't say for certain that she was "clear," but he found nothing to incriminate her either. Using transactional analysis techniques, he tested her at various "levels"—as an adult, a child, a parent. Most stress was in the adult and parent categories.

But many things can give skewed results. If an issue that is touched upon in the interview makes someone feel nervous, even if for a completely extraneous reason, the needles that monitor the voice response wave up and down dramatically. The results bothered Chapman because he had interrogated people in many cases, and he did not get the sense that Esther Houk was involved in the murder. Yet initially he could find no explanation for indications of stress on certain nonimplicating questions. Many years later he had an idea about why some of her responses showed nervousness, and the idea came from her former window washer, Richard Eberling. Eberling tried to implicate Esther. For Chapman, Eberling's statements had the opposite effect. It eased his conscience about the PSE responses by offering an explanation for unrelated stress, and pointed to her noninvolvement.

Journalist Dalrymple knew that Sheppard's 1966 defense team and members of the Sheppard family were suspicious of the Houks. Steve Sheppard wrote in 1993 that he could not "disregard" the Houks "because of their strange behavior during and after the investigation."

After his interviews with the then-elderly Spen and Esther, Dalrymple didn't agree. "I don't think Spen and Esther had anything to do with this," he said. Esther and Spen, he thought, were a couple of plain Midwestern folks, simple, straightforward, pretty banal; "nothing devious." Neither had a history of nefarious activities—nothing even as serious as a traffic violation. He certainly didn't think they were murderers.

Andy Tuney, an investigator for F. Lee Bailey, didn't buy the Houk theory either. "Too far-fetched for me," he said. He didn't disagree with the idea that Spen Houk would have gone into the Sheppard home to pursue Marilyn, if he thought Dr. Sam was out. But then what? "The wife [Esther] is supposed to come in and catch him with Marilyn or something, and she beats up on her. What's the husband do while she's beating her over the head? . . . You couldn't convince me in a hundred years that Houk could run down those stairs at the clip he did, knock Sam down twice. Sam would have picked him up and shook him like a chicken."

There was no deathbed confession of John Spencer Houk when he passed away on August 27, 1981, in Fort Myers, Florida, at the age of sixty-nine. Nor was there one of Esther Houk, when she died on July 6, 1982, in Cincinnati, Ohio, also sixty-nine. Nor did, as some media people reported, Dr. Sam Sheppard utter the name of the Houks as he lay dying in Columbus, Ohio, in 1970.

In 1980 Esther had at least found wisdom about the case. She knew that, despite her hopes and wishes, the Sheppard case wouldn't be content to lie peacefully inside her trunk of memorabilia. "I think I've got every paper, every magazine, every book. And Lare [Larry] accused me of being paranoid. . . . And I said, maybe I am, but boy, I said, the way they have swung this around, I want to see what they come up with next."

Unfortunately, she did not live to hear the story of her former window washer, Richard Eberling. He was about to present a new and different version of the murder of Marilyn Sheppard, featuring none other than Esther Houk.

SIXTEEN

Encounters

For Sam R., the years of coexisting with the tragedy had been filled with constant, churning activity. A voice inside him was alive, but he rarely spoke about the murder. The topic didn't seem appropriate. Other people might already know too much and find it boring, or they might think it was too out of the ordinary, or figure that he was some kind of martyr or freak. They might suddenly become cool, like the woman in the riding club who seemed to cycle off abruptly after someone mentioned his mother, his father, murder.

In an unanticipated way, work against the death penalty and on prison reform and victim reconciliation was activating him, connecting Sam R. to the real world and to the voices inside. He was learning, realistically, how to make sense out of all this experience that had stacked up within him but had found so little outlet before.

The first letter from Richard Eberling, return address in care of an Ohio correctional institution, Sam R. read again and again. "Sam, yes I do know the entire story . . ." Could it be, after all these years, there was someone who had a secret, had kept it, was now willing to tell? Could this former window washer at his parents' house, a figure on the West Side who had amassed property and money over the years, have real information? Sam R. was not going to hope for too much, but, still . . .

Beginning with that first letter in the fall of 1989, Sam R. kept up correspondence. He wrote. Eberling wrote back.

The letters came, in October, November, December. Richard Eberling supplied little particles of information, trying to convince Sam R. that he had private, previously undisclosed knowledge. Always, his sentences were fractured, his language fragmented, just like the pieces of the story that he told.

"Remember one summer morning. Your Mother dropping you off at [your uncle] Richards to spend the day. I was asked to keep a eye on you and your cousin. That was a big mistake on my part, by agreeing. . . . As you bounded across the drive, neat as a pin. You cut quite a figure. As well as your mother. A perfect American family we read about. Except you were one pain in the butt to me an hour later."

He sent a drawing of the property, architecturally accurate, with more detail than those of the investigators, showing the location of furniture, windows, and doors, including those to the basement.

Still, his answers only provoked more questions, such as, Why now? The reason, he said, that he had waited until 1989 to tell his story, when he was already in prison for life, was that he had previously promised Dr. Sam not to tell. "I think they [the Sheppards] considered me family," he explained in an interview later. Plus, at the time, he had not wanted to hazard losing any window-cleaning accounts. Dr. Sam, he said with dark undertones, asked him to "leave it alone." "He had his reasons. So began a nightmare in hell that lasted for years. Because I knew who the guilty person was."

Powerful stuff. The guilty person, he said, was Esther Houk, who died in 1982. "The true facts of Marylin [his spelling] Sheppards' murder have remained a secret to the public, reason being it could injure the reputations or careers of living persons. My reason for speaking out now. Is to help her son to understand what truly happened. This being the events leading up to the murder. The murder itself, and the cover up. Events in part that lead to [Dr.] Sam Sheppards early death."

His letters were spackled with little digs, pinpricks intended to hurt. With one finger he called Sam R. forward in an enticing gesture; with other fingers he poked at Sam R. and pointed in every direction, up, down, in odd places, making unusual claims about the murder of Mrs. Marilyn

Sheppard: "But her death was not intentional so to speak. The pressure build up caused temporary insanity. Then your father was sold a rotten bill of goods."

Eberling wrote again in January 1990, and again in February. Finally, Sam R. decided to make a trip to Lebanon State Prison in Ohio to hear in person what the former window washer, turned millionaire, turned convicted murderer, had to say. Sam R. had talked to people about his ordeal in the past year, had heard tales about his mother's murder. But all of it had been by telephone or by letter. This would be Sam R.'s first face-to-face meeting with someone who claimed to have information about the murder that occurred thirty-six years earlier, when Sam R.'s favorite activities were flying toy airplanes and collecting Native American paraphernalia.

Getting ready to go into Lebanon Prison in March 1990, Sam R. was nervous. There was a slight snafu. He discovered it at the hotel early in the morning, as he was about to go to the prison, twenty miles north of Cincinnati, with a camera crew trailing him. Greg Cook had also shown up for a scheduled visit to see Richard Eberling. Greg, a nephew of Eberling's friend and codefendant Obie Henderson, was handling some of their personal affairs. Under prison rules, another scheduled visit might mean that Sam R., who had laid out a substantial sum to fly from Boston to Cincinnati, might be shut out.

Sam R. talked to Greg. They agreed. Sam R. could have the visiting time for the day. One session in the morning, another in the afternoon.

Arranging a prison visit is not as simple as making airline reservations. Every prison has a slightly different set of rules and regulations. First, there was a visitor's form to fill out. It was up to the prisoner to agree to see someone first, so at Lebanon, a visitor could apply to visit only if the prisoner sent out a form first. If the prisoner was lazy or confused, or too depressed to do anything, as Richard often was, then no visit could be arranged. After receiving the form, the visitor had to answer a series of personal questions about his or her relationship to the prisoner, any convictions in the visitor's record, how the visitor knew the prisoner, and for how long. After the form was screened by prison officials, the visitor was then supposed to appear for a personal interview by prison officials. Since Lebanon is in remote farm country located between Columbus, Dayton, and Cincinnati, this meant a journey for almost everyone. Fortunately, the interview was waived for Sam R., since he was coming from out of state.

Lebanon was a maximum-security prison. Layers of razor wire fences surrounded acres of flat grasslands, with guard towers poking above. There were no trees. In the center of this geographical blankness was the prison, a plain, three-story brick edifice. The only entrance available to visitors had huge wrought-iron gates, which were pulled open only during visiting hours. The waiting room was typical, with pews for people to sit and wait, a desk, and a bureaucratic aroma. Embedded in the floor was the great seal of the state of Ohio: a sun rising over mountains, presumably the Appalachians, field in front with bundled wheat standing, waiting. Waiting with the great stamp of the state: Sam R. remembered it well.

Before entering the prisoner visiting area, visitors removed everything from their pockets, went through a metal detector, and took off their shoes and shook them out. They could take in a handful of change for the vending machines inside, but that was about it. After going through three electronic gates, visitors entered an area set up not unlike a junior high school cafeteria, with square Formica tables and molded plastic chairs. There were none of the little booths with screened windows that the movies always show. At one end of the room, on a raised dais, sat a guard who checked in visitors and kept track of activities. Sam R. took a seat.

Prisoners, who entered through a separate electronic gate after a strip search, had to wear "blues" for visiting—blue work shirts and pants. Sounds of people chattering, children squawking filled the room. On two sides of the room stood vending machines, dispensing candy and coffee in cardboard cups with miniature playing cards printed on the side. The sheer unhealthiness of the diet upset Sam R., and especially, he thought, for the kids who had come so far to see a dad or an uncle or a brother.

Finally, a man came into the room. He was balding, shaved, thin, a bit decrepit-seeming. Richard Eberling. His walk was far from a smooth gait—his body leaned forward from the waist and he loped, as if his tall physique was too much for him to support. Carrying some documents, he sat down across from Sam R. Eberling's arms were long, and sometimes he moved his forearms up and down like cranes as he talked; other times, one hand hugged the other arm at the elbow. He was prepared to talk about the Houks.

Eberling looked very different from the pictures Sam R. had seen. After running a business as a window washer, he had become an interior decorator and turned profits on a slew of deals and real estate. In Cleveland he had become known as a patron of the arts, a benefit giver, a figure in a tuxedo, toeing around the edges of society circles. The pictures from his trial for the murder of Ethel Durkin in 1989 showed a man in an open shirt, with straight dark hair combed down and swept across his forehead. A toupee to be sure, but it gave him a completely different shape, making it seem that his chin was jutting out, his eyebrows more noticeable. Now he was bald on top except for places where flimsy white threads of hair dared to grow. Age spots were visible on his scalp. His face was elongated without the toupee, and his body extended high, seemed uncontrollable. He was already sixty, Sam R. thought, fourteen years older than Dr. Sam when he died in 1970.

How amazing it seemed, to be meeting this man here, under these conditions.

The story Sam R. listened to was delivered by a man who was calm, even congenial. Richard Eberling's voice was well modulated, a pleasant baritone that, with training, might have been that of an emcee or a radio announcer. He liked to talk, diverting pointed questions to rambling stories about well-positioned people he met or knew, or seemingly irrelevant details of his trial.

He explained that he was not guilty of the murder for which he was in prison. In fact, the primary basis of his defense was that there had been no murder, that the supposed victim, Ethel Durkin, had died because of an accidental fall. He was seeking new legal counsel for an appeal, having lost his considerable fortune to lawyers, involuntary bankruptcy, the IRS, and the relatives of the woman who died. And he was especially concerned about his codefendant, Obie Henderson, serving time in another prison. But because of things brought to light about his background during the trial, he had decided to tell Sam R. what he knew.

What lay between the lines? Sam R. steeled himself to get through the rest of the day in the visiting room.

Over the next five years, Richard Eberling would meet in nearly a dozen sessions with Cynthia Cooper, and send over two hundred and thirty pages of letters. Eberling spun out stories that he said gave him personal knowledge of events in or surrounding the Sheppard murder. The perpetrator, he said, was Esther Houk, but Spen and Dr. Sam together were involved in a cover-up.

He had, it seemed, the story of the Houks, Scene 3.

The pieces of his tale veered from time to time. The harder part would come later, and that would entail trying to determine what, if anything, he said was valid. What he had to say was this:

Richard Eberling's company, called Dick's Cleaning Service, had an assignment at the home of Dr. Sam and Mrs. Marilyn Sheppard for Friday, July 2, 1954, said Richard Eberling. At the time, Eberling was twenty-four years old, and this was approximately the sixth time his company had been to the Sheppard home. Although on other occasions he had sent an employee to the house, this day, Eberling said, he personally went to the home.

"The second of July, I arrived about ten of eight. He [Dr. Sam] opened the library door." Eberling said he was invited to have coffee and a sweet roll with Dr. Sam and Marilyn, the only two people there. Young Sam, he said, was not around. They had fresh-squeezed orange juice.

"We were seated not more than five minutes when Spen Houk rapped on the door and said, 'Yoo hoo.' Sam was wearing a light summer suit—one of those white-and-blue things, seersucker, with matching jacket and pants." Spen brought in fresh meats and put them in the refrigerator, remarking that he had worked all night and had several more deliveries to make.

"Spen and I bitched in our business it was always a killer before holidays. Sam said it was just the opposite for doctors; holidays were always hell."

A red convertible pulled in. Marilyn said that the driver was there to pick up young Sam but that he had already been picked up. Dr. Sam said he was on his way out and would tell her.

* * *

Eberling went on about his cleaning work.

"I went upstairs to finish the windows. Meantime, Spen left, when I don't know. Marilyn came up to change the beds and I heard a voice and Marilyn talk back. I was in the inner bedroom. I heard this voice scream out, 'If you don't leave him alone, I'll kill you.' Then I walked by, and Marilyn said very calmly to me, 'Richard, will you do these windows next?' Esther Houk turned and looked at me." Marilyn took Esther downstairs and offered her a cup of tea.

Question: What did you think when you heard Esther's statement?

Eberling: I was shocked and dumbfounded. I laughed it off—two women having a bitch fight. You don't hear that kind of conversation. Marilyn was not upset or emotional. She held everything very nicely.

While he was working there, Eberling saw that Marilyn's slippers were on the side of the bed in the room that had two beds—he called it the guest room. He described details of the room: two "spool" beds, rounded at the corners, with wooden headboards and footboards and white washable bedspreads. There were, he said, Priscilla curtains, a gray carpet, an unremarkable nightstand with a white doily. The slippers he saw on the side of the bed were red satin. "It told you there was trouble in the household, 'cause she was sleeping in the guest room. . . . That's their business. Those are just little things you pick up."

Eberling also said that he was quite clear at this time that Dr. Hoversten was not staying there.

Eberling: I only saw him after the murder. I knew nothing about him until the trial. I'm not even sure he stayed at the house.

Question: Would you have known if he had?

Eberling: In that time frame, yeah. 'Cause Marilyn wouldn't have left her slippers in the guest room. It was the first time I'd noticed it. I didn't assume that [Dr.] Sam was using [the guest room]. Marilyn had the first bed coming in. That would have been the husband's place.

Question: Says who?
Eberling: That was the way things were in those days.

———

Question: Who was sleeping in the master bedroom?
Eberling: Who was in there? *Nobody.*
Sam was sleeping downstairs on the couch. . . .
Question: Are you sure about the date?
Eberling: There is not any possibility I am confusing
the dates. It must have been Friday. The meat was
brought for the Fourth of July.

After working upstairs for some time, Eberling heard
Marilyn call out to him. She had prepared lunch, he said.
"I went down and had lunch. She explained that Esther
was unbalanced, that it was difficult being 'first lady.' Marilyn said she [Esther] was on medication and drinking quite
a bit. Also said she was a sweet gal."

Lunch lasted an hour and a half, during which time Marilyn talked about not only Esther but also herself and Dr.
Sam. The conversation roamed from Dr. Sam being on the
West Coast and the "damn car" he had bought to her need
for a vacuum cleaner. Dr. Sam was unhappy at the hospital,
where they were trying to make him into something he
wasn't; he and Marilyn were thinking seriously about moving back to the West Coast. Dr. Sam was "undergoing a
living hell." Worst of all: Dr. Sam was a workaholic.

Marilyn, according to Eberling, elaborated on Esther
Houk's entry that morning. "Esther saw Spen's car there
in the morning. Spen had worked all night. Esther thought
something was going on. Esther had crazy ideas in her
head. . . . [Marilyn] talked about Spen being a playboy.
With him being mayor, the neighborhood understood. Esther was hysterical and not able to control herself, she said.
It was so easy to call the butcher shop and the order would
be delivered. Spen would come over and shove it in the
freezer. She said she would have to stop. Their house was
in broad view.

"A day and half later Marilyn was murdered. It was
just weird."

Eberling said that he did not know that Mrs. Sheppard was
pregnant until he read about it after she was murdered.
When asked in 1991, he paused, and paled at the thought,

answering slowly. "She didn't show. I'm looking right now, she didn't show. Marilyn wore very California-type clothes—a blouse, a pair of shorts."

Following lunch, Eberling said, he went back to work. And that is when he cut his hand.

> *Question:* Where did you cut it?
> *Eberling:* On the kitchen window, on the lock—damnable lock. There were cheap inserts. I had to grip the inserts to get it off. The pliers came loose. I was bleeding. When I was going upstairs, the blood dripped. It was my index finger of my left hand, along the side. I was dumping it in water. I don't baby myself. I left it alone. I was angry at the situation. The kitchen sink counter was higher than the sink. I had to get the window up and then had to get it to a certain height to get it out. It was early afternoon.

> *Question:* So you had finished with the upstairs?
> *Eberling:* I had to go upstairs. I had one window to do.
> *Question:* What window?
> *Eberling:* The bathroom window. I had to go back up and do it. The door was closed when I was upstairs earlier. My hand was bleeding as I went up the steps.
> I wiped it up.
> *Question:* Was the maid there?
> *Eberling:* No. I went upstairs to do the bathroom window.

On another occasion, Eberling said that he had never been in the upstairs bathroom. In any case, he said that he did not, at that time, go into any other rooms on the second floor, including the murder room.

After Mrs. Sheppard was murdered, Eberling said he confronted Dr. Sam Sheppard with the information about Esther Houk's statement "I'll kill you." During the week of Marilyn's funeral, Eberling said that he was washing windows at the home of Richard and Dorothy Sheppard, Dr. Sam's brother and sister-in-law, who lived next to Bay View Hospital. He is not sure of the day, but it was not a Friday. He had coffee with Richard Sheppard in the morning. Dr.

Richard then went to work, and Eberling began his maintenance jobs. Although Dorothy was there, he said he didn't really see her. "You could get lost in that house. It was big and grand. We didn't run across one another."

Toward the end of the day, Eberling said, Dr. Richard Sheppard brought in Dr. Sam from the hospital where he had been convalescing. Dr. Sam entered the library, where Eberling happened to be working at the moment. Dr. Sam was wearing his orthopedic collar, a suit, no tie, and was walking without a cane.

Eberling took the opportunity to speak to him. "I offered my condolences. Said I was sorry to hear about Marilyn's death. He mumbled something. He asked how I was. I told him, I said I was concerned about Mrs. Houk and her threat. He said, 'Don't let that be a problem. It's all taken care of.' *Richard, leave it alone*—that's what I took it as. I took it as an order. I wasn't the boss. I wasn't going to argue with a customer."

A calendar diary kept by Dr. Richard Sheppard contained sketchy day-by-day notes and makes no mention of the encounter. Nor did Dr. Sam, in his voluminous writings, memoirs, letters or trial notes, make mention of it.

There was another secret that Eberling claimed to know, and which he added to this combustible mixture. Spen Houk was gay, he said. Dr. Sam Sheppard was gay or bisexual, too. And they were having a homosexual affair.

Richard Eberling said he knew about the affair through an employee of his named Ed Wilbert. "He caught them at the Hotel Sterling. Shacked up. He was washing windows there. He told me about it. 'Who do you think I saw?' he told me, like gossip. In the summer of 1953."

On another occasion, Eberling said that all his window-washing clients in the early 1950s were on the West Side. The Sterling Hotel, by contrast, was on the East Side, and had a less than salubrious reputation.

This same employee, Eberling wrote in a letter, had allowed Spen Houk and Sam Sheppard to use his Lakewood apartment for liaisons. "This fellow worked the month before at Sheppards home. He knew Marylin [his spelling] he was checked out by the police and was outa state when the murder occurred. A true honest alibi! . . . Sam used the Sterling Hotel for wild sex. My employee always ended up there when he went on a drunk. . . . Hell, they even had threesomes: three men; two men, one gal."

Eberling claimed that Bay Village police officers came out to his home to talk to him after the murder. Another time, he thought they might have been Cleveland officers. One time, he said it was the summer and the officers stood outside; another time, he said it was in the winter. A review of police records shows no such interview, and officers who in 1959 looked for a 1954 police interview could find nothing either. "I told them the library door and the basement door were not locked."

The evening of Saturday, the third of July, Eberling said, he was at home. He hadn't gone to see fireworks that night; the next night, he was out with his foster brother John, and they went to a movie.

"We had tenants. Vrabec. They said I had been home." Eberling said he went to bed in a second-floor bedroom, although he gave two different times for doing so. "There was no way I had that I could get out. Mother had the house made into a double. I couldn't climb out of the room I was in." Eberling said on another occasion that after 1946 he had slept on the first floor, where a front porch had been converted into a glassed-in room. It had a door that exited directly to the outside.

Eberling further stated that, when questioned by police, he said nothing about the statements he heard by Esther, his supposed knowledge about homosexuality, or the interaction he had with Dr. Sam. "I wasn't concealing. [Dr.] Sam told me to leave it alone. I was taught that what's in one house, you leave it in the house. You don't carry tales. Had I been asked, I would have been very glad to tell. When the police came out, they didn't ask about the Houks. They stood in the hot sun smiling."

Question: Did they ask any personal questions?
Eberling: No.
Question: Did you volunteer anything?
Eberling: What's to volunteer? What's to say? They asked me when was the last time I was there and I told them. . . .
Question: They didn't ask anything else?
Eberling: No.

Question: They asked, "When was the last time you were there?" And that was it?
Eberling: Yes.

As events unfolded, Eberling was disturbed by certain elements of the story that Dr. Sam gave. Specifically, he was upset about the steps to the beach.

"This thing worked on me. There was something wrong there. What [Dr.] Sam said was not correct. You can't do what he said. You can't run out of the house and down the steps without going *through* the steps [because they were in disrepair]. No men could run down those steps like Sam said they did. Sam lied. He didn't chase a man down the steps."

He said he told Dr. Sam about the rotten steps when he saw him at Dr. Richard's house, and "he was fully aware."

But Dr. Sam knew that the steps down to the beach on the Sheppard property had been renovated as part of the reconstruction after a fire in 1953.

Eberling said he made a similar statement to police. No such statement is on record.

Eberling: "Something very silly that the police thought up was that the weapon was a cast cutter. If [Dr.] Sam was going to do it, he would have done it different. And why would he have a cast cutter? If he was going to murder, he'd strike with his fists. Or he'd have had to go get it. I could see if there was a shoe horn next to the bed, he might reach out in a rage and grab it. Cast cutter I don't buy."

Although the Houks were his customers, Eberling said, he never mentioned a word to them about the interaction he had seen. On another occasion, he said that the Houks were not his customers at the time of the murder, but in years following. He said that Esther misunderstood the situation—that Spen was having an affair not with Marilyn but with Dr. Sam.

Question: Did you ever ask Esther about what you saw?
Eberling: No. I considered that family and left it alone. If you're in a neighborhood situation, do you confront

her? Where's it going to go? Go and cry out in denial?
What purpose would it bring?

Why were Sam and Spen so close—out water skiing,
out boating? It was nothing to go swimming together.
They were always together. Should I say, "You dumb
broad, you got a queer husband"? All you do is express
sympathy for the Sheppards and what happened. I think
I was considered as family.

Question: Really?

Eberling: And when things happen, they don't expect
that [you'll go talking about it]. They can trust you.

Eberling said that he had solved yet another piece of the
puzzle. After Dr. Sam's acquittal in 1966, possibly the summer of 1969 or 1970, Eberling said, he ran into Dr. Sam
Sheppard at Sell's ice cream store, on the West Side. It was
midday. Dr. Sam, dressed in trousers and a T-shirt, had
grown out of shape. He told Eberling to sit down, and the
two men talked for about forty minutes. Then they went
on a walk down to an archery range by the lake.

Eberling had been interviewed by F. Lee Bailey and his
investigator Andy Tuney prior to the 1966 trial. They had
even considered calling him as a witness, but "only as a
potential witness to some doors," said Bailey. Ultimately,
he was not called to testify before the jury. Now Dr. Sam
decided to "dump" his story, said Eberling.

"[Dr.] Sam told me who murdered Marilyn. There were
three or four people there. Spen Houk came over after the
Aherns left. Esther was half-bombed. Esther snuck over.
Sam went to sleep. [Spen] gave a hug. Esther just went
wild.

"It was Esther calling 'Sam,' yelling, 'Help me.' Esther
went into his arms."

Dr. Sam, who had never told this story to any other
person, chose to tell Eberling because of "the hell I had
gone through," said Eberling. "Sam never thought they
would get caught. Spen promised immunity. Spen was going
to take the heat off. Sam, being dumb and naive, as a busi-
nessman, he went along with it. I was there when Esther
Houk came in raving mad [on July 2]. This is weird. This
is another world. It jolted me. I didn't pay any attention.
It didn't bother Marilyn. After thirty years, I never told
anybody. I wanted it to die."

From Dr. Sam, Eberling said, he learned that "Esther became insanely jealous. She called him after the deed had been done. She was momentarily insane. It was Spen who sprung the tale about an outsider coming in. [Dr.] Sam was a doctor, but he was not the smartest man on earth. Spen misled him. Got Esther cleaned up, changed clothes. The reason why Sam called so early—it was preconceived. So they could check everything they'd set."

Question: Why would Dr. Sam cover up?

Eberling: That was Spen Houk's doing. Sam wasn't a very bright man. I think it was a shock and surprise. They thought it was a clean route out. No one would ever doubt it.

———

Question: Why would Esther Houk do this?

Eberling: She thought Marilyn was having an affair. Saw Spen Houk there. Spen was supposed to be working all night. Minds work funny.

I think she went over there to beat her up. The tool she had was more like a hammer device. It was a long metal rod attached to an iron mold. A patty shell iron— that's what Sam told me. According to Sam, a person didn't have to have a lot of strength to kill with it. . . . It was anguish. Rage. When she [Esther] came to, she called Sam up. What Sam saw—Esther.

———

Eberling: It cleared my life up when [Dr.] Sam and I talked. I was able to get rid of something that nagged at me. It was a gut feeling.

———

Question: Did you feel sorry for him [Dr. Sam]?

Eberling: No, I felt he made his bed and he had to lie in it. It just happened to be.

The episodes that he had witnessed bothered him intensely, Eberling said. "It bugged me. It drove me nuts. It gave me a lot of hell. Even to this day. I put it out of my mind for twenty-six years. I knew that he told a lie."

On one occasion, while talking about this distress and the possible reason for the fire at the Houks' that morning, Eberling interrupted himself. "Why do women fight back when they are raped?" he asked.

* * *

The weapon—the patty or pastry shell iron—was from Esther's kitchen, Eberling said.

> *Question:* Do you remember the weight room?
> *Eberling:* Yes.
> *Question:* Could a weight have been the weapon?
> *Eberling:* It would have squashed her head open like a squash.
> *Question:* A shoe?
> *Eberling:* No. She could have fought it off.
> When she was hit, she was stunned, wasn't able to respond. She didn't fight back. I don't think so.
> [That's] what Sam meant when he said it didn't take much force to lunge with the instrument. She was stunned or knocked out. Then whoever was doing the murder was hitting a puddle of blood. Sent the blood all over.

Eberling explained the disarray of Marilyn's pajamas, a puzzling aspect of the case, more difficult to understand with regard to Esther Houk.

> *Question:* How does that fit with Esther Houk?
> *Eberling:* Sexual and jealous—she could have been ready to hit those parts. I don't know what goes through the mind . . .
> Going back to the pajamas. That could have been a setup. They set the scene up for attempted murder.
> *Question:* Who said that?
> *Eberling:* I did.
> Sam said they set up the scene. Spen figured out things. He thought no one would look any further into it. . . .
> It couldn't have happened when she was throwing her legs around. She'd be twisting and turning her body. I think anyone trying to rape her would have raped her and done it. What a ghastly mess. That would have to be somebody sick. . . .
> *Question:* In this scenario, how did Dr. Sam get hit?
> *Eberling:* Spen Houk hit Sam over the head. Remember—he was a butcher. He has muscle. He did it upstairs.
> *Question:* Who said so?
> *Eberling:* Sam and a newspaper said it. He was knocked out upstairs in the hallway.

Eberling did not reconcile this statement with an earlier one that Spen was at home, and that Esther, alone, had committed the murder.

On one occasion, Eberling said, Esther Houk had gone on to him about what an ordinary housewife Marilyn Sheppard was, and Esther didn't understand what all the fuss was about. Esther, in contrast, had a "wonderful," happy, glamorous life, he said.

Spen, he said, had played with fire because he was playing with her emotions. She couldn't help herself. "She was drinking and she was on medication. Her mind went like a merry-go-round. When she had done it and stood there with the weapon, Dr. Sam embraced her, felt sorry for her. Her mind was racing. All that thinking about Spen and Marilyn, going on all evening. She had suspicions before. That night she got on a merry-go-round. It was accidental. It was not a planned murder. Just frustration coming out."

This, he said, explained why there were so many blows. "She just beat and beat and beat. Just this insane moment in it. I think she exhausted herself with the blows. She spent her energy, trying to beat something out, a devil or a demon that she had in her mind."

> *Question:* How could she live with it?
> *Eberling:* I don't know. Strong people can fight it.

Dr. Sam lied initially about Esther Houk, Eberling said, and once he had lied, there was no way to go back and tell the truth. "He told a lie because of an affair he had with Spen Houk. All I could think of was, you poor damn fool. He had intercourse at his house and other places—the butcher shop. Spen Houk was anything but an attractive man. That filled in the missing part. Everyone accused Marilyn of having an affair with Spen Houk. I just didn't see it."

In a handwritten document, long and difficult to read, in pencil that barely left its lead on the page, Eberling wrote out for Sam R. the story that Eberling said he had received personally, firsthand, from Dr. Sam. This time, he wrote an account as if he were Dr. Sam, providing a first-person narrative.

According to Eberling, Dr. Sam woke up hearing his

name called. He went upstairs and saw a form in the bed-room—Esther Houk. Sobbing, she sank into Dr. Sam's arms, saying she didn't know what she was doing.

Dr. Sam took her downstairs to the kitchen and ran back to check on his wife. She was dead. He went back and made Esther take off her sweater, which was torn where Marilyn had tried to bite her, and gave her an injection to calm her. He called Spen and told him to come over, quick, and to enter quietly through the library door. He made tea and gave Esther a cup. Her dress and slip were ripped, and blood was in her hair and on her face.

As Spen arrived, Dr. Sam worried about young Sam awakening, so he gave him a tranquilizer, too. When Sam returned downstairs, Esther explained that she had had a fit of jealousy, because she had heard Spen tell Marilyn that he would come over after the Aherns left. She spied on them and saw Spen kiss Marilyn on the forehead. Esther spun into a rage, but went back home.

After Spen had returned and retired to bed, Esther had a few drinks. Suddenly she couldn't take it. She decided to teach Marilyn a good lesson—to stay away from Spen. She left the house, taking the iron mold out of the kitchen drawer. She entered the Sheppard home through the library, went upstairs, and was completely blank about the beating. Yet, in the middle of it all, she became aware of its happening, knew what she had done, and called out for Sam.

Spen took off Esther's clothes, and found a duster of Marilyn's for her to wear home. Spen washed himself off with a couple of towels. The clothes, towels, and Dr. Sam's pants and T-shirt were stashed in a grocery bag, along with the iron mold. Spen took the bag and Esther home, then returned with his plan. Spen would burn the clothes in the fireplace, taking the buttons and zippers off first. They would set up the pretense of robbery and murder, and hide the jewelry. Spen put Dr. Sam's watch in the green boat bag, smearing it with Marilyn's blood and tossing the bag on the lake bank. Eberling claimed the T-shirt was planted on the beach. Dr. Sam, shaken, just sat and listened, as Spen gave instructions to call them first. Dr. Sam trusted his friend, a man successful in politics and business. The set-up, break-in, confrontation, murder, robbery, and es-cape all sounded realistic at the time. Dr. Sam failed to realize that the actual evidence and real proof that would have vindicated him were gone. There was no proof that the Houks were involved. Unable to change his story, he pinned his hopes on being found not guilty. Nobody would have believed him if he had changed his story and told the truth at a later time.

Eberling, writing in first person from the point of view of Dr. Sam, ended his recitation with: "I felt as guilty as the person who killed my wife. Because like a fool, had broken down. Allowed people to use me to save themselves. I in turn brought a long lasting hellish nightmare on my family."

According to what Eberling said Dr. Sam told him, the one and only person who knew the truth was Eberling—because of the threat to Marilyn that he had supposedly heard Esther make on July 2, 1954.

Eberling was certain that Dr. Sam Sheppard had not committed the murder. "I don't think he was smart enough to murder. He was pampered enough he could walk out."

After listening to Eberling in prison, Sam R. was frustrated. Eberling meandered, was alternately nasty and sensational. Sam R. did not believe his father was gay or bisexual. In fact, his overaggressive heterosexuality seemed to be what had caused so much difficulty. Spen and Esther Houk *had* been considered suspects, and his father and uncles had mentioned their names, so there was no attempt to cover up for them. If anything, the Sheppards had been accused of Houk bashing.

By the time Sam R. left the prison, he was mentally exhausted. Media people who had come along, expecting a big scoop that would "solve" the case, urged him to feel duped by a man who seemed to prey on his despair. Yes, Sam R. had drained his financial resources and his emotions. But he felt satisfied that he had made the right decision in coming. Eberling was talking in circles, but maybe if Sam R. let him talk enough, his words and letters would reveal their true nature.

Sam R. returned to Boston. This was not going to be the end of the case, as he had once hoped in a moment of fantasy. More questions were raised than answers given. So many of the principals had died—what could possibly be known? Was it true that Esther Houk had screamed, "I'm going to kill you"? And did that have any bearing on the murder? Had Eberling talked to Dr. Sam about it? Had Dr. Sam even met Eberling in 1954? Did his father participate in a cover-up to protect Spen and Esther Houk? This idea, Sam R. thought, was ridiculous, but he recognized that inferences, no matter how crazy, could be twisted into character assassination that would damage the case. The challenge was, somehow, to test Eberling's statements against the facts, those known, those that could be learned.

The Houk family, too, did not welcome the comments of Richard Eberling. A couple of articles appeared in Ohio after the visit. Cindy Leise wrote one in which the police doubted Eberling's story. The Houks' children, still in Ohio, were in their fifties with grown children of their own. They had kept Esther's trunk and were not likely to forget the memories of the murder episode in their lives. But neither did they need to be reminded.

Dr. Lawrence Houk, son of Spen and Esther, was reached in Cincinnati by Leise. Houk also thought that Eberling's story was totally absurd. He had little doubt that his thrice-married father was heterosexual. His mother, he said, had in no way committed murder.

Esther's grandson was quoted by reporter Jim McCarty in 1994 in the *Plain Dealer* as saying that his grandmother may have made a comment like "I'm going to kill you," but that it was in the context of a card game.

An entirely different response came from criminalist Jim Chapman, who had participated in interviews with Esther Houk in the early 1980s. After testing Esther on a PSE machine, Chapman had been bothered by her responses. Chapman did not think her guilty, but he could never understand why she had reacted with stress to certain seemingly innocent questions. He thought Eberling, perhaps, had hit on one key. Eberling may have heard Esther say, "I'll kill you," or make some other offhand, jaded comment about Marilyn Sheppard at some time or another. "If she made that statement—even innocently—it would explain why Esther Houk had that nervous reaction. She said, 'Spen you're making a fool of yourself' If she had a confrontation with Marilyn Sheppard, if she made the threat 'I'm going to kill you' and then lied about it, she's gonna react, no question about it," he said.

Far from indicating guilt, the pinpointing of underlying

stress, if accurate, wiped away questions about Esther that Chapman had carried for years. Esther's comment, even if in jest, could have tormented her and caused the unusual reaction to the PSE test. Had he known Esther was carrying that burden, Chapman would have phrased questions differently.

But Chapman did not mean that whatever else Richard Eberling was saying was also true. Each statement had to be tested on its own merit. And Chapman was suddenly riveted by something else: Richard Eberling and the possible motive of someone who went to such great pains to provide information that he deemed to be damning to a "suspect" in this murder.

Andy Carraway, the director of investigations for AMSEC, concentrated closely but made few notes when he read over Eberling's statement. He barely paid attention to the comments about the Houks—skimmed through them as if they were so many jumbled hieroglyphics. He didn't really care if anyone was heterosexual or homosexual. His attention was elsewhere.

"This man," he later said, "has made a lot of statements about bleeding at the scene of a murder. This was a bloody murder. He's trying to give an alternative reason for why his blood might be found there."

Carraway had two questions: "Why?" and "Why was no one in authority in Bay Village or Cleveland or Cuyahoga County or Ohio taking a serious look into this man's claims?"

Who was Richard George Eberling, anyhow?

SEVENTEEN

Harbingers

Feel it is never proper to lie. But one can side step.
—*Richard George Eberling*

Before Sam R. had even left Ohio to return to Boston, Eberling had written him another letter, with its usual flaws in spelling and grammar.

Dear Sam:

It was indeed a pleasure to meet you once again.

Sincerely hope you aren't to disappointed by coming to meet me. Am most sorry couldn't give you strong proof. Surely you didn't expect me to have Esther's dress, and patty shell iron. Just kidding! . . . What you do is up to you. Remember one thing, your parents were good people. But they were victims of mental instability among their friends. . . .

Am sorry, but I was studying you the entire time you were here. . . . Your eyes, face are your dads. The complete honesty. Is your Mother, your nails, neatness, but casual dungarees, again are your mother. . . . Admire your wanting to help broken people. Hope you succeed in final results.

Soon he was writing considerably less pleasant letters to Sam R. and others. He had few kind things to say, especially about Dr. Sam. "There is a big difference between [Dr.] Sam Sheppard and ourselves," wrote Eberling "Sam was a pompous ass, who was very selfish. He was given two great opportunities and blew it all. Even ruined his own son's life."

On other occasions, Eberling projected, with gloom, that he never expected to leave prison alive. He felt nothing but disgrace, he said, until he should die. "Now with the Sheppard bull, even in death there can be no peace." Later he would make even more dire comments: "They said you were going to put me in the electric chair. . . . If they put me in the chair, I don't care. I have no opinion about that."

For Sam R., the task at hand was trying to get a fix on the information Richard Eberling was providing, and on the man himself. Soon, like mysterious sinkholes, contradictions would slowly begin to soften the ground under Eberling's statement, even as other parts stood solid as rock. Richard George Eberling would become curiouser and curiouser.

Richard George Eberling in 1954, in a certain pose, had an uncanny resemblance to Dr. Sam Sheppard. People remarked on it many times, Eberling told his client Dorothy Sheppard, Dr. Sam's sister-in-law, in the late 1950s after Dr. Sam was in prison.

Dorothy, the wife of Dr. Sam's oldest brother, Richard, was the first Sheppard to hire Richard Eberling's company, Dick's Cleaning Service. And Dorothy recommended Eberling to Marilyn Sheppard.

The company operated out of the Westlake farmhouse where Richard lived with his foster mother, Christine. Richard started Dick's Cleaning Service before graduating from high school in 1949, and he continued to build the business afterward. He hired other men, usually on a seasonal or part-time basis. By 1954, when Eberling was only twenty-four years old, the business had become an enterprise. A block ad in the Cleveland Yellow Pages for that year had a picture of an old oak bucket and carried copy offering the company's services.

a bucket isn't enough for . . .
A GOOD JOB OF
WINDOW & WALL
CLEANING
IT TAKES
EQUIPMENT

"KNOW HOW" & EXPERIENCE
WALLS • FLOORS • WOODWORK
WALLPAPER CLEANING
SANITAS WASHED
HOUSE CLEANING
MONTHLY WINDOW SERVICE
SERVING WEST SIDE
& SUBURBS
FULLY INSURED
DICK'S CLEANING SERVICE

At the time, Eberling was slightly bigger than Dr. Sam. Dr. Sam was six feet tall and weighed 170 pounds; Eberling was six feet one inch, about 180 to 190 pounds. Eberling's work required him to lift and carry heavy storm windows and screens, ladders, and equipment. His work took strength, Richard said, and he was particularly agile. At twenty-four, Eberling tended to look older than he was. His hair had thinned rapidly, and it bothered him so much to be "bare on top" that he had already picked up the habit of wearing a wig or toupee on certain occasions.

If there were any similarity in the appearances of Richard G. Eberling and Dr. Sam Sheppard, little in their backgrounds was alike. Richard Eberling was an orphan, abandoned by his father and his birth mother. He had no real family to call his own. In fact, Eberling was not even his real name.

His mother, Louise Lenardic, was a nineteen-year-old Yugoslavian immigrant when she gave birth in 1929. She grew up in Cleveland's "Little Croatia," an ethnic neighborhood on the near East Side. From there, the Terminal Tower, just being completed in 1929, was visible as a hazy structure. The lake was only two blocks away, but access was elbowed out by railroad tracks and factories.

Louise's father, Charles Lenardic, rented an apartment on East Thirty-second Street in a slap-dash structure built of utilitarian asphalt tiles. Lenardic's wife died in 1916, after having given birth to seven daughters and two sons. Lenardic had no interest in family responsibilities, drank excessively, and hustled his children out to jobs as soon as possible.

In 1928 and early 1929 Louise was a live-in domestic worker for Richard A. Butler, a salesman for Stevens

Grease and Oil, and his wife. The Butlers lived a comfortable existence in Cleveland Heights.

In the early spring of 1929 Louise, still single, became pregnant. When she went into labor in early December, she went to St. Ann's Hospital, which had a ward for unwed Catholic mothers. The baby was born in a breech delivery on December 8, 1929, and weighed slightly under seven pounds.

By then, Lenardic was no longer with the Butlers, but listed her occupation as "factory work." In the space on the birth certificate where the father was to be listed, big, curvaceous letters said: "Unknown." But "Color or Race" of father was filled in as "W" for white. Something was known. Yet it was another entry that came to terrorize baby Lenardic throughout his life. That was the one that asked: "Legitimate?" The answer was crisp: "No." And perhaps in honor of her former employer, Richard A. Butler, Lenardic chose the name "Richard Lenardic" for the new infant.

What bothered Richard constantly, overwhelmingly, was the fact of his illegitimacy. His good friend Oscar B. Henderson III recalled how deep this feeling ran. "The fact that he was a bastard, he became devastated about that. Like when he was getting a passport, and they asked for parents' names, he just got mad: 'I don't see why they have to ask that!' It bothered him so much."

Many years later, Richard's worldview was still shaped by that childhood emptiness. "Shame my elegant parents just didn't have an abortion, be done with it," he wrote shortly before his sixty-second birthday, in 1991. "Truly not fair to saddle a unborn child with such problems." At other times, he prided himself for having "risen" above his circumstances by operating his own businesses and amassing over one million dollars in assets by 1988. "The odds were pathetic, being born a bastard, many foster homes and an orphanage. Wasn't easy! But come out a winner every time," he wrote.

Always, Richard imagined how much easier life would have been with a mother and a father. He fantasized about families and had grand visions of the importance of the man who fathered him: a world leader, a powerful man of means and consequence. Depending on the occasion, Richard had many stories about his parentage. That they were not consistent or plausible did not bother him.

"Dick is somebody who has always wanted to be somebody with more grandeur. He takes facts and twists them or stretches them," said Peg Baker, his close friend and astrologer.

Later, Richard's heritage would become of major interest after a rumor circulated that he was the illegitimate son of Cleveland chief of police Frank Story, a major player in the Sheppard case. Suburban police circles originally floated the tale in 1959, when Richard, charged with larceny, was treated with a velvet touch. Connections were suspected. At the time Richard was born, Story was thirty-eight years old, married for twenty years, and had one child, Tom. When the Story suggestion was printed in a local newspaper in 1989, Eberling denied the relationship and Story was dead. No one ever asked remaining relatives. Grandson Tom Story, living in Arkansas, laughed about the idea. "Uncle Dickie?—No. He is no relative we ever heard of. . . . It sounds unlike my grandfather."

There may have been a police officer in Richard's family tree, but if so, it was George Anderson, a cop released from the suburban Cleveland Heights police force for intoxication. Anderson, who would have been twenty-nine at Eberling's birth, was tall, good looking, a womanizer, and sometimes considered too clever for his own good. He admitted having sexual relations with Louise Lenardic in April 1929, but unless the infant was premature, something doctors were unable to determine, he didn't think he could be the father.

Richard frequently said that if he were to release the name of his true father, it would "shock the people on earth." He hinted at Prince Edward. "If it were ever let out—every soap opera magazine would be out here. . . . My family is still in power. . . . This would leave the Sheppard murder in the dust."

In 1976 Richard swore in probate court records in New Jersey that a certain Bob was his father. This was also a fake and a lie, if successful and profitable. The documents related to the estate of a woman named Claire M., who died there, and was Bob's sister. Richard collected thirty-six thousand dollars and a host of figurines by stating he was Claire's nephew. Bob, deceased, was not the king of

England; he was a clerk and laborer in Cleveland and a sometimes rowdy fellow. Bob's family members at first believed Richard when he described a complicated scenario that explained how Bob had engendered him. But confidential documents collected afterward showed that Bob was indisputably and completely inaccessible for fatherhood in 1929. He could not have been Richard's father.

On other occasions, Richard had differing stories about the probate documents in New Jersey. Claire M., he said, was his real mother. This was also untrue. Claire M., Richard would say, disappeared at the time of his birth, and Louise Lenardic came in as a "subterfuge" to supply a name for his birth certificate. But a relative who lived in the same duplex as Claire M. in 1929 said that Claire, married at the time, had not been pregnant in any real or surrogate way. Nor did she disappear. She went to work every day and stopped by the relative's apartment every single evening to check in.

In fact, Richard had befriended Claire M. when she bought country property near his residence in Westlake. He called her "aunt." When Claire died without a will, attorneys found a "dear aunt" letter and assumed he was a relative. Happy to accept this windfall, Richard said under oath that it was true and let his imagination fill in where the facts did not.

"There are peasants," said Richard, "and there are royalty. You know where you fit in. I know who I am." But he may not have known at all.

Whoever fathered infant Richard hid in the shadows. He wanted no part of a baby. His mother made a choice, too: unwed and poor, she refused custody and care for the child, did not supply support, and would not sign adoption papers. Louise was considered uncooperative. Five years after the birth, Lenardic was briefly married to William Van Shoemaker, a thirty-three-year-old ballplayer from New Paris, Ohio. Later she married again and moved out of state. Although he often called her "that phony woman" who claimed to be his natural mother, Eberling went to meet her once when she was aged, alone, and in a nursing home in Oklahoma. "Her only question was 'What is a woman to do with a baby?' What could I say? Nothing. That was it. . . . I had no feeling whatsoever. I sat there in total disgust." Louise died in a hospital in 1987, after apparently choking on food.

Richard, as an infant, was channeled into the foster care system. He was placed in foster homes, not once, but five times before he was seven. His first placement, coming after he was kept in the hospital for over six months, lasted only two weeks. The "boarder baby" foster mother couldn't deal with him. As an adult, Richard could rattle off a list of other families, residences where he was moved, sent back, placed again. Child welfare reports that he had reviewed as an adult told the story. The Dynes—to age two and a half. The Hogans—East Ninetieth Street—gripping pains, couldn't walk, couldn't talk, to age four and a half. The Laceys of North Ridgeville—from four to seven years of age. A family in Clyde, Ohio—seven to eight years old.

Always he was rejected for one reason or another. He had blackouts. He was too old, or too young. He was trouble. He ran away. He was trotted out of each house as if he were a broken appliance, useless and not really worth the effort to repair.

He had severe temper tantrums or fits throughout his childhood. The episodes could not be adequately explained, and at age three, he was hospitalized because of them. He would hold his breath until he turned blue. Or he would throw himself on the floor, kicking and screaming, or become unconscious. During one period, he began to walk oddly and would throw his leg out. At times the blackouts seemed to be triggered by fear. When confronted with a new baby in one foster home, he had fourteen spells in nine days. He was possibly epileptic, but no final diagnosis could be made. One foster mother thought that the fits came on unexpectedly and that Richard tried to fight them off on occasion. A medical form completed when he was an adult said that Richard had been diagnosed with Saint Vitus' dance, or chorea. Medical books describe this disease as sometimes caused by rheumatism, resulting in tremors and jerky movements, heightened by emotional stress, and often accompanied by mental instability.

Saying he was born "mal petit," Richard could remember the fits. "I can remember being hurled across the floor. I had a seizure, blacked out. I don't remember anything immediately preceding it." The blackouts seemed to slow down, almost as if by will, at about age six.

Military records indicate that he was later classified as 4-F, physically unsuitable for military service, a classification that Richard attributed to the blackouts. He said that blackouts continued even in 1994, taking the form of dizziness, physical unsteadiness, confusion, his mind churning. What preceded them or caused them, he could not say. "It's like switching a light plate, a light switch," he said.

As a youngster, he did fine on intelligence tests, scoring 97 to 105 on I.Q. tests, although his schoolwork rarely reflected his measured abilities. His behavior was a problem. He was caught lying and stealing. He stole food, notepads, toys from other children, and even the money from a church collection basket. Teachers and foster parents found him to be very untruthful and said that he would never admit that he was lying even when confronted with facts that directly contradicted his story. One foster mother had not questioned his truthfulness because he always gave a reasonable explanation, but became concerned when other evidence constantly disproved him. He was considered uncooperative in school and was never afraid of punishment. He craved attention constantly. When left on his own at home, he would dress in women's clothes, and in one case, ruined his foster mother's shoes. With rare exceptions, teachers and foster parents were at a loss for what to do.

The ugliest side of human nature was revealed to him at the last home, in Clyde, he said, when he was seven. He was sick, from "nerves," he said. He had cramps and shakes. He'd black out. And, he said, he was tied up in the basement. First, he claimed, the family's daughter tied him up. "I can remember. I can see the bitch. I had to get on my hands and knees." Records show that the daughter, nineteen, was in nurse's training out of state most of the time while Richard lived there.

Worse was to come, Richard said. Richard told the story in nervous releases, his eyes focused on a distant scene that he seemed to be watching unfold in full color. His foster father took him to the basement and raped him.

"I was just a little servant boy. I was tied down by my hands and by my feet. No one else was home. They were very cold people. He used a clothesline rope. I don't know why I was tied down. I got a beating. That was how he subdued me. My underclothes and trousers were a mess with blood," Eberling said in an interview.

Afterward, he said, he ran away and hid inside a church. He curled up by the confessional. When he was found, he didn't know what had happened, how he got there. "It was horrible. I blacked it out."

He offered no explanation. Soon, he was ushered off to the Children's Aid Society (CAS), where troubled kids were sent. CAS records make no mention about the incidents he described. No one, he said, probed too deeply. If they had, he couldn't tell them. He compacted it and pushed it deep into some hidden section of his mind. Instead, in July 1938 the eight-and-a-half-year-old was institutionalized, placed in an orphanage that was, to him, the equivalent of a jail.

The whole incident in Clyde came back to him in high-speed recollections when Richard recovered his child welfare records in the 1980s. He never told anyone, he said, except one psychiatrist in Tennessee just as he was about to be arrested for murder in 1988. He never even told his closest friend, Obie Henderson.

"It [the record] just said that something happened at a church. That's when I remembered it. . . . I have never told anybody about Clyde, Ohio. I was in horrible pain and miserable. I can't stand to be confined. That was what scared the hell out of me and why I left the house. . . . I think that man [the foster father] was sick. The pain and the ropes were so offensive. I just had to remove myself. I don't consider it a homosexual act. Any man that would do that to a boy is sick. This man was depraved, he was sick."

Returning to the subject two more times, Richard added cryptically, "I don't think I'm that screwy. . . . I got hit with something so horrible that I can't deal with it. That [mental] compartment where the [Clyde, Ohio] stuff is. There's a lot there. It doesn't do any good to talk about it."

The Children's Aid Society in 1938 handled the hard cases, housing and working with about three dozen children who had experienced a variety of failures in previous placements. Through a tightly planned interdisciplinary program, CAS would try to put the children on a different path.

"I was troubled when I was born. I was troubled when I was five or six," Richard said.

Times at CAS were not particularly fun for kids. There

were no movies, no outings, no games; there were lots of rules. Everything was regimented. The smart kids learned to stuff their feelings, to hide whatever was bothering them, to project their dreams outside the facility. There was only one goal: getting out.

Sundays could be the hardest. For the luckiest of them, a couple might come by after church to take some kids out for the day. "That's where the pang of hurt and jealousy comes in. That's the only time. Years ago, I would have been depressed and hurt. . . . Sheer hell."

That pain never seemed to disappear completely. When Eberling was sentenced to the penitentiary for murder in 1989, fifty-one years later, CAS was right there. "When I started working the dining room [in the prison], a fellow stopped me and questioned me. He thought I might have been institutionalized some part of my life, before coming here. What's interesting, the fellow's a real flake. But he hit it on the head, about Richard," Richard wrote in a letter. Richard often referred to himself in the third person.

One who tried to adopt him from CAS, Richard insisted, was Ethel May Farrow Durkin. Durkin was the woman he was convicted of killing in 1989. Married, she was unable to have children. "Durkins—when they came it was a Sunday afternoon. . . . The [CAS people] told me to leave my clothes on after church. They brought a German shepherd with them," said Richard. Ethel would have been forty-six years old at the time. "Ethel Durkin looked me over for adoption. I wanted that so bad, I was crying. He killed it. Ethel was crying. I often wondered why put a child through that."

In a slightly different version of the same story, Richard said that his "surrogate" mother wouldn't sign off to allow the Durkins to adopt him. "Interesting what a web was spun. By all concerned!" Eberling later met Mrs. Durkin when she was sixty-seven years old and a widow; she recognized him as the CAS child, he said.

But Richard apparently did not share the adoption story with his closest friend. "I never heard that," said Obie Henderson, who held Durkin's power of attorney and shared a household with Richard Eberling for nearly thirty years. "It could be wishful thinking. He wanted to think that."

Ethel Durkin's niece, Arline Durkin Campbell, said that at that time her aunt and uncle were living and working in

Chicago and moved back to Cleveland only around 1939 or 1940.

CAS found Richard to be a tough client. They were troubled by his case history, and his behavior at CAS was problematic. Tall for his age, doctors noted that he had a long head ("dolichocephalic") but, worried that he was not masculine enough, gave him large doses of a growth hormone. He was generally disruptive in the dormitory, bothered other kids, had exhibitionist tendencies, and was considered self-centered, egocentric, and narcissistic. The staff team, including a social worker and a psychiatrist, conducted various tests. Drawings made by Richard were analyzed, not for artistic quality, but psychiatric insight. Together, staff members agreed that Richard showed signs of schizophrenia. "We may see this child develop a definite psychotic state, and there is nothing we can do at the present to help him," they concluded. Other than keeping him in an institution for the rest of his life, only a remote placement in an unpopulated setting would do.

Luckily, the Cuyahoga County Child Welfare Board came up with a placement that seemed like it might work. George E. Eberling and his third wife, the former Christine Klinkner, lived on a forty-acre farm in Westlake (then called Dover), a community far out on the West Side of Cleveland. George, sixty-nine, was getting on in his years, and he needed farm help. Good-size foster boys were a solution.

George's German Catholic father had settled the land in 1875. After owning a building contracting business, George turned to farming at age forty-five. Two wives predeceased him before he married Christine, seventeen years his junior. His own three children had grown children of their own by 1939.

Not only did foster parents get an allowance for taking in youngsters, but the boys could also work the farm. The Eberlings, with two teenage foster boys already, were convinced to add a third-grader, Richard Lenardic. He was taken out to 3961 Bradley Road.

After living in CAS for over a year, Richard had learned a lot. He left CAS with a small fortune—$2.85, more than any kid had amassed, saved from the quarters and nickels that were paid to children for cleaning chores. But the main thing was that at no cost did he want to go back to CAS.

If given one more chance at a foster home, he could cope. "Living in foster homes, you're subject to certain rules. I hate it. I live in a different world. My mind doesn't live in thoughts of yesteryear. I don't think in those terms. I woke up."

Nearly every student in the still-farmlike community of Westlake had a chicken-feeding job to do before heading off to school. As the youngest of the foster boys, Richard's work load was less than the others, but labor was meant to be part of life. Sometimes he envied kids with a life of play. "I hurt to have it. But I couldn't have it," he said.

If he had anger or rage, Richard learned to control it because, he said, that's the way an orphan is taught to behave. The most important thing he had on his mind was security. "That's been a gnawing thought since I've been old enough to think. Six years of age, I can remember people talking about rent, winter." All he ever wanted, he said, were "security and a home of my own."

Life on the Eberling farm would never be the same after Richard arrived. Eventually Richard, the foster child, would live there for nearly fifty years and own nearly all forty acres. He managed to accomplish this as the value of the property soared, and despite the inheritances of George Eberling's natural children.

"Some properties," he pondered, "seem to draw very strange happenings. The farm I spent the greater part of my life on was such a property."

John Eberling remembers when he first met Richard. John was a grandson of George's who eventually built a home by hand a few hundred feet away. He had been a paratrooper in the service and came back to find Richard at the home of his grandfather and stepgrandmother. "I said right then and there, 'that's bad news,' " said John in 1993.

The Eberlings were applauded for their generosity. A feature article in 1945 called Mrs. Eberling "Alias Santa Claus" for mothering three orphan boys. "The last of these boys, now 16 years old, came . . . from the Cuyahoga County Welfare Board. Pictures show him a ragged, pinch-faced youngster when he came to the Eberling farm some years ago. Today he stands over six feet and is a strong and healthy boy." The boy was Richard.

But another picture was forming at home. John Eberling

claims that small items would be missing. The son of a local day laborer, brought along to help in the picking season, was accused of stealing a tool, only to discover Richard had taken it. Gatherings of women, working on charity projects in one room, would find their purses and coats had been rifled in another room.

Then on July 9, 1946, at 11:30 P.M., George Eberling died at home. Although he had suffered from arterial hypertension for ten years and had been sick enough in the previous year to take to bed, George had died rather suddenly. On July 6 he experienced the sudden neurological incidence of cerebral apoplexy. Relatives whispered that someone had switched cough medicine with poison, producing the deadly event.

In 1994 Richard said, "I remember when dad [George Eberling] was dying, I breathed a sigh of relief. I was glad to see him go. Although he was very good to me, he was very strict."

But Richard had a new worry. He was afraid that if something happened to Christine Eberling, the other relatives would put him on the street. Insecurity mounted.

He began to make a plan to get his own property, something he would be able to accomplish because of the type of will George Eberling left. It set up a "life estate" in his wife's name. George left to Christine the use of his property for the rest of her life. Upon her death, the property was then to go to his three children. In addition, Christine was named as the executrix of the estate and was granted authority to manage, collect rents, make repairs, and even sell the property.

The value of George Eberling's property was not great, but it was substantial enough for the times. The land, thirty-nine acres, was valued at $15,600. The remaining assets were buildings on the land, worth only $2,800, and farm property, like a 650-pound black-and-white boar, sows, cultivators, plows, and the like.

Under this type of estate, the executor is to file an accounting once a year, explaining any income or any sale of assets. For twenty years Christine Eberling filed these "executor's accounts." For example, in the first year, Christine withdrew funds to pay for fire insurance and taxes. But in the next years, she began to sell off parcels of property in order to raise cash. The main purchaser was Richard George Eberling.

When George Eberling died, Richard Lenardic was not named as a relative in the obituary. He did not become an Eberling by invitation or adoption. "He's not related whatsoever," insisted John Eberling. In fact, Richard became an Eberling by usurpation.

Richard began using the Eberling name casually in school. Other foster children, such as John Antelic, made no such presumptive effort. Richard told schoolmates that his foster mother, Christine Eberling, was his grandmother. Then, in 1948, he changed his name legally to Eberling.

Although name changes are less complicated than many court actions, it was a sophisticated effort for a minor. At the time, anyone under the age of twenty-one had to have permission from a parent or guardian to take official legal action. John Eberling claims that no one in the family was aware of the change; Eberling said he did it because his foster mother wanted it.

Richard filed a petition in the Probate Court of Cuyahoga County in downtown Cleveland, on August 31, 1948, with "Alice Hart" named as "his guardian as next friend." John Eberling had never heard of her. No other probate court or juvenile court documents list Alice W. Hart as Richard Eberling's guardian. Eberling once suggested that she was a social worker with the county welfare department. On the form, Richard Lenardic said that "his name [Lenardic] is difficult to pronounce in English and being continually misspelled." He asked that his name be changed not merely to Richard Eberling but to Richard George Eberling. After formalities, such as legal advertising and notice, the petition was signed by a judge, and Richard officially became an Eberling, if not a "real" Eberling.

Within two more years, this change of name came to work nicely to Richard's benefit as he bought up the property that was once owned by George Eberling.

In high school, Richard Eberling was a loner, an outsider. "He stuck to himself," said Barbara Smith Moorman, who attended high school with him. There were only fifty-three students in Eberling's 1949 graduating class, then called

Dover High School and later Westlake. Everybody knew everybody.

In all the years of high school, Richard never had a date, to the memory of those who knew him best. He was nice enough, tall, thin, with decent looks. "Kind of chiseled features," said Phyllis Zemek Beyer. His dark hair was long in front, swept up in a high wave above his forehead; it was some time after graduating that he began to go bald and wear various sorts of toupees.

In his school courses, he used to get by, but that was about all. Although notably quiet, Richard flared up from time to time. "If a teacher questioned his answers and pressed him, he would lose his temper," recalled Beyer.

But sports were king at the school, and virtually every boy was drafted to participate. Athletes were not just the center of attention, they were the only recipients of attention. Eberling was not on any sports teams. "Compared to all the other boys, the athletes, he was the type you could consider a nerd," said Sally Hutcherson, a friend.

"I worked all my life. We didn't have time for sports. I would have liked to. I would have liked basketball, volleyball, track. I had fast legs. I ran in track and I did good in it. But I wasn't allowed to participate. Mrs. Eberling kept me from it . . . my mother. She was very possessive. Extremely possessive," said Eberling in 1993. "I feel gypped. I wasn't allowed to do much of anything. . . . I was not allowed to do anything social either. What can you do when you're an orphan? Nothing. I took it all. I didn't say anything. She [Mrs. Eberling] was bigger than I was. She was an adult and I was a school kid." He added: "I didn't object. I held it all inside. I was miserable. . . . I felt shortchanged."

In the meantime, Richard began to make his own way by starting his window-washing business. "I was interested in one thing—accounts receivable and how much money was in," he said.

And he began to turn to what became a major preoccupation, buying property, and specifically the Eberling farm. Richard says he bought property from Christine in high school. The first formal deed was filed in February 1951, shortly after Richard turned twenty-one. He had arranged a very good deal, purchasing a major subdivided tract from Mrs. Christine Eberling for a sum of nine hundred dollars.

The relationship with Christine was mixed. She wouldn't even give him a key to the house until he was twenty-eight years old, he said. Richard was high strung, and often fought her "tooth and nail." Yet his presence offered company to her, and she had no children of her own. By 1951 Christine was in her sixties. She was despondent and dependent. Income was a problem, and selling parcels of land was a solution. Richard quickly realized the potential in the widow's situation.

Christine signed over an "executor's deed under will." It showed Richard living at a different address, 30952 Center Ridge Road in Avon Lake, Ohio, perhaps to eliminate any odd questions that might arise. But he need not have worried. The name change was successful. No one thought to question a transfer of property from George Eberling to Richard George Eberling. Even experienced title searchers assumed was a natural heir who had inherited the land.

This initial purchase worked out so well that Richard repeated it. And repeated it. He filled transfers of ownership for tract 13 on July 13, 1956; tract 16 in January 1962; tract 14 in August 1965; and the original tract 6 with the house on the day after his birthday in December 1965.

"I don't know how Richard Eberling got his hands on my grandfather's property," said John Eberling, shaking his head. "A lot of shenanigans, a lot of shenanigans." Each slice of real estate that was sold off by an executor's deed under will was yet another piece of the Eberling estate that would not be passed on to the legitimate Eberling heirs.

The Eberling heirs were unaware that property was being transferred to Richard and subtracted from their inheritance. None had the time or inclination to make the arduous trip downtown and check county property or probate records. By July 1962, after Richard acquired his third major parcel, suspicions were aroused. For the most part, it was too late. An attorney, asked to look into the situation, reported back: "Mrs. Eberling is still living in the family home, with some small amount of land on which the home is built. The rest of the land has been sold; but she will continue to live in the home until her death, as the life tenant."

Even this matter went unheeded when Mrs. Eberling was placed in a nursing home by Richard very soon afterward. She was in her seventies, and senile. She did not live in the home as the "life tenant," but her foster son Richard and his friend Obie Henderson did. As of 1965, Richard also owned the house and the land surrounding it, buying it for sixteen thousand dollars. Christine Eberling died in 1969.

After the property was purchased by Richard, he and Obie Henderson transformed the old farmhouse into a showcase home, with antique reproductions and exquisite rugs. John Eberling was not impressed. "My two aunts used to come by on Thanksgiving, and they would walk down to 3961 where they grew up and say, 'It looks so nice, rugs and all.' I'd say, 'But where'd he get it?' "

The motto of Dick's Cleaning Service was: "We are expensive but we care." That, said Richard, brought in the trade he desired.

In addition to the Sheppards, Eberling worked for clients up and down Lake Road in Bay Village, including the Schueles and Bruscianos, directly to the west of Dr. Sam and Marilyn. He knew the neighborhood well.

Richard said all his clients were on the West Side in 1954. Most of his one hundred to two hundred accounts were homes, but he also had Interlake AlumLand, an office that sold gutters and siding; Danko Metal Products, a small fabricating company; Lifetime Distributors, a pots and pans firm; and at least three church parish houses. He used his own solution of water and hard brown vinegar, instead of ammonia, with a small dose of Blue Sheen carpet cleaner added. The cleaning business was booming.

In 1953 he purchased a new blue Ford station wagon and traveled to cleaning sites, carrying his own ladder in six-foot sections stowed in the back.

"From Day One, I had a call to do their windows," said Eberling of the arrival of Dr. and Mrs. Sam Sheppard in their Bay Village home. They first contacted him for window service in 1953, he said.

That was the same year that he first stole something from a client, according to statements Richard made in 1959 to Bay Village police and to a psychiatrist. His thefts from clients were more restrained in 1953 and 1954. From 1955 to 1959, though, cleaning out customers was a regular avocation. In 1959 he was finally arrested for grand larceny.

In May, when Marilyn called, Eberling first sent Ed Wilbert, someone who worked for him on and off for nearly ten years, and another fellow. "They came back and said there was a beautiful gal, cute. White girl, white shorts. They couldn't believe it. It was like a breath of fresh air," said Richard. "They said, 'Wow, what a dish.' She looked like the cover of a magazine. California influence—tan, a different manner of dress. Women were wearing cutoffs around their knees. Marilyn wore them up—tight."

Richard saw for himself when he went to get paid for the work that had been done. He collected personally after each job was complete. Mrs. Sheppard was girlish, more like a high school or college student, he thought.

He met Marilyn six times, he said. Marilyn showed him how to enter by the den door, which she said was left open so that young Sam could get in after school when she was at the high school coaching girls in basketball. The den door, hidden from the street, was next to the cellarway entrance, also unlocked. He explained: "There was a trap door to the basement—you go outside to go in; then you can go to the first floor. In those days, nobody locked the doors."

He met Dr. Sam in the fall of 1953, he said, when he went personally to do the winter changeover, going one day and returning the next to finish. "Sam was at the breakfast table. Chip [young Sam] was at the table. Marilyn introduced me to Sam. I had coffee with them. He had a tweed sports coat with a muffler. Chip was dressed for school. It was a sunny fall day. . . . I was a young kid. It was sort of you're interfering on a private family breakfast. . . . I was rather nervous. Sam sat there with a snarl on his face." It was nothing, Richard noted, like breakfast at the homes of his foster families. At the Eberlings', he could only remember huddling in the corner of the table. Here, there were just the three of them.

Question: Did it make you jealous?
Eberling: When I was a boy—It didn't make me jealous, it made me feel bad. I wanted that very badly. Wishing you could have had that, it's not jealousy. . . . Jealousy is when you're unhappy that somebody has something that you don't have. Jealousy is a horrible, horrible illness. . . . Once you're in somebody else's home, you find out it's not what it's cracked up to be.

For one thing, Richard said, he never liked Dr. Sam Sheppard. "He was arrogant. Condescending. An indifferent attitude. One of the problems I had, he used people and thought he was a gift to mankind. . . . He had a lot of arrogant mannerisms. . . . I thought, 'Who the hell does he think he is? Where is he coming from?' "

If Dr. Sam met Eberling, he didn't recall anything of it in notes that he made during the case, scouring his memory for landscapers, hospital workers, contractors. Marilyn Sheppard took care of organizing their household, hiring workers when needed, giving job assignments, and even paying them. Had Dr. Sam seen Eberling on the street in 1954, it is quite possible he would not have recognized him.

Marilyn Sheppard set the tone in the house, Eberling said, describing it as warm but not hospitable. He described her as "a little removed, but not arrogant. She had qualities of a fine groomed lady." He opined on another occasion that Marilyn was "one of the golden girls from the East Side," the women who were "highlights of the season," "the rare catches." Even though Marilyn's mother died when she was seven, Eberling pointed out that she was raised by aunts. "She was pampered and spoiled," he said, "pampered and spoiled."

His circumstances were different—unfairly so, he thought. "I was an orphan, she was a golden girl," he said. "I think she was class-conscious. The way she lived, the way she was raised on the East Side. The East Side was raised to think they were better. Just like Bay Village looked down on people in Westlake."

But, he said, Marilyn Sheppard was very lonely; he knew this, he said, because she talked to him.

The next job on the property was at Christmastime. He sent Ed, he said. And the next time he went back was around Valentine's Day. "She was getting ready for some kind of party," he said. "I went in the middle of the afternoon. It was too cold on the lake in the morning. I knocked on the library door. I let myself in. She came in later, she had [young Sam] with her. I went about my work. She was doing whatever. She wrote a check in Sam's office. Sam was on the West Coast—she bitched a little about that. It was ice gray."

Eastertime was his next visit to the Sheppards', he said.

The weather was beautiful. Young Sam was playing outside and was bugging Eberling. Marilyn came out with a tray of brownies and milk. "We went down to the beach. He [young Sam] was hanging on the railing. She warned him. She told me to be careful on the steps. They were dry-rotted. They told them when they bought it. She told me when I came in the summer I could use their pool house and go for a swim."

In a letter to Sam R., Eberling described this April story as occurring in June. It was one variation among many, written in his halting, stop-start style.

"In June. . . . You were giving me a hard time. Your Mother caught you, and we laughed. The three of us had cookies and milk. Then she took us down to the beach. You were not allowed to go down by yourself. Was told I could swim anytime. Bring a towel and suit. Change in the cabana. Of which was down near the lake. Your Mother warned us to be very careful. The steps were not secure, rotting away. She told you not to swing on the railing. That was a project in the future for your father. Only problem he turned a deaf ear. The entire stair and railing needed repair in the worst way."

Whenever this supposed walk to the beach took place, Eberling did receive a check dated June 24, 1954, from Mrs. Sheppard. Richard claims he returned again on July 2, 1954, the Friday before the holiday weekend. The check for this summer work was cashed nearly two weeks after it was signed, on July 7, 1954. That was the day of the funeral services for Marilyn Reese Sheppard, three days after she was murdered.

EIGHTEEN

Julys

Less than a year before he died, on July 8, 1969, Dr. Sam testified before a congressional committee about prison conditions. "Having spent a number of years in incarceration, I have become quite familiar with the destructive conditions that prevail," he said.

Dr. Sam turned back his memory to those painful years inside the Ohio pen, recalling an instance in which two prisoners had fought and one stabbed the other with a rough tool. The injured prisoner, a habitual criminal, was taken to the penitentiary hospital, where Dr. Sam worked. Sheppard supervised the hospital workers as they gave the man multiple quarts of blood, stabilized him, and were preparing him for surgery. A deputy warden, checking on the injured prisoner's condition, suggested to Dr. Sam that the man deserved to die. "He said 'retribution'—let the man die. And this sickened me as a physician and surgeon . . . to me this represents murder if it should be perpetrated."

At the hospital, they did the "proper" thing. The man did live, Dr. Sam reported to the committee. "And maybe this man could be saved. Who knows. He certainly could have been when he was a youngster."

On his first attempt to visit a prisoner in 1991 with the Family Awareness Program, Sam R. had been turned away. The initial attempt to go through gates similar to those he had known so well from ages eight to seventeen had gone awry. The dress code for visitors at the institution forbade jeans. Sam R. knew that the rules could be arbitrary, capricious, strict, and yet he had failed to check them. He wore jeans. It was a lesson and a reminder. He sat and waited while the other members of the group made the visit.

When he did meet with prisoners and later with death-row inmates in several states, Sam R. treated a prisoner's handshake with the greatest seriousness. The hands, Sam R. thought, had much to say.

He could remember his father's hands—healing hands, the hands of a surgeon. As a dental hygienist, Sam R. could be called upon to do intricate work with his hands, manipulating tools inside people's mouths, where nerves are extraordinarily sensitive.

The hands of the prisoners engrossed him, because hands, it seemed, did most of the work. Hands could do the caring, and they could do the killing. Often when he met with the prisoners, they did not want to discuss their crimes or the legal intricacies and appeals. They just wanted to talk. And yet Sam R. would wonder about their hands, if they had pulled the trigger on a dark night, or held knives, or clubs, or strangled, hurt, slapped, fought.

Delicate instruments, the hands were. They took orders unseen, from somewhere inside, Sam R. thought. And that led to the minds of the killers. The minds might be calculating, doing their killing and dirty work in the equations of business, drug profit and loss. But more frequently, the minds of the inmates he met reflected confusion, had acted in a haze of alcohol or narcotics or incomprehension. They were often shocked themselves that they had committed such acts of violence, and they sometimes persisted in denying them rather than face the grotesque reality. One prisoner, a multiple murderer, related the extreme mental torment he had suffered upon confessing, an action that required him to finally acknowledge the evil deeds that had occurred by his hand. It was, the inmate told Sam R., the hardest thing he had ever done; he thought suicide and death would have been easier. Sam R. did not excuse their acts; he wanted to understand why. They had ridden to the brink and, for some reason, could not put on the brakes and halt and turn back.

"I do not say any of these people are good guys," his father had said at the congressional hearing. But, his father believed, no matter what, each prisoner deserved to be treated humanely.

Similarly, the minds of killers that he met were not what people thought. People seemed to believe the prisoners had committed rational acts, made willful decisions. But more often, he was aware, when they touched palm to palm, that the prisoners were people in pain.

Richard Eberling did not tell the police in 1954 about cutting his hand at the Sheppard home, or about the Sheppard doors being unlocked, or about the basement entranceway, or about the path to the beach, or about the rotten back steps, or about the Houks. The police never questioned him. And Eberling did not volunteer.

A thorough search of police records collected through public information releases, attorney documents, writers, former Eberling employees, Sheppard files, and private sources revealed no officer who talked to Eberling in 1954. Eberling, who was ever conscious of money, did not present the information that he later claimed to have when a ten-thousand-dollar reward was offered by the Sheppard family.

When Eberling came to police attention for theft in 1959, he told Bay Village officers that he had been interrogated in 1954. According to Bay Village files released in 1994, "Lt. Hubach checked but could not find any record or statement that Eberling had been questioned or given this information to anyone."

Many things had happened to Richard Eberling from 1954 to 1959. Eberling's life had indeed taken strange and unusual turns. The month of July, in particular, had brought Eberling in touch with peculiar events, just as it had when he was first sent to the Children's Aid Society in July 1938.

On July 23, 1955, the year after the murder of Mrs. Marilyn Sheppard, a flash fire mysteriously burned the barn of Eberling's foster mother, Christine Eberling. Richard had just driven home.

A newspaper account said that the fire destroyed the barn, chicken coop, and garage. Mrs. Eberling was treated for shock. Firemen arrived three minutes after the alarm, but found the barn burning out of control.

"Mrs. Eberling's son, Richard, 25, arrived home at 1:30 A.M., parking his car near the barn," the article said. "A few minutes later the barn roof burst into flames."

Richard explained. "The cause of the fire was heat. Combustion. Hay in the loft. It was in the evening, 10–11 o'clock. I had just gotten in and the barn broke out. I went out and moved the car. I am the one who called the fire department."

The fire destroyed everything in the barn, including landscaping equipment kept there by John Antelic, another foster son. Insurance paid off, but relatives grumbled that the proceeds went to Richard and not Antelic.

"When that barn burned down, he made a hell of a lot of money," said Ronald DuPerow, a police officer who was part of a theft investigation of Eberling in 1959. DuPerow believed that Eberling had stored furniture in the barn and made insurance claims on it. What piqued the curiosity of police was the statement of a paperboy who, delivering newspapers early on the morning before the fire broke out, saw someone loading furniture onto a truck, as if the barn was being emptied. When questioned about it in 1959, DuPerow said Eberling became belligerent.

The fire stopped dead the efforts of Mrs. Eberling to keep her deceased husband's farm in operation. She began offering hay that grew on the property to anyone who would come and cut it and take it away.

July 1956 was even more traumatic for Eberling. On July 5, 1956, two years after the murder of Mrs. Sheppard, he was involved in an incident that would affect him for years. Eberling and a woman whom he was dating, Barbara Ann Kinzel, left for a holiday outing in eastern Michigan, one hundred miles away.

Kinzel, a nurse who worked for an oral surgeon in downtown Cleveland, was three years younger than Eberling and lived with her mother and five younger siblings in Avon Lake, another West Side suburb. "I started seeing Barbara after Marilyn died," Eberling explained. Like Marilyn Sheppard, she was dark-haired and pretty. An honors student, Barbara had been awarded a full scholarship to a Cleveland nursing school, and had graduated third in her class. She was hardworking, serious, and very concerned about doing everything right, said her sister, Nancy Espy.

Eberling met Barbara when he accompanied his foster mother to the wake for Kinzel's father in December 1955. The Kinzels lived on a farm about a mile from the Eberlings', and Barbara's father had helped out on the property from time to time. In January 1956, Eberling asked Barbara out. "Someone told me, 'You found her, don't let her get away,'" Eberling said. Later, it was common for him to exaggerate the duration of their dating by years and to describe Barbara as his fiancée. Barbara's sister said the relationship was far from a serious one.

Early on the morning of July 5, Richard and Barbara left for Michigan, to avoid the heavy holiday traffic. They rode in Barbara's car, a 1954 red two-door Ford convertible that she had recently purchased with her own earnings. At 11:25 that night, Richard was driving. Richard said, variously, that they had gone sailing at the Grosse Point Yacht Club, or that they had gone to the Cinerama and were trying to find Lake Erie's western shore. They were cruising south along the Dixie Highway, U.S. 25 in Monroe County, Michigan. A two-way paved highway, it was heavily traveled but unlit and rural in this area. Skies were cloudy, but there was no precipitation; roads were dry.

Barbara was reading the map, trying to find the way, when Richard suddenly saw the back end of a stationary White truck. One time he said he was driving thirty-five miles per hour; another time he said fifty to fifty-five miles per hour. The truck, a southern fruit transporter, was parked on the asphalt drive of a closed gas station, off to the right of the road. There was no shoulder. The left tail of the truck stuck out onto the highway, said Eberling. In the darkness, and without lights visible on the back of the truck, Eberling didn't see the vehicle. The headlights on the car he was driving were low, said Eberling. There was a blinding of lights, he said. Suddenly, his car rushing forward, he saw the truck. Too close. He swerved. A head-on crash was avoided. Still too late. The right side of the car smashed into the rear left of the truck.

"I hit the windshield myself and I was stunned. I reached over for Barbara. And she was down on the floor. I was bruised on my head, my forehead and cheeks," said Eberling. "I looked over and saw darkness. I touched her, got nothing. I called her, got nothing, no response. I wasn't scared. I didn't see any blood. There was no blood on me."

The rest was a haze. He hailed traffic. People stopped. He wandered into a field, then was piled into an ambulance, and next awoke in a local hospital. Police reports said he had a "bump" on his head. He asked a doctor what happened. The car was totaled, the doctor said, and Barbara Kinzel had been killed. She was twenty-three years old. "It was a jolt. It was unbelievable. I called my mother [Mrs. Eberling] from the hospital. . . . I told her we had an automobile accident and Barbara had died. She was horrified. . . . I asked her to go see Barbara's mother and tell her and she did."

The truck driver, Ira McConnell of Hammond, Louisiana, said that the vehicle was parked six feet off the highway, and denied that it hung out onto the road.

Kinzel, according to the death certificate, died of a "basal skull fracture." The traffic incident report mentions lacerations. Exactly how the basal skull fracture was caused was left unexplained. "Barbara broke her neck hitting the upper part of the windshield," said Eberling.

In Monroe County at the time, autopsy records were kept only by the funeral director who was authorized to conduct the autopsy. Central records were not maintained. An autopsy on Kinzel was authorized by Harold Maurice, the proprietor of a funeral home and also county coroner at the time. The old Dixie Highway had many accidents, said Daryl Bennett, who took over Mr. Maurice's funeral home in 1965. Autopsies were conducted in traffic accident cases only if there were something unusual at the scene that made the coroner suspicious of foul play. "If you go out and somebody's head is crushed and you can see the crushing of the head and that it was sufficient to cause death," no autopsy would be conducted, Bennett said. Maurice, who went to the scene, decided an autopsy was necessary. Afterward, he marked "accidental" as the cause of death. His full records were not kept after he retired.

The official traffic accident report filed by the Monroe County Sheriff's Department was exceptionally limited on details. The officer stated that the initial point of impact of the car with the truck appeared to be on the road, four feet from the edge, as Eberling had said. Eberling, who had many minor traffic infractions on his record in suburban Cleveland communities, was not cited with any violation.

"She was killed instantly. He walked off, just a couple of scratches," recalled Barbara's sister, Nancy. Richard said that after Barbara's funeral on July 9, Mrs. Kinzel went through photographs and gave him ones that he wanted.

"It would have been a good marriage," said Eberling, who never married. "Mother liked Barbara."

Eberling claimed that he returned to Michigan for an inquiry into the other driver. No charges were filed. Still, the truck's insurer rushed through a settlement of $5,025 to Mrs. Kinzel for the car, funeral expenses, and wrongful death claims, securing in return a full release from any and all damages. The death was so hurtful to Mrs. Kinzel, also recently widowed, that she never looked into the accident too deeply, said Barbara's sister.

Afterward, Eberling said that he just coped. "That's the way Germans do," he said, referring to the ancestry of his foster father, George. "They just go on, live with their misery and sorrow." By July 13, 1956, Richard was coping well enough that he was able to record the purchase of tract 13 of the Eberling farm, his second major purchase.

In July 1954, two years to the day before her death, Barbara Kinzel had been employed at the Sheppards' Bay View Hospital, according to records found in 1994 among those kept by attorney Bill Corrigan. Despite the hours that Richard Eberling spent talking about the Sheppard case in the 1990s, and proclaiming at the same time his irreplaceable love for Barbara, giving descriptions of her family, taste, car, education, and job, he never once mentioned that she had worked for the Sheppards.

As it happened, on July 6, 1954, Barbara, only twenty-one, had been the attending nurse for the recuperating Dr. Sam Sheppard. And on July 4, 1954, Barbara was the nurse on duty, just finishing up the night shift when the hospital faced an early morning emergency. She watched as Dr. Sam was rushed in. Barbara later gave her own verdict on the Sheppard case to her sister: "I don't think he did it," Barbara said. "He was so beaten up."

The years from 1956 to 1959 were tumultuous for Eberling. "Hot fingers" is how Dick Eberling described himself in those years of the late 1950s.

"I got my butt in trouble after Barbara had died and this Marilyn Sheppard murder. I started lifting small items from my clients. I was trying to draw attention to myself, to come out without the truth. Instead of staying all locked up inside," Richard said in 1991.

In 1994, Richard recalled these events again.

Question: Do you remember stealing?

Eberling: Very vaguely, yes. As fast as it [the memory] came in, I put it out.

When I was arrested for one item, I told about all. And then I put it out of my mind. I was trying to get caught and then to be forced to have to tell about the Sheppard affair.

In 1959 Eberling went to see a psychiatrist, Dr. Louis Karnosh, at the Cleveland Clinic, because of the thefts. The doctor, Eberling said in 1991, "was an evil, ugly man. . . . I wanted to jump out the window, he put me down so bad." The doctor "told me I was hiding something and till it came out, I wouldn't have peace."

Question: Didn't the psychiatrist put you in touch with your feelings?

Eberling: Not really. He shook me up.

Dr. Karnosh said I was suppressing Marilyn Sheppard's murder and I was doing the stealing to have a showdown.

He told me it was not my nature. It's not me. It's not what I am about. It's most unusual for me.

He tried to explain on yet another occasion: "I was trying to draw attention about this murder of Marilyn Sheppard. I knew who murdered her. With what happened to Sam and family, it drove me nuts. . . . [Dr.] Sam wouldn't let me say anything. . . . I was told by Sam Sheppard to keep your mouth shut. . . . What I knew had a bearing. When I brought it out to Sam, he told me to leave it alone. . . . I never liked Sam Sheppard and yet I had that damn feeling of caring."

Yet despite all this internal pressure, the desire for "a clean house," as he called it, Eberling admitted that he did not tell all and clear the slate. "Even when I was arrested I felt a sigh of relief, but I still didn't come out with it. I can't explain it," he said.

When first arrested in November 1959 on charges of grand larceny, Richard Eberling voluntarily pulled out a vast collection of items that he had stolen and gave them to officers George Jindra of Rocky River and Harold Wilbert of Westlake.

Eberling had been suspected in West Side suburban

thefts for several years. In 1956, after four complaints from citizens, Bay Village police used marked money to try to catch him, but the bait money was not taken. Officers from Fairview Park, another West Side suburb, recorded many complaints of money and property missing in homes he had worked in, but stated that they never found "sufficient evidence" to press charges.

Cash, gold pins, wristwatches, rings, jewels, diamonds, sterling silver spoons, sterling serving dishes, a piggy bank, Steuben glass, Royal Doulton figurines—all went from the shelves and the drawers and the dressers of his clients into his bucket or pocket and out the door. They were small items, easily concealable, no mess, no fuss. Eberling did not rip apart property, leaving piles on the floor. He stole nothing with serial numbers, nothing that could be traced with ease to the owners. There were no cars, no checks, no keys, no wallets with identification. If anything, he tried his best to put things back where they were, so that people wouldn't notice that something was gone. Sometimes he would steal an expensive rug or a Doulton and replace it with a less valuable but similar item.

At times, people did notice missing items. Eberling would express his concern. In one instance, Eberling was washing windows in a suburban house when the gas meter reader came. When Eberling was done with his job, the householder went to pay him and found her pocketbook emptied of cash. Eberling politely suggested that he thought the gas man had done something funny. The woman called the police, and the gas man was picked up, strip-searched, and questioned before being let go.

On another occasion, a man who worked for Eberling, Donny, was accused of stealing a diamond ring, until the police realized that Eberling had probably done it. At one Bay Village home, Eberling inquired whether a particular item was a Royal Doulton figurine. The woman said it was. When the figurine disappeared with him, the woman called his home, and a man answered and said, "Dick was always misplacing things like that and it would probably turn up in the next few weeks." Eberling sent back another worker to search for it. "I related to a friend that maybe [she] was right that Dick couldn't be trusted," the woman told police.

Finally, in 1959 Detective Jindra had a call about the window washer stealing ninety dollars in cash. The man who called had been downstairs, lying on the couch and watching a football game, when he heard a creak on the floorboard upstairs. He found the money missing from his wallet, left on an upstairs dresser. The only other person around had been the window washer, who had set a ladder against the outside of the house and, it seemed, climbed in. There was, noted Jindra, only one logical suspect. Once before, Jindra had gone out to talk to Eberling after a Rocky River minister complained about a missing diamond tie tack. Christine Eberling had started screaming at Jindra and threatened to sue.

This time, Jindra went out with Harold Wilbert, an officer in Westlake who had distant family ties to the Eberlings. Eberling confessed. Figurines were located around the house; jewels were stashed away, removed from their settings. Eberling knew exactly where each had come from, the name and address, and when he had taken it. In addition to money, which he kept, some officers believed that he fenced property in the area of Michigan in which he had the car accident that killed Barbara Kinzel. Two truckloads of stolen items were carted away from Eberling's home, according to Officer Ronald DuPerow of Bay Village. One canvas pouch was filled with diamonds that had been plucked from their settings. All told there were tens of thousands of dollars of valuables, enough to close more than one hundred larceny cases in West Side suburbs.

Even the officers were surprised at one item Eberling pulled out from the back of a drawer. He kept it apart from his other stash. Wrapped in tissue and hidden away was a ring that had belonged to Marilyn Sheppard.

"I had it probably a couple years," Eberling said. The ring, one diamond with several diamond chips, was valued at several hundred dollars. It had been stolen from property stored after the murder at the home of Dr. Sam's brother Richard. Dorothy Sheppard, Richard's wife, said that she missed the ring about six months earlier, but had not considered that it was stolen. She thought that Dr. Sam had requested her husband place it elsewhere.

Eberling explained in 1993:

> *Question:* Did you take Marilyn's ring?
> *Eberling:* I took Marilyn's ring.
> *Question:* From where?

Eberling: From Richard's home.

Question: Did you know it was hers?

Eberling: I didn't know.

Question: Why did you take it?

Eberling: I think I knew it was her ring.

Question: Why did you want her ring?

Eberling: I don't know.

Bay Village was the site of dozens of Eberling thefts, including ones at the homes of the next-door neighbors of Dr. Sam and Marilyn and of Dorothy and Richard Sheppard. The Bay Village police were very interested in talking to Eberling, and they wanted, among other things, to know more about the theft of Marilyn Sheppard's ring.

Eberling told Bay Village police that in the spring of 1957 he had stolen a silver dish and a Belleek china vase and pitcher from Dorothy and Richard. "No one was home and I just walked out with them."

Then, in March 1958, he was called again to do some cleaning at Dorothy and Richard's house.

I went to the house with my employee, Ed Wilbert. I started and finished washing the walls and closet in the master suite. . . . I ran across several boxes containing the personal belongings of Marilyn Reese Sheppard. I found one box containing two diamond rings which I removed and put them in my pocket. This box had writing on it which said "Marilyn Reese Sheppard personal property." It was an old cardboard box. I replaced the boxes back on the shelf as I had originally found them. Then I took the rings home with me and I took the smaller ring and took the stones out of it and I discarded the setting by throwing it in the trash can at home. Then I took the big stone out of the bigger ring and saved the setting with the remainder of the stones intact. These stones about which I am talking are diamonds. I saved the stones and also the bigger setting because I did not have time to dismantle the other stones in this bigger ring. I put them in a bag and then put them in my dresser behind the drawer. . . .

Question: Had you ever seen these rings before you took them from Dr. Richard Sheppard's home?

Eberling: Yes. I had seen the large dinner ring lying

on Marilyn Sheppard's dresser in Dr. and Marilyn Sheppard's home before she was murdered. I believe it was the fall before she was murdered. . . . I admired this ring at that time but I didn't take it.

When questioned further by Lieutenant Jay Hubach and other Bay Village officers, Eberling said that he had worked for Dr. Sam and Marilyn Sheppard in the last week of June 1954. Eberling said that he was at the house alone, and that he washed the windows and inserted the screens.

> *Question:* Do you recall what date you performed this work?
> *Eberling:* It was the early part of the week of the Sunday preceding her death.
> *Question:* Did anything happen to you while you were there?
> *Eberling:* Yes, I cut my finger in an effort to take the storm window out of the window by the kitchen sink and in doing so I went about my work throughout the house and down into the basement and at various times dripped blood in various parts of the house.

Bay Village officers were mildly alarmed. They wanted to know where Eberling was on the night that Mrs. Sheppard was murdered. Eberling, living on Bradley Road with Christine, said there were guests at his house that evening who left about eleven-thirty P.M. Eberling said he then went upstairs. He "shut the door and looked out the window, opened it and went to bed."

Although Dr. Sam stood convicted for five years, Chief John Eaton, still at Bay Village, could not forget this most trying moment. He had been stung by the arrogant attitude of the Cleveland police department, by the cocky way that a reporter had described Chief Eaton's only duty as following the school buses around. Even though he had testified for the prosecution, questions had always remained. Officer Jay Hubach, now Lieutenant Hubach, had actively disagreed with the prosecution of Dr. Sam.

Eberling's statements were far different from those of others in the police files on the Sheppard case. Eaton and Hubach knew the little-acknowledged fact that many things had been stolen on the night of the murder, even though the newspapers and prosecution had always emphasized what was *not* stolen. Dr. Sam and Marilyn did not have Royal Doultons or fancy silver trays. Their mementos, valuable only to them, such as the athletic trophies, were smashed on the floor. What items of value that they did have were taken, sometimes off bodies. In addition to the theft of money from Mrs. Sheppard's purse and Dr. Sam's wallet, Dr. Sam's watch was pulled from his wrist, Mrs. Sheppard's watch was pulled from her wrist after she was killed, and the chain with the onyx ring and gold charms was ripped from Dr. Sam's pants. The only visible items of value that were not stolen were Mrs. Sheppard's rings, and someone had seemingly tried to remove them from her fingers. The rings had been pulled up to the knuckles, leaving bruises, but the rings didn't or wouldn't come off.

Eberling's spontaneous statements about bleeding in the house—although he described a date nearly a full week before the murder—were unusual. And Chief Eaton may have noticed the arrest and identification record on Eberling, which recorded a half-inch scar on the inside of his left wrist. A suicide attempt? A cut on an artery or vein, the type of bleeding wound that would drip steadily, possibly unnoticed in the dark?

On November 11, 1959, according to police reports obtained in 1994, Eberling was questioned for a second time by Bay Village police about his relations with Marilyn and Dr. Sam Sheppard. Patrolman Ronald B. DuPerow wrote a report: "After stating that he cut his finger about four days prior to the murder and had dripped blood all over the downstairs of the Sheppard home *he changed his statement,* that he was all over the house with his finger dripping blood. He also said that he went to bed at 11:30 P.M. the night of the murder and *changed his story* and said that it was after 1:00 A.M. He said that he told two Cleve. Detectives this and also that Sam and Marilyn never kept the house locked. Lt. Hubach checked but *could not find any record or statement that Eberling had been questioned* or given this information to anyone" (emphasis added).

The officers asked Eberling if he would take a lie detector test. He agreed. Lieutenant Hubach arranged to transport Eberling to Shaker Heights, on the East Side, where one of the few decent polygraph operators in northeastern Ohio was located. When Bay Village officers arrived in

Shaker Heights, the polygrapher told them he was not allowed to give the test. His chief said they didn't want to get involved. County approval was needed.

Bay Village was miffed. Officers took a formal statement from Eberling and delivered it to Cuyahoga County Prosecutor John T. Corrigan. Corrigan didn't even look up. Officer DuPerow wrote: "11-12-59. Thurs. County Prosecutor Corrigan told us to drop the whole thing."

Chief Eaton perhaps felt he had been pushed around enough, and he wasn't going to stop there. He went straight to the top, Coroner Sam Gerber. Dr. Gerber said he wanted to talk to the man. "I remember him very clearly standing over me to talk to me," recalled Eberling.

DuPerow's official police report stated: "At 1:00 P.M. this date [11-12-59] Lt. Hubach and myself took Eberling to Gerber's office and he talked to him until 4:30 P.M. and then had Eberling dictate a statement. Gerber stated that he would arrange to have a Lie Detector test set up, or possibly a Sodium Pentathol test."

But things changed by the next day: "11-13-59. Gerber notified us that he had decided to not give the test. He said he believed Eberling and didn't think he was involved in the murder."

Whatever happened between the twelfth and the thirteenth of November obviously had had a riveting effect on the coroner. He, like other Cleveland officials, was going to hold the line.

Frustrated, Bay Village officers continued to seek a polygraph operator. Officers settled for a test by the Ohio State Bureau of Criminal Identification and Investigation, and one was arranged at a prison in London, Ohio, for November 19, 1959.

Two years earlier, in 1957, when the Sheppard murder was only three years old, Dr. Gerber had vociferously objected to the polygraph testing of Dr. Sam that Erle Stanley Gardner wanted to conduct in the Ohio prison. His objection was that since three years had passed, a polygraph test would not be valid.

A test was conducted on Eberling by A. Kimball, and a report was sent to Chief Eaton by Hugh Leggett, superintendent of the Bureau of Criminal Identification and Investigation. The report found no deception on questions "relevant" to murder; Bay Village authorities were so skeptical about the actual test and analysis, however, that a reevaluation of the polygraph was ordered in 1989. The interpretation was dramatically different. The expert conducting the new evaluation, head of the prestigious Polygraph Institute of the Department of Defense, was certain that the test was no good and was not to be trusted. The physiological data were insufficient to render a diagnosis of truth or deception, the expert said. Technical problems were rife. Three critical questions related to Eberling's knowledge of the crime scene were too ambiguous for evaluation. Too many questions had the blood pressure cuff inflated at an unacceptable level. And on several questions a deep breath was taken at or after the question.

The exact technique used on a lie detector test is significant. How a question is posed is as critical as the subject of the question. If a question is imprecise, a person can answer with no reaction. For example, a polygrapher might ask, "Did you steal?" But in the subject's mind, he borrowed, intending to return an object. He answers "no," and no reaction appears. If he were asked, "Did you take . . ." the reaction might be entirely different.

The 1959 test of Eberling was too poor to be evaluated because reactions were not "specific, significant and consistent." The test was not merely inconclusive, but completely useless.

Even Eberling said that he was hiding a substantial amount of information that he claimed to know. He mentioned nothing about the steps to the beach, Esther Houk's threat, the supposed homosexuality of Spen Houk or Dr. Sam, or Eberling's confronting Dr. Sam. "I wasn't concealing," he insisted in an interview. "Sam told me to leave it alone."

Bay Village police didn't need a lie detector test to know that Eberling was lying. He lied directly to the investigators. He came in and told different stories on multiple points: the date at which he was at the Sheppard home; what he did there; his activities on the evening of her murder. A polygraph test is only supposed to tell the investigators what areas to pursue in their interrogation. Polygraphs don't give answers; they point to areas for inquiry, like scents for a police dog to trail. It is the follow-up that counts, and that can happen with or without a polygraph.

With few resources at its disposal, Bay Village did no

more. No effort was made to check on any other aspect of Eberling's story, according to police documents released in 1994. Corroboration of where he was, people who worked for him, records, neighbors—nothing further was sought.

"When someone asks me why didn't we arrest Eberling," said Fred Drenkhan, a member of the police force at the time, trying to reach back, "it wasn't a high point." Eberling was passive, compliant. They didn't think he was "clever" enough. "He was a sneak thief, a small-time operator. Faced with this stuff, he grabbed it and took it," said Drenkhan.

And what else could they do in a suburb with limited authority? Ultimately, it came back to the county. Bay Village couldn't prosecute a felony—only the county could do that, and that meant Dr. Sam Gerber and John T. Corrigan. Gerber had said no, and he would be in office for the next twenty-six years. John T. Corrigan had said no, and he would be in office for the next thirty-two years.

For whatever reason, Bay Village officers decided in less than a week—in less time than was spent interviewing Dr. Sam Sheppard on virtually any single day of the month in every week of July or August 1954—to forget about Richard Eberling. Dr. Richard Sheppard was advised to pick up the rings of his former sister-in-law, Marilyn. Eberling was dismissed.

For Eberling, it was a watershed. "If I had been the slightest guilty," he reasoned in 1994, "they would have pulled me in." That was the end of Richard Eberling's name in Bay Village files until 1988.

In November 1959 Dr. Louis Karnosh adjudged Eberling to have an immature personality, obsessive-compulsive neurosis, and to be "in dire need of prolonged psychiatric care."

An indictment for grand larceny was sought on the ninety-dollar Rocky River theft and was issued on December 8, 1959, Eberling's thirtieth birthday. On December 15 he plead not guilty and posted bond. Eberling's attorney wrote to thirty-three individuals and jurisdictions, said Eberling, offering restitution. Officers didn't make a big fuss about filing charges, so long as cases were cleared off their books.

When the county prosecutor suggested a plea agreement

to the Rocky River police, officer Jindra objected. The one charge represented many thefts. Still, it went forward on a plea. On February 5, 1960, Judge Charles W. White in Cuyahoga County accepted a plea to the lesser included offense of petit larceny and recommended probation. On April 1, 1960, Eberling was sentenced to a fine of three hundred dollars, plus costs, and ninety days in the workhouse. The ninety days were suspended.

Eberling, for his part, said in a 1991 interview that he didn't lose a single customer over the incident, including Dorothy and Richard Sheppard. His customers were his family, his friends. They understood, he insisted.

Dorothy Sheppard remembered differently. "Naturally I did not contact him for window care . . . after the police called re the theft," she wrote.

The whole incident might have gone by completely unnoticed if it were not for two minor paragraphs printed in the newspapers in November 1959. One was headlined: "Admits Stealing Ring of Marilyn Sheppard." After the theft charge, Richard Eberling was trying to get his life together. In 1960 he had one fortuitous turn of events. He met at a party Oscar B. Henderson III, known as Obie.

Both Richard and Obie were alone. Both were talkers. "They could sell you about anything," recalled one acquaintance. Obie talked about having sent a gal in Boston a plane ticket to Cleveland; she instead cashed it in and flew to California. Richard talked about the car crash in which Barbara was killed. "We were in the same situation. His was more tragic, of course," said Obie, years later.

Obie was about Eberling's age, only four months younger. But he was more worldly, better educated. He had a college degree and had been in the navy for four years, ending in September 1954, and had served on the USS *Newport* carrying the Sixth Fleet in Europe. He then worked for the Chesapeake and Ohio railway, which transferred him to Cleveland in 1957. He decided to stay in Cleveland, switching to a clerical job with the Norfolk and Western railway, he said.

Raised in Tennessee and the midsouth, Obie presented a jovial "good ol' boy" charm. He could talk to everyone, tell jokes, wriggle an unwilling smile out of the reluctant and gloomy. He played tennis and handball, did calisthenics, lifted weights. Where Richard was tall and angular,

Obie was stockier, filled out and not as tall. Where Obie had residual religious roots, Richard's deepest beliefs were in astrology. Eberling wore a scarf tie or a bandanna and sometimes looked like a bumpkin; Obie was a perfectionist as a dresser, sharp and stylish. Eberling had a "bunch" of wigs, at least a half dozen, different ones, different styles for casual and conservative, mostly expensive ones of real woven hair purchased at top dollar from PermaHair on the East Side. Obie had plenty of his own hair, usually cropped short, sometimes with a tussled boyish look, and sometimes underscored with a frothy mustache.

They hit it off right away. Richard bought Obie a dog. Obie and the dog moved out to Bradley Road, occupying the upstairs rooms. For the next thirty years, Dick and Obie were to be friends and companions: living together; traveling together to Mexico, Japan, and Ireland; entertaining together; buying property together; writing wills naming each other. "I think Dick showed a lot of respect for me . . . because I do have a formal education and he doesn't," said Obie. "I think he and I are affable."

Imprisoned in separate institutions in 1993, both had fond recollections of the other and their years together. Obie recalled one time when they were taking a car trip together with Obie's four schnauzers. At the time, Dick and Obie had a substantial amount of money. They stopped at a motel, and the clerk asked how many. "I said, 'Two people and four dogs.' He wouldn't rent us a room. He said the dogs would urinate on the carpet. Dick said to him, 'Listen, this place is a comedown for the dogs. They normally sleep on couches. They each have their own.' " Obie chuckled at this memory. "We stayed there."

While Dick could get depressed, Obie packed optimism in his bag. "I picked up 'crepe-hanging,' " said Richard, always expecting the worst, as people in the old world did when they hung black crepe on their door when a death occurred. "I learned quickly from Henderson to get off it." Dick's friendship with Henderson helped him overcome possessiveness and envy, he said. "Obie—he loves to laugh; very disciplined, a perfectionist." Richard, in talking about Obie, could hardly hold back tears. He didn't deserve to be in prison, Richard insisted.

Both say that they are not homosexual or bisexual and were particularly offended by a magazine article that made it seem that they were. "They don't know. That's just an assumption. They don't care if it's true. It doesn't bother me. They don't know and that's what kills them. They get by with writing it and they don't need to prove it," Obie said. When asked directly, Obie answered firmly: "We didn't have a gay relationship. Richard is my friend."

Eberling described their life together: "He does the laundry, I do windows and cleaning. He goes his way, I go my way. Either one would fix supper, otherwise back on your own. He pays utilities, I pay groceries, so we don't fight over money. If he wants to have a party, I pitch in and help. If I want to, he pitches in and helps. . . . We just share."

The closest he has ever been physically to Obie, Richard said, is a handshake. He described the many women who had an interest in Obie, including Patricia Bogar. After Barbara Kinzel died, Richard said, he never found a true love.

If they sometimes had spats and tiffs in the presence of company, and some people assumed that they were a couple, mostly they traveled the same roads without much hassle. They were a linked pair, housemates with intertwining personal, social, business, and investment ties—a duo allied beyond a mere "Odd Couple" scenario.

Whatever the nature of their relationship, Obie and Dick developed a tight emotional connection. Upon this they agreed. Richard often referred to Obie as "Obie my brother," even though they were not related and Richard, as he seems to have sometimes told people, was not at one time a foster child in the home of Obie's parents. Obie explained: "I'm the only family he's got. He's got absolutely no one. No kinship." He added: "I have a good bond with the world. . . . I try to give him encouragement."

Despite their closeness over a thirty-year period, they also kept secrets. Obie didn't know about Richard's burglary record until many years later, when articles about Eberling's history came up at the same time that his competence as a designer for City Hall was questioned. "I'm not a prober," Obie said. "I'm interested in people, but only if they tell me. If people want you to know something, they will tell you. If not, they will lie."

Obie had known Richard for three or four years before the Sheppard case came up, and then Richard just said that he knew the Sheppards back in 1953–54. Nor was Obie aware that Richard had seen a psychiatrist in the 1950s or that he was so distraught. "I think he keeps things locked away," Obie said.

For his part, Obie never mentioned that he had been married when he was younger or that he had a son. "It was something that happened very fast. It's not part of my life. I didn't think I had any reason to share it," Obie said. "I'm a very independent person. So is he. He purchased his own clothes. So did I. We traveled together. We're both individuals. We shared a house. I didn't try to run his business and he didn't try to run my business."

Richard, when he heard about Obie's marriage and son and grandchild, was flabbergasted. He couldn't understand why a father wouldn't want to see his child. But it was Obie's business, he decided.

With Obie nearby, Eberling became more refined, sophisticated, acculturated. Richard had a way of soaking in and incorporating the ideas and personal mannerisms of others. And with Richard's knack for building up monetary reserves, the two of them were able to live well. Richard brought endless ideas on how to support a luxurious lifestyle; Obie brought his comfortable ability to befriend others.

On the day after his thirty-sixth birthday, in 1965, Richard completed the purchase of all the remaining land in George Eberling's estate. Dick now owned the farm. Together with Obie, Richard transformed the old farmhouse into a showpiece. Reproductions of antiques, which Eberling considered more valuable than antiques as an investment, were placed liberally. Charcoal or red wallcoverings, antique silk draperies, a crystal chandelier, Oriental rugs, and exquisite china created an atmosphere that put it on a "unique homes" tour. A writer on the Westlake Garden Club house tour described "the elegance of a 19th Century French salon." A Japanese garden and reflecting pool were added outside. They called it "The Hermitage" and had special stationery printed up.

As entertainers, they made a terrific pair. "People loved those guys—they thought they were great," said Mike Roberts, former editor of *Cleveland Magazine* and former reporter at the *Plain Dealer*. Obie, who worked as chief copy boy and then assistant to the managing editor at the newspaper, was well liked, competent, and fastidious. His sense of humor was notable. Although Richard was "nice enough," people were more wary of him; his manner was sometimes off-putting.

"Dick was a con artist. And he was very good at it," said Peg Baker, an astrologer and one of his closest friends. "A professional con artist. We knew it. He was a nice guy. You knew you didn't want to get into business with him. He could be a fun person. He could be caring and giving."

Eventually Dick and Obie both became close to a client of Richard's, Ethel May Durkin. Eberling became her personal caretaker; Obie held her power of attorney and handled her business affairs.

Two decades of mystery, intrigue, and murder began to surround Ethel May Durkin and her sisters in the 1960s. "They were very nondescript," reflected Richard Eberling of the elderly women. "But wow, what happened to them."

Richard met Ethel May Durkin when he was trying to think of ways to expand Dick's Cleaning Service. The exact date Eberling began to work for Ethel Durkin is unclear, but it was some time after 1957, when her husband, William Durkin, died. The first time Eberling went to the house, Durkin assigned him a job that he found distasteful, requiring him to snake through a crawl space. He was furious. But then, homey-like, she sat him down, made him a sandwich, and offered him a drink. "Ethel," he once described, "was very shy and afraid of people. But once the ice was broken, you have a friend for life." Or as he said another time, "Once she met and broke the ice, she wouldn't shut up."

Durkin lived in a grand house at 1052 Maple Cliff Drive in Lakewood, a large West Side suburb. The house was at the end of a street, and one of its special features was a screened-in porch that had a magnificent view overlooking Lake Erie.

The Durkins had moved back to Cleveland from Chicago in 1939 or 1940. William Durkin had been the vice president of Whitmore Manufacturing, a specialty oil firm that served the Great Lakes region. From 1917 to 1940 Ethel was his secretary. She was business-savvy, outspoken, brash, and, as often as not, doted on by her husband. At Ethel's insistence, William held on to stock he had received as compensation. When the company was sold, the stock's value was half a million dollars, which he left to her when he died.

They had never had any children, although Ethel had suffered a miscarriage at one time. Neither of Ethel's two sisters had any children either. The oldest sister, Sarah Belle Farrow, born in 1891, remained unmarried and was as mousy as Ethel was tough. After retiring from her job as a sales clerk at a department store, Belle moved in with Ethel. The youngest sister, Myrtle Fray, born in 1898, moved to an apartment near Ethel's house in 1961, but on the Cleveland side of the suburban border. Fray had retired from work as a telephone operator, and her husband, Bert, died when Fray was in her early sixties. Unlike Belle, Myrtle held her own with Ethel, willing to spar and not mincing words.

Eberling became friendly with Ethel, undertaking more and more household chores. If nothing else, in his years of living with Christine Eberling, Richard had learned about widows. They had plenty of household work to be done; they were needy, dependent, and isolated; and they loved attention. That he could provide. Windows and widows made a good combination.

"She was lonesome and she could pay for him," said Ethel Durkin's niece Arline Durkin Campbell.

Helen Hodge, a widow herself, had been married to a Durkin relative and thought that Dick Eberling was a nice fellow who was good to Ethel and gave her much-needed help. Hodge moved to Duluth, Minnesota, about five years before Ethel died.

Durkin loved to talk about her money. She found a willing listener, a kindred spirit, in Richard Eberling, who had an intense interest in money. Unfortunately, the small newspaper articles about his larceny charge in 1959 and sentence in 1960 had not gone unnoticed. This was not exactly the type of advertising that Eberling wanted.

As Richard's presence in the household grew, so did discomfort about him. "I didn't care for him at all," said Durkin's cousin Willis Corlett. Arline Campbell, a mother and local schoolteacher, had looked in on Ethel for years. Arline said she got to a point at which she would not even talk on the telephone to Aunt Ethel if Eberling was there.

Corlett and Campbell agree that Ethel's sister Myrtle Fray also thought Richard Eberling was a "creep," in Corlett's words. Arline could recall one particular conversation in 1962 in which she joined the three sisters on Ethel's porch while Eberling worked around the corner in the kitchen. Myrtle started railing at Ethel about Eberling.

According to Campbell, Myrtle told Ethel, "You've got to get rid of him. He's a crook. He's been convicted. He's taking you. Why do you want someone like that around here?" Ethel replied, "He's over all that. All that business is done with." Myrtle retorted, "They don't come like that." Ethel tried to hush her, indicating that Richard was in earshot. "I don't care if he hears me or not," shouted Myrtle.

For his part, Eberling said on some occasions that he never met Myrtle Fray and that he did not work for Durkin until the fall of 1962; on other occasions, he said he began working for Durkin in 1960. Campbell thought he began shortly after William Durkin died in 1957. At any rate, Myrtle Fray suffered her own disaster in the spring of 1962.

Ethel was the first one the Cleveland police called when they found Myrtle Irene Fray in her second-floor apartment at 10911 Lake Avenue. The call came at about eight-forty A.M. on Sunday, May 20, 1962. Fray, they said, had been beaten to death in her bed in predawn hours. As Richard Eberling said later: "She died the same way that Marilyn Sheppard died. Her face was beaten in."

Fray, ten days shy of her sixty-fourth birthday, was hefty. When found dead, she was five feet seven inches tall and weighed 190 pounds. Her hair, brown-gray, was wrapped in curlers. Her body was mostly nude, partially covered by a blue nightgown, which had been ripped down the front, one of the shoulder straps completely torn off. Her face and hair were coated with blood.

Neighbors recounted how screams had penetrated the calm as Saturday night unfolded into Sunday morning. At about four-thirty A.M. the custodian, John Yetson, seventy-two, was awakened by them. And a tenant who lived on the second floor next door to Fray phoned Yetson: he heard a woman screaming. Yetson and his wife, Hannah, went outside into a courtyard of the apartment building with a flashlight, listening, trying to figure out who or what or where. Other tenants poked out their heads. They agreed: someone had screamed bloody murder for about ten minutes. Then it had stopped. Quiet again and seeing no cause for action, Yetson and his wife went back to bed.

But in the morning Yetson went door to door in the complex. When he knocked at apartment 203 at eight o'clock, he got no answer and called the police. When police arrived, they found Myrtle Irene Fray lying in bed in the north bedroom, her face covered with a pillow. When they removed the pillow, they saw only blood. She had been murdered.

Although correct police protocol calls for the police to leave a body where found and call the coroner's office for an on-site investigation, the mobile patrol had the body of the obviously deceased woman taken to St. John's Hospital. She was pronounced dead on arrival at 10:15 A.M. The body was then removed to the county morgue.

The county's chief pathologist, Dr. Lester Adelson, viewed the body of Mrs. Fray at 11:20 that morning. Rigor mortis had set in. According to the autopsy, the cause of death was "asphyxia due to compression injury of neck with fracture of thyroid cartilage with extensive vocal cord hemorrhage, submucosal esophageal and pharyngeal hemorrhages, and intramuscular and fascial cervical hemorrhages. Multiple impacts to face with fracture of nasal bones, focal subarachnoid hemorrhages, and aspiration and swallowing of blood." The death was ascribed to "homicide (by assault)." Myrtle Fray died from being beaten around the face and head and chest, strangled and smothered.

A fuller description of the injuries showed upper and lower eyelids so swollen that they could barely be opened. The scalp had multiple small hemorrhage spots, called petechiae. The dura over the brain was not penetrated. Her nose was broken. The thyroid was fractured.

The fingernail scrapings showed nothing of significance. A vaginal smear was taken, but no microscopic testing for sperm was conducted; there apparently was not a similar examination of other bodily openings. Laboratory tests found zero alcohol or barbiturate content in the body. No other evidence was collected by the coroner's office. She was given autopsy number M-17829.

Cleveland police officers were called to the scene. They noticed blood splattered on the east wall and window curtain. They made no further analysis of it. "The night chain on the kitchen door leading to the main hallway was bro-

ken. This apparently was point of entry or exit or both,"
they wrote in a report. Because only the "night chain" was
broken, police and relatives believed that the assailant may
have been known to Fray. Some neighbors reported hearing a man's voice shortly before the screaming.

Contents of the apartment were not disturbed, wrote the
officers—"apparently nothing stolen." Finding no evidence
of any weapon, they concluded that the "injuries [were]
probably inflicted by use of hands." A bloody fingerprint
was found on a windowsill, and there was evidence that the
assailant had washed his hands in the bathroom sink.

Officers searched the courtyard, incinerator, garage, and
rubbish cans, but were unable to find anything to aid in the
investigation. Fray mostly associated with her sisters, and
no motive could be determined. Police theorized that the
killer might have been a burglar who then got frightened
off.

The conclusion: "No Suspects—No Arrests."

The Cleveland detectives didn't bother with luminol light
testing, and the coroner made no analysis of the pillow case
or wax reconstruction of the face. The bloody fingerprint
was never matched to anyone, and, in reality, little attempt
to do so was made. Myrtle Fray was written off.

With scant more effort, the homicide investigation into
the death of Myrtle Fray ended. For this woman, there was
no demand for an inquest, no sensational hype. There was
a single editorial, "This Mustn't Become 'Unsolved
Slaying.'"

Who would murder a sixty-three-year-old widow, retired,
living in a quiet residential neighborhood? Eberling had
some thoughts. Myrtle and her deceased husband, Bert, had
been involved with bookies, gambling, horse racing, and
someone to whom she owed money might have committed
the murder, he thought.

"Myrtle and Ethel never got along. Both had smart
mouths," he said. Eberling said that Ethel thought the jani-
tor had been involved. On another occasion, Eberling asserted that Ethel believed a woman had committed the
murder—a theory that he privately shared. "It had to be a
woman," he said. He also described the murder weapon.
"It was," he said, "the leg of the kitchen table that butch-
ered her."

The woman, he said, could not have been her sister,

Ethel. "I don't think she had the strength in the arms to carry it out." Nor would Ethel have hired someone because, he said, "her place in the community wouldn't have given her access to such a fellow. Or person." He knew of no motive for a woman to kill Fray, unless it was the wife of someone to whom she was indebted.

The reason it had to be a woman, said Eberling, was that Fray lived on the second floor and it would be hard for a man to get out without being spotted by the neighbors. Richard knew the neighborhood because, in addition to his extensive West Side business contacts, his friend Obie Henderson had lived seven blocks away at an apartment on West 116th Street for several years. If the killer was a man, speculated Eberling, he dressed in women's clothing in order to escape undetected, left in the morning about the time people might be going about their business, and slipped out the side door of the building.

In a letter, he described in detail the likely events of the murder night, as related to him, he said, by Ethel Durkin:

> First off Myrtle would never let a man in her home. With her hair in curlers, nightgown on only, no housecoat. Believe her teeth were in a glass soaking. Bottle of booze and two shot glasses (used) sitting on the coffee table, with race results. Her biggest concern, the murder weapon was a item from the kitchen. Like a wooden meat tenderizer, or a rolling pin. Ethel felt it was a woman (relative) because thats only way. They could have gained entrance to the apartment. The biggest reason for Ethels concern. Who ever killed Myrtle had to be very dirty from the splashing blood. Very carefully the person washed up. Then changed clothes wearing the dead womans out, into the public. As per Ethel, who would walk out into a public hall in a disarray? But a spotless person would pass unnoticed. Carried all evidence in a shopping bag.

Fray was laid to rest on May 24, 1962, at the Knollwood Cemetery in Mayfield Heights, Ohio, the same cemetery where Marilyn Sheppard was buried.

On May 29, 1962, Cleveland attorney Francis X. Feighan filed a probate court application for Fray's estate, the first of those he would file for the three sisters. Feighan was sometimes known as the "darling of probate court" because he handled so many estates. The Feighan family was practically an institution in Cleveland, a well-connected web of politicians and lawyers .

The estate total came to $25,179 and was divided equally between the two remaining sisters, Sarah Belle and Ethel. After expenses, each got $10,924. Fray was not in debt, as Eberling claimed, but had a fair amount of money in stocks and savings.

The case ended as quickly as it began. It was indeed another unsolved murder in Cleveland.

Ethel Durkin's older sister, Sarah Belle Farrow, was next among the sisters to die. She died March 10, 1970, a short while after she suffered a painful freak accident, which was less ominous than that of her younger sister, Myrtle.

Many people assumed that Ethel was the oldest because she was the bossiest. But Belle was three years her senior. Living with Ethel on Maple Cliff, Belle fell down a flight of steps to the basement, breaking both her arms and legs. Arline Campbell thought that perhaps the woman, frail and of poor eyesight, missed the landing and took a tumble. Belle, body wracked, was placed in the Wright Nursing Center in Lakewood, Ohio. She died within months, said Willis Corlett, a cousin. She was seventy-nine at the time.

"She was hanging a dish pan on a nail," said an incarcerated Richard Eberling of the incident that doomed Belle. As an aside, he later added, "If I wanted to get rid of Ethel, I'd get on the landing and push her."

Francis X. Feighan handled Belle's estate as he had done for Myrtle Fray. Belle had written a will in 1965, leaving small bequests to twenty or so friends and relatives, with the remainder of about ten thousand dollars and forty-three shares of A.T.&T. stock going to Ethel. The bequest was of little consequence to Ethel, who had amassed a minifortune. Now, more than ever, though, she was left alone.

With Belle gone, Eberling readily stepped into a broader role at Durkin's. He had become obsessive about using his cleaning business as a window of opportunity, moving from putting up screens and storms to securing a place inside people's homes.

"People have a secret side," he said. "A lot of people

never show it, ever. They trust you. They need to talk to somebody. People with no family or close friends seem to go for an outsider who will listen. . . . People say things they don't realize and you can put it in a computer bank."

The 1970s were his best years, Richard said. He would look after property while people were out of town, plan parties, buy supplies, help oversee building projects. He helped furnish homes, collecting both a fee from the owner and a commission from antique or home furnishing dealers. He managed new housing developments, caretaking their model homes. He joined a partnership to open a flower shop at the Cleveland Airport. Richard preferred to describe himself as an interior designer, with the company name R. G. Eberling & Associates. As a child, Richard said, he would take himself into another world by imagining redoing a room. Obie said he had a natural affinity for it.

His main interest, he conceded, was "my pocketbook." Sometimes he would have a brush with the law. Russ Sherman, who was local co-counsel with F. Lee Bailey in Dr. Sam's acquittal in 1966, had a problem with Eberling on a probate case. Eberling had removed rugs from an estate, supposedly to get them appraised, and Sherman had to threaten legal action. The victimized client was homosexual and had thus wanted to keep everything quiet.

Eberling counseled people on how they might turn a profit. One such person, Russ Zapach, met Eberling at a "club." Zapach had a foster mother and Eberling tried to explain to Zapach how he could get his name on her will. "I wouldn't do that," said Zapach. Eberling said he had tried to help Zapach with problems.

Everywhere, he found money-raising schemes. For Bev and Dale Scheidler, he devised a plan to syndicate a racehorse and sell shares at a Tupperware-like party. For Patricia Bogar and others, he came up with insurance swindles, faking a burglary and making a phony claim on the stolen property. Eberling himself received a windfall of $36,000 when he falsified documents relating to the death of his "aunt" Claire M.

"Richard was always hustling," said his friend Peg Baker. Jack Baker, her husband and also an astrologer, added, "Dick would help and help and help, and then he'd turn around and say, 'I want a favor returned.'"

In the 1970s Richard and Obie also found themselves

involved in city politics. Both began working, in different capacities, for Cleveland mayor Ralph Perk. Perk was a Republican West Sider who targeted his message to white ethnic groups. With little dynamism, and a base rooted in bowling alleys and beer joints, Perk ascended to office as an outsider in a city characterized by voracious political infighting.

Upon hearing that Perk planned to remodel the mayor's office in 1972, Eberling wrote to him. Perk liked his ideas and appointed a Commission for the Preservation of City Hall with Richard G. Eberling as its chair. It was, said Eberling, the most "significant event" of his life. For an abandoned boy once shipped off to Children's Aid Society, he was finally earning recognition. In 1974 Obie became Perk's executive secretary.

Eberling's appointment kicked up a controversy among more established designers. His qualifications were challenged. A front-page newspaper article in April 1973 reported that the major design associations had never heard of Eberling and that R. G. Eberling & Associates was not listed in the phone book. When approached about his background by reporter Brent Larkin, Eberling abruptly demanded, "Why are you asking all these questions?" Larkin's article also mentioned Eberling's larceny conviction in 1959.

Although Perk and the mayor's commission came to his defense, Eberling said he broke down in tears because of the article. He stayed on, but new allegations arose in July 1973 asserting that he was misspending city money, buying tens of thousands of dollars' worth of supplies and materials without competitive bidding or accounting. The mayor's executive commissioner put the brakes on. The mayor again came to Eberling's defense and eventually released seventy thousand dollars in city funds for redecorating, bronze gates, tapestry, and marble. The job wasn't completed until 1976. Costs rose to one hundred thousand dollars. But Eberling had one coup: the work was declared an aesthetic success.

Thinking the problems were past, Perk sent through an approval to pay Eberling fifty thousand dollars in a noncompetitive bid to supervise another eight-hundred-thousand-dollar renovation of city space. This time the uproar didn't die. After Perk was booted out of office in 1977, one of the first acts of the next mayor was to cancel the agreement with Eberling. Richard had already been paid thirty-six thousand dollars and demanded the remainder.

But through their connections, hosting benefits, doing favors, Richard and Obie continued to befriend society writers and city politicians. They accompanied single women to the ballet and other cultural events. They became known. Eberling set up a gala honoring all the former mayors of the city and their families. He finally had a taste of the kind of prestige he craved. Everywhere he went, Eberling would describe himself as a member of the mayor's cabinet. He basked.

Much later, Lakewood police sergeant Vince Kremperger found other spoils of office in Eberling's possession, including a monogrammed silver plate presented to the city of Cleveland by the city of Cleveland, England, and a large elegant portrait of a man, twelve feet by twelve feet, in a gilded frame. Eberling said it was an Eberling ancestor. Kremperger traced it to the basement of City Hall.

The world of politics had other side effects. Obie volunteered on the campaign of Republican George Voinovich for mayor in 1979, and there he met another volunteer, Patricia Bogar. She was a small-time entrepreneur, in her midforties. Bogar and Obie began to date. Usually when they went out, said Bogar, it was as a threesome. Obie would come to the door with flowers and with Richard. Still, she enjoyed herself on their benefit-and-party circuit.

Like cars on the Go-Kart track that Bogar had once owned, their paths would eventually cross lanes, bump, and crash. Bogar would come to have a long-term and not very pleasant influence on the lives of Obie Henderson and Dick Eberling and their client Ethel Durkin. "Judas" was one of the nicer names Richard and Obie later called Bogar.

Richard simultaneously built his other money-making ventures. Ethel Durkin was one of the biggest. As he moved into interior design, he began decorating the inside of her house for Christmas, with an extravagant display of greenery and ornaments. "He was soaking the devil out of her," said Durkin's cousin Willis Corlett, "but she enjoyed it."

According to Jack Baker, a friend of Eberling's, Eberling took care of "four or five old ladies." He'd bring their astrological charts to Jack or his wife, Peg, for a reading.

"He was always looking for old ladies to take care of. He'd be really nice to them. If you'd be nice to them, they'll be nice to you."

Ethel turned eighty in 1973. Her mind was as brisk as the midnight winds off the lake. Headstrong, she handled all her own finances, paid her bills, dickered with lawyers until they backed down, made investments, and taunted her relatives, none of whom had fared as well as she. "She would dangle ten cents in front of them. Only to give them a wooden nickel, or a dirty penny," wrote Richard, mocking the relatives as a "strange" group.

But physically, Ethel was deteriorating. At five feet three inches and two hundred pounds, she had a lot to carry around. Her knees were weak. Eberling flattered her. He called her "Twinkletoes," even as her mobility grew increasingly limited.

"He was soft-soaping her," said Arline Campbell, who derisively refers to Eberling as "Dickie boy." Ethel fell for it "hook, line, and sinker."

Ethel's world narrowed after the deaths of Myrtle and Belle. She was the only family member of her generation left. Helen Hodge became a close friend after marrying a Durkin relative, but she moved away in the late 1970s. Later, after Durkin's death, Helen would say, "Whatever happened, I don't know. If I had stayed, it would not have happened, everybody says."

When his work for Perk came to a close in 1978, Eberling had even more time to spend at the Durkin home. He referred to Ethel as the "Duchess" because she never lifted a finger cooking, cleaning, doing the dishes, or shopping. Richard did that. Placed on an hourly salary, Richard attended to her, listened to her stories, the same ones, over and over again until he knew them by heart.

And the subject she enjoyed the most happened to be one close to his heart, too. "Money was the main topic of conversation, and Dick kept feeding that," said Campbell. She loved to talk about her will, too. She would change her will constantly and call her lawyer, Francis Feighan, with yet another version of the will. "She lived to change her will," Arline mused.

Eberling would warn Ethel that her relatives were fortune hunters. Relatives felt that he was out to short-circuit the family, and they urged Ethel to put her money in a trust fund.

Beginning in 1978, the Corletts had dinner with cousin Ethel once a week. Dick would be there, cooking; Obie sometimes fixed her hair. "Oh, they'd come in and kiss her and tell her how pretty she'd look. They'd jolly her up." Willis Corlett thought they were using her grocery store tab to charge expensive items that they would take home. Dick would turn around and tell Ethel her relatives were robbing her. "He was always accusing me of stuff," said the elderly Corlett.

Eberling took Ethel out to dinner at restaurants, such as her local favorite, Miller's. She paid, and he was paid by the hour. If she was being taken for a ride, at least she enjoyed the view.

Somewhere, visiting on Maple Cliff Drive, Dick began fantasizing about his own past connection to Durkin. It was then that he came to believe that she had tried to adopt him as a child.

From 1979 to 1982 Ethel suffered a series of falls. Arline thought some of them odd. "He was always there when she fell." She thought Eberling gave Ethel double cocktails, against the doctor's orders, and then Ethel would stand up, light-headed, and fall.

Around 1979 it became apparent that Ethel needed around-the-clock care. She had fallen and injured her knee. Arthritis in her legs worsened, and she was supposed to use a cane but sometimes would not. She moved into a downstairs bedroom to avoid the stairs. Linda Dunderman Newton, a young cousin of Durkin's who lived on the East Side, started working as a private duty nurse. Other caretakers came and went over the next years, and Richard began to take charge of overseeing them. He put in a shift every afternoon, preparing an early dinner for Ethel at three-thirty.

In June 1982 Ethel had a serious tumble. In trying to break the fall, she put out her arms, and they were badly injured and bruised. "I was with her that afternoon and called the paramedics," Richard said. Arline Campbell and her husband, John, had just left for a vacation in Alaska. The situation worried Ethel.

Ethel decided to get more help with the day-to-day activities. Obie began to handle her business affairs, doing bank chores, writing checks to the nurses and others. In case she became totally incapacitated, Ethel signed a power of attorney, naming Obie. She made Obie the executor of her will.

Richard claims that she also signed a life care contract, drawn up by attorney Feighan, putting Eberling in charge of her personal care decisions. The idea for it was Mrs. Durkin's, he said, because she didn't want to go to a nursing home. "I might have told her about it. I had a battle with the heirs in '79 and I said I was powerless. She thought about it and decided it was a good idea."

The actual life care contract, Eberling said, was taken by police officers when they searched his house in 1988, and it never returned. "I never heard of it. There was no such animal as far as I'm concerned," said Marvin Koblentz in 1994, who was eventually assigned by the Cuyahoga County Probate Court to handle Durkin's estate.

These events, Cuyahoga County prosecutors came to charge later, were part of "years of emotional and financial manipulation" of Durkin. This manipulation resulted in Eberling's, "for all practical purposes, isolating Mrs. Durkin from her relatives, gaining control of her household and daily life as well as her financial affairs," wrote assistant prosecutor George Rukovena.

At times there were second thoughts. Arline claims that Ethel told her that she couldn't "cross" Richard because he had a "terrible temper." He had raised a fist one time when she questioned calls placed on her phone. But Ethel didn't want to fire him. He filled a void. By then she knew him and it was easier to put up with him than to train someone new.

Eberling said that he had only one fight with Durkin. "She told a nurse not to pay attention to me. I overheard it. I let her have it," said Richard. "She told people later, 'He was right.'"

Usually, though, he treated her royally. In 1982, he said, she refused to leave the hospital until he and Obie returned from a trip to Ireland, just after the Fourth of July. Her whims were indulged. He played cards with her. He had her sign her name on some pieces of paper to get her handwriting analyzed. He also tried to interest her in investing in some of his pet schemes, like Dale and Bev Scheidler's horse syndication. Ethel allowed him to engage in talk about it, but she wouldn't invest.

Richard gave a gala birthday party for her when her ninetieth year came around on May 15, 1983. The Scheidlers were among those who attended, but mostly relatives and close friends were invited. Ethel was thrilled.

Richard "loved that woman," said Obie, "and she loved him, and people could not stand that because money was involved. The hours involved . . . made me sick. He loved taking her out and all. . . . People—he tried to help them and they turned against him."

Eberling did order people around, sometimes obnoxiously. Linda Newton finally threw in the towel on November 1, 1983. She objected to the way Eberling was running things, resigned, and went on vacation for two weeks. "She quit," Richard recounted. "She couldn't get along with anybody. Linda was jealous of me. Afraid I'd get some money she was going to get."

This action opened a dam. That was, according to prosecutor Rukovena, the beginning of "the emotionally charged turmoil" that culminated on November 15, 1983.

Ethel, it seemed, became frantic when Linda resigned. This was exactly the kind of change and disruption in the household that she had been trying to avoid. Ethel had known Linda and doted on her since she was a small girl. At times over the next couple of weeks, Ethel was left alone. She hated that. She wanted Linda back, and Dick did not. When Linda returned from vacation on November 13, Ethel was on the phone to her immediately. There were calls and conversations back and forth to Linda, to Obie, to Dick, to Arline, to the Corletts, to another nurse, named Nila.

Ethel finally pleaded with Linda to come back, promising, "I'm the boss of the household." Linda agreed to show up for work again on November 14.

After midnight, Ethel called Linda again, crying—it wasn't going to work out, after all, Ethel said. "Richard says no." According to Nila, who got a call at home from Durkin on the fourteenth, Ethel was upset. The next morning, Tuesday, November 15, Nila arrived at work at seven o'clock. When Richard arrived later in the day, he was agitated. His temperament was different; he frightened Nila. Richard and Ethel argued. Linda was the subject. At about five o'clock in the afternoon, Richard drove Nila home. He was high-strung, demanding information, edgy.

"Interesting," wrote Eberling when sitting in Lebanon Correctional Institution and writing as if he were both "I" and "Richard," "had I told Ethel Durkin to take it and shove it, wouldn't be here. Something very wrong with Richard am afraid. Of course if I had to do it all over again, would do no different."

NINETEEN

Nightmares

The Lakewood rescue squad arrived at 1052 Maple Cliff Drive at seven P.M. on November 15, 1983. Richard Eberling met them at the door and his hands pointed to the living room floor. Paramedics Martin Mace and Al Davis entered with Lakewood police officer Thomas Geiger. Ethel May Durkin was lying on her face, unconscious, but alive. They noticed that blood had dried around her mouth.

She was very old—nearly ninety-one, Eberling said. She needed a walker, especially with her weight. She had fallen, Eberling explained. He was the only person in the house with her. He had been in the kitchen, fixing something to eat. He heard a thud. Ethel May was down.

With little fanfare, the paramedics put Durkin in an ambulance and took her to Lakewood Hospital. The officer filled out a short report, calling it "transportation to the hospital."

Older than most, Lakewood is by far the largest suburb on the West Side, with a population of over sixty thousand in 1980. Bordering right on Cleveland and with a full complement of bars and commercial enterprises, the suburban atmosphere of Lakewood could be interrupted with urban woes such as crime. To counteract the problem, Lakewood built a sizable police force of eighty officers and bragged about being tough.

Vince Kremperger joined the Lakewood police force in 1956. He was the burly type who would have been an asset

338

on a school football team, but in reality had to go to work to help out his mother instead. "Kremp," as just about everybody called him, was fair if people were square with him. But if someone crossed him, he didn't play around.

Cops in Lakewood went through special training, unlike those on a lot of the little suburban forces around. There were challenges in Lakewood crime fighting, even homicides.

For example, at the time that Durkin was whisked to the hospital, Lakewood officers were still puzzling over the murder of another old lady. Two years earlier, in October 1981, seventy-eight-year-old Ruth McNeil was killed in Lakewood. "We hadn't had a homicide in I don't know how many years," Kremperger said sadly.

McNeil, a widow for eleven years, lived alone in a house at 2071 Baxterly Avenue in Lakewood. On Tuesday, October 6, 1981, a daughter-in-law stopped by in the morning to drop off some laundry and found Mrs. McNeil dead.

Mrs. McNeil was lying between the living room and the dining room. She had been dead for more than a day, at least thirty hours, the coroner's office later estimated. She was wearing a yellow housecoat and a short nightgown underneath; no undergarments.

"You get something like that, you bust your butt trying to solve it," said Kremperger.

After an autopsy conducted by Dr. Lester Adelson, Coroner Sam Gerber ruled that the cause of death was "multiple blunt impacts to head with skull fractures, multiple cerebral contusions, and subarachnoid hemorrhage." In essence, she was beaten to death.

At five feet two inches and 184 pounds, McNeil suffered from multiple lacerations of the scalp, all of which had "abraded" edges. There were at least seven blunt impacts to the head, causing several skull fractures. The lacerations were on the upper face—nasal bridge, eyebrow, forehead. A metal band was on the left ring finger, but there was a bruise over the joint of the left ring finger, as if someone had tried to remove a ring, and the joint was swollen. McNeil was coated in caked blood. It was an ugly scene.

The only unusual activity that anyone in the neighborhood could remember was the barking of a neighbor's dog at 9:50 P.M. on Sunday, October 4. The last anyone had recalled talking to McNeil was on Saturday at 6 P.M. The only sign of struggle was a toppled television table. "We didn't find anything stolen," said Kremperger. Officers thought perhaps a burglar had been surprised by McNeil, struck her, and then been frightened off. No weapon was found.

A back window was broken, but it did not seem to be the means of entry. "I think it was broken *out*," said Kremperger. Police suspected that the intruder was someone she knew who came through the front door. Because the blows were not extremely powerful, they suspected for some time an elderly woman who lived in the neighborhood. No weapon was ever recovered.

A next-door neighbor reported that McNeil had complained for months that someone was trying to break into her home. McNeil told her that she thought the person was someone who had worked for her and had stolen her wedding ring. The neighbor had brushed McNeil off. Later, she couldn't shake the images. She had nightmares about it and finally moved from the neighborhood.

Specially trained in fingerprinting technique, Kremperger went through the entire house with special equipment, lifting prints. But he found nothing that he could match to existing prints on file. "We never solved that one. That one bothered me. We spent hours and hours there," said Kremperger. Lakewood officers didn't have many unsolved cases. Baxterly Road was one of the few.

As for Ethel May Durkin or Richard Eberling, Kremperger didn't even hear the names until nearly four years after the ambulance had logged Durkin's ride from Maple Cliff to Lakewood Hospital.

"I went through hell about my cousin. It was bad memories," said Linda Newton about the events surrounding Ethel May's fall on November 15 and the aftermath in the months and years to follow. "Makes me sick to think about it."

Upon arrival at the hospital, Ethel was found to have two broken cervical vertebrae. Her face was severely bruised on the right side, the result of hitting the floor on the forward fall, doctors decided Dr. Manuel Valera had treated Ethel after other falls and believed this one to be similar, if worse. He did not consider any foul play.

Durkin was placed in traction to stabilize the neck, a

technique almost like fastening her head with bolts to a large wooden frame to prevent any movement. A tracheotomy was done, placing tubes through her throat. She was paralyzed from the neck down. She couldn't speak at all.

"I called Linda and the rest of the relatives that night and told them what happened," Richard said in an interview in 1991. He explained that after he arrived at about three-thirty that afternoon, Ethel had had a cocktail, an old-fashioned. He hadn't argued with her, he said. "Then Ethel said, 'I'm hungry.' I went to the kitchen and put the tea kettle on. She was between the dining room and living room. I heard a thud. We had been talking in the living room. . . . She got up and turned. As she turned, she blacked out, hit her head above the eye. . . . I struggled with her. She laid prone on the floor. I called nine-one-one." This happened at six-thirty P.M., he said, although the times did not match up exactly. He didn't try to pick her up because he was present during a previous fall, and Ethel had said to just leave her be until the paramedics came. On another occasion, Eberling explained: "I think she blacked out that day and then she flew into a chair."

Nila, the nurse on duty, said that Eberling called her three times that evening: first to say that Ethel was angry, second to say that she had fallen, third to say that she was in the hospital.

That night, Obie Henderson was at the Bradley Road farmhouse, working with Bev and Dale Scheidler. The Scheidlers had gone there at Eberling's suggestion, arriving between seven and seven-thirty P.M. Eberling, from whom they had borrowed thirty thousand dollars on the failed horse syndication plan, had a new plan regarding the training of an Arabian horse. Henderson was helping them frame a letter to an Arizona horse farm. That night, Obie typed a one-page letter about the horse, Easter Bask, then refined and retyped it several times. At nine-thirty P.M., Bev Scheidler said that Obie answered the telephone, listened, and then said, "What's done is done." He hung up and told them the caller was Richard. Bev and Dale were soon ushered out.

Ethel regained consciousness by the next day. But because of the tubes, she could not speak. At times Ethel could respond to questions, sometimes by blinking or making a face.

Linda visited Ethel on November 16. Dick was there, too. Linda asked her elderly cousin if she remembered how she fell. Durkin seemed to nod. No further information was elicited.

On November 20, according to hospital records, nurse Blanchemari Collister completed a form about Durkin: "Questioned on her fall at home (has a large bruised bump on her forehead about the size of a quarter in circumference just R of center). Nodded 'no' to whether she was dizzy prior to, and nodded 'yes' whether she had slipped."

Her face looked horrendous, thought Arline Campbell, as if it had been smashed in. She too asked Aunt Ethel how she fell. She was suspicious. Ethel indicated that she didn't know how. She registered that her neck hurt. Another time, Arline asked Ethel if she wanted to go home with Richard, where he could be there to cater to her needs. She screwed up her face in an alarmed no, Arline thought. She seemed to try to speak. Arline thought about getting someone who could read lips to come in.

Cousin Willis Corlett wondered about the fall, too. When Ethel had fallen before, she had bruised and broken her arms trying to break the fall, a natural reaction. This time there was none of that.

Ethel's condition was not improving. Dr. Valera suggested removing the life supports. Obie, who held her power of attorney, said no. He pointed out that he had a pleasant interaction with Durkin when he took in Christmas cards for her to pick out. Richard also said no.

Unable to speak, Ethel's last utterances had been during the tearful dramas of November 14 and 15. Her condition was dire. On January 3, 1984, at 11:40 A.M., Ethel May Durkin, age ninety, was officially pronounced dead at Lakewood Hospital. Because she died in a hospital, by law, her body was taken to the coroner's office on Adelbert Road on the East Side.

There Dr. Gerber was still in command, empowered to make decisions about life and death that could affect other people's lives forever. Eberling became frantic when the autopsy was mentioned. He called Arline Campbell at the school where she taught, insisting that the school officials get her out of her classroom, rules be damned. When she got to the phone, he was panic stricken: "They're going to do an autopsy," he said. She was relieved. At last, some attention to the concerns that she had.

Later, Arline wished that she had called the coroner's office and told of her suspicions. It probably would not have made much difference.

In fact, no autopsy was done. No detailed analysis of the cause of death was made. The body was examined in a cursory way, and the necessary forms were filled out. But the serious examination that comes from actually opening the body and looking at possible areas of injury and making a decision about how the injuries came about was rejected as unnecessary.

Did Dr. Sam Gerber notice the name of the person who reported the incident on the typed reports given to him? Did he pay attention to the part about Ethel being found face down on the carpeted floor? Did Dr. Gerber's mind click back as he signed the statement that said "she was found by a friend, Richard Eberling of 3961 Bradley Road"? Did he recall that, at the insistence of Officer Jay Hubach at the Bay Village police department, he had spoken to Richard Eberling in his office for three hours in 1959 about another case, a case in which an autopsy had been conducted, an inquest convened, a case that towered over the coroner's office more than any other case in its history, the murder of Marilyn Sheppard? Did he remember that he had at first suggested further investigation of Richard Eberling, even though Dr. Sam Sheppard was in prison for the murder and he, Dr. Gerber, had been one of the principal people to put him there? And did he even shift in his seat at the recollection of how, abruptly, adamantly, he called back the Bay Village police the next morning and said to forget it, he wasn't interested after all?

The coroner was in command of the final decision. And in the death of this woman, he decided to do nothing. The coroner's verdict signed by Dr. Sam Gerber said, "Death in this case was the end result of a blunt impact to head with fracture of cervical vertebrae, due to a fall and was accidental in nature." Two words were in bold above his signature: ACCIDENTAL FALL.

Still years away from the Durkin case, these two words would stand like walls to be scaled for Vince Kremperger.

Richard and Obie planned a memorial service at Maple Cliff Drive, and then Ethel was to be buried in the Buffalo area, near her husband's grave. The obituary read: "Ethel M. Durkin (Née Farrow), beloved wife of the late William M., dear sister of the late Sarah Belle, Myrtle I. Fray, devoted friend of Linda Newton and Richard G. Eberling. . . . Family suggest contributions be made to The Ethel M. Durkin Memorial Fund c/o Obie Henderson."

Richard decked out Maple Cliff Drive royally for the "Duchess." He brought Oriental rugs and placed them all through the house. There were flowers. The casket was filled with letters from her husband, and Ethel herself was clad in her precious fur coat with her initials embroidered on the tag. "She wanted to be so beautiful in her casket," said Helen Hodge, who was sick and unable to attend. "She used to say, 'Put lipstick on me, and mascara.' " Her wishes were Richard's guide.

At the memorial, Arline Campbell went up to attorney Francis Feighan and asked if Ethel's will was intact. He nodded; no problem. Soon afterward, Bev Scheidler approached Feighan and introduced herself. Arline Campbell recalled seeing her exactly once before, at the ninetieth birthday party for Ethel that Richard had given the previous spring. Arline said that at that party, Bev had come up and thrown her arms around Ethel. As she walked away, Ethel had turned around and said, "Who the hell is that?" Now Bev held out an envelope to Feighan. It was Ethel's will, she said. Ethel was afraid that it would be stolen from Maple Cliff Drive and had asked Bev to keep it for her, she explained.

Feighan was as surprised as anyone. Year after year, Ethel had called him to change or update her will. He knew nothing about this one.

There were more surprises. Ethel May had named Obie Henderson as executor and had left him 4 percent of her estate. Her attorney, Feighan, and his wife were to get 5 percent of the estate, in addition to whatever attorney's fees were collectable. Ethel had made various other bequests to relatives, including a large one to Linda Newton, a substantial one to her church, and smaller ones to other cousins, nephews, nieces.

And 70 percent of her estate she left to her "good friend and adviser" Richard Eberling. In the will that Bev Scheidler had carried, Durkin wrote glowingly about Richard. He was "a gentleman who to me was the son I always wished for. Who has saved my life and gives me the greatest happiness and comfort." The syntax created choppy, fragmented sentences. The substance, style, and even the typing were also completely unlike that in any of her previous wills.

Durkin's estate of stocks, savings, and house were valued at about $1.4 million. The will was dated May 7, 1982, and three witnesses had signed it: Bev Scheidler, Dale Scheidler, and Patricia Bogar.

Bogar was not at the memorial service. She had given up on any kind of serious relationship with Obie and decided to try warmer pastures. In May 1982 she had moved to Florida. Before the relocation, in April, Dick had staged a burglary at her condominium in Strongsville, Ohio, by breaking a window screen and creating signs of theft. Then he assisted in collecting receipts for a phony insurance estimate that netted thirty-two thousand dollars after his 10 percent. He also facilitated her move, even driving a rental truck to Florida.

The relatives, who had had reports as regular as the Dow Jones from Ethel May Durkin on the status of their bequests, were astonished and none too happy. Several believed that Eberling had used undue influence to get Durkin to sign the will. Others questioned the circumstances surrounding her death. And some asked whether this will, which looked so very different from every other will of Ethel Durkin's, could be real.

In previous wills, Ethel had made bequests to Dick and Obie, but nothing like this. Relatives pointed out that in a 1980 codicil, or amendment, to her will, she had added Eberling, leaving him five thousand dollars. In a 1981 amendment she left Henderson thirty shares of General Motors stock and named him co-executor with Feighan. Feighan had little to say about it; he just put the will presented by Scheidler into motion in probate court.

If Feighan didn't question the will, no one at probate court would think to question Feighan. And Feighan certainly had no reason to turn his back on the bequest by Durkin, a sometimes stubborn woman whom he had served dutifully over the years. But others wondered about Feighan. Burt Fulton, along with his associate James Speros, came to represent some of the Durkin family members. "Franny was a nice guy," said Fulton. "But he was over the hill and shouldn't have been practicing law."

The world of probate court is a bit arcane, a mystery to all but a small group of lawyers who practice in that area. On April 18, 1984, a hearing was held in front of referee John W. Widder. Bev and Dale Scheidler testified about witnessing the signing of the will, and the will was admitted for probate. That was stage one in the probate process.

On May 21, 1984, referee Thomas Giurbino appointed Obie Henderson executor of the estate. The will would now be "administered"—assets accounted for and distributed to the beneficiaries who were named. That was stage two in the probate process, and everything was going smoothly.

Robert Steely represented Linda Newton, who had been given a fairly reasonable share under the will. At first, Steely just sat back while the will was processed. But then the money from the estate started disappearing. "The executor and the main beneficiary . . . were bilking the estate," said Steely.

Estate losses began to grow. Eberling cashed several checks signed by Durkin. They were paychecks he had stacked up, he said, and he felt they were owed to him. Lawyers complained that before he was approved as executor, Henderson made many payments to Eberling ranging in the thousands of dollars.

On March 29, 1984, when the assets had not yet been appraised, the house on Maple Cliff Drive was burglarized. Eberling reported it. When police arrived, four windowpanes were broken out in the sun room, the door was open, and there were large footprints in the snow. Eberling, whose big feet were so legendary that they were mentioned in his high school yearbook, pointed out that Willis Corlett had very large feet.

To the police, Eberling reported only a few small items missing, such as liquor and figurines. To the Allstate insurance adjuster, the list was much longer, including a fancy Rubina epergne, a Tree of Life dinner set, silverware, Hummels, rugs. A check for $17,552.87 was issued to Obie Henderson, as executor, although he was not yet executor. He put it into his own account; Obie said he merely followed Feighan's instructions. But the sum was not reported to, or added to, the estate.

As executor, Obie had the authority to write checks and

handle all of Ethel's money. Henderson had accounts with a hundred thousand dollars in her name changed to his, signing the bank's power-of-attorney forms that said she was alive. He said he didn't know that it was improper, and that he did everything with Feighan's guidance.

Long distance calls made from Ethel's home were charged to the estate. So was gas for her car. The car itself was sold on an insider "sweetheart deal," said attorney Steely. When an appraisal of the property was done, the appraiser was surprised at how empty the house was. Many items seemed to be missing.

Later, the executor, Obie, sold the house to Eberling for $65,000. Eberling undertook remodeling and fix-up repairs. Expenses for tree trimmers and landscapers were paid out of the estate funds. In September 1987, after owning the house for a year and a half, Eberling sold the property for $184,000, a profit of nearly $120,000. Obie stated consistently that any errors he made as executor were unintentional, and based on the advice given by attorney Feighan.

Steely began to object to expenditures from the estate. The checks were being cashed at a rate that would drain the estate before the heirs could take their share, reducing their percentage to beans. And he had a bad feeling about the main beneficiary. "I thought Richard Eberling was a snake from the first time I saw him. He gives off those vibes," he said.

Jim Speros began to make objections, too. Speros represented the interests of a half dozen heirs, including Willis Corlett and Arline Campbell. Speros wondered about the authenticity of the will itself. "From my perspective, all the spacing was wrong. We had copies of the prior wills and they all looked professional, as was appropriate for someone with her assets. This one seemed amateurish, like someone would do at home. Something seemed wrong with it."

Speros called Dr. Philip Bouffard, a forensic document examiner with a Ph.D. in chemistry. Forensic document examiners are nothing like hand-writing analysts who say they can describe a person's psychological makeup by examining characteristics of his or her writing. They are scientists who study paper, ink, and typewriting on documents for any kind of clue to solve the problem at hand.

Bouffard went to the Cuyahoga County Probate Court

with his microscope. The paper was an erasable bond—not quite right. The typewriter was unusual for the document, too. There was an odd two-inch gap in the typing at the top. He looked at the signature: "Ethel May Durkin." Yes, he thought it was her signature.

Then he noticed the *y* in the handwritten "May." Some of the typed letters crossed with the low part of the *y*. Was the typewritten part on the paper first so that the signature was merely written over it, which would have presented no concern? Or was the typewritten part placed on the paper after the signature, which would have indicated some impropriety? He noted that the typewriting was done with a correctable ribbon that works by a plastic film transfer. If the typing had been over the signature, the typed letters could practically be scratched off. If the ink of the signature was on top, there would be a difference in the reflection of the light. The ink would cause a disturbance in the type.

He concentrated on that *y* with his stereomicroscope. "My conclusion was that the typing came after it was signed," said Bouffard.

Bouffard wrote up a report, noting the improper crossing of letters, but the court refused to release the will for more extensive testing. "And that was the last I heard of it for four years," said Bouffard.

Speros decided to go one step further and to check out the suspicions of his clients about the cause of death. Had there been foul play? He contacted Dr. Lester Adelson, the forensic pathologist who testified in the Sheppard case, on a consulting basis. "Dr. Adelson related that the injuries—a broken neck—were not atypical for a woman of her age and were not a matter to be pursued."

A senior attorney at the firm where Speros worked, Burt Fulton didn't believe that foul play was likely either, but for a very different reason. "I figure a guy like that could steal by just being kind to her. . . . She was going to die anyway. Why would he want to kill her? He had control over her."

And Jack Baker, Eberling's astrologer, agreed. "Dick wouldn't have killed her," he said. "He was getting impatient. I said, 'Wait, she'll be dead in a couple months.' "

Without the support of the forensic pathologist, and not wanting to get involved in a crazy chase for a nonexistent golden goose, Speros and Fulton opted for a settlement. A series of meetings were scheduled at the probate court to work out an agreement for all the beneficiaries. One problem occurred. Eberling kept bringing different attorneys to each meeting, hiring and firing them. "To me it was an obvious ploy to siphon off money and to keep anything from happening," said Speros.

Richard and Obie, for their parts, found the process aggravating. They felt as if they were watching slow-motion theater, with greedy relatives picking at a dead woman's body. Ethel, said Eberling, warned him that the relatives would "never give up." Obie wrote to the probate court that those contesting the will were "failures" who did not know "how to cope with life." Durkin, he said, left money in her will to "those that were most beneficial and made her happiest."

The tension was heavy. Three years after Durkin's death, with the estate proceedings plodding on, Richard Eberling checked into the Cleveland Clinic in December 1986, as he celebrated his fifty-seventh birthday. He was diagnosed as suffering from alcohol abuse. A long history of alcoholism was noted, and he was transferred to a chemical detoxification program. Abruptly, Eberling withdrew from the program and asked to be discharged from the hospital.

Finally, on April 26, 1987, a settlement was reached. Referee Giurbino personally mailed checks distributing assets from Ethel May's estate. Various cousins received $5,657.72 apiece. St. James Catholic Church received $15,973.19; Henderson was granted $25,000; Linda Newton got a sum about double that; and the main beneficiary, the "son she never had," received $491,000. These amounts did not account, however, for the "side deals" that had been swung, like the profit on the sale of the house. In total, attorneys later estimated, Eberling received between $750,000 and $1.5 million from the "Duchess."

With the probate saga finally over, or so it seemed, Richard and Obie packed up to move to Tennessee. Before leaving, they made generous donations. Dick wrote a check for $10,000 in Obie's name to a college. He gave a horse supposedly valued at $35,000 to a local benefit auction.

Eberling sold some of the Bradley Road property. The Westlake Board of Education bought a chunk in 1985, paying about $500,000 for tract 13, about five hundred times what Eberling paid in July 1956. The old farmhouse was sold on June 12, 1987, for $140,000.

"It was time to move on," said Obie. "I'd been wanting to go back south." The two bought a ritzy $200,000 house in the wealthy community of Lookout Mountain, Tennessee. They could lounge, swim in their backyard pool, dabble in investments. Each of them had a Cadillac to drive. In October 1987 Dick bought the West End Shopping Center, a forty-five-thousand-square-foot complex with twenty stores in Rome, Georgia, for $1.7 million and made Obie its operations manager.

They also left some people hanging in Cleveland, such as Carl Andreano, a civil engineer who provided services to Eberling when he was subdividing the farmland and then got stuck with the bill. "Like a deadbeat, you know?" said Andreano.

This was typical of the trail the two left behind them, said Peg and Jack Baker. "Everybody in town wanted to get Dick Eberling and Obie. Dick was one of these guys, he'd bleed you for something. He did some wheeling and dealing," said Peg. "He was always hustling . . . everyone gets pissed off."

About that time, Peg read Richard's astrological chart for him. Saturn was appearing, she told him. The second time it appears in your life, she explained to him, is when you have all the trouble. It happens when you're twenty-nine, returns when you're fifty-eight. But, she said, don't worry unless you've done something bad.

"Richard became very upset," she recalled.

Richard ended up in a Tennessee mental institution in November 1988, just as his fifty-eighth year was coming to a close. The general psychiatric diagnosis by Dr. Mark W. Peterson was "extreme disturbance of behavior and mood." The cause of his disturbance could be traced directly to the coming together of two people who, under ordinary circumstances, were completely unlikely to be friends of any sort: Sergeant Vincent Kremperger and Patricia Bogar.

They were, in fact, not friends. When Pat Bogar called the Lakewood police department in September 1987, Kremperger answered. It was the type of call that a lot of cops would blow off with a bunch of "uh-huh's," making a note on a station message pad, and then snapping the pad shut for good.

"I was going to retire," said Kremperger, who had been on the force for thirty-two years, "when I got this stupid call."

"This woman calls me up. 'You're gonna think I'm crazy. I've got a suspicious death and a forged will,' " said Kremperger. She mentioned the name Ethel May Durkin. "I'm thinking, every crime report comes through here, I read it. I read them every day. . . . I'm thinking I would have known about a suspicious death and a forged will," said Kremperger.

Kremperger followed through. "I look upstairs. Sure enough, she's dead." He found the report "transport to hospital."

Bogar was not on a mission of mercy—quite the opposite. She had followed the Durkin probate case from a distance. In 1982 Dick Eberling had promised her 10 percent of his inheritance if she would sign her name as a witness to two blank sheets of paper he intended to make into a will. "I was not a goody two-shoes. I *knew* what it was about," said Bogar. Eberling planned to get Ethel's signature by offering to have her handwriting analyzed, but he didn't mean the type of analysis that Dr. Phillip Bouffard would conduct years later.

Bogar had left the Buckeye state for the Sunshine one, but she had not forgotten her little investments. In need of money, she decided to cash in. She called Richard and Obie's home in Lookout Mountain, Tennessee, and said she wanted to borrow some money. She figured she was entitled to ninety thousand dollars, about 10 percent of what Eberling got as beneficiary to Ethel May, but she asked for only ten thousand dollars.

Obie recalled later in an interview:

> *Obie:* She called one day and talked to me and made a threat. And I said I didn't know what she was talking about. And she said I'm sure you know what I'm talking about. I didn't know anything that was going on. Dick just said, "Aw, she's crazy." . . . Richard was a friend of mine. I trusted Richard. . . . If I had ever encountered any wrongdoing, I would have said, hey, you gotta quit. Or I would have severed the relationship.

Question: Is there part of Richard you don't know?
Obie: It's possible.

Eberling had a short answer for Bogar. He had cleared all the hurdles. It had taken years and attorneys and worry and anxiety. Having to deal with the will contest, putting Obie through all that hubbub. But the will was probated, the payments had been made. He was the lawful heir, and he was rather enjoying the lush life. There was no going back.

This was not the answer Bogar wanted. "I went to Dick for help. He made excuses," she said.

"She says, 'I signed a blank piece of paper. They were supposed to pay me,'" Kremperger remembered. "She says, 'I'm gonna screw 'em. I'm gonna show how it's done.'"

The initial police report from November 15, 1983, Kremperger thought, was shoddy. It irritated him. He found the death certificate: "blunt impact; accidental fall." It intrigued him. He went down to the probate court in downtown Cleveland to see this piece of paper Bogar was supposedly talking about.

That's when he saw the report of Dr. Philip Bouffard. She wasn't lying. There really was something here.

Kremperger wanted to get Bouffard to conduct more tests on the will, but the court balked. "The probate court was telling me it was *done*. If it was fraud, if it was phony, all the heirs signed it. I said this is a criminal matter, not civil." Dr. Bouffard was finally allowed to perform tests. He soon knew what he had suspected before, that the typing was over the signature; whatever Durkin had signed, it wasn't typed on there when she had signed it.

Clenching this information, Kremperger pulled in detective Kurt Fensel to give him a hand. They started checking out the details. After months of work, in February 1988 Kremperger was feeling confident that he could make a case on a forged will when he decided to do one last interview of Bogar. He asked her what Eberling had on her that might be a surprise. "She says, 'Yeah, well.' I says, 'Yeah, what?' She says, 'I reported a burglary in Strongsville. He took all the stuff.'"

Kremperger cringed. A fake burglary. A fraudulent insurance report. "That kind of takes the wind out of your sails."

Bogar said that when she had called and demanded money from Eberling, he challenged her with a hey-Pat-whatever-happened-to-all-that-property-"stolen"-from-your-place-in-Strongsville?

The officer went back to the file. The Scheidlers were the other element. They were witnesses to a will that was no good, and they had testified in probate court in 1984. That might mean perjury as well as forgery, but they weren't talking. Kremperger decided to play hardball.

On July 1 he had the Scheidlers arrested. This was another July that was not looking good for Richard Eberling.

The cops booked Bev and Dale Scheidler in Lakewood. They were photographed and fingerprinted. Before the police knew what was happening, an attorney representing Eberling appeared, saying he was there as counsel for the Scheidlers. The move backfired. "She was pissed," Kremperger recalled. Bev decided she was not going to jail and began to talk.

Eberling, in a 1994 interview, related, "Dale called and told me, 'I told what I had to tell.' Meaning, he confessed." Eberling stopped, then added awkwardly, "Meaning, 'I told them what they wanted to hear.'"

The girders that Kremperger needed to hold tight his forgery case began to fit in place. Bev Scheidler described how Eberling had had her come to Maple Cliff Drive with a typewriter on January 6, 1984. Durkin was already dead. Richard handed her two sheets of paper, blank except for the signatures of Ethel Durkin and Pat Bogar, and asked her to type two wills. Scheidler protested mildly before going ahead. The two documents, when typed, were identical except for the signatures: one had "Ethel M." and the other had "Ethel May." Eberling decided to go with the one that had "May" because he thought it looked more homespun, as if Ethel had typed it herself. It was a bad choice: the one with "M." instead of "May" did not have any overlap onto type. Then, alternately coaxed and goaded by Eberling, Bev and Dale agreed to sign as false witnesses. They were promised part of the take. Bev was set up to give the will to Francis Feighan at the wake.

As the day in probate court rolled around, Eberling met with the Scheidlers to help them prepare their testimony.

He had little scripts typed up that they were to memorize. They did that, and they also kept the scripts. Kremperger took them as evidence.

Eberling offered the Scheidlers a sweetener for their trouble. The week before they were to testify in probate court, he suggested that they could stage a burglary, describing the burglary at the Durkin home to show just how easy it could be. The Scheidlers went out to dinner, and when they came home, voilà, they had been burglarized. Richard helped them gather receipts and get appraisals to fill out a false insurance claim that brought them fifty thousand dollars.

The case was presented to the grand jury later in July, and Eberling, Henderson, and Bev and Dale Scheidler were all indicted for forgery, perjury, tampering with evidence, and tampering with records. Dick and Obie were also charged with several counts of grand theft and aggravated grand theft, and the Scheidlers with complicity in committing theft. Richard and Obie were arrested on July 13, 1988, in Tennessee. Obie was removed as executor of Durkin's estate; attorney Marvin Koblentz was named to replace him.

Eberling pointed out, endlessly, that Patricia Bogar was not even in the Cleveland area on the day that the will was dated: May 7, 1982. He was with her, driving her van to Florida, and he could prove it. What she was saying, Eberling said, was a lie. That the date on the will could have been faked like everything else never seemed to faze him: he harangued about this useless detail for years afterward.

Dick and Obie were convinced that they were the victims of political intrigue and conspiracy. "Can not say how far this case will reach. Once the truth starts to flow," wrote Richard.

Eberling publicly scoffed at the arrests, but his hands told a different story. They were peeling, the skin coming off in layers. When police tried to take fingerprints, they were utterly worthless. One officer thought he had a skin disease.

"The reason was nerves," said Eberling later. "I was picking at my fingers." He thought the police were trying to take his fingerprints, possibly a palm print, for comparison in some other case.

While held in jail that summer, Richard had an unusually violent nightmare. The whole world shook around him.

After the July indictment on will forgery, Kremperger still had suspicions about Durkin's demise. But he had no proof.

At the urging of Cuyahoga County prosecutor George Rukovena, Kremperger was running down everything he could. For their parts, Richard and Obie refused to talk to Kremperger. In fact, they rather despised him.

Lakewood officers got a search warrant in August 1988 for Richard and Obie's twenty-seven-room home in Lookout Mountain, Tennessee. Ed Hoover, a criminal investigator with the district attorney's office in the Chattanooga area who helped execute the search warrant, described the house as lavish, filled with an amazing amount of silver and china, drawers upon drawers of it. "They knew the quality things of life," he said.

Officers found items of great interest to them, including the Rubina epergne and Tree of Life dinnerware supposedly stolen from Ethel Durkin's home in 1984; the will of the deceased husband of a woman on the West Side with whom they had become friendly; a Fisher stereo rack system claimed to have been stolen from the Scheidlers; a rug claimed on an insurance form by Bogar; and a silver plate and portrait painting that seemed to belong to the city of Cleveland.

The thirteen-hour search, videotaped, was the subject of a legal motion to suppress evidence later. But like many things that seemed to be slipping away, Richard and Obie lost the challenge to the search.

Kremperger continued questioning the Scheidlers. They were under indictment and they were scared. And they were constantly coming up with eye-openers. First the typing of the will. Then the phony signing. Then the presentation of the will at the wake. Next the dummied-up burglary and insurance scam, and the scripts of perjured testimony.

A polygrapher had Bev Scheidler hooked up in one room when he called Kremperger in. Bev broke down and she was telling the truth, the polygrapher said. Kremperger heard the next installment. In April 1985 Bev had had dinner with Eberling at a West Side favorite, The Dock, formerly known as The Blue Fox. Dale was in the hospital at the time. As they drank and ate, Bev remarked that it was a shame that a fall like Durkin's could actually kill someone. According to Bev, Eberling smirked and said, "She didn't fall; I hit her."

Kremperger moved quickly. He got documents flying to Coroner Elizabeth Balraj, Sam Gerber's successor, for an order to disinter the body.

"I'm angry with Bev Scheidler," Eberling said. "She said I told her I hit Ethel. I'd never tell anybody such a thing. I wasn't born yesterday."

The incredible power of the coroner in Cleveland once again became apparent. Balraj ordered that Durkin's body, buried near Buffalo, be dug up and brought back to the coroner's morgue on the East Side of Cleveland.

On September 10, 1988, Dr. Balraj personally conducted an autopsy. The body was covered with a greenish moss and exuded a foul odor. The body was photographed, removed from the casket, and undressed.

Balraj prepared an amendment to the original coroner's verdict of three and three-quarters years earlier, finding, in addition to the contusion of the right forehead and fractures of the cervical vertebrae, other medical evidence of injuries: a one-quarter-inch segment of the spinal cord around the vertebrae that was soft and collapsed, and "a dull brown oval area of subscapular contusion 2" x 1" in dimension" in the left rear scalp.

In essence, what the coroner was saying was that she found a previously unidentified bruise to the back of the head. "A big hematoma in the front," explained Kremperger, slapping the top of his head, "and in back," slapping the back of his skull.

The cause of death on the original coroner's verdict, signed by Gerber, and the cause of death on the amended coroner's verdict were the same: "Blunt impact to head with fracture of cervical vertebrae." But two words on the original document were slashed out and were replaced with a single word. Where it had read ACCIDENTAL FALL, the coroner's verdict now read HOMICIDE.

More than merely describing injuries, the coroner made conclusions. Since Durkin had been found face down, the coroner decided that the newly discovered injuries were inconsistent with the explanation provided about the fall. The coroner now claimed that Ethel May Durkin had been killed by being hit with a blunt object, at least once on the back of her neck, or possibly several times on the front and back of her head.

With that one swoop, the entire Durkin case changed. One year, a woman died and the cause of death was an accidental fall. Now, years later, the power of the coroner's office was manifested anew as the cause of death was changed to homicide.

Had the coroner been derelict the first time around? Or incorrect the second? In an appellate brief, defense attorney Beverly Pyle took the process to task, arguing that an independent examination should have been conducted. The attorney claimed that the autopsy had contained major errors, including a statement that the female genitalia were in place when, by most accounts, Durkin had had a hysterectomy and the uterus thus was not in place. There was also the possibility that, buried in the ground, blood had settled or injuries might have changed over time. Why had hospital X rays not shown any injury? An independent expert pointed out in 1995 that a bruise from mid-November, when Ethel was taken to the hospital, would probably have healed by January when she died. Was there a bruise inflicted closer to the date of death? he wondered. "That was not murder. It was a settlement of blood," said Eberling. "The embalming blows out blood in the veins."

Based on the new autopsy findings, Richard George Eberling and Oscar Buford Henderson were indicted for murder. On October 13, 1988, a grand jury returned charges against them: one charge of aggravated murder, which was added to eight charges relating to the will, probate, financial management, burglary, and insurance fraud.

As he admitted himself to the HCA Valley Hospital in Chattanooga in November 1988, Eberling was in a panic. "When first being arrested, that was a horrible jolt. But later being indicted for murder, that was the straw that broke my back. Simply couldn't handle, took a nose dive into depressation [his spelling] and liquor (manic)."

Political maneuvering and insatiable relatives engineered the charge of murder as a means to invalidate the will, Richard and Obie believed. In interviews later, while he sat in prison, Eberling described his disgust. If Ethel were alive, he said, "She'd blow her stack. She'd tell her relatives off in a hurry. Tell the Lakewood police off. She loved a good fight. Then she'd turn around and clap. She'd be so damn disgusted. Ruining someone's life—she wouldn't buy that."

One more surprise awaited the Durkin relatives after the photographs were developed from the exhumation. Such photos are rarely pleasant. These were downright grue-some—"more horrendous than the best efforts of Holly-wood special effects horror films," wrote appellate defense attorney Pyle. Later, the Court of Appeals of Cuyahoga County agreed with her and held that photographs of Mrs. Durkin's moss-covered body should not have been intro-duced in court, but would not change the guilty verdict on that basis.

Relatives who had been at the memorial service observed something different when they looked at the photos. Ethel May Durkin had been buried in her fur coat. When the casket was dug out of the ground, there was no fur coat on her body.

Kremperger knew by then what had happened to the fur. In fact, he had it. And he had gotten it from Bev Scheidler. After Ethel Durkin's wake, Richard tossed it to her and said it was partial payment for typing the will. "Isn't this supposed to go in the casket?" she supposedly asked. "They'll never know if it is or not," he responded.

"They got caught," said Robert Steely, the attorney who represented Linda Newton, and himself a former prosecu-tor, "because of their own cheapness. Their getting caught was a matter of sheer outright greed."

Later, in the course of an interview of Eberling about the Durkin case, the question arose: "Would you do anything differently?" He thought for a bare moment. "Yeah," he said. "I'd have the body cremated."

When Eberling did not show up for a court appearance in December 1988 because he was in a Tennessee psychiatric institute, the court revoked his bail bond and ordered him brought to Cleveland on a fugitive warrant. After that, Eb-erling lived in custody.

One of the things that bothered Richard the most was how Obie was being treated. "It's terrible to ruin a person. And when it affects somebody else," he said. "I put *myself* into it. It was my doing that he got involved with her in the first place."

In fact, the murder charge against Henderson, rooted in complicity to commit murder, was later overturned, along with other charges of forgery, tampering with records, and grand theft. Four charges were confirmed, the most serious being two theft charges based on the transfer of funds from Durkin's accounts and the cashing of the seventeen-thousand-dollar check from the insurance company to pay for losses from the burglary on Maple Cliff Drive. The prosecutor had argued that Obie was guilty of murder because the homicide was the culmination of a chain of events, and that Obie signaled his participation in them when he answered the phone on November 15, 1983, and said, "What's done is done." The appellate court reasoned that only Richard Eberling had been present when Ethel May Durkin fell, and only he was guilty of murder.

The jury that initially sat on their joint trial judged them harshly, though, and July 1989 turned out to be another bad month for Eberling. The trial lasted for a month; there were two hundred exhibits and sixty witnesses. Obie testified; Richard did not. Each had separate lawyers, although not those hired originally. After receiving instructions from Judge Donald C. Nugent, the Cuyahoga County jury deliberated for eleven and a half hours over two days before returning its verdict on July 7, 1989. Richard George Eberling was found guilty of aggravated murder, forgery, three counts of grand theft, one count of aggravated grand theft, tampering with evidence, and complicity to commit perjury. The charges against Eberling stuck on appeal.

Eberling was sentenced to life imprisonment plus a term of years. The life sentence didn't begin until after time was served on two other sentences of five to fifteen years and thirteen years. He was ordered to pay massive restitution, and a condition was included in his sentencing that he and Obie be placed and kept in two different prisons throughout their incarceration. Obie's initial sentence was later reduced to approximately fifteen years.

Obie: Just lies. The principal witnesses committed perjury. . . . It was all political. It bothers me. So much suppressed evidence. Getting the coroner to exhume the body. . . . All this evidence they wouldn't allow. . . .

Richard: The hospital records were never read. Obie read them. Mrs. Durkin said she slipped—fell. That's how it happened—she had an accident. That was said by a nurse who didn't know anybody.

Obie: Feighan—I called him to testify. The judge said it would not be in the best interests of the client. I should have never listened.

Richard: I did things just the opposite of what Richard Eberling does. I usually go for the very best. We thought there was nothing to it. [But I felt] . . . You know they have nothing on you. You know you're innocent."

Obie: I think I'm a victim of circumstance. I shared a house with someone and they said I had to know what was going on. Everyone was lying and making one big thing out of another.

Richard: They made us look like a bunch of thieves—take an old lady. They don't look at the other side.

Obie: I was straight up on the witness stand. I was ignorant and naive at the age of fifty-nine. I heard fabrications, nothing but perjured testimony. And the sentences the judge gave were the maximum because of what he heard. I've had two traffic tickets in my life. He said, "It's obvious you have no respect for the law." . . . What if I had been a criminal? How could he say that?

Richard: I didn't take the stand. I wanted to. My attorney wouldn't let me. I was too naive to ask him, I didn't know how the court system worked. It was like a Grimm's fairy tale.

Obie: I thought I had really good friends but no one came to my defense.

Richard: Obie, he said to me, "We're in this together; we'll go down together and we'll rise together."

More things were going down than up. The new executor for the Durkin estate, in order to collect any money that belonged to the rightful heirs, took strong legal steps to strip Richard and Obie of their amassed fortune. Eberling was forced into involuntary bankruptcy. The shopping center and Lookout Mountain house were taken and sold. Any money that could be found was snatched up. The IRS came calling with claims and notices.

Attorney Francis X. Feighan, already in a nursing home by the time the murder trial was held, died not too long afterward. Kremperger retired. The Scheidlers, because of their cooperation, were sentenced to only five years' probation on the will forgery charges; Patricia Bogar was not charged. And the winding up of Ethel May Durkin's estate dragged on and on, with no closure in sight. Lakewood had one more solved homicide.

With or without her fur coat, Ethel May Durkin might have been surprised to learn that her resurrection was also bringing back to memory the phantoms that another prosecutor had spoken about so derisively decades earlier. A phantom burglar. A phantom murderer. A bushy-haired man. An intruder. There were a lot of phantoms in the Sheppard house, the prosecutor railed sarcastically in 1954. Now the conviction of Richard Eberling was reviving them.

"I think Eberling is a big bullshitter. You don't know what the hell he's going to say," said Lakewood's Kremperger. "You gotta admit a lot of the people around him suffered some unusual fate."

Eberling said, "Lakewood brought the Sheppard case back to life. I wish it would die. It's tiresome. It's a burden to talk about. . . . I feel like when I die I will have it on my tombstone."

TWENTY

Windows

Vern Lund was not expected. When he contacted Sam R. in 1990, his was not a name that had surfaced in any file of the Sheppard case. No police officer or lawyer or family member knew who he was. Now Vern Lund was beginning to pry the lid off the picture that Richard Eberling presented.

Lund had been prompted to write Sam R. by the newspaper articles following Sam R.'s visit to Eberling in prison. What bothered Lund was not the threat that Eberling said he heard from Esther Houk, or how Eberling said he had cut his hand on that same day, but the date that Richard Eberling gave for all this activity. Lund knew that Eberling did not work at the Sheppard home that week. Vern Lund knew this because he had worked as a window washer for Dick's Cleaning Service. On the Friday before Mrs. Sheppard's murder, it was Lund, not Eberling, who had washed the windows at the Sheppard home.

The dates that Eberling gave were critical. And even Bay Village police officers had noticed in 1959 that he changed them frequently. Now Vern Lund was saying that it was a fabrication in whole: Eberling wasn't there on July 2, 1954, or any other day that week.

As Lund described this history in 1990, he added that he was sick with cancer and didn't have long to live. He had to get this off his chest.

Sam R. understood the import. Perspective on Eberling from a different frame of reference was essential. What Eberling himself said snaked in circles, was contradictory, cryptic. He gave one story and then another. He blended, fused, mixed, and crossed paths.

In one letter to Sam R., Eberling lamented about himself and how he had "paid one helluva price for your mother's death." Was he trying to get sympathy? Attention? Did he have any concept about the "price" of a murder? Or was something about the murder of Marilyn Sheppard eating at him, putting pressure in a private place, or on a hidden persona? At times, Eberling spoke from a first-person point of view but as if he were in someone else's skin, as if he were a fiction writer projecting his personality on others, such as Dr. Sam or Esther Houk. At other times, he spoke about himself in the third person, as if inside that one lanky frame lived another Richard, another Dick, a Lenardic and an Eberling.

When asked, Eberling had an opinion about everything related to the Sheppard case.

> *Question:* Harold Bretnall, another detective hired by the Sheppards in the 1950s—did he ever talk to you?
> *Eberling:* Never talked to me.
> *Question:* Bretnall was very interested in those slippers that you mentioned that were under the bed.
> *Eberling:* The slippers were pink satin. They were on the floor. I don't know how they could have had blood on them. I don't think there's that much blood to drop out, that could be dripping down there.

In Sam R.'s reinvestigation, the slippers had reappeared. Opening a ragged box, Sam R. found himself staring at his mother's red-pink satin slippers, with their simple embroidered pattern on the toes, slightly flattened, but otherwise still in pristine condition, as if they had been a recent gift. There was no visible blood on the slippers.

The slippers had been kept in a box marked "important" by author Jack Harrison Pollack. These were the slippers that had been presented to the Dutch psychic, Croiset. Pollack had secured them from detective Harold Bretnall, who had, in turn, collected them from Dr. Sam's brothers. All that was left from Bretnall were the slippers.

And there was a memo about Bretnall's findings from author Paul Holmes. Neither Holmes nor Pollack published the information in the memo, which described Bretnall's assessment of the likely murder suspect. Bretnall, the memo said, "leaned to the 'window washer' theory. . . . But when the man was arrested he gave everything back and the Bay Village police gratefully dropped charges against him."

The old files, when reviewed by new eyes, showed Eberling's name obscurely tucked away. Vern Lund was never mentioned.

Jay Hubach, a Bay Village officer who never felt that Dr. Sam got a fair shake, tried to explain the Eberling connection to Jan Sheppard Duvall in 1982, but she had no access to records that would further flesh out the story.

Andy Tuney, Bailey's investigator, searched out Eberling in 1966, after hearing that police had once questioned him. "They secretly gave him a polygraph test—it was inconclusive. . . . They kept it hush-hush. They didn't want anyone to think that they would consider anyone else [than Dr. Sam]." The police, recounted Tuney, never did anything to check into Eberling's peculiar story about having cut his hand on the Sheppard property just days before the murder.

Even people who were not supporters of Dr. Sam had comments about Dick's Cleaning Service. One newspaper reporter wrote vehemently anti-Sheppard articles through the years. Yet, in a telephone conversation with criminalist Jim Chapman in 1982, she brought attention to one man:

> *Reporter:* I'm surprised you didn't ask me about the bushy-haired man.
> *Chapman:* Well, you know . . .
> *Reporter: (Laughs)* 'Cause I know who the bushy-haired man is.
> *Chapman:* Who's the bushy-haired man?
> *Reporter:* Well, his name is Dick Eberling and he was a window washer, but he also had light fingers and he stole . . .
> *Chapman:* Oh, the ring . . .
> *Reporter:* The ring . . .
> *Chapman:* Wait a minute, but that's not the same night, is it?
> *Reporter:* No, no, it wasn't. No, no. It was months before. There were many thefts out in Bay Village that were later traced to Dick Eberling . . .

Chapman: I'm sorry. I'm not quick enough. In other words, the bushy-haired man that Sam Sheppard "dreamed" up . . .

Reporter: That Bill Corrigan dreamed up . . .

Chapman: Oh, Bill Corrigan dreamed it up?

Reporter: Yes, you'd better believe it. Steve dreamed him up first.

Chapman: You think so?

Reporter: Oh, I know so. 'Cause I know Dick Eberling, and Dick told me the whole story, and Pat Gareau knows it, too.

Chapman: What story?

Reporter: That, this, they dreamed up the . . . the bushy-haired man was Dick Eberling, the window washer, as, you know, another possible suspect, and this was what Corrigan kept saying, you know, they had this evidence, the bushy-haired man, if they'd just find him, and they kept picking up hitchhikers and everything else. Well, the bushy-haired man turns out to be this kid in Bay Village who had a window-washing business. He just had a love for beautiful things, and when he'd be washing windows, if he was in the home alone, he'd just lift things from the dresser or table.

Chapman: Uh-huh.

Reporter: And take 'em home.

The subject was dropped after that, unfortunately, without delving into the explanation as to who had dreamed up Eberling's frequent comments about dripping blood on the steps.

So many aspects of Eberling's story were disjointed, hard to follow. And his story kept changing. No point could be verified or checked or discounted, if everything was a moving target.

Finally, the team working with Sam R. focused on three documents from Eberling. They organized Eberling's comments so that they could be worked with. First, Eberling wrote by hand a version of events that detailed what he believed had occurred on the night Marilyn Sheppard was murdered. Second, he drew an architecturally sound drawing of the interior of the house that indicated all the doors, including those to the basement. Third, in a statement framed like an affidavit, Eberling consolidated his comments and signed his name, saying it was an accurate reflection of his account.

With these materials there were definite points that could be tested:

- In 1954 he had a contract to wash the Sheppard windows and on July 2, 1954, he was on-site at the Sheppard home and had coffee with Dr. Sam and Marilyn Sheppard.
- There was a cellarway entrance to the house that was not locked.
- The steps to the lake were in disrepair.
- On July 2 he heard Esther Houk screaming at Marilyn Sheppard that she was going to "kill her."
- He cut his left index finger on a window in the kitchen.
- He spoke with Dr. Sam in the first days after the murder—approximately July 8, 1954, and told him what he had heard; he did not tell police, lawyers, or Esther Houk.
- He had heard from Ed Wilbert, an employee, that Dr. Sam Sheppard was having a homosexual affair with Spen Houk.
- In 1969 or 1970 Dr. Sam Sheppard told him that Esther Houk had committed the murder using a kitchen implement—patty shell iron or pastry maker, and that Dr. Sam and Spen Houk had covered it up.

Each point on the statement had its own peculiar set of challenges. Some were easier to deal with than others. A contract to wash windows at the home of Dr. Sam and Marilyn Sheppard could be verified. Dorothy Sheppard confirmed that easily enough, and a check from Marilyn Sheppard to Dick's Window Cleaning that was dated June 24, 1954, verified it. The fact that he worked for Dr. Sam and Marilyn seemed not in doubt, but it was not so clear that Dr. Sam had had much contact with him or had even met him. Eberling's interactions were with Mrs. Sheppard; Dr. Sam did not get involved in housekeeping activities.

And then there were points on the opposite end of the scale, such as the supposed homosexual relationship. It was virtually impossible to know for certain what people who had been dead for decades had done for sexual pleasure, unless a child resulted. But one huge reason that Dr. Sam

Sheppard had been convicted in 1954 was because of his heterosexual activities. He had had affairs, flings, flirtations, all with women. On this, his closest friends—Reverend Alan J. Davis; his second wife, Ariane; Bailey's investigator Andy Tuney; police officers; other doctors who worked with him; friends of Marilyn—generally agreed. Dr. Sam was quite heterosexually inclined.

And ultimately, the question of sexuality was a red herring, although a gay affair created a tempting 1990s version. It could derail those intent on solving the case, just as the information about Dr. Sam's affairs with Susan Hayes had thrown police investigators so wildly off course in the first place. Who was sleeping with whom, straight or gay, did not solve the murder. It answered nothing about who had attacked Mrs. Sheppard, disrobed her, and beat her.

The other points that Eberling raised needed to be checked and cross-checked, comparing them to Eberling's other statements and those of others. The task was time consuming and daunting. No wonder investigators were not eager to pick up the case and run.

Finding people who might have known something about Richard Eberling in 1954 was not easy. For example, John Eberling, a grandson of Richard's foster father, lived a few doors from Richard and recalled that by 1954, Richard had begun wearing a hairpiece. But because of his deep dislike for Richard, John had limited interaction with him.

The appearance of Vern Lund was exceptional. Lund located Sam R. through a newspaper reporter who had published a Sheppard story. Lund was originally from North Ridgeville, Ohio, a small town just south of Westlake. When he wrote to Sam R., he was convalescing in Oklahoma, living at his daughter's home. He emphasized that he was not well.

Lund related that he had entered the Air Force in July 1954, at the age of eighteen, and retired twenty years later. "Before I joined the Air Force I worked for Mr. Eberling as a window washer. . . . I was the one who washed your folks windows on the 3rd of July, 1954. I remember that there was a weight room in the house if that helps win your confidence. I need your forgiveness for not stepping forward in 1954 to testify against Eberling."

Lund said that once, in 1975, he had tried to tell his story to the Bay Village police, but they didn't seem interested. Then, in 1989 he contacted them again, and an officer talked to him.

Lund was disappointed because the officers didn't do anything with the information he provided. "I couldn't figure that out," he said. Doctors told him he had only months to live. He wanted to go to his Maker in a "state of grace." And, Lund wrote, he also wanted to be totally honest with young Sam. He had suffered from mental problems and nervous breakdowns.

But Sam R. saw a straightforwardness, a simple line of honesty and earnestness in his letter. Unlike many people who wrote with complicated stories, involving long scenarios and people who were dead, he had one simple point that he wanted to make. That Richard Eberling was lying about washing the windows and cutting his hand on the days before the murder of Mrs. Sheppard.

"I would like to see justice served," he wrote. "I expect the public opinion to demand a new trial to do the job. Marilyn Sheppard and her son deserve that much and I feel I owe it to them to do my part."

Was this Lund for real, or not? How much information did he have? What did he know? Did he have any reason to fabricate, lie? How specific could he be? Like Eberling's statements, Lund's information would have to be checked and cross-checked as well.

But his one clue about the date could be important. It seemed imperative that someone visit Vern Lund in Oklahoma City.

A constantly shifting date for the window-washing job was an indication that Eberling might be making it up, and had trouble remembering which version was correct. Given the intensity of the events that occurred early on Sunday, July 4, 1954, the day of Friday, July 2, would not have been forgotten by anyone close to the scene.

Suppose Eberling had placed another date on his version of events? An earlier date, more distant from the murder, would undermine the significance of his account. If Esther Houk made a threat right before the murder, that could be serious. But every minute, hour, day that intervened between the comment and the murder made it harder to find any relevant link.

The date also bore on Eberling's claim that he had cut his hand in the house. Was this a reality? Or was he trying to explain why his blood might have been found at the murder scene, to create a plausible reason why it should not be considered suspicious?

The Sheppard home was full of people, with more expected for the Fourth. Most people don't like to see blood. If any is spilled, they clean it up right away, for squeamish and sanitary and aesthetic reasons. If a worker in a household drips blood up and down the steps, he probably will wipe it up, especially if his reason for being there is cleaning. And if the Sheppards had found the window washer's blood on their steps, they surely would have cleaned it up, too. Elnora Helms, the part-time domestic worker at the Sheppard home, said that Marilyn Sheppard was especially swift to clean up when the dog bled in the house.

Eberling did not come forward with his story in 1954, despite the incredible public attention focused on the blood trails. Prosecutors in 1954 would have scoffed at any story suggesting that the blood trails had landed on surfaces and floors throughout the house in a way unconnected to the murder. Still, when Eberling finally made his claims to police, he gave several different versions of when and how he had cut his hand.

First questioned by Bay Village police in 1959, Eberling said that he had cut his hand at the Sheppards' house "four days" before the murder, which would have been Wednesday, June 30, or Thursday, July 1. In his second statement, he said that he performed the work early in the week before Mrs. Sheppard was murdered, which would have been Monday, June 28, or Tuesday, June 29. A check written to Dick's Cleaning Service by Marilyn Sheppard eleven days before the murder indicates that work had been done on or before June 24. By 1990 Eberling seemed to have settled firmly on the date of Friday, July 2, 1954, as the date upon which he had worked at the Sheppard home.

Even without talking to Lund, Eberling's story left several gaps. Eberling was absolutely certain that Dr. Hoversten was not staying there on the day that he cut his hand. But Dr. Hoversten was definitely staying at the Sheppard home on July 1 and 2. Part and parcel of Eberling's story was that he had had breakfast with Dr. Sam and Marilyn that morning. But in fact, Dr. Sam and Hoversten had breakfasted together, and then Dr. Sam had gone to the hospital, followed by Hoversten. When first questioned in 1959, Eberling was asked who was present on the day he cut his hand. "I was alone," he responded.

A right-handed man under normal circumstances, Eberling gave different versions of how he had cut a finger on his left hand. He told Bay Village officers that he had cut his finger in an "effort to take the storm window out of the window by the sink." July is late to be taking storm windows out for the summer, but if this had happened, Eberling would have taken the window to the basement and would not have gone upstairs, as he later described.

Ed Wilbert, a former Eberling employee located and interviewed by AMSEC, remembered a statement that Eberling made to him after the murder. Eberling said that he expected to be contacted by police because he had cut his hand storing windows in the basement, but Eberling mentioned nothing of this before the murder.

In a letter written to Sam Reese Sheppard, Eberling wrote: "I cut my finger on dumb cheap window. The backsplash was 4 inches high and presented a problem removing the storm sash." In more recent statements, Eberling was very specific and offered a slightly different version. He had cut his finger on a "damnable lock" on the kitchen window. In one interview, asked when he was last in the basement, Richard answered: "In June. The screens were downstairs. I put up the screens in June." Quickly, he added, "I was down there in July, for a second time."

Where he went after he cut his hand seemed to be a matter of confusion to Richard as well. Bay Village police officers in 1959 noted that he changed his story on this subject. First he said that he went down to the basement. Later, he changed this story and said that he also went upstairs.

In one interview, Eberling described having already completed the windows upstairs when he cut his finger in the kitchen. He said he walked down to the basement, but upon questioning, quickly modified his statement to add that he had also gone back upstairs to wash the bathroom window. In a letter to Sam R., he wrote in a sentence unadorned with punctuation: "Was never in the bathroom don't know why except saved money washing the window."

The only person who put Eberling's blood on the scene

of the murder was Richard Eberling. Articles printed about Eberling after his arrest in the Durkin case stated that Eberling's blood had been found at the Sheppard house, but that nothing had come of it. There was no truth in this because Richard Eberling's blood was *not* found; no one had the slightest idea of whose blood was on the blood trails or in the murder room. The blood had not ever been typed, even into broad ABO categories.

If the police or coroner had typed the blood, the police theory of the case would have evaporated. Only if the blood had been typed as O would the police have had any support for their contention that the blood was Marilyn Sheppard's and was transported on clothing or a weapon. The facts indicated that the blood had dripped from a wound. If the blood was type A, it might have matched Dr. Sam's blood type, but because he had no bleeding wounds, it could not have been his. Richard Eberling made several statements from 1989 to 1993 that his blood type was O positive. But medical records obtained in 1994, if correct, indicate that Eberling's blood type is A positive, the same as Dr. Sam's. If type A blood had been found, the prosecution's case against Dr. Sam would have crumbled. The prosecution fared far better by staying in the realm of inference.

All this background only made the timing of Eberling's statements more curious. Blood trails in the house had been sensationalized in 1954. But, the fact that the blood came from a bleeding wound on the killer's hand or arm was not publicly revealed until Dr. Kirk entered the case in 1955. Still, Kirk's findings were largely ignored by the media. The first real attention to Dr. Kirk's scientific work came in 1961 when Paul Holmes described the cut hand and blood trails in a few pages of his book. Yet upon his arrest in 1959, Eberling blurted out to the police that he had cut his hand in the Sheppard home. This statement suggested information about the manner in which the murder had been committed that could not have been picked up from the media. Eberling had an uncanny grasp of details that the experts had ferreted out only through sophisticated tests. This was underscored again by his 1989 description of the murderer (Esther Houk in his view) and his statement that Marilyn Sheppard had tried to bite the killer on the arm.

When it came to the how and why of cutting his hand, Eberling had conflicting things to say.

He said that he cut his hand and had dripped blood up and down the stairs.

He said at a different time that he had dunked his hand in his bucket, presumably to staunch or wash off the blood.

He said on another occasion that his blood had dripped, but that he had wiped it up.

The owner of Dick's Cleaning Service, whose motto was "we are expensive but we care," seemed to care not at all if he bled all over the house of a customer. Or so he seemed to be saying.

Lavern Leslie Lund was fifty-four in October 1990, when he sat with Cynthia Cooper in front of a video camera in his daughter's Oklahoma City living room to make a statement. His daughter, Julie Schofield, also listened in. She was a married mother who held a job and spent off-hours time writing children's stories. She had made over a small bedroom on the ground floor of their modest home for her ill father. The neighborhood was very much Oklahoma, with sparse vegetation and dry ground.

Vern, as he preferred to be called, was not a healthy-looking man. In moderately cool weather, he wore long underwear and a robe, and his body shrank into a stuffed rocker, legs pulled up to his chest, making him look smaller than his height of five feet nine inches. In good health he weighed between 165 and 180 pounds; now he looked a mere 120 pounds. His breathing was heavy as he explained that he had cancer of the stomach and lymph nodes.

With forthrightness, Lund stated that he was taking Prolixon for a "nervous condition." But the drug did not impair his ability to think; in fact, it helped him think more clearly. He spoke slowly, often taking a moment to absorb a question before answering. Smoking a cigarette and sipping on a giant glass of water, he answered willingly but with a midwestern spareness of words, never offering too much, answering each question squarely without adding more. He was a religious person, describing himself as a Roman Catholic charismatic.

Lund had moved to the North Ridgeville, Ohio, area in about 1948 with his parents and one brother. In 1954, when he was in the eleventh grade, Lund dropped out of high school and went to work for his father, a machinist. In the evenings Lund went to the Elyria Rollerina or other roller skating rinks, where he and his best friend, Marty Eskins, mastered speed skating. Eskins and Lund sometimes traveled in Marty's old car to out-of-state skating competitions. Marty knew that Vern, eighteen, wasn't happy working for his father, and in the late spring of 1954 he mentioned that a Mr. Eberling was looking for some window-washing help. Marty learned about the job because he was working in landscaping for John Antelic, a former Eberling foster son who kept his equipment in the barn on Bradley Road.

Lund hitchhiked to the Bradley Road farmhouse and Mr. Eberling—Lund really knew Richard only as "Mr. Eberling"—hired him to start in June. From his eighteen-year-old perspective, Eberling was "middle-aged." He described him as quite tall, over six feet, generally wearing jeans and a T-shirt, and as "normally masculine." The pay was eighty to ninety dollars a week—"good money back then"—and he would be paid in cash.

Lund worked five days a week. After hitchhiking to the Bradley Road house in the morning, he rode in Eberling's car to various window-washing or wall-cleaning jobs. Most of their job sites were private homes, but Lund remembered a cleaning job at the parish house of a church because Eberling had rifled through a desk and pulled out "girlie" magazines, confiscated from a wayward confessor, Lund imagined. Lund also recalled a job at a machine shop. "The windows were covered with oil," said Lund, "and he expected me to get it off with vinegar and water." Eberling later described the same jobs and the same formula for cleaning.

Lund remembered the job on the Friday before the Fourth of July. He'd been paid for the week later in the day, so he knew it was Friday. The murder that happened afterward helped to fix the event in his mind. "I will never forget that day as long as I live," said Lund.

But that morning, as they headed to the Lake Road home, an entirely different aspect of the work etched the day in his mind. On the way, Mr. Eberling made an announcement: Lund was going to do this house all by himself, a first. Every other day that week, Lund had worked side by side with Eberling, and they had not been to the Sheppards'. Mr. Eberling also told him to do the inside of the windows, as well as the outside. Lund had never done that before either, he said.

Eberling dropped Lund off at the Sheppard home, the ladders were unloaded, and Eberling drove away. "I knocked on the door and the lady of the house answered." The woman who answered the door had brown hair, was somewhat shorter than he was, weighed about 110 pounds, and was "very pretty". She was very nice to him. Later, she came out and offered him a soda—"the only person ever to give me a soft drink." Lund had no doubt it was Mrs. Sheppard.

He did his best with the cleaning assignment, and with one or two exceptions, the day went smoothly. There was one difficulty that he'd had to deal with, and one other matter that he felt guilty about.

The difficulty was a wasp. "I was on the roof, the porch roof. . . . I went to wash the windows and this one wasp went *buzz* right in front of my eyeballs. And I skeedaddled down the ladder. And was unable to do that window," recalled Lund. As he was leaving, he apologized to Mrs. Sheppard about the window with the wasp. "I explained to her and she was very sympathetic with me and understood that I couldn't wash the window."

And then there was the weight room. Lund, from a far less affluent background, had never seen anything quite like it. In the "dressing room next to the master bedroom, which Lester Hoversten was occupying, Dr. Sam had set up exercise weights. The temptation was too much for Lund. "I hefted one of the weights," he confessed. He raised it and then put it back on the rack.

Vern Lund never cut his hand anywhere—it was kind of hard to do with a bucket and a chamois, he said. His boss, Eberling, picked him up, drove him back to Bradley Road, and paid him. Lund hitched a ride home. Lund remembered having a normal weekend. He went to the roller rink with his friends and saw fireworks with his parents in Elyria. He didn't pay attention to the news.

The next week, he went back to work. When he climbed into his boss's car, Eberling stunned him with the information that Mrs. Sheppard had been murdered. "I was in shock. I was actually shocked. She was such a nice person. I wondered why anyone would want to kill her," he said. He did not see a cut on Eberling's hand and Eberling did not mention one. "And then in the next breath, he said that he was bisexual. And that was another shock."

Why Eberling was telling him this, Lund did not know, but bisexuality was something that frightened him. In early adolescence, an older man had lured Lund into sexual encounters and Lund was deeply conflicted about it because of his religious upbringing. He had married twice, but bisexual leanings had followed and bothered him for much of his life, Lund explained the next day, outside the presence of his daughter.

Lund didn't work for Eberling much longer. Later in the week, he quit and immediately left town. Eskins, Lund, and another friend decided to take off "for unknown places." Driving a 1947 Chevy, they lived a life of small adventure, driving and sleeping in the car. They got as far west as Iowa, where their car broke down. Funds depleted after the repair, they headed back to Ohio.

As soon as they returned, Vern and Marty Eskins went to the air force recruiting center and enlisted. They had been sold on a "buddy system" where young recruits could train and serve together. But after basic training in Florida, the two were split up and didn't see each other in the service again. Lund signed up for a four-year tour of duty as an aircraft worker. By July 29, 1954, according to his military records, Lund was out of Ohio at basic training.

Vern Lund was never questioned by the police in 1954, nor did he go to the police. Through the years, he would tell people he had worked for Mrs. Sheppard. He didn't know that he had something to offer in terms of solving the murder until much later.

In 1956 Lund married an English woman, with whom he would have five children. He didn't return to Ohio again until 1958, when he spoke with Eberling to find out what work might be available. But within a few weeks he decided to rejoin the service and left Ohio again. Lund served as an air frame repair technician, maintaining an E-6 status, and served 353 days in Vietnam in 1972. After leaving the service in 1974, Lund had a series of mental breakdowns, which he explained as a "chemical imbalance." In 1976 Lund and his wife divorced; he remarried in 1987; his second wife died within two years.

In October 1990, the day after making a taped statement, Lund signed an affidavit in front of an Oklahoma notary.

Earlier, he had thought he'd worked at the Sheppard home on July 3. But that date was an error; he was absolutely certain that he had been there on the Friday before the murder, or July 2, 1954. That was the statement that he signed.

Records secured in 1994 verified that Lund did go to the Bay Village police in July 1989 and tell them what he knew of Eberling. That part of his story was true. And he was consistent, giving essentially the same story: that he worked for Eberling, whom he described as a "middle age bald heavy set male who was a window washer." He described Eberling as living on Bradley Road near Lakewood Country Club. According to the police statement taken of Lund in July 1989, "He stated that he washed the windows in the Sheppard residence on 7-3-54 and was alone when he did so having been dropped off by his employer. On Monday following the murder of Marilyn Sheppard, he was told by his employer that he had washed the windows in the Sheppard home the week before." The officers showed Lund a 1959 mug shot of Eberling and he immediately identified him. Lund also told about various paranoid fears that he had about Eberling trying to set him up and make it seem as though he had committed the crime. Had the occasion arisen for police to investigate Lund, he felt that he would have been in a prime position to be blamed for theft or other nefarious activities.

Vern Lund died on August 8, 1991.

Marty Eskins moved back to Elyria, Ohio, where he lived with his wife, Pauline. In 1993, both of them recounted in an interview those days of 1954. Pauline was dating Marty then, and she, like Marty, was a friend of Lund's. She especially remembered the Sheppard case because Dr. Sam had treated her and she had great admiration for him.

Marty said he and Lund had traveled together and signed up for the service in 1954. Much bulkier than Lund, Marty recalled that he had been doing landscaping for John Antelic, no longer living. He remembered that Lund worked for Eberling and washed windows at the Sheppards'.

"I know Vern cleaned the windows, and it was just around the time she was murdered," said Marty. "I remember that he washed the windows just before we went into the service." Police never talked to either Eskins or Lund, he said.

One thing Pauline and Marty Eskins were both certain about: Vern Lund would not lie. Vern had a "close relationship" with the Lord, they said. "I don't think Vern would fabricate anything," said Pauline. "And if he didn't know, he told you," added Marty.

There was one other way to verify Vern Lund's statements: ask Richard Eberling. The basic facts that Lund gave about the type of work and some of the work sites were, in fact, confirmed by Eberling's own statements. Eberling, in describing his business, verified the machine shop and church where Lund said he had worked. Eberling said he used a vinegar-based solution. He described how he carried the ladders in his car and that ladders were necessary to reach the exterior of the Sheppard windows, just as Lund had said.

And then there was an opportunity to get right to the point by asking about Vern Lund. Did he remember him? Eberling was unnerved, suddenly visibly agitated. He began gesticulating with his arms, leaning forward, pointing, punctuating his words with a hard tap to the table. First he said that the Scheidlers, who had testified against him in the Durkin case, must know this guy and had dragged this up to try to get him. Soon he proceeded to other explanations. "He worked for John [Antelic] in landscaping, if for anyone," and he knew the Bradley Road property because John kept his equipment there. Then: Eskins never worked for John, and Lund never worked for Eberling, Richard announced.

"He didn't work for me. It's very easy to prove it. Bank records." Check stubs would prove it, Eberling said, although another former employee, Ed Wilbert, also said that Eberling often paid in cash.

Speaking both rapidly and in a rambling fashion, Eberling said that someone named Frank was the only person from North Ridgefield whom he had ever employed. If Lund worked for him at the Sheppards', ask him to draw a layout of the house. Anyhow, Eberling said, he couldn't afford to send someone else to do the Sheppard windows because the Sheppards didn't pay enough, even though earlier Eberling had said that Ed Wilbert had worked at the Sheppards'.

"Wouldn't they have checked those men?" he demanded. Wilbert confirmed that the police never spoke to him.

Eberling continued to froth about the Scheidlers, about his records, and launched into a genuine rant: "Evidently the Scheidlers are going to pass out some bull. If they can't get me here, they can't get me there. Do you realize what it cost? They're going to have to restore my monies. All this is going to . . . We live in a gestapo state. The Houks—why would you have a fireplace going? Why did the young Houk boy find the bag so easily? That shows that [Dr.] Sam was a brilliant man but was stupid. He let them make a fool of him."

In letters and a subsequent interview, Lund came up again. Eberling asserted that Lund didn't work for him. Then he said that Lund worked for him but that it was in 1953, or that it was May, or that it was part-time. Other times, he became caustic, asserting Lund was a "buffoon" or a "goofball" and interviewing him was "idiocy, to say the least."

> *Question:* Why would Lund say this?
> *Eberling:* Why do people call in and say they were responsible for the [World Trade Center] tower explosion? A fruitcake. He wants a claim to fame. If Lund has something to say, why did he wait to come forward?
> *Question:* I don't know; the same might be said about you.
> *Eberling:* I didn't come forth. It will probably haunt me to my grave. The Lakewood police just jumped on it.

Several things were clear about Lund. Vern Lund had worked for Richard Eberling. Vern Lund had mental problems, but when he made his videotaped statement, he could think clearly. He gave the same statement to the Bay Village police. He was known as an honest man who spoke the truth. He begged to tell his story to clear his conscience at a time when he was ill and dying. A religious person, he wanted to release himself of sins and burdens. And Lund had a simple story. There was only one point to it: he, not

Richard Eberling, had worked at the Sheppard home on July 2, 1954.

Richard Eberling's versions of events, in that case, could not stand. It left unexplained when and how he had cut his hand in the house, if indeed he did. And if he had not cut his hand, why was he going to such extremes to say that he had?

After Vern Lund died, Eberling sent out one letter from the prison in which he referred to the "fellow who died" without using a name. In the letter, Eberling threw around a number of threats and said that no one should involve him in the Sheppard murder. He said he would deny everything that he had said. And anyhow, he added, surely there would be enough information from the "fellow who died."

No matter how much was added up about Eberling, there were blanks to be filled in. Everyone wanted answers quick and easy, like an instant novel, like a teleplay.

In 1994 *Plain Dealer* reporter James McCarty was planning a story on Eberling and the Sheppard case. Eberling had been brought to Cleveland from the prison in southern Ohio for a perfunctory court appearance on restitution. Visiting rules were less complicated at the jail than the prison. After hearing the same story about Esther Houk, McCarty wanted to arrange a lie detector test. Eberling agreed. He hoped that it would result in a more lenient sentence for Obie Henderson on the grand theft and other charges that had not been overturned on appeal.

A polygraph test could not fill in blanks: a person is merely asked to say yes or no to a series of regulated questions. Sam R. was skeptical that a good polygraph test could be done of Eberling and, if done, could be useful. But when asked, he suggested two things: that the polygrapher be from out of state, and that the polygrapher do a pretest to see if the subject was actually testable. He suggested to McCarty the name of Morris Ragus of Pittsburgh, a man recommended by AMSEC because he used a special pretest exam to evaluate whether a candidate was a fit subject for a polygraph.

Ragus went to Cleveland to conduct the examination on March 1, 1994. Eberling, who had grown a wild white beard, was taken to the designated room, where he told McCarty that he had changed his mind, based on the advice of his attorney. While McCarty searched for the attorney, Ragus talked with Eberling and learned that he was being medicated for depression with Prozac, lithium, and tranquilizers. This was a bad sign. Drugs that affect the central nervous system, such as those, could have an adverse effect on the physiological responses being recorded by the polygraph. Ragus did a pretest evaluation, using cards of various colors, and saw that Eberling was having trouble with simple instructions. Upon McCarty's return, he and Eberling got in a fierce argument about a photograph of the bearded Eberling. Richard got up and walked out. It didn't matter. Ragus concluded that he would not be a suitable candidate for a polygraph and that no examination would be valuable at that time.

That didn't stop the same attorney who advised Eberling not to take a polygraph from arranging for Eberling to take one on the Sheppard case only two days later. The attorney, paid by the state to represent Eberling on his Durkin appeals, had absolutely no connection to the Sheppard case and had not contacted or spoken to Sam R. Sheppard or any of his family members. He said he was reading all the old books about the case. He did work out an arrangement for a local freelance journalist, who was trying to sell the Sheppard story, to videotape Eberling. Eberling's attorney lined up a local polygrapher. Eberling was walked down the hall, flanked by two cameras. No pretest exam was conducted. Although preparation by the examiner is critical to a good test, the examiner's knowledge was based on dusty surface knowledge of the case, not any of the new information that had been tediously collected. After the test was completed, the journalist got a copy of the results, but they were not otherwise released.

Eberling wrote from prison afterward that he was pleased with the results of the polygraph test: "Now I can be left alone in peace, dam thing about drove me crazy. Thank God its all behind me. *Dead!* Should never have said a thing about the murder in the first place. But the Lakewood police started it. When we were first arrested down in Tenn. The F.B.I. brought it up before the federal judge. Frankly who gives a good dam who did it."

Later, Eberling said that his attorney told him that he had flunked part of the test. The test was useless and meaningless, given Ragus's determination. But it also muddied the waters. Lost was the opportunity to seriously approach Cleveland authorities about talking to Eberling about the Sheppard murder and urging them to take advantage of his return to Cleveland in order to seek real information to fill in the blank spaces. No one in authority had yet bothered to do so.

Meanwhile, Sam R. and those working with him knew that the only way to evaluate Eberling was the old-fashioned way, slowly digging, reviewing, checking small points, reconsidering—footwork.

Other points that Eberling offered gratuitously needed to be examined. Eberling said that he had been at home the night that Marilyn Sheppard was murdered. Then, in describing his home circumstances, he volunteered that once he was in the house, he couldn't even climb out a window. Another time, he related how, before retiring, he had looked out the window and then had gone to bed. Why was he bothering to mention the window at all? On yet another occasion, Richard related that blackened windows frightened him and that his mind sometimes became hyperactive at night. He said that after 1946, he slept on the glassed-in front porch of the Eberling home, from which a door led outside.

Eberling gave Bay Village police in 1959 two different times for his bedtime. One was 11:30 P.M., the other was 1:00 A.M. The Sheppard home was less than five miles from the Bradley Road farmhouse.

One part of Eberling's story relied on the knowledge of tenants who he said were then living in an upstairs apartment at the Bradley Road house and knew that he was at home. He identified the tenants as Stanley and Dolores Vrabec. Exactly when the Vrabecs lived at the Bradley Road address is unclear. Christine Eberling, Richard's foster mother, had to file accounts showing any rental income with the probate court every year. The reports ran from July through June. The report beginning with July 1955, and each report for nearly every year thereafter, specifically listed rental income from the upstairs apartment. The report beginning with July 1954 did not list any rental income. There appears to be a strong possibility that no tenants were living at the Eberling house that July. Stanley Vrabec was located by AMSEC in North Carolina in 1995. But the man who answered flatly refused to speak. Whether Vrabec could further support Eberling's version of events was unknown.

Slowly Sam R. was trying to search out the people who knew Eberling in 1954. Ed Wilbert was a name that kept cropping up. Eberling mentioned Ed Wilbert, his "long-time" employee, time and time again. Ed Wilbert worked for him in 1954. Ed Wilbert was distantly related to the Eberlings. Ed Wilbert had been the first person from Dick's Cleaning to meet Marilyn Sheppard. Ed Wilbert, according to Eberling, had the inside information on various affairs of Spen Houk and others.

In a letter, Eberling wrote: "When you review my past records a full time employee will appear. . . . This fellow worked the month before at Sheppards home. He knew Marilyn. He was outa state when the murder occurred. A true honest alibi! . . . His name wasn't brought up when Sam told me who the real murderer was."

Several times Eberling claimed that he had an account at the Sterling Hotel, which had something of a low-life reputation, and that Ed Wilbert had seen men and women having affairs there. Or, he said, there was a hell of a lot of spice" around this fellow. Wilbert was a source of information on Eberling's business, life-style, and contact with the Sheppards.

Somehow, it felt important to contact Ed Wilbert, but no one knew where he was. Eberling thought he was dead. "Saw him ten to twelve years ago. He stopped off to visit. Unfortunately, everyone in my life is dead."

Ed's cousin, Harold, had been an officer on a West Side suburban police force and had been part of the team that arrested Eberling for larceny in 1959. Harold had retired. In the early 1990s, he was not well and his memory was fading. He couldn't remember where Ed was, let alone whether he had—well, maybe yes, he had—worked for Eberling.

When AMSEC joined with Sam R., investigators immediately agreed that Ed Wilbert might be an important link, since he had firsthand knowledge of Eberling in 1954, and because he was so frequently mentioned by Eberling himself. Using the type of computer tracking data employed in corporate background checks, they learned that Wilbert was not dead, as Richard Eberling had thought. He was very much alive and living in Florida. In 1993, Edmund William Wilbert was already seventy-nine years old, and time was not to be wasted.

By phone, Wilbert was reluctant. "There's not much I can tell you on him. I mean, I worked for him for a short while. I can tell you that much. I finally quit and, well, moved out of Cleveland altogether. Most of this was done, I never even realized it. You know. Then of course a lot of this was done, I didn't have anything to do with him anymore, I never saw him anymore."

Wilbert said he worked for Eberling on and off from 1951 to 1958. "From then on, I never saw the man." He'd been in St. Louis and Washington, D.C., where he made money buying, renovating, and selling real estate. He then owned a successful dairy cream store near an air force base and in 1970 moved to Florida.

When he cleaned windows for Dick's Cleaning, Eberling would tell him where the sites were and Ed traveled there on his own. The jobs were mostly in Westlake or Rocky River. He had never washed windows at the Sterling Hotel; he said he had never heard of it. Yes, he had worked for Dr. Sam and Marilyn, but didn't know either of them very well. "I guess I saw them once or twice in all that while. I wasn't working there at that time [of the murder]. I was working a different job when that happened."

> *Question:* Eberling says that there were a lot of things that he told you or you told him about Sheppard.
>
> *Wilbert:* No, that's nothing. That's not anything. No. I don't go along with any of that.
>
> *Question:* You think he's bringing your name up to—
> *Wilbert:* Just forget about it.
>
> *Question:*—to make this up.
> *Wilbert:* Yeah . . . yep. Evidently. That's about all I can tell you.
>
> *Question:* When you worked at the Sheppards', was Eberling alongside?
> *Wilbert:* Not necessarily, no.
>
> *Question:* Ever meet Mrs. Sheppard?
> *Wilbert:* Oh, she was in the house when I was working there, yes. Same as all the rest of the customers. Yeah,

well, I'm not going to waste any more time on this, so
I'll just say good-bye.

Three months later, at a strategy meeting with three
AMSEC investigators, Wilbert's name came up again.
"Where is he?" asked Allen E. Gore, a retired New York
police detective and former commander of the Bronx district attorney's detective squad, now working for AMSEC.

"Fort Myers Beach."

"I'll stop by there next week," Gore said.

Gore went to the address in Florida in December 1993.
Gore, in his late fifties, is unprepossessing in appearance,
wears glasses of a not especially popular style, and, under
a dangling and slightly out-of-date sports jacket, carries a
gun in a holster. Shocks of hair can easily dangle in his
eyes without his noticing it. Instead of taking over a conversation, his style is to listen, to become an invisible cipher
and slowly try to shift the conversation to the topics of
concern to him.

When he arrived at the address, Gore saw a man sitting
in a deck chair on the patio, and a For Sale sign in the
yard. Unobserved, he took a couple of pictures and then
decided to ask about the house as a way of feeling out
the situation.

The man was not Ed Wilbert, but a housemate, Joe
Malik. He too was from the Cleveland area, and he and
Wilbert had lived together for nearly forty years. Wilbert
was inside and eventually joined the conversation as Gore
toured the property. The two men, although older, lived
comfortably in well-toned middle-class circumstances and
definitely took good care of themselves.

After easing himself into the house, Gore told them what
his real interest was. He said he was representing Sam
Reese Sheppard, and he wanted to talk to them about
Richard Eberling. The conversation slowed, even shut
down for a while. They didn't really want to talk. Malik
mentioned that he too knew Eberling. They were hesitant.
Slowly, just as he had worked his way into the house, Gore
engaged them in a three-way conversation.

Wilbert had a slight hearing defect, and Malik was the
more garrulous of the two. He would often take over the
conversation, deflecting questions directed to Wilbert, in-
terceding if necessary. But Malik had his own thoughts

about Richard Eberling, and they were not kindly. His shorthand description: "conniver, con man, liar, and vicious if pushed."

Slowly, Wilbert began to say more. He had worked for Eberling for several years, was paid in cash or sometimes by check. On several occasions, he went to the Sheppard home to clean windows or remove or replace storm windows. Often, no one was home, he said, and a door would be left unlocked for entrance. Kokie, the dog, might be there, but was pitiful as a guard dog and never barked at Wilbert or at strangers at all. Once, he announced that he was there to wash the windows, and a woman called down and said that he should come in and help himself.

He remembered the other means of entry: the basement door. The outside cellarway entry to the basement was always unlocked, he said.

Eberling, he thought, was a social climber. He had somehow wriggled his way into a membership at the prestigious Cleveland Yacht Club, said Wilbert. Dorothy Sheppard had mentioned that, as well. One time, Wilbert said, Eberling tried to bar Dr. Sam and Marilyn from coming into the club because they supposedly appeared in "dirty attire."

After Marilyn Sheppard was murdered, Wilbert was never interviewed by the police or any law enforcement person. He had talked about the case informally with his police officer cousin, Harold, but no Cleveland or Bay Village cop or Cuyahoga County sheriff or coroner's representative ever came to talk to him. Eberling said to him one time, "Guess they'll want to speak to me. I cut my hand storing storms in the basement the day before the killing and dropped blood on the basement stairs." Nobody talked to Eberling. Wilbert never saw any cut on Eberling's hand.

People in Bay Village knew Eberling was a crook, said Wilbert. For some reason, in the polite pastoral suburban venue in which they lived, many people, usually the women of the house who had direct contact with Eberling and whom he seemed to charm in some way, let it pass and tolerated his thievery rather than confront him.

But there was one exception, one person who wouldn't tolerate his stealing. "You know," said Wilbert, "Marilyn was going to blast him, and told him so. She didn't like him." Marilyn Sheppard, he said, had caught Eberling trying to steal.

When AMSEC sent out Gore's report to Sam R., its style was straight-forward, unpretentious. These words practically burned through the paper.

Had Marilyn Sheppard known in 1954 that Richard Eberling was stealing? Eberling was never even under police suspicion in Bay Village until 1956. He was not arrested for his thievery until the end of 1959, after it had reached outrageous levels, and when a man, at home that day and hearing an odd noise, called the police. Yet in 1959 Eberling himself told Bay Village police and a psychiatrist at the Cleveland Clinic that he had begun stealing from clients in 1953.

In an interview in 1994, Eberling was asked to respond to Wilbert's comment. He had a moment of wonderment that Ed Wilbert was alive and had been located. "Where did you find him?" he asked.

As for Marilyn Sheppard having caught him in the act of stealing, he scrunched his face like a small child. "Nope. Nope. Nope. There was nothing in that house to steal. That house was bare." Yet when he had been confronted by Bay Village police about Marilyn Sheppard's ring in 1959, he admitted that he had seen it on a dresser at the home of Dr. Sam and Marilyn before she was murdered and had admired it then, but had not stolen it.

Ed Wilbert, Eberling said, would not have "bad-mouthed" him. He became perturbed. "Did he say how good I was to him?" Eberling demanded. "How would he know that Marilyn Sheppard hated me? . . . She wouldn't sit on the step and talk to me if she hated me." He continued, "He was not aware I was stealing. . . . I never discussed my clients with him. How would he know that I took something out of the Sheppard house? . . . Maybe it's jealousy on his part. Because he never made it. . . . I think it's gossip that he heard. And it's taking on color. If Marilyn Sheppard caught me stealing, she would have fired me. She would not have had me. I'm very clear on that," said Eberling.

Richard Eberling had two things on his mind: money and security. If he were exposed by someone like Marilyn Sheppard, as popular and well known in the community as she and her husband and their relatives were, then his business could be wrecked. Things could be taken away. He thought of them as family and now she was turning her back, the same way he had been treated as a CAS orphan. The arrogance of someone who had everything threatening to take away the small opportunities of someone who had struggled so hard could be overwhelming.

Who was Richard Eberling?

Slowly a picture emerged. Richard Eberling was a complex man, whose personality had sides that were layered and crisscrossed and sometimes well cloaked.

Who was Richard Eberling?

He was in prison for the murder of a woman for whom he had been a caretaker, a murder he said he did not commit.

He was in prison at the same time for aggravated theft, setting up false burglaries at three sites, helping to collect and organize false receipts for the stolen property, and defrauding insurance companies.

He was in prison at the same time for forging the will of an elderly woman and usurping the money that would have rightfully gone to relatives and heirs of the woman and her husband—a scheme that he had planned and carried out over a period of years.

He was in prison at the same time for complicity to commit perjury by encouraging and aiding lying under oath, in sworn testimony before the probate court.

He was a thief convicted of larceny, having admitted to over forty burglaries at residential properties in the West Side suburbs of Cleveland, and having been suspected of three times that number.

He was illegitimate, abandoned by his mother.

He was a foster child who had been shifted around to six homes and the Children's Aid Society.

He was not an Eberling by birth or adoption, but had changed his name to Eberling from his birth name of Lenardic.

He was sexually abused as a child by a foster parent, he claimed.

He wore toupees, and ones that, by the account of a friend, gave him a "bushy-haired" appearance in 1954.

He was a large man: six feet one inch tall and, when in his twenties, weighed between 180 and 190 pounds.

He had a large head, so much so that it had been medically designated as such (dolichocephalic).

He had blackouts as a child even to the point of unconsciousness, and suffered from dizzy spells and racing thoughts as an adult.

He suffered from Saint Vitus' Dance as a child, a disease that causes physical spasms, is heightened by emotional stress, and is accompanied by emotional instability.

He had problems as a child involving stealing and inability to tell the truth; he had signs of schizophrenia and was seen to be developing into a psychotic.

He was described by a psychiatrist who saw him in his twenties as needing prolonged psychiatric care.

He was classified 4-F by the Selective Service.

He said he had O positive blood; medical records showed he had A positive blood.

He had worked at the Sheppard home in 1954 as a window washer.

He said he had worked at the Sheppard home on the Friday before Mrs. Sheppard was murdered, but this was not true.

He knew the Sheppard property extremely well, and was able to make a detailed drawing of it.

He knew about a cellarway entrance to the property that was always unlocked and opened into the basement, and at which site a police investigator found "fresh tool marks," although evidence of this was suppressed.

He thought that the steps to the Sheppard beach were not safe in 1954, although they had been repaired in 1953; and a parallel path through the brush had been found the morning of the murder, along which path the green bag was found.

He was familiar with the docile nature of the dog at the Sheppard home.

He was not questioned by the police in 1954.

He drove a blue Ford station wagon in 1954.

He was familiar with many of the Sheppard neighbors along Lake Road and knew the neighborhood very well.

He was first questioned by the police in 1959, when Dr. Sam Sheppard had been incarcerated for over five years.

He was not allowed to participate in athletics as a young person, something that he resented.

He resented pampered members of the upper-middle class. While living with his elderly foster mother, he was able to convince her to transfer to him, for small amounts of money, property that had been left to the heirs of the family that homesteaded and built it, for which he was later able to obtain over three-quarters of a million dollars.

He drove home and parked by the Bradley Road barn, possibly emptied of certain stored property earlier in the day, moments before it burst into flames and was consumed by fire.

He lied.

He lied about his parentage.

He lied to commit fraud in insurance swindles.

He lied under oath in a New Jersey court to obtain an inheritance from someone of no relation.

He devised a plan to get other people to lie in probate court, and coached them to do so.

He lied to police officers in 1959 and changed his story about the Sheppards.

He stole small items that had no marking or identification, such as watches, rings, cash, jewels, and also expensive collector-style figurines; but not checks, cars, or items with identification numbers.

He stole Marilyn Sheppard's rings from the home of her brother-in-law, picking them out from a box of items stored in a closet, and marked "Marilyn Sheppard property."

He kept Marilyn Sheppard's rings wrapped and hidden in a manner and style different from that of other items he stole.

He had been the driver of a vehicle when, in an unusual accident, he smashed one side of the car into a stationary vehicle, killing the young woman riding with him.

He did not go to police with information that he claimed to have about the murder of Marilyn Sheppard at any time; nor did he seek any cash reward.

He did not testify in any trial involving Dr. Sam Sheppard, although he had been interviewed and considered as a potential witness about unlocked doors for Dr. Sam's 1966 trial.

He was unmarried, and lived for thirty years with a bachelor friend.

He was arrested in 1988, but his fingerprints could not be taken because of severely flaking skin, which he ascribed to nervous picking.

He took drugs for depression, suffered migraines and headaches, and was diagnosed as suffering from alcohol abuse in 1986.

He frequently changed stories about what he saw and heard and did at the Sheppard home.

Who was Richard Eberling? On the surface, he was congenial and most comfortable when he could tell stories in which he fared well or had succeeded. He had an exterior personality that persuaded and charmed many people. Sometimes, though, a door would open—a window, unwashed—and another Richard Eberling would appear.

He wrote letters with choppy phrases serving for sentences, and in them, he spoke out on a range of subjects—his admiration of Hitler's economic success, his revulsion at those who had "betrayed" him, his opinion that women were inferior to men, his theories of the political conspiracy that had engulfed his own case, his belief in astrology and how people are "recirculated" after they die, and his long list of those he intended to sue. He would be alternately friendly and vitriolic, threatening and boastful. Sometimes he would attempt to raise a fist inside a linguistic glove, such as, "When you speak to [him], please tell him I am so happy he is no longer drinking," or, "You are too nice to sue." He would switch from a first-person "I" to a third-person "Richard" within a paragraph. Frequently he gave answers that went well beyond the question asked, and that provided insight into his perception.

Who was Richard Eberling? His own words described him best.

Question: What would you like to be remembered for?
Eberling: Actually, nothing. I'd like to dry up and go away. I'd like to be remembered for good things. I helped people out. I've been very considerate of people.

Eberling: I'm a pretty self-reliant person.
Question: Meaning?

Eberling: That means I can cope on my own. Even in here [prison].

Question: Is that part of the problem?

Eberling: I cope with that also. I think I can control myself.

Question: Well, yes, but can you control events around you?

Eberling: Probably. Like I know I'm gonna be out of here. I'll kick and scream until I get out. The only thing I know [is] it takes time.

Question: What do you do when you get mad?

Eberling: I don't normally get mad. In here, I've learned more patience than ever. I ride over it.

Question: Where does the anger go?

Eberling: It's just held within. It wastes itself out. It just works itself out.

Question: What did you think of Marilyn Sheppard?

Eberling: Marilyn had trouble up till the day she died. She was a lovely lady. A very fine lady. She was very respectable. I think she was lonesome because she let a lot of family dirt out to me.

Question: Would you have dated Marilyn Sheppard if you had met her before [Dr.] Sam?

Eberling: I probably would have dated her once or twice.

[Shaking his head.] Probably not.

I was an orphan, she was a golden girl. A golden girl looks for position, and me, being a nobody . . . I wasn't good enough.

Eberling: (Referring to a claimed rape, unrelated to the Sheppard case): If she paraded for him like she paraded for me, she asked for it. She was all dolled up in the middle of the afternoon for the window washer. Put on all that feminine charm.

Question: Why do you say, "She asked for it"?

Eberling: Beguiling ways. Built the heat up. A man doesn't walk into a woman's house and rape her unless something provoked him. I place the blame on her. She decorated that place like a cheap whorehouse. . . . The way the house was decorated it set a provocative mood.

Question: You're saying that a man . . .

Eberling: I know that does not call for raping a woman. None of that calls for raping a woman. . . . Rape—usually it's an intentional thing. I can't understand how a man can enter a woman's home and rape her. Unless the husband went someplace . . .

Question: Do you know about an attempted rape of Marilyn Sheppard?

Eberling: I don't believe there was an attempt to rape. Rape was not as common as today. For a neighbor to go in that would not have made sense. That would have closed off all social avenues.

————

Question: A prisoner wrote and said that he met a man who worked for a hospital in a bar outside Cleveland, this was in the seventies, and the man said he had murdered Mrs. Sheppard.

Eberling: If Sam had hired someone to kill Marilyn, it would be a different story. I don't know why anyone would say that. Some things you tell and some things you don't tell. Why would anyone sit in a bar and claim that?

————

Question: A detective named Howard Winter wrote an article in the fifties, and he thought the murderer was someone who had been watching Mrs. Sheppard, maybe knew her casually, and was emotionally disturbed or unstable in some way, confused about his sexuality.

Eberling: Nobody in the neighborhood fits that.

————

Question: What did you mean you said Esther Houk's mind was on a merry-go-round?

Eberling: I think that's what happened. The more she thought the more she thought. After the deed was done, Spen thought he could cover it up.

Question: That merry-go-round, is that like what happens to you?

Eberling: Yep. My mind goes a mile a minute.

————

Question: What would happen if you were in touch with your feelings?

Eberling: I think I have feelings. I have feelings. Like this place [prison] I consider my home. The guards I consider babysitters.

Question: Is that a feeling?

Eberling: That's a feeling. So I don't hate it; I just adjusted to it.

———————

Eberling: I've never thought about my feelings and "do I love myself." When it comes up, I don't think about it. I don't expel on it.

———————

Eberling: I have a staying power. I hurt. My mind just churns around.

———————

Question: How would you feel if you did something that you didn't know about?

Eberling: I would be lost in another world. If you are referring to my blackouts, I don't honestly think that I ever went into another personality.

Question: What happens when you go into blackouts?

Eberling: It just hits me. . . . I can't recount every moment leading up to this feeling. It's like switching a light plate. A light switch.

———————

Eberling: To understand Richard a bit better. He always looks to tomorrow and feels the streets are littered with gold. Meaning all one has to do is to stoop over and pick it up.

———————

Question: Why do you refer to yourself in the third person, such as, "Richard thinks this," or "Richard says that"?

Eberling: I go through my writings and take the *I*'s out on purpose. It's too pretentious.

Question: But why the third person like this . . . Richard believes"? *(showing him)*

Eberling: I do write strange. I know that. I don't know why. Sometimes I treat myself as a subject. Have I done that before?

They're trying to take things away from me. Things that have happened to me are most abnormal. I'm a very arrogant individual. I learned I come across as arrogant— but I'm not really. The average person's never gone through this journey in life. The journey I embarked on— it's good, it's interesting. It's not dull by any means.

———————

Eberling: People have a secret side—a lot of people never show it, ever. . . . I am very much to myself.

———————

Eberling: On Sheppard . . . it'll go to my grave. And I hate it.

———————

Eberling: If you are my downfall, I really don't care. If I go to the electric chair, that's no problem. It isn't important any more. Life isn't important any more.

———————

Eberling: The Sheppard answer is in front of the entire world. Nobody bothered to look.

TWENTY-ONE

Chances

Richard Eberling, a convicted killer, sat in prison in Ohio, still writing letters, claiming to have inside knowledge of the Sheppard murder. If the Sheppard affair "would pop up," he said, "I am, it seems, a marked man."

In March 1994 Eberling was sent back to the Cleveland jail. He and Obie Henderson were brought from their respective prisons to appear at a somewhat perfunctory court hearing on the Durkin case. Riding in a van to the city, Eberling and Henderson saw each other for the first time in four and a half years. Obie barely recognized Richard.

Prison had been rough on Eberling. He had lost weight. Now sixty-four years old, he had grown an unruly, long beard. He was so severely depressed that prison doctors, usually reluctant to prescribe medication, put him on heavy doses of anti-depressants and sleeping pills. He suffered from blackouts and dizzy spells. During the previous summer, he had fallen flat on his face while walking outside on the prison track and, unconscious, was rushed to the infirmary. He described himself as being "deathly ill."

While in the Cleveland jail, Eberling was visited by journalists interested in the Sheppard story. Reporters, not cops, were his most frequent visitors. No investigator from the Bay Village police or from the Cleveland police or from the sheriff's office or from the coroner's office or from the prosecutor's office had interrogated him about the Sheppard case. No one had sought a blood sample, a psychiatric

395

evaluation, a palm print. No official had held even a casual conversation with him about the Sheppard case since November 1959 when John T Corrigan flatly closed the door, the coroner canceled plans to interrogate him, and Bay Village gave up.

Around that same time, Sam R. read a newspaper story on a different aspect of the criminal justice system in Ohio that gave him the smallest inclination to feel hopeful that Cleveland had changed. Had not the Sheppard name also appeared in the story, he might never have been aware of it. The story was about the 1951 disappearance of a ten-year-old Cleveland girl, Beverly Potts. It was an unsolved case. After all those years, a letter had been discovered hidden under the carpet of a Cleveland home in which a woman confessed that her husband committed the crime. Two police detectives tracked down the woman in Kansas City and flew there to interview her. As it turned out, the confession was a fabrication, if a sad one. The woman explained that she had been a victim of battering by her husband. She took to writing confessions that connected him to various crimes, reasoning that they might expose his violent behavior if she were killed. As it happened, she had divorced the man in 1955. She had another confession for the detectives: they might find a letter that implicated her husband in the murder of Marilyn Sheppard. It, too, was fabricated.

Sam R. was struck by two things. One was how this modest woman had suffered from 1950s violence, just as he had. But there was another impressive point. The prosecutor of Cuyahoga County had actually initiated the reinvestigation, requesting that the police officers go and talk to her.

For the first time, Sam R. and his team were able to focus on one very salient fact. There was a new prosecutor in Cuyahoga County. For thirty-four years, since 1957, there had been one prosecutor in Cuyahoga County: John T. Corrigan. He was known to local citizens as a tough guy, aggressive, warring. He was known to Sam R. Sheppard as the man who had represented the county in the U.S. Supreme Court when his father's case was heard and who, after he lost there, had decided to try his father again and who, after he lost there, had declared that his father was guilty anyhow. He was the man who had refused even to interview Richard Eberling or any other suspect in the Sheppard case.

When Corrigan retired in the middle of his last term, his successor was to be selected by the central committee of the county Democratic Party, and Corrigan made no secret of his preference: his son, Michael J. Corrigan, then a common pleas judge. In a surprise move, Cuyahoga County Democrats said no. A common pleas judge was named as prosecutor in January 1991, but it was Stephanie Tubbs Jones.

Often described as charismatic, Jones became the first woman and the first African American to hold the top prosecutor's job. She had an impressive career, attending Case Western Reserve University Law School, doing a brief stint in John T. Corrigan's office, and working for the Equal Employment Opportunity Commission. She had been a municipal court judge and was then elevated to the common pleas bench, the first African-American woman to serve there. She truly signaled a changing of the guard in the prosecutor's office.

Sam R thought that if she had reached out on the 1951 Potts case, maybe she understood something about the pain of victims, about their unanswered questions. She was about Sam R.'s age, even younger, and might not have all the old Sheppard baggage to distract her. Perhaps, after all these years, the refusal to do anything could not be assumed. Maybe, if presented with the information that had been gathered—the cellarway entrance, the blood on the stairs, the psychological profile, the statements of people who had not been questioned previously—she would take action. Maybe now was the time.

Time seemed to favor the chances of actually securing once-elusive answers. Forensic analysis operated in a new world of advanced technology. Answers that were previously unattainable could be determined with certainty—if authorities would cooperate.

The blood vial that contained the wood chip on prosecution exhibit 84 was critical. DNA testing could be done on it or on other samples, if they existed.

But DNA testing is worthless in isolation. The value of this kind of genetic profiling is in comparing the microscopic evidence found at a scene with its possible sources.

Collecting source material would be necessary, too. Criminalist Dr. Peter De Forest believed that before any testing should be scheduled, all available source material needed to be gathered, including samples from Dr. Sam and Marilyn Sheppard. If the blood on the stair was that of the victim, as the prosecution had contended with its false "weapon-dripping" theory, the testing would show it. If the blood on the sample was, by any chance, Dr. Sam's (even though he had no bleeding wounds), that too could be definitely determined. And if the blood was that of a third person, that could be discovered as well.

Getting cell or blood samples from Sam R.'s parents was problematic. Their bodies could be disinterred, but it was an expensive and distasteful process that would need the approval of authorities. Another option would be to find existing cell samples. The coroner's office certainly once had samples of Mrs. Sheppard's blood, as well as tooth chips and hairs, which could also be used for DNA typing. The New York Medical Examiner's Office, for example, said it kept all blood samples through the years, but the Cuyahoga County Coroner's Office would not say what it had. The prosecutor could demand that information.

Finding samples for Dr. Sam would be more difficult. Ideas could be explored—what about a shock of hair from Dr. Sam's baby book? There was another option, suggested Dr. Robert Shaler, head of the forensic biology lab for the Office of the Medical Examiner in New York City. Sam R.'s blood could provide substitute information. Each person's cells contain genes from both parents. With a cell sample from Sam R., clues could be gathered in reverse. The question would be to sort out the maternal genes on the DNA from the paternal. Possibly in combination with a blood sample from Mrs. Sheppard, a sample from Sam R. could solve this riddle and reveal the DNA of both his parents. Paternity tests were routinely done using these techniques. One process for DNA testing, known as mitochondrial DNA typing, shows the mother's DNA pattern in her child. Testing Sam R.'s cells in this way would indicate Mrs. Sheppard's DNA. The Y chromosome traces solely to the father, so if DNA probes could identify that in Sam R.'s sample, his father's DNA pattern could be known. Or it might be possible, Dr. Shaler explained, to use cells from Sam R. in conjunction with cells from Dr.

Sam's brother to sort out the paternal DNA characteristics on the Y chromosome, which the three males would share. With both parents' DNA identified, each could be compared to the DNA pattern extracted from blood on the wood chip.

Sam R. didn't hesitate for a moment to agree. He would readily give a blood sample to facilitate DNA testing. Absolutely.

That filled in only part of the puzzle. Getting blood or cell samples from suspects was necessary, too. And there, again, was a stumbling block. How to get other samples? For example, Richard Eberling at one point in 1994 had agreed to provide a blood sample and had even given Cynthia Cooper a signed statement to that effect. Immediately afterward he rushed off a letter saying that he had changed his mind—"I ask for why in Gods name." Even if he had not switched gears, the logistics of a private citizen's getting a blood sample from someone in prison presented a labyrinth of obstacles. The assistance of someone in authority was necessary.

The politics that could entwine his mother's murder still confounded Sam R. Why was it so hard for someone in Cleveland to step forward on the Sheppard case?

Would Stephanie Tubbs Jones finally crack the wall? She was described as a rising political star. There was one worrisome note. She backed away from difficult decisions, the *Plain Dealer* charged, pointing out that she had failed to present a controversial police brutality case to the grand jury and that matters that implicated local politicians in shady financial dealings seemed to be treated lightly. The paper wondered if she could "turn in tough performances on highly publicized cases." As if to prove the paper wrong, Jones presented a grand jury case against the county treasurer for dereliction of duty.

John Lenear, senior editor of the *Call and Post,* Ohio's respected African-American newspaper, said Jones's strength was her consistent fairness and leniency. As a prosecutor, this meant that she was less inclined to rush forward and seek indictments. This change was a breath of fresh air for the prosecutor's office, said Lenear, but left her open to criticism. "She's too laid-back for her own good," he said. He predicted that she would be under severe pressure by the time of the next election, noting that one potential candidate even switched his party affiliation to Republican to assure a general election ballot. That was Michael J. Corrigan.

Still, by the end of 1994, everybody working on the team with Sam R. agreed. As private individuals, using journalism, law, investigative techniques, they had come to an impasse. Only people inside law enforcement could finish the job. They needed to find out if Stephanie Tubbs Jones would be any different on the Sheppard case from all the people in the prosecutor's office who had preceded her.

AMSEC began the massive task of compiling all the information that had been gathered into a single report for the prosecutor's office. A binder of 160 pages was organized, with 80 exhibits that took up another 200 pages. Terry Gilbert arranged an appointment for mid-March 1995. Sam R. thought sitting through the meeting was more than he could bear. Andy Carraway and Cynthia Cooper arranged to participate.

With an appointment set for early afternoon, Carraway and Cooper joined Gilbert in his law office's conference room in the morning. Gilbert put finishing touches on a letter to the prosecutor, outlining eight specific steps that she could take—"areas of investigation that cannot be pursued from the private sector," he wrote. They included securing, for once and all, the evidence at the coroner's office, getting blood samples for a DNA test, and seeking the assistance of a forensic psychologist or behavioral science specialist. The three of them skipped lunch to review any final details. As the time for the meeting with Jones drew near, they sat in a ponderous silence. The solemnity of the event, its momentousness, settled on each of them.

Had those in the prosecutor's office never considered "what if?" What if someone had entered the Sheppard home early on July 4, using the unlocked cellarway door and prying open the sticky basement door? What if he had walked through the basement, up the stairs to the kitchen and to the second floor, avoiding the day bed? What if Mrs. Sheppard had bitten his hand, causing him to yank it away so rapidly that two of her teeth were pulled out and his hand was cut and bleeding? What if, after striking her, he knocked Dr. Sam unconscious, and walked to the basement, dripping blood? What if he stripped his victims of their jewelry, smashed their athletic trophies, and rifled the drawers? What if, interrupted, he ran down to the beach through the brush, dropping the bag on the way, and, encountering Dr. Sam again, knocked him into the water? What if he had carried this secret for forty-one years? Getting official attention on this case after so long—a case that had evoked sharp responses from so many, attracted such enormous public attention, established legal precedent, and created tragic personal aftershocks—was a challenge unlike one that any of them had ever had.

They walked across the street to the Justice Center, where Jones's ninth-floor office had a wall of windows that looked out to Lake Erie.

Jones promised to get back to them with a decision soon. Sam R. got a briefing by telephone the next day from Andy Carraway, who summarized the two-hour session with Jones and her first assistant, Carmen Marino. By agreement, none of the details were to be released to the media. Andy's description made Sam R. elated, ebullient. But what would Jones do?

Three days later, Sam R. absorbed more about the encounter when he met in person with Cooper. Sam R. was in New York City as part of a long-distance walk to oppose the death penalty; Cooper had just returned from Ohio. As they sat in the midtown Edison Coffee Shop, Sam R. saw for himself a copy of the binder given to the prosecutor, with its organized subsections, documents, transcriptions, affidavits, nine-page index, and cover page that read, "Confidential, Homicide Investigation Report, Marilyn Sheppard." He leafed through the expandable brown legal jacket filled with numbered exhibits. This was outstanding. No one, he thought, could ignore this.

The team had done its part. They had amassed the evidence. They had verified their points. They had provided the information, respectfully, to the appropriate authorities in a most professional way. They had done so calmly, without grandstanding, away from hype and publicity. The chances for getting action seemed real.

After listening to high points of the Cleveland meeting, Sam R. headed to Times Square to participate in an anti-death penalty demonstration by the Living Theater. Actors, dressed in black, began a 1960s-style street performance.

Huge neon billboards above created an eerie stage, blinking on and off. Would the prosecutor act? Or not? Once more, the suspenseful anxiety of waiting washed over him.

Five weeks later, Sam R. put in a call to Jones's office. He called again. And again. After the fifth call, Sam R. had still not spoken to prosecutor Jones. Officialdom, it seemed, was not going to respond. He steeled himself for the inevitable disappointment. Little, it seemed, had changed about the prosecutor's office when it came to the Sheppard case.

Terry Gilbert picked up the first whispers of hope after a couple more weeks. The prosecutor's office called him, asking for particular details. Something was afoot, Gilbert thought. Then another call came. And another. In low-rolling waves, the historic flow of the Sheppard case was being reversed.

In July, the prosecutor's office wanted to meet again. Gilbert, Carraway, and Cooper appeared at the Justice Center. Although not present, Jones authorized a statement, meant to be bold and unambiguous. "We're reviewing all the facts and evidence. We're doing something on it. We're serious." The tone of the meeting matched the statement. The prosecutor's office described the activities under way. Almost all the points in Gilbert's letter to Jones were being addressed. This was anything but frivolous. A final comment from Jones underscored the import: "We have a definite course of investigative action that we are going to take."

Gilbert, Carraway, and Cooper left, convinced that the prosecutor's office was sincere, committed, broaching the case anew. Forty-one years after the murder of Marilyn Sheppard, the seemingly impossible had happened. They dared to believe that the case had been reopened.

TWENTY-TWO

Living

Souvenirs were collected by various people when the old Sheppard house was torn down in 1993. Some people called young Sam or the phone line and said that they had crept onto the property in the middle of the night and collected part of a door or a piece of a fixture or even the demolition permit.

Most did so not out of ill will or malice, but because the murder of Marilyn Sheppard and the subsequent wrongful incarceration of Dr. Sam had touched them in some way. It had been the topic of conversation over dinner. Or the murder had been the first to fracture the idyllic image of suburbia. Or they had watched as the events unfolded daily through the new medium of television on summer nights in 1954.

Sam R. Sheppard didn't need a piece of the house. Memories were his souvenirs, memories arising at the oddest moments, the least expected.

A certain twist of a smile from a stranger might remind him of his dad and his ironic, half-satisfied, half-childish look when he asked for the clipboard. The clipboard, aluminum, sleek, had belonged to Sam R., a prized possession. With pen pressed to paper upon it, he had written meaningful diary entries and high school letters to his dad in prison. He had carried the clipboard on his sailing trip, and brought it back from India before the Supreme Court hearing. Then, during the months after the hearing while his father anxiously awaited the Supreme Court's decision, he asked Sam R. for the clipboard. In prison, Sam R.'s father said, if someone was your friend he would give you his most precious possession. When he did, the item doubled in value. And aren't you my friend? his father had asked. Sam R. handed the clipboard to his dad. And a few months later, as Sam R. was about to head to Boston for college, his father gave the clipboard back. A simple clipboard had now tripled in value. It shimmered with memories.

Ambling by the water, Sam R. might glimpse a shell with a particular combination of pink and white and pearl colors, and he would see the image of his mother in California, walking across the sand, seeking an abalone shell. He couldn't have been very old when they made the trips, maybe three or four. Standing alone, his toes sunk in the sand, perhaps with a bucket and a shovel beside him, digging, he would stretch his eyes to see her bending down to caress a special find. And yet she seemed so very far away.

They all wanted a resolution—the reporters and the television writers and the agents and the editors. What's the resolution? What's the third act? What's the solution? Will you name a killer? Who will it be? Something to end the story. That's what we need, something to put a nice cap to the end.

Real life is so much harder than they want it to be. The pain, the process, the meaning of "resolution."

In 1966, nineteen years old, Sam R. thought it was over. The resolution. The end. Fini! He had literally danced the night away.

The tension in advance had been almost unbearable. Everyone was tense.

He was living in Miles Standish Hall at Boston University, learning to be on his own in the city. His father's attorney, F. Lee Bailey, lived in Boston and had encouraged Sam R. to move there. Bailey invited him to spend weekends at his home and gave him free access to his motorcycle or car. Sometimes there were parties at Bailey's home and investigator Andy Tuney would corner him and poke at him, kid him about studying to be the "next Bailey."

As the date approached, anxiety grew. Bailey and Tuney and the rest left for the trial in Cleveland. He was to stay in Boston, attending his classes. He had not appeared in the first fiasco; it looked like he would not appear in this trial. But he was to be ready.

He kept pretty much to himself. A few select friends would learn something, make a comment. But mostly he plodded on, studying when he could concentrate, worried as hell. There was no one to talk to, not really. He held his own counsel.

The call came from one of Bailey's secretaries: tomorrow was the day. He flew to Cleveland from Boston, got a cab, stepped into the courthouse building in time to be called as a "surprise" witness after the lunch recess. He was sworn in. Bailey asked for his full name. He gave it. Bailey asked where he had spent his summer. He replied with his dad's address.

No further questions.

No cross-examination.

In a blur, it was over. He stepped down to a brief recess, giving his dad a handshake and a hug. Cameras were in the hallway and on the courthouse steps. The judge this time had taken care to keep the media from overrunning the courtroom. Cameras clicked and people shoved. He was whisked away and out to the cab, back to the airport, back to Boston.

Alone, he waited for the verdict. On Friday afternoon the case went to the jury. He had supper by himself, then sat by the radio in his room. A friend stopped by. Already it was after nine at night, and the friend convinced him that no verdict would come in that night. Why not come to a party on Beacon Hill? They doubled up on the motorcycle borrowed from Bailey.

When they arrived, a fellow walked up and held out his hand. "Congratulations," he said. "Just heard on the car radio on the way over.

Not guilty. The verdict had come in. His dad had finally, after twelve years—the time that a kid spends in elementary and junior high and high school and traveling around and the first year of college—finally been found not guilty. He was in Boston, and they were in Cleveland. But like the perfect wind filling the sails of a boat on Lake Erie, floating across the waves, a burden was magically lifted from him.

There was time now, perhaps, to get on with his life, without the case weighing him down.

But it had not been so. An end, yes. But there had been no real resolution.

And now, when the events were all so long ago, so far away, he had taken them up again.

With the help of others, he had exposed the corruption of the police and high authorities. He had discovered, through the reinvestigation, documents that showed the police had lied, that they had covered up the key evidence, that people in authority aided and abetted and colluded.

Officials knew that his dad was innocent and that there were signs of forced entry. The pilings under the prosecution case would have been washed away. The prosecution argued over and over again: there was no evidence of forced entry; Dr. Sam Sheppard was in the house; Dr. Sam must have done it. But police had found forced entry and they had lied.

They knew that there were signs of a third person in the house. They knew that the blood trails had to have come from a bleeding wound. They knew his dad did not have a bleeding wound. They failed to type the blood. They had covered up so much more, matchstick details that when bound together became the bonfire to burn his dad.

They had not seriously attempted to search out the real killer. And it is possible, in that failure to act, that a crime was committed against other people as well, that there were other victims, that there were others having to live with their sorrow.

His dad had known it, had written in 1955: "In recording for my boy what I have been subjected to, it will be necessary to make known American injustice perpetrated not by the laws of our land, but by those who have sworn themselves to uphold those laws. . . . A frightening breach of American rights has taken place, and the important point is that the breach has happened here in America, not who it has happened to." And he, the boy his father had referred to, had found the help, and they had proved that breach.

Officials had had real, live criminals sitting in their offices, telling stories that would have aroused suspicion in the minds of reasonable people, and they had done nothing, knowing that another man was in prison serving time for a crime he did not commit. They had quietly buried this information, too.

They had lost their moral compass, and he had suffered for it.

And he had discovered and disclosed how excessive power had been granted to the coroners' offices in Ohio: more power than in any other jurisdiction in the country. The power was unchecked, power accountable to no authority. The coroner had been able to hold a McCarthy-like inquest and to slant evidence in his dad's case precisely because the system was ripe for abuse. In a position shielded from public view, there was—and is—no curb to the coroner's power. What some would consider to be an obscure elected position holds the power of life and death. Sam R. knew this firsthand. Elsewhere, elected coroners' offices had been abolished for that very reason and medical examiners' established in their place. Elsewhere the potentially abusive powers had been limited, checks and balances established; in Ohio and in Cuyahoga County, they had not.

He could give them that resolution:

An injustice was done.

He had proved it.

The police had lied, covered up, hid, fabricated.

An agency of government—the coroner—had excessive power, a situation still unremedied.

His dad, whom he had always known was innocent, was indeed innocent.

Crimes had been committed against his father, himself, the memory of his mother.

And he had run down every available detail that was within his power, or the power of those who worked to help him, to find the murderer. They had told the authorities what they had discovered.

Those who needed a resolution could dramatize that, run the screen version. There could be an investigator rising to click open the briefcase, remove the file folder, and then, with that firm look in the eye, tenderly pass it over to the authorities.

They could have that resolution.

These were the clichés that they wanted. The snap of handcuffs, the slam of bars, the closing of a coffin.

But so much of the case was buried in clichés, entwined with the sheer lack of imagination that sought the simplest target, the easiest solution, that refused to admit error and failed to acknowledge the complications of the human mind. Quick and easy. Don't worry about the consequences. Don't fret over the inconsistencies. Get it over with, get it out of the headlines, get it past.

Life is not a television drama. The experience of survivors, of victim families, of persons wrongfully incarcerated, is not fiction. Even if a clean ending closes the story, it will never be neat. The reality is that it's ragged. The repercussions and ripples will continue. And the wounds can never heal completely as long as the expectation exists that the stories of victims of injustice will slot together nicely in the end like Lego pieces.

Over twenty-two thousand murders occur in this country every year. In a ten-year period, victims and victim families easily mount to one million people. Those affected in some way by a murder—friends, neighbors, colleagues—remain an unknown quantity.

Criminologists say that in 44 percent of the murder cases, no one is ever arrested. In another 27 percent, an innocent person is arrested and acquitted, or charges are dropped. In another 10 percent or more, an innocent person is arrested and convicted.

More than half the murders in the country are unsolved.

Myrtle Fray. Ruth McNeil. Marilyn Sheppard.

Members of victim families lie awake at night, wonder, agonize. They may have a handwritten shopping list—the last thing written by their loved one—a vial with a blood sample, a favorite shirt, or a pair of slippers. Mostly they have their memories to live with, their what-ifs and could-it-have-beens.

Markers are hard to come by when reconciliation and healing are sought. Finally, a little connection, an insight, a small thing happens, and that part of the mind can rest. Each moment may take years.

Sam R. understands what it means to be a victim: the pain, bewilderment, isolation, and unquenchable loneliness. But he believes he has managed to surmount some of the obstacles. He sees himself not as a victim but as a survivor. That alone is an achievement, rarely acknowledged. He is a survivor of violence that society lets pass too readily and injustice too frequently tolerated. He is a survivor of murder, of the criminal justice system, of the prison system, of the death penalty. He is a survivor of a selling game. He has been searching for healing, for home, for understanding.

The resolutions, big and small, keep coming.

In the process of reinvestigating his mother's murder, he has found someone else, and it is himself. He has found a way to take all these years of hurt and confusion and turn them into solutions and forward motion, into ways to help others. He is asked to speak to a college class, and he assents. He addresses a group of police officers without the quake of nerves. He takes the microphone at an anti-death penalty forum, and a woman he knows distantly comments that he is much more confident. The photographer from the Associated Press wants to take a picture. Sam R. looks right into the camera.

The murder victim families are being ignored at a rally in Georgia where the governor is having a press conference on criminal justice issues. As the governor concludes, Sam R. tucks away the scarf given to him by an inmate executed in Florida. Maybe you remember my dad, Dr. Sam Sheppard, he says. The governor looks. Won't you consider abolishing the death penalty and putting the funds into helping murder victim families? The governor makes an apology, but the cameras capture the moment. The reporters now take a new interest in the families. Sam R. moves away, feeling the strength of action, from the reinvestigation to this, rising inside him.

He believes that this is a resolution.

Organizers call and ask if he can help. He says yes. He takes charge of the planning for a major anti-death penalty march in Arkansas, a death penalty state and the president's home. With urgency, he knows that the killing must stop, and that killing affects the children the most—whether the killing occurs on the street or in the home or in the state's execution chamber.

He believes that this is a resolution.

The activists are marching against the very core of violence. Some people shout them down, with anger and with hatred. He responds by walking forward, searching for healing, for nonviolence. He is trying to stand against the myths. The murders mount, the tabloid headlines continue, the selling of gore and bloodshed and revenge escalate, and even in high-resolution living color on television, murder looks nothing like it does in day-in, day-out actuality.

The resolution is within reach, but so very far away.

Afterword
New Beginnings

Prosecutor Stephanie Tubbs Jones issued a press release on October 13, 1995:

> The Cuyahoga County Prosecutor's Office is reviewing all of the facts and evidence, including information submitted by Cynthia L. Cooper and Sam Reese Sheppard, son of Dr. Sam and Marilyn Sheppard, authors of *Mockery of Justice: The True Story of the Sheppard Murder Case*. An investigation is in progress.

The simple announcement lifted the Sheppard case to a new life. Years of investigation and struggle had finally pried open an official door.

The focus of this investigation soon became obvious: Richard George Eberling.

Sam R. also started on a fresh path, moving to Oakland, California. While the Sheppard team—Cooper, Gilbert, AMSEC—sizzled with excitement about activities on the case, Sam R. knew better than the others to expect setbacks. He had lived through years of setbacks. Yet even he succumbed momentarily to the fantasy that maybe, just maybe, results would come quickly or easily.

Prosecutor Jones turned over the Sheppard case to Carmen Marino, first assistant prosecutor. Marino ranked high on the list of top trial attorneys in Cleveland. Known as both tenacious and forthright, he directed the lawyers' day-to-day work. He had pursued a career in law only after serving a year in Vietnam and working his way through law school. His experience with murder cases now spanned twenty-four years.

Marino didn't shy away from difficult cases: he thrived on them. A solidly built man in his fifties, he sat in an inauspicious office, dispensing advice to the 155 assistant prosecutors or scribbling notes on one of the 18,000 felonies that came under the office's purview. At night he raced up and down the basketball court, playing three-on-three half-court in an amateur league, Hoop It Up, as the city's oldest player-member.

He was a native Clevelander from the West Side, and the old stories on the Sheppard case needed no stirring for him: he remembered them well. Like almost everyone in the prosecutor's office, he had believed in Sheppard's guilt. Now he dug into the new evidence presented by AMSEC.

Marino changed his mind.

Dr. Sam would not have been charged with murder at all had the case originated during his watch—no matter what the newspapers wanted.

Four things specifically bothered Marino. First, the charges against Dr. Sam had been rushed. Marino presses charges only when he can say the evidence is as strong as it will ever be. Had the prosecutors followed this simple rule, Eberling would have surfaced, and the case would have taken a "harsh turn," he said.

Second, Marino could find no motive. Sheppard had no history of violence. The evening had been amiable. And why, he asked, would a man so exhausted from a long day's work that he fell asleep on the couch while entertaining guests arise in the middle of the night and murder his wife? He didn't buy the worn-out notion that an extramarital affair automatically equals motive.

Third, the police failed miserably by not interviewing every person who had access to the house. Had they done so, Eberling would have emerged, as would have Vern Lund, his employee, who could have quickly shattered Eberling's false alibi.

Finally, Marino's attention zoomed in on the blood trail. The blood on the stairs and elsewhere throughout the house was surely connected to the murder. Someone had bled. That could not have been Dr. Sam Sheppard. His injuries—neck contusion, swollen eye, distended lip—did not include an open wound, a bloody cut.

So where had the blood come from? Marino didn't think much of the old claim by the prosecution that the blood belonged to the victim—highly unlikely. If the blood did not come from the victim, then it had to be the blood of a third person—an intruder, a murderer. Ignoring the source of this blood was fatal to the prosecution's case.

If the state had made a mistake, Marino decided to rectify it. He considered it his duty as a prosecutor. "First I look at what's moral, and then I look at what's legal," he said. "Usually they are the same."

Fortunately, Marino was freed from what he called "the ignorance of 1954." Forensic science had undergone a revolution, including the development of DNA testing.

Not everyone in the establishment appreciated Marino's stance. Nerves jumped—some of them important.

In Cleveland, loads of people had opinions on the Sheppard case, as if it were a kind of game. Every family had a memory of someone who knew someone. People speculated endlessly. In speculation, consequences seemed distant, rumor served as well as fact—sometimes even better. The truth actually presented obstacles: it could end the game.

And Cleveland basked in a different euphoria in the fall of 1995. The Rock 'n' Roll Hall of Fame opened to national attention. Ground was broken for a high-tech science museum on the lakefront. For the first time since 1954, Cleveland's baseball team entered the World Series. Fans exuded wild enthusiasm. Clevelanders certainly did not want to dwell on mistakes from 1954.

Brent Larkin, a top editor at the city's sole surviving daily, the *Plain Dealer,* admitted that he hadn't bothered to read any of the new evidence when he freely opined that Sheppard was guilty and always would be. Michael Corrigan, son of the former prosecutor, turned to public commentary, saying that Dr. Sam was guilty despite a "not guilty" verdict in 1966. A Cleveland police officer pulled in on the case by Marino found a dozen reasons not to investigate. In one meeting the officer blurted out: "You don't understand—I'm going against my department in investigating this case."

Marino moved forward anyhow, even if the resources available to him were limited. In early October, he called on Richard Eberling at the Orient Correctional Institution in Columbus. Eberling, almost sixty-six, was transferred to Orient's hospital facility because of continuing blackouts and other mysterious physical ailments, including an inability to walk. Marino took with him the Cleveland police officer who proclaimed that it was "against" his department's policy and Lieutenant James Tompkins of Bay Village. Lieutenant Tompkins' previous role in solving the murder of Marilyn Sheppard had been to block access to Bay Village's files.

The trio didn't get far. Tompkins reported: "Eberling denied being involved in the Sheppard murder in any way. He stated the reason he did not divulge that he overheard conversations between Marilyn Sheppard and Houks [in early July 1954] was because he told [Dr.] Sam Sheppard what he had heard a short time after the murder and Sam told him to 'Forget it. I'll take care of it.' He also stated that Vern Lund had never worked for him."

Eberling soon described the scenario differently in a letter to Cooper. He had been visited, he said, by Marino and "his henchmen"—he also called them "rotten devils" and "wicked" men. "They felt I should come clean. Before I met my maker— Hogwash, I say. I said that!" he wrote. He added, "Wish to be left alone period. . . . Besides, you or [Sam R.] can handle the [media] interviews." In closing, he put in a singular note: "Hope you folks weren't too cruel on me."

Marino didn't worry about Eberling's responses. He was working behind the scenes, and the visit was merely a prelude to his next step. In January 1996, Marino first spoke publicly when Peter Finn of the *Washington Post* coaxed a comment. Marino revealed that he was seeking a blood sample from Richard Eberling for a DNA test. "I think he did it," Marino said. "My personal opinion is that he is a serial killer."

Momentum on the Sheppard case built elsewhere, too. While the criminal investigation progressed, Terry Gilbert filed a civil court action. Gilbert wanted to force the state to admit that it had made a mistake. A pursuit for a "declaration of innocence" began.

Peculiar to Ohio, the procedure created a means of recourse for innocent people wrongfully convicted of a crime. Dr. Sheppard had never been compensated for his years in prison. At the time the procedure was byzantine—petitioning the entire state legislature. The law changed in 1986 because of outrage over an African American doctor convicted of rape, later discovered to be innocent when the actual rapist was arrested. A new procedure was created to remedy such injustices in the "declaration of innocence" law.

Gilbert saw the law as an entree to a proper forum. Under the law, a wrongfully convicted person applies to a civil court for a declaration of innocence. If successful, the person may petition the Ohio Court of Claims for compensation. The action would get the Sheppard facts before a judge. Sam R. might eventually get some of the compensation denied his family, enabling him to fulfill his vision of a foundation for the children of victims or offenders, helping to ease the trauma they suffer.

Soon the case landed in the court of Judge Ronald Suster. New to the bench, Judge Suster had distinguished himself as a state legislator, earning respect for his leadership and thoughtfulness. A Democrat, he had been appointed to the court vacancy by a Republican governor.

Although recently seated, Judge Suster got into gear without delay. He ordered all public officials to turn over their files, documents, and physical evidence on the Sheppard case to him. The prosecutor's office now had to admit publicly what it had said previously in Cooper's freedom of information lawsuit: it had no idea what had happened to the files on the Sheppard case. They had last been seen in the late 1980s, before Prosecutor John T. Corrigan retired. Bay Village did deliver its documents. And the coroner's office was strangely quiet. It requested more time.

Then a court date was announced: February 22, 1996. For the first time in nearly thirty years, since Dr. Sam had been found not guilty, the Sheppard case would find its way onto a court calendar. For six years Sam R. and the Sheppard team had gathered information, piling up more and more documentation. Now it could be aired apart from the odd prejudices of some people in the local media. Although Sam R. could not be present, Reverend Alan Davis, special administrator of the Sheppard estate, sat at the table, along with Andy Carraway from AMSEC and Cynthia Cooper. In a curious twist, the prosecutor's office had to defend the state on this action, and Carmen Marino appeared as respondent with two assistant prosecutors from the civil division. Print and broadcast reporters filled the jury box.

The bailiff announced Judge Suster's entry into the courtroom. At long last, the Sheppard case was called to order.

Gilbert kicked off the hearing, offering into evidence the thick binders prepared by AMSEC investigators and a copy of *Mockery of Justice*. To win at this first stage, Gilbert needed to meet unusual standards—to prove actual innocence, a more stringent standard than not guilty in a criminal trial. That meant showing that Sheppard had no part in committing the crime—by demonstrating, for example, that someone else had committed the crime.

With a vast range of evidence at hand, Gilbert gave Judge Suster three distinct reasons why the declaration of innocence should be granted—massive misconduct by the state; evidence that entirely excluded Sheppard; and the revelation of a more likely prime suspect—Richard Eberling.

Gilbert listed dozens of points to support each of these grounds, a litany of powerful items: the state's misconduct in hiding evidence of a break-in, failing to type the blood trail, not interviewing potential suspects, cutting down a path through the brush, presenting misleading testimony about the weapon. "Not a single piece of evidence ever linked Dr. Sheppard to the murder," Gilbert said, pointing out that Dr. Kirk had found the blood of a third person in the murder room.

Richard Eberling had uncanny insights into the crime, he said, introducing Carraway and Cooper to explain investigative findings. The duo explained Eberling's nearly two dozen statements of a confessional nature, his use of a false alibi, his physical resemblance to the intruder, knowledge of the premises, his theft of Marilyn Sheppard's ring, his troubled background and psychiatric problems, his odd comments about bleeding at a bloody crime scene, his familiarity with the basement door that was forced open, and his angry response to being caught stealing by Marilyn Sheppard, as described by his former employee Ed Wilbert.

The prosecutors said nothing to contest Dr. Sheppard's innocence. They briefly raised obscure procedural issues, a tactic which the assistants would soon employ with tedious, case-stalling repetition.

Judge Suster continued the case, an acknowledgment that this hearing was merely the beginning of a process that would last for many months. With that, the session ended. Unlike the carnival trial of 1954, this hearing carried an aura of calm and equanimity that Dr. Sam Sheppard had rarely experienced.

The old hysteria of the Sheppard case still lingered. As the session ended, a small group sitting in the back row of the courtroom popped up. Cooper recognized one man as "Mason," an "operative" of the elusive Monsignor, who at one point had followed her in Cleveland while she did research. Monsignor had continued to poke and probe into the Sheppard case. Mason flew into the hallway, marching back and forth as people exited, occasionally shouting obscenities.

Joining "Mason" was a man who described himself as a pastor and spokesman for Richard Eberling. The pastor usually held forth on a community radio program, spinning a series of conspiracy theories mixed with fundamentalist theology. Sometimes Monsignor or his "operatives" joined as guests. Brow sweating, the pastor read a list of demands to television cameras: Sam R. Sheppard should submit to a lie detector exam; the fetus of Marilyn Sheppard should be tested by DNA. He offered no rationale for these demands. Monsignor later ventured to confide his latest theory on the Sheppard case to a British reporter. The evidence would show, Monsignor was quoted as saying, that the murderer was definitely not Dr. Sam Sheppard, but that the deadly weapon was wielded by none other than young Sam, seven years old.

A prison van delivered Eberling to the Justice Center in the last week of February. At the request of Marino, Judge Suster signed an order requiring the Cuyahoga County Sheriff to take a blood sample from Richard Eberling.

Criminalist Peter De Forest thought his mentor, Dr. Kirk, would have enjoyed this moment had he been alive. Dr. Kirk had predicted that gene study and DNA technology would change the face of forensics, and he was right. Now its exciting developments were being applied to the very case Dr. Kirk had pioneered.

Forensic DNA testing had emerged as a sophisticated

tool for crime solving. What makes DNA so valuable to criminalists is that it differs in every person and yet can be easily deposited at a crime scene by the culprit. DNA is found in virtually invisible cell tissue inadvertently left by the criminal—in hair, saliva, sweat, semen, tooth chips, blood, fragments of skin.

DNA actually is a chemical compound found inside the forty-six chromosomes, which themselves are in the nucleus of each human cell. The function of DNA in the body is to carry the private code that tells each cell how to reproduce itself. A person's DNA repeats six billion times in each cell. Much DNA material is the same in everyone, passing on basic information about bodily functions. What makes DNA unique is contained in four substances identified by the letters A, T, G, C, and which create a distinctive combination. Forensic DNA typing seeks to identify that combination—like cracking the lock on a safe.

Since the whole DNA code is so extensive, forensic scientists concentrate on evaluating critical fragments that limit the people who could have this DNA to a small group. While standard ABO blood testing matches blood to over 20 percent of the population, DNA analysis links samples to 1 percent of the population or less. The scientist can then determine if a suspect's DNA falls into that same 1 percent. Better yet, the DNA tester can readily tell if someone does *not* fit, and that person can be eliminated as a source of the DNA.

As Eberling was let out of the van in Cleveland, he threw the hood of a sweatshirt over his head. He sat in a wheelchair, but otherwise he looked healthier than he had in years. Previously, Eberling had indicated that he had no problem giving a blood sample. He had even signed a consent form for Cooper at one point. Now, faced with the reality of a nurse ready to draw blood, Eberling refused. He would not allow it.

Responsible for carrying out the judge's order, the Sheriff's Office promptly arranged to take Eberling to a hospital, where the blood could be safely drawn even if he objected. After talking with a lawyer, Eberling finally relented. On March 1, several lawyers stood by as the nurse took a blood sample in a matter of minutes.

The prosecutor and Gilbert consulted with Dr. De Forest. Eberling's DNA could now be compared to the blood on the wood chip that was in De Forest's custody. The tricky part would be removing the blood from the wood chip in a way that it could be tested for DNA. With crime scene evidence this old, the extraction took special expertise. Yet money for testing was in short supply. De Forest suggested proceeding with the tests in the lab of the Cuyahoga County Coroner's Office, but under the guidance of an independent expert. He recommended Dr. Mohammad Tahir, head of the DNA and Serology Lab of the Forensic Services Agency for Indianapolis and Marion County, Indiana.

By mid-March, Dr. Tahir was en route to Cleveland, ready to get a testing protocol established. Highly regarded in the field, Tahir knew a lot about DNA, but very little about the Sheppard murder. From time to time Sheppard had been mentioned in seminars on blood-splatter analysis at forensics conferences, but that was it. Tahir held multiple degrees in forensics, biochemistry, and microbiology. Prior to setting up the Indiana lab, he had headed blood testing analysis for the Chicago science lab of the Illinois State Police. He served as the DNA coordinator for the Midwestern Association of Forensic Scientists, winning its Distinguished Service Award for significant contributions to the advancement of forensic science. He was on the cutting edge of DNA, defining the protocol for working with unbelievably small amounts of DNA and for testing old samples of DNA with results free from contamination. He, too, was blissfully free of contamination on the Sheppard case, having moved to the U.S. from Pakistan around the time that Dr. Sam died.

At the Cuyahoga County Coroner's Office, Tahir encountered some surprises. He learned that the coroner's office did testing only for the prosecution. Tahir's own lab did scientific analysis for the prosecution or the defense: neutrality guided it. His job, as he saw it, was not only to point to a guilty person, but also to exclude innocent people. In 31 percent of his cases, DNA testing resulted in the release of innocent suspects. "The role of the lab is to get to the truth," explained Tahir.

Tahir discovered other problems at the coroner's office. A quality DNA test demands accurate and precise equipment. Conducting a sample test with blood deposited on a blanket in 1955, Tahir got a zero reading—nothing. How, then, could it test evidence from 1954? More sophisticated equipment was necessary, and Cuyahoga County was sadly lacking. Tahir could not recommend proceeding in Cuyahoga County under any circumstances. He left Ohio, DNA plans seemingly scuttled.

Back in Indiana, Tahir approached the administrator of the county's crime labs. Tahir had designed the DNA facility with a budget of a half-million dollars, and he was justifiably proud of it. Only thirty of the three hundred forensic labs in the country could claim similar capabilities for indepth DNA testing. Spreading out through fifteen rooms and alcoves, the lab included a darkroom, exam table, radiation room, prep rooms, computer systems, work stations, and all the latest equipment. Equipment was inspected on a daily basis—refrigerators had to be at the right temperature, heating devices in working order. Tahir maintained rigorous standards, employing a staff of eight people, half of whom held Ph.D.'s. By comparison, Cuyahoga County had one person to conduct DNA testing.

What about doing the Sheppard testing in his lab? Tahir asked. The administrator consented, but only if Tahir did all the work on his own time. Tahir agreed. He contacted Cuyahoga County, making yet another offer: he would provide his expertise at no charge. With a stroke of luck, DNA testing could continue in Indiana.

Soon County Coroner Elizabeth Balraj made a different announcement. She had discovered some Sheppard materials. In fact, she suddenly had located a *vault* of Sheppard materials. There were so many items that she could not give a proper accounting of them.

The coroner's office held, she declared on the night before the judge's deadline, boxes and boxes of Sheppard materials. In them were hundreds of documents, photographs, and trace evidence reports. And, it turned out, there were dozens of items of physical crime scene evidence—items that might be testable for DNA.

Possibilities grew. So did a new task. The files were a giant mess. Before the DNA tests could proceed, someone had to dig through them and pull out the evidence.

                    *   *   *

Kathie Collins, a home health-care manager in Florida, was far removed from DNA testing and the coroner's office and Cleveland, her hometown. But as soon as she heard a televised story about the planned DNA test, she got on the phone. "I heard the name Dick Eberling," Collins said, "and chills ran up my spine."

More and more information had arisen about Richard Eberling. Additional child-welfare reports revealed details of his distressed childhood. Growing up as the orphaned Richard Lenardic in various foster homes, the boy had had monthly visits from social workers. When caseworkers had arrived at the Eberling home, his foster parents joked: "Oh, Dick, pack your bag, the social workers are here to take you away." Foster father George Eberling had been severe. After George's death, caseworkers counseled foster mother Christine against her habit of allowing Dick, an adolescent, to sleep in bed with her.

Social workers also fretted about what they saw as an unhealthy ambition held by Richard. He insisted that he wanted to be a doctor, for which he had neither scholastic aptitude nor financial resources. They tried again and again to dissuade him. Finally, after years of effort, Dick renounced his long-standing desire.

Information relevant to Eberling's possible involvement in the Sheppard case mounted. And sometimes it slipped away. In the fall of 1995, reporter Cindy Leise ran two Sheppard stories in Elyria, just southwest of Cleveland, breaking details of new evidence and once again trouncing the backsliding Cleveland daily. A woman from Elyria who read the stories had known Eberling, as had her husband. She responded to the articles with a phone call in which she privately described an evening she had spent at a bar with Richard Eberling. He had downed a couple of drinks. Without prompting, he had turned the subject to the Sheppards, and began to brag that he had murdered Marilyn Sheppard. The woman, a witness in the Durkin murder case, was nervous about saying anything further. Although the tip was promptly passed on to Cleveland authorities, they delayed four months before contacting her. By then she had clammed up, and would say nothing.

Still, the woman's statement had an unintentional ripple effect. Andy Carraway of AMSEC lightly described the woman in a television interview. It was this moment that

Kathie Collins overheard while fixing dinner for her kids. She exclaimed, "Oh, my God!" That night she raced to a local bookstore to get a copy of *Mockery of Justice*. There weren't any. Kathie took the name of the publisher. She didn't think she could wait until a copy of the book came in.

The next evening, Collins explained on the phone to Cooper that she knew Eberling. In 1983, at the age of twenty, she had been hired by Eberling to work as a caretaker for Ethel Durkin. For about six months, Kathie stayed with Durkin on the night shift, 11:00 P.M. to 7:00 A.M. Sometimes Eberling was there and talked into the night. One conversation had made a distinct impression.

Before the week ended, AMSEC sent Allen Gore to Collins' home to videotape a statement. This time solid information would not be frittered away in foot shuffling. Gore was impressed with Kathie's memory and command of detail. In rapid-fire and animated tones, Collins described how she had met Eberling while doing volunteer work at the Cleveland Ballet, where Eberling roamed prominently among the patrons. Kathie admired his worldliness and smooth style. When he offered her a job as a caretaker for a "woman friend," she readily accepted.

Her assignment was not difficult. She helped Mrs. Durkin to bed and spent the night there, sleeping on a cot in case an emergency arose. On some occasions, when Kathie couldn't do her shift, her mother filled in.

Eberling personally worked the shift before Kathie's and generally was at the Durkin home when she arrived. If Durkin had already fallen asleep, he would lead her into the kitchen and regale her with stories, something at which he was known to excel. Eberling poured himself scotch and water, while Kathie, a nondrinker, sipped a Coke.

On occasion he enticed her with promises, saying he would be taking Ethel on a big trip, and Kathie would be invited, too. He rolled out tales of his work for the mayor, his own window-washing business, his childhood, Obie, his property purchases, his interior decorating, Satanic worship, his thefts of jewelry and money and silver place settings and figurines from his clients. "He had a very loose mouth," she said.

One night the conversation veered. Kathie mentioned

that she had seen a violent movie about Vietnam. Eberling observed that killing could be extremely exciting.

"Have you ever killed anyone?" he asked her.

Kathie responded in the negative: of course she hadn't.

"Well, I did," he said. "Have you ever heard the name Marilyn Sheppard?"

The whole Sheppard case was well before Kathie's time, and she said no again.

"Well, I did her," he said.

"You mean 'killed her'?"

"Yeah," he responded. "I got off and somebody else paid the bill."

Her boss continued, saying that the Sheppards had acted like they were better than other people. He described hitting her husband on the head. And he announced, "The bitch bit the hell out of me."

After he seemed to have exhausted himself, he turned to Kathie. "You didn't hear any of that, did you?" he prompted. "You're not going to say anything, now, are you?"

She responded with a noncommittal "Okay." Mostly she was beginning to wonder if this Dick Eberling was the same man whom she had admired at the ballet. This Dick Eberling seemed nuts.

Kathie couldn't put the conversation entirely out of her mind. She asked her mother if the name Marilyn Sheppard meant anything to her, and her mother gave a thumbnail sketch of the Sheppard case. In 1996, her mother recalled Kathie's inquiry, too. "Kathie said that Richard Eberling had told her that he had killed Marilyn Sheppard. I told her not to listen to Dick because he was crazy," she said.

Kathie left it at that: the ranting of an unbalanced man. Only years later did she begin to reconsider her conclusion.

At the time of the conversation with Eberling, Kathie had worked at the Durkin home for nearly six months, with more or less the same routine. In the next two weeks, life changed drastically. Weird things kept happening. Property of hers disappeared during the night while she slept. Noises in the basement awakened her, but when she rose to listen more carefully, the sounds stopped. Then one night Eberling sent her down to the basement to get something. Durkin's basement was dingy and unfinished, not unlike the Sheppard basement. While in the cellar, the lights were abruptly switched off. The door at the top of the steps suddenly slammed shut, the lock turned. Kathie gathered her wits and searched her pockets for a lighter. Flicking it on, she found her way up the steps and banged on the door, yelling loudly. Eberling stood on the other side and laughed. Finally he opened the door. Kathie was unnerved.

The next week, she arrived for work and Eberling fired her. He said liquor was missing. Kathie protested that she didn't drink. She puzzled over it, but in a way she was relieved. Within days Ethel Durkin suffered a fall in the living room that years later was designated as homicide.

In the Durkin murder trial in 1989, Kathie's name had come up, however briefly, when Obie Henderson named the people who had worked at the Durkin household. Kathie was one; her mother another. Documents collected for the Durkin probate estate included thirty-one weekly paychecks written to Kathie and several paychecks for one-night services to her mother.

By 1989, Collins had been in Florida for five years. Her mother had moved to California. Both had taken the last names of spouses. Even as hometown events faded, Kathie sometimes skimmed through a *Cleveland Magazine* to keep in touch. There she read a story about Richard Eberling's arrest for murder. "I became worried that maybe the things Eberling told me about murdering Mrs. Sheppard were true," she said. Alarmed, she called the Cleveland police department and spoke with a detective, describing her vivid encounter with Eberling. The detective said Eberling was suspected in several murders and that she should be thankful he fired her. "He could have taken you and her out and made it look like a burglary," she remembered him saying. Collins offered to be available and left her number.

Cleveland police had no intention of following up on the Bay Village murder. Sergeant Vince Kremperger of Lakewood, the dogged investigator on the Durkin case, also ran into stonewalling about Sheppard at the Justice Center in the years when Prosecutor John T. Corrigan still reigned. "It was a matter of common knowledge that John wouldn't reopen the Sheppard case," Kremperger said.

Collins, indeed, never heard from Cleveland again. She next heard about the Sheppard murder on TV in 1996. In fact, she believed Andy Carraway was referring to her as the woman who had come forward, but that the police had refused to disclose her name. That was why she called.

Although outspoken and spirited, Collins experienced nightmares after recounting her story to Allen Gore. She cried. Over and over she recalled the moment when Eberling had locked her in the basement. Had Eberling thought about killing her? Was his firing of her intended to get her out of the way so that he could kill Durkin? Could her evidence have solved the Sheppard case earlier? Would Eberling somehow come after her now?

Despite her fears, Collins agreed to go to Cleveland at her own expense to talk with prosecutors in April. She believed it was her civic duty. Left to meet with various assistants and office investigators because Marino was out, she bristled at their huffy attitude. They grilled her. They doubted her. They claimed they didn't understand her job at the Durkin household. They said they certainly would have gone to Florida to interview her, although they had lagged ruinously in contacting the other woman in Elyria.

Beleaguered, Collins felt frustrated. "One thing I know— *I* didn't murder Marilyn Sheppard. I wasn't even born," she said later. "Have they spent this much time interrogating Dick Eberling?" The answer was no.

Faced with a continually unraveling story, Eberling sent out obliquely threatening letters. He had information, he claimed, that would damage the Sheppard family.

He had, he said, an affidavit from a man in prison named Jack who had explosive information about Dr. Sam Sheppard. As a fellow prisoner, Sheppard had treated Jack as a sex slave, engaged him in various nefarious activities, and, incidentally, also confessed to murder, Eberling said.

To Sam R., Eberling wrote for the first time in several years "to inform you of what filth lies ahead." Eberling's advice: "(Q)uietly pull down your tents."

A check with Ohio corrections officials traced Jack's incarceration history. He first entered prison, it turned out, in 1976—six years after Sheppard had died.

The coroner's vault yielded a vast reservoir of telling information. In these files rested the graying original of Dombrowski's report pointing to a break-in in the basement. The question about whether powerful people had

known about a break-in was answered. Coroner Dr. Sam
Gerber had known.

The original report by Detective Harold Lockwood, in
which he tried to explain away the blood throughout the
house, was there. He theorized that the victim had been
assaulted downstairs and then ran up to her bed. Police
obviously understood that the blood on the stairs came
from freshly bleeding wounds, and Sheppard had none. Dr.
Gerber knew that, too.

There was other information never seen before. A report
by Ray Keefe, the investigator for Dr. Gerber, described
the murder scene shortly after noon on July 4. The police
had not interviewed witnesses, gathered evidence, or written a single report. An autopsy had not yet been conducted.

"I then went around to the front of the house. . . . Dr.
Gerber advised Chief Eaton to station a policeman at the
door to Dr. Sheppard's room at Bay View Hospital and to
permit no one to talk to the doctor *and to place the doctor
under arrest.* Chief Eaton walked over to Mayor Houk and
informed him of Dr. Gerber's suggestions and request.
Mayor Houk said, 'Oh no, not Sam!' " [emphasis added]
Now it was absolutely clear that Gerber had targeted Dr.
Sam before the investigation was even off the ground.

Photographs showed the large amount of blood on the
stairs, much of it on the vertical backs of risers. The blood
could not have landed there easily except from a bleeding,
swinging hand. The blood could be seen as falling on the
left if someone was walking down, matching a wound on
the left hand.

The files had an unsigned statement of Richard Eberling—apparently one taken by Dr. Gerber in 1959, before
abruptly canceling further interrogation. Eberling gave yet
another version of cutting his hand. In this narrative Eberling said, "Mrs. Sheppard called and asked that we do her
windows the latter part of June"—not July 2, as he later
declared. He said that when he told her the amount of the
bill, she said she would mail a check—which, if it occurred,
would put him at the Sheppard home before June 24, 1954,
the date of the check Mrs. Sheppard wrote to him. In contrast to his other statements, Eberling then said he had cut
his hand when a screwdriver slipped.

And in this version he also made reference to the basement door—which surely must have alerted Dr. Gerber,

who knew about the tool marks there. Eberling described the basement door as "hard to open and shut."

Finally, an original Bay Village police report lay in the coroner's files. The report had not been in the files released by Bay Village—possibly because the only copy had been secured by Dr. Gerber.

The August 2, 1955, report by Bay Village Police Chief John Eaton described a call from Karl Schuele, a Sheppard neighbor. The ripped T-shirt found after the murder in 1954 had washed up into Schuele's Lake Erie pier.

Thirteen months after the murder, Schuele found something else on his beach. Buried in the sand twenty feet from the shore in eighteen inches of water, he uncovered a flashlight. Chief Eaton reported:

"This light is a *3 cell flash light* and appears to be an Eveready. There is no glass in the reflector and the bottom cap is broken out. *The light has been damaged by striking something repeatedly* and the case has been dented on the side about where a person's thumb would come. Batteries are still in the light which *appears to have been in the water for some time.*" [emphasis added]

Eaton immediately connected the flashlight to the Sheppard case. So did Adelbert O'Hara, a Cleveland homicide officer. And so did Dr. Sam Gerber, who had placed the report and the flashlight with the files of Marilyn Sheppard's murder.

Yet no mention of finding this flashlight had ever been made to the police or the media or the forensic scientists. According to Dr. Steve Sheppard, no word of a flashlight was ever made known to the Sheppard family, to Dr. Sam, or to F. Lee Bailey.

There were good reasons to hide the item. It was exactly the type of weapon described by Gerber's nemesis, Dr. Paul Kirk, when he analyzed the Sheppard case. He described the weapon as an industrial-sized flashlight with the glass missing. Flashlights of this type had red paint on them, and Kirk had matched the red chips found in the murder room to this type of paint.

Criminalist Jim Chapman, reviewing the case in the 1980s, had thought about flashlights, too. "I was convinced that was the murder weapon," he said. Chapman recalled the type of three-cell flashlight referred to by the Bay Village report—it consisted of three D-size batteries, lined up vertically, making the whole flashlight 10 or 12 inches long. It had a big flange on the end. It was heavy. The glass came out easily; Chapman could recall having one in which it popped out. Red lacquer was on it, too.

A flashlight presented an entirely different set of clues about the murder. An intruder was likely to carry a flashlight to see his way around. A burglar was likely to carry a flashlight. A killer, carrying a flashlight used as a weapon, was likely to discard it. "If you just killed somebody, why would you want to carry the weapon?" asked Chapman. "You would bury it in the sand."

Whatever happened to the flashlight was an unknown. On the side of the report stashed away in the Sheppard files was a handwritten note in red: "Discarded." The date on it was March, 1986—shortly before Dr. Sam Gerber retired.

AMSEC continued to pursue Sheppard leads, and John Burkholder, an AMSEC investigator and former ATF agent, found his curiosity whetted by the 1957 prison confession of Donald Joseph Wedler. Burkholder reinitiated an effort to find Wedler, running computer name searches. He looked for Wedler at his last known address in Washington, D.C. No luck—the entire neighborhood was gone.

Burkholder then got a printout of all the Wedlers in the United States, ready to go through them one by one. He used Washington, D.C., as his epicenter, and first picked a number for a Wedler in Maryland. An elderly woman answered. Did she, by any chance, know a Donald Joseph Wedler? Burkholder asked cautiously. "Donny?" the woman responded. Yes, she knew a Donny Wedler. In fact, she was Donny's stepmother. A former government employee, she had married Wedler's father, Lester, in the 1960s. She had heard plenty about Wedler's arrest in Florida, his prison history, and his claim to have been in Cleveland on the night of the Sheppard murder. Burkholder probed gently, asking what she knew about Wedler's current whereabouts.

She recounted how Wedler had moved to the capital after his release from prison. He married and had a daughter. About the time that his daughter turned four, in the late 1960s, Donny got caught up in a nasty incident on the streets when a shoot-out erupted over drugs. Wedler was shot. He died as a result. Wedler was currently buried in southwest Washington, D.C.

Burkholder hung up, ending at least the mystery of Wedler's disappearance.

All physical evidence collected from the coroner's office landed in the lab of Dr. Tahir in Indiana. To his disappointment, the material was in shambles, poorly marked, barely documented. Tahir was not used to this kind of evidence mishandling. Every item brought into his lab is labeled, logged, photographed, and tracked. Witnesses observe testing and attest to its accuracy. A sign hanging in a corner of the sprawling lab carries the word "Assume" with a slash through it—Assume Nothing.

Coming in at five in the morning to do Sheppard testing before he started his regular duties, Tahir worked patiently. Good testing took time. The Sheppard case, he soon realized, was going to take an exceptional amount of time. No one had ever conducted DNA testing on crime-scene evidence this old. "Every step of the way involves research," Tahir said. "You have to stop and think: what to do next, what can you do."

Meticulously, over several weeks, Tahir began to plow through ninety-one evidence envelopes, a dozen vials, and forty-nine slides of microscopic material, trying to discover any that contained something capable of being analyzed by DNA testing. Many of the envelopes were empty; others unidentifiable. The chances of locating anything else that could be tested seemed bleak.

For example, AMSEC investigators had drawn attention to the pocket area of Dr. Sam's trousers, where a smear of blood had been found. Keys had been torn from the pocket. If a bleeding killer had reached into Dr. Sam's pocket and deposited blood there, it would be a very revealing piece of evidence. Lab technician Mary Cowan had seen this blood but never tested it at all. The trousers were missing. All that remained were tiny squares, an eighth of an inch in size. From what part of the pants the fabric came was unclear. Dr. Sam had described leaning against the murder bed, so the knee area might have absorbed Marilyn Sheppard's blood. If it was not Marilyn's DNA, it would point to a third person at the crime scene.

In time Dr. Tahir located other useful items. He found

a swatch of the green bag tossed in the yard. He discovered a blood droplet preserved on a slide and collected from the porch area on the lake side of the house, the direction in which Dr. Sam had chased the intruder. Richard Eberling, in his varying descriptions of cutting himself at the Sheppard home, had never mentioned walking on the porch. Two slides of vaginal swabs from the coroner's office, never tested, were also in the files. With Exhibit 84, the wood chip, Tahir had several crime-scene samples on which he could work.

On this evidence Tahir planned to use a DNA technology known as PCR or polymerase chain reaction. PCR testing could be done with minute samples of DNA—smaller than one-billionth of a gram, entirely invisible to the eye. Part of the process involved multiplying or amplifying the DNA—essentially photocopying it. The mechanisms of the body were simulated so that the DNA cloned or replicated itself, as it did naturally in cells. A batch could be made that measured 200 billion times the size of the original sample, and exactly identical to it. After amplification any number of comparison tests to suspects could be conducted.

The extreme sensitivity of PCR testing also means that it could show DNA left on the sample from other sources, such as from handling at the crime scene or lab. For example, detectives and technicians in 1954 didn't wear gloves. Sweat from their hands could transfer to a sample and be amplified, along with the DNA of the original source. In such cases testing would show two DNA types. Fortunately, the appearance of a second DNA did not corrupt the integrity of the first DNA typing.

Even a single PCR test is complex—this is not a simple litmus test. The test involves three stages. In the first stage the DNA is extracted, a detailed procedure in which the blood or saliva is physically transferred to a cotton swab and treated in several solutions. This is followed by the equally difficult process of amplification. The protocol for amplification alone calls for about eighty individual steps—adding chemicals, heating, stirring, washing. DNA typing comes in the third stage. This is accomplished by comparing the amplified DNA to certain standard measures, known as probes. In PCR testing the probes are contained on thin white strips with a series of dots. When the DNA sample correlates to a known DNA measure, the dot turns blue.

Before extracting blood from the crime-scene samples, Tahir turned his attention to the other side of the equation—to whom would he attempt to match the blood on the crime-scene evidence? Richard Eberling offered one source of comparison, but Tahir wanted the victim's DNA so that he could eliminate the possibility that any blood on the scene was hers. If the group of DNA could not be connected to Marilyn Sheppard, then the prosecution of Dr. Sam would be proven completely bogus. It clearly meant that a third person shed the blood.

Since incontrovertible facts showed that Dr. Sam had not been bleeding, he could be eliminated as a source of blood. For this reason, prosecutor Marino argued forcefully that any testing for Sheppard's DNA would be an absolute waste of time. Still, with research in mind, Tahir decided at least to try to get Sheppard's DNA.

Since both Dr. Sam and Marilyn were dead, finding their DNA turned out to be a formidable task. Exhuming bodies, a costly last resort, was not really feasible. Tahir ruled out using the mitochondrial DNA of Sam R. for scientific reasons, and he began to look for other solutions.

He could obtain Marilyn Sheppard's DNA from many sources. The teeth found on the bed would offer excellent samples, but the coroner's office couldn't find them. Tahir tried a swatch from the quilt that Sam R. had kept. No DNA appeared in testing, possibly because Sam R. had dried it in the sun, Tahir guessed. Tahir continued to search. He found hairs taken from the victim's head during the autopsy. Since the roots were intact, they might yield DNA. After extracting cells from the hair roots, Tahir could tell that he had a sufficient quantity of DNA for testing, and he moved quickly to do the DNA typing. But when he did, two DNA codes showed up. Sloppy autopsy procedures had seemingly left someone else's blood or sweat on the hairs. Finally, he found hairs of Marilyn Sheppard removed from her mattress with a portion of the scalp attached. From these Tahir was able to determine Marilyn Sheppard's DNA.

Getting Dr. Sam's DNA involved more obstacles. No blood samples had been preserved. DNA testing on baby hairs would be futile, since the curls were cut and had no roots. Tahir prodded the Sheppard team. Wasn't there anything else? Was there a shirt with sweat on the collar, a razor with skin cells, a toothbrush with saliva? None could be found. Then Tahir asked: what about envelopes Sheppard had sealed? Letters, in fact, had been saved by family members.

Tahir planned to look for cells deposited by saliva in the glue flaps on the backs of envelopes or underneath the stamps. Saliva testing had yielded successful results in several of his cases. In the murder case of a cab driver, a beer bottle was discovered on the backseat. Extracting cells from the rim of the bottle, Tahir gathered enough DNA to type it and match it to a suspect.

Letters were among the memorabilia that Sam R. had collected. His father had been a steady correspondent while away at college in 1942–43, writing frequently to sweetheart Marilyn Reese in Cleveland in the years before they married. The letters all began "Marilyn Darling" and had a breezy style—"hi kid," "take it easy," "all my love for always." Marilyn had carefully saved the letters, folding them neatly into their envelopes with their three-cent stamps still affixed on them. Tahir soaked the stamps to extract any cells, concentrating on the area between the stamp and the envelope. He amplified the DNA. Unfortunately, each of his results showed the presence of more than one DNA source, probably, he felt, from the paper absorbing tiny particles of sweat when fingered over the years.

Although the envelope testing proved unsuccessful, Tahir satisfied himself that he had tried every available measure. He could move forward now with his two comparison samples—DNA of Marilyn Sheppard and DNA of Richard Eberling. He turned his attention to the crime-scene samples and conducting comparison tests.

National media articles about the Sheppard case proliferated, but Judyth Ulis became increasingly agitated by the commentary about Richard Eberling. She was especially irked by accounts that referred to Eberling as serving time in prison for an "unrelated murder." Unrelated to whom? she would ask. After all, Judyth *was* related to murder victim Ethel Durkin.

Judyth had fond memories of Ethel. Ethel and Judyth's grandmother (niece and aunt who were actually the same age) had grown up in the same household. Not long before Ethel was killed, Judyth had visited with her and listened to tales from those childhood years. Judyth fumed when *Plain Dealer* editor and Sheppard accuser Brent Larkin proclaimed that Eberling had committed only crimes of greed, not violence. Killing a defenseless ninety-year-old woman wasn't violent? Ulis wondered. Beating an old lady, completely vulnerable and alone, to death?

Ulis was also haunted by the violent endings of Ethel's two sisters, Myrtle Fray and Belle Farrow. Myrtle had been bludgeoned to death in her bed, and police had done virtually nothing to find the murderer. Belle had taken an unaccounted fall down the basement steps, with little inquiry into the cause. Two, and possibly three, of the women related to her had been victims of murder.

In 1989, Ulis observed the murder trial of Richard Eberling from the spectator section of the courtroom. She recoiled at testimony about Eberling's temper tantrums and outbursts at the Durkin home. Witnesses expressed fear. Yet in court Eberling reacted by making faces and behaving peculiarly. An elementary school principal, Ulis associated him with ten-year-old boys who were dragged into her office because of their uncontrollable conduct. Later, she was upset by his bizarre statement to Cooper and the accumulating information about his knowledge of the deaths of the sisters. Why wasn't anyone official looking into this?

Judyth talked with her father. Together they wrote a letter to the prosecutor's office. Myrtle Fray, they noted, had died after a "horrific beating," yet for thirty-four years family members had been denied the consolation of seeing the killer brought to justice. This was especially disconcerting, given new details of Myrtle's murder coming to light. They asked the prosecutor to reopen the case of Myrtle Fray's unsolved homicide.

Carmen Marino called back immediately. He said the prosecutor's office would get to work on it.

AMSEC also prepared a request for Marino. Convinced that the most fruitful clues to the murder lay inside Richard Eberling's mind, AMSEC worked up a preliminary psychological profile on him. From Eberling's troubled childhood, abandonment, blackouts, difficulties with telling the truth, epilepsy, psychiatric incidents, alcohol consumption, and pattern of constantly shifting statements, a picture emerged that seemed to make Eberling an excellent candidate for further study by a behavioral scientist or forensic psychologist who studied personality types and crime patterns. They might get results that a Cleveland police officer could not.

Marino also believed that psychiatric know-how could present insights into the case. He consulted with a local psychologist who had helped the prosecutor's office in the past. Marino planned to bring him into the Sheppard case. Just as he was ready to do so, the man passed away unexpectedly.

What about a request to the FBI Behavioral Science Unit? AMSEC asked. In a meeting in June 1996 Marino agreed to check into the FBI unit. He picked up the phone and called an agent with the unit in Quantico, Virginia. The agent said the FBI would consider the case if documentation was sent down.

Meanwhile, after months of effort, Dr. Tahir prepared to complete the final experiments. Could he extract DNA from the crime-scene samples? Would comparison tests of the blood show links to Marilyn Sheppard? Or would they eliminate the possibility that the blood on the scene was hers and instead point to a bleeding killer that would unequivocally establish the innocence of Dr. Sheppard? Would the tests show that Richard Eberling could be excluded as the source of the blood? Or, to the contrary, would they show that the blood might be his and further implicate him? Spurred by media reports, people across the country awaited the results.

So much had happened in a year. The Cleveland Browns left Cleveland, but ultimately without the Browns name. Michael Corrigan decided not to run for prosecutor but for a court of appeals office. The reelection of Stephanie Tubbs Jones was secure. Judge Suster, up for his first election, won handily.

Change was under way. The Sheppard team continued its pursuits, now bolstered by the efforts of critically placed people who, one by one, were making a difference—a prosecutor, a judge, a forensic scientist. However slowly it moved at times, the Sheppard case sped along compared to the years of nothing.

Sam R. also adjusted to changes. In moving to California, he reconnected with the cousins who had become his immediate family after his mother died. He and his Uncle Steve grew closer than they had been in years. At the same time, blood relatives on his mother's side in Cleveland openly offered support. Strangers called and wrote with words of encouragement.

More uncomfortable, though, were media accounts that made Sam R. the sole focus of the Sheppard case, repeatedly describing him on a "quest," as if he were Don Quixote. They skipped the big picture. Erased were the six years of investigative effort, the long hours of those working on the case. Eliminated was the exposé of gross misconduct. Overlooked was the frightening failure of the justice system.

In mythologizing Sam R., media stories reduced the case to elements so simple that they missed genuine problems. If this could happen to his father, a middle-class white man, how could the justice system be trusted to treat others fairly? If the investigation and prosecution of his mother's homicide could be handled so disgracefully, what did it say about the treatment of victims and women?

They missed that the Sheppard case was not merely about Sam R. but about an entire generation that had believed in its leaders, in government, in the media—and was thoroughly misled. It was about a whole community and, by extension a national audience, that had been shockingly deceived. Sam R. had suffered, but thousands of others were victims, too.

Or perhaps the commentators reduced the story to Sam R. because the real question that begged to be answered was so impossible. Why? Why had this happened? Cleveland had had 93 homicides in 1954. Why had this one case become so twisted?

Were officials concerned with quelling fear over an unknown assailant roaming the community? Had they a personal dislike for Sheppard? Did a zeal to sensationalize overwhelm rationality and a search for the truth? Was a willingness to overlook the evidence a face-saving need to win at all costs?

Barbara Greenberg, executive director of the Cuyahoga County Bar Association, pointed to the power of former *Cleveland Press* editor Louis Seltzer. "If he liked you, your name was in the headlines once. If he didn't like you, it was in for days," she said.

Terry Gilbert thought that once the initial accusation of

guilt was hurled, it became impossible to retract. "Once that railroad train starts going," he said, "it's hard to stop."

Marino believed that the coroner's office wrongly usurped the jobs of the police and prosecutor, throwing the checks and balances of the justice system off-kilter.

Or perhaps only a volatile combination of causes set off the Sheppard case like so many Fourth of July firecrackers lit all at once.

Richard Eberling spoke little during the year, although he kept up his correspondence. Letters ranged from angry and menacing to desperate and heartrending. He repeatedly insisted that people were trying to execute him, even though by Ohio's law the death penalty was not a possibility (it had been suspended for crimes in certain years). No one other than Eberling had ever mentioned the death penalty. The irony, of course, was not lost on Sam R., whose anti-death penalty activities continued and even increased on the West Coast.

At other times Eberling's comments dropped into a seeming death wish. One letter he sent to Cooper in June said:

> But by the saving grace of God it will all be over soonest. Thank God for the hangman's noose. My so-called life on this planet will cease to be. Peace at long last. Saddest part of all, they should have let me die when I was a baby. Then there would have been no Eberlings nor Durkin and lastly Sheppard. How sad that it was to be. Hopefully my future will be that I can be put [to] sleep soonest.

Finally, in January 1997 Dr. Tahir had preliminary conclusions. Given the age of the evidence, his results are remarkable. Tahir successfully extracted DNA from three crime-scene samples: the wood chip from the basement stair; the trousers; the blood from the porch. In addition, he subjected vaginal swabs to DNA testing, yielding some findings.

Tahir ran in to some of the same problems he had previously encountered with material handled at the coroner's office. Two DNA types appeared on certain items, for example, the trousers and wood chip. The blood from the porch—better preserved on a slide—revealed, in very small amounts, only one person's DNA.

Compelling details emerged. Marilyn Sheppard's DNA was not on *any* of the crime-scene samples. Even the trousers did not have her DNA. Blood on the stair at the crime scene, on the path of escape, and on clothing worn by Sheppard all came from some other person—some *bleeding* person. The intruder was real.

There were other riveting conclusions. In each test the DNA did *not* exclude Richard Eberling. Whether one DNA appeared or two, Eberling could have been its source. Nothing removed Eberling from the murder scene. Blood on the stair and trousers and even sperm from a vaginal swab included his type. And, most convincing, the sole DNA on the porch implicated Richard Eberling or someone in his DNA category—a group that includes less than one-tenth of one percent of the population (0.07 percent). After forty-two years DNA now furnished new clues to solve the murder of Marilyn Sheppard.

In the end, Sam R., working with others, had managed to roll back the Sheppard case to its beginning, to the central facts. On the day after the murder in 1954, before accusations became contorted by rumor and misrepresentation and suppressed evidence, an Akron, Ohio, newspaper had carried a simple report:

> CLEVELAND—A jewel thief clubbed the wife of a suburban doctor to death Sunday when she discovered him in her home and severely injured her husband when he came to her rescue. . . . Sheppard told a grim tale of battling his wife's attacker. . . . Police found a bag of family jewelry on the steps leading to the beach where the burglar had evidently dropped it.

After all these years the Sheppard case had returned to that one salient story. A new beginning ascended independently from the tattered memories.

The Sheppard case, at long last, held the possibility of being transformed from a mockery to a model. The entire case might not be resolved, but a few people, aiming only for the truth, had been able to overcome four decades of a deplorable past. For Sam R., this alone offered a semblance of hope.

NOTES

Prologue

5   Cameras, press . . . : "Get That Killer!," *Cleveland Plain Dealer,* July 22, 1954; "Somebody Is . . . ," *Cleveland Press,* July 20, 1954, p. 1; "Why Isn't . . . ," *Cleveland Press,* July 30, 1954, p. 1.

6   A cross between Henry Fonda . . . : Dorothy Kilgallen, reporter for the Hearst newspapers, in *Our Living Bill of Rights: Free Press v. Fair Trial: The Sheppard Case,* Encyclopedia Britannica Film (Educational Corporation, 1969).

6   Dear Sir . . . : personal files of Dr. Sam Sheppard and Sam Reese Sheppard, hereafter cited as Sheppard Files.

6   As if the notoriety . . . : "The Fugitive" television series originally aired on ABC from 1963 to 1967, with a two-part ending in August 1967. The story was of a doctor who, wrongfully convicted of killing his wife, escapes en route to the execution chamber and begins to search for the true murderer, a one-armed man. In the meantime, authorities search for the doctor. The series was conceived by Roy Huggins, Martin Quinn was the executive producer, and David Janssen starred as Dr. Richard Kimble. The movie *The Fugitive,* released in 1993 by Warner Brothers, was produced by Arnold Kopelson and starred Harrison Ford as Dr. Kimble and Tommy Lee Jones as the marshal who pursues him.

        The television show was a consistent winner in audience share surveys and ran in seventy countries (*Magazine of the Academy of Television Arts* 4, no. 6 [November–December 1982]: 42). In 1993 *Entertainment Weekly* ranked shows produced before 1980 and listed "The Fugitive" as the sixth best series of all time (July 30, 1993). When the show went off the air, the *New York Times* wrote that "viewer interest may have started to drop last November when Samuel H. Sheppard, the former osteopathic surgeon, was acquitted in a second trial in Ohio of murdering his . . . wife" (November 29, 1971). F. Lee Bailey, who represented Sheppard from 1961 to 1966, noted that it was common knowledge that "The Fugitive" was based on the Sheppard case (F. Lee Bailey with Harvey Aronson, *The Defense Never Rests* [New York: Stein & Day, 1971], p. 67; Jane Gaibraith, "Dr. Richard Kimble, Meet Dr. Sam Sheppard" *Los Angeles Times,* September 13, 1993). Roy Huggins and those involved with the show have denied that the show was based on the Sheppard case (ibid.). John Greenya, who co-wrote *For the Defense* with F. Lee Bailey, said that in a personal conversation Huggins told him that the Sheppard case was the model for "The Fugitive" (interview by C. Cooper, 1993).

8   "One of the most common . . .": Edward Radin, *The Innocents* (New York: Morrow, 1964), p. 7.

8   "Countless men and women . . . : Michael L. Radelet, Hugo Adam Bedau, Constance E. Putnam, *In Spite of Innocence: Erroneous Convictions in Capital Cases* (Boston: Northeastern University Press, 1992), p. 271.

9   "Don't try to solve . . .": Dorothy Kilgallen, "When Justice Took the Day Off," in *Murder One* (New York: Random House, 1967), pp. 231, 234 (published after Kilgallen's death in 1965).

9   The case had been . . . : Erle Stanley Gardner, "Are the Sheppards Telling the Truth?" *Argosy Magazine,* August 1957, pp. 15, 95.

10   He types . . . : *Sheppard v. Maxwell* (No. 490, 1965 Term), 384 U.S. 333, 86 S. Ct. 1507 June 6, 1966), opinion by Justice Tom Clark.

10   "Few are willing . . . : Radelet, Bedau, and Putnam, *In Spite of Innocence,* p. 11.

Chapter 1 • Deeds Will Rise

12   Cleveland is a city . . . : For general information on Cleveland, see Carol Poh Miller and Robert Wheeler, *Cleveland: A Concise History, 1796–1990* (Bloomington: Indiana University Press, 1990); historical perspectives from *The Cleveland City Directory* (Cleveland: Cleveland Directory Co., 1929, 1954).

12   The Sheppards had opened . . . : Bay View Hospital was located at 23200 West Lake Road, in Bay Village, Ohio.

13   Now Gerber's name . . . : The Cuyahoga County Coroner's Office is located in the Gerber Building, 2121 Adelbert Road, Cleveland.

18   "The fact that . . .": Dr. Sam notes, Sheppard Files.

18   "Strive for greater learning . . .": Sheppard Files.

19   Cindy Leise . . . : Cindy Leise, interviews by C. Cooper, 1993–94.

20   The homicide of Ethel May Durkin . . . : *State v. Eberling and Henderson,* No. CR-232316, Court of Common Pleas, Cuyahoga County, transcripts, appellate briefs, and opinions; letters and interviews as noted below in chapter 19.

21   "My father believes . . .": Judge Michael Corrigan, interview by C. Cooper, 1993.

21   Cleveland reporters . . . : " Free Press and Fair Trial," *Toledo Blade,* December 22, 1954: "At this distance, some 100 miles

from Cleveland, it looks to us as though the Sheppard murder case was sensationalized to the point at which the press must ask itself if its freedom, carried to excess, doesn't interfere with the conduct of fair trials.

"The hue and cry raised in Cleveland newspapers after Marilyn Sheppard was found murdered could not help but inflame public opinion even as it pointed the finger of suspicion. One of the papers, which virtually demanded the arrest of Dr. Sheppard, almost had a vested interest in his conviction."

21   "Is this . . .": Sheppard Files.

22   The paper waited . . . : Cindy Leise's articles included "Sam's Brother: Reopen the Case," *Chronicle-Telegram*, July 24, 1989, p. 1; " 'I Know Who Killed Marilyn . . . ,' " *Chronicle-Telegram*, August 7, 1989, p. 1; and the series "Shadowed by Death," *Chronicle-Telegram*, beginning August 10, 1989.

22   *The New York Times* . . . : "Sheppard Murder Case Attracting New Interest," *New York Times*, August 14, 1989.

22   A judge had once . . . : *State v. Sheppard*, 165 Ohio St. 293, 294 (1956), decision by J. Bell.

22   In 1960 Adelson . . . : Dr. Lester Adelson, *New England Journal of Medicine* 262, no. 5 (February 4, 1960): 229.

Chapter 2 • Emergency

24   Bay Village police . . . : In 1943 the bodies of murdered thirteen-year-old twin brothers were found in the woods in Bay Village, but the case was handled by the Cleveland police, who were investigating the suspect on another charge (*Cleveland Plain Dealer,* August 14, 1943, p. 1).

24   In June 1954 . . . : These and other details based on unreleased interviews of Esther Houk by Janet Sheppard Duvall, Richard Dalrymple, and Jim Chapman, 1980–81, hereafter cited as Esther Houk interviews. Other details are drawn from interviews of Spen Houk, Larry Houk, and the former Lyn Houk by Richard Dalrymple and Janet Sheppard Duvall, 1980–81, from statements made to the police and released under Ohio's public records law, and from transcripts of Sheppard's trials, the inquest, or hearings.

24   Sheppard would hop in a jeep . . . : Statements, testimony and writings of Dr. Sam Sheppard, Sheppard Files.

25   A medical-school chum . . . : Hoversten information drawn from private files of Dr. Sam Sheppard, documents released by police under Ohio's public records law, evidence kept in the 1954 trial and turned over to Dr. Sam Sheppard and held in Sheppard Files, Hoversten's 1954 diary and court testimony, and interviews about Hoversten in 1992–94, as described in notes to chapter 14.

27   Dr. Sam converted . . . : James Redinger, interviews by C.

Cooper, 1993, 1994 (hereafter cited as Redinger interviews); Larry Houk, inquest testimony, July 1954.

27   Even workers . . . : Drawn from extensive interviews and letters of Richard Eberling, as described in notes to chapters 17–20.

27   *Strange Holiday* . . . : Ephraim Katz, *The Film Encyclopedia* (New York: Perigee Books, 1979), pp. 869, 944–45; *The Magill Movie Guide* database (1993) and *McGill's Survey of Cinema* database (Salem Press, 1994).

30   When Roy Huggins . . . : Ed Robertson, *The Fugitive* (Pomegranate Press, 1993). A retrospective in the *Plain Dealer* on January 5, 1992, published an incorrect caption under a photo of Dr. Sam: "Dr. Sam Sheppard: Wearing a neck brace in 1954 after he said a one-armed man hit him and murdered his wife."

Chapter 3 • *Sounding Out*

33   Three days of events . . . : Sam Reese Sheppard, personal diary. Sample articles include Joe Dirck, "Dr. Sam's Son Says He Denied Mom's Death," *Plain Dealer,* October 25, 1989, from Lordstown, Ohio; Associated Press, "Son Says Father Feared Re-Imprisonment . . . ," October 25, 1989, from Youngstown, Ohio; Felix Hoover, "Sheppard, Adams Say 'No Death,' " *Columbus Dispatch,* September 27, 1989.

34   Adams's own ordeal . . . : *The Thin Blue Line* (1988), directed by Errol Morris, produced by Mark Lipson; Randall Dale Adams and William and Marilyn Mona Hoffer, *Adams v. Texas* (New York: St. Martin's Press, 1991).

35   Monsignor proceeded to read . . . : Letter from Dr. Stephen A. Sheppard to Hon. Frank J. Merrick, dated January 7, 1965, filed January 8, 1965, In Re Guardianship for Samuel Reese Sheppard, Cuyahoga County Probate Court, no. 513–077.

37   But later, when AMSEC . . . : See chapter 11.

37   He was not registered . . . : New York Department of State, Division of Licensing, 1994; Ohio Department of Commerce, Division of Consumer Finance, 1994.

37   He once said . . . : Records department, University of Dayton, 1993.

37   William Corrigan . . . : William J. Corrigan Papers, 1920–64, MSS 4464, microfilm edition, Western Reserve Historical Society, Cleveland, Ohio; hereafter cited as William J. Corrigan Papers.

37   Mrs. Nellie Kralick . . . : Interview by C. Cooper, 1994.

37   Court records indicated . . . : Case no. 138481, Court of Common Pleas, Cuyahoga County, Ohio; also Cuyahoga County case nos. 81CVF2330, 81CVF2341, 81CVF79373, 82CVF919151, and others.

40   The writing . . . : Richard Eberling, letter to Sam Reese Sheppard.

Chapter 4 • Red Dye

42   His case was being heard . . . : The oral arguments before the Supreme Court were originally set for the week of February 21–24, 1966, and later changed to February 28, 1966 (U.S. Supreme Court Calendar).

43   The opinion by Judge Weinman . . . : Sheppard v. Maxwell, 231 F. Supp. 37, 59 (D.C. S.D. Ohio, July 15, 1964). "This Court now holds that the prejudicial effect of the newspaper publicity was so manifest that no jury could have been seated at that particular time in Cleveland which would have been fair and impartial regardless of their assurances."

43   Almost ten years . . . : Judge Weinman added a coda to his opinion, which he recognized as "somewhat atypical," that ordered Dr. Sam's immediate release. Dr. Sam was released on July 16, 1964, but immediately had to fight to stay free when Ohio appealed on July 17, 1954, and asked that he be reincarcerated. He was left free upon the posting of a bond ("Sheppard Gains in Freedom Plea," New York Times, July 23, 1964).

43   In May 1965 . . . : Sheppard v. Maxwell, 346 F. 2d 707 (6th Cir., May 5, 1965, rehearing den. July 14, 1965).

43   Miraculously . . . : "Sheppard Gets Stay for Appeal," New York Post, July 27, 1965.

44   The Supreme Court doesn't take . . . : Supreme Court Watch, 1993.

44   The American Civil Liberties Union . . . : Sheppard v. Maxwell, No. 490, 1965 Term, U.S. Supreme Court; "Motion for Leave to File and Brief of Amici Curiae, American Civil Liberties Union and Ohio Civil Liberties Union," Bernard Berkman (Cleveland, Ohio) and Melvin Wulf (New York), National Archives. Also see Philip B. Kurland and Gerhard Casper, eds., Constitutional Law, vol. 63, Landmark Briefs and Arguments of the Supreme Court of the United States (Arlington, Va.: University Publications of America, 1975–   ).

45   "Much reaction . . . : Sheppard Files.

45   Corrigan objected . . . : Transcript of the trial of Dr. Sam Sheppard, 1954; also cited in Sheppard v. Maxwell, 346 F. 2d 707, 743–44 (dissent by J. Edwards). Further portions of the court encounter were as follows:

Corrigan: I would like the record to show that inside the bar . . . is a table . . . that extends over the width of the courtroom; that this courtroom is 26 by 48 feet; that the table runs east and west, and the west end of the table is within six inches of the seat of the thirteenth juror and approximately two feet from the end of the jury box; that there has been assigned to that table representatives of . . . news agencies [listing fifteen news representatives to be seated at the table]. . . .

We also wish to note in the record that there are in this courtroom three loudspeakers and a microphone which stands in front of the witness chair. . . . I now move that the table be taken from inside the bar and removed from this courtroom; that the signs [assigning three of the four rows of spectators' benches to the press] be removed . . . and that the court rescind the order whereby the only admission to this courtroom is by card issued by him. I so move.

Judge: Overruled.

(Transcript, *State v. Sheppard,* No. 64571, Court of Common Pleas, County of Cuyahoga, State of Ohio, 1954.)

45   Marshall Perlin . . . : Interview by C. Cooper, 1993.

45   Dr. Sam registered . . . : Sheppard Files.

45   The judge himself . . . : *Sheppard v. Maxwell,* 231 F. Supp. 37, fnn. 7, 72; 64 (1964); Dr. Edward Murray (son of Edward T. Murray), interview by C. Cooper, 1993.

46   Kilgallen . . . : *Sheppard v. Maxwell,* 231 F. Supp. 37, 64–65; Lee Israel, *Kilgallen* (New York: Delacorte Press, 1979), pp. 252–53, 363–65; briefs on file, National Archives, Great Lakes region, Chicago, Ill.

46   Although every court on appeal . . . : The Ohio Court of Appeals in 1955 said: "[T]he case, from the date of Marilyn Sheppard's death . . . received unusual coverage by the press, radio and television. No case in this community ever attracted such public interest or received so much attention by the news disseminating agencies. Some of such publicity unquestionably was intended to spur on the investigation and was highly critical of the defendant and went so far in some instances as to have been designated by other newspapers as an attempt to try the case in the public press before the defendant was indicted" (*State v. Sheppard,* 100 Ohio App. 345, 355 (Ohio Ct. App. 1955), opinion by J. Skeel, denying Sheppard's appeal). Other Ohio decisions are found at 97 Ohio App. 487 (1955); 100 Ohio App. 399 (1955); 165 Ohio St. 428 (1956); 165 Ohio St. 293 (1956).

46   Bill Corrigan had even tried . . . : The Supreme Court denied the petition for cert. in 1956. Justice Felix Frankfurter wrote a short opinion, an unusual step: "Such denial of his petition in no wise implies that this Court approves the decision of the Supreme Court of Ohio" (*Sheppard v. Ohio,* 352 U.S. 910, 77 S. Ct. 118 [November 13, 1956]).

46   In 1961 Paul Holmes . . . : *The Sheppard Murder Case* (1961; New York: Bantam, 1962), p. 243.

46   In one decision after another . . . : *Miranda v. Arizona,* 384

U.S. 436 (1966) (right to an attorney and to be advised of right to remain silent); *Wong Sun v. US.,* 371 U.S. 271 (1963), *Mapp v. Ohio,* 367 U.S. 643 (1961) (material seized illegally not to be admitted as evidence).

47   The hearing began . . . : see Kurland and Casper, *Landmark Briefs,* p. 537; Russell Sherman, interview by C. Cooper, 1994; Sheppard Files.

49   "We have concluded . . .": *Sheppard v. Maxwell,* 384 U.S. 333 (1966).

49   By the 1990 . . . : WESTLAW, *West* Publishing Co.

50   Upon being released . . . : *Our Living Bill of Rights,* Encyclopedia Britannica Film.

51   "Dearest Mother . . .": Sheppard Files.

51   The Court repeated . . . : *Sheppard v. Maxwell,* 384 U.S. at 351.

51   In 1994 Neil Postman . . . : Postman, a professor of culture and communications, "Defending Ourselves against the Seductions of Eloquence," lecture at the New School for Social Research, New York City, February 16, 1994.

Chapter 5 • Circumstances

52   Now he had some questions . . . : These conversations took place over a period of time.

52   Even their neighbor . . . : Esther Houk interviews.

53   "Will you tell me . . .": Transcript of inquest, July 1954.

53   Esther and Spen Houk . . . : Description of events is based on transcripts, police records released under Ohio's public records law, public documents, and interviews, as described in chapter 2.

54   A fingerprint officer . . . :

Corrigan: Now, [the prosecutor], during his examination, asked you constantly about unidentified fingerprints. Did you understand what he was asking you?

Grabowski: Yes, sir.

Corrigan: Well, did you find some fingerprints that were not identifiable?

Grabowski: Are you talking of a specific—are you talking about the desk itself?

Corrigan: I am talking about the question that was given to you by [the prosecutor] and which you answered a number of times, that you did not find any identifiable fingerprints at certain places where you made examinations.

Grabowski: He specified the places, if I recall correctly.

Corrigan: Well, did you in those places that were specified in his question find any fingerprints that were not identifiable?

Grabowski: Yes.

Corrigan: So you found fingerprints?

Grabowski: Yes.
Corrigan: But you didn't identify them?
Grabowski: That's right.

(Transcript of *State v. Sheppard*, 1954.)

54   When Sam R. . . . : Peter De Forest, interviews by C. Cooper, 1993–94.

54   And, as it turns out . . . : Paul Holmes, letter to Jack Harrison Pollack, 1964, files of Jack Harrison Pollack.

55   The Houks immediately . . . : Esther Houk interviews, 1980.

57   There was a void . . . : Philip W. Porter, "Porter on Murder Case: Fouled Up Bay Village Investigation Points to Need for Metropolitan Police Authority," *Cleveland Plain Dealer*, July 17, 1954.

58   Before the crowds . . . : Fred Drenkhan, court testimony; reports filed with Bay Village Police Department and released under Ohio's public record laws, 1994, hereafter cited as Bay Village Files; interviews by AMSEC, 1993, and C. Cooper, 1994.

59   They piled Sam R. . . . Statements to Cuyahoga County Sheriff's Office, Sheppard Files; inquest transcript, July 1954.

59   Forensic scientists . . . : Charles R. Kingston is a professor at John Jay College of Criminal Law in New York City; interview by C. Cooper, 1993.

60   An animal writer . . . : Maxwell Riddle, "Dog's Failure to Bark No Factor in Bay Case," *Cleveland Press*, July 27, 1954. Riddle's byline described him as Press Dog Editor.

60   Richard Eberling . . . : Interview by C. Cooper, 1991.

60   But later, in an unpublished interview . . . : Esther Houk interviews.

60   A woman's watch . . . : *Sheppard v. Ohio*, "Assignments of Error and Brief of Defendant-Appellant," appeals from the Court of Appeals of Cuyahoga County, nos. 34615 and 34616 to *Supreme Court of Ohio*, by William J. Corrigan, Arthur E. Petersilge, and Fred W. Garmone, filed October 15, 1955, in National Archives.

61   A Bay Village officer . . . : Noted in report of Sergeant Harold Lockwood and Detective Doyle, Cleveland Police Department, July 25, 1954, obtained by Sam Reese Sheppard from confidential source, 1993; hereafter cited as Lockwood report.

61   Hubach and others . . . : Reports of Jay Hubach, Bay Village Files; Hubach, interview by Jan Sheppard Duvall and Jim Chapman, 1982.

63   Esther Houk saw it . . . : Esther Houk interviews, 1980.

64   Only the police . . . : Don Ahern, statement to Bay Village police, July 5, 1954, Bay Village Files.

64   "This should have been . . .": John Burkholder, interview by C. Cooper, 1994.

65 Ray Keefe . . . : Report from July 1954, made available for viewing by Cuyahoga County Coroner's Office to C. Cooper, 1993.

65 "The investigation for . . .": David Kerr, "Investigation of the Homicide Scene," in *Criminal Investigation and Interrogation,* ed. Samuel R. Gerber and Oliver Schroeder (Cincinnati: Anderson, 1962), pp. 143–44.

65 John H. B. Troon . . . : Interview by C. Cooper, 1993.

67 "Murderers have been run . . .": *State v. Sheppard,* "Assignments of Error," p. 195.

67 One reporter said . . . : "Was Dr. Sam Sheppard Condemned by the Newspapers?," broadcast debate, WHK, October 18, 1954, transcript, William J. Corrigan Papers. The standard today is completely different. As stated by one court: "In no situation . . . do we feel the mere act of hiring an attorney is probative in the least of the guilt or innocence of defendants." *Bruno V. Rushen,* 721 F. 2d 1193, 1194 (9th Cir. 1983).

67 One of the key players . . . : Mary Cowan, interview by Jan Sheppard Duvall, 1981.

67 "You guys are out . . .": Article by Bill Tanner, *Cleveland Press,* synopsized in Sheppard Files.

67 Captain David Kerr . . . : Kerr, while not referring to the Sheppard case, made another telling admission. "I would like to point out another dangerous mistake that investigators make: they jump to conclusions too readily. A lot of us are guilty of this weakness; I know I am" ("Investigation of the Homicide Scene," p. 173).

69 "A philanderer may have. . . .": "If defendant did have such propensities for peacefulness, as this evidence indicates, such evidence would be evidence of a circumstance tending to indicate that defendant did not commit the crime of violence in the instant case. . . . A violent crime by the defendant would be entirely out of character and inconsistent, not only with the events in his home during the preceding evening, but also with everything known about defendant's previous life and his family background" (*State v. Sheppard,* Judge Kingsley Taft, dissenting opinion, 165 Ohio St. 293, 308).

69 An editor . . . : Letter responding to Mrs. William Higer, September 2, 1954, Sheppard Files.

69 Rumors were passed off . . . : Review of calls, letters, and reports to and by police in the Bay Village Files shows the pervasiveness of these rumors at all levels.

69 The fantasy of television . . . : *Editor & Publisher,* January 8, 1955, p. 12, repeated the opinion of editors on an American Society of Newspaper Editors panel. Ten of fourteen said that the coverage of the murder of Marilyn Sheppard was the "most overplayed" story of 1954. Next on the list were the McCarthy

hearings and the short-lived marriage of Marilyn Monroe and Joe DiMaggio.

70   The path . . . : Lockwood report.

70   In the brush . . . : Redinger interviews.

71   The watch in the bag . . . : Questions about the testing of blood on the watches created controversy throughout the appeals. See, e.g., 165 Ohio St. 293, 307 (dissent); also *Sheppard v. Alvis*, No. 35777 (Ohio Supreme Court, 1958), Ohio Supreme Court Library, Columbus, Ohio. This issue and those of the key chain and pants were also prominent in forensic analysis by Dr. Paul Kirk (see chapter 8), and in the 1966 trial of Dr. Sam Sheppard (see chapters 9–10).

Chapter 6 • Inquisition

74   The students were waiting . . . : Bill Mintz and Frank Klimko, "TDC Prisoner Executed by Injection," *Houston Chronicle*, December 7, 1982; George Kuempel, "Convicted Killer Brooks Executed," *Dallas Morning News*, December 7, 1982.

74   The headline . . . : "State Asks Death for Dr. Sam," *Cleveland Press*, December 15, 1954.

79   The public was barely aware . . . : One author wrote as long ago as 1889 that "the powers and duties of the county coroner are far more important and deserve much greater attention from the public than citizens are generally aware of. . . . Perhaps there is no public office so little understood. . . . There is much opportunity for abuse of authority" (Robert H. Vickers, *The Powers and Duties of Police Officers and Coroners* [Chicago: T. H. Flood, 1889]).

79   The coroner's office held the power . . . : Ohio Code, section 313.11 et seq.

79   Gerber's early medical career . . . : "Did You Know?," *Cleveland Medical Society Bulletin*, 1976; Curriculum vitae, candidate questionnaires, *Cleveland Press* archives, Cleveland State University, Cleveland, Ohio.

80   The new coroner described the killer . . . : Samuel Gerber, *The Coroner and the Law in Ohio* (n. p., 1950), p. 56 (available at Cleveland Public Library) .

81   Even in England . . . : Vickers, *Power and Duties*, pp. 165–74; Phil Scranton and Kathryn Chadwick, *In the Arms of the Law: Coroners' Inquests and Deaths in Custody* (London: Pluto Press, 1987); "The Coroner and Medicolegal Investigation," Franklin County Coroner's Office, Columbus, Ohio, n.d.

81   In 1937 . . . : *Cleveland Plain Dealer*, January 30, 1937.

81   A coroner had vastly more . . . : Cyril Wecht, *U.S. Medicolegal Autopsy Laws* (Arlington, Va.: Information Resources Press, 1989); "Medicolegal Investigation into Sudden and Unexplained Deaths in Different Countries," in *Gradwohls' Legal*

Medicine, ed. Francis E. Camps, Ann E. Robinson, and Bernard G. B. Lucas (Chicago: Wright, 1976), p. 57; Henry W. Turkel, "Merits of the Present Coroner System," *JAMA* 153, no. 12 (November 21, 1953): 1086; Dr. R. Gibson Parrish (co-author, with D. S. Combs and Dr. Roy Ing, of *Death Investigation in the United States and Canada 1992* (Atlanta: U.S. Dept. of Health and Human Services, Centers for Disease Control, National Center for Environmental Health, 1992), interview by C. Cooper.

81 "Why No Inquest . . .": *Cleveland Press,* July 21, 1954, p. 1.

81 Gerber was friends . . . : Pat Riebau, interview by C. Cooper, 1993. Seltzer became the editor of the *Cleveland Press* in 1928. He was "known as Mr. Cleveland and 'king maker in Ohio politics,' " and allowed no debate about the innocence of Dr. Sam, wrote Don Bean in "Hosts of Ghosts over Dr. Sam's House," *Plain Dealer,* June 25, 1993. The *Press* was a flagship paper of the Scripps-Howard network, owned by the E. W. Scripps Company, and in addition to his *Press* role, Seltzer was made editor in chief of Scripps-Howard Newspapers of Ohio. A vast syndicate, Scripps-Howard owned United Press International wire service and in 1950 purchased the *New York Sun* from the Hearst Corporation. Scripps-Howard also owned radio and television stations and began WEWS-TV in Cleveland in 1947, a practice of local cross-media ownership now prohibited by the Federal Communications Commission (except by congressional authorization). Tom King, Scripps-Howard, interview by C. Cooper, 1993; "What Is Scripps-Howard, And How It Operates," handbook, at New York Public Library; "Historical Highlights of the E. W Scripps Company" (Cincinnati: Scripps-Howard Corp.); see also Louis Seltzer, *The Years Were Good* (Cleveland: World, 1956).

82 They are not often conducted . . . : Dr. Robert Challener, chief medical examiner of the Cuyahoga County Coroner's Office, interview by C. Cooper, 1993. "We do them very rarely," said Thomas A. Stettler, director of the Franklin County Coroner's Office in Columbus, Ohio, in an interview by C. Cooper in 1993.

82 Coroner's inquests, in particular . . . : "The inquisitional nature of a coroner's proceedings placed a suspect in a position of considerable disadvantage" (Scranton and Chadwick, *In the Arms of the Law,* p. 37).

82 If the inquest system . . . : "The system is certainly subject to abuse. . . . For the most part it is hidden. It gets very little press, gets very little attention" (Parrish, interview). Even those who defend the idea of inquests admit that problems are rife. Henry W. Turkel, a California coroner, said problems with inquests arise because of the incompetence of individual coro-

ners, not because of the system. "Any departure from . . .
procedure can only be the result of a lack of interest or integrity
on the part of the particular coroner" ("Merits," p. 1091). Herb
Buzbee, international secretary-treasurer of the International
Association of Coroners and Medical Examiners, called the
Ohio system "atypical" (interview by C. Cooper, 1993).

82   Ohio, unlike virtually . . . : Historical studies show how unusual
it is for the coroner to have the extent of powers found in
Ohio. One of the earliest reported cases from Great Britain
stated, "The coroner ought to hear evidence on both sides" (2
Hale Cr. 62, 157, cited in Vickers, *Powers and Duties,* p. 173).
This was not necessary in Ohio.

    It was also recognized that the person accused should be
allowed to present an adequate defense at an inquest hearing.
"The principle is undeniable that a person accused of a felony
at a coroner's inquest may defend himself by testimony. To
offer that testimony without counsel would be worse than useless in many, perhaps most, cases. No person can be required
to sit still and hear himself accused, and be denied explanation
or defense, especially when the accusation involves his arrest
and detention and the severe consequences . . . an accused
person and his counsel, at least one, have the right to be present
and cross-examine witnesses" (ibid., pp. 205–6). After the Sheppard trial, Gerber traveled to Great Britain and seemed surprised to learn that British coroners had to convene a jury, just
like a judicial court. "Finds Our Dr. Gerber Studying Scotland
Yard," *Cleveland Press,* February 6, 1955.

83   Ohio's coroners . . . : "A bad feature of the American coroner
was the persistence of the electoral system of appointment. This
imparted a distinctly political flavor to the office" and was part
of its fall into disrepute (Gavin Thurston, *Coronership* [Great
Britain: Rose, 1980], p. 16).

83   Dr. Gerber scurried out . . . : Subpoenas in Bay Village Files.

83   A report by . . . : Rossbach report, released by confidential
source, 1993.

84   Gerber played to the crowd . . . : Transcript of inquest, made
available for viewing by Cuyahoga County Coroner's Office to
C. Cooper, pursuant to Ohio public records law, 1993. A newspaper reporter, Doris O'Donnell, told criminalist Dr. James
Chapman in an interview in 1982 that the U.S. Supreme Court
had it wrong when it described the trial of Dr. Sam as a
"Roman circus": "See, a lot of people confuse the inquest with
the trial. . . . This is where . . . the Roman holiday phrase came
into it, which carried all the way up to the Supreme Court. It
was not the trial at all."

84   "We returned to find . . .": A statement released by Kreke at
the time; copy in Sheppard Files.

84　　As the sole questioner . . . : Authorities hold that cross-examination, not permitted here, is necessary "to ensure that justice is done" ("Medicolegal Investigation," p. 61).

84　　Elkins concluded that Dr. Sam. . . : Drenkhan report, Bay Village Files.

84　　He pursued hearsay . . . : Inquest transcript. Houk testimony, Mrs. Ethel Sheppard.

84　　Larry Houk . . . : Ibid.

85　　Dr. Sam's mother . . . : Ibid.

85　　Newspapers geared up . . . : "Doctor in Tears," *Cleveland Press,* July 23, 1954, p. 1; "Doctor Relates," *Cleveland Press,* July 23, 1954, p. 8; "I Heard Her . . .," *Cleveland Press,* July 23, 1954, p. 9.

85　　For five hours . . . : Inquest transcript.

86　　After all . . . : "Although the coroner has long claimed an arbitrary right to exclude persons at his pleasure, yet he has no such right by any law, ancient or modern" (Vickers, *Powers and Duties,* p. 205).

86　　"Remove him . . .": Inquest transcript.

86　　"I was mortified . . . ": Kreke statement, Sheppard Files.

87　　"Carnival-like four-year spree . . .": David Halberstam, *The Fifties* (New York: Villard Books, 1993), p. 52.

87　　The words are reminiscent . . . : *Sheppard v. Maxwell,* 384 U.S. 333 (1966).

87　　Those called in private . . . : Inquest transcript.

88　　"It is to be remembered . . .": Gerber, *The Coroner and the Law,* p. 25.

88　　"Accidental in nature . . .": *State v. Eberling;* Autopsy verdict on Ethel May Durkin, Cuyahoga County Coroner's Office, January 4, 1983.

88　　Bill Corrigan repeatedly demanded . . . : Transcript, *State v. Sheppard,* Court of Common Pleas, 1954.

88　　Even in 1993 . . . : Cuyahoga County Coroner Elizabeth Balraj refused to release all the documents that she held, after receiving a public records request filed by C. Cooper, and personally refused to permit copies of any records to be made. Ohio Public Records Law sec. 149.43 (B) states: "Upon request, a person responsible for public records shall make copies available at cost, within a reasonable period of time."

Chapter 7 • Mistrial

90　　"The family was under . . .": Kralick interview.

90　　Any trick was used . . . : Articles and editorials in this time period included: "This Is Murder, Why Be So Polite?" *Cleveland Press,* July 20, 1954; "Sheppard Set for New Quiz: Getting Away with Murder," *Cleveland Press,* July 20, 1954, p. 1; "Get That Killer!" *Cleveland Plain Dealer,* July 22, 1954; "[Police

Captain] Kerr Asks Doctor's Arrest," *Cleveland Press,* July 26, 1954, p. 1; "Why Don't the Police Quiz No. 1 Suspect?" *Cleveland Press,* July 28, 1954, p. 1; "Why Isn't Sam Sheppard in Jail?" *Cleveland Press,* July 30, 1954, p.1.

91   In the first week . . . : Activities described here are documented in Sheppard Files, William J. Corrigan Papers, Coroner Files; Bay Village Files, police documents provided confidentially .

91   A few resisted . . . : George Serb, interview by C. Cooper, 1994.

91   Bad press dogged . . . : The "Papa Joe Cremati vice scandal," which broke in January 1954, continued to be publicized even in July 1954; see, e.g., "Police Lawyers Seek to Drop 'Neglect' Charge," *Cleveland Press,* July 20, 1954.

92   "A crowd . . . Others jabbed me . . .": Sheppard Files.

93   "There is no physical proof . . .": James McArthur, Report of testimony before the grand jury, Sheppard Files; *Cleveland Press,* August 17, 1954.

93   The names of grand jurors . . . : Pictures, names and addresses of grand jury members were published in the *Cleveland Press,* August 16, 1954; Winston's comments were repeated at a pre-trial bail hearing before Judge Blythin on September 22, 1954, and reprinted in *Sheppard v. Ohio,* Appendix to Petition for a Writ of Certiorari, U.S. Supreme Court, 1956, p. 176a.

93   "It's obvious . . .": *Cleveland News,* August 30, 1954.

93   Police officers were dispatched . . . : Inspector James McArthur told people at a national police gathering later: "I uncovered a lot of Dr. Sam's 'extra-curricular' activities, after many trips to the West Coast. And he had plenty. He was quite the ladies' man and wasn't too discreet about it. . . . Actually, a lot of Dr. Sam's extra-marital affairs would never have been permitted as testimony in court if his brothers and close friends had not tried to paint him as a virtuous and loving husband. This gave us an opportunity to disprove his character witnesses" (*Knoxville News-Sentinel* [Tenn.], August 25, 1955).

93   According to Esther Houk . . . : Esther Honk interviews.

94   Dr. Lester Hoversten . . . : Hoversten's letters, diary and testimony, along with relevant police statements and previously unreleased police reports are documented in chapter 14.

94   The officer suggested . . . : Lockwood report.

95   Swabs were not taken . . . : The autopsy description by Dr. Lester Adelson refers to vaginal smears in his "microscopic description, " but there is no indication that the vagina, other bodily cavities, or the smears were tested for sperm or evidence of sexual assault, nor was there any indication on the trace-evidence report viewed by C. Cooper in 1993 that vaginal or other smears from bodily cavities were presented to lab technician Mary Cowan for testing in 1954. Dr. A. J. Kazlauckas, a former deputy coroner who reviewed the autopsy for William

Corrigan in 1954, wrote, "What was found in the vagina? No tests are recorded that sperm was either found or not found in the vaginal secretions" (William J. Corrigan Papers).

95   Finally, the prosecution . . . : Tom Weigle, interview by Jan Sheppard Duvall, 1981.

95   "Sam Called . . .": *Cleveland Press*, November 24, 1954, p. 1.

96   On the morning of July 23 . . . : Henry Dombrowski, interview by C. Cooper, 1994; also transcripts from *State v. Sheppard*, Court of Common Pleas, 1954; police documents provided confidentially to C. Cooper in 1993.

96   In other areas of the house . . . : Kerr, "Criminal Investigation," p. 182. Kerr also described the dangling light fixture, p. 182.

97   Richard Eberling . . . : Drawing by Richard Eberling given to Sam Reese Sheppard, 1992; also comments from letters and interviews 1989–95 (see chapters 16, 19–20).

98   Officers who went . . . : Report of Dave Yettra and Carl Rossbach, Cuyahoga County Sheriff's Department, in police documents sent to C. Cooper, 1993, from confidential source.

98   Cowan also went to the trouble . . . : Transcripts of *State v. Sheppard*, 1954. In addition to identifying exhibit 84 and other blood samples, Cowan was asked about the blood typing by defense attorney Corrigan:

Corrigan: Did you type any of the blood stains in the house of Sam Sheppard that were found on the stairs?
Cowan: No, sir. The quantity was insufficient.
Corrigan: I didn't hear you.
Cowan: The quantity was insufficient in any single spot. . . .
Corrigan: Now, then, it is possible, is it not, Miss Cowan, by a correct analysis of the type of blood that may be at the scene of a crime, if it is the blood of a criminal that is picked up, that that blood may be typed and you may be able to reduce the number of people in a group that have that type of blood to a very small number?
Cowan: If there is a sufficient amount of blood, yes, sir.

The trace-evidence report at the coroner's office, viewed in 1993 by C. Cooper, states that stains on the basement steps "produced positive results for blood but the blood was not typed."

99   Scientific analysis . . . : Kirk's findings are reported in chapter 8. Captain Kerr understood the implications of the blood. He wrote: "The scientific examiners discovered blood stains going down the stairs which must have dripped from the body of the assailant. . . . the assailant, dripping blood and fleeing from his crime, knew enough to walk around this light. . . . whoever committed this kind of burglary was also dripping blood." "Criminal Investigation," p. 182.

99   Mrs. Sheppard, who was . . . : Lockwood report.

99   He was injured . . . : Medical reports, Sheppard Files; testimony, *State v. Sheppard*, 1954, 1966; police reports, Bay Village Files; William J. Corrigan Papers; Russell Sherman trial notebook; Dr. Murray, interview by C. Cooper, 1993.

100   The evidence was totally overlooked . . . : "Bloodstains were taken as synonymous with murder, and they incriminated Sheppard because everyone had already decided that he was the killer" (Jürgen Thorwald, *Crime and Science: The New Frontier in Criminology,* trans. Richard and Clara Winston [New York: Harcourt, Brace & World, 1967], p. 145).

100   "I think it would be wise . . .": Sheppard Files.

100   "Find Killer's . . .": *Cleveland Press,* August 3, 1954, p. l.

101   Documents released in 1994 . . . : Bay Village; further documents obtained pursuant to Ohio's public records laws and through releases signed by Richard Eberling (see chapters 18, 20), hereafter cited as Bay Village Police Documents.

101   Not until 1963 . . . : *Brady V. Maryland,* 373 U.S. 83, 87 (1963).

101   Only by accident . . . : The Knitters' statement was made on July 14, 1954, according to records obtained in 1994 by C. Cooper from Bay Village Police Department under Ohio public records law, hereafter cited as Bay Village Records. Officer Larry Adler of the nearby suburb of Lakewood made the drawing.

101   "It was one of the most . . ." : Kralick interview.

102   When a second fingerprint expert . . . : Officer Jerome Poelking testified on cross-examination that he found a palm print and fingerprints on the bedroom door that belonged to Cleveland police detective Carmen Naso. A thumbprint of Dr. Sam's was supposedly found on the bed, and a partial palm print on a downstairs desk was said to be Sam R.'s.

102   The coroner's office removed . . . : A report marked "Property inventory re: Marilyn Sheppard case" and viewed at the Cuyahoga County Coroner's Office by C. Cooper in 1993 lists "2 white painted doors" among items removed from the premises. When defense co-counsel Fred Garmone took a property inventory on September 28, 1954, the doors were neither shown to him nor mentioned as having been removed and returned, although other items were (Sheppard Files) .

102   Thousands of people . . . : *Time,* August 30, 1954.

102   "I did not interfere . . . : Sheppard Files; Affidavit of Arthur Petersilge, *State v. Sheppard,* No. 64571, April 1954; testimony of Petersilge on motion for a new trial reprinted in *State v. Sheppard,* Assignments of Error to Supreme Court of Ohio, October 1955, pp. 488–93; see also *Sheppard v. Maxwell,* Petition for Cert., U.S. Supreme Court, 1965, by F. Lee Bailey, in Kurland and Casper, *Landmark Briefs,* p. 43.

103   Officials conducted . . . : Report by Captain David E. Kerr,
       Cleveland Police Department, August 4, 1954, provided to C.
       Cooper in 1993 by confidential source; David Kerr, "Criminal
       Investigation."

103   Ray DeCrane . . . : DeCrane is quoted in "Tip Turned to
       Bloody Work" by Jim Bebbington, *Lorain Journal*, (Ohio) Au-
       gust 20, 1989; DeCrane refused to comment when contacted by
       C. Cooper in 1993.

103   Criminalist and professor . . . : Kingston interview. After the
       1954 trial, criminalist Dr. Paul L. Kirk also discussed this so-
       called demonstration and described two points: "1. Dr. Sam
       does not know how long it was after the screams, or outcry,
       before he roused himself to rush upstairs—and neither does
       anyone else. 2. There is no evidence whatever to prove that
       Marilyn was beaten to death before Sam arrived. If she were
       unconscious at that time, and if Sam too, was knocked out, the
       final beating could have taken place after, as well as before, he
       made an appearance" (unpublished manuscript, Dr. Paul L.
       Kirk); see chapter 8 of this volume.

104   The trial strategy . . . : It is precisely because of police willing-
       ness to use tactics like this that most defense attorneys tell their
       clients to say absolutely nothing to the police, to remain silent,
       to offer no explanations. Because Dr. Sheppard made extensive
       voluntary pretrial statements, the police were able to utilize
       this technique.

104   Reporters had a debate . . . : See, e.g., WHK, October 18, 1954.

104   One writer . . . : Sidney Andorn, October 22, 1954, reprinted
       State v, Sheppard, No. 23,400, Assignments of Error before Su-
       preme Court of Ohio, pp. 313–14.

104   All but one . . . : *State v. Sheppard*, 1954, transcript; also synop-
       sized in William J. Corrigan Papers.

106   After twenty-eight days of testimony . . . : This description is
       based on transcripts of *State v. Sheppard*, 1954; trial notebook
       excerpting and synopsizing testimony made available by Russell
       Sherman, the Elyria attorney who was co-counsel with F. Lee
       Bailey in *Sheppard v. Maxwell* before the U.S. Supreme Court
       and in *State v. Sheppard*, Cuyahoga County Court of Common
       Pleas, 1966; Sheppard Files; original studies, photographs, and
       analyses by Dr. Paul Kirk, hereafter cited as Kirk Files; William
       J. Corrigan Papers.

106   Years later, Esther . . . : Esther Houk interviews.

107   The coroner didn't really . . . : The transcript shows the follow-
       ing interaction between Blythin and Gerber:

       Judge: I understood you to say it was the impression of a
       surgical instrument. Is that what you said?
       Gerber: Yes, sir.

Judge: All right. Do I understand you to say, then, that it could not have been made by anything other than a surgical instrument?

Gerber: No, sir.

Judge: You didn't mean that?

Gerber: No, sir, I did not mean that.

Judge: Could it have been made by another instrument?

Gerber: Similar to this type of surgical instrument.

108   Records released . . . : Police report by F. Drenkhan, Bay Village Files.

108   Doris Bender . . . : Statement in reports by Deputy Sheriff Carl Rossbach, dated July 7, 1954 (Bay Village Files) and July 23, 1954 (obtained from confidential source) indicate that Mr. and Mrs. Bender gave differing accounts of lights when first interviewed, and that Mrs. Bender said they were "almost" positive about the date.

108   Teenagers who had . . . : Bay Village Files. Significantly, Huntington Park was not patrolled by Bay Village, even though it was squarely within Bay Village's boundaries, because it was part of the Metropolitan Park System, which had separate governance countywide.

109   A red frayed fiber . . . : Information from Mary Cowan's trial testimony; the trace-evidence report, which C. Cooper viewed in the coroner's office in October 1993, was never released to Dr. Sam or his attorneys.

109   "My track trophy . . .": Notes made during the 1954 trial, Sheppard Files.

110   His frustration . . . : Transcripts, *State v. Sheppard*, Court of Common Pleas, 1954.

111   A member of the jury . . . : Howard Barrish, *New York Journal American*, December 22, 1954; 1993 comments by William Lamb, "Juror in Sheppard Case Wants to Tell His Side of Story," June 17, 1993, *Lakewood Sun Post*; also see "Verdict on Dr. Sam," *Plain Dealer*, February 13, 1995.

114   And the *Cleveland Press* . . . : *Newsweek*, January 3, 1955, quoting Louis Seltzer. From March 1953 to March 1954, the Press had suffered a circulation decline, according to *Editor & Publisher*, July 1954. In the January 8, 1955, issue, *Editor & Publisher* reported "extraordinary" circulation gains by all three Cleveland newspapers during the Sheppard trial.

Chapter 8 • *Scientific Track-Down*

116   "I realized . . .": Dr. Sam notes, Sheppard Files.

119   With bachelor's . . . : Paul L. Kirk, résumé, Sheppard Files; obituary, *New York Times*, June 6, 1970.

119   "Wherever [the criminal] steps . . .": Paul L. Kirk, *Crime Inves-*

tigation: Physical Evidence and the Police Laboratory (New York: Interscience, 1953), pp. 3–11.

120   When he was first . . . : Dr. Kirk's observations on the Sheppard case are based on several primary resources: Paul L. Kirk, "Report in the Matter of the Murder of Marilyn Sheppard," March 1955, in Sheppard Files, hereafter cited as Kirk report; Affidavit of Dr. Paul Leland Kirk, *Sheppard v. Maxwell*, Court of Common Pleas, April 1955, hereafter cited as Kirk affidavit; Kirk Files; letters by Dr. Kirk in the Sheppard Files and William J. Corrigan Papers; notes on the Sheppard case by Dr. Paul L. Kirk, written between 1956 and 1961, hereafter cited as Kirk notes; also, trial preparation notes of Russell Sherman; Thorwald, *Crime and Science,* pp. 149–55; other sources where indicated below.

121   Lockwood listed . . . : Lockwood report.

121   Mary Cowan . . . : Interview by Jan Sheppard Duvall, 1981.

124   Detective Henry Dombrowski . . . : Dombrowski's testimony under cross-examination in Sheppard's 1954 trial was as follows:

> *Corrigan*: Did you find any blood spots on the carpet [in the murder room]?
>
> *Dombrowski*: We did not check for blood spots on the carpet.
>
> *Corrigan*: Well, you didn't test for blood spots on the carpet in Marilyn's room?
>
> *Dombrowski*: That's right, sir.
>
> *Corrigan*: Wouldn't it be that, as a scientist, making an investigation, wouldn't that be the very first place you would make a test?
>
> *Dombrowski*: We didn't think so, because there was obviously so much blood in the room.
>
> *Corrigan*: Then may I assume, Mr. Dombrowski, that you did not examine the carpet because you assumed, because of the condition of the murder, and the amount of blood that had been spilled, that there was blood on the carpet in Marilyn's room?
>
> *Dombrowski*: That, plus the fact that it would be of no significance to prove whether there was or wasn't. . . .
>
> *Corrigan*: Did you cover [with luminol spray to test blood spots] the room in which Marilyn was murdered?
>
> *Dombrowski*: Not for detailed test. Just to check our solution.
>
> *Corrigan*: Well, why did you avoid that particular room?
>
> *Dombrowski*: Well, it was our opinion that it was—
>
> *Corrigan*: What?
>
> *Dombrowski*: It was our opinion that just from the appearance of the blood in the room, it would add nothing to the investigation. . . . It was just there so far as we were concerned.

126   Attorney Arthur Petersilge . . . : Letter to appellate attorney Paul Herbert, April 1956, Sheppard Files; see also William Corrigan, letter to Paul Herbert, February 1956, William J. Corrigan Papers.

127   Dr. Gerber had said something similar . . . : Bay Village police officer Jay Hubach, interview by Jim Chapman and Jan Sheppard Duvall, 1982.

128   Dr. Charles Kingston . . . : Edgar Marburg Lecture on Forensic Science delivered at the American Society for Testing and Materials Conference of Technical Committee Officers, October 2, 1972, printed in *Standardization News* 1, no. 4 (April 1973): 8; Kingston, interviews by C. Cooper, 1993.

129   Documents viewed . . . : At the Cuyahoga County Coroner's Office by C. Cooper, 1993.

130   Today, capable forensic scientists. . . : Dr. Owen Lovejoy, interview by C. Cooper, 1993.

132   Victim's pajamas . . . : Kirk report; Kirk affidavit.

132   Mary Cowan . . . : Microscopic analysis report, released in 1954; also trace-evidence report and Cowan's work cards viewed by C. Cooper in 1993; Transcript of *State v. Sheppard*, 1954.

133   Gerber claimed on July 7 . . . : *Cleveland Plain Dealer,* July 7, 1954.

134   A report secured . . . : Report by Bay Village police officer G. H. Deutschlander, July 19, 1954, released 1994, pursuant to public records request and lawsuit.

135   "She was so happy . . .": Dr. Sam notes, Sheppard Files.

137   Dr. Roger Marsters . . . : Affidavit filed in *State v. Sheppard*, 1954; counter affidavit by Dr. Paul L. Kirk responding to Marsters affidavit; Sheppard Files and Kirk Files.

137   Dr. Peter De Forest . . . : Interview by C. Cooper, 1994. Dr. De Forest, who studied under and worked for Kirk, is a professor of criminalistics at John Jay College of Criminal Justice in New York City, an international lecturer and consultant, author of dozens of abstracts, author or co-author of chapters in five forensic science texts, and co-author with R. Gaensslen and H. Lee of *Forensic Science: An Introduction to Criminalistics* (New York: McGraw-Hill, 1983).

137   The doors . . . : Documents viewed at Cuyahoga County Coroner's Office by C. Cooper, 1993.

138   "Reread Kirk's report . . .": Dr. Sam notes, Sheppard Files.

138   Blythin denied the motion . . . : Blythin's ruling and the decision upholding it are reported in *State v. Sheppard,* 100 Ohio App. 399, July 20, 1955, Opinion of J. Kovachy.

138   "That the court . . .": Paul L. Kirk, letter to William Corrigan, June 1956, William J. Corrigan Papers.

138   The scientific understanding . . . : See, e.g., Thorwald, *Crime and Science;* Peter A. Pizzola, Steven Roth, Peter R. De Forest,

"Blood Droplet Dynamics," *JFSCA* 31, no. 1 (January 1986): 36–49.

139   The academy decided . . . : De Forest, interviews by C. Cooper, 1993, 1994.

Chapter 9 • Enduring

140   The letters . . . : Sheppard Files; some of the original letters used Sam R.'s childhood nickname of "Chip" instead of Sam.

141   "Father's day card . . .": Dr. Sam notes, Sheppard Files.

143   Two separate appeals . . . : The legal history is as follows: On January 3, 1955, the trial court denied a motion for a new trial based on errors during the trial. On May 9, 1955, the trial court denied a new trial based on newly discovered evidence and the affidavit of Dr. Kirk. On July 20, 1955, the Court of Appeals of Cuyahoga County agreed with the January 3, 1955, decision of the trial court, denying a new trial based on claimed errors (Skeel opinion, 100 Ohio App. 345). On July 25, 1955, the Court of Appeals of Cuyahoga County agreed with the May 9, 1955, decision of the trial court, denying a new trial based on newly discovered evidence (Kovachy opinion, 100 Ohio App. 399.) On January 11, 1956, a motion to allow an appeal from the court of appeals decision on newly discovered evidence was denied (164 Ohio St. 428), ending consideration of that matter. On May 31, 1956, the Ohio Supreme Court affirmed the decision of the Court of Appeals on the issue of trial errors (165 Ohio St. 293). A rehearing by the Ohio Supreme Court was denied July 5, 1956. On November 13, 1956, the U.S. Supreme Court decided not to hear the case (352 U.S. 910); a petition for rehearing was denied on December 19, 1956.

144   A former investigator . . . : Harold B. Bretnall letters to Sheppards, Sheppard Files; Mrs. William Bretnall, interview by C. Cooper, 1994; notes by Steve Sheppard.

144   Bretnall was convinced . . . : Paul Holmes, letter to Jack Harrison Pollack, February 3, 1964. Pollack was the author of many articles on the Sheppard case, as well as books on Sheppard and the Dutch psychic, Croiset. His daughters, Susan Pollack and Debbie Pollack, turned over his files to S. R. Sheppard in 1993; hereafter cited as Pollack Files.

144   He also challenged a claim . . . : Bretnall, letter to Sheppards, November 26, 1957, Sheppard Files.

146   The evidence on the blood . . . : Kirk notes, Kirk affidavit; Cowan testimony; Kirk, *Crime Investigation;* De Forest interviews, 1993–94.

146   Cowan had tested . . . : Mary Cowan, notes, viewed at Cuyahoga County Coroner's Office by C. Cooper, 1993.

146   Cowan worked with Roger Marsters . . . : Letter from Marsters in Coroner Files; affidavit of Marsters, Kirk Files; testimony of

Marsters, *Sheppard v. State,* 1966, Sheppard Files; Thorwald, *Crime and Science,* p. 155.

146   In testimony . . . : Cowan's testimony concerning the blood grouping analysis in the trial of Dr. Sam Sheppard in 1954, according to the transcript, was as follows:

Prosecutor: Now, did you attempt to type that blood, Miss Cowan, that was found on the watch?

Cowan: I attempted a crust typing with the OAB group, and it was inconclusive. Then it was typed with anti-M and anti-N serum to determine the M factor, and the M factor was found to be present.

Prosecutor: And I think you had previously stated that the M factor was found to be present in Marilyn Sheppard's blood, is that correct?

Cowan: That's right.

On cross-examination, Cowan switched from one grouping methodology to the other, but Corrigan did not catch the point.

Corrigan: Now, you typed the blood and you discovered— am I correct in this as to your testimony — you discovered that the type of blood that Marilyn Sheppard had and the type of blood on the two watches was the same.

Cowan: They had one factor in common.

Corrigan: Well, I understood you, and am I mistaken in this, that when you typed the blood of Marilyn Sheppard, you found it was an O type. . . . And you found that the type of blood on the watches was the same type as Marilyn Sheppard's blood, type O?

Cowan: No, sir.

Corrigan: You did not. Well, then, I misunderstood your testimony. Your typing of Marilyn Sheppard's blood revealed O?

Cowan: Yes, sir.

Corrigan: And that was done on July 4th or the 5th?

Cowan: 5th.

Corrigan: And your typing of the man's watch was what day? You may refer to your notes, if you want to.

Cowan: On the 16th of July.

Corrigan: On the 16th of July. And when you typed that blood, you found it to be what type?

Cowan: M.

Corrigan: M?

Cowan: Yes.

Corrigan: And you typed the blood on the lady's watch, and . . . you found that to be what type?

Cowan: M.

Corrigan: Now, you had a different type of blood, then, in regard to Marilyn and the two watches.

Cowan: No, sir. Marilyn Sheppard's blood also had the M factor in it.

Corrigan: Well, the two watches didn't have the O factor in it?

Cowan: That I couldn't say. The typings for the OAB grouping were inconclusive.

One scientific observer said that Cowan's testing of the watches yielded a strange result" that suggested lack of experience and proved the analysis "totally valueless"; Thorwald, *Crime and Science,* p. 142.

146   Corrigan was adamant . . . : *Sheppard v. Alvis,* Reply Brief of Relator on Motion for Return of Exhibits, No. 35777, Sup. Ct. of Ohio; Supreme Court of Ohio Library, Columbus, Ohio.

146   This new legal effort . . . : *Sheppard v. Alvis,* 170 Ohio St. 551, 167 N.E. 2d 94 (Ohio Supreme Court, 1960).

147   Even in 1956 . . . : Dr. Sam notes and letters, Sheppard Files.

148   When Sloan-Kettering . . . : See Tetsuo Itoh and Chester M. Southam, "Isoantibodies to Human Cancer Cells in Healthy Recipients of Cancer Homotransplants," *Journal of Immunology* 91 (October 1963): 469; Dr. Chester Southam, letter to Dr. Sam Sheppard, February 1964, Sheppard Files, see also Cindy Cooper, "The Test Culture: Medical Experimentation on Prisoners," *New England Journal on Prison Law* 2, no. 2 (1976):261.

148   People began writing . . . : Mrs. Erle Stanley Gardner, letter to C. Cooper; "Just Justice," brochure by Gardner; survey of correspondence on Wedler and Sheppard, Gardner Archives, Harry Ransom Humanities Research Center, University of Texas at Austin; Gardner, letters in Sheppard Files and Pollack Files; letter from Harry Steeger to writer Frank Harvey, 1960, Pollack Files; *Argosy* articles, 1957–63, including "Are the Sheppards Telling the Truth?" by Erle Stanley Gardner, August 1957; "The Human Side of the Sheppard Case," by Erle Stanley Gardner, September 1957; Gardner, foreword to Holmes, *The Sheppard Murder Case.*

149   When these developments . . . : Samuel Gerber, letter to Dr. Richard N. Sheppard, July 22, 1957, Sheppard Files: "I read in the daily newspapers . . . that you have requested the 'Court of Last Resort' to inquire into the conviction of your brother. . . . These mediums of information further state that you have asked to take a lie detector test . . . you, of your own volition, have injected yourself into this matter. . . . I therefore ask that you voluntarily permit a lie detector test to be done by a local polygraph expert."

149   Donald Joseph Wedler . . . : See chapter 13.

149   Frustrated with Ohio politics . . . : Erle Stanley Gardner, letter to Mrs. William Higer, October 7, 1957, Sheppard Files.

149   *"The Case . . . :* Sheppard Files.

150   As described . . . : Jack Harrison Pollack, *Croiset the Clairvoyant* (New York: Doubleday, 1964), pp. 82–83; also described in correspondence and notes in Pollack Files.

150   Holmes, who had covered . . . : Paul Holmes, letters, Pollack Files, Sheppard Files; Mrs. Miriam Holmes, interview by C. Cooper, 1994.

150   Permission was denied . . . : See *State ex. rel. Sheppard V. Koblentz,* 174 Ohio St. 120, 187 N.E. 2d 40 (1962).

150   Dr. Sam Gerber . . . : Doris O'Donnell, "Parole Sam Sheppard, Dr. Gerber Urges State," *Plain Dealer,* February 25, 1964.

151   Gerber had also had some encounters . . . : See chapters 13, 18.

151   To these ends . . . : Andy Tuney, interview by C. Cooper, 1993; interview by Richard Dalrymple and Jan Sheppard Duvall, 1981.

152   But some of the evidence . . . : Trial strategies described in F. Lee Bailey, interview by C. Cooper, 1993; Russell Sherman, interview by C. Cooper, 1994; Russell Sherman trial notebook; partial transcripts, *State v. Sheppard,* 1966 trial.

152   This time, though . . . : Portions of Cowan's testimony are reproduced in Paul Holmes, *Retrial: Murder and Dr. Sam Sheppard* (New York: Bantam Books, 1966), pp. 173–97.

154   "Lee summed it . . .": Tuney, interview by Dalrymple, Sheppard; Bailey describes the trial in his own words in *The Defense Never Rests.*

154   Soon after the acquittal . . . : F. Lee Bailey, letter to Fred Drenkhan, Chief of Police, Bay Village, November 23, 1966, Sheppard Files.

155   The grand jury heard . . . : William Pringle, interview by C. Cooper, 1993; "2 Witnesses Heard by Sheppard Jury," *New York Times,* December 7, 1966.

156   Dr. Sam testified in Congress . . . : "Testimony of Dr. Sam Sheppard Before the Senate Subcommittee to Investigate Juvenile Delinquency," July 8, 1969, 5584 *Congressional Record* 1969.

156   After the acquittal . . . : Dr. Sam Sheppard, *Endure and Conquer* (Cleveland: World, 1966).

156   When his right to practice . . . : Sheppard's license to practice was reinstated by the State Medical Board of Ohio on December 15, 1967.

157   "Massive pervasive prejudicial . . .": *Sheppard V. Maxwell,* 384 U.S. 333 (1966).

157   On April 6, 1970 . . . : Death certificate, Dr. Samuel Holmes Sheppard, Bureau of Vital Statistics, Ohio Department of Health.

158   Jack Harrison Pollack's . . . : *Dr. Sam: An American Tragedy* (Chicago: Regnery, 1972); *Guilty or Innocent: The Sam Sheppard Murder Case*, written and produced by Harold Gast, filmed by Universal TV and first aired on NBC-TV on November 17, 1975, "Monday Night at the Movies"; "American Justice: Dr. Sam Sheppard," hosted by Bill Kurtis, Nugas/Martin Productions, first airing on Arts & Entertainment Network, November 1992; Thorwald, *Crime and Science*. Anthology inclusions abound; see, e.g., *Crimes of the 20th Century, A Chronology* (New York: Crescent Books, 1991), pp. 179–82.

158   On November 17, 1982 . . . : Based on Bay Village Files, Federal Bureau of Investigation Files, released pursuant to public records and freedom of information requests, including Peter Gray, report, November 1982; FBI letters, December 2, 1982; December 22, 1982; March 23, 1983.

159   Jan Sheppard Duvall . . . : Notes, 1980–82; essay, 1994.

159   Jan, the older daughter . . . : Dr. Stephen Sheppard, with Paul Holmes, was the author of *My Brother's Keeper* (New York: McKay, 1964).

160   But as often . . . : Richard Dalrymple, letter to Jim Chapman, 1981.

160   Jim Chapman was intrigued . . . : Chapman, interviews by C. Cooper, 1993–94.

Chapter 10 • Suppressed

166   Ohio's law was broad . . . : Ohio Rev. Code, sec. 149.43; see also David L. Marburger, "Tapping Officials' Secrets: The Door to Open Government in Ohio," Reporters Committee for Freedom of the Press, 1989.

166   Gilbert went ahead . . . : *State of Ohio ex. rel. Cynthia L. Cooper v. City of Bay Village and City of Cleveland and County of Cuyahoga*, Case No. 92-9609, Supreme Court of Ohio, filed December, 1992 (a writ of mandamus, asking that government officials be ordered to open their files pursuant to Ohio's law).

167   Old-time employees . . . : Mary Ellen Leycock, interview by Richard Dalrymple, 1980.

168   Whatever information . . . : De Forest interview.

168   These statements were coming . . . : Eberling, letters (see chapter 16).

169   The use of . . . : Paul Holmes said that the prosecutor emphasized the corduroy jacket in his opening statement in Dr. Sam's 1966 trial, saying that when the Aherns left, Dr. Sam was "asleep on a couch wearing a corduroy jacket." Holmes noted, "It was to be one of the state's supposedly strong points" (Holmes, *Retrial*, p. 153).

169   *Police:* Did you . . . : Bay Village Files, Statement taken by Esther Aldrich, 6:05 P.M., July 5, 1954, at the Bay Village City Hall.

170   Bay Village documents . . . : Eaton, Statement, July 8, 1954, Bay Village Files. After several more days of searching, the chief found another $20.50 hidden in a desk drawer. This information was completely altered by the time the case reached the Ohio Court of Appeals, which wrote that money in various places "was easily discovered by the chief of police" (100 Ohio App. 345, 381).

170   On July 7, 1954 . . . : F. Drenkhan, Supplementary Offense Report, 54-194, July 7, 1954, Bay Village Files.

171   For example . . . : Deutschlander, Police reports, July 19, 1954, Bay Village Files.

171   Some were made available . . . : Trace Evidence Report, viewed by C. Cooper, 1993, at Cuyahoga County Coroner's Office; and lab cards, viewed and hand-copied at Cuyahoga County Coroner's Office by C. Cooper, 1993; microscopic and lab analysis, Sheppard Files; property inventory, viewed at Coroner's Office.

173   "Yes," Gerber replied . . . : Transcript, *State v. Sheppard*, 1954.

173   A plain manila envelope . . . : This group of documents, from an unknown source, are hereafter cited as Confidential Documents.

173   One document . . . : Lockwood report.

173   Cleveland police officer Pat Gareau . . . : Dr. Steve Sheppard, letter, in William J. Corrigan Papers.

174   Dr. Kirk had insisted . . . : Kirk notes, Kirk Files.

176   Dr. Sam and his defense team . . . : The information that evidence of forced entry had been discovered and documented by the Cleveland police, that a report of it existed, and that a cast of the markings had been made was thoroughly withheld from defense attorneys, to the extent that they had to argue around this damaging point. This element was pervasive throughout the case even to its present day. William Corrigan wrote in one appellate brief: "Throughout the trial the State represented that . . . there was no evidence of forcible entry from the outside, and that in this tightly secured house only one person, [Dr. Sam], was capable of committing the crime charged" (*Sheppard v. Alvis*, No. 35777, Amendment to Petition). F. Lee Bailey, representing Dr. Sam in 1966, wrote: "There was no sign of forcible entry, as you know" (letter to Bay Village police chief Fred F. Drenkhan). Juror James Barrish reported immediately after the trial that the jury voted for conviction because there was no evidence that anyone else had entered the house (*New York Journal American*, December 22, 1954). In 1993, one reporter wrote: "As for me? I feel deeply that when Marilyn died there were only three people in that home. Marilyn, Sam and a 7-year-old son. . . . And I don't think the son did it." Don Bean, "Hosts of ghosts over Dr. Sam's house," *Plain Dealer*, June 25, 1993.

177   Gertrude Bauer Mahon . . . : Quoted in a letter from Bill
       Corrigan to Paul Herbert, 1956, William J. Corrigan Papers.
177   John T. Corrigan . . . : Holmes, *Retrial*, p.154.
177   And Mary Cowan . . . : Interview by Jan Sheppard Duvall, 1981.
177   There were no windows . . . : Ann Leusch, interview by C.
       Cooper, 1994.
178   He made a drawing . . . : Drawing by Eberling sent to Sam
       R. Sheppard, 1992; also letters, interviews with Eberling (see
       chapter 16).
178   A man who worked . . . : Ed Wilbert, interviews by AMSEC,
       1993–94.
178   On July . . . : Statement of Dr. Steve Sheppard, July 6, 1954,
       Bay Village Files.
178   Lights in the basement . . . : This could have explained the
       testimony of Mrs. Bender that she saw a vague light in the down-
       stairs at approximately two-thirty A.M. In the original police re-
       ports, released by Bay Village, Mrs. Bender admitted her
       uncertainty about the information.
179   The tool described . . . : Jim Chapman, interviews by C. Cooper,
       1993–94. Dr. Virgil Haws, D.O., of Detroit, Michigan, made an
       external examination of Mrs. Sheppard's body on July 6, 1954,
       after embalming. Three of the scalp wounds, he noted, were
       relatively unchanged by the embalming and "suggest the instru-
       ment to be a dull edged unyielding instrument for example, an
       automobile tire tool or a so-called jim (pry-bar)" (Haws, letter,
       July 10, 1954, William J. Corrigan Papers). Haws tempered his
       observations because of "unsatisfactory conditions" presented
       by the autopsy.
179   Henry Dombrowski . . . : Interview by C. Cooper, 1994.

Chapter 11 • Who
185   "Can American citizens . . .": Kirk notes.
186   As Sam R.'s connection . . . : AMSEC's name comes from the
       firm's original name, American Security Services Corporation.
       AMSEC is now a division of Gallagher Bassett Services, Inc.
187   A close look inside . . . : Transcript, *State v. Sheppard*, 1954;
       testimony of Mary Cowan.
187   Dr. Peter De Forest . . . : interviews by C. Cooper, 1994, 1995.
188   In multiple statements. . . : For example, Sheppard, statement
       at sheriff's office, July 10, 1954.
188   One description by Mr. and Mrs. Richard Knitter . . . : Police
       reports, statements, Bay Village Files; transcript, *State v. Shep-
       pard*, 1954; Russell Sherman trial notebook; William J. Corri-
       gan Papers.
188   Dr. Kirk believed . . . : Kirk report; Kirk Files.
189   The disfigurement . . . : See John E. Douglas et al., *Pocket
       Guide to Crime Classification Manual* (New York: Lexington
       Books, 1992).

190   Most sex murders . . . : Douglas et al., *Pocket Guide.*

190   William J. Walker . . . : Letter to Dorothy Kilgallen, William J. Corrigan Papers.

190   Howard Winter . . . : "Not Guilty As Charged," *Man's Magazine,* October 1955, pp. 17, 62.

190   In the early 1990s . . . : Douglas et al., *Pocket Guide* provides a synopsis of the full manual.

191   Jim Chapman . . . : Interview by C. Cooper, 1993.

191   This view was even adopted . . . : See *State v. Sheppard,* 100 Ohio App. 345, 382.

191   Gerber later dropped . . . : *State v. Sheppard,* transcript, 1954. Dr. Sam Sheppard, upon hearing about the psychiatric analysis of a "passion killer," wrote to his attorneys from his jail cell, suggesting that he be examined by a psychiatrist, whose evaluation would show how inconsistent the description of "passion killer" was with his psychological makeup (Notes, Sheppard Files). No such test was made.

192   Some see differences . . . : John Dawson, Barbara Boland, "Murder in Large Urban Counties, 1988," Bureau of Justice Statistics Special Report, U.S. Department of Justice, May 1993. The report finds that men were defendants in murder cases at a rate of nine times that of women. The FBI Uniform Crime Report for 1993 shows a ratio of known offenders of one woman to nearly ten men. In murder cases, 64.3 percent of the arrests were of male defendants, 6.6 percent of female defendants, with no arrest in 29.1 percent of the cases, with the killer's gender unknown.

192   Although women kill less often . . . : Violence between Intimates," Bureau of Justice Statistics Special Report, U.S. Department of Justice, November 1994. Intimates commit approximately 13 percent of the total violent victimizations, according to the National Crime Victimization Survey, cited in the special report.

192   British author . . . : Anne Campbell, *Men, Women, and Aggression* (New York: Basic Books, 1993).

192   Canadian forensic psychologist . . . : Robert Hare, *Without Conscience: The Disturbing World of the Psychopaths among Us* (New York: Simon and Schuster, 1993); also excerpted in "Predators," *Psychology Today* 55 (January–February 1994).

192   Dr. Joel Norris . . . : *Serial Killers* (London: Arrow Books, 1990); *Walking Time Bomb* (New York: Bantam Books, 1992); discussion with C. Cooper, 1993. The twenty-one behavior patterns that Norris designates are ritualistic behavior, masks of sanity, compulsivity, search for help, severe memory disorders and a chronic inability to tell the truth, suicidal tendencies, history of serious assault, deviate sexual behavior and hypersexuality, head injuries or injuries incurred at birth, history of

chronic drug or alcohol abuse, alcohol- or drug-abusing parents, victim of physical or emotional abuse or of cruel parenting, result of an unwanted pregnancy, products of a difficult gestation for the mother, interrupted bliss or no bliss of childhood, extraordinary cruelty to animals, arsonal tendencies without obvious homicidal interest, symptoms of neurological impairment, evidence of genetic disorders, biochemical symptoms, and feelings of powerlessness or inadequacy (*Serial Killers,* p. 291).

192   Some researchers . . . : See Norris, Serial Killers, p. 236.

192   The possible relationship . . . : William J. Corrigan Papers.

193   Among the more sophisticated . . . : Dorothy O. Lewis et al., "Neuro-psychiatric, Psychoeducational, and Family Characteristics of 14 Juveniles Condemned to Death in the United States," *American Journal of Psychiatry* 145, no. 5 (May 1988); Dorothy Lewis, "Intrinsic and Environmental Characteristics of Juvenile Murderers," paper delivered at a meeting of the American Academy of Child and Adolescent Psychiatry, May 1988; M. Feldman, K. Mallouh, D. Lewis, "Filicidal Abuse in the Histories of 15 Condemned Murderers," *Bulletin of the American Academy of Psychiatry Law* 14, no. 4 (1986): 345–52.

Chapter 12 • Confessors

196   Anonymous, woman . . . : Transcripts of selected calls to the Sheppard phone line, July 1993–September 1994.

196   The inventory of police . . . : The information in this chapter, unless otherwise indicated, is from Bay Village Files.

196   Coroner Sam Gerber . . . : "Check Shotgun in Murder Probe," *Cleveland Press,* July 19, 1954, p. 1.

196   Helen K . . . : Report of Deputy Sheriff Rossbach, July 11, 1954, Confidential Documents.

197   George Ennis . . . : "Murder Plot Story False, Drifter Says," *Cleveland Press,* July 15, 1954, p. 1.

197   Louis Winner . . . : Statement, August 1, 1954; Jay Hubach and Fred Drenkhan, supplementary offense report, August 1, 1954.

198   A tip from Trenton . . . : Report taken from Dr. Stephen Sheppard by J. Hubach, September 10, 1954, and reported by Hubach to Cleveland police; see also Sheppard with Holmes, *My Brother's Keeper,* p. 152.

198   Tree trimmers . . . : Statement of Mrs. Schuele; Jay Hubach and Fred Drenkhan, supplementary offense report, August 2, 1954, on trip to Lorain, Ohio, Police Department; report of Deputy Sheriff Rossbach, July 18, 1954, on interview of M.W.G., tree expert, Confidential Documents; Report from Bay Village, July 12, 1954, on M., a landscaper.

198   A man by the name of Henry F. . . . : Report of Thomas J. Fitzpatrick, Jr., chief of police, Elmwood Place, Ohio, Novem-

ber 21, 1954; statement of Henry F.; reports of Bay Village police; police court affidavit and warrant signed by J. Spencer Houk, FBI report; see also Sheppard Files.

199   A woman who . . . : Paul Kirk, letter to Mrs. Richard N. Sheppard, October 1955, Sheppard Files.

200   A man who had . . . : Jay Hubach and Fred Drenkhan, supplementary offense report, August 2, 1954, about a man who died in an accident in Loudenville, Ohio. The officers were seeking a palm print. Also, Paul Kirk, letter, October 18, 1955, Sheppard Files.

200   Another man did commit . . . : Jay Hubach and Fred Drenkhan, supplementary offense report, August 4, 1954, about man from Avon Lake, Ohio, who shot himself in the stomach in Vermillion on the Lake, Ohio.

200   A woman in Oklahoma . . . : Mrs. G. C., letters to Bay Village police, 1980.

200   Even in 1993 . . . : Transcripts of selected calls to the Sheppard phone line, July 1993–September 1994.

201   Marilyn's cousin . . . : Jay Hubach and Fred Drenkhan, supplementary police report, July 20, 1954; see also Sheppard Files.

201   One-time Bay Village . . . : Interview by Jan Sheppard Duvall and Jim Chapman, 1982; "Barry C[.] Is Turned Loose after 9 Years, Suspect in 1950s Unsolved Killings," *Chicago Tribune,* September 20, 1967.

201   Russell Sherman . . . : Interview by C. Cooper.

201   And then there was James F . . . : Letter to Police Chief Fred Drenkhan, January, 1967, from Bellevue, Ohio.

Chapter 13 • Strangers

203   Donald Joseph Wedler . . . : Source materials include statement of Donald Wedler taken by E. W. Clapper and Sheriff Rodney Thursby, De Land, Florida, July 15, 1957; statement of Donald Wedler before William J. Corrigan and Fred Garmone, July 29, 1957, and Corrigan's notes, William J. Corrigan Papers; Harold Bretnall, letter to Steve Sheppard, July 29, 1957, and Sheriff Thursby, letter to Gene Lowall, 1963, Sheppard Files; arrest record, Donald J. Wedler, Florida; interview, Florida State System of Parole, 1993; interview, Florida State Department of Corrections, 1993; and others, as indicated.

204   Gardner described him . . . : "The Sheppard Case Breaks Wide Open," *Argosy,* October 1957; letter to Mrs. William Higer, October 1957, Sheppard Files; letter to Jack Harrison Pollack, 1964, Pollack Files.

208   Meanwhile, Erle Stanley Gardner . . . : *Argosy,* October 1957; Gardner letters, comments (see chapter 9).

208   More things started to fall . . . : Ibid.; see also Gardner, letter to Ellie Fryfogle, statement of Ellie Fryfogle, William J. Corrigan

Papers; *The Lowdown* magazine, November 1957; "Sailor Puts Finger on Wedler," *Cleveland Plain Dealer,* July 24, 1957.

208   "Naturally I have . . ." : Dr. Sam Sheppard, letter to William Corrigan, William J. Corrigan Papers.

209   As was Bill Corrigan . . . : "Corrigan Will Seek Extradition of Wedler," *Cleveland Plain Dealer,* July 30, 1957.

209   Cleveland officials . . . : "Verbal Blast by M'Arthur Irks Gardner," *Cleveland Plain Dealer,* July 23, 1957.

209   Portions of Wedler's story . . . : Harold Bretnall, letter to Steve Sheppard, Sheppard Files.

209   There was only the house . . . : Alternatively, Wedler could have initially driven past the Sheppards', parked to the west of their house and walked back east, then escaped by running west on the beach, where several houses were situated on the embankment above the lake.

210   Politically connected . . . : Letter to Corrigan, August 3, 1957, William J. Corrigan Papers.

211   On April 9, 1963 . . . : Florida Department of Corrections; letter from Thursby to Lowall, Pollack Files; Florida State System of Parole; response from FBI to Freedom of Information request by C. Cooper, 1994, information request by C. Cooper, 1993.

212   Sheriff Thursby . . . : Thursby died in November 1992, according to Mrs. Louis Thursby, Sr., a cousin contacted by C. Cooper in 1994.

Chapter 14 • Friends

214   "Many people live . . .": Dr. Sam letters, Sheppard Files.

215   The letter that . . . : Dr. Thomas S., letter to Cleveland chief of police, three pages, postmarked Dayton, Ohio, August 7, 1954, Sheppard Files.

215   Lester Tillman Hoversten . . . : Sources for this chapter include statement of Lester Hoversten, July 6, 1954, before Deputy Sheriffs Carl Rossbach and Dave Yettra, Bay Village Files; trial notes and letters of Dr. Sam, Sheppard Files; diary of Dr. Lester Hoversten, sent to C. Cooper, 1994; testimony of Dr. Lester Hoversten, transcript, *State v. Sheppard,* Court of Common Pleas, 1954; police reports, Bay Village Files; report of Deputy Sheriff Rossbach, July 10, 1954, Confidential Documents; Russell Sherman trial notebook; and others as indicated.

216   "You could talk . . .": Bob Bailey, interview by C. Cooper, 1993.

216   "He stayed . . .": Dr. Edward Murray, interview by C. Cooper, 1993.

217   A confidential local informant . . . : Letter to Bay Village police, August 3, 1954, Bay Village Files.

219   In late fall of 1951. . . : Dr. Sam Sheppard, letter to Lester Hoversten, October 1951, Sheppard Files.

219   By July 1952 . . . : "Custody and Maintenance" agreement signed July 9 and 17, 1952, in Los Angeles County, filed with Petition for Divorce, Court of Common Pleas, Cuyahoga County, No. 652673.

219   According to neighbor . . . : Esther Houk, interview by Richard Dalrymple, 1980.

220   One doctor said . . . : Thomas S., letter to Cleveland Chief of Police.

221   In the meantime . . . : Court of Common Pleas hearing, February 23, 1954, no. 652673.

221   In February . . . : Hoversten diary.

223   In a letter . . . : Lester Hoversten, letter to Dominic Aveni, June 15, 1954, contained in evidence folder turned over to Dr. Sam Sheppard in 1966, Sheppard Files; Jay Hubach and Fred Drenkhan, supplementary offense report, August 3, 1954, Bay Village Files.

229   A report by Cleveland detective . . . : Patrick A. Gareau, "Police Department, Departmental Information," July 4, 1954, Confidential Documents .

229   As soon as he arrived . . . : letter to Steve Sheppard, August 10, 1954; letter to Dr. William S., August 6, 1954; letter to Mabel Moyers, postmarked July 24, 1954, Sheppard Files.

232   "Hoversten Tells More . . ." : *Cleveland Press,* August 12, 1954; "Family Points to Bay Man As New Suspect As Hoversten Talks," *Cleveland Plain Dealer,* August 13, 1954; "Susan, Dr. Hoversten to Testify Tomorrow," *Cleveland Press,* August 16, 1954.

233   The fliers . . . : Hoversten diary; copies of fliers in Sheppard Files and William J. Corrigan Papers.

234   Once he took . . . : Transcript, *State v. Sheppard,* Court of Common Pleas, 1954.

236   "He disappeared . . .": Murray, interview.

236   But in 1956 . . . : Dorothy Sheppard, letter to Dr. Sam Sheppard, Sheppard Files; Britain research by Lyn Date, 1993.

237   In 1958 he wrote . . . : Notes, Sheppard Files.

237   Dr. Bob Bailey . . . : Bailey interview.

237   In 1975 . . . : Information from California Board of Medicine, 1993; Ohio Medical Board, 1993; California Board of Osteopaths, 1993; California Osteopathic Society, 1993.

237   In 1987 . . . : Certificate of Death, State of California; obituary, *San Jose Mercury News,* December 13, 1987. Hoversten's body was cremated.

237   Buried deep . . . : Western Union telegram, dated November 17, 1966, Sheppard Files.

238   In 1994 . . . : Correspondence from Hoversten's son to C. Cooper, January 1994.

Chapter 15 • Neighbors

239   *A man* . . . : Transcripts of calls to Sheppard phone line, 1993–94.

240   The names of the Houks . . . : Sources for this chapter include the following: statement of J. Spencer (Spen) Houk, July 5, 1954, and statement of Esther Houk, July 6, 1954, Bay Village Files; testimony of Spen Houk, Esther Houk, Larry Houk, transcript of inquest into the murder of Marilyn Sheppard, July 1954; testimony of Spen Houk, Esther Houk, Larry Houk, transcript, *State v. Sheppard*, 1954; testimony of Spen Houk and Esther Houk, transcript, *State v. Sheppard*, 1966; notes of bail hearing, 1954, *State v. Sheppard,* Sheppard Files; Larry Houk, interview by Richard Dalrymple, July 1980; Spen Houk, interview by Richard Dalrymple and Jan Sheppard Duvall, March 1981; Lyn Houk E., interviews by Richard Dalrymple, October 1980; Esther Houk, interviews by Richard Dalrymple, Jan Sheppard Duvall, and Jim Chapman, including Psychological Stress Evaluator (PSE) exams, July 1980, September 1980, March 1981, April 1981, June 1981, November 1981; Redinger interviews by C. Cooper, 1993-94; public records of death, divorce; and others as noted.

241   "I impulsively grabbed . . .": Esther Houk, interview by Dalrymple, 1980.

241   Dr. Sam saw . . . : Dr. Sam Sheppard, inquest testimony, July 1954.

242   The Houks were three doors . . . : Their address was 29104 Lake Road, Bay Village. To the west of their home was a cemetery, and past that, the home of the Aherns.

244   "The Houks were carefree . . .": Richard Eberling, interview by C. Cooper, 1993.

245   Dr. Sam learned . . . : Larry Houk, inquest transcript, July 1954.

246   A couple of weeks later . . . : Dr. Sam notes, Sheppard Files.

247   "It wasn't unusual . . .": Jim Redinger, interviews by C. Cooper, 1993–94.

247   The most controversial . . . : Dorothy Sheppard, interview by Jan Sheppard Duvall, 1982; notes, William J. Corrigan Papers.

247   Jack Krakan . . . : F. Lee Bailey, letter to Fred F. Drenkhan, November 23, 1966, Sheppard Files; Andy Tuney, interview by Richard Dalrymple and Jan Sheppard Duvall, March 1981.

248   A babysitter . . . : Bailey, letter to Drenkhan, Sheppard Files.

248   Out of a sense of personal honor . . . : Dr. Sam notes, Sheppard Files.

249   "Jeez, I used to . . .": Spen Houk, interview by Dalrymple and Duvall, 1981.

251   Yet on the day . . . : Esther Houk, interview by Dalrymple, 1980.

252   Was it then . . . : Jay Hubach, interview by Jan Sheppard Duvall and Jim Chapman, 1982.

254   Allegations began flying . . . : "Story Calls Houk Suspect,"
        Cleveland Press, August 13, 1954; " 'Lies, Lies,' Cried Houk at
        Dr. Steve," *Cleveland Press,* August 14, 1954; Dr. Sam notes,
        Sheppard Files; notes, William J. Corrigan Papers; attorney
        notes, Sheppard Files.

254   Years later, a man . . . : Notes by Dr. Steve Sheppard, files of
        Jan Sheppard Duvall.

254   She didn't see what purpose . . . : Esther Houk, letter, June 1,
        1955, files of Jan Sheppard Duvall; interviews.

255   In June 1955 . . . : Copy of letter provided to Dalrymple and
        Duvall, 1980.

255   After Sheppard's acquittal . . . : Bailey, letter to Drenkhan. See
        chapter 8 for left-handed analysis.

255   In 1994 her grandson . . . : Todd E. son of Lyn, interview by
        C. Cooper, 1994.

256   Another piece of evidence . . . : Report of Detective Patrick
        Gareau, July 4, 1954, Bay Village Files.

256   Paul Kirk discovered . . . : Kirk notes.

256   Esther said in 1981 . . . : Interview by Janet Sheppard Duvall
        and Richard Dalrymple, 1981.

256   Spen and Esther Houk had divorced . . . : Petition for Divorce,
        No. 742822, January 17, 1962, Court of Common Pleas, Cuya-
        hoga County.

257   Through Bailey's skillful cross-examination . . . : Transcript,
        State v. Sheppard, 1966.

258   Bailey also believed that motive . . . : Bailey, letter to
        Drenkhan.

258   Esther admitted that . . . : Interviews with Dalrymple, 1980–81.

259   A grand jury . . . : William Pringle, interview by C. Cooper,
        1993; "2 Witnesses Heard by Sheppard Jury," *New York Times,*
        December 7, 1966.

260   Jim Chapman participated . . . : Interviews by C. Cooper,
        1993–94.

261   Steve Sheppard . . . : Letter to C. Cooper, 1993.

261   "I don't think . . .": Richard Dalrymple, conversation with C.
        Cooper, 1994.

261   Andy Tuney . . . : Interview by Duvall and Dalrymple, 1981.

261   There was no deathbed confession . . . : Todd E., interviews
        by C. Cooper, 1993–94.

261   Nor did . . . : B. Strickland, conversation with Sam R. Shep-
        pard, 1991.

261   In 1980 Esther had . . . : Interview by Dalrymple and Duvall,
        1980.

Chapter 16 • *Encounters*

263   Beginning with that first letter . . . : Richard Eberling, letters
        to Sam R. Sheppard, 1989–90.

268   Over the next . . . : Information in this chapter is taken from
       the following sources: Richard Eberling, interview by Sam R.
       Sheppard at Lebanon State Prison, March 1990; ten interviews
       by C. Cooper at Lebanon Prison, August 1991, March 1993,
       September 1994, and at Cuyahoga County Jail in Cleveland,
       Ohio, March 1994; 56 pages of letters to Sam R. Sheppard; 180
       pages of letters to C. Cooper; two statements, 6 and 4 pages;
       a drawing with comments; and other sources as indicated.

268   What he had to say . . . : These comments, culled from more
       than one writing or conversation, are provided in their original
       context. Space breaks indicate a change in source material.

272   A calendar diary . . . : William J. Corrigan Papers. Dr. Richard
       Sheppard died in 1980. In a letter to Sam R. Sheppard in 1994,
       Dorothy Sheppard said she had no recollection one way or the
       other about window washing that week.

273   Officers who in 1959 . . . : Report by Officer Ronald B. DuP-
       erow, Bay Village, November 12, 1959, Bay Village Police
       Documents.

275   Eberling had been interviewed . . . : F. Lee Bailey, interview
       by C. Cooper, 1993; Andy Tuney, interview by C. Cooper, 1993;
       Russell Sherman, interview by C. Cooper, 1994.

275   Ultimately, he was not . . . : Whether or not Eberling testified
       at the 1966 trial has been variously reported both by Eberling
       and by newspaper reporters. Russell Sherman did not recall
       any testimony from Eberling before the jury. In 1966 Eberling
       had an arrest record, and the prosecution would have been
       entitled to cross-examine him about it. Mike Roberts covered
       the trial, writing "color" features, and knew Eberling. Roberts
       does not recall his testifying. Akron Beacon Journal reporter
       Keith McKnight uncovered a file story from 1966 that refers to
       Eberling testifying about the basement door. Eberling himself
       stated in interviews that he did not testify; on other occasions
       he said that he had a "brief appearance" on the stand. Notes
       from some trial participants found in the Sheppard Files seem
       to indicate that Eberling may have been asked to take the stand
       while the jury was out, and that the judge ruled his testimony
       inadmissible. Full court records that might clarify this point
       could not be located.

281   A couple of articles . . . : Cindy Leise, "Eberling Says: Mayor's
       Wife Killed Marilyn," Chronicle-Telegram, March 3, 1990, quot-
       ing Lawrence Houk; "Cop Pooh-Poohs Eberling Story," Chron-
       icle-Telegram, March 5, 1990.

281   Esther's grandson . . . : "Grandchildren to the Defense," Plain
       Dealer, July 4, 1994.

281   An entirely different . . . : Jim Chapman, interview by C. Coo-
       per, 1994.

282   "This man . . .": Carraway, interview by C. Cooper, 1995.

Chapter 17 • Harbingers

283   "Feel it is . . .": Letter to C. Cooper. Sources for Eberling's comments are listed in the notes for chapter 16.

284   People remarked on it . . . : Dorothy Sheppard, letter to Sam R. Sheppard, 1994.

284   A block ad . . . : Cleveland Ohio Business Telephone Directory for 1954, on microfilm, Cleveland Public Library.

285   His mother, Louise . . . : Birth certificate, Department of Vital Statistics, Ohio; marriage records, Cuyahoga County; child welfare records released with permission; *The Cleveland City Directory*, 1928, 1929.

286   His good friend . . . : Oscar B. (Obie) Henderson III, interviews by C. Cooper at Marion Correctional Institution, Ohio, March 1993, September 1994.

287   "Dick is somebody . . .": Peg Baker, interview by C. Cooper, 1993.

287   "Uncle Dickie? . . .": Tom Story, interview by C. Cooper, 1994.

287   There may have been . . . : Child welfare records released with permission.

287   In 1976 Richard swore . . . : In the Matter of the Estate of Claire M., Bergen County Surrogate's Court, State of New Jersey; interviews with the attorney who handled the estate by C. Cooper, 1993; interview by C. Cooper with relative of Claire M. who spoke on condition of anonymity in greater Cleveland, 1994; property records, Cuyahoga County.

287   Bob . . . : Name changed at the request of family members, and the exact nature of the confidential documents shown to the author has been excluded. Claire, raised by Bob's mother, was unrelated.

288   His mother . . . : Child welfare records released with permission; marriage records, Cleveland, Ohio; certificate of death, May 14, 1987, State of Oklahoma, Department of Health, for Louise Harter; Order Appointing Successor Guardian and other probate documents, District Court of Oklahoma County, No. P-82-1003.

289   He had blackouts . . . : Information in this section based on child welfare records released with permission; medical reports released with permission; Eberling, interviews by C. Cooper, 1991–94.

290   Military records . . . : Selective Service System Classification Records for Birth Year 1929.

290   As a youngster . . . : Child welfare records released with permission.

291   "I never heard . . .": Henderson interviews.

292   Ethel Durkin's niece . . . : Arline Durkin Campbell, interview by C. Cooper, 1994.

293   CAS found Richard . . . : Child welfare records released with permission.

293   Westlake (then called Dover) . . . : Westlake is described in general in *A History of Westlake, Ohio, 1811 to 1961,* book 1 by William D. Ellis, book 2 by Mary Ellen Wobbecke (Westlake, Ohio: n.p., 1961).

294   John Eberling remembers . . .": John Eberling, interviews by C. Cooper, 1993, by AMSEC, 1994.

294   "The Eberlings were applauded . . .": "Alias Santa Claus: She Mothers Four Not Her Own," *Cleveland Press,* December 12, 1945.

295   The son of . . . : Philip Kinzel, interview by C. Cooper, 1995.

295   Then on July 9 . . . : Death certificate, George Eberling, Ohio Department of Vital Statistics; Richard Eberling interviews.

295   It set up a . . . : Estate of George Eberling, Probate Court of Cuyahoga County, Case No. 385421.

296   Richard began using . . . : School yearbooks, Dover schools, Porter Library, Westlake, Ohio.

296   Richard told schoolmates . . . : Sally Hutcherson, interview by C. Cooper, 1994.

296   Then, in 1948 . . . : In re Richard Lenardic, a minor, petition for change of name, Probate Court, Cuyahoga County, No. 412732 (August 31, 1948).

296   In high school . . . : High school yearbooks, Dover High; Barbara Smith Moorman, interview by C. Cooper, 1994; Hutcherson interview; Phyllis Zemek Beyer, interview by C. Cooper, 1993.

297   The first formal deed . . . : Property records, Cuyahoga County; records of the county recorder, Cuyahoga County; estate of George Eberling, Cuyahoga County. See, e.g., Recorded Deeds, vol. 7217, p. 460, "Executor's Deed under a Will, Cuyahoga County."

298   By July 1962. . . . : Letter, probate file, estate of George Eberling.

299   As of 1965. . . : Probate file, estate of George Eberling; Cuyahoga County property records; Eberling interviews; Christine Eberling death certificate, Ohio Department of Vital Statistics.

299   "My two aunts . . .": John Eberling, interview by C. Cooper, 1993.

299   That was the same year . . . : In a statement signed before Bay Village officers on November 10, 1959, Eberling states: "I first started to steal in a Rocky River home in 1953." Bay Village Police Documents. A letter written by psychiatrist Dr. Louis Karnosh, who saw him on November 11, 1959, states, "Since 1953 he has been subject to compulsive stealing" (Cleveland Clinic Files, released with permission).

302   Eberling did receive a check . . . : The check was for thirty dollars (see William J. Corrigan Papers).

Chapter 18 • Julys

303   "Having spent a number of years . . .": Congressional testimony, July 8, 1969, cited in notes to chapter 9.

305   When Eberling came . . . : Report by Officer Ronald B. DuPerow, November 12, 1959, Bay Village Police Documents.

305   Many things had happened . . . : For general sources of Eberling comments, see Eberling, interviews and letters, cited in notes to chapter 16.

305   On July 23, 1955 . . . : "Flash Fire Burns Barn in Westlake," *Cleveland Press,* July 23, 1955; Eberling interviews; John Eberling interview; Ronald DuPerow, interview by C. Cooper, 1995; annual reports of Executrix, estate of George Eberling; "Westlake: Woman Offers 30 Acres of Hay to Anyone Who'll Harvest It," *Cleveland Press,* June 27, 1960.

306   July 1956 was even more . . . : Monroe County, Michigan, Sheriff's Department, official traffic accident report, July 5, 1956; certificate of death, Barbara Ann Kinzel, Michigan Department of Health; obituary, July 8, 1956, Necrology Files, Cleveland Public Library; "Delayed Trip to Avoid Traffic But Nurse Dies," *Cleveland Press,* July 6, 1956; Eberling interviews; Nancy Espy, interview by C. Cooper, 1995; Philip Kinzel interview.

308   In Monroe County . . . : Monroe County Medical Examiner's Office, 1993; Daryl Bennett, interview by C. Cooper, 1993.

308   The official traffic . . . : Review of the document by Dr. John Plunkett, Dakota County, Minnesota, 1995, confirmed that the description of injuries provided no possible insight into the nature of the accident. Interview by C. Cooper.

308   Eberling, who had many minor . . . : For example, in Lakewood, one of many West Side suburbs, Eberling had four moving violations in the years 1952–55, for speeding, careless driving, and passing left of center (Lakewood police reports released under Ohio's public record law).

309   Eberling claimed that he returned . . . : In a search by C. Cooper in 1993, no official records were located.

309   Still, the truck's insurer . . . : Estate of Barbara Kinzel, Probate Court of Lorain County, Ohio, Case No. 34499.

309   As it happened . . . : The document, in the William J. Corrigan Papers, lists all the nurses at Bay View who had come in contact with Sheppard while he was hospitalized with injuries after the murder. Kinzel, listed at her mother's Avon Lake address, is included, with a brief note: "Only contact was Tues 10 A.M. He [Dr. Sam] appeared tired, gave sedatives the Dr. ordered. Attend Dr. Elkins when he gave puncture."

310   In 1959 . . . : Dr. Louis Karnosh, letter "To Whom It May Concern," November 11, 1959, confirms that he examined Eberling (Cleveland Clinic Files released with permission).

310 When first arrested . . . : Sources include George Jindra, interview by C. Cooper, 1994; Harold Wilbert, interview by AMSEC, 1994 (Wilbert was reportedly a cousin of George Eberling's second wife, who died before he married Christine Eberling, Richard's foster mother); Ronald DuPerow, interview by C. Cooper, 1995; Fred Drenkhan, interviews by C. Cooper, 1993; by AMSFC, 1994; police reports, Rocky River, Ohio, Police Department, Fairview, Ohio, Police Department, Bay Village Police Documents; statement of Richard G. Eberling November 10, 1959, taken by Officer Jay Hubach, Bay Village Police Documents; Jay Hubach, interview by Jan Sheppard Duvall and Jim Chapman, 1982.

312 Dorothy Sheppard . . . : Letter to Sam R. Sheppard, 1994; Report of John Eaton, November 12, 1959, Bay Village Police Documents.

313 Bay Village was the site. . . : Bay Village Police Documents; DuPerow interview.

313 Then, in March 1958 . . . : Statement of Richard G. Eberling with reference to larceny from the home of Dr. Richard Sheppard, at 23346 Lake Road, November 10, 1959, Bay Village Police Documents.

315 And Chief Eaton may have noticed . . . : Identification no. 167, Bay Village Police Documents.

315 Patrolman Ronald B. DuPerow . . . : Supplementary offense report 55-95 et cetera by Ronald B. DuPerow, Bay Village Police Document, and "Summary of Investigation" and letter by Lt. James R. Tompkins, Bay Village Police Department, March 21, 1989, Bay Village Police Documents.

316 A test was conducted . . . : Official polygraph report, Ohio State Bureau of Criminal Identification and Investigation, London, Ohio, November 20, 1959, BCI File No. 9283; letter to James R. Tompkins, April 28, 1989, by an unidentified reviewer, Bay Village Police Documents; Bay Village supplementary report 54-194, 3-21-89; expert testimony in 1989 by Dr. William J. Yankee.

317 "When someone asks . . .": Fred Drenkhan, interview by C. Cooper, 1994.

318 In November 1959 . . . : Karnosh, letter, Cleveland Clinic Files.

319 On February 5, 1960 . . . : *State v. Eberling,* Court of Common Pleas, Cuyahoga County, Case No. 72182 (1960).

319 "Naturally I did not . . .": Dorothy Sheppard, letter, 1994.

319 After the theft charge . . . : Sources include Eberling interviews and letters; Henderson interviews; and others as indicated.

319 On the day . . .": Property records, Cuyahoga County; "How They Live and Entertain," *Cleveland Press,* June 1, 1974; "Strollers Will View West Side Beauties," *Plain Dealer,* July 18, 1976; "Homes on Tour Are Exceptional," *Cleveland Press,* October 15, 1977.

322   "People loved . . .": Mike Roberts, interview by C. Cooper, 1994.

323   "Dick was . . .": Peg Baker, interview by C. Cooper, 1993.

323   Richard met Ethel . . . : Sources include Eberling interviews and letters; Arline Durkin Campbell, Willis Corlett, Helen Hodge; interviews by C. Cooper 1993–94; obituary, William Durkin; other sources, as indicated.

325   Ethel was the first . . . : Sources include those above and certificate of death, Myrtle Fray, Ohio Department of Health; report of autopsy and coroner's verdict, Myrtle Fray, Case No. 103423, Cuyahoga County, May 20, 1962; probate court file 625698, Cuyahoga County; homicide report, complaint 12637, Cleveland Police Department, May 20, 1962.

327   With scant more effort . . . : "Screams Ignored, Woman Is Slain," *Plain Dealer,* May 21, 1962; "Fingerprint Found Near Bed of Slain Lake Ave Widow," *Cleveland Press,* May 21, 1962; "Police Seek Clues in Widow's Slaying," *Plain Dealer,* May 22, 1962.

327   There was a single . . . : "This Mustn't Become 'Unsolved Slaying,' " *Cleveland Press,* May 23, 1962: "There's a lack of clues in the slaying of the Lake Ave. widow in her apartment early Sunday but there will not be peace of mind in many homes until the killer is locked up."

329   She died . . . : Certificate of death, Sarah Belle Farrow, Ohio Department of Health; probate records, Cuyahoga County; Campbell, Corlett interviews; Eberling interviews.

330   Russ Sherman . . . : Sherman interview.

330   Eberling counseled . . . : Russ Zapach, interview by C. Cooper, 1994.

330   For Bev and Dale . . . : Transcript, *State v. Eberling,* Cuyahoga County Court of Common Pleas, No. CR-232316 (1989).

330   For Patricia Bogar . . . : Patricia Bogar, interview by C. Cooper, 1994, interview with AMSEC, 1994; transcript, *State v. Eberling*

331   Eberling himself received . . . : Circumstances surrounding probate case of Claire M. are described in chapter 17.

331   "Richard was always . . .": Peg Baker and Jack Baker, interview by C. Cooper, 1993.

331   Eberling's appointment . . . : Brent Larkin, "Window Washer Is Boss of Redoing Perk's Offices," *Cleveland Press,* April 3, 1973; "Designer Is Window Washer: City Hall Preservation Chief Backed," *Cleveland Press,* April 4, 1973.

331   He stayed on . . . : Thomas Brazaitis, "City Spends $28,000 on Perk Office," *Plain Dealer,* July 5, 1973; Brent Larkin, "Private Funds Lacking for City Hall Project," *Cleveland Press,* July 15, 1973.

331　Thinking the problems . . . : Brent Larkin, "Perk Home Decorator Will Redo City Hall," *Cleveland Press,* March 31, 1976; "Design Society Questions Perk on Office Project," Cleveland Press, June 19, 1976.

331　After Perk was booted . . . : "City Owes Him $16,000, Perk's Decorator Says," *Plain Dealer,* December 20, 1979.

332　But through their connections . . . : "International Night Hosts Will Be on Toes for Benefit," *Plain Dealer,* May 20, 1979; "Perk Invites Stokes" *Cleveland Press,* August 22, 1973: "Yale, City Hall Get Together," *Cleveland Press,* December 6, 1976; "Up with the Lights! Palace Glitters Again," *Plain Dealer,* September 7, 1977; "Beautiful Place for Party," *Cleveland Press,* March 14, 1977.

332　The world of politics . . . : Eberling interviews and letters; Henderson interviews; Patricia Bogar interview by C. Cooper, 1994, interview by AMSEC, 1994.

332　Richard kept his money-making . . . : Sources include Corlett, Campbell, Hodge interviews; Transcript, *State v. Eberling*

332　According to Jack Baker . . . : Interview by C. Cooper.

335　"I never heard . . .": Marvin Koblentz, interview by C. Cooper, 1994; Rich Koblentz, interview by C. Cooper, 1993.

335　These events . . . : Transcript, *State v. Eberling;* brief of state (appellee), Eighth District Circuit Court of Appeals, Ohio, Case Nos. 58559, 58560, p. 5.

336　Linda Newton finally . . . : Transcript, *State v. Eberling.*

Chapter 19 • Nightmares
338　The Lakewood rescue squad . . . : Files, Lakewood police; transcript, *State v. Eberling.*

338　Vince Kremperger . . . : Interviews by C. Cooper, 1994; by AMSEC, 1994.

339　McNeil, a widow . . . : Kremperger interview; a neighbor who, although identified, asked to remain anonymous, interviews by C. Cooper, 1993–94; autopsy report, autopsy verdict, and report of laboratory findings, Ruth McNeil, autopsy no. M-47775, October 6, 1981, Cuyahoga County Coroner's Office; death certificate, Ohio Department of Health; "Lakewood's Police Seeking Clues in Slaying of Widow," *Plain Dealer,* October 8, 1981; "Clue Hunt Continues in McNeil Homicide," *Lakewood Sun Post,* October 15, 1981.

341　"I went through hell . . .": Sources for this chapter include: Eberling interviews and letters; Henderson interviews and letters; *State v. Eberling and Henderson,* CR-232316, Court of Common Pleas, Cuyahoga County, briefs, court files; appellate decisions and briefs, *State v. Eberling and Henderson,* Nos. 58559, 58560, 1992 WL 74227 (Ohio App. 8 Dist., April 9,

1992); Ohio Supreme Court 92-990 (January 13, 1993); review of Lakewood police records by AMSEC; death certificate, Ethel May Durkin; autopsy report and verdict and amendments, Ethel May Durkin; obituary of Ethel Durkin, *Plain Dealer,* January 14, 1984; estate of Ethel May Durkin, File Nos. 968546 and 961017, Cuyahoga County Probate Court; Campbell, Hodge, Corlett, Bogar, Bakers, Robert Steely, Marvin Koblentz, Rich Koblentz, Burt Fulton, James Speros, Vince Kremperger, Dr. Phillip Bouffard, Linda Newton, Bev Pyle, Donald Green, Ed Hoover, interviews by or conversations with C. Cooper, 1993–94; and others as indicated.

347   Jim Speros . . . : Speros, Bouffard interviews; transcript, *State v. Eberling.*

349   Eberling sold . . . : Property records, Cuyahoga County.

350   In October 1987 . . . : "West End Complex Changes Hands," *Rome* (Georgia) *News-Tribune,* October 15, 1987; Koblentz, Bakers interviews.

350   They also left . . . : *Andreano v. Eberling,* SR41213659, Cuyahoga County Court, closed by arbitration decree, November 23, 1987; Carl Andreano, interview by C. Cooper, 1994.

350   The general psychiatric . . . : Dr. Mark W. Peterson, letter "To Whom It May Concern," November 10, 1988, court documents, Cuyahoga County criminal courts, *State v. Eberling.*

355   Lakewood officers got . . . : Ed Hoover, interview by C. Cooper, 1994; Kremperger interviews; inventory list, 219 West Brow Oval, Lookout Mountain, Tennessee, *State v. Eberling;* search warrant, Hamilton County, Tennessee; court files, Hamilton County.

356   On September 10, 1988 . . . : Elizabeth Balraj, report of autopsy, M-57321, amended coroner's verdict, originally dated January 3, 1984, amended September 15, 1988; Balraj, affidavit of correction of death certificate of Ethel May Durkin, September 16, 1988.

356   In an appellate brief . . . : Beverly Pyle, brief on behalf of Oscar B. Henderson, No. 58560, Court of Appeals for Cuyahoga County, p. 17. Pyle represented Henderson, but not Eberling, on appeal.

357   An independent expert . . . : Dr. John Plunkett, Hastings, Minnesota, reviewed the autopsy; interview by C. Cooper, 1995.

358   These were downright gruesome . . . : Pyle, brief, p. 33; 1992 WL 74227, (Ohio App. 8 Dist.) (April 9, 1992).

359   The prosecutor had argued . . . : Henderson was charged not with conspiracy to commit murder, but with complicity, which was defined as soliciting or aiding in the crime (1992 WL 74227, 7).

359   The charges against Eberling . . . : One count of tampering

with records was vacated on appeal. In addition, the appellate court ordered a new hearing on restitution issues and vacated that portion of the sentence that ordered defendants Eberling and Henderson to spend one day a year, the anniversary of Durkin's death, in solitary confinement. The decisions had no impact on Eberling's term of incarceration. No. 58559; 1992 WL 74227 (Ohio App. 8 Dist.) (April 9, 1992), 92-990 (Ohio Sup. Ct., January 13, 1993).

360   The new executor . . . : The amount awarded to Eberling and Henderson under Durkin's will was forfeited, and the probate court issued a judgment against Eberling for "concealing and having been in possession of $769,760.74 belonging to Ethel M. Durkin" plus a 10 percent penalty of $76,976.07, interest, and costs (In re Ethel M. Durkin, judgment entry No. 96017, September 20, 1989). The judge presiding over the probate matter was Judge Francis J. Talty, who had been the judge in Dr. Sam Sheppard's 1966 acquittal.

Chapter 20 • Windows

362   The dates that Eberling gave . . . : Primary sources are listed in notes to chapters 16 and 18.

363   When asked, Eberling had . . . : Eberling interviews.

363   The slippers . . . : Jack Harrison Pollack, who died in the late 1980s, had the slippers in one of several boxes of stored Sheppard materials. The Pollack Files were transferred to Sam R. Sheppard and C. Cooper by Pollack's daughters, Susan Pollack and Debbie Pollack, in 1993. Holmes's letter to Pollack was dated February 4, 1964, not long after Bretnall died. In 1982 Jan Sheppard Duvall spoke to Pollack, who mentioned that this letter would be an important aid, although she did not see a copy of it. J. Pollack, interview by Duvall, 1982. In a letter to Cynthia Cooper in 1993, Dr. Stephen Sheppard confirmed that Bretnall had, indeed, believed in the "window washer" theory.

364   Jay Hubach . . . : Interview by Jan Sheppard Duvall and James Chapman, 1982.

364   Andy Tuney . . . : Interview by C. Cooper, 1993.

364   One newspaper reporter . . . : Conversation with Jim Chapman, January 1982.

365   Finally, the team working with Sam R . . . : The dates of the three documents are the version of events, 1990, the drawing, 1992, and the statement, March 1993.

367   The appearance . . . : Lund first contacted Sam R. Sheppard in 1990.

367   Elnora Helms . . . : Notes, William J. Corrigan Papers.

367   Articles printed about Eberling . . . : "Blood of [Eberling's] type was discovered inside the home . . ."("Sheppard Murder

Case Attracting New Interest," *New York Times,* August 14, 1989); "Drops of Eberling's blood indeed were found in the Sheppard home." (James McCarty, "Mystery Witness," *Plain Dealer Sunday* Magazine, May 15, 1994, pp. 6, 18); "Eberling's blood was found in the Sheppard home in 1954 . . ." (Mary Mihaly, *"The Fugitive Redux," Ohio Magazine,* February 1995, pp. 39, 77).

371 But medical records . . . : According to lab analysis by the Cleveland Clinic, September 17, 1984.

371 The first real attention . . . : Paul Holmes, *The Sheppard Murder Case,* pp. 172–73.

372 Lavern Leslie Lund . . . : C. Cooper interviewed Lund in Oklahoma City in October 1990. Lund supplied pictures of himself as a young man. He signed the sworn affidavit in front of an Oklahoma notary the next day. After Lund died, in 1991, his son provided C. Cooper with official documents, additional photographs, and Mr. Lund's writings.

376 Records secured in 1994 . . . : A supplementary report on 54-194, the murder of Marilyn Sheppard, written by Bay Village police lieutenant James R. Tompkins, indicates that Lund called the Bay Village station on July 24, 1989; that on July 28, 1989, Tompkins and Detective Cleary interviewed Lund and showed him the mug shot; and that on August 17, 1989, Lund went to the Bay Village Police Department at his own request. (Bay Village Documents) .

376 Marty Eskins moved back . . . : Marty Eskins and Pauline Eskins, interviews by C. Cooper, 1993.

377 Another former employee, Ed Wilbert . . . : Interview by C. Cooper, 1993.

379 He hoped that it would result . . . : The charges against Henderson for aggravated murder, forgery, and tampering with records were overturned by the Court of Appeals of Ohio, Eighth District, and the Ohio Supreme Court, No. 92-1004, 66 Ohio St. 3d 1219 (May 12, 1993). Four charges were not overturned: aggravated grand theft, the most serious; complicity to commit perjury; tampering with evidence; and grand theft.

379 Ragus went to Cleveland . . . : Report by Morris Ragus, April 1994.

381 He said he was reading . . . : Conversations with attorney and polygrapher by C. Cooper, 1993–94; conversations with journalist by Terry Gilbert, 1993–94; Eberling interviews.

381 Eberling gave Bay Village . . . : Report by Bay Village Officer Ronald B. DuPerow, Bay Village Police Documents.

381 Christine Eberling . . . : Executrix accounts, estate of George Eberling

382 Ed's cousin, Harold . . . : Sources include Eberling interviews;

Harold Wilbert, conversations with C. Cooper, 1992–93, with AMSEC, 1994.

383   He was very much alive . . . : Ed Wilbert, interviews by C. Cooper, 1993, and by AMSEC on three occasions, 1993–94.

390   His own words describe him best . . . : Eberling's comments, and the context in which they were made, are excerpted from Eberling interviews and letters. Space breaks indicate shifts from one source to another.

Chapter 21 • Chances

395   If the Sheppard affair . . . : See notes to chapters 16 to 19.

395   Obie barely . . . : Henderson, interview by C. Cooper, 1994.

396   The story was about the 1951 . . . : Douglas Montero, "Fiction of Fear," *Plain Dealer,* March 8, 1994: Detective Richard Martin, interview by C. Cooper, 1994.

397   When Corrigan retired . . . : "Race to Replace J. T. Corrigan: Campaigning for Tomorrow's Vote Heats Up amid Charges," *Plain Dealer,* January 11, 1991; "County Prosecutor Stephanie T. Jones Spends Eventful First Day," *Plain Dealer,* January 15, 1991.

397   Often described as charismatic . . . : "Stephanie T. Jones Topples Old Guard, Prosecutor Contest Ends Corrigan Era," *Plain Dealer,* January 13, 1991; Brent Larkin, "Stephanie T. Jones Win Ends Local Party Legend," *Plain Dealer,* January 13, 1991; "Jones for Prosecutor," *Plain Dealer,* September 18, 1992; Mary Strassmeyer, "Jones Ready to Try on That Glass Slipper," *Plain Dealer,* February 26, 1995; *Profiles of Ohio Lawyers, Vol. I, Cleveland and Vicinity,* ed. Lynn M. LoPucki (Cincinnati: Anderson, 1989), p. 237.

398   Criminalist Dr. Peter DeForest believed . . . : Peter De Forest, interviews by C. Cooper, 1993–95.

398   There was another option . . . : Dr. Robert Shaler, interview by C. Cooper, 1995.

399   She backed away . . . : Steve Luttner, "Jones Getting Reputation for Dropping Ball," *Plain Dealer,* February 13, 1993.

399   John Lenear . . . : John Lenear, interview by C. Cooper, 1995.

Chapter 22 • Living

406   His dad had known . . . : Sheppard diary, Sheppard Files.

408   Over twenty-two thousand . . . : According to the Bureau of Justice Statistics at the Justice Department, which cites the FBI's *Crime in the U.S.,* there were 22,250 murders in 1992.

408   Criminologists say . . . : The FBI's 1993 Uniform Crime Report states that no arrest is made in 44 percent of the murder cases, according to the Bureau of Justice Statistics. "Murder in Large Urban Counties, 1988," a special report of the Bureau of Justice Statistics, reports that in 27 percent of the

murder arrests, an innocent person is arrested and acquitted or charges are dropped. Estimates on the number of innocent persons who are convicted comes from a conversation by Sam R. Sheppard with Michael Radelet, author of *In Spite of Innocence.*

Afterword • New Beginnings

412   "Marino didn't shy away . . .": Carmen Marino, interview by C. Cooper.

412   "Marino could find no motive": Marino states that as a prosecutor he was not obliged to prove motive.

413   "Brent Larkin . . .": John Blades, "Presumed Guilty," *Chicago Tribune,* October 25, 1995; "Burden of Proof," CNN, January 31, 1996; Brent Larkin, "Consensus on murder," *Plain Dealer,* March 3, 1996. For a response to the latter, see Terry H. Gilbert and Cynthia L. Cooper, "No Sheppard consensus," *Plain Dealer,* March 8, 1996.

413   "Michael Corrigan . . ." Brian McGrory, "Murder revisited," *Boston Globe,* March 4, 1996; "Dateline," NBC, February 7, 1996.

413   "A Cleveland police officer . . .": Meeting with Terry Gilbert, Andy Carraway, Cynthia L. Cooper, July 17, 1995.

414   "Tompkins reported . . .": Report of October 2, 1995, in Bay Village Police files, in custody of Cuyahoga County Common Pleas Court.

414   "Eberling soon . . .": Letter to C. Cooper, October 15, 1995.

414   "Marino first spoke publicly . . .": Peter Finn, "Blood Will Tell," *Washington Post,* January 28, 1996.

415   "A new procedure . . .": Ohio Wrongful Imprisonment Act, Ohio Revised Code 2305.02 and 2643.48 (1986).

415   "Soon the case landed . . .": *Alan J. Davis, Administrator of the Estate of Samuel H. Sheppard v. Ohio,* Case No. CR 64571 (original caption *Sheppard v. State*) (Cuyahoga County, Court of Common Pleas, October 19, 1995). Later, because of objections by assistant prosecutor Marilyn Barkley Cassidy, the case was refiled and received a new case number: 96 CV 312322 (Cuyahoga County, Court of Common Pleas, July 24, 1996).

415   "The prosecutor's office now had to admit . . .": See James F. McCarty, "Sheppard murder files missing," *Plain Dealer,* February 22, 1996.

416   "To win at this stage . . .": The standard of proof in the "declaration of innocence" action is not "beyond a reasonable doubt," as it would be to convict someone of a crime, but a lower standard. To succeed here, the wrongfully convicted person only has to prove innocence by a "preponderance of the evidence," the same standard required by plaintiffs in all civil cases.

416   "The prosecutors said nothing . . .": In the next months assistant prosecutors Marilyn Barkley Cassidy and David Zimmerman raised an array of technical complaints that delayed the case, arguing that the case should have been filed while Dr. Sam was alive, that the time had passed for filing such an action even though the law had no time deadline or statute of limitations, and most incredibly, that the prosecutors were at a disadvantage because they had lost their files. Arguments challenging the truth of the claims in the petition for the declaration of innocence were not presented.

417   "Monsignor later ventured . . .": Quoted by Russell Miller, "In pursuit of the truth," (London) *Times Magazine*, July 28, 1996.

417   "Criminalist Peter De Forest . . .": Taken from comments written by De Forest in October 1995.

420   "Conducting a sample test . . .": The blanket had been used for testing by former lab technician Mary Cowan, who had deposited her own blood on it.

421   "Kathie Collins . . .": Interviews with Cynthia Cooper; interviews with Allen Gore of AMSEC and other AMSEC investigators; videotape statement of Collins, March 1996; two affidavits signed by Collins in April, 1996; also see James F. McCarty, "Eberling admitted killing Sheppard, nurse says," *Plain Dealer*, April 29, 1996.

421   "But as soon as she . . .": *Inside Edition*, March 18, 1996.

421   "Additional child welfare . . .": Reports of Department of Children and Family Services, Cuyahoga County, released with permission.

421   "In the fall of 1995, Cindy Leise . . .": Cindy Leise, "New evidence reopens Sheppard controversy," *Chronicle Telegram*, October 18, 1995; Cindy Leise, "New evidence can clear dad, says Dr. Sam's son," *Chronicle Telegram*, October 19, 1995.

423   "In 1996, her mother . . .": Interviews by AMSEC, affidavit by Virginia H., August 12, 1996.

424   "In the Durkin murder trial . . .": Transcript, *State v. Eberling and Henderson*, CR-232315, Court of Common Pleas, Cuyahoga County, see Chapter 19.

424   "There she read a story . . .": Evelyn Theiss, "The Dark Secrets of Darling Dick," *Cleveland Magazine*, December, 1988.

424   "Sergeant Vince Kremperger . . .": Interview by C. Cooper, 1996; with reference to the Sheppard case, Kremperger is quoted by writer Mary Anne Sharkey as saying, "I was told to leave it alone." See "Richard Eberling's Trail of Corpses," *Cleveland Magazine*, June 1996.

425   "To Sam R. . . .": Letter from R. G. Eberling to S. R. Sheppard, postmarked March 12, 1996.

425   "A check with . . .": Ohio Department of Corrections, March, 1996, research by C. Cooper.

425   "The coroner's vault . . ." David Zimmerman, Terry Gilbert, and Andy Carraway went through the coroner's files in March 1996, compiling a 10-page raw list. In June and August 1996 Cynthia Cooper reviewed documents that were set aside as particularly pertinent.

425   "The graying original of Dombrowski's . . .": July 23, 1954, report of Henry Dombrowski, Cleveland Police Department; see Chapter 8.

426   "Report by Harold . . .": Report of Sergeant Harold Lockwood, Cleveland Police Department; see Chapter 7.

426   "A report by Ray Keefe . . .": July 4, 1954, report by Ray Keefe, Office of the Cuyahoga County Coroner.

427   "Finally, an original Bay Village . . .": Bay Village Supplemental Report by Bay Village Police Chief John Eaton, August 2, 1995; report by Cleveland Police Department Detective Adelbert O'Hara to David E. Kerr, August 4, 1955, headed: "Investigation of the Homicide of Marilyn Sheppard, July 4, 1954."

427   "He described the weapon . . ." Affidavit, report, by Dr. Paul Leland Kirk, see Chapter 8.

427   "Criminalist Jim Chapman . . .": Interview by C. Cooper, 1996.

428   "On the side of the report . . .": The comment was written on the side of the Cleveland Police Department report by Detective O'Hara.

428   "Donald Joseph Wedler": See Chapter 13 for a full description of Wedler.

428   "Burkholder reinitiated . . .": Report by J. Burkholder for AMSEC International.

429   "All physical evidence . . .": Interviews with Dr. Mohammad Tahir by C. Cooper.

432   "National media articles . . .": A review of articles in general includes: Fox Butterfield, "After Life of Notoriety and Pain, Son Tries to Solve His Mother's Murder," *New York Times,* March 26, 1996; Stephanie Saul, "Sam Sheppard Revisited," *Newsday,* March 14, 1996; Tom Curly, "The 'Fugitive' murder sequel," *USA Today,* March 7, 1996; Judy Pasternak, "Son's Evidence Revives Sheppard Case of 1950s," *Los Angeles Times,* March 18, 1996; Michael Taylor, "In the Name of the Father," *San Francisco Chronicle,* April 7, 1996; Roger Vozar, "New evidence presented by Sheppard book authors," *Lakewood Sun Post,* October 26, 1995; Thom Weidlich, "Will Blood Tell Who Did It?", *National Law Journal,* February 12, 1996; R. Joseph Gelarden, "Dr. Sheppard's Revenge," *Indianapolis News,* April 11, 1996; Michael von Glahn, "Let the Truth Be Told," *Cleveland Magazine,* November 1995; Marc Peyser & Gregory Beals, "Hunting 'The Fugitive' " *Newsweek,* February 12, 1996; "A Son's Crusade," *People,* April 8, 1996; "The Fugitive and the Truth," *Guardian* (U.K.), May 13, 1996; Richard Woods and

          Christopher Goodwin, "Court reopens the Fugitive murder
          case," *Sunday Times* (UK), May 3, 1996.

432–4   "But Judyth Ulis . . . :" Interviews with Judyth Ulis by C.
          Cooper.

432   "Brent Larkin . . . :" "Burden of Proof," CNN, January 31,
          1996.

433   "Together they wrote . . . :" Letter dated June 28, 1996.

434   "In a meeting . . . :" Meeting with T. Gilbert, C. Cooper, John
          Burkholder and another AMSEC investigator, and Sam R.
          Sheppard on June 25, 1996.

436   "One letter . . . :" Letter from Richard Eberling to Cynthia
          Cooper, dated May 23, 1996.

437   "CLEVELAND . . . ." *Akron Beacon Journal,* July 5, 1954, quoted
          by and with special thanks to: Keith McKnight, "Haunting
          Questions: The Sam Sheppard Case, Eight Part Series," *Akron
          Beacon Journal,* June 30, 1996—July 7, 1996.

INDEX